ISBN 978-1-332-29539-5
PIBN 10310511

# 1 MONTH OF
# FREE
# READING

at

## www.ForgottenBooks.com

By purchasing this book you are eligible for one month membership to ForgottenBooks.com, giving you unlimited access to our entire collection of over 1,000,000 titles via our web site and mobile apps.

To claim your free month visit:

www.forgottenbooks.com/free310511

English
Français
Deutsche
Italiano
Español
Português

# www.forgottenbooks.com

**Mythology** Photography **Fiction**
Fishing Christianity **Art** Cooking
Essays Buddhism Freemasonry
Medicine **Biology** Music **Ancient**
**Egypt** Evolution Carpentry Physics
Dance Geology **Mathematics** Fitness
Shakespeare **Folklore** Yoga Marketing
**Confidence** Immortality Biographies
Poetry **Psychology** Witchcraft
Electronics Chemistry History **Law**
Accounting **Philosophy** Anthropology
Alchemy Drama Quantum Mechanics
Atheism Sexual Health **Ancient History**
**Entrepreneurship** Languages Sport
Paleontology Needlework Islam
**Metaphysics** Investment Archaeology
Parenting Statistics Criminology
**Motivational**

# A REPORT

OF THE

# RECORD COMMISSIONERS

CONTAINING

## BOSTON BIRTHS, BAPTISMS, MARRIAGES, AND DEATHS. 1630–1699.

BOSTON:

ROCKWELL AND CHURCHILL, CITY PRINTERS,

No. 39 ARCH STREET.

1888.

# CITY OF  BOSTON.

## REPORT

# RECORD COMMISSIONERS.

The Record Commissioners of the City of Boston herewith offer the ninth volume printed under their charge. It wa intended and is believed to contain every entry of birth, death, and marriage recorded as happening in the town of Boston in the first seventy years of its existence, and now found in the office of the City Registrar, and every entry of baptism on the records of the First Church for the same period.

A few words are all that it is necessary to say of the latter. The records are perfect, and for most of the time remarkably well kept. The volume containing them was probably not in use in 1630, as the baptisms for the early years seem t have been all recorded together, but apparently before 1640 Where the mother of a child is named alone or first, it is be cause she was a member of the Church, while the father wa not. It was not thought necessary to include the baptisms at other churches before 1700, for the following reasons : those recorded at the Second Church begin only about 1690, and are already in print; those of the Baptist Church ar very few indeed; and those of the Old South will probabl soon appear in print, under the care of a member of that church.

The Town Records require much longer notice. The authorities of the Colony of Massachusetts intended from the beginning to provide for a complete record of all children born within its limits, and of all deaths and marriages ; and at various times took action to secure such record. In September, 1639, the General Court ordered, "That there bee records kept of all wills, administrations, & inventories, as also of the dayes of every marriage, birth, & death of every person within this jurisdiction." In June, 1642, we read that "Whereas, at the Generall Cort the 4th 7th mo. 1639 there was provision made for the recording of severall particulers, amongst which it is observed that birthes, deathes, & marriages are much neglected in many townes,—

"It is therefore ordered, that hearafter the clarks of the writts in severall townes shall take especially care to record all birthes & deathes of persons in their townes; & for every birth & death they so record they are to have alowed them the summe of 3ᵈ, & are to deliver in yearely to the recorder of the Cort belonging to the jurisdiction where they live a transcript thereof, togeather with so many pence as there are births & deaths recorded, & this under the penalty of 20ˢ for every neglect; & for time past it is ordered, they shall do their utmost indeavor to find out in their severall townes who hath bene borne, & who hath died, since the first founding of their townes, & to record the same as aforesaid.

"Also the magistrates & other persons appointed to marry shall yearly deliver to the recorder of that Cort that is nearest to the place of their habitation the names of such persons as they have married, with the dayes, months, & yeares of the same; & the said recorders are faithfully & carefully to inrolle such birthes, deathes, & marriages as shall thus bee committed to their trust." [1]  In May, 1657, it was found necessary to go farther, and "This Court, taking into theire consideracon the great damage that will unavoydeably aerne to the posteritie of this common wealth by the generall neglect of observing the lawe injoyning a record of all births, deaths & marriages within this collony, doe therefore order, that hencforth the clarks of the writts in each towne respectively take due care for effecting the same according to the intent of the aforesaid lawe : and in case any person or persons shall neglect theire duty required by the said lawe more then one month after any birth, death, or marriage, the clarke of the writts shall demand the same, with twelve pence a name for his care and paynes ; and in case any shall refuse to sattisfy him, he shall then retourne the names of such person or persons to the next magistrate or commissioners of the toune where such person dwells, who shall send for the party so refusing, and in case he shall persist therein, shall

---

[1] The action of the Selectmen of Boston upon this order may be seen on page 71 of the second volume of the Record Commissioners.

give order to the counstable to levy the same. And if any clarke of the writts shall neglect his duty hereby injoyned him, he shall pay the following penalty; *i.e.*, for neglect of ᴀ yearly retourne to the County Court, five pounds, and for neglect of retourning the name of any person retourneable by this lawe, whither borne, married, or dead, more then thirty daies before his retourne to the County Court, five shillings. And that no future neglect may be heerein, the recorder of each County Court is hereby injoyned from time to time to certify the County Courts respectively the names of all such clarks as shall neglect to make their yearely retourne according to this lawe, who, uppon notice given, shall send for such clarke, and deale in the case according as lawe requireth."

For most of the years before 1700 the record of births seems to be quite full and complete; but sometimes, as in 1675, nearly all was lost by some chance. The years 1647–50 are also evidently imperfect. The deaths and marriages are less regularly recorded, and there is a long break in each. No deaths were recorded 1665–88, and no marriages 1663–79.

The contents of this volume are found in five volumes of manuscript. In the first volume are the following, viz.: "A register of the Births & Deaths in Boston from the yeare 1630 untill the first of the first month 1644," sixteen pages and a half in one general alphabetical arrangement; "Boston Register from (8) 1643 unto the (1) 1646," three pages and a half in one general alphabetical arrangement; "Boston births and burialls," 1646–50, four pages in the same form; "Boston Birthes" 1651–57, forty pages and a half, "by Jonathan Negus Clarke of the Writts in Boston, 28. 8. 1657;" "Deaths," 1651–57, nine pages also by Jonathan Negus; "Boston Marriages," 1651–57, fourteen pages also by Jonathan Negus 28 December 1657; "Boston Birthes" 1658–62, twenty-seven pages, "Boston Deathes" 1658–62, nine pages, "Boston Marriages" 1658–62, ten pages and a half, all by Jonathan Negus; "Boston Births" 1657–66, seventeen pages and a half, and "Boston Deathes" 1567–64, six pages. Probably a leaf at the end is missing.

The second volume contains a copy of all the births recorded in the first, and the births 1666–89, those of each year being arranged alphabetically.

The third volume contains Births 1689–92, in one alphabetical arrangement, with the following statement, "Whereas the Births within the Town of Boston entered by Mr. Joseph Webb deceased dureing the time of his being Clerk of the Writts for the County of Suffolke have since his deccace been misslayd so as that they came not to hand untill this present

year the which Births being then found contained in severall
wast Books on file with the Records of the sd. County Are
now digested into Alphabetticall Order and in this and the
sixteen foregoing pages are recorded being with the said wast
Bookes carefully compared & Exam^d. in the year 1709 p.
Joseph Prout Town Clerk; " " Sundry Births Recorded outt
of Season," half a page; "Sundry more Births as entered
in the Townes waste Book kept by Capt. Ephraim Savage
when he was Clerk," half a page; Births from March 1693 to
1696, eighteen pages in one arrangement; "Boston Births
being transferr'd out of a Waste book kept by Mr. William
Griggs while he was Town Clerk being such Births then
brought in to him & belonging to preceeding years," one page
and a half; Births for 1697, 98, 99, each year alphabetically.

The fourth volume contains Marriages 1689–95, twenty
pages in one arrangement, (Webb's record), with statement by
Joseph Prout similar to the first in third volume; Marriages
1693, 94, 95, 96, three pages, (Savage's record), with statement nearly as in third volume; Marriages for 1697, 98, 99.

The fifth volume contains Deaths 1689, 90, 91, 92,
seven pages in one arrangement (Webb's record), with statement by Prout similar to first in third volume; Deaths for
1696, one page; Deaths 1693, 94, 95, 96, three pages and a
half in one arrangement; and Deaths for 1697, 98, 99. The
number of misplaced entries in every class is very great in
each volume.

Every entry on Town Records and Church Records has
been compared with the original, and it is believed that the
exact meaning is expressed in the printed copy, though the
wording has been often changed for the sake of brevity.
The editing Commissioner claims no infallibility in reading
old manuscript, but has had the advantage of long experience.
In some cases an equally practised person might read the
name differently, at least in one or two letters : but most of
the mistakes were made by the writer of the original manuscript. No exact rule has been followed as to duplicate
entries, but generally only one has been printed; in some
cases intentionally, and in a few accidentally, both entries
appear in this volume. It is hoped that the Index will be
approved. The various spellings, evidently intended for the
same name, have been generally grouped under the form
most often or most correctly used ; but sometimes it has been
thought best to do otherwise, especially when it is not easy
to say which is the standard or correct form.

Readers will kindly note these two marriages as belonging
to 1699, and accidentally omitted : —

Joseph Shaw & Mercy Cross were married by Mr. Cotton Mather Feb. 22.

Richard Smith & Mary Clay were married by Mr. Cotton Mather Feb. 9.

The charge of this volume, since it was put in the printer's hands, has been entirely with the junior Commissioner, who alone is responsible for all mistakes since the preparation of copy.

Respectfully submitted,

WILLIAM H. WHITMORE,<br>WILLIAM S. APPLETON,<br>Record Commissioners.

BOSTON, October, 1883.

## BIRTHS AND BAPTISMS.

### 1630.

#### TOWN.

Edward son of Wm and Elizabeth Aspinwall born 26 day of 7th month and died 10th day of 8th month.

#### FIRST CHURCH.

| | |
|---|---|
| Joy & Recompence dangᵗˢ of John Milles | 8 mo. |
| Pittie daugʳ of Willᵐ Baulstone | 8 mo. |
| Increase of Increase Nowell [1] | 21 day 9 mo. |

### 1631.

#### TOWN.

Hannah of Wm & Elizabeth Aspinwall born 25 day of 10th month.
Jerusha of Edward & Margaret Gibbons born 5th day 8th month.
Elizabeth of Matthias & Anne Ijons born 15th day 2nd month.

#### FIRST CHURCH.

[The following entries are dated 1631, but undoubtedly belong to 1632. —W. S. A.]

| | |
|---|---|
| Abigail of Increase Nowell [1] | 3 day 4 mo. |
| Samuel son of Raph Sprage [1] | 3 day 4 mo. |
| Phebe daughter of Ezekiel Richardson [1] | 3 day 4 mo. |
| Lidya daugʳ of John Perkins [1] | 3 day 4 mo. |
| John of Henry Harwoode [1] | 3 day 4 mo. |
| John of John Milles | 3 day 4 mo. |
| Mary of Richard Gridley | 10 day 4 mo. |
| Josiah & Mary of Edward Raynsford | 17 day 4 mo. |
| Willᵐ of John Winthrope Governor | 26 day 6 mo. |
| Mary of Thomas French | 23 day 7 mo. |

### 1632.

#### TOWN.

Anne of Wm & Anne Beamsley born 13th day of 12th month.
Jacob of Jacob Eliott born 16th day 10th month.
Mary of Richard & Grace Gridley born 14th day 2nd month.
Mary of Edward & —— Rainsford born 1st — 4th month.
Joshua of Edward & —— Rainsford born 1st — 4th month. & died 7th month.
Wife of Edward Rainsford died 4th month.

---

[1] Not called "our brother," i.e., not member of this Church.—W.S.A.

FIRST CHURCH.

| | |
|---|---|
| John of Will<sup>m</sup> Cheesebrough | 11 day  9 mo. |
| Ruth of John Foxalls [1] | 11 day  9 mo. |
| Jacob of Jacob Elyott | 16 day 10 mo. |

## 1633.

### TOWN.

Elizabeth of Wm & Elisabeth Aspinwall born 30th day of 7th month.
Seaborne of John & Sarah Cotton born 12 day 6 month.
Jotham son of Edward & Margaret Gibbons born 6th day 8th month.
Nathaniel of William & Susan Hudson born 30th day of 11th month.
John of Thomas & Anne Leverit born 7th day 7th month.
Jeremy son of Walter & Rebecca Merry born 11th month & died soon after.
Hannah of John & Hannah Newgate born 1st day 6th month & died in the
     11th month.
Nathaniel of Mr Thomas Oliver died 9th month.
Mary of Mr John & Elizabeth Wilson born 12th — 7th month.
Timothy of Richard & Judith Tapping born & died.

### FIRST CHURCH.

| | |
|---|---|
| James of James Pennyman. | 26 day  1 mo. |
| William of William Balstone. | 15 day  2 mo. |
| John of John Sampford | 26 day  4 mo. |
| Hannah of Anne Newgate | 6 day  6 mo. |
| Seaborne son of John Cotton | 8 day  7 mo. |
| John of Anthony Colby. | 8 day  7 mo. |
| Mary of John Wilson | 15 day  7 mo. |
| Elizabeth of William Aspinwall. | 22 day  7 mo. |
| Jotham of Edward Gibbon | 27 day  8 mo. |
| Thomas of Thomas Mattson | 27 day  8 mo. |
| Elizabeth of George Ruggle | 8 day 10 mo. |
| Timothy of Richard Topping | 15 day 10 mo. |
| Nathaniel of William Hudson | 19 day 11 mo. |
| Mary of Lettysse Button | 23 day 12 mo. |

## 1634.

### TOWN.

Sarah of Nathaniel & Alice Bishop born 20th day 1st month.
John of Jacob Eliot born 28th day 10th month.
John of Thomas & Mary Fairewether born in the 8th month.
Sarah of Richard & Grace Gridley born 14th day 2d month.
Mary of William & —— Pell born 30th — 4th month.
John of Edward & Elizabeth Rainsford born 30th — 4th month.

### FIRST CHURCH.

| | |
|---|---|
| Mary of William Coddington | 2 day  1 mo. |
| Mary of Thomas French | 2 day  1 mo. |
| Thomas of Samuel Dudley, grandchild to our brother John | |
|      Winthrop Gov. | 9 day  1 mo. |
| John of Richard Palsgrave | 9 day  1 mo. |
| John of Richard Bulgar | 20 day  2 mo. |
| Sarah of William Browne | 11 day  3 mo. |
| Sarah of Richard Grydley | 1 day  4 mo. |
| Sarah of John Winthrop. the Elder | 29 day  4 mo. |

---

[1] Not called "our brother," *i.e.*, not member of this Church. — W. S. A.

| | | |
|---|---|---|
| John of Edward Ransford | 27 day | 5 mo. |
| John of Edward Hutchinson the Elder | 31 day | 6 mo. |
| Mary of William Balstone | 14 day | 7 mo. |
| Mary of William Pell | 14 day | 7 mo. |
| John of Thomas Fairewether | 21 day | 7 mo. |
| James of Robert Houlton | 5 day | 8 mo. |
| Elyakim son of Thomas Wardall | 23 day | 9 mo. |
| Samuel of Oliver Mellowes | 7 day | 10 mo. |
| Jeremiah of Waters Merry | 15 day | 10 mo. |
| John of Jacob Elyott | 28 day | 10 mo. |
| Hannah of Richard Brockett | 4 day | 11 mo. |
| Barnabas son of Richard Brenton | 24 day | 11 mo. |
| Lydia of James Pennyman | 22 day | 12 mo. |
| Daniel of Lettysse & Mathias Button | 22 day | 12 mo. |

## 1635.

### TOWN.

Samuel son of Wm & Elisabeth Aspinwall born 30th day of 7th month.
Elizabeth daughter of Miles & Mary Awkley born the ———
Grace of Wm & Anne Beamsley born 10th day of 7 month.
Sarahjah daut. of John & Sarah Cotton born 12 day 7th month.
Abigail daut of Wm & Mary Davies born 31th day 8th month.
Thomas of ——— Dincley born 9th day 11th month.
Rebecca of Walter & Rebecca Merry born 11th month & died soon after.
Hannah of John & Hannah Newgate born 1st day 6th month.
John of John & Margaret Odlin born 30th day 4th month. and died soon after.
Anne wife of Mr Thomas Oliver died 3rd month.
Joanna of Nicholas & Anne Parker born 1st day 4th month.
Thomas of John & ——— Parker born 2d — 8th month
Lazarus of Philemon & Susan Pormort born 28th — 12th month.
Elizabeth of Richard & Elizabeth Sherman born 1st — 10th month.
Elishua of Robert & ——— Walker born 14th — 12th month.
Shoreborne son of William & Patience Wilson born 6th — 6th month
Alexander of Alexander & Elizabeth Baker born 15th — 11th month.
Judith wife of Richard Tapping died.
Hannah of Angel & Catherine Hollard born 8th — 8th month.
Peleg of William & Mary Salter born 15th — 1st month.
John of Elizabeth & William Wen born 22nd — 9th month.
Eliakim of Thomas & Elizabeth Werdall born 9th month.

### FIRST CHURCH.

| | | |
|---|---|---|
| Charity daug<sup>r</sup> of Jonn Baker | 12 day | 2 mo. |
| Hananeel daug<sup>r</sup> of John Coggeshall | 3 day | 3 mo. |
| Jabez son of Will<sup>m</sup> Cheesebrough | 8 day | 3 mo. |
| Samuel of John Sampford | 21 day | 4 mo. |
| John of Samuel Dudley grandchild to our br. John Winthrop the Elder | 28 day | 4 mo. |
| John of John Audley | 28 day | 4 mo. |
| Freegrace son of Edward Bendall | 5 day | 5 mo. |
| Hannah of John Newgate | 19 day | 5 mo. |
| Jonathan of John Mylles | 30 day | 6 mo. |
| Shoreborne son of William Wilson | 13 day | 7 mo. |
| Sariab of John Cotton Teacher | 20 day | 7 mo. |
| Samuel of William Aspinall | 20 day | 7 mo. |
| Grace of William Beamsley | 20 day | 7 mo. |
| Mary of Thomas Alcocke | 8 day | 9 mo. |
| Samuel of William Dyer | 20 day | 10 mo. |
| Edward of Edward Gibbon | 3 day | 1 mo. |
| Mary of George Ruggle | 3 day | 11 mo. |
| Constance daug<sup>r</sup> of Richard Fairebancke | 10 day | 11 mo |
| Benjamin of John Mylam | 10 day | 11 mo |

| | |
|---|---|
| Lydia of Richard Palsgrave | 17 day 11 mo. |
| Thomas of Will<sup>m</sup> Dyneley | 17 day 11 mo. |
| Mehetabel of Will<sup>m</sup> Balstone | 24 day 11 mo. |
| Elizabeth of John Underhill | 14 day 12 mo. |
| Elishuah daug<sup>r</sup> of Robert Walker | 28 day 12 mo. |

## 1636.

### Town.

Hannah of Edmund & Martha Jackson born 1st day 1st month.
Ethlan son of Wm & Elisabeth Aspinwall born 1st day of 1st month.
Free Grace son of Edw: & Anne Bendall born 30th day of 7th month.
Elhanan son of Rich: & Elizabeth Cooke born 30th day 4th month & died Nov:
Annah of John Coggan born 7th day 9th month.
Thomas son of Wm & Mary Davies born 15th day 1st month.
Eleaser son of Nathaniel & Elizabeth Eaton born 22 day 7th month.
Hannah of Jacob Eliot born 29th day 11th month.
Mary of Thomas & Mary Fairewether born in 9th month.
Zachary of Benjamin & Anne Gillom born 30th day 7th month.
Hannah of Richard & Grace Gridley born 10th day 2d month.
Elizabeth of George & Alice Griggs born 14th day 3rd month.
Abraham of Thomas & Hannah Hawkins born 1st day 11th month.
Joseph of Richard & Joan Hogge born 10th month.
Jonathan of Edward & Elizabeth Rainsford born 8th month.
Elizabeth of Mr John & Elizabeth Winthrope born 24th — 5th month.
Sarah of Henry & Sarah Linn born 20th — 6th month.

### First Church.

| | | |
|---|---|---|
| Martha of Oliver Mellowes | 6 day | 1 mo. |
| Lazarus of Philemon Pormort | 6 day | 1 mo. |
| Zuryell daug<sup>r</sup> of Will<sup>m</sup> Hutchinson | 13 day | 1 mo. |
| Hannah of Richard Grydley | 24 day | 2 mo. |
| Bedaiah son of William Coddington | 1 day | 3 mo. |
| Ezekiel of James Everill | 15 day | 3 mo. |
| Elizabeth of James Fitch | 15 day | 3 mo. |
| Elvezar of Will<sup>m</sup> Townsend | 12 day | 4 mo. |
| Elizabeth of John Winthrop the younger | 3 day | 5 mo. |
| John of Thomas Matson | 10 day | 5 mo. |
| Elhanan son of Richard Cooke | 17 day | 5 mo. |
| Wayto daug<sup>r</sup> of John Coggeshall | 11 day | 7 mo. |
| Eleazar son of Nath<sup>l</sup> Heaton | 2 day | 8 mo. |
| Jonathan of Edward Ransford | 23 day | 8 mo. |
| Zechariah son of Benja. Gillam | 23 day | 8 mo. |
| Hannah of Anne & John Cogan | 6 day | 9 mo. |
| Rebecca of Waters Merry | 18 day | 10 mo. |
| John of James Pennyman | 15 day | 11 mo. |
| Thomas of Jane & John Parker | 22 day | 11 mo. |
| Hannah of Jacob Elyott | 29 day | 11 mo. |

## 1637.

### Town.

Returno daughter of Richard & Grace Gridley born 14th day 1st month.
Eliakim son of Thomas & Alice Marshall born 1st day 1st month.
Mercie son of Wm & Anne Beamsley born 9th day (10th) month.
Anne wife of Edw: Bendall died 25th day (10th) month
Joseph Blanchard died in the 10th month.
Thomas of George & Anne Burden born & buried 1 day (2d) month.
Thomas of Thomas & Anne Buttolph born 12 day (6th) month.
Elisha of Richard & Elizabeth Cooke born 16th day 7th month.

Elizabeth of John & Sarah Cotton born 9th day 10th month.
Abigail of ——— Dineley born 10th month.
Sarah of George & Alice Griggs born 15th day 3d month.
Sarah of Hugh & Elizabeth Gunnison born 14th day 12th month.
Zuriell son of Ralph Mason born 14th day 2nd month.
Jeremy son of Walter & Rebecca Merry born 11th month & died soon after.
Hannah of John & Margaret Odlin born 9th day 12th month & died soon after.
Daniel of Mr. Thomas Oliver died 4th month.
Another born & died 14th day 4th month.[1]
Elishua daughter of Arthur & Elizabeth Perry born 20th December.
John of David & Sarah Phippeni born and died 5th month.
Joshua of Robert & Elizabeth Rice born 14th — 2nd month.
Philip of Samuel & Grace Sherman born 31st — 10th month.
Mary of John & Elizabeth Spurre born 20th — 1st month.
Elizabeth of William & Elizabeth Ting born 6th — 12th month.
Moses of Gamaliel & Grace Waite born 4th month.
Zachary of Robert & ——— Walker born 15th — 7th month.
Meribah daughter of William & Alice Werdall born 14th — 3rd month.
Jonathan of Thomas & Rebecca Wheeler born 20th ——— 8th month.
Mary of William & Patience Wilson born 11th — 11th month.
John of Robert & Joan Wing born 22nd 5th month.
Mary of Richard and Mary Woodhouse born & buried 11th month.
Samuel of Alexander & Elizabeth Baker born 16th — 11th month.
Job of Job & Sarah Judkins born 10th — 3rd mo. died 24th — 3rd month.
John of Henry & Alice Stevens born 10th — 7th month.
Martha of Thomas & Elizabeth Werdall born 6th month.

### FIRST CHURCH.

| | | |
|---|---|---|
| Abiah daut[r] of Thomas Grubbe & it dyed that night | 5 day | 1 mo. |
| Deliverance daut[r] of Robert Potter member of Rocksbury Ch. | 5 day | 1 mo. |
| Mary daut[r] of Thos. Faireweather | 5 day | 1 mo. |
| Hannah of Edmund Jackson | 5 day | 1 mo. |
| Ethlannah son of Will[m] Aspenall | 12 day | 1 mo. |
| Edward of Edward Gibbon | 26 day | 1 mo. |
| Jabez of Robert Houlton | 2 day | 2 mo. |
| Meribah of Willam Balstone | 9 day | 2 mo. |
| Joshua of Robert Royce | 16 day | 2 mo. |
| Peter & John } of Richard Brockett | 7 day | 3 mo. |
| Patience of Will[m] Townsend | 28 day | 3 mo. |
| Elisha of Will[m] Cheesbrough | 4 day | 4 mo. |
| Mary of John Wheelwright | 25 day | 4 mo. |
| Meribah of Will[m] Wardall | 25 day | 4 mo. |
| Jonathan of Elizabeth & Will[m] Tuttell | 2 day | 5 mo. |
| Bedaiah son of John Coggeshall | 30 day | 5 mo. |
| Ichabod of Edward Hutchinson the Elder | 3 day | 7 mo. |
| Martha of Thomas Wardall | 3 day | 7 mo. |
| Moses of Gamaliel Wayte | 3 day | 7 mo. |
| Hannah daut[r] Tho[s] Hasard | 10 day | 7 mo. |
| Zacharias son of Rob[t] Walker | 1 day | 8 mo. |
| Abigail of William Dyneley | 8 day | 8 mo. |
| Hannah of Rachel & Francis Newcombe | 15 day | 8 mo. |
| Elishua dant[r] of Edward Hutchinson the younger | 5 day | 9 mo. |
| Elishua son of Richard Cooke | 5 day | 9 mo. |
| Jonathan of Thomas Wheeler | 12 day | 9 mo. |
| Marie of Alexander Winchester | 19 day | 9 mo. |
| Elizabeth of John Cotton Teacher | 10 day | 10 mo. |
| Elizabeth of Thomas Alcocke | 10 day | 10 mo. |
| Mercie of William Beamesley | 10 day | 10 mo. |
| Eliphal dau. of John Sanford | 10 day | 10 mo. |
| Stephen of Elizabeth & Robert Meares | 10 day | 10 mo. |

---

[1] This refers to a child of Nicholas and Anne Parker. — W. S. A.

John of George Ruggle                              31 lay 10 mo.
Marie of William Wilson                            21 day 11 mo

## 1638.

### Town.

Hannah of Valentine & Frances Hill born 17th day 1st month.
Elizabeth of John & Jane Lugg born 7th day 1st month.
Moses of Gamaliel & Grace Waite died 1st month.
Miles son of Miles & Mary Awkley was born 1st day of 2nd month.
John son of Thomas Bell. born & died 24 day (6th) month.
John Bill died the 10th month.
Elisha of George & Anne Burden born the 4 day (12th) month.
Grace wife of John Button died 9th day 1st month.
Deliverance daugtr to Wm Courser born 4th day 1st month.
Thomas son of Wm & Mary Davies died 24th day 5th month
Aaron of Wm & Mary Davies born 20th day 5th month.
Thomas of Wm Davies died 5th month.
Fathergone son of ——— Dinely born 25th day 10th month.
Hannah of Madit & Joan English born 2d day 1st month.[1]
Mary of Thomas & Mary Fairewether died in 9th month.
Thomas of Thomas & Mary Fairewether died in 6th month.
Elizabeth of Wm & Alice Francklin born 3rd day 8th month.
Hannah of Benjamin & Anne Gillom born 9th month & died soon after.
John Goordley. servt to Rich. Tuttle died 10th month.
William of George Griggs buried in 10th month.
John of Thomas Grubb born the 6th month.
John of Edmund and Martha Jackson born 20th day 8th month.
John of Matthias & Anne Ijons born 16th day 7th month.
John of William & Elizabeth Winborne born 21st day 7th month.
Joseph of Francis and Alice Loyall born 10th day 8th month.
Stephen of Robert & Elizabeth Meere born 25th day 10th month.
Constance of John & Christian Milom born 25th day 10th month.
John of John & Elizabeth Oliver born 21st day 9th month.
Joseph of Richard & Anne Parker born 1st day 6th month & died 30th day
    9th month.
Noah of John & ——— Parker born 3d — 2d mo.
Nathaniel of William & ——— Pell born 10th — 6th month & died 9th month.
Anna of Philemon & Susan Pormort born 5th — 2nd month.
Ranis daughter of Edward & Elizabeth Rainsford born 4th — 4th month.
Abijah of Thomas & Faith Savage born 1st — 6th month.
Nathaniel of Robert & Elizabeth Scott born 6th month.
Melatiah son of Thomas & Milcah Snow born 30th — 7th month.
Hannah of Miles & Sarah Terne born 8th month.
David of David & Susanna Sellick born 11th — 10th month.
Isaac of Richard & Elizabeth Waite born 9th — 6th month. & died 21st —
    6th month.
Grace of Gamaliel & Grace Waite born 10th — 11th month.
Ruth of Nathaniel & Mary Williams born ———.
Mary of Richard and Mary Woodhouse born 14th — 11th month.
Pfitz-John Son of Mr John & Elizabeth Winthrop born 14th — 1st month.
Samuel of Job & Sarah Judkins born 27th ——— 9th month.
Elizabeth of Angel & Catherine Hollard born 5th month.
Elizabeth of Henry & Sarah Linn born 27th — 1st month.
John of John & Elizabeth Oliver born 21st — 5th month.

### First Church.

Hannah of John Awdley                             4 day 1 mo.
Deliverance daut^r of William Coursar             4 day 1 mo.
Sarah of Hugh Gunnyson                            4 day 1 mo.

---

[1] Only found in second MS., the bottom of leaf of oldest MS. being worn away. — W. S. A.

| | | |
|---|---|---|
| Peleg of William Salter | 25 day | 1 mo. |
| Noah of Jane & John Parker | 8 day | 2 mo. |
| Returne dant<sup>r</sup> of Rich<sup>d</sup> Gridley | 8 day | 2 mo. |
| Marie of Henry Elkyn | 8 day | 2 mo. |
| Eliakim son of Thomas Marshall | 15 day | 2 mo. |
| Anna of Philemon Pormort | 15 day | 2 mo. |
| Nathaniel of William Pell | 29 day | 2 mo. |
| Anna of Christopher Marshall | 13 day | 3 mo. |
| James of John Milles | 3 day | 4 mo. |
| Ragnis daut<sup>r</sup> of Edward Ransford | 10 day | 4 mo. |
| Bethiah dautr of Richard Palsgrave | 8 day | 5 mo. |
| John of John Olyver | 29 day | 5 mo. |
| Abiah son of Thomas Savage | 12 day | 6 mo. |
| Nathaniel of Robert Scott | 19 day | 6 mo. |
| Mary of Oliver Mellowes | 26 day | 6 mo. |
| Restored daut<sup>r</sup> of Zachariah Bosworth | 26 day | 6 mo. |
| John of Thomas Grubbe | 2 day | 7 mo. |
| Constance of John Mylam | 16 day | 7 mo. |
| John of Matthew Ines | 30 day | 7 mo. |
| Metsathiell son of Edward Gibbon | 7 day | 8 mo. |
| John of Edmund Jackson | 28 day | 8 mo. |
| Coneniah daut<sup>r</sup> of James Everill | 4 day | 9 mo. |
| Deliverance of Henry Sandys | 6 day | 11 mo. |
| Fathergone son of William Dyneley our gone brother | 6 day | 11 mo. |
| John of Richard Swanne | 13 day | 11 mo. |
| Grace of Gamaliel Wayte | 20 day | 11 mo. |
| Elisha of George Burdon | 3 day | 12 mo. |
| Esther of Griffyn Bowen | 10 day | 12 mo. |
| Mary of Martha Bushnall widow | 17 day | 12 mo. |

## 1639.

### TOWN.

Seth of Arthur & Elizabeth Perry born 7th — 1st month.
Dorcas daughter of Wm & Elizabeth Aspinwall born 14th day of 12th month.
John of George & Anna Balden born 25th day of 8th month.
Wm Barrell died 20th day of 6th month.
Mary of Nicholas & Anne Baxter born 12th month.
Mary the wife of Alexander Beck died 2nd day 3rd month.
Reforme son of Edw: & Marah Bendall born 18 day (8th) month.
Ruth of Nathaniel & Alice Bishop born 14 day (2d) month.
John of Thom: & Anne Buttolph born 28 day (12th) month.
Lidia of John Coggan born 14 day 5th month.
John of John & Sarah Cotton born 15 day 1st month.
Cornelius of Thomas Clarke born 10 month.
Joannah of Wm Courser born 9th day 12th month.
John of John & Alice Crabtree born 25th day 8th month.
John Cramwell died ———[1]
Aaron of Wm & Mary Davies died the 31st day 8 month.
Abigail dautr of Wm & Mary Davies died 24th day 12th month.
Jacob ot James & Joanna Davies born 11th day 5th month.
Samuel of Francis & Mary East born 11 day 1st month.
Nathaniel of Nathaniel & Elizabeth Eaton born 31st day 6th month.
Abigail of Jacob Eliot born 7th day 2d month.
Mary of Daniel Fairefield buried 5th month.[1]
Elizabeth of Thomas & Margaret Fowle born 14th day 1st month.
John of Arthur & Agnes Gill born 16 th day 9th month.
Hannah of Benjamin & Anne Gillom born the 11th month.
Mary of Samuel & Francis Greames born 27th day 2d month.
Sarah of Abraham & Elizabeth Hagborne born 24th day of 10th month.
John of George & Jane Harwood, born 4th day. 5th month.

---

[1] Only found in second MS., the bottom of leaf of oldest MS. being worn away. — W. S. A.

Sarah, of John & Abigail Jackson born 15th day 6th month.
Samuel of Thomas & Joan Joy born 26th day. 12th month.
Hannah of John & Anne Kenrick born 9th day 12th month.
Joseph of Francis & Alice Loyall died 10th day 12th month.
Benjamin of Francis & Alice Loyall 1st day 11th month.
Benjamin of John & Christian Milom died 15th day 12th month.
Dorothy wife of Thomas Munt died 12th month 28th day.
Elizabeth of John & Elizabeth Oliver born 28th day 12th month.
Elishua daughter of Arthur & Elizabeth Perry died April 10th.
Thomas of Thomas & Katherine Painter born 4th — 3rd month & died 36th
　　— 7th mo.
William of Thomas & Katherine Painter died 30th — 7th month.
Nathaniel of Robert & Elizabeth Rice born 1st —2nd month.
Thomas of Thomas & Joan Scotto born 11th month.
Martha of Samuel & Grace Sherman born 5th — 7th month.
Anna of William & Elizabeth Ting born 6th — 11th month.
Ephraim of Robert & Penelope Turner born 13th — 10th. month.
Hopestill daughter of John & Mary Vyall born 14th — 6th month.
Returne son of Richard & Elizabeth Waite born 8th — 5th month.
John of Robert & ——— Walker born 22nd — 7th month.
Vsal son of William & Alice Werdall born 7th — 2nd month.
John of William & Patience Wilson born 11th month.
Hannah of Robert & Joan Wing born 14th — 12th month.
Luce daughter of John & Elizabeth Winthrop born 28th — 11th month.
Joseph of George & Jane Kenrick born 12th month.
Ephraim of Henry & Sarah Linn born 16th — 11th month. .
John of John & Elizabeth Oliver died 27th — 1st month.
Elizabeth of John & Elizabeth Oliver born 28th — 12th month.
Mary of Peter & Margaret Henrickson born 21st — 1st month.
Elizabeth of William & Mary Salter born 16th — 2nd month.
Benjamin of Thomas & Elizabeth Werdall born 12th month.
Job of Henry & Mary Walton born 29th — 7th month.

## FIRST CHURCH.

| | | | |
|---|---|---|---|
| Elizabeth of William Tinge, | 10 day | 1 mo. | |
| Hannah of Valentine Hill, | 17 day | 1 mo. | |
| Nathaniel of Robert Royce, | 24 day | 1 mo. | |
| Elizabeth of Jane & John Lugge, | 24 day | 1 mo. | |
| David of Elizabeth & William Tuttell. | 7 day | 2 mo. | |
| Abigail of Jacob Elyott. . | 7 day | 2 mo. | |
| John of Anthony Harker | 14 day | 2 mo. | |
| Mary of John Spour | 21 day | 2 mo. | |
| Hannah of Sarah & Myles Tarne | 21 day | 2 mo. | |
| Joseph of Thomas Mekyns the younger | 5 day | 3 mo. | |
| Eliphalet of Anne & Thomas Hett | 26 day | 3 mo. | |
| Ruth of Nathaniel Willyams, aged about 1 year | 2 day | 4 mo. | |
| Lydia of Anne & John Cogan | 14 day | 5 mo. | |
| Returne son of Rich^d & Eliz^b. Wayte member of Newberry Ch. | 14 day | 5 mo. | |
| Samuel of Samuel Dudley, grandchild to our br. John Winthrop the Elder | 11 day | 6 mo. | |
| John of John Hurde, | 18 day | 6 mo. | |
| Joseph of Richard Hogge, aged about 1 yr 8 mos. | 25 day | 6 mo. | |
| Nathaniel of Nathaniel Heaton, | 1 day | 7 mo. | |
| Joseph of James Pennyman | 29 day | 7 mo. | |
| John of Robert Walker | 29 day | 7 mo. | |
| Thomas of Thomas Buttall | 29 day | 7 mo. | |
| Joseph of Francis Lysle, aged about 1 year | 6 day | 8 mo. | |
| Rachel of Richard Brockett | 3 day | 9 mo. | |
| Elizabeth of Edward Hutchinson the younger | 10 day | 9 mo. | |
| Reforme daut^r. of Edward Bendall | 24 day | 9 mo. | |
| Zachens son of Rich^d. Fairebancke | 8 day | 10 mo. | |
| Thomas of Thomas Scottcwe . | 8 day | 10 mo. | |
| Ephraim of Robert Turnor | 22 day | 10 mo. | |

Benjamin of Francis Lyslo        5 day 11 mo.
Anna of William Tinge        12 day 11 mo.
Anna of Benjamin Gillam        12 day 11 mo.
Luse daut[r] of John Winthropp the younger        2 day 12 mo.
Jonathan of Nicholas Parker from the Ch. of Roxbury        2 day 12 mo.
John of William Wilson        9 day 12 mo.
Hannah of John Kenricke        9 day 12 mo.
Johanna of William Courser        9 day 12 mo.

## 1640.

### TOWN.

Mary of Jeremy & Esther Houtchin born 18th day 1st month.
Thomas of Edmund & Martha Jackson born 1st day 1st month.
Benjamin of Francis & Alice Loyall buried 1st day 1st month.
Hannah of Edward & Mary Ting born 7th — 1st month.
Elisha son of John and Margaret Odlin born 1st day of 5th month.
Samuel of Wm & Anne Beamsley born the 31st day 10th month.
Habbakuk son of Wm & Anne Beamsley born the 31st day 10th month.
Ephraim son of Alexander & Elizabeth Beck born 1st day (4th) month.
Deliverance Beck born 1 day (4th) month.
Strange Beck born 1st day (4th) month.
Joan daughter of Thomas Bell born and died 4th day (1st) month.
Nehemiah son of Nehemiah & Hannah Bourne born 10 day (4th) month.
Elizabeth of Zaccheus & Anne Bosworth born 24th day (5th) month.
Jonathan of Wm & Goodith Copp born 23 day 6th month.
Samuel of Richard and Alice Croychley born 25th day 10th month.[1]
John of Wm Davies died 20th day 1st month.
Sarah of Edmund & Sarah Dennis born 6th month.
Elizabeth of Daniel & Elizabeth Fairefield born 30th day 8th month.[1]
Beleeve son of Richard & Grace Gridley born 1st day 3rd month.
Elizabeth Griggs aged 4 years died in 3rd month.
Elizabeth of Hugh and Elizabeth Gunnison born 25th day 2d month.
Abigail of William & Joane Harvie born 25th day 2d month.
Deliverance son of George Harwood died 12th month.
Hannah of Thomas & Hannah Hawkins born 20th day 11th month.
Job son of Thomas & Hannah Hawkins born 20th day 11th month.
John of Valentine & Francis Hill born & died 1st day 7th month.
John of Robert and Elizabeth Howen born 4th month.
Elizabeth of Francis & Mary Hudson born 13th day 8th month.
George Hunne died 4th month.
Samuel of Edmund & Susan Jacklin born 19th day 2d month.
Mary of James & Margaret Kade born 4th day 8th month.
Elizabeth of William & Elizabeth Kirby born 20th day 10th month.
Hudson son of John Leverit born 3rd day 3rd month.
Mary of Francis & Alice Loyall born 14th day 12th month.
John of Ralph Mason born 15th day 8th month.
John of John & Christian Milom horn 18th day 7th month.
Elizabeth of Benjamin & Elizabeth Negoos born 14th day 2nd month.
Elisha of John & Margaret Odlin born 1st day 5th month.
Jonathan son of Nicolas & Anne Parker born 1st day 12th month.
Elizabeth of Thomas & Katherine Painter died 24th — 2nd month.
Richard Tuttle died 8th — 3rd month.
Moses of Gamaliel & Grace Waite born 7th month.
Joseph of Thomas & Rebecca Wheeler born 15th — 3rd month.
Elizabeth of Nathaniel & Mary Williams born 21st — 8th month.
John of Alexander & Elizabeth Baker born 20th — 4th month.
James of Henry & Alice Stevens born 10th — 2nd month.
Hannah of William & —— Pell born 14th —— 11th month.
John cf David & Sarah Phippeni born and died 5th month.

---

[1] Only found in second MS., the bottom of leaf of oldest MS. being worn away. -- W. S. A.

Pedajah son of Philemon & Susan Pormort born 3rd — 4th month.
Margery wife of Richard Sanford died.
Thomas of Thomas & Faith Savage horn 28th -- 3rd month.
Elizabeth of Robert & Elizabeth Scott born 10 — 10th month.
Samuel of John & Grace Seaberry born 10th — 10th month.
Hannah of William & Anne Semond born 7th month.
Mary of Walter & Mary Sinet born 19th — 9th month.
John of John & Dorothy Synderland born 10th month.
Sarah of Robert & Penelope Turner born 11th — 1st month.

### First Church.

| | | |
|---|---|---|
| John of Thomas Buttall | 1 day | 1 mo. |
| Elizabeth of John Olyvar | 8 day | 1 mo. |
| Philip of Samuel Sherman, born 31st day 10 mo. 1637 | 8 day | 1 mo. |
| Martha of Samuel Sherman born 5th day 7th mo. 1639 | 8 day | 1 mo. |
| Seth of Arthur Purye | 15 day | 1 mo. |
| Samuel of Francis East | 15 day | 1 mo. |
| John of John Cotton, our Teacher | 22 day | 1 mo. |
| Elkanah son of Richard Cooke | 12 day | 2 mo. |
| Elizabeth of Hugh Gunnyson | 19 day | 2 mo. |
| Samuel of Edmund Jacklyn | 26 day | 2 mo. |
| Elizabeth of William Salter | 26 day | 2 mo. |
| Beleive son of Richard Gridley | 3 day | 3 mo. |
| Hudson son of John Leveritt. aged 8 days | 10 day | 3 mo. |
| Joseph of Thomas Wheelar | 10 day | 3 mo. |
| Thomas of Thomas Savage | 17 day | 3 mo. |
| Ephraim & Deliverance of Alexander Becke | 7 day | 4 mo. |
| Elisha of John Audlyn | 5 day | 5 mo. |
| Naomi dautr of William Copp | 5 day | 5 mo. |
| Cornelius of Thomas Clarke | 19 day | 5 mo. |
| Elizabeth of Zachariah Bosworth | 26 day | 5 mo. |
| Isaac of Johanna & Isaac Willey | 2 day | 6 mo. |
| Sarah of Edward Dennys | 9 day | 6 mo. |
| Benjamin of Anthony Stoddard. aged 11 days | 23 day | 6 mo. |
| Jonathan of William Copp | 23 day | 6 mo. |
| Moses of Gamaliel Wayte | 23 day | 6 mo. |
| Hannah of Maudett Inglys born. 2d 1st mo. 1639 | 6 day | 7 mo. |
| Hannah of Marie & Edward Tinge, born 7d 1st mo. 1640 | 6 day | 7 mo. |
| John of John Mylam | 13 day | 7 mo. |
| Thomas of Thomas Painter, born 4th day 3rd mo. 1639 | 13 day | 7 mo. |
| Sarah of Abigail & John Jackson born about middle 6th mo. 1639 | 13 day | 7 mo. |
| Hannah of John Hurde | 20 day | 7 mo |
| Elizabeth of Nathaniel Willyams | 18 day | 8 mo. |
| Elizabeth of Robert Scott. aged 13 days | 13 day | 10 mo. |
| Hannah of William Pell. aged 7 days old | 20 day | 10 mo. |
| Samuel & Habakuk, of William Beamsley aged about 14 days | 7 day | 12 mo. |
| Elizabeth of Margaret & Thomas Fowle | 14 day | 12 mo. |
| Mary of Francis Lysle, aged, about 4 days | 14 day | 12 mo. |

## 1641.

### Town.

Samuel of Wm & Anne Beamsley died the 2nd month.
Habbakuk son of Wm & Anne Beamsley died the 2d month.
Tabitha of Tho: Bell born 24th day (1st) month.
Hopefor son of Edw: & Marah Bendall born 7th day (8th) month.
Hannah of Nehemiah & Hannah Bourne born 10th day (9th) month.
Samuel of Zaccheus & Anne Bosworth born 4th day (1st) month.
Ezekiel of George & Anne Burden born 28 day 1st month.
Mary of Richard & Anne Carter born 3rd day 5th month.
Sarah daughter of John & Joan Cole born 15 day (11th month.
Elkanah son of Richard & Elisabeth Cooke born 14 day 2d month.

Rebecca of Wm & Goodith Cop born 6 day 3d month.
Mariah of John & Sarah Cotton 16th day 12th month.
Deliverance of John & Alice Crabtree born 3d day 7th month.
Susannah of Jacob Eliot born 22 day 5th month.
John of Thomas & Margaret Fowle born 1st day 5th month.
John of Edward & Margaret Gibbons born 30th day 1st month.
Elizabeth of Benjamin & Anne Gillom born the 11th month.
Samuel of Thomas Grub — born 5th day 10th month.
Thomas of William & Joane Harvie born 18th day 10th month.
Elizabeth of Valentine & Francis Hill born 12th day 10th month.
Mary of Richard Hogge born ———
Hannah of Wm & Anne Hudson born 16th day 2d month & died 20th day 3d month.
Richard of William & Susan Hudson died 26th day 8th month.
Abigail of John & Abigail Jackson born 24th day 6th month.
John of Thomas & Joan Joy born 10th day 8th month.
John of John & Anne Kenrick born 3rd day 8th month.
John of John Leverit born 1st day 4th month.
Samuel of Robert & Elizabeth Meere born 7th day 4th month.
Hope son of Mingo. a neger born 19th day 3rd month.
John of Henry Messenger born 25th day 1st month.
Benjamin of Benjamin & Elizabeth Negoos born 7th month.
John of John & Margaret Odlin born 3rd day 12th month.
Hannah of John & Elizabeth Oliver born 3rd day 1st month.
Abiel son of Nicholas & Anne Parker born 15th day 11th month.
Sarah of Richard & Anne Parker born 8th day 5th month.
Abigail of Bartholomew & ——— Pasmer born 4th month.
William Pierce died 13th — 5 month.
Katherine wife of Thomas Painter died.
Nathan of Edward & Elizabeth Rainsford born 6th month.
Joshua of Joshua & Lydia Scotto born 30th — 7th month. & soon after buried.
Thomas of Thomas & Johan Scotto born 4th month & then buried.
Jonathan of David & Susanna Sellick born 20th— 3rd month.
Deliverance of Miles & Sarah Terne born 30th —7th month.
Jane of Evan & Jane Thomas born 16th — 3rd month.
Bethiah daughter of William & Elizabeth Ting born 17th — 3rd month.
Mary of Edward & Mary Ting born 17th — 2nd month.
Hannah of William & Hannah Townsend born 4th — 2nd month.
Mary of John & Mary Vyall born 30th — 9th month.
Hannah of Richard & Elizabeth Waite born 14th — 7th month.
Moses of Gamaliel & Grace Waite died 7th month.
Samuel of Gamaliel & Grace Waite born. ———.
Sarah of Robert & ———Walker born 15th 9th month.
Joseph of Robert & — Williams born 5th month.
Waite-still son of John & Elizabeth Winthrop born 27th —12th month.
John of Richard & Mary Woodhouse born 9th — 2nd month.
Joseph of Robert and Rachel Woodward born 24th —8th month.
Job son of Job & Sarah Judkins born 30th —4th month & died 4th month.
Thomas of Angel & Catherine Hollard born 7th —3rd month & lived 20 weeks.
Hannah of John & Elizabeth Oliver born 3rd — 1st month.

### FIRST CHURCH.

| | | |
|---|---|---|
| Thomas of Edmund Jackson | 7 day | 1 mo. |
| Sarah of Robert Turner | 14 day | 1 mo. |
| Tabetha of Anne & Thomas Bell | 4 day | 2 mo. |
| Hannah of William Townsend | 11 day | 2 mo. |
| Jonathan son & ⎫ of Thomas & | 11 day | 2 mo. |
| Eunice daut' ⎭ Elizabeth Tart, member of Ch. of Sittuate. | | |
| John of Edward Gibbon | 18 day | 2 mo. |
| Elizabeth of Matthew Ines | 18 day | 2 mo. |
| Abigail of Griffyn Bowen | 18 day | 2 mo. |
| Ezekiel of George Burdon | 25 day | 2 mo. |

| | | |
|---|---|---|
| Hannah of William Hudson the younger | 25 day | 2 mo. |
| John of Sarah & Henry Messinger | 25 day | 2 mo. |
| Mary of Edward Tinge | 2 day | 3 mo. |
| Hopestill dautr of John Vyall | 9 day | 3 mo. |
| Jane of Evan Thomas | 16 day | 3 mo. |
| Bathinh of William Tinge | 23 day | 3 mo. |
| Samuel of Eliz^b. & Robert Mears | 13 day | 4 mo. |
| John of Robert Howyn | 20 day | 4 mo. |
| John of John Leveritt, aged about 4 days | 4 day | 5 mo. |
| John of Margaret & Thomas Fowle. aged about 10 days | 11 day | 5 mo. |
| Sarah of Richard Parker aged 2 days | 11 day | 5 mo. |
| Susanna of Jacob Elyott. aged about 6 days | 22 day | 5 mo. |
| Mary of Richard Hogge aged about 6 days | 22 day | 5 mo. |
| Nathan of Edward Ransford. aged about 8 days | 1 day | 6 mo. |
| Samuel & } of Sarah & Job Judkyn. | 15 day | 6 mo. |
| Job } | 15 day | 6 mo. |
| Abraham of Hannah & Thomas Hawkins. aged about 4 yrs. 30 wks | 22 day | 6 mo. |
| Hannah daut } of Hannah & Thomas, aged about 30 wks | 22 day | 6 mo. |
| Job son, } Hawkins aged about 30 wks | 22 day | 6 mo. |
| Abigail of Abigail & John Jackson aged about 5 days | 29 day | 6 mo. |
| Hannah of Richard Wayte, aged about 6 days | 12 day | 7 mo. |
| Melita of Thomas Snow, aged about 3 years | 12 day | 7 mo. |
| Deliverance of Sarah & Myles Tarne aged about 8 days | 19 day | 7 mo. |
| Samuel of Johanna & Thomas Jay, aged about 1 yr. 7 mos | 19 day | 7 mo. |
| Elizabeth of Wentworth Day aged about 8 days | 26 day | 7 mo. |
| Elizabeth of Henry Shrimpton. aged 10 days | 3 day | 8 mo. |
| Elizabeth of James Everill aged 3 days | 3 day | 8 mo. |
| John of John Kenricke aged 2 days | 3 day | 8 mo. |
| John of Joan & Thomas Jay. aged about 8 days | 17 day | 8 mo. |
| Mary of Anthony Harker aged about 5 days | 17 day | 8 mo. |
| Hoptfor son of Edward Bendall. aged about 2 days | 31 day | 8 mo. |
| Samuel of Gamaliel Wayt. aged about 7 days | 7 day | 9 mo. |
| Joseph of Rachel & Robert Woodward | 7 day | 9 mo. |
| Hannah of Nehemiah Burne from the Ch. of Dorchester aged about 3 days | 14 day | 9 mo. |
| Elisha of Edward Hutchinson the younger. aged about 13 days | 28 day | 9 mo. |
| Sarah of Robert Walker aged about 6 days | 28 day | 9 mo. |
| Elihu of William Wardall | 5 day | 10 mo. |
| Mary of John Vyoll | 5 day | 10 mo. |
| Samuel of Thomas Grubb. aged about 8 days | 12 day | 10 mo. |
| Elizabeth of Valentine Hill. aged about 6 days | 19 day | 10 mo. |
| Nathaniel of Samuel Sherman. aged about 12 days | 19 day | 10 mo. |
| Elizabeth of Benjamin Gillam, aged 4 days | 9 day | 11 mo. |
| John of Edward Bates, aged about 14 days | 23 day | 11 mo. |
| John of John Audlyn, aged about 7 days | 13 day | 12 mo. |
| Maria of John Cotton our teacher aged about 5 days | 20 day | 12 mo. |

## 1642.

### TOWN.

Tremble son of Richard & Grace Gridley born 14th day 1st month.
Joseph of Francis & Alice Loyall born 14th day 1st month.
Nathaniel of Francis & Isabel Baker born 27 day of 1st month.
Thomas of Thos Bell born 3 day (6th month.
Joseph of Nathaniel & Alice Bishopp. born 14 day (5th) month.
Hannah of Wm Briggs born & buried 28 day (6th) month.
Daniell of Wm Brisco died the 3 month.
Abigail of Tho: & Anne Buttolph born 18 day (12th) month.
Joseph of Richard & Elizabeth Cooke born 1st day 3d month.
Jacob of Thomas Clark born in 3d month.
John of Wm Courser born 8th day 3d month.
Trine son of Wm & Mary Davies born 10th day 6th month.
Josebeth dau. of James & Joanna Davies born 20 day 6 month.

Mary of Edmund & Sarah Dennis born 4th month.
Elizabeth of Francis & Katherine Douse born 20 day 6 month.
Mary of Francis & Mary East born 25 day 1st month.
Deborah of Gabriel & Elizabeth Fish born 20th day 10th month.
John of Ralph Greene born 22nd day 10th month.
Isaac of Edmund & Katherine Grosse born 1st day 8th month.
Deborah. of Hugh and Elizabeth Gunnison born in 8th month.
Joseph of John & Prudence Guttridge horn 1st day 8th month.
Isaac of Abraham & Elizabeth Hagborne born 3rd day 8th month.
Mehetabel of George & Elizabeth Halsall. born 15th day 9th month.
Joanna of George & Jane Harwood born 10th day 10th month.
Mary of George & Anne Hide born 3rd day 6th month.
Israel of Robert & Elizabeth Howen was born ————
Thomas of Thomas & Joan Joy born 3rd day 1st month ————
Elizabeth of William & Elizabeth Kirby died 12th day 5th month.
Samuel of Richard & Dinah Knight born 18th day 12th month.
Jacob of John & Elizabeth Ferniside born 28th day 5th month.
Mary of John & Jane Lugg born 6th month.
Eleasaph son of John & Christian Milom born 30th day 7th month.
John of Arthur & Elizabeth Perry born 26th — 2nd month.
Hannah of Peter & Alice Plaise born 20th — 11th month.
Susan wife of Philemon Pormort died 29th — 10th month.
Patience of Robert & Elizabeth Rice born 1st — 2nd month & buried 8th —
  2nd month.
Nathaniel of Simon & ———— Rogers born 14th — 12th month.
Mary of Robert & Elizabeth Scott born 28th — 12th month.
Thomas of Thomas & Joan Scotto born 1st month & then buried.
Elizabeth of John & Mary Seavorne born 21st — 8th month.
Nathaniel of Samuel & Grace Sherman born 19th — 10th month.
Elizabeth of Walter & Mary Sinet born 23rd — 4th month.
Ebenezer of John & Elizabeth Spur born 3rd — 3rd month.
Thomas of Thomas & Martha Stanberry born 15th ——— 8th month.
John of Anthony & Mary Stanion born 16th — 5th month.
Mary of John & Dorothy Synderland born 12th — 1st month.
Dorcas daughter of Evan & Jane Thomas born 5th — 12th month, & died
  the 28th — 12th mo.
Deborah of Benjamin & Deborah Thwing born 17th — 3rd month & died 6th
  month.
Mercie daughter of William & Elizabeth Ting horn 13th — 11th month.
Joshua of Alexander & Elizabeth Baker born 30th — 2nd month.
Deborah of Cotton & Jane Flack buried 3rd month.
Hester of William & Hester Hilyard born 25th — 1st month.
Hephtzibah daughter of Angel & Catherine Hollard born 10th — 6th
  month.
John of Peter & Margaret Henrickson born 22nd — 12th month.
Mary of William and Mary Salter born 10th — 6th month.
Jonathan of Edward & Mary Ting born 15th — 10th month.
Peter of William & Hannah Townsend born 26th — 8th month.
John of Robert & Penelope Turner horn 1st — 10th month.
Elihu son of William & Alice Werdall born 9th month.
Nathaniel of Nathaniel & Mary Williams born 16th — 7th month.
Jacob of Robert & Joan Wing born 31st — 5th month.
Nathaniel of Robert & Rachel Woodward born ? 30th — 8th month.
Samuel of Richard & Dinah Knight born 9th — 11th month.
Joseph of Henry & Alice Stevens born 1st — 7th month.
Hannah of William and Mary Briggs born 6th month.
John of William & Joanna Francklin born 14th — 5th month.
Sarah of Robert & Sarah Willis born 10th — 11th month.

### First Church.

| | | |
|---|---|---|
| Waitstill of John Winthropp, the younger aged about 8 days | 6 day | 1 mo. |
| Hannah of John Oliver, aged about 4 days | 6 day | 1 mo. |
| Hannah of Johanna & Isaac Willey | 6 day | 1 mo. |

| | | |
|---|---|---|
| Abiah son of Nicholas Parker, from the Ch. of Roxbury aged about 9 wks | 27 day | 1 mo. |
| Mary of Francis East, aged about 3 days | 27 day | 1 mo. |
| Mary of Samuel Grame, aged about 3 years | 27 day | 1 mo. |
| Thomas of Thomas Scottoe, aged 1 day | 10 day | 2 mo. |
| Joseph of Robert Williams | 17 day | 2 mo. |
| John of John Underhill aged about 13 days | 24 day | 2 mo. |
| John of Arthur Pury. aged about 3 days | 1 day | 3 mo. |
| Samuel of Richard Chichley | 1 day | 3 mo. |
| Joseph of Richard Cooke. aged about 6 days | 8 day | 3 mo. |
| Ebenezer of John Spurre aged about 6 days | 8 day | 3 mo. |
| John of William Courser aged about 4 days | 8 day | 3 mo. |
| Jacob of Thomas Clarke, aged about 5 days | 22 day | 3 mo. |
| Samuel of Sarah & John Seaberry, aged about 1 yr 6 mos | 22 day | 3 mo. |
| Strange of Alexander Becke, aged about 5 days | 5 day | 4 mo. |
| Marie of Edward Dennys. aged about 6 days | 3 day | 5 mo. |
| Elizabeth of Anne & John Stockbridge. member of Ch. of Situate aged about 2 yrs. 6 mos | 10 day | 5 mo. |
| John of John Hurd, aged about 4 days | 17 day | 5 mo. |
| Elizabeth of Francis Dowse aged about 2 days | 17 day | 5 mo. |
| John of Anthony Stanyon member of Ch. of Exeter aged about 6 days | 24 day | 5 mo. |
| Anne of Samuel Poole aged about 8 days | 7 day | 6 mo. |
| Thomas of Anne & Thomas Bell, aged about 9 days | 7 day | 6 mo. |
| Hannah of Richard Bellingham aged about 7 days | 14 day | 6 mo. |
| Israel of Robert Howin aged about 7 days | 14 day | 6 mo. |
| Phœbe of Phœbe & William Blanton aged about 5 days | 21 day | 6 mo. |
| Johoshabeath dau of James Davisse, aged about 8 days | 28 day | 6 mo. |
| Nathaniel of Nathaniel Williams, aged about 6 days | 25 day | 7 mo. |
| Deborah of Hugh Gunnyson, aged about 7 days | 25 day | 7 mo. |
| Mary of Jane & John Lugg, aged about 4 days | 25 day | 7 mo. |
| Isaac of Abraham Hackborne, aged about 7 days | 2 day | 8 mo. |
| Joseph of John Guttrige, aged about 8 days | 2 day | 8 mo. |
| Eleazer of John Mylam, aged about 4 days | 2 day | 8 mo. |
| John of Robert Winge, aged about 5 ys 3 mos | 16 day | 8 mo. |
| Hannah of Robert Winge, aged about 2 yrs. 8 mos | 16 day | 8 mo. |
| Jacob of Robert Winge, aged about 9 weeks | 16 day | 8 mo. |
| Peter of William Townsend, aged about 6 days | 30 day | 8 mo. |
| Mary of William Salter. aged about 3 days | 30 day | 8 mo. |
| Nathaniel of Rachel & Robert Woodward. aged about 4 days | 30 day | 8 mo. |
| Joseph of William Wilson aged about 5 days | 13 day | 9 mo. |
| John of Robert Turner aged about 4 days | 4 day | 10 mo. |
| Deborah of Gabriel Fish from the Ch. of Exeter. aged about 8 days | 11 day | 10 mo. |
| Jonathan of Edward Tinge aged about 4 days | 18 day | 10 mo. |
| Mehetabell of George Halsall from the Ch. of Dorchester aged about 13 days | 1 day | 11 mo. |
| Mercy of William Ting aged about 14 days | 5 day | 12 mo. |
| Dorcas of Evan Thomas, aged about 11 days | 5 day | 12 mo. |
| Thomas of Matthew Ines. aged about 18 days | 5 day | 12 mo. |
| Samuel of Richard Knight, aged about 4 days | 12 day | 12 mo. |
| Abigail of Thomas Buttall, aged about 2 days | 19 day | 12 mo. |

## 1643.

### Town.

Lidia daughter of Roger and Sarah Amadowne born 27th day of 2nd month.
John of George & Anna Balden died the 6th month.
George Barrell died 11th day of 7th month.
Joseph & Benjamin sons of George & Anne Burden born 1 day 2d month & died in 2d mo.
John of John and Joan Cole born 17 day 9th month.

John Cooke died 3d month.
Ruth of Wm Copp born 24th day 9th month.
Deliverance of John & Alice Crabtree died in 4th month.[1]
Joseph son of Richard & Alice Croychley born 3rd day 3d month.[1]
Elizabeth of Nathaniel & Elizabeth Eaton born 13 day 8 month.
Mary of Daniel & Elizabeth Fairefield born 7th day 5 months.[1]
Lidia daugtr of Richard & Lidia Floud.
Margaret of Thomas & Margaret Fowle born 13th day 2d month.
Elizabeth daughter of Strong & Ellenor Furnell, born 7th day 3d month.
John of Robt. & Mary Garret born 2d day of 4th month.
Mehetabel of George & Elizabeth Halsall died in October.
Hope daughter of Thomas & Hannah Hawkins born 2d day 2nd month.
Elizabeth of Valentine & Francis Hill died. 9th day 2nd month.
Elizabeth Haugh vx: Atherton Haugh died 14th day 8th month.
Jeremy of Jeremy & Esther Houtchin born 20th day 2nd month & died soon
    after.
Mary of Francis & Mary Hudson born 18th day 6th month.
Lidia of James & Anne Hudson born 27th day 2d month.
Hannah of William & Anne Hudson born 12th day 1st month.
Joseph of William & Patience Wilson born 10th — 9th month.
Hannah of Richard & Mary Woodhouse born 15th — 1st month.
Hannah of William & Anne Beamsley born 10th month.
John of Garret & Mary Bourne born 30th — 5th month & died 30th — 6th
    month.
Peter of William & Mary Bridg born 11th mo.
John of Richard & Joan Hogg born 4th — 1st month.
Anne of Edward & Katherine Hutchinson born 18th — 9th month.
Joel of Job & Sarah Judkins born 30th — 7th month.
Samuel of Richard & Dinah Knight buried 25th — 7th month.
John of John & Abigail Manning born 25th — 3rd month.
John of Abel & Anne Porter born 27th — 9th month.
Onesimus son of John & Sarah Stevenson born 26th — 10th month.
Susannah of Edmund & Susan Jacklin born 27th day 2d month and died
    10th day 8th month.
John of John & Abigail Jackson born 26th day 4th month.
Samuel of Edmund & Martha Jackson born 27th day 4th month.
Thomas of Matthias & Anne Ijons born 18th day 4th month.
Margaret wife of James Johnson died 28th day 1st month.
Hannah of John Leverit born 16th day 2nd month.
Thomas of Christopher & Elizabeth Lawson born 4th day 3rd month.
Sarah of Henry Messenger born 12th day 1st month.
Mary of Benjamin & Elizabeth Negoos. born 7th day 8th month.
Joseph of Nicholas & Anne Parker born 26th day 1st month.
John of John & Elizabeth Pierce born 16th — 4th month.
Elizabeth of John & Elizabeth Pierce born 16th — 4th month.
John of Abel & Anne Porter born 27th — 9th month.
Henry Poole died 14th — 7th month.
Hannah of Thomas & Faith Savage born 28th — 4th month.
Joshua of Joshua & Lydia Scotto born 12th — 6th month.
John of David & Susanna Sellick born 21st — 2nd month.
Jonathan of Sampson & Abigail Shoreborne born 12th — 4th month.
John of Walter & Mary Sinet born 10th — 5th month.
Mr. Symons buried 14th — 7th month.
Sarah of Robert & ———— Walker buried 19th — 10 month.
Rebecca of Thomas & Rebecca Wheeler born 17th — 4th month.
Phebe of Richard Williams born 6th mo.
Sarah of Thomas & Sarah Webber born ————
Benjamin of William & Joanna Francklin born 12th — 8th month.
Sarah of Bezaleel & Mary Paiton born 9th — 6th month.
Samuel of Thomas & Elizabeth Werdall born 16th — 3rd month
Adam of Henry & Mary Walton born 8th — 3rd month.

---

[1] Only found in second MS., the bottom of leaf of oldest MS. being worn away. — W. S. A

FIRST CHURCH.

| | | |
|---|---|---|
| Mary of Robert Scott, aged about 6 days | 5 day | 1 mo. |
| John of Jane & George Harwood, aged about 3 yrs. 8 mos | 5 day | 1 mo. |
| Johanna of Jane & George Harwood. aged about 14 wks | 5 day | 1 mo. |
| Sarah of Sarah & Henry Messenger aged about 6 days | 12 day | 1 mo. |
| Jeremiah of Jeremiah Howchen member of Ch. of Dorchester | 12 day | 1 mo. |
| Thomas of Joan & Thomas Jay. aged about 10 days | 12 day | 1 mo. |
| Samuel of Zachariah Bosworth, aged about 6 days | 12 day | 1 mo. |
| Nathaniel of Simon Rogers, member of Ch. of Concord aged about 20 days | 12 day | 1 mo. |
| Hannah of William Hudson the younger. aged about 8 days | 19 day | 1 mo. |
| Hannah of Alice & Peter Place, aged about 8 wks | 19 day | 1 mo. |
| Joseph of Francis Lysle, aged about 4 days | 26 day | 1 mo. |
| Joseph of Susan & Sylvester Evylith. aged about 1 yr & 9 mos | 26 day | 1 mo. |
| Tremble son of Richard Gridley. aged about 7 days | 2 day | 2 mo. |
| Hope of Hannah & Thomas Hawkins, aged about 8 days | 9 day | 2 mo. |
| Marie of Thomas Fowle. aged about 4 days | 16 day | 2 mo. |
| John of John Sinderland, aged about 2 yrs. 6 mos | 16 day | 2 mo. |
| Marie of John Sinderland, aged about 1 yrs. 6 wks | 16 day | 2 mo. |
| John of Susan & David Sellick. aged about 3 days | 23 day | 2 mo. |
| Hannah of John Leveritt. aged about 8 days | 23 day | 2 mo. |
| Lydia of Anne & James Hudson. aged about 6 days | 23 day | 2 me. |
| Lydia of Roger & Sarah Hannadowne member of Ch. of Waymouth. aged about 6 days | 23 day | 2 mo. |
| Joseph of George Burden, aged about 8 days | 30 day | 2 mo. |
| John of Anthony Harker, aged about 10 days | 30 day | 2 mo. |
| Susannah of Edmund Jacklyn, aged about 5 days | 30 day | 2 mo. |
| Hannah of Anne (now Porter) & William Simmons. aged about 2 yrs. 8 mos. | 30 day | 2 mo. |
| Joseph of Richard Critchley aged about 4 days | 7 day | 3 mo. |
| Joseph of Nicholas Parker aged about 6 weeks | 14 day | 3 mo. |
| Elizabeth of Strong Furnell aged about 6 days | 14 day | 3 mo. |
| Mary of Mary & Richard Woodhouse, aged about 4 yrs 4 mos | 14 day | 3 mo. |
| John of Mary & Richard Woodhouse, aged about 2 yrs. 5 wks | 14 day | 3 mo. |
| Elizabeth of Benja. Negoose aged about 3 yr. 2 mos | 11 day | 4 mo. |
| Benjamin of Benjamin Negoose aged about 1 yr. 7 mos | 11 day | 4 mo. |
| Jonathan of Samson Shore aged about 7 days | 18 day | 4 mo. |
| Deborah of Mary & Francis Hudson | 18 day | 4 mo. |
| Elizabeth of Mary & William Burnell | 18 day | 4 mo. |
| John of Alice & Henry Stevens, aged about 5 yrs. 9 mos | 18 day | 4 mo. |
| James of Alice & Henry Stevens, aged about 3 yrs 10 weeks | 18 day | 4 mo. |
| Joseph of Alice & Henry Stevens, aged about 9 mos. 3 weeks | 18 day | 4 mo. |
| Samuel of Henry Shrimpton, aged about 26 days | 25 day | 4 mo. |
| Rebecca of Thomas Wheeler, aged about 9 days | 25 day | 4 mo. |
| Samuel of Edmund Jackson, aged about 6 days | 2 day | 5 mo. |
| John of Abigail & John Jackson, aged about 6 days | 2 day | 5 mo. |
| Hannah of Thomas Savage, aged about 5 days | 2 day | 5 mo. |
| Jarratt of Jarratt Burne, aged about 26 days | 6 day | 6 mo. |
| Wentworth of Wentworth Day, aged about 6 days | 13 day | 6 mo. |
| Sarah of Bezaliel & Mary Payton, she sometime called Mary Grenow from the Ch. of Sandwitch | 13 day | 6 mo. |
| Joshua of Joshua Scottoe, aged about, 7 days | 20 day | 6 mo. |
| Mary of Mary & Francis Hudson, aged about 5 days | 20 day | 6 mo. |
| Phœbe of Robert Williams, aged about 8 days | 3 day | 7 mo. |
| Joel of Sarah & Job Judkyn, aged about 9 days | 17 day | 7 mo. |
| More Mercy of Edward Bendall. aged about 2 days | 24 day | 7 mo. |
| Solomon of Anthony Stoddard aged about 4 days | 1 day | 8 mo. |
| Elizabeth of Nathaniel Heaton, aged about 3 days | 8 day | 8 mo. |
| Mary of Benjamin Negoose aged about 8 days | 8 day | 8 mo. |
| Hannah of Susan & Sylvester Evylith | 8 day | 8 mo. |
| Hannah of John Audlyn, aged about 8 days | 29 day | 8 mo. |
| Nathaniel of Richard Wayte. aged about 11 days | 5 day | 9 mo. |

Anne of Edward Hutchinson, the younger. aged about 2 days    19 day 9 mo.
John of Abel Porter, aged about 7 days    19 day 9 mo.
Ruth of William Copp. aged about 2 days    26 day 9 mo.
Hannah of William Beamesly aged about 4 days    17 day 10 mo.
Rowland of John Cotton, Teacher. aged about 6 days    24 day 10 mo.
Sarah of Peter Oliver, aged about 6 days    7 day 11 mo.
Thomas of Thomas Marshall. aged about 5 days    7 day 11 mo.
Elijah of John Kenricke, aged about 6 days    21 day 11 mo.
Deborah of Gamaliel Wayte, aged about 4 days    21 day 11 mo.
Jonathan of Samuel Sherman, aged about 3 days    11 day 12 mo.
John of Robert Turner born 28 day last 2nd. mo 1643    18 day 12 mo.

## 1644.

### TOWN.

Hannah of Capt. Thomas Hawkins born 8th month.
Hannah wife of Thomas Hawkins baker died 27th — 3rd month.
Joseph & Benjamin sons of Valentine & Frances Hill born 29th — 4th month & died 6th month.
Zebulun son of Nicholas Huet born 11th mo.
Mehetabel of Jeremy & Ester Houtchin born 4th month.
Deborah of James Hudson born 3rd — 8th month.
Mary of Francis & Mary Hudson born 22nd — 6th month.
Joseph of John & Mary Hurd born 10th — 7th month.
Timothy of George & Anne Hyde born 6th month.
Susan of Edmund & Susan Jacklin buried 1st — 8th month.
Rebecca of Matthew & Anne Jjons born 26th — 12th month.
Joseph of James & Abigail Johnson born & buried 27th — 7th month.
Jone daughter of Thomas & Anne Dutchfield born & buried 5th month.
Isaac of Isaac & Anne Addington born 22nd — 11th month.
James Alexander servant to Theodore Atkinson died 19th — 6th month.
Theodore of Theodore & Abigail Atkinson born 10th — 2nd month.
Hopestill daughter of Thomas & Anne Bel born the 2nd — 6th month.
Mary wife of Edward Bendall buried 3rd month.
Benjamin of Nathaniel & Alice Bishop born 31st — 3rd month.
John of William Bornell born 8th mo.
Mary wife of Garret Bourne 30th — 3rd mo.
Peniel son of Griffith & Margaret Bowen born 10th — 3rd month.
Moses of Robert & Martha Bradford born 2nd — 1st month.
Hannah of Alexander & Elizabeth Baker born 29th — 7th month.
Stephen of Stephen & Judith Winthrop born 7th — 9th month.
John of Robert and Rebecca Winsworth born 10th — 12th month.
John of Nathaniel & Mary Williams born 6th month.
Samuel of Edward & Elizabeth Weeden born 6th month.
William Webb buried 10th month.
Elizabeth of Robert & Joan Wing born 5th mo.
Smith of Robert & Rachel Woodward born 6th mo.
Elizabeth of David & Ursula Yale born 3rd month & died 30th — 6th month.
Hannah of Thomas & Milcah Snow born 2nd month.
Hannah of George & Susan Allen born 10th — 1st month.
Elizabeth of Lancelot & Judith Baker born 13th — 10th month.
Ebenezer of William & Phebe Francklin died 24th — 8th month.
Hannah Lathrop servant to Richard Waite died 30th — 9th month.
John of Richard & Abigail Lippincot born 6th — 9th month.
Abigail wife of John Manning buried 25th — 3rd month.
Mary of John & Abigail Manning born 3rd — 4th month.
Jacob of Ralph & Anne Mason born 12th — 2nd month.
James of Robert & Elizabeth Mers born 9th — 1st
Samuel of John Milom born 6th month.
Sarah of Joseph Phippeni born 11th mo.

John of William & Anne Pollard born 4th — 4th month.
Elizabeth of Peter & Alice Plaise born 29th — 7th month.
Sarah of Arthur & Elizabeth Perry born 30th — 9th month.
David of Edward & Elizabeth Rainsford born 7th month.
Deliverance of Henry & Sibla Sands born 6th month.
John of Thomas & Joan Scotto born 2nd — 3rd month.
Mary of John & Mary Severne born 15th — 7th month.
Jonathan of Sampson & Abigail Shore born 16 — 3rd month and buried
    3rd mo.
John of Francis & Elizabeth Smith born 30th — 6th month.
Hannah of John Synderland born 8th mo.
Mary of Thomas & Alice Spaule born 7th month.
John of Benjamin and Deborah Thwing born 21st — 9th month.
John of Robert & Elizabeth Turner buried 19th — 3rd month.
Joseph of Robert & Penelope Turner born 7th — 7th month.
Hannah of Thomas & Alice Venner born 11th month.
Jacob of Robert Walker born 21st — 1st mo.
Isaac of Isaac Walker born 7th month.
Mary of William Werdall born 2nd month.
Deborah of Cotton & Jane Fflack born 5th — 8th month
Hannah of John Gallop Junior born 14th — 6 month.
Thomas of Arthur Gill born 8th month.
Joseph of Benjamin & Ann Gillam born 7th month.
Susan of Edmund & Katherine Grosse born 6th month.
John of Thomas & Anne Grubb born ———— & died 6th month.
Elizabeth of Thomas & Anne Grubb born 5th month & died 8th month.
Joseph of George & Elizabeth Halsall born 3rd — 10th month.
Experience daughter of William & Joan Harvie born 4th — 1st month.
Mary of William & Mary Chadbourne born 10th month.
Benjamin of Richard & Elizabeth Cooke born 6th month.
John of Lawrence & Martha Douce born 8th month.
Mary of William & Mary Davies born 3rd — 8th month.
Martha of Edmund & Sarah Dennis born 1st — 3rd month.
Martha wife of Lawrence Douce buried 8th month.
John of William & Martha Dinsdale born 3rd month.
Elizabeth of Frances & Mary East born 1st — 9th month.
Marie of Madit & Joane Engles born 9th mo.
Robert of Robert & Deborah Ffen born 4th mo.
Abel of Gabriel & Elizabeth Ffish born 15t \ — 10th month.
Mary Ffitch servant to Richard Waite died 24th — 8th month.
Mary of William & Hester Hilyard born 7th — 4th month.
John of John & Elizabeth Oliver born 15th — 2nd month.
Mary of Thomas & Luce Saxton born 2nd — 11th month.
Elizabeth of Jacob & Margaret Sheafe born 1st — 8th month.
Seth of Robert & Margaret Woodmansey born 26th 1st month.
Thomas of Angell & Catherine Hollard born 8th — 8th month.

## FIRST CHURCH.

| | | |
|---|---|---|
| Hannah of Mary & Richard Woodhouse, aged about 5 days | 3 day | 1 mo. |
| Moses of Robert Bradford, aged about 10 days | 10 day | 1 mo. |
| John of Richard Hogge, aged about 7 days | 10 day | 1 mo. |
| Experience of Joan & William Harvy, aged about 7 days | 10 day | 1 mo. |
| Sarah of Arthur Clarke, aged about 7 days | 17 day | 1 mo. |
| Onesimus of John Stevenson, aged about 13 wks | 24 day | 1 mo. |
| Jacob of Robert Walker, aged about 4 days | 24 day | 1 mo. |
| James of Elizabeth & Robert Meares, aged about 4 days | 31 day | 1 mo. |
| Marie of William Wardall, aged about 9 days | 14 day | 2 mo. |
| John of John Oliver. aged about 7 days | 21 day | 2 mo. |
| Elisha of Nathaniel Woodward, aged about 6 days | 21 day | 2 mo. |
| Rich-Grace Simons of Henry Simons from the Ch. of South Hampton. aged about 3 days | 21 day | 2 mo. |
| Hannah of Thomas Snow. aged about 5 days | 21 day | 2 mo. |

| | | |
|---|---|---|
| Mary of Francis Dowse aged about 6 days | 21 day | 2 mo. |
| Theodore of Theodore Atkinson, aged about 9 days | 28 day | 2 mo. |
| John of Thomas Scottoe, aged about 4 days | 5 day | 3 mo. |
| Martha of Edward Dennys aged about 6 days | 5 day | 3 mo. |
| John of Robert Feilde aged about 4 days | 26 day | 3 mo. |
| Benjamin of Nathaniel Bushopp. aged about 3 days | 2 day | 4 mo. |
| John of John Vyoll, aged about 5 days | 2 day | 4 mo. |
| Deborah of William Pell aged about 6 days | 2 day | 4 mo. |
| Deborah of Thomas Clarke. aged about 6 days | 9 day | 4 mo. |
| Robert of Robert & Deborah Fenne, from the Ch. of Salem aged about 3 days | 16 day | 4 mo. |
| Joseph & Be'ijan'ii } of Valentine Hill aged about 4 days | 23 day | 4 mo. |
| Mehetabel of Jeremiah Howchin aged about 7 days | 30 day | 4 mo. |
| Elizabeth of Thomas Grubb. aged about 6 days | 30 day | 4 mo. |
| Hopestill daut' of Anne & Thomas Bell, aged about 3 days | 21 day | 5 mo. |
| John of Jane & John Lugg. aged about 2 days | 4 day | 6 mo. |
| Benjamin of Richard Cooke aged about 5 days | 4 day | 6 mo. |
| Smyth son of Rachel & Robert Woodward, aged about 5 days | 4 day | 6 mo. |
| Elizabeth of Robert Winge aged about 8 days | 4 day | 6 mo. |
| Elizabeth of Mary & John Seborne | 11 day | 6 mo. |
| Samuel of John Mylam, aged about 3 days | 18 day | 6 mo. |
| John of Nathaniel Willyams aged about 3 days | 18 day | 6 mo. |
| David of Edward Ransford aged about 3 days | 1 day | 7 mo. |
| Mary of Nicholas Baxter | 1 day | 7 mo. |
| Mary of John Winthropp jun aged about, 9 days | 15 day | 7 mo. |
| John of Robert Turnor. Shoemaker aged about 7 days | 15 day | 7 mo. |
| Joseph of Robert Turnor, Inholder. aged about 8 days | 15 day | 7 mo. |
| Joseph of John Hurde, aged about 7 days | 15 day | 7 mo. |
| Mary of Mary & John Seborne. aged about 7 days | 22 day | 7 mo. |
| Joseph of James Johnson, aged about 8 days | 29 day | 7 mo. |
| Hannah of John Sinderland | 29 day | 7 mo. |
| Elizabeth of Alice & Peter Place. aged about 7 days | 6 day | 8 mo. |
| Joseph of Benjamin Gillam. aged about 9 days | 13 day | 8 mo. |
| Deborah of Cotton Flacke aged about 8 days | 13 day | 8 mo. |
| Thomas of Arthur Gill. aged about 8 days | 20 day | 8 mo. |
| Deborah of Anna & James Hudson, aged about 8 days | 20 day | 8 mo. |
| Stephen of Stephen Winthrop, aged about 3 days | 10 day | 9 mo. |
| Hannah of Thomas Hawkins. aged about 1 day | 10 day | 9 mo. |
| Elizabeth of Francis East. aged about 4 day | 10 day | 9 mo. |
| John of Richard Lippincott. member of Ch. of Dorchester aged about 4 days | 10 day | 9 mo. |
| Thomas of Angell Hollard. member of Ch. of Waymouth aged about. 5 wks | 10 day | 9 mo. |
| Mary of Maudit Inglys aged about 4 days | 17 day | 9 mo. |
| Joseph of Thomas Bumstead. member of Ch. of Rocksbury aged about. 7 days | 24 day | 9 mo. |
| Mary of William Townsend. aged about 7 days | 24 day | 9 mo. |
| John of Benjamin Thwing aged about 7 days | 1 day | 10 mo. |
| James of Thomas Fowle aged about 5 days | 8 day | 10 mo. |
| Joseph of George Halsall | 8 day | 10 mo. |
| Sarah of Thomas Webber aged about 3 days | 8 day | 10 mo. |
| Sarah of Arthur Pury aged about 7 days | 15 day | 10 mo. |
| Abel of Gabriel Fish member of Ch. of Exeter. aged about 8 days | 23 day | 10 mo. |
| Joseph of Richard Webb. aged about 4 years | 12 day | 11 mo. |
| Nehemiah of Richard Webb aged about 3 years | 12 day | 11 mo. |
| Isaac of Isaac Addington. aged about 5 days | 26 day | 11 mo. |
| Samson of Samson Shore aged about 14 days | 26 day | 11 mo. |
| Anna of ——— Venner member of Ch. of Salem aged about 18 days | 2 day | 12 mo. |
| John of Mary & William Burnell | 2 day | 12 mo. |
| Sarah of Joseph Phippeny member of Ch. of Hingham. aged about 5 days | 9 day | 12 mo. |
| John of Rebecca & Robert Windsore. aged about 7 days | 16 day | 12 mo. |

## 1645.

### TOWN.

Rebecca of Henry & Sarah Linne born 15th — 12th month.
John of John & Sarah Marshall born 10th — 10th month.
Thomas of John & Elizabeth Oliver born 10th — 12th month.
Abraham of Abraham & Mary Page born 7th — 1st month.
Susan wife of Henry Pease buried 25th — 10th month.
Samuel of William & Anne Pollard born 24th — 11th month.
Isaac of Isaac & Susanna Walker died 30th — 8th month.
William of Henry & Mary Walton born 29th — 7th month.
Elizabeth of George & Mary Michell born 26th Aug.
Mary of Henry & Ellinor Shrimpton born 6th month.
Deborah of Henry & Alice Stevens born 25th — 2nd month.
John of John & Sarah Stevenson born 7th m.
John of Thomas Stanberry born 15th — 7th m.
Temperance wife of John Sweete died 11th mo.
Joseph of Richard & Alice Tapping born 30th — 7th month & died 14th — 8th
    mo.
Grace of William & Grace Toy born 23rd — 6th month.
Deliverance of Edward & Mary Tyng born 6th — 6th month.
John of Hezekiah & Frances Usher buried 10th month.
Elizabeth of Hezekiah & Frances Usher born 1st — 12th month.
Benjamin of Richard Williams born 6th mo.
Newgrace son of William Wilson buried 6th month.
John of Robert & Mary Wright buried 1st mo.
David of David & Ursula Yale born 18th — 7th month.
Posthumus son of Thos: & Anne Dutchfield born 6 month.
Thomas Dutchfield buried 24th day 2 month.
Elizabeth of Nicholas & Catherine Charlet born 15th — 5th month & buried 7th
    month.
Thomas of John & Susan Collens born 15th — 8th month.
Benjamin of Richard & Elizabeth Cooke buried 3rd month.
Joseph of Richard & Alice Critchley buried 6th month.
Alice the wife of Richard Critchley buried.
John of Lawrence & Martha Douce buried 6th month.
Thomas of William & Mary Davies born 3rd — 7th month.
John of George Dell born 8th month.
Ebenezer of Robert & Dorothy Moone born 7th — 8th month.
Faith of Thomas & Faith Munt born 24th — 2nd month.
Samuel of Benjamin & Elizabeth Negoos born 17th — 10th month.
Leonard Pitts servant of John Burrell died 13 Feb.
Ruth of William & Ruth Parson born 3rd — 8th month.
Timothy of Timothy Pront born 10th — 1st month.
Elisha of William Rex born 6th mo.
Ephraim of Thomas & Faith Savadge born 2nd — 5th month.
John of Robert Scott born & buried 6th mo.
Lydia of Joshua & Lydia Scotto born 5th month.
Nathaniel of David & Susan Selleck born 5th month.
Deborah of John & Mary Severne born 26th — 12th month & died 6th — 1st
    mo.
Hannah of Edmund & Susan Jacklin born 12th — 9th month.
Hannah of John Jackson born 2nd — 5th mo.
Jeremie of Edmund & Martha Jackson born 5th month.
Abigail of James & Abigail Johnson born 25th — 9th month.
Joseph of Thomas & Joan Joy born 1st — 2nd mo.
Sarah of Job & Sarah Judkin born 7th — 10th month.
Caleb of John & Mary Lake born 27th — 3rd mo.
Mary of Christopher & Elizabeth Lawson born 27th — 8th month.
Ester of William Ludkin buried 8th mo.
Joseph of Richard & Dinah Knight born 15th — 3rd month.
Simeon of Henry & Sarah Messenger born 1st month.
Elizabeth of George & Mary Michel born 20th — 6th month.

Amander of James & Mary Minort born 7th month.
Mary of Alexander & Mary Adams born 19th — 11th month.
Nathaniel of Theodore & Abigail Atkinson born 28th — 9th month.
Samuel of Godfrey & Sarah Armitage 7th — 8th month.
John of John & Mary Barrel born 6th month.
Hannah of John & Hannah Bateman born 10th — 1st month.
Manasseh of Alexander & Elizabeth Beck born 8th — 8th month.
Mary of William & Phebe Blantaine born 5th month.
John of John & Sarah Bodman born 6th month.
Sarah of Zaccheus & Anne Bosworth died 5th month.
James of James & Grace Browne born 7th month.
Martha of Robert & Martha Bradford born 9th — 9th month.
Benjamin of Nicholas & Anne Shapley born 7th month.
Abigail of William & Martha Beamsley born 8th — 12th month.
Mary wife of Wm. Burnell died 16th — 9th month.
John of John & Mary Barrell born 6th — 6th month.
John of Henry & Elizabeth Bridgham born 7th month.
Thomas of Thomas & Anne Bayes born 1st month.
Mary of William & Phebe Blantaine born 4th — 6th month.
John of Jonathan & Mary Baulston born 8 month.
Alice wife of Richard Critchley died 26th — 1st month.
Thomas Cook mariner died 12th month.
Hannah of Francis & Catherine Douce born 7th — 11th month.
Deborah of Robert & Deborah Fen born 15th — 11th month.
Caleb of Thomas & Hannah Rawlins born 8th — 1st month.
Lydia of Simon & Susan Rogers born 1st — 10th month.
Lydia of Joshua & Lydia Scotto born 30th — 4th month.
Sampson of Anthony Stoddard born 3rd — 10th month.
Stephen of Walter & Mary Sinet born 12th — 9th month.
Hopestill of Edward & Sarah Wells born 13th — 8th month.
Mary of Richard & Elizabeth Waite born 15th — 12th month.
Heman son of Thomas & Anne Grub born 21st — 12th month.
Mary of Mark & Avery Hannds born 15th — 12th month.
George Hide mariner died.
Susan of Francis & Mary Hudson born 15th — 10th month.
Samuel of John & Hannah Hanniford born 1st — 3rd month.
Joseph of William & Joan Harvie born 8th — 10th month.
James of Samuel & Isabel Hayward born 16th — 10th month.
Susan of James & Mary Hawkins born 13th — 12th month.
Sarah of Job Judkin born 3rd — 10th month.
Elisha of John & Anne Kenrick born 18th — 8th month.
Timothy son of Thomas & Mary Keisar born 15th — 12th month.
Susanna of Henry & Anna Largin born 16th — 11th month.
John of Edmund & Sarah Dennis born 18th — 12th month.
Posthumus son of Thomas and Anne Ditchfield born 6th month.
William of William Dugias born 1st — 2nd month.
Mehetabel of Jacob & Margerie Eliot born 2nd month.
Eliezer of William & Phebe Ffrancklin born 4th — 8th month & buried.
Marie of Strong & Elliner Ffurnell born 5th month.
Elizabeth wife of Hugh Gunnison died 25th — 11th month.
Mary Hammon servant to Mr. Cotton died 7th month.
Mary of Mark & Avery Hands born 15th — 12 month.
Rebecca of Thomas Hawkins baker born 28th — 5 month.
Frances wife of Valentine Hill died 17th — 12th month.
Jabesh son of William & Mary Salter born 6th month.

## FIRST CHURCH.

| | | |
|---|---|---|
| Rebecca of Matthew Ines aged about 4 days | 2 day | 1 mo |
| Newgrace of William Wilson aged about 4 days | 23 day | 1 mo |
| Timothy of Timothy Pront aged about 10 days | 23 day | 1 mo |
| Simeon of Sarah & Henry Messenger aged about 4 days | 23 day | 1 mo |
| Isaac of Edmund Grosse aged about 2 yrs 6 mos | 23 day | 1 mo. |
| Susannah of Edmund Grosse aged about 6 mos. | 23 day | 1 mo. |

| | | |
|---|---|---|
| Samuel of Lawrence Dowse aged about 2 yrs 14 wks | 23 day | 1 mo. |
| John of Lawrence Dowse aged about 22 wks | 23 day | 1 mo. |
| Mary of Elizabeth & George Orrys aged about 1 yr. 7 mos | 23 day | 1 mo. |
| Elizabeth of John Spoure aged about 6 days | 30 day | 1 mo. |
| Joseph of Joan & Thomas Jay aged about 13 days | 13 day | 2 mo. |
| Deborah of Alice & Henry Stevens aged about 3 days | 27 day | 2 mo. |
| Mehetabell of Jacob Elyott deacon aged about 9 days | 4 day | 3 mo. |
| Hannah of George Burden aged about 20 days | 4 day | 3 mo. |
| John of Thomas Rashley aged about 6 weeks | 18 day | 3 mo. |
| Joseph of Richard Knight aged about 4 days | 18 day | 3 mo. |
| Caleb of John Lake aged about 5 days | 1 day | 4 mo. |
| Rebecca, of Mary & Thomas Keysar aged about 4 yr. 7 mo | 15 day | 4 mo. |
| Thomas of Mary & Thomas Keysar aged about 2 yr. 5 wks | 15 day | 4 mo. |
| Mary of Anne & George Hyde aged about 2 yr. 10 mo. | 15 day | 4 mo. |
| Timothy of Anne & George Hyde aged about, 10 mo 2 wks | 15 day | 4 mo. |
| Lydia of Joshua Scottoe aged about 6 days. | 29 day | 4 mo. |
| Deliverance, of Edward Ting aged about 8 days · | 13 day | 5 mo. |
| Jeremiah of Edmund Jackson aged about 6 days | 20 day | 5 mo. |
| Elizabeth of Nicholas Charlett aged about 5 days | 20 day | 5 mo. |
| Ephraim of Thomas Savidge aged about 6 days | 27 day | 5 mo. |
| Nathaniel of David Sellick aged about 9 days | 27 day | 5 mo. |
| Sarah of Zacharias Bosworth aged about 3 days | 27 day | 5 mo. |
| Hannah of Abigail & John Jackson aged about 4 days | 27 day | 5 mo. |
| John of John Barrell aged about 3 days | 3 day | 6 mo. |
| Mary of William Blanton aged about 8 days | 3 day | 6 mo. |
| Mary of Henry Shrimpton aged about 13 days | 10 day | 6 mo. |
| Mary of Strong Furnell aged about 8 days | 10 day | 6 mo. |
| Jabez of William Salter aged about 8 days | 17 day | 6 mo. |
| John of Robert Scott aged about 4 days | 24 day | 6 mo. |
| Grace of William Toy aged about 3 days | 24 day | 6 mo. |
| Thomas of William Davisse aged about 5 days | 7 day | 7 mo. |
| James of James Browne aged about 8 days | 7 day | 7 mo. |
| John of Robert Willyams | 7 day | 7 mo. |
| Benjamin of Sarah & John Bodman | 7 day | 7 mo. |
| Joseph of Richard Topping aged about 4 days | 28 day | 7 mo. |
| John, of John Stevenson aged about 5 days | 28 day | 7 mo. |
| Eleazer of William Francklyn aged about 1 day | 5 day | 8 mo. |
| Sarah of Jane Stertt widow of William aged about 1 yr. 46 wks | 5 day | 8 mo. |
| Alexander of Alexander Baker aged about 9 yr² 9 mo⁵ | 5 day | 8 mo. |
| Samuel of Alexander Baker aged about 7 yr. 9 mo⁴ | 5 day | 8 mo. |
| John of Alexander Baker aged about 5 yr. 15 wk | 5 day | 8 mo. |
| Joshua, of Alexander Baker aged about 3 yr. 5 mo | 5 day | 8 mo. |
| Hannah, of Alexander Baker aged about 1 yr 6 days | 5 day | 8 mo. |
| Manasseh son of Alexander Beck aged about 5 days | 12 day | 8 mo. |
| Isaac of Isaac & Susanna Waker from the Ch. of Salem aged about 15 days | 12 day | 8 mo. |
| Ruth of William Parsons aged about 7 day | 12 day | 8 mo. |
| Samuel of Godfrey Armitage from the Ch. of Lynne aged about 6 day | 12 day | 8 mo. |
| Elisha of John Kenricke aged about 2 day | 19 day | 8 mo. |
| Martha of Robert Bradford aged about 8 days | 16 day | 9 mo. |
| John of Gamaliel Wayte aged about 3 days | 16 day | 9 mo. |
| Hannah of Edmund Jacklyn aged about 7 days | 16 day | 9 mo. |
| Abigail of James Johnson aged about 4 days | 30 day | 9 mo. |
| Nathaniel of Theodore Atkinson aged about 4 days | 30 day | 9 mo. |
| Mary of Mary & Edward Kibby aged about 5 yr. 7 mo 2 wks | 30 day | 9 mo. |
| James of Mary & Edward Kibby aged about 3 yr 6 mo. | 30 day | 9 mo. |
| Elisha of Mary & Edward Kibby aged about 10 mo. 10 d. | 30 day | 9 mo. |
| Thomas of Martha & Thomas Stanbury aged about 3 yr⁴. 7 wks | 30 day | 9 mo. |
| John of Martha & Thomas Stanbury aged about 1 yr. 11 wks | 30 day | 9 mo. |
| Samson of Anthony Stoddar aged about 5 day | 7 day | 10 mo. |
| Lydia of Simon Rogers aged about 4 day | 7 day | 10 mo. |
| John of Elizabeth formerly Lothrop now wife of John Skuddar | 7 day | 10 mo. |
| Sarah of Sarah & Job Judkyn aged about 8 days | 14 day | 10 mo. |

Joseph of Joan & William Harvy aged about 5 day      14 day 10 mo.
Joseph of Henry Bridghamaged about 8 days      14 day 10 mo.
Hannah of Mary & Francis Hudson aged about 7 days      21 day 10 mo.
Hannah of Robert Button from the Ch. of Salem aged about
     5 days      21 day 10 mo.
Samuel of Benjamin Negoose aged about 16 day      4 day 11 mo.
Hannah of Francis Dowse aged about 5 day      11 day 11 mo.
William of Edward Hutchinson jun aged about 1 day      18 day 11 mo.
Mary of Mary & Alexander Adams aged about 6 days      25 day 11 mo.
Deborah of Robert and Deborah Fenne from the Ch. of Salem
     aged about ½ day      8 day 12 mo.
Elizabeth of Hezekiah Usher from the Ch. of Cambridge aged
     about 7 day      8 day 12 mo.
Abigail of William Beamesley aged about 2 day      8 day 12 mo.
Timothy of Mary & Thomas Keysar aged about 5 day      15 day 12 mo.
Heman of Thomas Grubbe aged about 2 day      22 day 12 mo.
John of Edward Dennys aged about 5 day      22 day 12 mo.
Mary of Richard Wayte aged about 6 day      22 day 12 mo.

## 1646.

### TOWN.

Susanna of Samuel & Anna Davis born 4th **May.**
Thomas Werdall died 10th December.
Joseph of Robert & Sarah Walker born 5th month.
Susanna wife of Isaac Walker died 30th — 7th month.
John of Robert & Mary Wyar born 1st — 9th month.
Mary of Nathaniel & Mary Williams born 30 — 9th month.
John of Mr. Stephen Winthrope born 24th — 3rd month.
Joseph of Robert & Joanna Wing born 13th — 8th month.
Robert of Robert & Rachel Woodward born 14th — 9th month.
Cornelius of William & Elizabeth White born 7th — 11th month.
Mercy of Thomas & Ann Bell born 14th Jan.
John of Henry & Sibil Sandis born 28th — 6th month.
Joseph of Francis & Elizabeth Smith born 24th — 6th month.
Elizabeth of Thomas & Elizabeth Smith born 6th — 9th month.
Elizabeth of Thomas & Mary Spaule born 29th — 7th month.
John of John & Martha Shaw born 16th — 3rd month.
Daniel of Daniel & Lydia Turell born 16th — 6th month.
Benjamin of Robert & Penelope Turner born 6th — 1st month.
Rebecca of Edward & Mary Tyng born 23rd — 1st month.
James of William & Hannah Townsend born 15th — 11th month.
John of Richard & Mary Tailor born 2nd — 12th month.
Leah of William & Alice Werdall born 7th — 10th month.
Abigail of James & Abigail Johnson born 12th — 12th month.
Sarah of Arthur & Jane Kynde born 9th month.
Deborah of George & Jane Kenrick born 16th — 6th month.
Abigail of Richard & Abigail Lippincot born 17th — 11th month & died 9th —
     1st month.
Ebenezer of John & Christian Milom born 6th — 3rd month.
Sarah of Richard & Abigail Montague born 15th — 4th month & died 19th ---4th
     month.
Daniel of Dermin & Dinah Mahoonne born 4th — 10th month.
John of John & Judith Marble born 10th — 9th month.
John of George & Elizabeth Oris born 1st — 1st month.
Peter of John & Margaret Odlin born 2nd — 6th month.
Mary of Bezaleel & Mary Paiton born 7th — 3rd month.
Anne of Isaac & Ann Addington born 10th — 1st month.
Naomi daughter of George & Susan Allen born 26th — 10th month.
Manaoh son of John & Sarah Bodman born 6th — 1st month.
Mary of John & Mary Barrell born 16th — 1st month.
James of Richard & Penelope Bellingham born 2nd — 3rd month.
John of Nathaniel & Alice Bishop born 31st — 11th month.

Samuel of Nathaniel & Alice Bishop died 7th — 1st month.
Lydia of William & Goodith Copp born 5th month.
William of William & Anne Cotton born 31st — 3rd month.
Rachel of Thomas & Elizabeth Clarke born 6th — 5th month.
John of Hugh & Lydia Drury born 2nd — 3rd month.
Joseph of Peter & Alice Plaise born 19th — 8th month.
Elizabeth of Arthur & Elizabeth Perry born 28th — 11th month.
Abraham of Abraham & Mary Page died 30th — 1st month.
Jane of Thomas & Margaret Robinson born 16th — 7th month.
Mary of William & Grace Rex born 4th — 1st month.
Rebecca of Robert & Hannah Read born 29th — 7th month.
John of William & Susan Reade born 25th — 7th month.
Timothy of Robert & Eunice Roberts born 7th — 6th month.
James of John & Dorothy Synderland born 18th — 1st month.
Thomas of Thomas & Joan Scotto born 3rd — 1st month.
Nathan of Thomas & Martha Stanberry born 25th — 10th month.
David of Francis & Mary East born 26th — 11th month.
Joanna of Strong & Eleanor Furnel born 26th — 12th month.
Mary of John & Elizabeth Ferniside born 8th — 7th month.
Mary of Mark & Avery Hannds died 7th — 4th month.
Hannah of George & Elizabeth Halsall born 11th month.
Sarah of Angel & Catherine Hollard born 5th — 1st month.
James of James & Anne Hudson born 25th — 6th month.
Joseph of Edward & Eleanor Harrison born 20th — 3rd month.
Martha of Job & Frances Hawkins born 26th — 1st month.
Mary of Richard & Joan Hogg born 3rd — 11th month.
Ephraim of Thomas & Joan Joy born 7th — 12th month.
Sarah of Anthony & Mary Harker born 30th — 7th mo.

Herman Atwood & Ann Copp married 11th — 6th month.
John Tuttell was married to Mary Holyoacke dau. of Mr. Edward Hollyoacke
    of Lynne Feb. 10.

### FIRST CHURCH.

| | | |
|---|---|---|
| Mary of Peter Oliver aged about 8 days | 1 day | 1 mo. |
| Deborah of Mary & John Sebborne aged about 4 days | 1 day | 1 mo. |
| Thomas of John Oliver aged about 26 day | 8 day | 1 mo. |
| Abraham of Abraham & Mary Page from the Ch. of Braintree aged about 1 day | 8 day | 1 mo. |
| Elizabeth of William Duglas born 26d 6 mo. 1641 | 8 day | 1 mo. |
| Sarah of William Duglas born 8 day 2 mo. 1643 | 8 day | 1 mo. |
| William of William Duglas born 1 day 2 mo. 1645 | 8 day | 1 mo. |
| Elisha of Grace & William Bickes | 8 day | 1 mo. |
| John of John Leveritt aged about 5 days | 22 day | 1 mo. |
| Susanna of John Collens aged about 3 yr. 12 day | 5 day | 2 mo. |
| Thomas of John Collens aged about 7 mo. | 5 day | 2 mo. |
| Nathaniel of Nathaniel Woodward aged about 7 day | 12 day | 2 mo. |
| James of Richard Bellingham aged about 7 day | 10 day | 3 mo. |
| Ebenezer of John Mylam aged about 4 day | 10 day | 3 mo. |
| John of George Clifford | 10 day | 3 mo. |
| Mary of Bezaleel Payton aged about 8 days | 17 day | 3 mo. |
| John of Stephen Winthropp aged about 8 days | 31 day | 3 mo. |
| Mary of Samuel Davis aged about 26 days | 31 day | 3 mo. |
| John of Elizabeth & Francis Smith aged about 1 yr ¾ | 31 day | 3 mo. |
| Mary of Agnes & William Keayne aged about 7 yr & ½ | 31 day | 3 mo. |
| John of Agnes & William Keayne aged about 3 yr 10 mo. | 31 day | 3 mo. |
| Lucy of Abraham Hackborne aged about 4 days | 14 day | 4 mo. |
| Sarah of Abigail & Richard Mountague aged about 2 days | 28 day | 4 mo. |
| Samuel of Richard Davenport from the Ch. of Salem aged about 11 day | 5 day | 5 mo. |
| Peter of John Audley aged about 9 day | 12 day | 5 mo. |
| Rachel of Thomas Clarke aged about 6 day | 12 day | 5 mo. |
| Joseph of Robert Walker aged about 5 day | 19 day | 5 mo. |
| Samuel of Thomas Buttall aged about 3 day | 19 day | 5 mo |

| | | |
|---|---|---|
| Lydia of William Copp aged about 3 day | 9 day | 5 mo |
| Joseph of Valentine Hill aged about 8 day | 26 day | 5 mo. |
| Nathaniel of John Vyoll aged about 3 day | 26 day | 5 mo. |
| Timothy of Thomas Robert member of Ch. of Rocksbury aged about 1 day | 9 day | 6 mo. |
| John of Robert Scott aged about 20 day | 16 day | 6 mo. |
| Joseph of Elizabeth & Francis Smith aged about 5 day | 30 day | 6 mo. |
| James of ——— wife of James Hudson aged about 6 day | 30 day | 6 mo. |
| John of Jarvis & Mary Gould member of Ch. of Hingham aged about 33 days | 30 day | 6 mo. |
| Deborah of George Kenricke member of Ch. of Situate aged about 6 wks | 13 day | 7 mo. |
| Submit daut of Thomas Clarke member of Ch. of Dorchester aged about 1 day | 20 day | 7 mo. |
| John of William Reade member of Ch. of Waymoth aged about 4 day | 27 day | 7 mo. |
| Elizabeth of Gabriel Fish member of Ch. of Exeter aged about 5 day | 4 day | 8 mo. |
| Susanna of Isaac Waker aged about 8 day | 11 day | 8 mo. |
| Sarah of Anthony Harker aged about 23 days | 11 day | 8 mo. |
| Solomon of John Blacklidge from the Ch. of Salem | 18 day | 8 mo. |
| Martha of Thomas Foule aged about 7 days | 25 day | 8 mo. |
| Solomon of Edward Ransford aged about 8 days | 25 day | 8 mo. |
| Joseph of Peter Place | 25 day | 8 mo. |
| Joseph of Robert Winge aged about 7 day | 1 day | 9 mo. |
| Samuel of Arthur Clarke aged about 4 day | 1 day | 9 mo. |
| Rebecca of Robert Reade member of Ch. of Exeter aged about 29 days | 1 day | 9 mo. |
| Mary of John Hurd aged about 7 days | 8 day | 9 mo. |
| Robert of Rachel & Robert Woodward aged about 2 days | 8 day | 9 mo. |
| Mary of Nathaniel Willyams aged about 1 day | 6 day | 10 mo. |
| Leah of ——— wife of William Wardall | 6 day | 10 mo. |
| Abigail of Abel Porter aged about 2 days | 13 day | 10 mo. |
| Hannah of George Halsall aged about 4 days | 10 day | 11 mo. |
| James of William Townsend aged about 2 days | 17 day | 11 mo. |
| More-Mercie of Anne & Thomas Bell aged about 3 days | 17 day | 11 mo. |
| Abigail of Richard Lippincott aged about 6 days | 24 day | 11 mo. |
| Elizabeth of Arthur Pury aged about 4 day | 31 day | 11 mo. |
| John of Nathaniel Bishopp aged about 2 day | 31 day | 11 mo. |
| Mary of Richard Hogg aged about 5 day | 7 day | 12 mo. |
| Abigail of James Johnson aged about 8 day | 21 day | 12 mo. |
| John of Elizabeth & George Orrys aged about 4 day | 21 day | 12 mo. |
| Benjamin of Robert Turnor late Inholder aged about 3 day | 28 day | 12 mo. |
| David of Francis East aged about 3 day | 28 day | 12 mo. |
| Joanna of Strong Furnell aged about 5 day | 28 day | 12 mo. |
| Ephraim of Joan & Thomas Jay aged about 22 day | 28 day | 12 mo. |

## 1647.

### TOWN.

Abigail of Theodore & Abigail Atkinson born 24th — 6th month.
William son of Alexander & Elizabeth Baker born 15th — 3rd mouth.
Robert of Robert & Francis Burnam born 25th — 7th month.
Jane of Richard & Jane Critchley born.
Samuel of George & Abigail Dell born 31st — 6th month.
Robert of Robert & Mary Field born 30th — 9th month.
Heman son of Thomas & Anne Grub died 29th — 7th month.
Mary of Edmund & Martha Jackson born 17th — 2nd month.
John of John & Martha Mellowes born 8th — 2nd month & died 19th — 2nd month.
Hannah of Ralph & Anne Mason born 23rd — 10th month.
Susanna of Timothy & Margaret Prout born 26th — 2nd mouth.
Susanna of John & Susanna Sweete born 3rd — 2nd month.

Jabesh *of* William & Mary Salter born 7th month.
Habbakuck son of Robert & Elizabeth Turner born 18th — 2nd month.
Joseph of Peter & Mary Thornton born 5th — 2nd month.
John of Christopher & Ann Holland born 1st Feb.
Joseph of Joseph & Mary Bastarr born 29th Sept.
John of Thomas & Luce Saxton born 29th June.
David of David & Elizabeth Kelly born 18th Dec.

### FIRST CHURCH.

| | | |
|---|---|---|
| Samuel of Mauditt Inglys aged about 9 days | 7 day | 1 mo. |
| Thomas of Thomas Scottoe aged about 5 days | 7 day | 1 mo. |
| Sarah of Angell Hollard member of Ch. of Waymonth aged about 4 days | 7 day | 1 mo. |
| Mary of Grace & William Rickes aged about 4 days | 7 day | 1 mo. |
| Manoah of Sarah & John Bodman aged about 3 days | 7 day | 1 mo. |
| Anne of Isaac Addington aged about 5 days | 14 day | 1 mo. |
| Abigail of Samson Shore aged about 7 days | 14 day | 1 mo. |
| Mathias of Mathias Ines aged about 6 day | 14 day | 1 mo. |
| Rebecca of Edward Ting aged about 6 day | 21 day | 1 mo. |
| Mary of John Barrell aged about 6 day | 21 day | 1 mo. |
| Jane of Richard Critchley aged about 6 day | 21 day | 1 mo. |
| James of John Sinderland aged about 4 day | 21 day | 1 mo. |
| David of Joseph Phippeny member of Ch. of Hingham aged about 7 wks. | 4 day | 2 mo. |
| Deriah of Griffin Bowen aged about 6 days | 11 day | 2 mo. |
| Nathaniel of John Gill | 11 day | 2 mo. |
| Susanna of John Sweete aged about 7 days | 11 day | 2 mo. |
| Habbakkuk son of Robert Turnor Shoemaker aged about 5 days | 18 day | 2 mo. |
| Samuel of Hannah & John Hannifall aged about 36 wks | 18 day | 2 mo. |
| William of Alexander Baker aged about 4 days | 18 day | 2 mo. |
| Mary of Edmund Jackson aged about 2 days | 18 day | 2 mo. |
| Jonathan of Mary & Richard Woodhouse aged about 9 day | 25 day | 2 mo. |
| Susanna of Timothy Prout aged about 7 day | 2 day | 3 mo. |
| Ebenezer of Anne & John Manning aged about 10 wks 3 days | 16 day | 3 mo. |
| Mary of William Cotton aged about 5 yr 5 mo. | 16 day | 3 mo. |
| John of William Cotton aged about 3 yr 5 mo | 16 day | 3 mo. |
| William of William Cotton aged about 11 mo. 16 d. | 16 day | 3 mo. |
| Patience of Mary & George Dodd aged about 1 yr. 35 d. | 16 day | 3 mo. |
| Sarah of Sarah Gunison late w. of Henry Lynne dec. aged about 10 yrs 6 mo. | 23 day | 3 mo. |
| Elizabeth of Sarah Gunison late w. of Henry Lynne dec. aged about 9 yr. 2 mo. | 23 day | 3 mo. |
| Ephraim of Sarah Gunison late w. of Henry Lynne dec. aged about 7 yr. 4 mo. | 23 day | 3 mo. |
| Rebecca of Sarah Gunison late w. of Henry Lynne dec. aged about 5 yr 3 mo. | 23 day | 3 mo. |
| Hannah of Joanna & Hugh Northend she form. Copp aged about 5 days | 30 day | 3 mo. |
| Mary of Mary & Waters Sennitt aged about 6 yr 6 mo 11 d | 30 day | 3 mo. |
| John of Mary & Waters Sennitt aged about 3 yr. 10 mo 18 days | 30 day | 3 mo. |
| Stephen of Mary & Waters Sennitt aged about 1 yr. 6 mo. 18 days | 30 day | 3 mo. |
| Mary of Thomas Savidge aged about 8 days | 6 day | 4 mo. |
| Joshua of Rebecca & Robert Windsore aged about 7 day. | 13 day | 4 mo. |
| Martha of Sarah & Richard Mountague aged about 4 day | 20 day | 4 mo. |
| Vigilant son of Samuel Oliver aged about 7 day | 27 day | 4 mo. |
| Borshua daut of Philemon Pormort member of Ch. of Exeter | 4 day | 5 mo. |
| Benjamin of Benjamin Thwing aged about 4 days | 18 day | 5 mo. |
| Samuel of Robert Scott aged about 4 days | 1 day | 6 mo. |
| Elizabeth of Joshua Scottoe aged about 2 day | 1 day | 6 mo. |
| Samuel of Thomas Buttall aged about 8 day | 15 day | 6 mo. |
| Hannah of Edmund Grosse aged about 8 day | 15 day | 6 mo. |
| Maryah of Sarah & Henry Messenger aged about 7 day | 15 day | 6 mo. |
| John of Valentine Hill Deacon aged about 8 day | 22 day | 6 mo. |

| | |
|---|---|
| Thomas of Thomas Clarke aged about 4 days | 22 day 6 mo. |
| Mary of Marmaduke Mathews member of Ch. of Yarmouth aged about 11 mo. | 29 day 6 mo. |
| Abigail of Theodore Atkinson aged about 7 days | 29 day 6 mo. |
| Samuel of Jeremiah More | 29 day 6 mo. |
| Anna of William Davisse aged about 8 days | 5 day 7 mo. |
| Daniel of Lydia & Daniel Turell | 5 day 7 mo. |
| Peter of Abigail & John Jackson aged about 6 days | 12 day 7 mo. |
| Mary of Catharine & Nicholas Charlett aged about 5 days | 3 day 8 mo. |
| John. of Hermon Atwood aged about 5 days | 10 day 8 mo. |
| Elizabeth of Mary & Mark Haines aged about 5 days | 10 day 8 mo. |
| Isaac of Isaac Waker aged about 6 days | 17 day 8 mo. |
| Adam of Adam Winthropp aged about 16 days | 31 day 8 mo. |
| Paul of John Stevenson aged about 3 days. | 31 day 8 mo. |
| Persis daut of John Lake aged about 13 days | 31 day 8 mo. |
| Sarah of Francis Dowse aged about 6 day | 7 day 9 mo. |
| Deborah of Mary & Edward Kibby | 7 day 9 mo. |
| John of William Toy aged about 5 day | 21 day 9 mo. |
| Elizabeth of George Burden aged about 5 wks 4 days | 28 day 9 mo. |
| Maria of Sarah & James Jempson | 28 day 9 mo. |
| Sarah, of Jacob Elyott Deacon aged about 6 days · | 5 day 10 mo. |
| Robert of Robert Feild aged about 6 days | 5 day 10 mo. |
| Jonathan of William & Mary Alford member of Ch. of Salem aged about 6 days | 5 day 10 mo. |
| Elizabeth of Robert & Deborah Fenne from the Ch. of Salem aged about 4 days | 26 day 10 mo. |
| John of James Pemerton | 26 day 10 mo. |
| Mary of Mary & Amos Richardson | 26 day 10 mo. |
| John of Mary & Amos Richardson aged about 29 days | 26 day 10 mo. |
| John of George & Faith Bennett she formerly Newell aged about 4 days | 2 day 11 mo. |
| Mary of John & Dorothy Downam member of Ch. of Braintree aged about 10 days | 2 day 11 mo. |
| Hannah of Hannah & William Blanchard aged about 7 days | 9 day 11 mo. |
| Elizabeth of Gamaliel Wayto aged about 5 days | 16 day 11 mo. |
| Sarah of Robert Button from the Ch. of Salem aged about 6 days | 16 day 11 mo. |
| Elizabeth of John Mylam aged about 9 days | 30 day 11 mo. |
| Peter of Peter Place aged about 3 days | 30 day 11 mo. |
| John of Richard Taylor aged about 4 days | 6 day 12 mo. |
| Johanna of David Sellicke aged about 2 days | 13 day 12 mo. |
| Hester of Hugh Gunison | 20 day 12 mo. |

## 1648.

### Town.

Susan of Alexander & Mary Adams born 14th — 3rd month.
Ruth of George & Susan Allen born 3rd — 8th month.
Joseph of Edmund & Sarah Dennis born 13th — 4th month.
Martha of William & Martha Dinsdale born 10th — 11th mouth.
John of Abraham & Lydia Dible born 7th — 5th month.
Lydia of James & Anne Hudson born 15th — 1st month.
Peleg son of James & Mary Hawkins born 9th — 1st month.
Susan of Edmund & Susan Jacklin born 16th — 11th month.
Honour of Dermin & Deiner Mahoone born 29th — 8th month.
Hannah of William & Anne Pollard born 10th — 11th month.
Martha of John & Elizabeth Spoore born 26th — 1st month & died 19th — 7th month.
John of Hezekiah & Frances Vsher born 17th — 2nd month.
Peter of Richard & Sibil Bennet born 18th — 11th mouth.
Mercy of George & Mary Michell horn 25th Aug.
Mary of Matthew & Tabitha Abda born 24th May.
John of Thomas & Sarah Stevens born 15th May.

## FIRST CHURCH.

| | | |
|---|---|---|
| Joseph of Mary & Waters Sennitt aged about 9 days | 12 day | 1 mo. |
| Sarah of William Cotton aged about 1 day | 19 day | 1 mo. |
| John of Lydia & Hugh Drewry aged about 1 yr ¾ & 7 wks | 19 day | 1 mo. |
| Martha of John Spoure aged about 3 days | 26 day | 1 mo. |
| Samuel of Margaret & Jacob Sheafe aged about 4 days | 9 day | 2 mo. |
| Jabez of Benjamine Negoose aged about 9 days | 9 day | 2 mo. |
| Temperance of Michael Wills member of Ch. of Dorchester | 9 day | 2 mo. |
| John of Hezekiah Usher from the Ch. of Cambridge aged about 7 days | 16 day | 2 mo. |
| Nathaniel of Mary & Francis Hudson aged about 7 day | 16 day | 2 mo. |
| Elizabeth of John Collens aged about 8 days | 16 day | 2 mo. |
| Susanna of Rebecca & Christopher Clarke aged about 8 day | 23 day | 2 mo. |
| Mehetabel of Anne & Thomas Hett | 23 day | 2 mo. |
| Mehetabel of William Salter aged about 4 day | 30 day | 2 mo. |
| Catharine of Edward Hutchinson jun. aged about 2 days | 14 day | 3 mo. |
| Sarah of Hannah & George Baldin she now wife of Richard Bradly aged about 3 yr & ½ | 14 day | 3 mo. |
| John of Hannah & John Bateman aged about 3 yr. 5 mo. | 14 day | 3 mo. |
| Hannah of Hannah & John Bateman aged about 2 yr. 2 mo. | 14 day | 3 mo. |
| Elizabeth of Hannah & John Bateman aged about 7 mo. 2 wks | 14 day | 3 mo. |
| Elisha of Benjamin Gillam aged about 8 days | 21 day | 3 mo. |
| Susanna of Alexander Adams aged about 8 days | 21 day | 3 mo. |
| John of Edward Harryson member of the Ch. at Virginia | 21 day | 3 mo. |
| Hester of Joseph & Miriam Wormall member of Ch. of Concord | 21 day | 3 mo. |
| John of Robert Shrimpton aged about 6 wks | 28 day | 3 mo. |
| Susanna of Samuel Davis aged about 3 days | 28 day | 3 mo. |
| Ephraim of Edward Bendall aged about 2 days | 11 day | 4 mo. |
| Joseph of Richard Tappin aged about 14 days | 11 day | 4 mo. |
| Joseph of Edward Dennys aged about 6 days | 11 day | 4 mo. |
| Elizabeth of Eunice & Thomas Robert aged about 2 days | 11 day | 4 mo. |
| Elizabeth of Robert Turner shoemaker aged about 5 days | 18 day | 4 mo. |
| Elizabeth of Richard Cooke aged about 5 wks 6 days | 25 day | 4 mo. |
| Joseph of Thomas Rawlings from the Ch. of Waymouth aged about 11 days | 25 day | 4 mo. |
| Samuel of Richard Wayte aged about 20 days | 9 day | 5 mo. |
| John of Abraham Deeble from the Ch. of Dorchester aged about 9 days | 16 day | 5 mo. |
| Sarah of John Leverett aged about 4 days | 16 day | 5 mo. |
| Grace of Anthony Stoddar aged about 2 day | 16 day | 5 mo. |
| Abigail of Bezaleel Payton aged about 5 days | 23 day | 5 mo. |
| John of Simon Rogers aged about 5 days | 23 day | 5 mo. |
| Sarah of Joan & Thomas Jay aged about 31 days | 23 day | 5 mo. |
| Sarai of Richard Bellingham aged about 2 days | 30 day | 5 mo. |
| Bethiah of Elizabeth & George Orrys aged about 6 days | 30 day | 5 mo. |
| James of John Sinderland aged about 7 day | 6 day | 6 mo. |
| John of William Browne from the Ch. of Salem aged about 4 day | 13 day | 6 mo. |
| John of Strong Furnell aged about 5 days | 20 day | 6 mo. |
| John of Godfrey Armitage from the Ch. of Lynn aged about 4 days | 20 day | 6 mo. |
| Benjamin of John Hurd aged about 7 day | 27 day | 6 mo. |
| Elizabeth of Edward & Margaret Lambe member of Ch. of Watertowne aged about 11 days | 27 day | 6 mo. |
| Solomon of John Blacklidge from the Ch. of Salem aged about 2 days | 3 day | 7 mo. |
| John of Sarah & James Jempson aged about 2 day | 3 day | 7 mo. |
| Maria of John Kenricke aged about 1 day | 10 day | 7 mo. |
| John of Anne & John Manning aged about 4 day | 24 day | 7 mo. |
| Barthsheba daut of Thomas Webber aged about 3 day | 24 day | 7 mo. |
| Mary of Eliah Parkman member of Ch. of Winsor aged about 4 day | 24 day | 7 mo. |
| Mercy of Rachel & Robert Woodward aged about 6 day | 1 day | 8 mo |

| | | |
|---|---|---|
| Isaiah of William Townsend aged about 3 day | 5 day | 9 mo. |
| Samuel of Thomas Buttall aged about 10 days | 12 day | 9 mo. |
| Abigail of Peter Oliver aged about 1 day | 19 day | 9 mo. |
| Hannah & } dautr's of John Maynard { aged about 4 days | 26 day | 9 mo. |
| Lydia } from the Ch. of Duxbury { aged about 4 days | 26 day | 9 mo. |
| Samuel of Valentine Hill Deacon aged about 2 days | 10 day | 10 mo. |
| John of Grace & William Rickes aged about 2 days | 10 day | 10 mo. |
| Joshua of John Winthropp Governor aged about 5 days | 17 day | 10 mo. |
| Thomas of Thomas Clarke aged about 5 days | 17 day | 10 mo. |
| Jeremiah of Jeremiah More | 17 day | 10 mo. |
| John of Hannah & John Hannifall aged about 12 day | 7 day | 11 mo. |
| Hannah of Nathaniel Willyams aged about 9 days | 7 day | 11 mo. |
| Margaret of Michael Powell from the Ch. of Dedham aged about. 8 days | 14 day | 11 mo. |
| Sarah of James Pemerton aged about 6 wks | 28 day | 11 mo. |
| Deborah of Robert Read member of Ch. of Exeter aged about 3 days | 28 day | 11 mo. |
| Palti dautr of William Parker member of Ch. of Watertowne aged about 1 mo. | 4 day | 12 mo. |
| William of Hannah & William Hanbrough member of Ch. of Plimwoth aged about 6 days | 11 day | 12 mo. |
| Hannah of Nathaniel Bishop aged about 7 days | 11 day | 12 mo. |
| John of Timothy Prout aged about 8 days | 11 day | 12 mo. |
| Edward of Matthew Ines aged about 3 days | 11 day | 12 mo. |
| Mehetable of Thomas Scottoe aged about 4 days | 11 day | 12 mo. |
| Benjamin of Robert Wing aged about 7 day | 18 day | 12 mo. |
| Nathaniel of Elizabeth & Francis Smith aged about 5 day | 18 day | 12 mo. |
| Susanna of Edmund Jacklyn aged about 33 day | 8 day | 12 mo. |
| Jonathan of Samuel Oliver aged about 7 day | 25 day | 12 mo. |
| Elizabeth of Edward Ransford aged about 7 days | 25 day | 12 mo. |
| Abel of Abel Porter aged about 3 day | 25 day | 12 mo. |
| Mary of Edward Devotion aged about 4 days | 25 day | 12 mo. |

## 1649.

### TOWN.

Margaret Grimsted widow died 20th — 11th mo.
Joseph of Hugh & Sarah Gunnison born 31st — 1st month.
Elihu of Hugh & Sarah Gunnison born 12th — 12th month.
Stephen of Thomas & Mary Lake born 13th — 12th month.
Dorothy of Christopher & Rebecca Clark born 6th — 11th month.
Joseph of George & Abigail Dell born Feb.
John Gallop died 11th month.
Jolliff Rudock died 7th month.
Bridget of Christopher & Anne Holland born 14th March.
Timothy of Richard & Mary Hicks born 2nd May.
Martha of John & Martha Bundy born 2nd Nov.
Mary wife of John Biggs died 10th — 11th mo.
Richard of Richard & Dorothy Norton died 10th — 12th month.
John of John & Ruth Ingolsby died 3rd — 6th mo.
Rebecca of Edward & Mary Ting died 16th — 1st mo.

### FIRST CHURCH.

| | | |
|---|---|---|
| Submit of Thomas Clarke aged about 19 days | 4 day | 1 mo. |
| John of Lydia & Daniel Turell aged about 6 days | 4 day | 1 mo. |
| Rebecca of Isaac Addington aged about 4 days | 11 day | 1 mo. |
| Elizabeth of George Halsall aged about 10 days | 11 day | 1 mo. |
| Jonathan of Richard Knight aged about 8 days | 11 day | 1 mo. |
| Martha of Martha & Thomas Stanbury aged about 6 days | 11 day | 1 mo. |
| Marie of John Vyall aged about 7 days | 18 day | 1 mo. |
| Lydia of Anne & James Hudson aged about 3 days | 18 day | 1 mo. |

| | | |
|---|---|---|
| Joseph of Jarvis & Mary Gould from the Ch. of Hingham aged about 14 days | 25 day | 1 mo. |
| Edward of Edward Ting aged about 6 days | 1 day | 2 mo. |
| James of John Barrell aged about 4 days | 1 day | 2 mo. |
| Joseph of Hugh Gunnyson aged about 3 days | 1 day | 2 mo. |
| John of Hannah & Richard Bradley aged about 6 days | 1 day | 2 mo. |
| Joseph of Robert Woodmansey member of Ch. of Ipswich aged about 4 days | 1 day | 2 mo. |
| John of John Ingolsby aged about 2 days | 1 day | 2 mo. |
| Joseph of Alexander Baker aged about 3 days | 8 day | 2 mo. |
| Deliverance of Alice & Henry Stevens aged about 4 days | 15 day | 2 mo. |
| Thomas of Robert Walker aged about 10 days | 22 day | 2 mo. |
| Mary of Robert Walker aged about 10 days | 22 day | 2 mo. |
| Elizabeth of James Johnson aged about 8 days | 29 day | 2 mo. |
| Jonathan of Samson Shore aged about 6 days | 29 day | 2 mo. |
| John of Robert Scott aged about 15 days | 6 day | 3 mo. |
| Samuel of Thomas Snow | 6 day | 3 mo. |
| Joseph of Joseph Phipeny member of Ch. of Hingham aged about 7 days | 6 day | 3 mo. |
| Sarah of Sarah & John Bodman aged about 1 day | 13 day | 3 mo |
| John of Angell Hollard member of Ch. of Waymouth aged about 6 day | 27 day | 3 mo. |
| Mehetabell of Hezekiah Usher member of Ch. of Cambridge aged about 6 days | 27 day | 3 mo. |
| Mary of John Lake aged about 4 days | 3 day | 4 mo. |
| Susanna of Edward Hutchinson aged about 22 days | 10 day | 4 mo. |
| Daniel of George Parkhurst member of Ch. of Watertowne aged about 11 days | 10 day | 4 mo. |
| Peter of Peter Place aged about 2 days | 17 day | 4 mo. |
| William of Jeremiah Howchin aged about 3 days | 1 day | 5 mo. |
| Deborah of Arthur Pury aged about 4 days | 1 day | 5 mo. |
| John of John Wilson Pastor of Ch. of Dorchester aged about 2 days | 8 day | 5 mo. |
| Mary of Anne & Thomas Hett | 15 day | 5 mo. |
| Temperance of John Sweete aged about 5 days | 5 day | 6 mo. |
| Samson of John Mylam aged about 2 day | 12 day | 6 mo. |
| Mercy of Anthony Harker aged about 10 day | 12 day | 6 mo. |
| Sarah of Joanna & Samuel Northend aged about 4 day | 12 day | 6 mo. |
| Sarah of John Leverett aged about 17 days | 19 day | 6 mo. |
| Benjamin of William Davisse aged about 2 days | 19 day | 6 mo. |
| Frances dau. of Robert Turner shoemaker aged about 6 days | 26 day | 6 mo. |
| Ezechiell of Joel Jenkins from the Ch. of Braintree | 16 day | 7 mo. |
| Sarah of Richard Davenport from the Ch. of Salem | 30 day | 7 mo |
| Sarah of Hannah & John Bateman aged about 8 days | 7 day | 8 mo |
| Elizabeth of Thomas & Elizabeth Ryder member of Ch. of Waymouth | 14 day | 8 mo. |
| Elizabeth of Thomas Harryson Pastor of the Ch. at Virginia aged about 7 days | 28 day | 8 mo. |
| Timothy of Robert Turner Inholder aged about 6 days | 4 day | 9 mo. |
| Mary of Abigail & John Jackson aged about 6 days | 4 day | 9 mo. |
| Sarah of Francis East aged about 2 days | 11 day | 9 mo. |
| Bethiah of Hannah & William Blanchard aged about 5 days | 2 day | 10 mo. |
| Elizabeth of Richard Bellingham aged about 3 days | 9 day | 10 mo |
| Restore of Edward Bendall aged about 17 day | 30 day | 10 mo. |
| Mary of Rebecca & Robert Winsore aged about 11 day | 30 day | 10 mo. |
| Sarah of Sarah & Gamaliel Phipeny aged about 6 days | 30 day | 10 mo. |
| Mary of Valentine Hill Deacon aged about 1 day | 30 day | 10 mo. |
| Dosithea of Thomas Savage aged about 1 day | 30 day | 10 mo. |
| Samuel of Anthony Stoddar aged about 6 day | 20 day | 11 mo. |
| Amos of Mary & Amos Richardson aged about 6 day | 20 day | 11 mo. |
| Dorathie of Rebecca & Christopher Clarke aged about 14 days | 20 day | 11 mo. |
| Anna of Sarah & Henry Messinger aged about 13 days | 20 day | 11 mo. |
| Mercy of Thomas Bumstead member of Ch. of Roxbury aged about 5 days | 20 day | 11 mo. |

| | |
|---|---|
| Samuel of Thomas Venner from the Ch. of Salem aged about 11 day | 3 day 12 mo. |
| Eleazer of Theodore Atkinson aged about 8 day | 3 day 12 mo. |
| Elizabeth of Henry Fowning aged about 24 day | 3 day 12 mo. |
| Isaac of Edmund Jackson aged about 7 day | 10 day 12 mo. |
| Elihu of Hugh Gunnyson aged about 3 day | 17 day 12 mo, |
| Samuel of Robert Button from the Ch. of Salem aged about 4 day | 24 day 12 mo. |
| Samuel of Godfrey Armitage from the Ch. of Lynn aged about 2 day | 24 day 12 mo. |

## 1650.

### Town.

James of James & Christian Allison born 20th — 8th month.
Mary of Francis & Alice Bennet born 15th — 7th month.
Susanna of Richard & Sibil Bennet born 2nd — 12th month.
Dorothy wife of Simon Eyre died 11th — 6th month.
Hannah of John & Elizabeth Ferniside born 8th — 3rd month.
Samuel of Frances & Mary Hudson born 19th — 5th month.
John of John & Elizabeth Spoore born 16th — 10th month.
Elizabeth of Thomas & Anne Walker born 18th — 6th month.
Mr. Atherton Haugh died 11th — 7th month.
Daniel of Robert & Penelope Turner born 26th — 9th month.
Deborah of Thomas & Ann Bell born 29th Nov.
John of George & Mary Michell born 3rd June.
Elizabeth sonne of Edward & Jane Barker born 17th July.
Priscilla of Samuel & Anna Davis born 3d Aug.

William Phillips Jr. was married to Martha Franklin 24th — 8th month by William Hibbins.
Samuel Gallop was married to Mary Phillips 20th — 11th month by Richard Bellingham.

### First Church.

| | |
|---|---|
| Isaac of Jonathan Negoose aged about 10 days | 3 day 1 mo. |
| Isaiah of William Toy aged about 7 days | 10 day 1 mo. |
| Lydia of Edmund Grosse aged about 4 days | 10 day 1 mo. |
| William of Robert Feild aged about 3 days | 17 day 1 mo. |
| Rachel of Benjamin Thwing aged about 5 days | 17 day 1 mo. |
| Elizabeth of John Harwood aged about 4 days | 17 day 1 mo. |
| Samuel of Strong Furnill | 14 day 2 mo. |
| Thomas of Robert Woodward's wife | 14 day 2 mo. |
| John of Tho: Boyden member of Ch. of Watertowne | 21 day 2 mo. |
| Sarah of Edward Jackson member of Ch. of Cambridge | 21 day 2 mo. |
| Prissilla of George Kenniricke member of Ch. of Bastuble | 21 day 2 mo. |
| Sarah of Water Senit's wife | 28 day 2 mo. |
| Hannah of Mr. Fernide member of Ch. of Duxbury | 12 day 3 mo. |
| Benja: of Tho: Joye's wife | 12 day 3 mo. |
| Hannah of Howchin | 19 day 3 mo. |
| Mary of Sheaffe | 19 day 3 mo. |
| Lydia of Douse | 26 day 3 mo. |
| Nath: of Euins | 26 day 3 mo. |
| Sarah of Atwood | 26 day 3 mo. |
| Johana of Dawes of Braintry | 2 day 4 mo. |
| Hopestill of Richard Woodis' wife | 2 day 4 mo. |
| Joseph of Scott | 9 day 4 mo. |
| Mary of Richard Cooke | 23 day 4 mo. |
| Elisha of Burden | 8 day 5 mo. |
| Patience of Samuel Oliver | 8 day 5 mo. |
| Israel of Thorne | 14 day 5 mo. |

| | | | |
|---|---|---|---|
| Benjamin of | Tappin | 21 day | 5 mo. |
| Joseph of | Browne of Salem | 27 day | 5 mo. |
| Sarah of | Halsoll | 27 day | 5 mo. |
| John of | Keibye | 27 day | 5 mo. |
| Samuel of Francis Hudson's wife | | 27 day | 5 mo. |
| Martha of | Adams | 27 day | 5 mo. |
| Mary of Thomas Willyams' wife of Exeter | | 11 day | 6 mo. |
| Benjamin of | Blauge of Braintry | 18 day | 6 mo. |
| Deborah of | Townsend | 25 day | 6 mo. |
| John of | Dible | 25 day | 6 mo. |
| Timothy of | Waker | 1 day | 7 mo. |
| John of | Place | 1 day | 7 mo. |
| Sarah of | Read | 1 day | 7 mo. |
| Elizabeth of | Carr of Salisberry about 6 years old | 8 day | 7 mo. |
| John of | Inglesby | 15 day | 7 mo. |
| Priscilla of Samuel Davis | | 15 day | 7 mo. |
| Benjamin of | Dinnis | 22 day | 7 mo. |
| Obadiah of Joell Jenke of Braintry | | 13 day | 8 mo. |
| Thomas of | Clarke | 20 day | 8 mo. |
| Experience of Isaac Waker | | 20 day | 8 mo. |
| Samuel of George Davis | | 20 day | 8 mo. |
| Mary of John Hurd's wife | | 20 day | 8 mo. |
| Sarah of Hezekiah Usher | | 17 day | 9 mo. |
| Elizabeth of Richard Wait | | 17 day | 9 mo. |
| Gamaliel of Gamaliel Wait | | 17 day | 9 mo. |
| Samuel of Matthew Ines | | 24 day | 9 mo. |
| Daniel of Robert Tourner | | 1 day | 10 mo. |
| John of Richard Knight | | 1 day | 10 mo. |
| Deborah of Thos Bell's wife | | 1 day | 10 mo. |
| Bethiah daut of Robert Woodmansey | | 15 day | 10 mo. |
| John of John Spurr | | 22 day | 10 mo. |
| Hannah of John Honifford's wife | | 5 day | 11 mo. |
| Sarah of | Lewis of Situate | 5 day | 11 mo. |
| Hannah of Edward Rainsford | | 12 day | 11 mo. |
| John of Nathaniel Bishop | | 26 day | 11 mo. |
| Thomas of Thomas Weebber | | 2 day | 12 mo. |
| James of Sampson Shoore | | 2 day | 12 mo. |
| Joseph of Timothy Proute | | 9 day | 12 mo. |
| Mary of Jeremy Moore | | 16 day | 12 mo. |
| William of William Cotton | | 23 day | 12 mo. |
| Benjamin of John Jackson | | 23 day | 12 mo. |

## 1651.

### Town.

Sarah of John & Sarah Strange born 18th — 8th month.
Samuel of George & Barbary Davis born 17th Oct.
Hannah of Nicholas & Hannah Stone born 8th Jan.
John of John & Susanna Sweete born 8th Sept.
James of Francis & Alice Bennet born 14th Feb.
Sarah of John & Emm Coddington born 4th Oct.
Job of Hugh & Sarah Browne born 29th Mch.
William of William & Martha Harvey born 27th Aug.
Thomas of Thomas & Sarah Stevens born 28th Dec.
Elizabeth of Robert & Frances Burnam born 27th — 8th month.
Ann of Mr John & Ann Maning born 12th — 1st month.
Mary of Samuel & Mary Gallop born 4th — 12th month.
Jonathan of Jonathan & Mary Balston born 2nd March.
Joseph of Henry & Elizabeth Bridgham born 17th Jan.
Anne of John & Anne Maning born 13th March.
Sarah of John & Mary Viall born 14 March.
Elizabeth of Edward & Margaret Coalman born 28th — 11th month.
Abigail of Thomas & Milcha Snow born 10th — 1st mouth.

Joseph of John & Christian Milam born 26th — 12th month.
Mary of John & Christian Milam born 26th — 12th month.
James of Francis & Alice Benit born 17th — 12th month.
Samuel of Godfrey & Mary Armitage born 14th — 2nd month
Elizabeth of George & Elizabeth Waye born 19th — 1st month.
Matthew of Rice & Ann Jones born 30th — 4th month.
Hannah of Thomas & Milcah Snow born 10th — 1st month.
Elizabeth of John & Sarah Tuckerman born 5th — 12th month.
Hannah of John & Ann Kenricke born 20th — 1st month.
Asaph of Jacob & Margery Eliott born 25th — 8th month.
Anna of Richard & Anna Bradley born 16th — 10th month.
John of Thomas & Margery Alcocke born 2nd — 5th month.
Rebecca of Mr Edward & Mary Ting born 13th — 5th month.
Mary of Thomas & Mary Broughton born 5th — 5th month.
Sarah of John & Hannah Bateman born 6th — 3rd month.
Rachel of John & Hannah Bateman born 28th — 3rd mouth.
Samuel of Samuel & Joanna Norden born 8th — 9th month
Edward of Edward & Abigail Hutchinson born 3rd — 11th month.
Samuel of William & Mary Lane born 23rd — 11th month.
John of Humphrey & Sarah Cumby born 23rd — 11th month.
Sarah of Isaac & Anne Addington born 12th — 2nd month.
Hannah of John & Mary Barrell born 23rd — 2nd mouth.
Isaac of Edward & Martha Jackson born 22nd — 9th month
Jeremiah of Jeremiah & Easter Houchine born 5th — 9th month.
Deborah of Francis & Catherine Dowse born 1st — 11th mouth.
Samuel of John & Martha Shaw born 4th — 9th month.
Mary of William & Martha Demsdall born 24th — 7th month.
Nicholas of Isaac & Susanna Waker born 1st — 10th month.
David of Benjamin & Wilmat Phipeny born 6th — 9th month.
Thomas of Robert & Mary Feild born 1st — 10th month.
William of Edward & Rachel Rawson born 21st May.
Mehetabel of Thomas & Annis Buttolph born 26 — 8th month.
Sarah of John & Alice Tincker born 2nd — 11th month.
James of James & Sarah Jempson born 22nd — 10th month.
Deliverance of Elias & Bridget Parkman born 3rd — 6th month.
Elizabeth of Joseph & Elizabeth Rocke born 5th — 12th month.
Penn of William & Hannah Townsend born 20th — 10th month.
Deborah of Mr Samuel & Lydia Oliver born 1st — 12th month.
Anne of Michael & Anne Ines born 6th — 12th month.
William of Wm. Jr. & Martha Phillips born 13th — 11th month.
William of Edward & Margaret Preston born 30th — 11th month.
Isaac of George & Mary Dod born 3rd — 7th month.
Jonathan of Thomas & Frances Bojden born 20th — 12th month.
John of Christopher & Rebecca Clarke born 3rd — 12th month.
Theophilus of David & Urslye Yeale born 14th — 11th month.
Perez of Capt. Thomas & Faith Savage born 17th — 12th month.
Elizabeth of David & Susanna Selecke born 1st — 12th mouth.
Anna of Mr. Edward & Elizabeth Rainsford born 1st — 12th month.
Nathaniel of Peter & Sarah Olliver born 8th — 1st month.
Dorothy of John & Jane Bushnell born 19th — 12th month.
Gamaliel of Gamaliel & Sarah Phipeny born 12th — 1st mouth.
Robert of Robert & Rebecca Lord born 2nd month.
Anne of Ezekiel & Anne Woodward born 10th Aug.
Hannah of Samuel & Mary (?) Dunkin born 28th Apr.


Daniel of Robert & Penelope Turner died 4th — 2nd month.
Ama of William Vpshall died 7th — 9th mo.
Jeremiah of Jeremiah Houchine died 8th — 10th mo.
Hannah of Thomas Richards deceased & Weltham his wife died 10th — 9th
    month.
Joseph of Richard & Elizabeth Wayt aged 14 years died 20th — 9th month.
Richard of John & Anna Webb died 30th — 10th mo.
Sarah of George & Joan Hallsell died 16th — 10 mo.
Sarah of Henry deceased & Joan Swan died 23rd — 10th month.

Su·an of John & Anna Webb died 17th — 10th mo.
Joshua youngest son of the late John Winthropp Esq. died 11th — 11th month.
Mary of James & Sarah Astwood died 21st — 11th mo.
Faith wife of Capt. Thomas Savage died 20th — 12th mo.
Susan of Philip Phillips died 14th — 10th month.
Sarah of John & Elizabeth Purchase died 14th — 12th mo.
Mary wife of Mr John Coggan died 14th — 11th month.
Elizabeth of Job & Elizabeth Bishop of Ipswich died 27th — 12th month.
Margaret wife of Isaac Cullimore died 13th — 10th month.
Hannah of Robert & Abigail Button died 20th — 1st month.
Alice wife of Nathaniel Souther died 27th — 7th mo.
———— Pateson of Lyme in the County of Dorset died aboard the ship John &
     Sarah whereof was master Mr. John Greene 27th — 12th mo.


Nicholas Phillips was married to Hannah Salter 4th — 10th month by Richard
     Bellingham Esq.
William Philpot was married to Ann Hunn widow by Richard Bellingham
     Esq 16th — 10th mo.
John Cole son of Isaac Cole was married to Susanna Hutchinson daughter·of
     the late William Hutchinson of Road Island 30th — 10th month by Richard
     Bellingham Esq.
William Baker was married to Mary Eddington dau. of Edmund Eddington
     23rd 7th mo.
Edmund Madocks was married to Rebecca Munings 14th — 11th month by
     Thomas Dudley Dept. Governor.
Samuel Davis was married to Sarah Thayer daughter of Richard Thayer
     20th — 5th month by William Hibbins.
Joseph Brisco was married to Abigail Compton dau. of John Compton 30th —
     11th mo. by William Hibbins.
Ambrose Due was married to Ester Barker dau. of Nicholas Barker 10th —
     12th mo. by Wm. Hibbins.
John Coggan was married to Mrs Martha Winthrop by John Endicott Governor
     10th — 1st mo.
Peter Till was married to Elizabeth Nick 26th — 12th month by William
     Hibbins.
Isaac Cullimore was married to Margery Page 22nd — 11th month by Rich-
     ard Bellingham.
Thomas Saxton was married to Ann Atwood widow 10th — 1st month by Rich-
     ard Bellingham.
William Paddy of Plymouth was married to Mary Paiton of Boston widow
     3rd — 10th mo. by Richard Bellingham.


### FIRST CHURCH.

| | | |
|---|---|---|
| Mercy of Francis Smyth's wife | 9 day | 1 mo. |
| Samuel of James Johnson | 16 day | 1 mo. |
| Thomas of Matthew Barnes of Braintry | 16 day | 1 mo. |
| Elizabeth ⎫ | 23 day | 1 mo. |
| Sarah ⎬ daughters of William Hersy's wife | 23 day | 1 mo. |
| Hester ⎭ | 23 day | 1 mo. |
| Joseph of John Stevenson | 23 day | 1 mo. |
| Samuel of John Bodman's wife | 23 day | 1 mo. |
| Naomy of William Parsons | 6 day | 2 mo. |
| Sarah of Wm Hawghton's wife | 6 day | 2 mo. |
| James of James Pemerton | 13 day | 2 mo. |
| Joana of Michael Wills | 13 day | 2 mo. |
| Sarah of Isaac Adington | 20 day | 2 mo. |
| Elizabeth of Edward Devotion | 20 day | 2 mo. |
| Hannah of John Barrill | 27 day | 2 mo. |
| Elizabeth, of John Leverit | 4 day | 3 mo. |
| John of John Harrod | 4 day | 3 mo. |
| Ephraim of William Davice | 18 day | 3 mo. |
| Lydia of Thomas Roberts | 18 day | 3 mo. |

| | |
|---|---|
| Simion, of Anthony Stoddard | 25 day 3 mo. |
| Elizabeth, of Vall. Hill. | 25 day 3 mo. |
| Experience of George Orice's wife | 25 day 3 mo. |
| William of Rawson of Newberry | 25 day 3 mo. |
| Sarah of Alexander Baker | 25 day 3 mo. |
| Rachel of John Bateman's wife | 1 day 4 mo. |
| John of Richard Wilson's wife | 1 day 4 mo. |
| Sarah of William Stanbery's wife | 1 day 4 mo. |
| Mary of Strong Furnill | 1 day 4 mo. |
| John of William Blancher | 8 day 3 mo. |
| John of William Salter | 8 day 4 mo. |
| Deane of Deane Winthorp's wife | 15 day 4 mo. |
| John of Tho: Alcoke | 6 day 5 mo. |
| Rebecca of Edward Tinge | 20 day 5 mo. |
| Arthur of Arthur Perry | 27 day 5 mo. |
| Elizabeth of Simon Rogers | 3 day 6 mo. |
| Deliverance son of Elias Partman | 10 day 6 mo. |
| Jacob of Elizabeth Rider of Waymouth | 10 day 6 mo. |
| Richard of Goody Chapman of Braintry | 17 day 6 mo. |
| John of Benjamin Negoose | 31 day 6 mo. |
| Mary of Blacklech of Salem | 7 day 7 mo. |
| Humphry, of Daniel Turant. | 7 day 7 mo. |
| Mary of Angill Hollard | 14 day 7 mo. |
| Joanna of Samuel Sindall of Newbery | 21 day 7 mo. |
| John of John Sweete | 21 day 7 mo. |
| Edward of John Tuttill's wife of Linn | 21 day 7 mo. |
| Mehetabel of Thomas Buttole | 28 day 7 mo. |
| Mary of Henry Pownening | 5 day 8 mo. |
| Sarah of Strang's wife | 26 day 8 mo. |
| Asaph of Jacob Eliot our elder, dec. | 2 day 9 mo. |
| Jeremiah of Jeremiah Howchin | 9 day 9 mo. |
| Samuel of Samuel Norden's wife | 16 day 9 mo. |
| Isaac of Edmund Jackson | 23 day 9 mo. |
| Nicholas of Isaac Waker | 7 day 10 mo. |
| Thomas of Robert Feild | 7 day 10 mo. |
| Deborah, of Francis Dowse | 7 day 10 mo. |
| John of Robert Woodward's wife | 14 day 10 mo. |
| John of Richard Bradley's wife | 22 day 10 mo. |
| Penn of William Townsend. | 28 day 10 mo. |
| James of James Jemson's wife | 28 day 10 mo. |
| Edward of Edward Hutchison | 4 day 11 mo. |
| Elizabeth of Joseph Rocke | 8 day 12 mo. |
| Elizabeth of David Sellicke. | 8 day 12 mo. |
| Ann of Edward Rainsford. | 8 day 12 mo. |
| Deborah of Samuel Oliver | 8 day 12 mo. |
| Ann of Matthew Ines. | 8 day 12 mo. |
| John of John Clarke's wife | 8 day 12 mo. |
| Joseph } sons of | 8 day 12 mo. |
| Benjamin } Thomas Emans | 8 day 12 mo. |
| Pereez of Thomas Savage | 22 day 12 mo. |
| John of John Merion. | 22 day 12 mo. |
| Jonathan of William Boyden | 22 day 12 mo. |
| Naomy daut of George Allin's wife | 22 day 12 mo. |

## 1652.

### TOWN.

Mary of Edward & Jane Barker born 15th Feb.
Thomas of James & Sarah Pemberton born 17th Feb.
John of George & Barbary Davis born 3rd June.
Daniel of Francis & Mary East born 21st Sept.
Sarah of George & Mary Michell born 8th Dec.
Catherine of Edward & Abigail Hutchinson born 13th Feb

Joanna of Christopher & Anne Holland born 1st Feb.
Mary of Robert & Judith Ratchell born the last of Aug.
Tabitha of Matthew & Tabitha Abda born 24th Nov.
Hugh of Hugh & Sarah Browne born 16th July.
Thomas of William & Martha Harvey born 16th Aug.
Joanna of Henry & Mary Stevens born 28th May.
Hannah of Thomas & Elizabeth Sowell born 2nd Nov.
Joanna of William & Elline Furnell born 9th Dec.
Benjamin of Joseph & Mary Bastarr born 4th April.
Sarah of Nathaniel & Sarah Hunn born 8th July.
Elizabeth of Nicholas & Hannah Phillips born 24th Feb.
Daniel of Daniel & Esther Travis born 3rd Oct.
Mary of Jeremiah & Easter Fitch born 1st March.
John of John & Mary Barrell born 15th Mch.
Mary of Samuel & Joanna Sendall born 13th March.
William of Edward & Mary Ting born 3rd March.
William of William & Ann Pollard born 20th March.
Elizabeth of Thomas & Elizabeth Watkins born 27th Nov.
Mary of Thomas & Elizabeth Williams born 30th July.
Benjamin of Alexander & Elizabeth Baker born 16th March.
Elizabeth of Thomas & Elizabeth Pecke born 19th Jan.
Mary of John & Hannah Bateman born 16th Jan.
Isaac of John & Sarah Merion born 20th Jan.
Abiel of William & Grace Toy born 21st Jan.
Elizabeth & Mary twins & daughters of John & Judith Hull born 23rd Jan.
Joanna of Richard and Joanna Knight born 24th Jan.
John of John & Hannah Haniford born 29th Jan.
Rebecca of William & Ann Cotton born 30th Dec.
Alice of Mathew & Rebecca Barnes born 22nd Dec.
John of Alexander & Mary Adams born 26th Feb.
Sarah of Isaac & Ann Adington born 11th Feb.
Thomas of Robert & Mary Feild born 28th Nov.
John of Thomas & Anne Waker born 15th March.
Sarah of Anthony & Deborah Stoddard born 21st Oct.
Susanna of Strong & Elline Furnell born 14th Sept.
Elizabeth of Henry & Elizabeth Blake born 28th Oct.
Elizabeth of Thomas & Sarah Yeo born 1st Oct.
Judith of William & Cicilla Talbott born 24th July.
Elizabeth of Peter & Alice Place born 21st Oct.
Mary of John & Abigail Jackson born 25th Oct.
Edward of Benjamin & Deborah Thwing born 14th Nov.
Susanna of William & Susanna Hawes born 15th Oct.
James of James & Mary Hawkins born 3rd July.
Mehetabel of William and Martha Brenton born 28th Nov.
Maria of Mr Symon & Martha Aeirs born 26th — 1st month.
Mehetabel of William & Elizabeth Spowell born 31st — 1st month.
Rebecca of Nathaniel & Alice Bishop born 8th — 2nd month.
Rebecca of John & Abigail Leader born 10th — 2nd month.
Rebecca of Thomas & Catherine Downes born 22nd — 2nd month.
John of John & Persis Harrison born 2nd — 2nd month.
Mary of Humphrey & Mary Millam born 23rd — 3rd mouth.
Robert of Robert deceased & Elizabeth Turner born 17th — 3rd mouth.
Simon of Simon Jun. & Lydia Eire born 6th Aug.
John of William & Hannah Blanchard born 18th Sept.
Benjamin of George & Joan Hallsell born 18th Sept.
Samuel of Richard & Martha Thurston born 11th July.
Mary of Edmund & Ann Grosse born 9th Sept.
Jeremiah of Jeremiah & Sarah Merills born 22nd Augt.
Elizabeth of Capt. Richard & Elizabeth Davenport born 13th Sept.
Sarah of Jacob & Margaret Sheafe born 14th Sept.
Moses of John & Jane Huntley born 1st July.
Joseph of Philip & Anne Long born 16th Aug.
Joseph of Abraham & Elizabeth Hagborne born 8th Oct.
Rebecca of Joshua & Lydia Scottow born 10th Oct.

Wilham of William of Pulling pointe & Sarah Hasey born 15th Sept.
Benjamin of George & Abigail Dill born 27th — 2nd month.
Mary of William & Mary Baker born 16th — 3rd month.
Joseph of William & Friswit Osborne born 6th — 2nd month.
Mehetabel of Thomas & Sarah Webber born 10th — 4th month.
Rebecca of Henry & Sarah Messinger born 26th — 4th month.
Eliakim of Robert and Sarah Waker born 3rd — 5th month.
Elizabeth of Joseph & Dorothy Phipeny born 10th — 4th month.
Stephen of Amos & Sarah Richardson born 14th — 4th month.
Mary of John & Mary Phillips born 13th July.
Edward of Robert & Ann Knight born 5th Feb.
Susanna of George & Susanna Alline born 11th May.
Jeremiah of Jeremiah & Ester Houchine born 26th Nov.
Anne of Capt. John & Sarah Leveritt born 23rd Nov.
Benjamin of John and Mary Hurd born 28th Nov.
Mehetabel of Mark & Mary Hands born 21st Oct.
Thomas of Robert & Rebecca Winsor born 30th Sept.
Joseph of Thomas & Anne Dure born 24th June.
John of John & Hannah Anger born 16th Sept.
Michael of Michael & Millered Willis born 11th Nov.
Sarah of Joseph & Elizabeth Rocke born 17th Jan.
Mary of Thomas & Hannah Rawlins born 24th Nov.
Joshua of John & Martha Coggan born 15th Dec.

Mary of William & Mary Baker died 25th — 6th mo.
Sarah of John & Alice Tinker died 28th — 6th mo.
John of Robert & Sarah Waker died 22nd — 5th mo.
Sarah of Isaac & Ann Addington died 2nd — 6th mo.
John of John & Elizabeth Farnum died 26th — 6th mo.
Robert of Robert deceased & Elizabeth Turner died 21st — 6th month.
Zechary of Zechary & Elizabeth Phillips died 2nd — 7th month.
Philip of Abram & Bitteris Josline died 2nd — 6th mo.
Bozon Allen died 14th — 7th month.
William Ludkine drowned 27th — 1st month.
Samuel Olliver drowned 27th — 1st month.
George Bennet drowned 27th — 1st month.
David Nichols died 13th — 1st month.
Adam Winthropp Esq. died 24th — 6th month.
John of Robert & Rachel Woodward died 23rd — 6th month.
Ephraim of William & Margaret Davis died 2nd — 6th month.
William of William & Anne Cotton died 29th — 6th month.
Mehitabel son of Thomas & Sarah Webber died 7th — 7th month.
Samuel of John & Martha Shaw died 15th — 7th mo.
Joseph of Philip & Ann Long died 28th — 6th mo.
Nathaniel of Arthur Gill died 2nd — 7th mo.
James of Richard & Joanna Knight died 27th — 7th month.
Gamaliel of Gamaliel & Sarah Phipeny died 8th — 7th month.
William Ivery carpenter & inhabitant of Lynn died 3rd — 8th month.
Frances wife of Hezekiah Vsher died 25th — 2nd mo.
Zechariah of Zechariah & Elizabeth Phillips died 4th — 7th month.
Joseph of John & Sarah Stephenson died 10th — 7th month.
Martha wife of Edmund Jackson deceased 12th — 9th month.
Thomas of Thomas & Anne Dure died 3rd — 10th mo.
Ann wife of James Hudson died 3rd — 10th mo.
Matthew Parker died 19th — 7th month.
Thomas Standbury died 26th — 7th month.
Arthur Perry died 9th — 8th month.
William Blanchard died 7th — 8th month.
Mr John Cotton Teacher of the Church of Boston died 15th — 10th month.
Elizabeth of John & Judith Hull died 12th mo.
Mary of John & Judith Hull died 30th — 11th mo.
John of Francis & Sarah Pit'ney died 17th — 8th mo.
John Stark Scottishman servant to Lieut. William Hudson died 22nd — 3rd
    month.

Mercy of Francis & Elizabeth Smith died 4th —7th month.
John of John & Hannah Haniford died 7th — 12th mouth.
Capt. William Ting died 18th — 11th mouth.
Jane wife of Capt. William Ting died 3rd —8th mo.
Susan of Strong Furnell died 21st — 7th mo.
John of Robert & Mary Wright died 22nd — 4th mo.
Joanna of Christopher & Ann Holland died 1st — 3rd month.
Hugh of Hugh & Sarah Browne died 16th — 5th mo.
Ellinor of Henry & Mary Shrimpton died 9th — 1st month 1652?
Thomas Oddingsalls a stranger deceased at Mr. Rucks house at Boston in New
England 21st — 4th month.


John Cheeckley was married to Ann Eires daughter of Mr Symon Eires
5th — 1st month by William Hibbins.
Edward Allen of Boston was married to Martha Waye 7th — 3rd month by
Thomas Dudley.
Nath Gallop was married to Margaret Eneley 11th — 4th month by Richard
Bellingham.
Edward Yeomans was married to Elizabeth Joslin 21st — 4th month by Rich-
ard Bellingham.
Polus Lunerus was married to Margaret Clemons widow 1st — 5th month by
Wm Hibbins.
Joseph Howe was married to Frances Willey 16th — 5th month by William
Hibbins.
William Ballantine was married to Hannah Hollard daughter of Angel Hol-
lard 23rd — 5th mo by William Hibbins.
Silvester Harbert was married to Lucie Adams 21st — 7th month by William
Hibbins.
Capt Thomas Savage was married to Mary Simmes the daughter of Zechariah
Simmes Pastor of the Church of Christ in Charlestown by Increase Nowell
15 — 7th month.
Thomas Love was married to Hannah Thurston 23rd — 7th month by Richard
Bellingham.
Thomas Edzall was married to Elizabeth Ferman 16th — 7th month by
Richard Bellingham.
Edward Ellis was married to Sarah Blott daughter of Robert Blott of Boston
By Thomas Dudley Dept Govr 6th — 8th month.
Matthew Grosse was married to Mary Trott by Thomas Dudley Dept Govr
5th — 8th month.
Hezekiah Vsher was married to Elizabeth Simes daughter of Zechariah Simes
Pastor of the Church of Christ at Charlestown 2nd — 9th month by Increase
Nowell.
Nath Adams was married to Elizabeth Purmott daughter of Philemon Purmott
24th — 9th month by Richard Bellingham.
Edmund Jackson was married to Mary Gawdren widow 7th — 11th month by
Richard Bellingham.
James Burgesse was married to Lydia Meed 19th — 8th month.
John Mosse was married to Mary Jupe 24th — 10th month by Richard Bel-
lingham.
Thomas Robinson of Scituate was married to Mary Woodey widow 10th —
11th month by William Hibbins.
Edward Hull son of Robert Hull of Boston was married to Elinor Newman
20th — 11th month by William Hibbins.
James Hudson was married to Rebecca Browne daughter of William Browne
of Boston 3rd — 12th month by William Hibbins.
John Samuel was married to Lucie Wight widow 24th — 10th month by Rich-
ard Bellingham.
Thomas Bill was married to widow Elizabeth Nichols 14th — 11th month by
Richard Bellingham.
William Awbrey merchant was married to Rachel Rawson daughter of Edward
Rawson 18th — 11th month by Wm Hibbins.
Simon Lynde was married to Hannah Newgate daughter of John Newgate of
Boston 22nd — 12th month by William Hibbins.

William Hinckesman was married to Mary Philberd 20th — 11th month by Mr. Glover.

Peter Wittoms was married to Redgon Clarke 17th — 4th month by William Hibbins.

William Greenough was married to Elizabeth Vpshall daughter of Nicholas Vpshall of Boston 4th July by William Hibbins.

## FIRST CHURCH.

| | |
|---|---|
| Joseph of John Millam | 7 day 1 mo. |
| Mary of John Millam | 7 day 1 mo. |
| Jarat of Jarat Bourne | 7 day 1 mo. |
| Elizabeth of Anthony Harker | 7 day 1 mo. |
| Joshua of Parkis of Watertowne | 7 day 1 mo. |
| Nathaniel of Potter Oliver | 14 day 1 mo. |
| Abigail of Thomas Snow | 14 day 1 mo. |
| Gamaliel of Gamaliel Phipeny's wife | 14 day 1 mo. |
| Ann of John Manning's wife | 21 day 1 mo. |
| Joseph of Henry Bridgham | 22 day 1 mo. |
| Sarah of John Viall | 22 day 1 mo. |
| Thomas of Walter Sennet's wife | 28 day 1 mo. |
| Maria of Simon Ayres | 4 day 2 mo. |
| Rebecca of Nathaniel Bishop | 11 day 2 mo. |
| Elizabeth of Richard Waight | 18 day 2 mo. |
| Hannah of John Kenniricke | 18 day 2 mo. |
| Samuel of Godfrey Armitage | 18 day 2 mo. |
| John of John Harrisson | 25 day 2 mo. |
| Robert of Robert Turner | 23 day 3 mo. |
| John of George Davis | 6 day 4 mo. |
| Benjamin of George Dill of the New Ch. | 6 day 4 mo. |
| Susannah of Susannah & George Allin | 6 day 4 mo. |
| Mehetabel of Tho: Weebber | 13 day 4 mo. |
| Steven of Amos Richisson's wife | 20 day 4 mo. |
| Elizabeth of David Phipeny | 20 day 4 mo. |
| Rebecca of Sarah & Henry Messinger | 27 day 4 mo. |
| Eliakim of Robert Waker | 4 day 5 mo. |
| Samuel of Martha & Richard Thurston | 11 day 5 mo. |
| Ann of Richard Bellingham | 26 day 5 mo. |
| Benjamin of John Sunderland | 26 day 5 mo. |
| Joseph of Philip Long's wife | 22 day 6 mo. |
| Matthew of Dorcas a Negro of Dorchester | 12 day 7 mo. |
| John of William Blanchard | 19 day 7 mo. |
| Elizabeth of John Damford of Salem | 19 day 7 mo. |
| Mary of Edmund Groose | 19 day 7 mo. |
| Susannah, of Strong Furnill | 19 day 7 mo. |
| Benjamin, of George Halsoll | 19 day 7 mo. |
| Sarah of Jacob Sheafe | 23 day 7 mo. |
| Thomas of Rebecca & Thomas Winsor | 3 day 8 mo. |
| Elizabeth of Henry Blauge | 3 day 8 mo. |
| Elizabeth of Thos: Yoo's wife | 3 day 8 mo. |
| Rebecca of Josua Scotto | 10 day 8 mo. |
| John of Abram Hagbourne | 10 day 8 mo. |
| Susan of William Dawes | 17 day 8 mo. |
| William of William Asey's wife | 17 day 8 mo. |
| Eliza of Joan & Thomas Jay | 17 day 8 mo. |
| Sarah of Anthony Stoddard | 24 day 8 mo. |
| Sarah of John Jackson | 31 day 8 mo. |
| Elizabeth of Peter Place | 7 day 9 mo. |
| Mehetabel, of Marke Haines | 7 day 9 mo. |
| Edward of Benjamin Thwing | 14 day 9 mo. |
| Daniel of Francis East | 21 day 9 mo. |
| Ann of John Leaverit | 28 day 9 mo. |
| Jeremiah of Jeremiah Howchin | 28 day 9 mo. |
| Mary of Rawlins of Waymouth | 28 day 9 mo. |

| | |
|---|---|
| Calib of John Coggan | 26 day 10 mo. |
| Alce of Matthew Barnes of Braintry | 26 day 10 mo. |
| Rebecca of William Cotton | 2 day 11 mo. |
| Samuel of Samuel Damford pastor of Ch. of Roxbery | 16 day 11 mo. |
| Abihell of William Toye | 23 day 11 mo. |
| Sarah of Joseph Rocke | 23 day 11 mo. |
| Mary of John Bateman's wife | 23 day 11 mo. |
| Mary of John Hull | 30 day 11 mo. |
| Elizabeth of John Hull | 30 day 11 mo. |
| John of Hannah & John Honyford | 30 day 11 mo. |
| Isaac of John Meriam | 30 day 11 mo. |
| John of Alexander Adames | 13 day 12 mo. |
| Sarah of Isaac Adington | 13 day 12 mo. |

## 1653.

### Town.

Redemption of Robert & Elizabeth Scott born 2nd March.
James & John twins of James & Abigail Johnson born 7th March.
Abigail of John & Abigail Leader born 29th May.
Thomas of Mr. Thomas & Mary Broughton born 26th May.
Robert of Robert & Mary Wright born 16th June.
Maria of Jonathan & Jane Negus born 6th July.
John of John & Ruth Ingolesby born 10th July.
Joseph of Joseph & Frances Howe born 23rd June.
Mary of John & Alice Tincker born 2nd July.
Sarah of Capt. Thomas & Mary Savage born 25th June.
Martha of Philemon & Elizabeth Pormott born 16th June.
William of Lieut. William & Margaret Davis born 25th June.
Mary of Robert & Sarah Willis born 18th July.
Mary of George & Mary Dod born 5th July.
Lydia of John & Elizabeth Ferniside born 3rd April.
Benjamin of Benj. & Wilmot Phipeny born 6th April.
John of John & Ann Checkley born 21st April.
John of George & Mary Munjoy born 17th April.
Mary of William & Mary Holloway born 2nd April.
John of John & Jane Mavericke born 18th April.
Hezekiah of John & Elizabeth Harwood born 27th April.
Mary of John & Mary Tuttle born 28th April.
John of William & Mary Gilford born 14th May.
Thomas of Robert & Rebecca Lord born 18th May.
William of Timothy & Margaret Prout born 23rd May.
Samuel of Sylvester & Lucy Harbart born 12th June.
Martha of Matthew & Mary Grosse born 29th June.
Hannah of Gamaliel & Sarah Phipeny born 29th July.
. Peter of Samuel & Mary Johnson born 2nd July.
Martha of David & Mary Faulkner born 30th March.
Mary of Sargt Thomas & Mary Lake born 27th July.
John of Mordica & Alice Nichols born 18th Aug.
Eunice of Thomas & Eunice Roberts born 18th Aug.
Benjamin of Stephen & Jane Butler born 2nd Aug.
Sarah of Edward & Martha Alline born 22nd Aug.
John of William & Hannah Townsend born 3rd Sept.
Elizabeth of John & Persis Harrison born 2nd Aug.
John of Samuel & Mary Flacke born 12th March 1652–3.
Nathaniel of Nathaniel & Mary Adams born 10th Sept.
Mary of Edward & Margaret Coleman born 12th Sept.
Mary of John & Thomasine Scarlet born 21st Sept.
Jane of John & Thomasine Scarlet born 21st Sept.
Richard of Richard & Sibbell Bennet born 3rd Sept.
Elizabeth of Richard & Frances Woody born 19th Sept.
Martha of Robert & Ann Knight born 1st Sept.
Hannah of Benjamin & Elizabeth Negus born 2nd Oct.

John of William & Hannah Ballantine born 29th Sept.
Joseph of Thomas & Susanna Bumsteed born 24th Oct.
Naomi of Francis & Catherine Dowse born 26th Oct.
Robert of Robert & Mary Field born 11th Sept.
Samuel of Thomas & Ann Saxton born 8th Oct.
Sarah of James & Sarah Balston born 26th Aug.
Elizabeth of Richard & Jane Chritchley born 11th Nov.
Elizabeth of Edward & Margaret Cowell born 17th Aug.
Joseph of John & Sarah Bodman born 17th Oct.
Nathaniel of William & Mary Paddy born 5th Nov.
Samuel of Simon & Hannah Lynde born 1st Dec.
Nathaniel of Samuel & Joanna Norden born 27th Nov.
Deane of Deane & Sarah Winthropp born 6th Sept.
Sarah of Francis & Mary Hudson born 27th Nov.
Abigail of Sampson & Abigail Shore born 6th Dec.
John of James & Rebecca Hudson born 8th Nov.
Sarah of George & Elizabeth Oris born 16—
Joseph of Henry & Alice Largine born 23rd Nov.
Joseph of Thomas & Anne Bell born 1st Nov.
John of William & Mary Baker born 14th Dec.
Joanna of Angel & Catherine Hollard born 17th Dec.
Hannah of Hezekiah & Elizabeth Vsher born 29th Dec.
Mary of Edward & Margaret Preston born 1st Jan.
Joseph of Daniel & Lydia Turell born 27th Dec.
Stephen of Anthony & Barbary Stoddard born 6th Jan.
John of James & Mary Dennis born 6th Dec.
Mary of William & Ann Cole born 6th Dec.
John of Simon & Martha Eire born 19th Feb.
Constancy of Humphrey & Mary Milam born 15th Dec.
Sarah of Ezekiel & Anne Woodward born 21st Jan.
Hannah of Gamaliel & Sarah Phipeny born 25th July.
James of John & Sarah Stephenson born 1st Oct.
John of Strong & Elline Furnell born 28th Jan.
John of William & Mary Lane born 5th Feb.
Elizabeth of Mathew & Ann Grosse born 30th Jan.
Ebenezer of Jacob & Margaret Sheafe born 4th Feb.
Josiah of Nicholas & Hannah Stone born 4th Feb.
Thomas of John & Joan Baker born 12th Feb.
Mary of John & Susanna Sweete born 28th Jan.
Anna of John & Anna Chamberlin born 6th Feb.
John of Robert & Catherine Nanny born 16th Feb.
George of George & Deborah Burrell born 13th Feb.
James of Emanuel & Christian Fryer born 7th Oct.
Elnathan of George & Susanna Allen born 26th Dec.
Joanna of Christopher & Anne Holland born 13th Oct.
Sarah of Jeremiah & Ester Houchine born 10th March.
Ann of Robert & Judith Rachell born 4th Feb.
John of Ambrose & Mary Bennet born 19th Feb.
Jacob of Hope & Rachell Alline born 22nd Feb.
John of Richard & Rebecca Wayte born 1st Nov.
John of John & Martha Amey born 12th March.
Samuel of William & Joanna Whitwell born 15th March.
Mary of Henry & Julian Lamprey born 8th March.
John of Thomas & Elizabeth Watkins born 21st March.
John of John & Emm Coddington born 9th Feb.
Berachiah of Edward & Martha Arnold born 22nd Feb.
William of William & Mary Hinckesman born 29th Jan.
Martha of John & Martha Mellowes born 8th Feb.
Mehetabel of Edmund & Susanna Jackline born 15th Feb.
Sarah of Hugh & Sarah Browne born 16th Aug.
William of Anthony & Alice Shaw born 21st Jan.
Hannah of John & Hannah Buckman born 5th July.
Mary of Peter & Redigon Wittoms born 15th April.
Mary of John & Martha Bundy born 5th Oct.

Thomas of Thomas & Elizabeth Sowell born 13th July.
Joanna of William & Mary Smaledge born 15th April.
James of James & Mary Hawkins born 18th March.
Jonas of Thomas & Sarah Stevens born 27th Oct.
Sarah of Ezekiel & Ann Woodward born 14th July.
Samuel of John & Elizabeth Wilkey born 3rd April.
Elizabeth of Richard & Jane Critchly born 28th Nov.
John of Edward & Jane Barker born 15th Jan.
Rebecca of William & Elizabeth Ingram of Rumney Marsh born 26th **Sept.**

John of Henry & Mary Willis died 8th — 1st mo.
Jane wife of Augustine Lindon died 16th — 1st mo.
Samuel of Augustine Lindon died 26th — 1st mo.
John of James & Christian Alleson died 2nd — 2nd mo.
John of John & Mary Barrell died 27th — 3rd mo.
Clement Critchet servant of John Sunderland died 29th — 3rd month.
Rebecca wife of Walter Merry died 4th — 5th mo.
Margaret wife of Lieut. William Davis died 3rd —5th mo.
Jane wife of Richard Peacocke died 29th — 5th mo.
Lydia wife of Mr. Simon Eire died 10th — 6th mo.
Elizabeth of Joseph & Dorothy Phipeny died 14th — 5th mo.
Hannah wife of John Hanniford died 16th — 6th mo.
Mary of Thomas & Mary Lake died 1st — 7th mo.
Richard Walters mate of Dickory Carwithy died 3rd — 6th month.
Thomas Millerd of Newbery died 1st — 7th month.
Mary Fisher widow died 27th — 7th month.
Dickery Carwithen shipmaster died 6th — 7th mo.
Mary of George & Mary Dod died 4th — 8th mo.
Thomas of Robert & Rebecca Lord died 6th — 8th mo.
Lucie wife of John Andrewes died 1st — 7th mo.
Elizabeth Howen widow died 27th — 7th mo.
Susanna wife of William Read died 12th — 8th mo.
Robert Boltin of Saffron Walden in England a seaman was accidentally slain
    at Nantasket in New England by a ship gun 28th — 5th mo.
Paul Michell a fisherman living at Crafthold in England deceased at William
    Coursers house at Boston in New England died intestate 18th -- 9th month.
Hannah of Mr. John Olliver died 11th — 9th month.
Susanna of David Sellick died 10th — 9th month.
Henry Mason servant to James Everill of Boston died 10th — 9th month.
Elias Manyard mariner of Sidmouth in Devonshire died 4th — 9th month.
Susan of Edward Breecke of Dorchester servant to Mr. William Paddy
    deceased 11th — 9th month.
Richard neger servant of Capt. Robert Keayne died.
Sibbell wife of Richard Bennet died 13th — 7th mo.
David of David & Mary Evons died 2nd -- 9th month.
John Looe died 1st —10th month.
Malachy Browning died at Mr. Robert Scotts house 27th — 9th month.
Rachel of Thomas & Elizabeth Clarke died 16th — 9th month.
John of James & Joanna Davis died 13th — 9th mo.
Jonathan of Thomas & Elizabeth Wihorne died 10th — 10th month.
John Franckline kinsman to Wm. Franckline of Boston died 26th — 9th
    month.
Rebecca wife of James Hudson died 14th — 9th mo.
Joseph of Thomas & Ann Bell died 29th — 9th mo.
Peter of John & Abigail Jackson died 5th — 9th mo.
Benjamin of John and Abigail Jackson died 11 — 9th mo.
Ezra Cane of Fingworth in Lecestershire died 4th — 7th month.
John Robinson of Fiddingworth in Lecestershier died 7th — 7th month.
James of William & Hannah Browne died 15th — 9th month.
Richard Done neger servant to Capt. Robt. Keayne died 11th — 9th mo.
Richard of Richard & Mary Chapman died 17th — 9th month.
Elizabeth of James & Abigail Johnson died 11th — 9th month.
Mary of William merchant & Ann Cole died 23rd — 10th month.
Nathaniel Edwards merchant died 2nd — 11th mo.

John Whittingham son in law to Mr. Simon Eire died 7th — {th month.
Zacheus of Richard & Elizabeth Fairebanks died 10th — 9th month.
William King servant to George Hallsell died 14th — 10 month.
Elizabeth of Edward & Elizabeth Page died 19th — 9th month.
John of James & Rebecca Hudson died 21st — 16th mo.
Rebecca wife of Thomas Leader died 16th — 10th mo.
Patience of Samuel & Lydia Olliver died 26th — 9th month.
Isabel wife of William Caustine died 25th — 11th mo.
Richard of Richard & Sibbell Bennet died 26th — 12th mo.
Elizabeth of Francis & Alice Bennet died 17th — 11th month.
Naomi of William & Judith Cope died 8th — 8th month.
Ralph Waldren born in Barbadoes died 29th — 9th month.
Sarah of Mr. Robert Woodmansey died 10th — 9th mo.
William Dening died 20th — 11th month.
Robert Woodward died 21st — 9th month.
Jeremiah of Robert & Rachel Woodward died 26th — 9th month.
Joseph Shaw died 13th — 10th month.
Sarah of Hugh & Sarah Browne died 2nd — 11th mo.
Hannah of William Holloway died last 8th month.


Edmond Browne was married to Elizabeth Oklye 14th — 12th mo. by Richard Bellingham Dep. Govr.
John Lowle was married to Hannah Proctor daughter of George Proctor of Dorchester 3rd — 1st month by Wm Hibbins.
William Jaye was married to Mary Hunting daughter of John Hunting of Dedham? ———.
Samuel Mattocke was married to Constance Fairebanks daughter of Richard Fairebanks of Boston 30th — 1st month by William Hibbins.
Anthony Shaw was married to Alice Stanare 8th — 2nd month by Increase Nowell.
John Gilbert was married to Mary Eaton 5th — 3d month by Thomas Dudley Dep. Gov.
Jeremiah Beels of Hingham was married to Sarah Ripley daughter of William Ripley of Hingham at Boston 26th — 8th month by William Hibbins.
Habbacuke Glover was married to Hannah Eliott daughter of John Eliott teacher of the Church of Christ at Roxbury 4th — 3rd month by Thomas Dudley Dept. Govr.
Joseph Jewitt of Rowley was married to Ann Allen widow form. wife of Capt. Bozon Allen of Boston 13th — 3rd month by Richard Bellingham.
Isaac Bull was married to Sarah Parker daughter of John Parker 22nd — 4th month.
John Sandy was married to Ann Holmes 7th — 5th month by William Hibbins.
Ambrose Dart was married to Anne Adis daughter of William Addis of Cape Ann 24th — 4th month.
John Chamberline was married to Anne Browne daughter of William Browne of Boston 19th — 3rd month by William Hibbins.
George Manning was married to Mary Haroden 15th — 5th month.
William White & Phillip Wood were married 4th — 6th month.
Thomas Spaule & Marry Gutteridge were married 18th — 6th month by William Hibbins.
Abram Browne was married to Jane Skipper 19th — 6th month by William Hibbins.
Walter Merry was married to Mary Doling 18th — 6th month by Mr. Glover.
William Russell was married to Alice Sparrow widow 7th — 7th month.
Isaac Page was married to Damaris Shattock 30th — 7th month by William Hibbins.
Ambrose Bennet was married to Mary Simons 15th — 2nd month by William Hibbins.
Joshua Rogers was married to Ann Fisen 12th — 8th month by William Hibbins.
Andrew Cload was married to Elizabeth Bugby 29th — 7th month by William Hibbins.

Charles Pretious was married to Rebecca Martine 7th — 9th month by John Glover.

John Endicott son and heir to the worshipful John Endicott was married to Elizabeth Houchin daughter of Jeremiah Houchin of Boston 9th — 9th month by Richard Bellingham.

William Pittman was married to Barbary Evons 29th — 9th month by William Hibbins.

George Dobson was married to Mary Bostwicke[1] 24th — 9th month by John Glover.

John Gillet was married to Elizabeth Perry widow 22nd — 10th month by William Hibbins.

Robert Breck merchant was married to Sarah Hawkins the daughter of Mrs. Mary Hawkins widow 4th — 11th month by Richard Bellingham Dept Govr.

Samuel Bedwell was married to Mary Hodgkinson 2nd — 12th month by William Hibbins.

Richard Martine merchant was married to Sarah Tuttle daughter of John Tuttle of Boston 1st — 12th month by William Hibbins.

Theophilus Frery was married to Hannah Elliott daughter of Jacob Elliott of Boston deceased 4th — 4th month by William Hibbins.

John Lawrence was married to Elizabeth Adkinson 8th — 12th month by William Hibbins.

James Robbinson was married to Martha Buck 21st — 12th month by William Hibbins.

Nathaniel Sowther was married to Sarah Hill widow 5th — 11th month.

Joseph Shaw was married to Mary Sowther daughter of Nath Sowther 1st — 10th mo.

## FIRST CHURCH.

| | |
|---|---|
| William of Edward Tinge | 6 day 1 mo. |
| Deliverances[2] son of Robert Scott | 6 day 1 mo. |
| James of James Johnson | 13 day 1 mo. |
| John of James Johnson | 13 day 1 mo. |
| John of John Barrill | 27 day 1 mo. |
| Benjamin of Alexander Baker | 27 day 1 mo. |
| Tho: of James Pemerton | 27 day 1 mo. |
| Mary of Samuel Sindall of Newberry | 27 day 1 mo. |
| Samuel of Robert Reade of Exeter | 3 day 2 mo. |
| Benjamin of Benjamin Phipenny | 10 day 2 mo. |
| Abigail of        Furnisey of Duxberry | 10 day 2 mo. |
| John of John Chickley | 24 day 2 mo. |
| John of George Mungy | 24 day 2 mo. |
| Hezekiah of John Harrod | 1 day 3 mo. |
| William of        Innes | 1 day 8 mo. |
| Mary of John Tutle's wife of Linn | 8 day 3 mo. |
| William of Timothy Proute | 29 day 3 mo. |
| Tho: of Robert and Rebecca Lord of the New Ch. | 29 day 3 mo. |
| Martha of Philemon Purmit | 19 day 4 mo. |
| James of Christian Alisson sister | 19 day 4 mo. |
| Sarah of Tho: Savage | 26 day 4 mo. |
| William of William Davis | 26 day 4 mo. |
| John of Edward Cowell's wife | 26 day 4 mo. |
| Edward of Edward Cowell's wife | 26 day 4 mo. |
| Mary of Mary & John Tinker | 3 day 5 mo. |
| Maria of Jonathan Negoose | 10 day 5 mo. |
| John of John Inglsby | 10 day 5 mo. |
| Anna of Sarah & Gamaliel Phippeny | 31 day 5 mo |
| James of Elizabeth & Francis Smyth | 8 day 6 mo. |
| Mary of George Davis of the New Ch. | 14 day 6 mo. |

[1] This has been so read, but I am by no means sure that it is the true name. — W. S. A.

[2] Called Redemption on Town Records, one of the two names being evidently written from memory. — W. S. A.

| | | |
|---|---|---|
| Johanna of Henry Stevens | 14 day | 6 mo. |
| Eunice of Tho Roberts | 21 day | 6 mo. |
| Elizabeth of William Cowell's wife | 21 day | 6 mo. |
| Jeremiah of Rachel & Robert Woodward | 28 day | 6 mo. |
| Elizabeth of John Harisson | 28 day | 6 mo. |
| John of William Townsend | 4 day | 7 mo. |
| Elizabeth of Richard Woody of Roxberry | 25 day | 7 mo. |
| James of John Steevenson | 2 day | 8 mo. |
| Hannah of Edward Rawson of Newberry | 10 day | 8 mo. |
| Hannah of Benjamin Negoos | 10 day | 8 mo. |
| Joseph of Ann & Thos Bell | 10 day | 8 mo. |
| Samuel of Ann & Tho Saxton | 10 day | 8 mo. |
| John of Deane Winthorp's wife | 24 day | 8 mo. |
| Joseph of John Bodman's wife | 24 day | 8 mo. |
| Joseph of Tho Bomsteed | 31 day | 8 mo. |
| Naomye of Francis Dowse | 31 day | 8 mo. |
| Nathaniel of William Padye of Plimouth | 7 day | 9 mo. |
| John of Richard Wayt | 7 day | 9 mo. |
| Eliza of Rich. Chrichly | 13 day | 9 mo. |
| Sarah of George Oris's wife | 20 day | 9 mo. |
| Sarah of Francis Hudson's wife | 27 day | 9 mo. |
| Nathaniel of Samuel Norden's wife | 4 day | 10 mo |
| Nathaniel of Elizabeth Ridder of Waymouth | 4 day | 10 mo. |
| Abigail of Samson Shoore | 11 day | 10 mo. |
| Anna of Ezekiah Usher | 1 day | 11 mo. |
| Joseph of Daniel Turand's wife | 1 day | 11 mo. |
| Stephen of Anthony Stoddard | 8 day | 11 mo. |
| John of Simon Ayers | 22 day | 11 mo. |
| Elizabeth of Joseph Rocke | 29 day | 11 mo. |
| John of Strong Furnill | 29 day | 11 mo. |
| Ebenezer of Jacob Sheafe | 5 day | 12 mo. |
| Mary of John Sweete | 5 day | 12 mo. |
| Elnathan of Susan & George Allin | 5 day | 12 mo. |
| Katharine of Edward Hutchison | 19 day | 12 mo. |
| John of Mr Nanny of Hampton | 19 day | 12 mo. |
| Callib of Mr Parkis of Watertowne | 26 day | 12 mo |

## 1654.

### TOWN.

Mary of Charles & Rebecca Pretious born 16th March.
Elisha of William & Mary Salter born 7th March.
Martha of William a Mariner & Martha Phillips born 10th March.
Thomas of Thomas & Catherine Downes born 17th March.
Henry of Henry & Elizabeth Powning born 28th April.
Benjamin of Henry & Elizabeth Bridgham born 4th May.
Thomas of William & Grace Rix born 11th April.
Mary of Peter & Joan Garland born.
Mary of John & Mary Mosse born 20th April.
Henry of Henry & Eleanor Shrimpton born 26th April.
Simon of Simon & Susan Rogers born 28th April.
Aaron of John & Jane Huntley born 15th April.
Sarah of Rice & Anne Jones born 19th April.
Mary of Richard & Mary Hickes born Dec.
Samuel of Lyonell & Eleanor Wheatley born 29th April.
Elizabeth of Peter & Redigon Wittoms born 26th May.
Anne of Matthew & Ann Ines born 6th June.
Anne of William & Margaret Snelling born 7th May & baptized 17th **May.**
Peter of Christopher & Rebecca Clarke born 14th June.
Dorcas of William & Phillips White born 19th April.
John of John & Mary Tappine born 31st May.
Sarah of Edward & Sarah Ellis born 1st July.
Catherine of David & Catherine Hitchborne born 2nd June.
Rebecca of John & Rebecca Crumwell boru 20th July.

William of John & Mary Barrell born 28th July.
Hannah of William & Hannah Shattock born 8th July.
William of William & Elline Furnell born 29th July.
Eliazer of Robert dec. & Elizabeth Scott born 18th July.
Peter of Samuel & Isabel Howard born 4th Aug.
Jabes of Thomas & Elizabeth Hunt born 11th June.
John of John & Judith Hull born 3rd Nov.
Sarah of Thomas & Frances Boyden born 12th Oct.
Hannah of John & Elizabeth Gillet born 12th Oct.
Mary of Robert & Sarah Waker born 1st Nov.
Elizabeth of John & Ann Sandie born 15th Oct.
Elizabeth of Andrew & Elizabeth Cload born 13th Sept.
John of Thomas & Leah Baker born 1st Oct.
Edmund of Edmund & Mary Jackson born 30th — 8th month
John of Mark & Mary Hands boru 10th Sept.
Joseph of John & Mary Viall born 4th June.
Sarah of Edward & Jane Barker born 9th March.
Benjamin of Henry & Elizabeth Bridgham born 3rd May.
Patience of Ambrose & Ester Due born 1st Dec.
Rebecca of Edward & Rachel Rawson born 19th Oct.
Thomas of John & Abigail Leader born 19th Nov.
Nathaniel of Thomas & Mary Broughton born 5th Dec.
Hannah of Nicholas & Hannah Phillips born 25th Nov.
Susanna of Joseph & Mary Bastarr born 1st Sept.
Isaac of Walter & Mary Sennet born 22nd Sept.
Mary of Abraham & Jane Browne born 19th Dec.
Rebecca of Robert & Rebecca Winsor born 20th Dec.
Elizabeth of William & Anne Pollard born 13 Jan.
Abigail of Henry & Susanna Ambrose born 28th Dec.
Zechariah of Hezekiah & Elizabeth Vsher born 26th Dec.
Hannah of Samuel & Mary Gallop born 3rd Sept.
Sarah of James & Sarah Jemson born 2nd Jan.
William of Ambrose & Ann Dart born 1st Jan.
John of James & Sarah Balston born 3rd Dec.
William of William & Elizabeth Spowell born 18th Jan.
Elizabeth of Francis & Alice Bennet born 20th Dec.
Catharine of Amos & Mary Richardson born 6th Jan.
Gustavus of William & Mary Hambleton born 7th Augt.
James of Richard & Joanna Knight born 1st Feb.
Lydia of William & Mary Castine born 22nd Jan.
William of William & Anne Cotton born.
Benjamin of Benjamin & Wilmotte Phippeny born 19th Jan.
Elisha of Robert & Betteris Risdon born 25th Jan.
Mary of Peter & Mary Buttler born 21st Jan.
John of William & Martha Harvey born 5th Feb.
Joshua of Joshua & Anne Rogers born 20th Feb.
William of William & Ruth Read born 3rd Feb.
Priscilla of John & Elizabeth Clow born 28th Jan.
Rachel of Thomas & Elizabeth Pecke born 21st Jan.
Tabitha of John & Tabitha Blower born 12th Feb.
Dorothy of John & Jane Mavericke born 23rd Jan.
William of William & Mary Holloway born 11th Jan.
Nathaniel of William & Grace Toy born 23rd Feb.
Robert of Humphery & Sarah Cumby born 14th Feb.
Mary of David & Mary Faulkner born 10th Nov.
Anne of Thomas & Anne Waker born 27th Feb.
Josiah of Alexander & Elizabeth Baker born 26th Feb.
Elizabeth of Christopher & Anne Holland born 17th Feb.
William of Anthony & Alice Shaw born 24th Feb.
Asa of William & Sarah Halsey born 1st Jan.
Henry of Thomas & Elizabeth Edsell born 28th Feb.
Aaron of Thomas & Sarah Stevens born 28th Feb.
Samuel of Robert & Hannah Read born 28th Feb.
Thomas of Thomas & Sarah Yeo born 24th April.

Mehetabel of Thomas & Milcha Snow born 8th Feb.
John of Matthew & Sarah Barnard born 29th Sept.
Martha of John & Hannah Leeth born the last of Aug.
John of James & Mary Hudson born 26th Jan.
Benjamin of Francis & Joyce Burgesse born 11th Oct.
Jabesh of Samuel & Mary ? Dunkin born 24th Feb.

Joanna of Christopher & Ann Holland died 2nd — 1st month.
Joseph of Henry & Alice Largino died 14th — 1st mo.
Peter of Samuel & Mary Johnson died 19th — 1st mo.
Samuel of Robert & Hannah Read died 31st — 1st month.
Judith wife of Robert Hull died 29th — 1st mo.
John of James & Mary Dennis died 31st — 1st mo.
Sarah of Hugh Browne died 3rd — 2nd mo.
John of John & Susan Sweete died 3rd — 2nd mo.
Joanna of Angel & Catharine Hollard died 29th — 1st month.
William of Anthony & Alice Shaw died 25th — 1st mouth.
Jane wife of John Anderson died 4th — 3rd mo.
Ann wife of Thomas Trescott mariner died 10th — 3rd month.
Thomas Wheeler died 16th — 3rd month.
Samuel of Lyonell & Ellinor Wheatly died 20th — 3rd month.
Tabitha of Thomas & Ann Bell died 27th — 2nd mo.
Elizabeth of Peter & Redigon Wittoms died 25th — 3rd month.
Joseph of Daniel & Lydia Turrill died 10th — 3rd month.
Benjamin of Benjamin & Wilmot Phipeny died 28th — 3rd month.
Hannah the daughter Ireson of Lynn servant to Sibbella Sands widow deceased 5th — 9th month.
Martha a neger daughter of Matthew & Dorcas died 26th — 6th month.
William of Matthew & Ann Jyons died 1st — 9th month.
Mary of John & Hannah Bateman died 17 — 8th month.
Elizabeth Looe died 24th — 8th month.
John of Robert & Elizabeth Sanford died 23rd — 9th month.
Matthew Cenig died 4th — 10th month.
John of John & Judith Hull died 14th — 9th month.
Major General Edward Gibbons died 9th — 10th month.
Thomas of Thomas & Elizabeth Sowell died 7th — 10th month.
Isaac of Walter & Mary Sennot died 11th — 8th mo.
Thomas Dinely died 15th — 11th month.
Joshua of Joshua & Ann Rogers died 15th — 12 mo.
Mary Bigsby widow died 5th — 11th month.
Barnebas Farre died 13th — 10th mouth.
Hannah of Thomas & Elizabeth Sowell died 2nd — 11th month.
John of John & Joan Baker died 25th — 4th mo.
Sarah of John & Mary Philips Jr. died 29th — 4th month.
Hezekiah of John & Elizabeth Harwood died 25th — 4th month.
Zechariah of Zechariah & Elizabeth Phillips died 24th — 5th month.
Thomas of Robert & Rebecca Winsor died 8th — 5th month.
Samuel of John Anderson died 10th — 5th mo.
Phillipee wife of William White died 5th — 5th month.
Samuel Norton died 28th of June 1654.
James of Arthur & Jane Kind died 19th — 5th mo.
Sarah of Joseph & Elizabeth Rocke died 27th — 4th mo.
Hannah of Hezekiah & Elizabeth Vsher died 24th — 5th month.
Mary of Samuel & Joanna Sendall died 23rd — 5th month.
Anna of Matthew & Ann Jyons died 26th — 5th month.
Mr. William Hibbins died 23rd — 5th month.
Elizabeth of Peter & Alice Place died 8th — 6th mo.
Elizabeth of Edward & Margaret Cowell died 7th — 6th month.
John of William & Hannah Townesend died 17th — 6th mo.
Ann of John & Bridget Sanford died 26th — 6th month.
Mary of Samuel & Jane Wilson of Fairefeild died
Eliazer of Robert & Elizabeth Scott died 3rd — 6th mo.
Grace of Richard Bellingham died 3rd — 7th mo.
Thomas of Thomas & Mary Broughton died 1st — 7th montl

John of Robert & Catherine Nanny died 20th — 7th month.
Eliakim of Robert & Sarah Waker died 30th — 7th mo.
John Avery died 31st — 5th month.
Naomi of Francis & Catharine Douce died 14th — 7th mouth.
Lydia of Francis & Catharine Douce died 6th — 8th month.
Mary of Henry & Sibilla Sands died 14th — 8th mo.
Gustavus of William & Mary Hambleton died 27th — 11th month.
John of James & Mary Hudson died the first week in February.


William Read & Ruth Crooke were married 20th — 1st month by William
   Hibbins.
John Farnum & Susanna Arnold daughter of Thomas Arnold of Watertown
   were married 7th — 2nd month by Increase Nowell.
Richard Wilson & Sarah Hurst were married 7th — 2nd month by Richard
   Bellingham.
Joseph Gridley & Lydia Flood widow were married 9th June.
John Tappin & Mary Woodmansey daughter of Mr. Woodmansey of Boston
   were married 20th — 6th month.
Angolla a neger servant of Capt. Robert Keayne was married to Elizabeth a
   neger servant of Edward Hutchinson 20th — 2nd mo by William Hibbins.
John Richards & Elizabeth Winthrop widow were married 3rd — 3rd month
   by William Hibbins.
Robert Hubberd & Margaret Allen were married 2nd — 4th month by William
   Hibbins.
John Conney & Elizabeth Nash daughter of Robert Nash of Boston were
   married 20th — 4th month by Richard Bellingham Dep. G.
Capt. Robert Fen & Mrs. Mary Hawkins widow were married 26th — 4th
   month by William Hibbins.
Thomas Harwood & Rachel Woodward widow were married 7th — 5th month
   by William Hibbins.
Simon Roberts & Christian Baker daughter of Alexander Baker were
   married 18th — 5th month by Richard Bellingham.
John Peirce of Dorchester & Rebecca Wheeler of Boston widow were married
   10th — 6th month by Capt. Humphrey Atherton.
Richard Smith of Lancaster & Joanna Quarlls were married 2nd — 6th month
   by Richard Bellingham Govr.
Ezekiel Hamlen & Elizabeth Drake were married 8th — 6th month by Richard
   Bellingham Gov.
John Blake & Mary Shaw widow were married 16th — 6th month.
Richard Peacocke & Margery Shove widow were married 17th — 6th mo. by
   Richard Bellingham Gov.
John Hawkins & Sarah Damarill widow were married 15th September by
   Richard Bellingham Governor.
Samuel Bucknell & Sarah Bishop daughter of Nath Bishopp of Boston were
   married 18th — 7th month by Richard Bellingham Gov.
James Toung & Elizabeth Hagborne daughter of Abraham Hagborne of Boston
   were married 8th — 7th month by Capt. Humphery Atharton.
Edward Bobbet & Sarah Tarne, daughter of Myles Tarne of Boston were
   married 7th — 7th month by Capt. Humphery Atharton.
Isaac Bollard & Sarah Jones daughter of Thomas Jones of Dorchester were
   married 3rd — 11th month by Mr. Glover.
Robert Higgins & Susanna Westoe were married 2nd — 9th month by Richard
   Bellingham Govr.
Matthew Coy & Elizabeth Roberts were married 29th — 6th month by Capt.
   Humphery Atharton.
Jonathan Danforth & Elizabeth Powter the daughter of Good. Powter
   deceased of Billerky were married 22nd — 9th month.
John Aylett & Mary Hawkins daughter of Capt. Thomas Hawkins deceased
   were married 21st — 9th month by Capt. Humphery Atherton.
Thomas Jones & Lydia Sanderson daughter of Robert Sanderson of Boston
   were married 13th — 10th month by Richard Bellingham Gov.
John Willis & Hannah Elsse were married 11th — 11th month by Capt.
   Humph Atharton.

Jacob Elliott & Mary Wilcock widow were married 9th — 11th month by Capt. Humphery Atharton.

William Hambleton & Mary Richardson were married 7th — 6th month by Richard Bellingham Governor.

William Therrell & Rebecca Simpkins daughter of Capt. Nicholas Simpkins were married 29th — 11th month by Richard Bellingham Governor.

## FIRST CHURCH.

| | |
|---|---|
| Berekiah of Edward Arnoll's wife | 6 day 1 mo. |
| Sarah of Jeremiah Howchin | 12 day 1 mo. |
| Elisha of William Salter | 12 day 1 mo. |
| John of Robert Samford. | 19 day 1 mo. |
| Tho: of William Ricker | 16 day 2 mo. |
| William & Th?: } of Martha & William Harve | 23 day 2 mo. |
| Mary & Jaiene } of Tomeson & John Scarlet | 23 day 2 mo. |
| Mary of John Moos | 23 day 2 mo. |
| Henry of Henry Powning | 30 day 2 mo. |
| Simond of Simond Rogers | 30 day 2 mo. |
| John & Jain } of Jain & John Mavericke | 30 day 2 mo. |
| Benjamin of Henry Bridgham | 7 day 3 mo. |
| Joseph of John Viall | 21 day 3 mo. |
| Matthew Sarah } of Ann & Tho: Joanes | 4 day 4 mo. |
| Mehetable of        Edindin of Ch. of Situat | 4 day 4 mo. |
| Peter of Christopher Clarke's wife | 11 day 4 mo. |
| Ann of Matthew Jones | 11 day 4 mo. |
| Sarah of Sarah Elice | 2 day 5 mo. |
| Eliezer of Robert Scott | 23 day 5 mo. |
| Wm. of John Barrill | 30 day 5 mo. |
| Grace of Rich: Bellingham | 13 day 6 mo. |
| Sarah of John Leverit | 20 day 6 mo. |
| Richard of Capt: Savage | 27 day 6 mo. |
| John of Ann & John Anger | 27 day 6 mo. |
| Sarah of Wm. Davis | 3 day 7 mo. |
| Henry of Sara & Henry Messinger | 3 day 7 mo. |
| John of Mary & Mark Haines | 10 day 7 mo. |
| Isaac of Walter Sennet's wife | 1 day 8 mo. |
| Edward of Edward Rainsford | 15 day 8 mo. |
| Stephen of Isaac Waker | 15 day 8 mo. |
| Sarah of John Gillit's wife | 15 day 8 mo. |
| Ann of Edward Boyden of Ch. of Watertowne | 15 day 8 mo. |
| Thomas of Theodor Atkinson | 22 day 8 mo. |
| Rebecca of Edward Rawson of Ch. of Newberry | 29 day 8 mo. |
| Ann of John Saunders of Ch. of Watertowne | 29 day 8 mo. |
| John of John Hull | 5 day 9 mo. |
| Edmund of Edmond Jackson | 5 day 9 mo. |
| Mary of Robert Waker | 5 day 9 mo. |
| Zacharia of Hezckia Usher | 31 day 10 mo. |
| Rebecca of Rebecca & Thomas Windsor | 31 day 10 mo. |
| Sarah of James Jemson | 7 day 11 mo. |
| Elizabeth of Joan & Tho: Joy | 7 day 11 mo. |
| Kathrine of Ann & Amos Richison | 14 day 11 mo. |
| Abigail of Mrs. Costone of Ch. of Linn | 28 day 11 mo. |
| Benjamin of Mrs. Phipeny of the New Ch. | 28 day 11 mo. |
| Dorothy of Jaen & John Mavericke | 28 day 11 mo. |
| Wm. of Wm. Cotton | 4 day 12 mo. |
| Wm. of Wm. Read | 11 day 12 mo. |
| Mehetabel of Tho: Snowe | 11 day 12 mo. |
| John of sister Harvey | 11 day 12 mo. |
| Peter of Wm. Toy | 25 day 12 mo. |

## 1655.

TOWN.

James of Thomas & Mary Robinson born 14th March.
Eunice of Edward & Mary Ting born 8th March.
William of John & Hannah Bateman born 8th March.
Hannah of Thomas & Elizabeth Rider born 7th March.
Lydia of Francis & Catherine Dowse born 10th March.
William of William & Susanna Dawes born 8th March
Hannah of John & Elizabeth Harwood born 6th March.
Samuel of John & Mary Hurd born 14th March.
Hannah of Matthew & Rebecca Barnes born 14th March.
Rebecca of Joseph & Elizabeth Rocke born 16th March.
Mary of Joseph & Lydia Gridley born 22nd March.
Nathaniel of Thomas & Elizabeth Wyborne born 12th March.
Sarah of John & Jane Bushnell born 24th March.
Mary of William & Elizabeth Browne born 16th March.
Peter of Peter & Sarah Olliver born 3rd March.
Joseph of Daniel & Lydia Turell born 25th March.
Mary of Robert merchant & Sarah Brecke born 19th April.
Elizabeth of Capt. James & Abigail Johnson born 12th April.
Silvanus of Walter & Mary Merry born 8th April.
Sarah of Thomas & Sarah Moore born 26th Apr.
John of Simon & Christian Roberts born 27th April.
Samuel of John & Joan Baker born 16th Apr.
Robert of John & Mary Dawes born 29th March.
Deliverance of Richard & Anna Bradley born 3rd April.
Sarah of Samuel & Sarah Bucknell born 17th May.
John of Edmund & Ann Grosse born 21st April.
Catharine of Matthias & Ann Jions born 1st June.
Mary of Nathaniel & Mary Adams born 20th May.
Mary of William & Siscilla Talbott born 21st June.
Prudence of Jonathan & Mary Balston born 28th May.
Rachel of Thomas & Rachel Harwood born 20th June.
Nathaniel of Elias & Bridget Parkman born 24th June.
William of Edward & Margaret Cowell born 28th June.
Ann of Sargt Richard & Frances Woodee born 12th July.
Joseph of James & Sarah Pemberton born 2nd July.
Thomas of Matthew & Mary Grosse born 5th July.
Mary of Richard & Sarah Martine born 7th June.
Benjamin of Timothy & Margaret Prout born 16th July.
———— of Mr. Jacob & Margaret Sheafe born 25th July.
Ephraim of Capt. John & Ann Manning born 10th Aug.
Sarah of Jeremiah & Sarah Merrills born 14th Aug.
Joanna of William & Mary Davis born 16th Aug.
Mary of Henry & Mary Willis born 26th July.
Thomas of Thomas & Anne Dure born 26th Aug.
Sarah of John & Elizabeth Purchase born 10th Aug.
Martha of Edward & Margaret Coleman born 8th Aug.
Nathaniel of Nathaniel & Damaris Robinson born 29th Aug.
John of John & Susanna Farnum born 20th May.
Elizabeth of David & Mary Evans born 10th Aug.
John of John & Hannah Lowell born 26th Aug.
John of James & Mary Dennis born 4th Aug.
Martha of John & Martha Shaw born 16th Sept.
William of William & Hannah Ballantine born 22nd Sept
Simon of Simon & Hannah Lynde born 26th Sept.
Samuel of Thomas & Anna Rawlins born 1st Sept.
William of William & Mary Baker born 19th Oct.
Elizabeth of Robert & Elizabeth Sanford born 5th Dec.
Mary of Edward & Martha Arnold born 16th Sept.
John of John & Ruth Ingolsby born 2nd Oct.
John of John & Sarah Tuckerman born 8th Oct.

Mary of Mr. John & Mary Aylet born 8th Oct.
Mary of Jacob & Mary Eliott born 6th Oct.
Joseph of Hope & Rachel Allen born 4th Oct.
James of Arthur & Jane Kinde born 29th Oct.
William of William & Sarah King born 6th Nov.
Martha of Mr. Peter & Mary Duncan born 10th Nov.
Sarah of Richard & Joyce Staines born 16th Nov.
George of George & Hannah Munning born 24th Nov.
Hannah of Jacob & Anne Leger born 14th Nov.
Mary of William & Mary Hincksman born 20th Dec.
Rebecca of William & Rebecca Turell born 26th Dec.
Mary of Edmund & Rebecca Madock born 4th Jan.
Samuel of John & Sarah Miriam born 14th Dec.
John of John & Susanna Higgins born 15th Feb.
John of James & Lydia Burgesse born 21st Feb.
Martha of John & Martha Amey born 10th Nov.
Joseph of Robert & Mary Wright born 14th Nov.
Joshua of Thomas & Sarah Scottow born 23rd Dec.
Sarah of Joseph & Frances Howe born 28th Feb.
John of Mr. Jeremiah & Ester Houchine born 27th Oct.
Martha of John & Mary Gilbert born 8th Dec.
Elizabeth of William & Mary Hambleton born 13th Dec.
Thomas of Samuel & Mary Dunkin born 15th Jan.
Hopestill dau. of Nicholas & Hannah Stone born 7th Jan.
Joseph of James & Dorothy Wiseman born 24th Dec.
Josiah of Josiah & Ranis Belchere born 23rd Dec.
Mary of John & Elizabeth Wilkey born 17th Dec.
Joanna of John & Mary Anderson born 25th Dec.
Jaleham of Mr. William & Martha Brenton born 15th Nov.
Mary of John & Sarah Jeffes born 8th Jan.
John of John & Elizabeth Conney born 5th Jan.
Marah of Edward & Susanna Jackline born 15th June.
Jane of Lyonell & Elinor Wheatley born 28th May.
Mary of Capt. John & Sarah Leveret born 12th Feb.
Elizabeth of John & Elizabeth Lawrence born 9th May.
Sarah of John & Sarah Stephenson born 6th Feb.
Ezekiel of Ezekiel & Elizabeth Hamline born 2nd Nov.
Edmund of Clement & Mary Gross born 9th March
John of Nathaniel & Sarah Hunn born 16th Jan.
Hannah of Mr. William & Mary Paddy born 8th Jan.
Martha of Henry & Elizabeth Blake born 2nd Nov.
Margaret of Ezekiel & Ann Woodward born 24th Feb.
Daniel of Robert & Margaret Hubberd born 9th May.
Mary of Richard & Jane Critchly born 18th Jan.
Joshua of Thomas & Sarah Scottow born 23rd Dec.
John of John & Ann Chamberline born 1st May.
John of Mr. Robert & Catharine Nanny born 12th Aug.

Barbary wife of Mr. Anthony Stoddard died 15th — 2nd mouth.
Edmund Grosse died 1st — 3rd month.
Anne of Thomas & Anne Waker died 20th — 2nd month.
Susanna wife of Lieut. William Phillips died 16th - 4th month.
Sylvanus of Walter & Mary Mery died 16th — 4th.
Thomas Bell died 7th — 4th month.
Nathaniel Sowther died 27th — 4th month.
Mr. Robert Knight died 27th — 4th month.
Samuel of John & Joan Baker died 2nd — 5th month.
Hannah wife of Robert Read died 24th — 4th mo.
Robert of Robert & Margery Brooke died 11th — 5th month.
Margaret wife of Henry Feltch died 23rd — 4th mo.
Ester Cogsall decease at Godfry Armitages house 7th — 4th month.
John Speres master of the Barque May Flower an inhabitant of Virginia deceased at Evan Thomas his house 25th — 5th month.
Zakeus Bosworth deceased 28th — 5th month.

John Coddington deceased 18th — 6th month.
Thomas Bounty of Wappine or Redriffe in England deceased at Lieut. William Hudsons 26th — 6th month he died intestate.
John Foote a seaman of Manchester died 16th — 6th month.
John of James & Mary Dennis died 10th — 7th mo.
Benjamin of Benjamin & Wilmot Phipeny died 20th ⸱7th month.
William Davis a seaman living in Chadwell in England deceased at Isaac Cullimors house 20th — 7th month.
Richard of Capt. Thomas & Mary Savage died 23rd — 7th month.
Rebecca of Mr. Joseph & Elizabeth Rocke died 19th — 7th month.
Dorcas of William & Philip White died 30th — 7th month.
Chrestable wife of John Gallop died 27th — 7th month.
Elisha of William & Mary Salter died 14th — 7th month.
William of William & Hannah Balantine died 4th — 8th month.
Margaret Mathewes deceased 23rd — 9th month.
Mary of Arthur & Jane Kind died 27th — 8th mo.
John of John & Ruth Ingolsby died 15th — 10th mo.
Mary wife of Lieut. Joshua Hewes died 23rd — 6th month.
John Clemons seaman at a town near Lee in England deceased at Isaac Cullimors 13th — 8th month.
Elizabeth of Andrew & Elizabeth Cload died 17th — 7th month.
George Stevens a cooper in London died at Isaac Cullimors house 2nd — 9th month. .
Mary wife of Ralph Roote died 15th — 9th mo.
Mary wife of William Baker died 12th — 10th mo.
Lydia of Jonathan & Mary Balston died 6th — 11th month.
Judith of William & Scisly Talbot died 16th 11th mo.
Francis Bennet was drowned at Nodles Island dyed 4th — 10th month.
Em wife of Thomas Rawlins died 27th — 10th mo.
Mary of John & Hannah Keetch died 1st — 11th month.
Philip Sherman apprentice of John Blower died 12th — 10th month.
Elizabeth Rose servant to Hugh Williams died 20th — 11th month.
Simon of Mr. Simon & Hannah Lynd died 4th — 11th month.
Mary wife of Mr. Thomas Purchase died 7th — 11th mo.
Alice Fermase widow died 9th — 12th month.
Mary of Moses Maverick of Mablehead died 24th — 12th month.


Josias Belcher & Ranus Ransford were married 3rd — 1st month by Capt. Humphery Atharton.
George Manning & Hannah Blanchard widow were married 13 — 1st month by Richard Bellingham Governor.
Clement Corbet & Dorcas Buckmaster daughter of Thomas Buckmaster of Muddy River were married 7th — 1st month by Capt. Humphery Atharton.
John Merick & Elizabeth Wyborne daughter of Thomas Weyborne of Boston were married 3rd — 2nd month by Capt Humphery Atharton at Cambridge.
William Browne & Elizabeth Ruggles daughter of George Ruggles of Brantrey were married 24th — 2nd month.
John Griffine & Susanna Price were married 27th — 2nd month by Capt. Humphery Atharton.
John Browne & Ester Makepeace daughter of Thomas Makepeace of Boston were married 24th — 2nd month by Capt. Humphery Atharton.
Zachariah Buckmaster & Sarah Webb were married 7th — 1st month by Capt. Humphery Atharton.
Arthur Mason & Joanna Parker daughter of Nicholas Parker of Boston were married 5th — 5th month by Increase Nowell.
Richard Bennet & Margaret Gurgefield widow were married 11th — 5th month by Richard Bellingham Dep. Governor.
Abiel Everill & Elizabeth Phillips daughter of Lieut. Will. Phillips of Boston were married 6th — 5th month by Capt. Humphery Atharton.
Mr. Samuel Lee of Virginia & Elizabeth Bowland of Boston were married 2nd — 6th month by Capt. Humphery Atharton.
Samuel Sprague & Recuba Crawford were married 23rd — 6th month by Richard Bellingham Dept. Govr.

Joseph Waters & Martha Mellowes were married 13th — 7th month by Capt. Humphery Atharton.

Edward Morris & Grace Bett were married 20th — 9th month by Richard Bellingham Dept. Govr.

Mr. William Thompson & Catharine Treat daughter of Richard Treat of Wethersfield were married 19th — 9th month by John Endecott Governor.

Mr. Jeremiah Eggington & Elizabeth Cotton daughter of the late John Cotton deceased were married 12th — 8th month by Capt. Robert Bridges.

Emanuel Springfield & Mary Mellowes were married 13 — 7th month by Capt. Humphery Atharton.

Richard George & Mary Pell daughter of William Pell of Boston were married 1st — 9th mo. by Capt. Humphery Atharton.

Robert Twelues & Martha Bracket daughter of Peter Bracket of Brantrey were married 22nd — 9th month by Richard Bellingham Dept. Govr.

John Palsgrave & Mary Mavericke daughter of Samuel Mavericke of Nodles Island were married 8th — 12th month by John Endecott Govr.

Wm Pitts & Susan Aealy late widow of Philip Aealy were married 7th — 10th month by John Endecott Govr.

Edward Belcher & Mary Wormwood daughter-in-law to Edward Belcher Senior were married 8th — 11th month by Major Humphery Atharton.

John Brimblecombe & Barbara Davis the late widow of George Davis were married 14th — 11th mo. by Richard Bellingham Dept. Govr.

Abram Fort & Hannah Hutchinson widow were married 18th — 11th month by John Endecott Govr.

Oliver Callowe & Judith Clocke widow were married last of February by John Endecott Govr.

Matthew Clark & Abigail Maverick daughter of Elias Maverick of Winnesimett were married 4th — 4th month

John Hanniford & Abigail Dill widow were married 8th — 9th month by Capt. Wiggins.

## FIRST CHURCH.

| | | |
|---|---|---|
| Peter of Peter Oliver | 4 day | 1 mo. |
| Josiah of Alexander Baker | 4 day | 1 mo. |
| Asaph of Wm. Harsey | 4 day | 1 mo. |
| Eunice of Edward Ting | 11 day | 1 mo. |
| Anna of John Harrod | 11 day | 1 mo. |
| Wm. of Wm. Dawes | 11 day | 1 mo. |
| Lydia of Francis Douce | 11 day | 1 mo. |
| Wm. of John Bateman's wife | 11 day | 1 mo. |
| James of & Mary Robbinson | 18 day | 1 mo. |
| Rebecca of Joseph Rocke | 18 day | 1 mo. |
| Jacob of Ann & John Hurd | 18 day | 1 mo. |
| Eliashib of John Harisson | 18 day | 1 mo. |
| Anna of John Barnes of Ch. of Braintree | 18 day | 1 mo. |
| Joseph of Daniel Turant's wife | 1 day | 2 mo. |
| Deliverance of Rich: Bradley's wife | 8 day | 2 mo. |
| James of James Johnson | 15 day | 2 mo. |
| Sylvanus of Walter Merry | 15 day | 2 mo. |
| Mary of Mr. Brecke of Ch. of Dorchester | 22 day | 2 mo. |
| Anna of Mr. Anger's wife | 29 day | 2 mo. |
| John of Edmond Groose | 29 day | 2 mo. |
| Tho: of Tho: Yoo's wife of the New Ch. | 29 day | 2 mo. |
| David of Tho: Duer | 6 day | 3 mo. |
| John of Tho: Duer | 6 day | 3 mo. |
| Sampson of Tho: Duer | 6 day | 3 mo. |
| Tho: of Thomas & Martha Stocker of Ch. of Linn | 6 day | 3 mo. |
| Elizabeth of Thomas & Martha Stocker of Ch. of Linn | 6 day | 3 mo. |
| John of Alice Nichols | 13 day | 3 mo. |
| Rachel of Rachel & Thomas Harrod | 24 day | 4 mo. |
| Wm. of Edward Cowell's wife | 8 day | 5 mo. |
| Nathaniel of Elias Partman | 8 day | 5 mo. |
| Ann of Rich. Woody of Ch. of Roxberry | 15 day | 5 mo. |
| Benjamin of Timothy Proute | 22 day | 5 mo. |

| | | |
|---|---|---|
| Marcye of Jacob Sheaffe | 29 day | 5 mo. |
| Joseph of James Pemerton | 29 day | 5 mo. |
| Mary of Thorne | 29 day | 5 mo. |
| John of Mary & John Dinis | 5 day | 6 mo. |
| Ephraim of Ann & John Manning | 12 day | 6 mo. |
| John } of sister Pecke | 12 day | 6 mo. |
| Elizabeth } of sister Pecke | 12 day | 6 mo. |
| Rachel } of sister Pecke | 12 day | 6 mo. |
| John } of Sarah & John Marshall | 12 day | 6 mo. |
| Joseph } of Sarah & John Marshall | 12 day | 6 mo. |
| Samuel } of Sarah & John Marshall | 12 day | 6 mo. |
| Sarah } of Sarah & John Marshall | 12 day | 6 mo. |
| Hannah } of Sarah & John Marshall | 12 day | 6 mo. |
| Elizabeth of William Davis | 26 day | 6 mo. |
| Thomas of Thomas Duer | 2 day | 7 mo. |
| Mary of William Arnoll's wife | 16 day | 7 mo. |
| John of John Lowell | 16 day | 7 mo. |
| John of John Tinker | 30 day | 7 mo. |
| William of John Inglsby | 7 day | 8 mo. |
| Mary of Jacob Eliot | 14 day | 8 mo. |
| Martha of Henry Blauge | 28 day | 8 mo. |
| George of Hannah & George Manning | 25 day | 9 mo. |
| Anna of Wm Leauger | 25 day | 9 mo. |
| John of Jeremiah Houchin | 2 day | 10 mo. |
| Elizabeth of Robert Samford | 9 day | 10 mo. |
| Josua of Tho: Scotto | 9 day | 10 mo. |
| Samuel of John Meriam | 9 day | 10 mo. |

## 1656.

### TOWN.

Sarah of James & Mary Hawkins born 18th Mar.
Ambrose of Ambrose & Mary Bennet born 21st Mar.
Isaac of William & Ruth Read born 18th Apr.
William of William & Elizabeth Greenoe born 12th April.
George of George & Mary Munjoy born 21st April.
Benjamin of Sargt Thomas & Elizabeth Clarke born 4th May.
Abigail of John & Susanna Sweet born 4th May.
Lydia of John & Sarah Badman born 26th April.
Samuel of Alexander & Mary Adams born 7th May.
Thomas of John & Sarah Marshall born 11th May.
Mary of William & Mary Lane born 15th May.
Rebecca of Mr. Edward & Rachel Rawson born 21st May.
Sarah of John & Mary Milam born 6th April.
Joseph of Thomas & Ann Sexton born 9th May.
Hannah of Henry & Elizabeth Fowning born 8th April.
James of Abiel & Elizabeth Everill born 4th Apr.
John of John & Bridget Willford born 26th May.
William of Capt. Richard & Elizabeth Davenport born 11th May
Benjamin of Mr. Edward & Abigail Hutchinson born 2nd June.
Jeremiah of Thomas & Rachel Harwood born 4th June.
John of Robert & Margaret Hubberd born 18th May.
Nathaniel of John & Joan Baker born 4th April.
John of Thomas & Elizabeth Hunt born 11th April.
Sarah of Nathaniel & Christian Fryer born 20th July.
Walter of Walter & Mary Merry born 3rd June.
Benjamin of Samuel & Joanna Norden born 15th June.
Samuel of Thomas & Ann Waker born 26th June,
Elizabeth of Anthony & Alice Shaw born 21st May.
Mary of Ensigne Joshua & Lydia Scottow born 11th May.
John of Robert & Mary Feild born 9th June.
Anthony of Anthony & Christian Stoddard born 16th June.
Benjamin of William & Mary Holloway born 8th July.

Benjamin of Benjamin & Wilmott Phipeny born 15th July.
John of Rober & Sarah Waker born 14th July.
Rebecca of Francis & Mary East born 22nd July.
John of John & Elizabeth Purchase born 3rd Aug.
Stephen of Isaac & Susanna Waker born 13th Aug.
Mary of James & Mary Hudson born 27th July.
John of Robert & Catharine Nanney born 12th Aug.
Sarah of John & Abigail Haniford born 8th Aug.
Anne of Arthur & Joanna Mason born 10th Aug.
Elizabeth of Jeremiah & Elizabeth Eggington born 15th Aug.
Joseph of Thomas & Naomi Wells born 7th June.
Mary of Richard & Mary George born 22nd Aug.
Matthew of Matthew & Elizabeth Coy born 5th Sept.
David of William & Hannah Ballentine born 24th Aug.
Sarah of Isaac & Elizabeth Coussins born 31st Aug.
Thomas of David & Mary Faulkner born 26th Sept.
Samuel of Richard & Frances Woodee born 11th Sept.
Lydia of Jonathan & Mary Balston born 9th Oct.
Mary of John & Anne Sandy born 24th Oct.
Abigail of John & Mary Viall born 21st Oct.
Hannah of Samuel & Mary Flacke born 26th Oct.
John of Joseph & Elizabeth Rocke born 2nd Nov.
Elizabeth of John & Anne Chamberline born 25th Oct.
Martha of Thomas & Martha Fitch born 9th Nov.
Samuel of Capt. Thomas & Mary Savage born 16th Nov.
Samuel of John & Susanna Cole born 24th March.
Mary of Andrew & Elizabeth Cload born 22nd July.
William of Samuel & Sarah Davis born 4th Sept.
Elizabeth of John & Susanna Griffine born 26th Aug.
John of Lieut William & Bridget Phillips born 18th Sept.
Jeremiah of Samuel & Ester Travis born 9th Sept.
Henry of Henry & Mary Stephens born 20th July.
Lydia & Priscilla twins of Henry & Sarah Messinger born 22nd Nov
Exercise dau. of William & Hannah Shattocke born 12th Nov.
Jonathan of Henry & Eleanor Shrimpton born 18th Nov.
Sarah of Richard & Joanna Knight born 6th Nov.
Edward of Edward & Sarah Ellis born 26th Nov.
John of John & Hannah Andrewes born 21st Nov.
Mary of Capt. William & Huldah Davis born 3rd Dec.
Joseph of Thomas & Elizabeth Peck born 11th Dec.
Peter of Peter & Reddigan Wittoms born 15th May.
Mary of Edmund & Elizabeth Browne born 15th Dec.
Ebenezer of John & Ruth Ingolsby born 13th Dec.
Mary of William & Esther Peirce born 10th Dec.
Henry of Henry & Mary Phillips born 1st Oct.
Jonathan of William & Friswith Osborne born 16th Nov.
Henry of Henry & Ruth Keskeyes born 3rd May.
Elizabeth of John & Martha Mellowes born 15th Dec.
Ezekiel of William & Grace Rex born 30th Nov.
John of John & Elizabeth Gill born 11th Jan.
Samuel of George & Deborah Burrell born 10th Jan.
Richard of Richard & Mary Hicks born 20th Jan.
Elizabeth of Thomas & Mary Read born 28th Jan.
Sarah of William & Elizabeth Browne born 8th Jan.
Elizabeth of Edmund & Mary Jackson born 11th Feb.
William of William & Elizabeth Sumner born 9th Feb.
William of William & Mary Ingram born 9th Feb.
Rebecca of Besse the negro servant of Thomas Lake born 1st Feb.
Thomas of Mr. Thomas and Mary Lake born 9th Feb.
Thomas of Mr. Thomas & Mary Broughton born 23rd Dec.
John of John & Mary Barrell born
Jonathan of George & Elizabeth Oris born
Nicholas of Nicholas & Hannah Phillips born 26th Feb.
Rebecca of Gamaliel & Sarah Phipeny born 12th Feb.

Samuel of Samuel & Mary Gallop born 14th Feb.
Hannah of Francis & Joan Crocum born 15th Feb.
Ebenezer of Timothy & Mary Prout born 14th March.
Mehetabel of Thomas & Rebecca Hawkins born 27th Jan.
Joseph of William & Helen Furnell born 19th Jan.
Satisfaction son of Edward & Mary Belcher born 23rd Feb.
James of Edward & Margaret Coleman born 31st Jan.
Elizabeth of Peter & Mary Duncan born 28th Feb.
Mary of John & Dorothy Downes born 4th March.
Thomas of Tho: & Dorothy Bligh born 18th Oct.
Sarah of Edward & Elizabeth Page born 13th April.
Elizabeth of Nathaniel & Damaris Robinson born 24th Feb.
Abigail of Matthew & Abigail Clarke of Winisemet born 17th June.
Simon of Simon & Christian Roberts born 22nd Nov.

Judith Whittingham daughter-in-law unto Mr. Simon Eire died 27th — 1st mo.
Abigail son of John & Susanna Sweete died 16th — 3rd month.
Mary wife of William Lane died 2nd — 3rd mo.
Hannah of Mr. Edward & Rebecca Rawson died 27th — 3rd month.
Matthew of Matthew & Ann Jions died 13th — 3rd month.
Jarvis Goold died 27th — 3rd month.
Gershom of John & Elizabeth Mathew died —
John of John & Bridget Wilford died 12th — 4th month.
Thomas Johnson of Hingham drowned 29th — 3rd month.
Stephen of Isaac & Sarah Waker died 29th — 4th month.
Joanna wife of Samuel Norden died 29th — 4th mo.
Nathaniel of John & Joan Baker died 13th — 4th month.
John of Thomas & Elizabeth Hunt died 19th — 6th month.
Philip of Benjamin & Sarah Brisco died 16th — 6th month.
Sarah of Thomas & Sarah Moore died 25th — 6th month.
Susanna of Philip & Rachel Phillips died 15th — 6 month.
John Jellet died 13th — 6th month.
Zechariah of Mr. Hezekiah & Elizabeth Vsher died 23rd — 6th month.
Sarah of Francis & Catharine Dawse died 18th — 5th month.
Elizabeth of Clement & Mary Grosse died 1st — 7th month.
Sarah of Samuel & Sarah Bucknell died 25th — 6th month.
Elizabeth wife of Jeremiah Eggington died 31st — 6th month.
Ester wife of Jeremiah Fitch died 14th — 7th month.
John Jarvis merchant died 24th — 7th month.
Rachel of Thomas & Rachel Harwood died 27th — 7th month.
Thomas Wiborne died 2nd — 8th month.
Samuel Wilbore died 29th — 7th month.
Mrs. Ann Leverit died 16th — 8th month.
Sarah of John & Emm Coddington died 8th — 9th month.
Jeremiah of Daniel & Ester Travis died 1st — 9th month.
Hannah of William Read died 25th — 9th month.
Mary wife of Samuel Flacke died 6th — 9th month.
Anne wife of John Kenricke of Muddy River died 15th — 9th month.
Elizabeth wife of Isaac Coussnes died 14th — 10th month.
Dinah wife of Dorman Mahoon died 8th — 11th mo.
William of William & Mary Ingram died 19th — 11th month.
Capt. Robert Keayne died 23rd — 1st mo.
Thomas Buckminster died 28 September.

William Baker & Pilgrim Edye daughter of John Edye of Watertown were
    married 22nd — 2nd month by William Browne.
Isaac Woody & Dorcas Harper were married 20th — 1st month by Major
    Humph. Atharton.
Thomas Rawlins & Sarah Madocks of Roxbury a widow were married 2nd —
    3rd month.
John Jephson & Emm Coddington widow were married 7th — 3rd mo. by
    Major Humph. Atharton.
William Mullings & Ann Bell widow were married 7th — 3rd mo. by Richard
    Bellingham Dept. Govr.

Joseph Moore & Ruth Starr were married 21st — 3rd month by John Endicott Govr.

William Browne & William Parchmt were married 11th — 2nd month by Richard Bellingham Dept. Govr.

John Peirce & Ruth Bishop daughter of Nath Bishop of Boston were married 15th — 2nd month by John Endicot Govr.

Thomas Thorp & Rebecca Miluard were married 27th — 3rd month by John Endecott Govr.

William Ingram & Mary Bairstow were married 14th — 3rd month by Major Humph. Atharton.

John Davis & Returne Gridley daughter of Richard Gridley of Boston were married 9th — 2nd month by John Endecott Govr.

Mounsieur Christian Belvele & Lady Francis Hopkins were married 9th — 4th month by John Endicott Govr.

Richard Tozer & Judith Smith were married 3rd — 5th month by Richard Bellingham Dept. Govr.

Samuel Ruck & Margaret Clarke were married 22nd — 5th month by Richard Bellingham Dept. Govr.

Mr. John Thompson of Newhaven & Anne Vicaris were married 4th — 6th month by John Endicott Govr.

Ralph Hutchinson & Alice Bennet late wife of Francis Bennet were married 8th — 6th mo. by John Endicot Gov.

William Lane & Mary Brewer daughter of Thomas Brewer of Roxbury were married 21st — 6th month by Richard Bellingham Dept. Govr.

Mr. Richard Mather Pastor to the Church of Dorchester & Mrs. Sarah Cotton widow were married 26th — 6th month by John Endecott Govr.

John Senter & Mary Muzzy were married 27th — 1st month by Richard Bellingham Dept Govr.

Abner Ordway & Sarah Dennis widow were married 15th — 6th month.

Samuel Norden & Elizabeth Formott dau. of Philemon Pormott late of Boston were married ———

Lawrence Willis of Bridgwater & Mary Makepeace daughter of Thomas Makepeace of Boston were married 5th — 7th month by Major Humphry Atharton.

Michael Martine & Susanna Holliocke daughter of Edward Holliocke of Rumney Marsh were married 12th — 7th month by John Endecott Governor.

Thomas Goold & Frances Robinson were married 10th — 7th mo. by Major Humph. Atharton.

George May & Elizabeth Franckline were married 6th — 8th month by Richard Bellingham Dept Govr.

Michael Willborne & Mary Beamsley daughter of William Beamsley of Boston were married 17th — 8th month by Richard Bellingham Dept. Govr.

Henry Boyen & Frances Gill daughter of Arthur Gill of Boston were married 17th — 8th month by Major Humph. Atharton

Thomas Cooper of Rehoboth & Ann Bosworth widow were married 17th — 8th month.

William Ticknor & Hannah Stockbridge daughter of John Stockbridge were married 29th — 8th month by Major Humphery Atharton.

John Rogers of Scituate & Roda King daughter of Thomas King of Scituate were married 8th — 8th month by John Endecott Govr.

Edward Turner & Mary Sanford daughter of Richard Sanford were married 25th — 8th mo. by John Endicott Govr.

Moses Mavericke & Eunice Roberts widow of Thomas Roberts were married 22nd — 8th mo. by John Endicott Govr.

Francis Johnson & Hannah Hanbury were married 24th — 8th month by John Endecott Govr.

Mr. Robert Drue & Mrs. Jemina Clarke daughter of John Clarke of Boston were married 6th — 9th month by John Endecott Govr.

Jonathan Ransford & Mary Sunderland daughter of John Sunderland of Boston were married 29th — 9th mo. by Richard Bellingham Dept. Gov.

William Wardell & Elizabeth Jellet widow were married 5th — 10th month by Richard Bellingham Dpt. G.

John Mavericke & Catharine Skipper were married 9th — 2nd month by Richard Bellingham Dept. Govr.

Henry Kcskeyes & Ruth Graves daughter of Richard Graves were married
7th — 6th month.
Joseph Benham of Newhaven & Winifred King were married 15th — 11th month
by Richard Bellingham Dept. Govr.
William Hunter & Scissilla Corish were married 30th of January by Richard
Bellingham Dept. Govr.
John Hill & Elizabeth Strong were married 16th — 11th mo. by Major Hum-
phrey Atharton.
James Moore a Scottishman & Mary (?) Both were married 6th — 12th month
by Richard Bellingham Dept. Govr.
Henry Tite & Sarah Walton were married 11th — 12th month by Richard
Bellingham Dept. Gov.
James Sanford & Elizabeth Smith dau. of Francis Smith of Boston were mar-
ried ———
John Sanford & Sarah Potter widow were married 19th — 12th mo. by Major
Humph. Atharton.
Henry Bishop & Elizabeth Wilbore widow were maried 20th — 12th month by
Richard Bellingham Dept. Gov.
Mr. John Joyliffe merchant & Ann Knight widow were married 28th — 11th
month by John Endecott Gov.
Edmond Coussins of Pulling Point & Margaret Bird an Irish maid, servant to
John Grover of Rumney Marsh were married ———
Joshua Hewes & Alice Crabtree the Relict of John Crabtree were married
11th — 12th month.
Joseph Soper & Elizabeth Alcocke daughter of Thomas Alcocke were married
6th — 3rd mo. by John Endecott Govr.

### FIRST CHURCH.

| | | |
|---|---|---|
| Mary of Rich. Chrihly | 2 day | 1 mo. |
| Sarah of Francis Smyth's wife | 9 day | 1 mo. |
| Mary of John Leverett | 16 day | 1 mo. |
| Ann of William Padye | 16 day | 1 mo. |
| Hannah of Henry Fowning | 13 day | 2 mo. |
| Benjamin of Tho. Clarke | 20 day | 2 mo. |
| Isaac of William Read | 20 day | 2 mo. |
| John of Monioy | 27 day | 2 mo |
| Lydia of sister Bodman | 27 day | 2 mo. |
| Abigail of John Sweett | 4 day | 3 mo. |
| Samuel of Alexander Adams | 11 day | 3 mo. |
| Joseph of Thomas Saxton's wife | 11 day | 3 mo. |
| Thomas of John Marshall's wife | 11 day | 3 mo. |
| Mary of Josua Scottow | 18 day | 3 mo. |
| Wm. of Capt. Davenport of Ch. of Salem | 18 day | 3 mo. |
| Benjamin of Edward Hutchinson | 8 day | 4 mo. |
| Walter of Walter Merry | 8 day | 4 mo. |
| Jeremiah of Rachel & Tho. Harrod | 8 day | 4 mo. |
| John of Robert Feild | 15 day | 4 mo. |
| Abigail of Richard Waight | 15 day | 4 mo. |
| Anthony of Anthony Stoddard | 22 day | 4 mo. |
| Benjamen of Samuel Norden's wife | 22 day | 4 mo. |
| John of Robert Waker | 20 day | 5 mo. |
| Rebecca of Francis East | 27 day | 5 mo. |
| Henry of Henry Stevens | 27 day | 5 mo. |
| Stephen of Isaac Waker | 17 day | 6 mo. |
| John of John Nanny | 17 day | 6 mo. |
| Samuel of Rich. Woody | 19 day | 7 mo. |
| John of Wm Phillips | 21 day | 7 mo. |
| Henry of Henry Philips of Ch. of Dedham | 28 day | 7 mo. |
| Abigail of John Viall | 26 day | 8 mo. |
| John of Joseph Rocke | 9 day | 9 mo. |
| Martha of Tho. & Martha Fitch of Ch. of Watertowne | 16 day | 9 mo. |
| Samuel of Tho. Savidge | 23 day | 9 mo. |

| | |
|---|---|
| Lydia & ⎫ of Sarah & | 23 day 9 mo. |
| Priscilla ⎭ Henry Messinger | 23 day 9 mo. |
| Ezekiel of William Rickes | 30 day 9 mo. |
| Edward of Sarah Elise | 30 day 9 mo. |
| Marya of William Davis | 7 day 10 mo. |
| Joseph of sister Pecke | 14 day 10 mo. |
| Anna of John Harisson | 21 day 10 mo. |
| William of Benja. Thwing | 28 day 10 mo. |
| Ebenezer of John Ingolsby | 4 day 11 mo. |
| Samuel of Peter Oliver | 11 day 11 mo. |
| Thomas of Wm Cotton | 18 day 11 mo. |
| Jonathan of George Orrice's wife | 8 day 12 mo. |
| Elizabeth of Edmond Jackson | 15 day 12 |
| Joseph & ⎫ of Joseph How | 22 day 12 |
| Sarah ⎭ of Joseph How | 22 day 12 |
| John of John Barrill | 22 day 12 |

## 1657.

### TOWN.

Joseph of William & Anne Pollard born 15th March.
Sarah of Thomas & Elizabeth Watkins born 1st March.
Hester of Humphrey & Sarah Cumbee born 1st March.
John of John & Emm Jephson born 1st Mar.
Mary of Isaac & Dorcas Woody born 22nd March.
Lydia of William & Mary Salter born 24th March.
Zechariah of Zechariah & Elizabeth Phillips born 5th March.
William of John & Martha Amee born 24th March.
Grace of John & Returne Davis born 4th March.
Joanna of Richard & Joanna Richardson born 25th Feb.
John of Christopher & Elizabeth Pickett born 6th Sept.
Gamaliel of Simon & Susanna Rogers born 26th March.
John of Joseph & Mary Bastar born 25th March.
Mary of Capt. James & Abigail Johnson born 27th March.
Mary of John & Mary Dawes born 12th April.
Mary of William & Lydia Browne born 23rd April.
Mary of John & Tabitha Blower born 25th April.
Hannah of Samuel & Isabel Howard born 11th April.
Constance of Robert & Rebecca Winsor born 7th May.
Elizabeth of Edward & Martha Arnold born 7th May.
Elizabeth of George & Mary Dod born 5th April.
Thomas of Matthew & Sarah Barnard born 14th April.
Rebecca of Christopher & Rebecca Clarke born 4th May.
Edward of Edward & Elizabeth Yeomans born 6th May.
Anna of John & Mary Anderson born 5th May.
Samuel of Thomas & Hannah Tilee born 1st May.
Elizabeth of Samuel & Margaret Rucke born 11th
Thomas of Richard & Judith Tozer born 5th May.
Martha of David & Mary Evans born 28th May.
Samuel of Henry Jr. & Hanna Felch burn 3rd June.
Paul of Elias & Anne Mavericke born 10th June.
Sarah of William & Mary Lane born 15th June.
Leah of Hope & Rachel Allen born 16th May.
Rebecca of Edward & Mary Kibby of Muddy River born 1st May.
Abigail of William & Mary Smaledge born 28th May.
Sarah of Francis & Catharine Dowse born 2nd June.
John of Edward & Martha Allen born 8th June.
Rebecca of Henry & Elizabeth Blake born 5th July.
Sarah of William & Mary Hambleton born 7th April.
Sarah of Richard & Sarah Martine born 2nd July.
John of Henry & Jane Curtis born 2nd July
James of James & Sarah Balston born 22nd June.
Elizabeth of Sampson & Abigail Shore born 25th June.
Jeremiah of William & Grace Toy born 18th July.

Joseph of Mr. Edward & Mary Ting born 12th July.
Sarah of Amos & Mary Richeson born 19th July.
Joseph of William & Sarah Halsey born 29th May.
Henry of Henry & Mary Willis born 2nd Aug.
Joanna of William & Susanna Davis born 26th July.
Ruth of Josiah & Mary Cobitt born 6th Aug.
Richard of Henry & Mary Ley born 27th July.
John of John & Mary Stockbridge born 19th July.
Mary of Henry & Frances Bowen born 14th Aug.
Sarah of Nathaniel & Mary Adams born 9th Aug.
Joseph of Thomas & Leah Baker born 16th Aug.
Samuel of Capt. Thomas & Mary Savage born 22nd Aug.
Rebecca of James & Lettis Neighbour born 30th March.
Elizabeth of Joseph & Elizabeth Bowd born 20th Aug.
Anna of Samuel & Lydia Turrell born 20th Aug.
Anna of Thomas & Rachel Harwood born 26th Aug.
Elizabeth of John & Jane Bushnell born 30th Aug.
Thomas of Edward & Jane Barker born 23rd Aug.
John of John & Emm Brakenbury born 9th Aug.
Sarah of Peter and Alice Place born 3rd Sept.
Sarah of Thomas & Sarah Stevens born 31st Aug.
Sarah of Robert & Sarah Mason born 20th Aug.
Richard of Richard & Jane Deuce born 4th Sept.
Sarah of James & Dorothy Wiseman born 18th Sept.
Joseph of William & Secilla Talbott born 13th Oct.
Abigail of Theodore & Abigail Atkinson born 9th Dec.
Elizabeth of Mr. Edward & Rachel Rawson born 12th Nov.
Elizabeth of Samuel & Elizabeth Norden bern 2nd Sept.
Susan of Edward & Susan Haviland born 2nd Sept.
Joseph of Ezekiel & Elizabeth Hamlin born 18th Aug.
Sarah of Mr. Dean & Sarah Winthrop born 11th Feb.
Mary of Matthew & Mary Grosse born 17th Sept.
Sarah of Thomas & Sarah Seottow born 27th Sept.
Mehetabel of John & Susanna Sweet born 8th Oct.
John of William & Francis Parum born 24th Aug.
Sarah of John & Sarah Snelling born 4th Oct.
Samuel of David & Elizabeth Kelly born 9th Oct.
John of Josiah & Ranis Belcher born 9th Oct.
Theophilus of Theophilus & Hannah Frery born 20th Sept.
Hannah of Leift Joshua & Alice Hewes born 28th Oct.
Joseph of John & Martha Shaw born 11th Nov.
Elizabeth of Thomas & Elizabeth Barlow born 13th Nov.
Mary of Michael & Mary Willborne born 30th Oct.
Elizabeth of Nathaniel & Christian Fryer born 1st Nov.
Elizabeth of Ezekiel & Anna Woodward born 22nd Oct.
Sarah of Samuel & Sarah Davis born 19th Dec.
Join of Mr. Sinon & Hannah Lynde born 8th Nov.
Ephraim of William & Ruth Read born 23rd Nov.
Abigail of Jacob & Mary Eliot born 16th Dec.
Hannah of Richard & Grace Travis born 21st Aug.
Sarah of Mr. John & Martha Coggan born 25th Dec.
Mehetabel of John & Mary Hurd born 21st Dec.
William of William & Hannah Ballentine born 20th Dec.
Mary of John & Hannah Lowell born 7th Jan.
Jane of Abraham & Jane Browne born 9th Aug.
Sarah of William & Martha Dinsdall born 7th Jan.
Hannah of John & Mary Blake born 16th Jan.
Edward of William & Elizabeth Ingram of Rumney Marsh born 15th June.
Hannah of John & Hannah Andrewes born 20th Feb.
Abigail of Henry & Elinor Shrimpton born 3rd Jan.
Mary of Edward & Margret Cowell born 23rd Jan.
Elizabeth of Jos: & Lydia Gridley born 27th Jan.
Mary of Edw: & Mary Right born 19th Jan.
William of Wm. & Mary Ingram born 27th Jan.

Hanna of Tho: & Hanna Hull born 24th Jan.
Timothy of Daniel & Esther Trevis born 14th Jan.
Hannah of Mr. John & Judith Hull born 14th Feb.
Ann of Tho: & Frances Gold born 5th Feb.
Thomas of Wm. & Elizabeth Spowel born 14th Feb.
Hannah of Benj: & Sara Briscoe born 6th Feb.
Elizabeth of James & Sara Pemberton born 26th Dec.
John of Ric: & Jane Chrichley born 10th Feb.
Joseph of Mr. Jos: & Elizabeth Rock born 1st Feb.
Richard of Tho: & Rebecca Hawkinnes born 20th Feb.
Benj. of Mr. Wm. & Mary Paddy born 23rd Feb.
James of Jonathan & Mary Bolston born 18th Feb.
Sarah of John & Sara Tuckerman born 20th Nov.
Elizabeth of George & Hanna Manning born 19th March.
Daniel of Stephen & Elizabeth Greenleaf born 17th Feb.
Samuel of Leift. Wm. & Bridget Phillips born 16th March.
Sergant of Thos. & Elizabeth Bill born 26th Feb.
John of John & Thomasin Scarlett born 18th March.
John of Edmond & Rebeccah Maddoc born 12th March.
Jonathan of Edward & Jane Baker born 20th Feb.


Mehetabel of Thomas & Rebecca Hawkins died 14th — 3rd month.
Peter of Samuel & Isabel Howard died 31st — 1st month.
Nicholas Busby died 28th — 6th month.
Priscilla of Henry & Sarah Messinger died 21st — 4th month.
John of Jeremiah & Ester Houchine died 2nd — 5th month.
Sarah wife of John Lewes died 12th — 5th mo.
John Mosse died 26th — 3rd month.
Jonathan of Henry & Ellinor Shrimpton died 22nd — 5th month.
Hannah of Henry & Elizabeth Powning died 6th — 5th month.
John of John & Emm Jephson died 19th — 5th mo.
Nicholas of Nicholas & Hannah Phillips died 1st — 6th month.
William of William & Elizabeth Greenoe died 7th — 6th month.
John of Lieut. William & Bridget Phillips died 8th — 6th month.
Mehetabel of Henry & Ellinor Shrimpton died 29th — 5th month.
John of Joseph & Elizabeth Rocke died 13th — 6th month.
John of John Woodee of Roxbury and Mary his wife died 12th — 6th month
David of William & Hannah Balantine died 16th — 6th month.
John of John & Elizabeth Picket died 14th — 6th mo.
Stephen of Walter & Mary Sennet died 14th — 7th month.
John of Nathaniel & Sarah Hunn died 3rd — 7th month.
Joseph of Thomas & Leah Baker died 30th — 6th month.
Mary of Edward & Margaret Coleman died 6th — 7th month.
Leah of Hope & Rachel Allen died 9th — 7th mo.
Edward Arnold died 8th — 6th month.
Thomas of Thomas & Elizabeth Brattle died 5th — 7th month.
William of Samuel & Sarah Davis died 21st — 7th month.
Bartholomew Barlooe died 26th — 7th month.
Samuel of Capt. Thomas & Mary Savage died 22nd — 6th month.
Sarah of Thomas & Elizabeth Watkins died 26th — 6th month.
Samuel of Peter & Sarah Olliver died 9th — 7th month.
Ann of Arthur & Joanna Mason died 11th — 7th month.
John Stockbridge died 13th — 8th month.
Walter Merry was drowned 28th — 6th month.
Theophilus of Theophilus & Hannah Frery died 24th — 7th month.
Rebecca wife of Matthew Barnes died 19th — 7th mo.
Elizabeth of Henry & Hannah Feltch Jr. died 18th — 8th month.
William Rix died 13th — 9th month.
Thomas Alcock died 14th — 7th month.
Richard a neger servant of John Lowell died 7th —9th month.
Elizabeth of Sampson & Abigail Shore died 15th — 10th month.
Sarah wife of Job Judkine died 26th — 9th mo.
John of Robert & Sarah Waker died 3rd — 11th mo.
Mary wife of Wm. Holloway died 24th Jan.
Joseph Briscoe was drowned 1st Jan.

Wm. Weare died 11th Feb.

Sarah of Mr. John & Martha Coggan died 12th — 1st mo.

Experience dau. of Isaack & Susanna Walker died 11th Feb.

Thomas of Tho: Scottow & his late wife died 11th — 9th mo.

Hannah of Tho: & Hannah Hull died 9th — 12th mo.

Sarah of John & Sara Tuckerman died 4th — 10th mo.

Thomas Hokerson died at Phillip Longs intestate 11th Jan.

John Baker & Joan Swift daughter of Thomas Swift of Dorchester were married 5th — 9th month by John Winthrop Govr.

Thomas Hull & Hannah Townsend daughter of William Townsend of Boston were married 3rd April by John Endecott Governor.

Ferman Haddon was married to ———— 5th — 3rd month by Richard Bellingham Dept. Govr.

Edward Bunn of Hull widower & Elizabeth Mason were married 20th — 6th month by Richard Bellingham Dept Govr.

William Edmunds of Lynn & Ann Martine widow were married 1st — 7th month by Mr. Simons of Ipswich.

Joseph Hutchins & Mary Edmonds daughter of William Edmonds of Lynn were married 1st — 7th month by Mr. Simons of Ipswich.

Thomas Jones of Hull & Abigail Elithrop widow were married 25th June by Richard Bellingham Dept. Govr.

George Robinson & Mary Bushnell were married 3rd — 8th month by John Endecott Govr.

Samuel Clement & Hannah Ings daughter of Madit Ings of Boston were married 2nd — 5th mo. by Major Humph. Atharton.

Nath. Greene & Mary Houchine daughter of Jeremiah Houchine were married 22nd — 4th mo. by John Endecott Govr.

James Riseing & Elizabeth Ensdell daughter of Robert Ensdell of Meadfield were married 7th — 5th month by John Endicott Govr.

Joshua Carwithy & Elizabeth Farnam daughter of John Farnam of Boston were married 6th — 6th month by Major Humph. Atharton.

Samuel Stratton of Watertowne & Margaret Parker widow were married 27th — 6th month by John Endecott Govr.

John Harris & Hannah Briggs daughter of William Briggs of Boston were married 10th — 7th month by John Endecott Govr.

Mr. Samuel Torrey of Hull & Mary Rawson daughter of Edward Rawson of Boston were married 15th — 3rd month by Richard Bellingham Dept Govr.

James Breding & Hannah Rocke daughter of Joseph Rocke of Boston were married 9th — 8th month by John Endicott Govr.

John Lawrence of Muddy River & Sarah Buckmaster were married 30th September.

Edward Davis & Hannah Gridley daughter of Richard Gridley of Boston were married 16th — 7th month by John Endecott Governor.

Isaac Coussins & Ann Hunt formerly wife of John Edwards were married.

Elias Henly & Sarah Thompson were married 4th — 9th month by Richard Bellingham Dept. Govr.

Matthew Barnes & Elizabeth Hunt widow were married 4th — 9th month by Richard Bellingham Dept. Govr.

John Jackson & Jane Thomas daughter of Evan Thomas were married 14th — 9th mo. by John Endecott Govr.

Robert Thornton & Mary Merry late wife of Walter Merry were married 13th — 9th month by John Endecott Govr.

Joseph Sowther & Elizabeth Fairefeild daughter of Daniel Fairefeild of Boston were married 22nd — 8th mo. by John Endecott Govr.

Mr. Edward Lane & Hannah Keayne were married 11th — 10th mo. by John Endecott Govr.

Thomas Wiborne & Abigail Eliot daughter of Jacob Eliot deceased were married 16th — 10th month by John Endecott Govr.

Richard Travis & Grace Clements daughter of Francis Clements of Glassenbury in Sumersetshire were married 22nd — 10th month by John Endecott Govr.

Tristram Hedges & Ann Nickerson of Boston were married 20th — 10th month by John Endecott Governor.

Henry Crab & Hannah Emmons daughter of Thomas Emmons of Boston were married 1st — 11th month by John Endecott Governor.

Nath Reynolds & Sarah Dwite daughter of John Dwite of Dedham were married 30th — 10th month by John Endecott Governor.

James English & Joanna Farnum daughter of John Farnum of Boston were married 7th — 11th month by Major Humph. Atharton.

Edward Wright & Mary Powell were married 27th — 3rd month by John Endecott Gov.

## First Church.

| | |
|---|---|
| Rebecca of Gamaliel Phipeny's wife | 1 day 1 mo. |
| Ebenezer of Timothy Proute | 15 day 1 mo. |
| Mary of James Johnson | 22 day 1 mo. |
| Ann of William Salter | 22 day 1 mo. |
| Gamaliel of Simon Rogers | 22 day 1 mo. |
| John ⎫ of William Dinsdale | 5 day 2 mo. |
| Adam ⎪ of William Dinsdale | 5 day 2 mo. |
| William ⎬ of William Dinsdale | 5 day 2 mo. |
| Martha ⎪ of William Dinsdale | 5 day 2 mo. |
| Mary ⎭ of William Dinsdale | 5 day 2 mo. |
| Ann of Samuel Sindale of Ch. of Newberry | 26 day 2 mo. |
| Rebecca of sister Clarke | 10 day 3 mo. |
| Elizabeth of William Arnoll's wife | 10 day 3 mo. |
| Constance of Robert Winsor's wife | 10 day 3 mo. |
| Deborah of Edward Devotion | 17 day 3 mo. |
| Sarah of Deane Winthorp's wife | 24 day 3 mo. |
| Sarah of Francis Dowse | 21 day 4 mo. |
| Rebecca of John Kibby's wife | 21 day 4 mo. |
| Elizabeth of Sampson Shoore | 28 day 4 mo. |
| Joseph of Wm. Asey's wife | 28 day 4 mo. |
| Rebecca of Henry Blauge | 5 day 5 mo. |
| Joseph of Edward Ting | 19 day 5 mo. |
| Jeremiah of William Toy | 19 day 5 mo. |
| Sarah of Amos Richisson | 19 day 5 mo. |
| John of John Stockbridg of Ch. of Sittuat | 26 day 5 mo. |
| Johanna of William Dawes | 2 day 6 mo. |
| Mary of sister Harvey | 2 day 6 mo. |
| Philip of Mrs. Ann lock | 2 day 6 mo. |
| Ann of Daniel Turand's wife | 23 day 6 mo. |
| Ann of Tho: Harrod's wife | 30 day 6 mo. |
| Sarah of Peter Place | 6 day 7 mo. |
| Theophilus of Theophilus Frayry | 20 day 7 mo. |
| Sarah of Tho: Scottow | 4 day 8 mo. |
| Mehitabel of John Sweet | 11 day 8 mo. |
| John Bakon of Ann Pope aged 13 years | 18 day 8 mo. |
| Ephraim Pope & | 18 day 8 mo. |
| Elizabeth Pope | 18 day 8 mo. |
| Elizabeth of Mr. Rawson of Newbery | 15 day 9 mo. |
| Ephraim of William Read of Waymouth | 29 day 9 mo. |
| Abigail of Theodore Atkinson | 13 day 10 mo. |
| Abigail of Jacob Eliot | 20 day 10 mo. |
| Sarah of John Coggan of Ch. of Dorchester | 27 day 10 mo. |
| Mehetabel of Ann Hurd | 27 day 10 mo. |
| Sarah of William Dinsdale | 10 day 11 mo. |
| Mary of John Loell | 10 day 11 mo. |
| Ann of John Blaug of Dorchester | 17 day 11 mo. |
| Mary of William Cowell's wife | 24 day 11 mo. |
| Joseph of Joseph Rocke | 7 day 12 mo. |
| Hannah of John Hull | 14 day 12 mo. |
| Elizabeth of James Pemerton | 14 day 12 mo. |
| Benjamin of Mr. Pady | 28 day 12 mo. |
| Martha of Mrs. Duncan | 28 day 12 mo. |

## 1658.

Anna of Edmond & Sarah Ellis born 1st 5th day of Febr.
Mary of Francis & Catharine Dowse born 30th January.
William of Bartholmew & Elizabeth Stretton born 30th January.
William of Thomas & Hannah Hull born 23rd January.
John of John & Susanna Cole born 23rd January.
Bethshua of Robert & Elizabeth Sanford born 6th Jan.
Samuel of Simon & Christian Roberts born 18th March.
Rachel of Thomas & Leah Baker born 7th Feb.
Elisha of Edmond & Mary Jackson born 12th Feb.
David of William & Hannah Ballantine born 5th Feb.
Thomas of Joseph & Francis Howe born 7th Feb.
Benjamin of Stephen & Jane Buttler born 10th Feb.
Richard of Richard & Frances Woodde born 3rd Dec.
Bethia of Mr. Henry & Elinor Shrimpton born 30th Jan.
Mary of Nathaniel & Isabell Wales born 9th Feb.
Mary of Tho: & Martha Fitch born 17th Feb.
David of David & Martha Evans born 2nd Feb.
Oulando of Oulando & Sarah Bagly born 18th Feb.
Henry of John & Anne Chamberline born 3rd Feb.
John of John & Jane Jackson born 11th Feb.
Thomas of Richard & Joice Staines born 16th Aug.
Peter of John & Ruth Ingoldsby born 8th March.
Mary of Richard & Johannah Knight born 25th Jan.
John of Nathaniel & Sarah Hunn born 12th Feb.
Hannah of Christo: & Anne Holland born 7th Dec.
Mary of John & Susanna Cole born 6th Oct.
Dorothy of John & Dorothy Downes born 31st Jan.
John of John & Sarah Parker born 25th Dec.
Nathaniel of Samuel and Thomasin Mayo born 1st April.
Dinisha dau. of Henry & Ruth Kiskees born 31st Oct.
Christian daughter of Mr. Anthony and Christian Stoddard born March 22.
Edward of Edward & Elisabeth Page born March 20th.
William of William and Rebecca Thorull born March 16th.
Martha of Francis and Joice Burges born March 11th.
Josiah of George and Mary Munjoy born April 4th.
Benjamin of Francis and Elisabeth Smith born Aprill 10th.
Sarah of John and Sarah Miriam born Aprill 24th.
Sarah of John and Mary Gilbert born March 19th.
Job of Job and Francis Hawkins born Aprill 20th.
Joseph of Joseph and Ruth Moore born May 7th.
Elisabeth of John and Elisabeth Clough born May 10th.
Elisabeth of James and Mary Denis born May 20th.
Mary of John Bowhonno a Scotchman and Moer his wife & Irishwoman born May 9th.
Sarah of Benjamin and Wilmutt Phippen born Aprill 13th.
Hannah of Henry and Elisabeth Fowning born May 22nd.
Hannah of Mr. Edward and Abigail Hutchinson born May 16th.
Mchitabell of Mr. Jacob and Margret Sheafe born May 28th.
Emm of John and Emm Jepson born June 2nd.
Temperance daughter of Robert and Judith Rachell born June 8th.
George of George and Mary Robbinson born March 30th.
Joseph of Robert and Katherin Nanny born June 1st.
Nathaniel of Nathaniel and Margret Gallop born June 14th.
Martha of Richard and Lucresia Smith born June 16th.
Nathaniel of Peter and Mary Duncun born June 29th.
Elizabeth of Rice and Ann Jones born July 6th.
Mary of Jerem: and Sara Morrill born January 5th.
John of John and Jane Baker born July 17th.
Mary of Peter and Mary Felt born Aprill 17th.

Susanna of Alexander and Mary Addams born July 21st.
Robert of Robert and Sara Breek born June 24th.
Elisabeth of Robert and Mary Feild born June 17th.
Thomas of Mr. Thomas and Elisabeth Brattle born June 20th.
Thomas of Thomas and Mary Stevens born May 20th.
James the son of
Hopestil son of Henry and Elisabeth Bridgham born July 29th.
Nathaniell of Mr. Jeremiah and Esther Houchinne born July 27th.
Rebecca of Captain William and Hulda Davis born August 3rd.
Elisabeth of James and Hanna Brading born August 5th.
Mehittabel of Daniell and Mary Stone born August 1st.
Joseph of John and Hannah Bateman born August 21st.
Joseph of Joseph and Abigail Brisco born August 21st.
John of John and Hannah Harris born August 8th.
Richard of Mathew and Elisabeth Coy born September 6th.
Bethia of John and Persis Harrison born September 7th.
Hannah of John and Sara Jeffs born September 5th.
William of William and Elizabeth Greenowe born September 5th.
Hannah of Francis and Martha East born September 24th.
John of Theophilus and Hannah Frary born September 19th.
Martha of Andrew and Elisabeth Cload born September 18th.
Ruth of Edmond and Susan Jacklin born August 4th.
Lydia of Robert and Mary Right born August 24th.
Joseph of Joseph and Elisabeth Souther born August 20th.
Edward of Edward and Elisabeth Wanton born September 18th.
Nathaniel of Arthur and Jane Kind born August 1st.
Mary of Richard and Mary Seward born October 2nd.
Mary of Henry and Julian Lamprey born March 19th.
Elihu of James and Mary Hawkinnes born September 22nd.
Samuel of Edward and Hannah Davis born September 30th.
Lazarus of James and Mary Hudson born October 22nd.
Elisabeth of John and Elizabeth Ferniside born October 26th.
James of James and Joanna Englishe born October 15th.
Susanna of Richard and Anna Gridley born October 23d.
Joseph of Joseph and Elisabeth Swett born October 26th.
Timothy of Henry and Mary Phillips born September 15th.
Martha of Obadiah and Alice Emons born October 12th.
Ellen of David and Mary Faulkner born October 20th.
Experience daughter of Robert and Mary Thornton born November 2nd.
John of John and Ann Sandey born October 14th.
Martin of Joseph and Joanna Lellock born November 22nd.
Zechariah of Zechariah and Hannah Buckmaster born November 28th.
Jane of Thomas and Jane Young born November 28th.
John of William and Ann Alford born November 29th.
Nathaniel of Thomas and Ann Saxton born November 29th.
Faith of Thomas and Elisabeth Pecke born December 8th.
Samuel of Mordecai and Alice Nichols born December 9th.
Richard of Richard and Rebecca Wayte born December 16th.
Mary of Anthony and Alice Shaw born December 17th.
Thomas of Thomas and Katherine Warner born December 24th.
Hannah of Mr. Thomas and Mary Broughton born December 28th.
James of Ambrose and Mary Bennet born January 7th.
Abigail of Nicholas Stone born November 20th.
Jane of Edward and Patience Blake born September 29th.
Abigail of Thomas and Abigail Wyborn born January 6th.
Experience daughter of Edward and Sarah Grant born September 26th.
Richard of John and Sarah Tuckerman born November 27th.
Joseph of James and Lydia Burgess born January 7th.
Joseph of Joseph and Ruth Belknap born January 26th.
Samuell of Thomas and Dorothy Bligh born January 20th.
Ruth of Thomas and Joane Joy February 28th.

John of William & Anne Alford died 29th Jan.
Simon of Simon & Christian Roberts died last of January.

Elizabeth of Rice & Anne Jones died 31st Jan.
Samuel of late Henry & Sibella Sands died 20th Febr.
Joshua Newgate Senior died 12th November.
Mary of William & Hannah Townsende died 29th November.
John of John & Jane Jackson died 18th Jan.
Ezekiel of William & Grace Rix died 17th — 12th mo
James Wyborne deceased March 7th.
Elisabeth of Thomas and Mary Read March 28th.
Francis wife of Thomas Boyden died March 17th.
Hannah wife of Samuel Clement died Aprill 9th.
Edward of Edward and Sarah Ellis died April 9th.
Elisabeth wife of Thomas Bill died March 5th.
Mary of Jeremia and Sarah Morrill deceased January 16th.
Mathew Smith of Watertown son-in-law to Thomas Cooper of Boston
     drowned at Noddles Island May 21st.
Elisabeth of James and Mary Denis deceased June 5th.
Elisabeth wife of Thomas Williams deceased Aprill 30th.
Joseph of Robert and Katherin Nanny died June 21.
Elisabeth wife of Comfort Starr died June 25th aged 63.
Mr. John Coggan deceased April 27th.
Mary wife of John Center of Winnysimmet died July 25th.
Samuel of Samuel and Sara Bucknell died July 29th.
Elisabeth Lyon servant of Joseph Moore died July 18th.
Hannah of Benjamin and Sarah Briscoe died 7th of the 5th month.
Mehittabell of John and Susanna Sweet deceased July 27th.
Richard of Richard and Mary Hicks deceased July 27th.
John of Edward and Martha Allen died July 5th.
James of Jonathan and Mary Balston deceased Augt 26th.
Elisabeth Tilston servant of Captain Waldren died September 2nd.
Joseph of Edward and Mary Ting died July 30th.
Hanna of Henry and Elisabeth Fowning died July 23rd.
Anna of Daniell and Lydia Turell died August 8.
Lydia wife of Mr. John Miller minister of Yarmouth died at the house of
     Thomas Bumstead of Boston August 7th.
Mary wife of Daniell Stone died August 8th.
Sarah wife of James Pitney deceased August 14th.
Mary of Richard and Mary George deceased August 17th.
John Dawson servant of Samuel Norden died August 16th.
Sarah of Thomas and Sarah Stevens deceased June 29.
Mr. William Paddy merchant died August 24th.
George Munning deceased August 24th.
Mary of John Jr. and Mary Phillips deceased August 5.
Anna of Thomas and Rachel Harwood deceased August 15.
William Harvye deceased August 15th.
John Barrell deceased August 29th.
Mary wife of Mr. Richard Barrett of South Hampton upon Long Island died
     at the house of Robert Nashe August 25.
Samuell Whiting died at Mr. Thomas Lakes September 6.
Joseph of Joseph and Ruth Moore died August 14.
Ruth Mr. Joseph Moore's wife died September 3.
Addingstill daughter of Michaell and Mildred Willis died September 6.
Mary Gibbons deceased at Captain Oliver's September 5th.
John of Robert Sanderson deceased the 17th of the 7th month.
Martha of Mr. David and Martha Evans died the 8th of the 7th month.
Elisabeth of John and Elisabeth Ferniside died the 26th of the 7th month.
John of Richard and Jane Crichley died September 25th.
John of John and Thomasin Scarlet deceased September 13.
John of Orlando and Sara Bagly deceased August 31.
Ensigne William Beamesly deceased September 29th.
Thomas Rowell deceased at Richard Bradley's house in Boston Dec. 29.
Joseph Dawson servant to Henry Bridgham deceased the 12th of the 8th
     month.
John Minord deceased October 4th.
Abigail of Nicholas and Hannah Phillips died 2nd of 7th month.

Mr. Simon Eires deceased the 10th November.
Samuel of David and Elisabeth Kelly September 11th.
John of Richard Wayt deceased 5th of November.
Mary wife of Edmund Burfe deceased August 15th.
Robert Battle deceased December 23d
John of Robert and Katherin Nanny died 11th of the 10th month.
Joseph of Mr. John and An Newgate died 14th of the 10th month.
Experience daughter of Robert Thornton died 24th of the 10th month.
Enoch of Ephraim and Ebbott Hunt deceased January ——
Mary wife of John Smith deceased January 11th.
Hannah Richards servant to Rice Jones died January 21st.
Martha Stacye apprentice to Robert Waker died January 23d.
Jane wife of Evan Thomas deceased January 12.


Samuel Sheeres of Dedham & Ann Grosse of Boston widow were married
   15th — 6th month by Richard Bellingham Dept. Govr.
John Sunderland & Mary Vjall dau. of John Vjall were married 26th Jan. by
   Major Humphrey Atherton.
Thomas Boyden & Hannah Mosse widdow were married 3rd Nov. by Richard
   Bellingham Dep. Gov.
Nathaniel Barnard & Mary Lugg were married 11th Feb. by Richard Belling-
   ham Dep. Gov.
James Webster a Scotishman & Mary Hay an Irish maid were married 14th
   Feb.
Joshna Nash & Elizabeth Porter dau. of Edward Porter of Boston were mar-
   ried 23rd Feb. by John Endecot Gov.
John Megdaniell & Elizabeth Smith were married 17th May by John Endecott
   Gov.

## FIRST CHURCH.

| | | |
|---|---|---|
| Samuel of Wm. Philips | 21 day | 1 mo. |
| John of John Scarlet's wife | 21 day | 1 mo. |
| Elizabeth of George Manning's wife | 21 day | 1 mo. |
| Christian of Mr. Stoddard | 28 day | 1 mo. |
| Benjamin of Francis Smyth's wife | 18 day | 2 mo. |
| Sarah of John Meriam | 25 day | 2 mo. |
| Amos of John Tinker | 16 day | 3 mo. |
| Elizabeth of John Clough | 16 day | 3 mo. |
| Ann of Edward Hutchisson | 23 day | 3 mo. |
| Ann of Henry Fowning | 23 day | 3 mo. |
| Elizabeth of Mary Dinis | 23 day | 3 mo. |
| Mehetabel of Jacob Sheaffe | 30 day | 3 mo. |
| Joseph of Mr. Nanny of Hampton | 13 day | 4 mo. |
| Elizabeth of Robert Feild | 20 day | 4 mo. |
| Joseph of James Jemson | 20 day | 4 mo. |
| Zachariah of Tho. Savage | 4 day | 5 mo. |
| Nathaniel of Mrs. Duncan | 4 day | 5 mo. |
| Elizabeth of Rice Joanes' wife | 11 day | 5 mo. |
| Thomas of Henry Stevens | 11 day | 5 mo. |
| Thomas of Thomas Brattle | 25 day | 5 mo. |
| Elizabeth of Alexander Adams | 25 day | 5 mo. |
| Nathaniel of Jeremiah Howchin | 1 day | 6 mo. |
| Hopstill of Henry Bridgham | 1 day | 6 mo. |
| Rebecca of Wm. Davis | 8 day | 6 mo. |
| Elizabeth of Mr. Brayden of Newbery | 8 day | 6 mo. |
| Mehitabel of Mr. Stone of Cambridge | 8 day | 6 mo. |
| Joseph of John Bateman's wife | 28 day | 6 mo. |
| Joseph of Abigail Brisco | 28 day | 6 mo. |
| Bethya of John Harrison | 12 day | 7 mo. |
| Timothy of Henry Phillips | 19 day | 7 mo. |
| Wm. of Tho. Harwood's wife | 19 day | 7 mo. |
| John of Theophilus Frayry | 26 day | 7 mo. |
| Ann of Francis East | 26 day | 7 mo. |

| | |
|---|---|
| Samuel of        Davis | 3 day  8 mo. |
| Joseph of Joseph Swett of Ch. of Newbery | 31 day    Oct. |
| Elizabeth of Mr. Furnicee of Ch. of Duxbery | 31 day    Oct. |
| John of Mr. Alford | 5 day 10 mo. |
| Richard of Rich: Woody of Roxbery | 5 day 10 mo. |
| Samuel of sister Nichols | 12 day 10 mo. |
| Faith of sister Pecke | 12 day 10 mo. |
| Richard of Rich: Waight | 19 day 10 mo. |
| Grindall of Edward Rawson | 30 day 11 mo. |
| Naomi of Francis Dowse | 6 day 12 mo. |
| Ann of Edward Eellice's wife | 6 day 12 mo. |
| Thomas of Joseph How | 13 day 12 mo. |
| Elisha of Edmond Jackson | 13 day 12 mo. |
| Elizabeth of Thomas Fitch of Ch. of Watertowne | 20 day 12 mo. |

[The following births were all recorded in 1659, and are therefore printed together here. — W. S. A.]

William of William & Rachel Griggs born 2nd April, 1640.
Sarah of William & Rachel Griggs born 6th October, 1642.
Rachel of William & Rachel Griggs born 13th Oct., 1644.
Isaac of William & Rachel Griggs born 5th Oct., 1646.
Elizabeth of William & Rachel Griggs born 3rd October, 1648.
Jacob of William & Rachel Griggs born last Nov., 1658.

## 1659.

### Town.

Elizabeth of Clement & Mary Grosse born 5th March.
Sarah of John & Susanna Griffine born 10th March.
James of Peter & Sarah Olliver born 19th March.
Rebecca of Mr. William & Mary Paddy born 3rd Aug.
Lydia of Jeremiah & Sarah Murrells born 30th March.
Jonathan of William & Ruth Read born 23rd April.
Mehittabel of Samuel & Mary Gallop born 5th April.
Anne of John & Ann Checkly born 22nd April.
Mary of Lyonel & Ellinor Wheatly born 14th April.
Richard of John & Return Davis born 15th April.
Anne of Thomas & Anne Walker born 1st May.
Samuel of Tho. & Elizabeth Smith born 20th April.
James of Roger & Sarah Burges born 24th April.
Moses of Thomas & Sarah Stevens born 22nd April.
John of John & Sarah Seate born 14th April.
Mary of Mr. Thomas & Mary Lake born 1st May.
Mary of John & Mary Williams born 29th March.
Nathaniel of Nathaniel & Grace Sherman born 19th December.
Elizabeth of William & Alice Russell born 22nd April.
John of John & Elizabeth Brookin born 11th May.
Elizabeth of Will. & Elizabeth Browne born 5th May.
Elizabeth of John Jr. & Elizabeth Blackleach born 25th May.
Thomas of Thomas & Elizabeth Watkin born 10th May.
Priscilla of Henry & Sarah Messinger born ———
Martha & Mary twins of Hope & Rachel Allen born 15th June.
Nathaniel of Samuel & Sarah Bucknell born 1st June.
Mary of Edward & Mary Belcher born 4th April.
Hannah of William & Elizabeth Sumner born 10th June.
Susanna of John & Phillip Snell born 21st June.
Samuel of Daniel & Lydia Turrell born 14th June.
Thomas of Ensigne Joshua & Lydia Scottow born last June.
Elnathan son of Capt. Richard & Anne Waldren 6th July.
Elizabeth of Joshua & Elizabeth Carwithy born 6th June.
John of Edward & Martha Allen born 21st June.
Jacob of Jacob deceased & Margaret Sheafe born 23rd July.

Elizabeth of Richard & Mary Hicks born 25th July.
Martha & Mary twins of William & Ester Pearse born 26th May.
Sarah of Nathaniel & Sarah Reynolds born 26th July.
Sarah of Hen. & Elizabeth Fowning born 3rd August.
Sarah of Joseph & Sarah Sutton born last July.
Sarah of Tho. & Elizabeth Barlow born 18th July.
Thomasin daughter of Tho. & Sarah Scottow born 14th August.
Elizabeth of Gamaliel & Sarah Phipeny born 10th Aug.
David of Nathaniel & Mary Adams born 30th June.
Susanna of John & Hannah Andrewes born 12th August.
Joshua of Henry & Mary Stevens born 15th May.
Samuel of Robert & Catharine Nanny born 27th August.
Zecharia of Samuel & Sarah Doves born 29th July.
Hannah of Samuel & Ann Flacke born 21st August.
Elizabeth of Jonathan & Mary Bolston born 12th Aug.
Benjamin of Mr. Joseph & Elizabeth Rocke born 9th Sept.
Sarah of John & Mary Stone born 16th Sept.
Mary of John & Mary Kneeland born 6th Oct.
James of John a Scotishmā & Ruth Marshall born 29th Sept.
Thomas of Robert & Rebecca Winsor born 1st October.
John of Isaac & Dorcas Woodee born 18th Sept.
Joseph of William & Anne Clarke born 10th Sept.
Mary of William & Mary Hunter born 5th Sept.
Samuel of Samuel & Constance Mattocke born 15th October.
Lydia of Richard & Lydia Garrett born 10th Oct.
William of William & Mary Lane born 1st Oct.
Sarah of William & Ann Pollard born 20th October.
John of John & Elizabeth Megdaniell born 13th Sept.
Mary of Alexander Bogle born 17th Oct.
Anne of George & Lydia Nowell born 13th Oct.
Ebenezer of Richard & Thomasin Collicott born 6th Sept.
Sarah of Thomas & Abigail Bill born 18th Sept.
Ephraim of Daniel & Easter Travis born 13th Sept.
William of Ezekiel & Elizabeth Hamline born 9th Oct.
Mary of Robert & Mary Stroud born 11th Oct.
John of John & Tabitha Blower born 19th Oct.
Thomas of Arthur & Jane Kinde born 26th Sept.
James of James & Mary Webster born 16th July.
Susanna of William & Lydia Browne born 24th Oct.
Mary of Peter & Mary Duncan born 12th Nov.
Hannah of James & Abigail Johnson born 23rd Nov.
Nathaniel of Mr. Sinon & Hannah Lynd born 22nd Nov.
Thomas of Thomas & Frances Gold born 27th Nov.
Jonathan of John & Susanna Farnum born 13th Nov.
Thomas of Samuel & Margaret Rucke born 9th July.
John of William & Sarah Eustis born 8th Dec.
Nathaniel of Henry & Elizabeth Bridgham born 8th Dec.
Mary of George & Hannah Manning born 15th Dec.
Mary of John & Elizabeth Aldin born 17th Dec.
Huldah of Capt. William & Huldah Davis born 21st Dec.
Hannah of John & Mary Glover born 5th April.
Bethia & Abigail of James & Mary Hudson born 13th Dec.
John of John & Jane Bushnell borne 19th January.
John of Josiah & Ronas Belcher born 23rd Dec.
Samuel of Henry & Hannah Crab born 23rd Dec.
Thomas of Obediah & Alice Emmons born 7th Jan.
Susanna of Samuel & Elizabeth Norden born 26th Nov.
Hannah of John & Susanna Dawes born 7th Jan.
Jeremiah of Nathaniel & Mary Greene born 29th Dec.
Samuel of George & Elizabeth Orris born 20th Dec.
John of Charles & Abigail Stockbridge born 2nd Dec.
Grace of Tristram & Anne Hedges born 20th Aug.
Mary of Jonathan & Mary Ransford born 2nd July.
Elisha of John & Martha Mellowes born 16th Nov.

Mary of Joshua & Mary Atwater born 15th Jan.
Nathaniel of Robert & Sarah Mason born 23rd Dec.
Samuel of John & Isabel Pearse born 14th Jan.
Joseph of Joseph & Elizabeth Soper born 5th Jan.
Mehitabel of Mchallalaell & Hannah Munnings born 20th January.
Benjamin of Joseph & Elizabeth Sweete born 22nd January.
William of Lieut William & Bridget Phillips born 28th January.
Martha of John & Martha Amey born 23rd Febr.
Christopher of Mr. Christopher & Rebecca Clarke born 19th January.
Jeremiah of Jeremiah & Sarah Fitch born 5th Feb.
Elizabeth of Matthew & Mary Grosse born 3rd Feb.
Samuel of Amos & Mary Richardson born 18th Feb.
Mary of Samuel & Isabel Howard born 15th Sept.
Margaret of John & Mary Bowhonnon born 8th January.
Mary of John & Elizabeth Purchase born 3rd Feb.
Mehittabel of John & Susanna Sweete born 8th Dec.
Jonathan of John & Elizabeth Stutly born 8th Dec.
Hannah of Rice & Ann Jones born 4th May.
Deborah of Benjamin & Deborah Thwing born 13th January.
Thomas of Thomas & Mary Lambert born 6th November.
Sarah of James & Martha Robinson born 24th March.
Elizabeth of William & Hannah Ballantine born 8th March.
Michael of Michael & Susanna Martine born 10th Feb.
Rebecca of Elias & Ann Maverick born 1st January.
Matthew of Matthew & Estech Bunn born 9th June.
Joseph of Joseph & Elizabeth Bowd born 28th Oct.
Hannah of William & Elizabeth Ingram born 15th June.
Mary of Robert & Betteris Risdon born 15th June.
Sarah of David & Lydia Chapin born 3rd March.

Mary wife of Edmund Jackson died 18th Jan.
Jacob Sheafe died 22nd March.
Benjamin of Timothy & Margaret Prout died 5th April.
Martha of Henry & Gartred Pease died 15th April.
William of William & Elizabeth Greenough died 27th April.
Robert Raynolds died 27th April.
Ann of Thomas & Ann Walker died ———.
John of John & Joanna Baker died 23d May.
Richard Webb died 2nd July.
Sarah of Benjamin & Sarah Brisco died 26th June.
Lydia wife of Daniel Turell died 23rd June.
Jane Francklin widow died 16th July.
Jane wife of Martine Stebbins died 24th July.
Experience son of Nicholas & Dorothy Vpshall died 2nd Angus
Giles Kimball died 1st August.
Anne Burrell widow died 3rd August.
Jacob of late Jacob Sheafe died 4th August.
Thomas Walker died 11th August.
Elizabeth of Mr. Henry & Elinor Shrimpton died 12th August.
Jonathan of William & Ruth Read died 2nd July.
John of William & Elizabeth Holloway died 6th August.
Hannah of Francis & Mary East died 15th June.
John of John & Elizabeth Brookine died 16th Aug.
Abigail of Humphery & Mary Millam died 7th May.
Thomasine of Thomas & Sarah Scottow died 26th Aug.
Sarah wife of Matthew Barnard died 31st Aug.
Hannah of John & Mary Blake died 30th Aug.
Stephen Webb servant to Lieut. William Philips died 18th Sept.
Mary of Mr. Thomas & Mary Lake died 25th Oct.
Mrs. Sarah Pacy died 3rd November.
Samuel of Silvester & Lucy Harbert died 6th November.
Ephraim of Daniel & Ester Travis died 1st Nov.
Joshua of Henry & Mary Stevens died 10th Nov.
Mehalaliell of Mehalaliell & Hannah Munnings died 22nd Nov.

Mary wife of Richard Martine died 28th Nov.
Martha of William & Ester Pearse died 11th Dec.
Elnathan dau. of Capt. Richard & Ann Waldren died 10th Dec.
Martha of John & Martha Amey died 20th Dec.
Joshua of Thomas & Sarah Scottow died 8th January.
Lydia of Richard & Lydia Garrett died 28th Dec.
John of Samuel & Mary Flacke died 30th Dec.
William of Thomas & Rachel Harwood died 4th Dec.
Caleb of Richard & Jane Peacocke died 26th Sept.
Mr. Comfort Starr died 2nd January.
Grace of Tristram & Ann Hedges died 4th Jan.
Deborah Burnam servant to Benjamin Ward died 11th or 12th Sept.
John of John & Elizabeth Megdaniell died 4th Jan.
Ruth of Edmond & Susanna Jackson died 20th Jan.
Susanna wife of Robert Blott died 20th Jan.
John of Charles & Abigail Stockbridge died 1st Febr.
Dowsabell wife of Mr. Henry Webb died 28th Feb.
Mahalaleel Munnings was drowned 27th Feb.
Hannah of ——— & Susanna Dawes died 14th January.

Richard Barnard & Elizabeth Negus dau. of Benjamin Negus of Boston were
married 2nd March by Major Humphrey Atherton.
Richard Stabbs of Hull & Margaret Read were married 3rd March by Major
Humphrey Atherton.
Samuel Fisher & Milcha Snow dau. of Thomas Snow of Boston were married
22nd March by John Endecott Gov.
John Rosse & Mary Osborne dau. of John Osborne of Weymouth were mar-
ried 7th May by John Endecott Gov.
Thomas Shearer & Hannah Bumsteed dau. of Thomas Bumsteed of Boston
were married 18th April by Richael Bellingham Dep. Gov.
James Penniman & Mary Crosse were married 10th May by John Endecott
Gov.
Mr. William Blackston & Sarah Stephson widow were married 4th July by
John Endecott Gov.
William Shutt & Hopestill Viall dau. of John Viall of Boston were married
1st July by John Endecott Gov.
Zechariah Gillam & Phebe Phillips dau. of Lieut. Wm. Phillips of Boston
were married 26th July.
Richard Price & Elizabeth Crumwell were married 18th August by Major
Humphrey Atherton.
Philip Harding & Susanna Haviland widdow were married 23rd August by
John Endecott Gov.
Thomas Paine & Hannah Bray dau. of Thomas Bray of Newhaven were mar-
ried 25th August by John Endecott Gov.
Richard Hollingworth & Elizabeth Powell dau. of Mr. Michaell Powell of Bos-
ton were married 23rd August by John Endecott Gov.
John Morrell an Irishman & Lysbell Morrell an Irishwoman were married 31st
August by John Endecott Gov.
John Laughton & Johannah Mullings widdow were married 21st Sept. by
Richard Bellingham Dep. Gov.
Abraham Busby & Abigail Brisco widdow were married 23rd Sept. by John
Endecott Gov.
George Pearse & Mary Woodhouse dau. of Richard Woodhouse of Boston
were married by Richard Bellingham Dep. Gov.
Samuel Miles & Elizabeth Dowse dau. of Francis Dowse of Boston were mar-
ried 16th Oct. by John Endecott Gov.
Michaell Lambert & Elinor Furnell widdow were married.
Robert Portis & Alice Greenwood were married 3rd Nov. by Major Hum-
phrey Atherton.
Timothy Pratt & Deborah Cooper were married 9th Nov. by Major Atherton.
Roger Wheeler & Mary Stone widdow were married 23rd Nov. by Major
Humphrey Atherton.
John Lewis & Alice Bishop widdow were married 22nd Nov. by Major Hum-
phrey Atherton.

Joseph Cocke & Susanna Vpshall dau. of Nicholas Vpshall of Boston were married 10th Nov. by Mr. Tho. Danforth.

Henry Tewxbery & Martha Harvy widdow were married 10th Nov. by John Endecot Gov.

Nathaniel Hudson & Elizabeth Alford dau. of William Alford of Boston were married 1st Dec. by Mr. Tho. Danforth.

Samuel Smith & Susanna Read dau. of William Read of Boston were married 13th Dec. by John Endecott Gov.

William Norton & Susanna Mason dau. of Ralph Mason of Boston were married 14th Dec. by John Endecott Gov.

Daniel Turell & Mary Barrell widdow dau. of Elder William Colebron of Boston were married at Roxbury.

John Garretson & Alice Willey were married 5th Dec. by John Endecott Gov.

Mr. Antipas Boyce & Mrs. Hannah Hill dau. of Mr. Valentine Hill of Pascataque or Dover were married 24th Jan. by John Endecott Gov.

William Dennison of Pulling Point & Mary Parker were married 27th Oct. by Richard Bellingham Dep. Gov.

Edward Darby & Susanna Hooke were married 25th Jan. by Ri. Bellingham Dep. Gov.

John Matson & Mary Cotton dau. of Sargent William Cotton of Boston were married 7th March by Major Humphrey Atherton.

Thomas Woodward & Mary Guns were married 7th March by Major Humphrey Atherton.

Clement a negro servant to Mr. John Joyliffe & Mary a negro servant to the said Mr. Joyliffe were married.

David Cope & Obedience Topliffe dau. of Clement Topliffe of Dorchester were married 20th Feb. at Dorchester by Major Humphrey Atherton.

### FIRST CHURCH.

| | | |
|---|---|---|
| Elizabeth of David Chapin of Sprinkfield | 6 day | 1 mo. |
| Peter of John Inglesby | 13 day | 1 mo. |
| James of Peter Oliver | 20 day | 1 mo. |
| Rebecca of Wm. Padye | 3 day | 2 mo. |
| Ann of John Chickley | 24 day | 2 mo. |
| Jonathan of Wm. Read | 24 day | 2 mo. |
| Ruth of Joan & Thos. Joy | 1 day | 3 mo. |
| Priscilla of Henry Messinger's wife | 12 day | 4 mo. |
| Josua of Henry Stevens | 26 day | 4 mo. |
| John of Edward Devotion | 26 day | 4 mo. |
| Elnathan of Mr. Waldin | 10 day | 5 mo. |
| Tho: of Josua Scottow | 10 day | 5 mo. |
| Jacob of Mrs. Sheaffe | 24 day | 5 mo. |
| William, Isaac, Jacob, Elizabeth, Sarah, Rachel — Children of William Griges' wife | 31 day | July. |
| Sarah of Henry Fowning | 7 day | 6 mo. |
| Tomisen of Thomas Scottow | 15 day | 6 mo. |
| Elizabeth of Gamaliel Phipeny's wife | 15 day | 6 mo. |
| Christopher of John Marshall | 21 day | 6 mo. |
| Benjamin of Joseph Rock | 11 day | 7 mo. |
| Thomas of Rebecca Winsor | 9 day | 8 mo. |
| Samuel of Constance & James Mattock | 23 day | Oct. |
| Thomas, Mary, Sarah, Anna — Children of Mary & Crispus Brewer | 13 day | 9 mo. |
| Mary of Peter Duncan's wife | 20 day | 9 mo. |
| Anna of James Johnson | 27 day | 9 mo. |
| Nathaniel of Henry Bridgham | 11 day | 10 mo. |

| | |
|---|---|
| Mary of Hannah Manning | 18 day 10 mo. |
| Huldah of William Davis | 25 day 10 mo. |
| Samuel of John Peirce of Ch. of Wobourne | 22 day 11 mo. |
| Samuel of George Orice | 22 day 11 mo. |
| Benjamin of John Swett of Ch. of Newberry | 29 day 11 mo. |
| William of William Phillips of Ch. of Charlestowne | 5 day 12 mo. |
| Christopher of Christopher Clark's wife | 19 day 12 mo. |
| Samuel of Amos Richisson's wife | 19 day 12 mo. |

## 1660.

### TOWN.

Elizabeth of Alexander and Mary Adams born Oct. 1.
John of John & Eliza. Aldin born Novem. 20.
Martha of John and Hannah Andrewes born Decem. 5.
Elizabeth of John & Joanna Baker born June 26.
Elizabeth of Mr. Thomas & Elizabeth Brattle born Nov. 30.
Samuel of Henry & Eliza. Bridgham born Jan. 17.
William of Mr. James & Hannah Breding born Oct. 26.
Mary of John & Hannah Bateman born Sept. 4.
Sarah of Mr. Thomas & Mary Broughton born June 9.
Joseph of Henry & Elizabeth Blake born Sept. 2.
Samuel of Roger & Sarah Burgesse born Nov. 17.
Mary of Joseph & Ruth Belknap born Sept. 25.
Sarah of Oulando & Sarah Bagly born Jan. 14.
Elizabeth of John & Eliza. Brookine born May 26.
Sarah of Abraham & Jane Browne born June 16.
John of Edmund & Eliza. Browne born Oct. 9.
John of John Junr. & Eliza. Blackleech born Jan. 13.
Elizabeth of Jonathan & Mary Balston born Sept. 18.
James of James & Sarah Balston born Apr. 8.
John of Capt. Thomas & Mary Breden born Apr. 24.
Anna of Joseph & Mary Bastar born July 26.
Daniel of John & Ann Buckman born Mar. 29.
Ann of John & Susanna Cole born Mar. 7.
Rebecca of Isaac & Rebecca Coussins born Apr. 2.
Sarah of John & Eliza Conney born May 22.
Hannah of William & Ann Cotton born Sept. 4.
Sarah of Francis & Joan Crokum born Nov. 16.
Thomas of William & Martha Demsdall born Nov. 16.
Mary of James & Mary Dennis born Aug. 4.
Edward of Edward & Hannah Davis born Nov. 22.
Samuel of John & Mary Dawes born May 1.
Mary of Samuel & Anna Davis of Rumney Marsh born May 21.
Elizabeth of Thomas & Eliza. Dexter born Apr. 7.
William of Richard & Jane Druse born May 1.
Mehetable of George & Mary Dod born May 25.
Elizabeth of Robert & Jemima Drew born July 22.
Mary of Edward & Susanna Darby born Dec. 29.
William of William & Sarah Eustis born Feb. 25.
Hannah of Jacob & Mary Eliott born June 15.
Sarah of Robert & Mary Field born Oct. 20.
Theophilus of Theoph: & Hannah Frary born Dec. 4.
John of Daniel & Sarah Fairefield born Oct. 28.
Nathaniel of Emanuel & Christian Fryer born Dec. 9.
Hannah of William & Rachel Griggs of Rumney Marsh born 12th March.
John of John & Mary Gilbert born July 21.
Israel of William & Eliza. Greenough born July 27.
Joseph of Edward & Sarah Grant born Feb. 15.
John of John & Mary Glover born Feb. 1.
Miles of Nathaniell & Mary Greenwood born May 23.
Martha of Zachariah & Phoebe Gillam born June 2.
Edward of Edward & Joane Garretson born Sept. 22.

Hannah of Richard & Mary George born Jan. 21.
Abigail of John & Abigail Hanniford born March 8.
Rachel of Mr. Jeremiah & Esther Howchin born Dec. 16.
Ebenezer of John & Persis Harrison born May 31.
George of Nathaniell & Sarah Hunn born May 23.
Deborah of Christopher & Anne Holland born Mar. 8.
Jane of Philip & Susanna Harding born May 1.
America of William & Mary House born Apr. 30.
Susanna of William & Sarah Hasye born May 30.
Rachel of Thomas & Rachel Harwood born Feb. 28.
Timothy of William & Mary Ingram born July 2.
Joanna of James & Joanna Ingles born Oct. 18.
Sarah of Edmund & Eliza. Jackson born Sept. 24.
Richard of John & Emm Jepson born June 14.
Hannah of Mr. John & Anna Joyliffe born May 9.
Nathaniel of Abraham & Betteris Joslin born July 4.
John of John & Hannah Keene born Sept. 2.
Edward of Joseph & Joanna Kellocke born Oct. 1.
Mary of Richard & Johanna Knight born Feb. 13.
Anna of Edward & Anna Lane born Oct. 5.
John of John & Elizabeth Lowell born Apr. 7.
Abigail of John & Sarah Langdon born Aug. 25.
Mary & Martha Meiland daughters of ———
Benjamin of John & Sarah Marshall born Feb. 15.
Thomasin of John & Hannah Mirriam born Sept. 19.
Sarah of Thomas & Sarah Moore born May 5.
Jotham of John & Kathar. Maverick born Mar. 30.
Abigail of Humphry & Mary Milam born Oct. 10.
Sarah of Samuel & Thomasin Mayo born Dec. 19.
Elizabeth of John & Elizabeth Morse born Jan. 22.
Thomas of Joseph & Elizabeth Nash born Apr. 21.
John of William & Susanna Norton born Aug. 22.
Ruth of William & Frances Param born April 5.
David of Philip & Rachel Phillips born 1st March.
Mary of Ensign Henry & Mary Phillips born Nov. 28.
Nicholas of Nicholas & Hannah Phillips born May 12.
Sarah of Thomas & Eliza. Pecke born Jan. 13.
Mary of George & Mary Pearse born June 20.
Hannah of John & Ruth Pearse born June 30.
Benjamin of James & Sarah Pemberton born Apr. 26.
Thomas of Mr. Richard & Elizabeth Price born July 22.
Jonathan of Edward & Elizabeth Page born July 31.
Sarah of Mr. John & Sarah Paine born Aug. 14.
William of John & Sarah Parker of Muddy River born Dec. 5.
Timothy of Timothy & Deborah Pratt born Dec. 18.
Timothy of Wm. & Ruth Read born Aug. 11.
Mary of Nathaniell & Sarah Reynolds born Nov. 20.
Sarah of John & Mary Rosse born May 21.
Joseph of Richard & Luke Smith born May 2.
John of Joseph & Elizabeth Souther born Sept. 5.
Joseph of John & Ann Sawdy born Dec. 5.
Ruth of Anthony & Alice Shaw born Dec. 10.
Elizabeth of Mr. Henry & Ellener Shrimpton born Apr. 11.
Richard of Richard & Joice Staines born Dec. 3.
John of John & Sarah Skate born Apr. 25.
Thomasin of Thomas & Sarah Scottow born Aug. 18.
Lydia of Anthony & Christian Stoddard born Mar. 27.
Thomasin of John & Thomasin Scarlet born May 18.
Susanna of Sampson & Abigail Shore born May 20.
Ebenezer of Capt. Thomas & Mary Savage born May 22.
Nicholas of Pilgrim & Miriam Simpkins born Oct. 22.
John of John Jr. & Mary Sunderland born Jan. 22.
Abigail of David & Abigail Saywell born Feb. 4.
Lydia of Daniel & Lydia Turell born Nov. 30.

Hannah of Richard & Grace Trevis born May 28.
Stephen of Daniel & Ester Travis born Sept. 18.
Mary of Thomas & Hannah Tylee born Apr. 10.
Richard of Richard & Martha Twells born May 16.
Rebecca of John & Mary Tuttell born June 17.
Elizabeth of William & Grace Toy born June 25.
Elizabeth of Bartholmew & Damaris Threenedle born June 16.
Elizabeth of Henry & Martha Tereberry born Aug. 22.
James of Robert & Sarah Taylor born Jan. 17.
John of Richard & Rebecca Waite born Feb. 9.
Thomas of Thomas & Abigail Wiborne born April 2.
Esther of Capt. Richard & Anne Waldren born Dec. 1.
Prudence of Ezekiel & Anne Woodward born Apr. 4.
Abigail of William & Eliza. Wardell born Apr. 24.
Rebecca of Philip & Mary Wharton born May 5.
Hannah of Robert & Sarah Ward born May 6.
Margaret of Mr. Dean & Sarah Winthrop born July 25.
John of John & Josabeth Wing born Aug. 14.
Margaret of Mr. John & Margt. Woodmansey born Oct. 17.

Capt. Thomas Thornell died 11th March.
Anna of John & Mary Anderson died 12th March.
Elizabeth of Thomas and Elizabeth Barlow deceased the 17th of Aprill.
Josiah Robinson apprentice to Mr. Joseph Rocke deceased the 17th of Aprill.
Christopher Smith of Plymouth in England Carpenter of the ship Walsingam deceased the 10th of Aprill.
Abigaile wife of Thomas Wiborne deceased the 24th of Aprill.
Anne Norgrave widow deceased the 4th of Aprill.
Rebecca dau. of Phillip Wharton died the 10th of May.
Joseph of Joseph and Elizabeth Soper deceased the 28th of Aprill.
Thomas Rawlins deceased the 15th of March.
William of William and Hannah Ballantine deceased the 12th of May.
Nathaniell of Henry and Elizabeth Bridgham deceased the first of June.
George Griggs deceased the 23d of June.
Richard Sherman deceased the 30th of May.
Mary dau. of George Pearse deceased the 10th of July.
Ebenezer of John and Persis Harrison deceased the 11th of July.
Mary of John and Mary Kneeland died the 19th of October.
John of Theophilus and Hannah Frary deceased the 31st of July.
Hannah of Captain James and Abigail Johnson deceased the 3d of August.
Simeon of William and Elizabeth Holloway deceased the 17th of August.
Mr. William Paine deceased the 10th of October.
John of John and Josabeth Wing deceased the 26th of August.
Israel of William and Elizabeth Greenough deceased the 5th of September.
Joseph of Mr. Joseph and Elizabeth Rocke deceased the 10th of September.
Samuell Bitfield deceased the 10th of September.
Mr. Henry Webb deceased the 7th of September.
William of Thomas and Hannah Hull deceased the 27th of September.
Sarah Goodier deceased the 19th of November.
Elizabeth of Jonathan and Mary Bolston died the 26th of September.
Johanna of James and Johanna English deceased the 17th of November.
Miriam wife of Pilgrim Simpkins deceased the 10th of November.
Thomas of William and Martha Demsdall deceased the 13th of January.
Margaret Woodmansey wife of Mr. John Woodmansey deceased the 29th of December.
Charity White deceased the 28th of January.
Elizabeth of George and Hannah Manning deceased the 4th of February.
John of John and Susanna Cole deceased the 22nd of January.
George Broome died the 24th of February.
Daniell of Daniell Stone deceased the 27th of February.
Michaell of Michaell and Susanna Martine deceased the 14th of February.

John Aldine & Elizabeth Everill, widow, relict of Abiell Everill, deceased, were married 1st Aprill by John Endecott Gov.

Mr. Pelatiah Glover & Hannah Cullick were married 20th May.

Edward Garreson & Joan Pullen were married 29th August.

Mr. Samuell Coale & Anne Keayne widow were married 16th October by Richard Bellingham Dep. Gov.

Joseph Lowell & Abigail, daughter of ——— Procter, of Dorchester, were married 8th March by Major Humphrey Atherton.

Daniell Henricke & Mary Stockbridge widow were married 8th April by John Endecott Gov.

Mr. Abraham Browne & Rebecca Usher daughter of Mr. Hezekiah Usher of Boston were married first May.

Henry Adams & Mary Fitty daughter of William Fitty of Weymouth were married 10th May by Mr. Richard Russell Treasurer.

Isaac Willy & Francis Burcham daughter of Edward Burcham of Linne were married 8th June by Major Humphrey Atherton.

Samuell Moore & Abigail Hawkins daughter of Captain Thomas Hawkins deceased were married 13th May by Richard Russell Treasurer.

Clement Salmon & Johanna Riland were married 13 June by John Endecott Gov.

William Williams & Johanna Linn were married 19th July by Richard Bellingham Dep. Gov.

Peter Warren & Sarah Tucker daughter of Robert Tucker living within the limits of Dorchester were married first August by Major Atherton.

Richard Iggleden & Ann Prince were married 19th July by Captain Daniell Gookin.

David Saywell & Abigail Buttolph daughter of Thomas Buttolph were married 15th August by Richard Bellingham Dep. Gov.

Samuell Emmons & Mary Scott daughter of Robert Scott deceased were married 16th August by Richard Bellingham Dep. Gov.

John Parker & Mary Fairefeild daughter of Daniell Fairefeild of Boston were married 20th August by John Endecott Gov.

Thomas Matson & Mary Read widow were married 14th August by Mr. Thomas Danforth.

Richard Raser & Exercise Blackleech daughter of Mr. John Blackleech of Boston were married 24th August by Mr. Richard Russell of Charlestown.

Jasper Frost & Elizabeth Wakefeild daughter of John Wakefeild of Boston were married 20th August by John Endecott Gov.

John Hincksman & Elizabeth Emmons daughter of Thomas Emmons of Boston were married 10th August by Major Humphrey Atherton.

Eliphalet Het & Ann Douglas daughter of Henry Douglas of Boston were married first September by Richard Bellingham Dep. Gov.

Thomas Buttolph & Mary Baxter daughter of Nicholas Baxter of Boston were married 5th September by Richard Bellingham Dep. Gov.

John Veren & Mary Wiseman daughter of James Wiseman of Boston were married 12th June by John Endecott Gov.

David Carwithen & Francis Oldam widow were married 22nd September by Richard Bellingham Dep. Gov.

Mr. Francis Hooke & Mary Palsgrave widow were married 20th September by Major Humphrey Atherton.

Mr. Robert Gibbs & Elizabeth Sheaffe daughter of Mr. Jacob Sheafe deceased were married 7th September by Major Humphrey Atherton.

Myles Standish & Sarah Winslow daughter of Mr. John Winslow were married 19th July by Major Humphrey Atherton.

Richard Martine & Elizabeth Gay of Dedham daughter of John Gay were married at Salem by Major Hawthorne.

William Greenow & Ruth Swift the daughter of Thomas Swift of Dorchester were married 10th October.

Benjamine Gillam & Hannah Savage the daughter of Captain Thomas Savage of Boston were married 26th October by Major Humphrey Atherton.

John Faireweather & Sarah Turner daughter of Robert Turner of Boston were married 15th November by John Endecott Gov.

Edmund Jackson & Elizabeth Pilkenton were married 27th October by Mr Thomas Danforth.

Thomas Reape & Judith Rachell widow were married 30th November by John Endecott Gov.

Daniell Croeker & Sarah Balden were married 30th November by Richard Bellingham Dep. Gov.

John Benham & Margery Alcock widow were married 16th November by John Endecott Gov.

Richard Mason & Sarah Messinger the daughter of Henry Messinger of Boston were married 20th November by John Endecott Gov.

Clement Short & Faith Munt the daughter of Thomas Munt of Boston were married 21st November by John Endecott Gov.

Edward Loyd & Mary Wheelewright daughter of Mr. John Wheelewright late of Hampton were married 4th December by John Endecott Gov.

Samuell Mavericke & Rebecca Wheelewright daughter of Mr. John Wheelewright late of Hampton were married by Major Humphrey Atherton.

Benjamine Thurston & Elisha Walker daughter of Robert Walker of Boston were married 12th December by Richard Bellingham Dep. Gov.

John Tomline & Sarah Barnes daughter of Mathew Barnes of Boston were married 26th December by John Endecott Gov.

John Sowther & Hannah Read were married 11th January by Richard Bellingham Dep. Gov.

## FIRST CHURCH.

| | |
|---|---|
| Moses of Moses & Eunice Mavericke of Ch. of Salem | 4 day 1 mo. |
| Mehetabel of John Sweet | 4 day 1 mo. |
| Mary of Mr. Atwater of Newhaven | 11 day 1 mo. |
| Ann of Ann & Rice Joanes | 11 day 1 mo. |
| Lydia of Anthony Stoddard | 1 day 2 mo. |
| Anna of William Griges | 8 day 2 mo. |
| Mehetabel } of Edmond Jacklin<br>Mary | 8 day 2 mo. |
| Sarah of Henry Shrimpton aged 11 years | 15 day 2 mo. |
| Abigail of Henry Shrimpton aged 2 years | 15 day 2 mo. |
| Bethiah of Henry Shrimpton aged 1 year | 15 day 2 mo. |
| Elizabeth of Henry Shrimpton aged 5 days | 15 day 2 mo. |
| Tomisen of Tomisen & John Scarlet | 20 day 3 mo. |
| Ebenezer of Tho: Savage | 27 day 3 mo. |
| Hannah of Sampson Shore | 27 day 3 mo. |
| Ebenezer of John Harisson | 3 day 4 mo. |
| Hannah of Jacob Eliot | 10 day 9 mo. |
| Joseph of James Pemerton | 24 day 10 mo. |
| Elizabeth of Wm Toy | 1 day 5 mo. |
| Susan of William Hassy's wife | 14 July. |
| Mary of sister Dinnis | 5 day 6 mo. |
| Timothy of Wm Read | 12 day 6 mo. |
| Tomisen of Tho. Scottow | 19 day 6 mo. |
| Margaret of Dean Winthorp's wife | 2 day 7 mo. |
| Mercy of Mr. Bradford of Plymoth | 2 day 7 mo. |
| Hannah of William Cotton | 9 day 7 mo. |
| Joseph of Henry Blauge | 9 day 7 mo. |
| Mary of John Bateman's wife | 9 day 7 mo. |
| Tomisen of John Meriam | 23 day 7 mo. |
| Mary of Edmond Jackson | 30 day 7 mo. |
| Elizabeth of Alexander Adams | 30 day 7 mo. |
| Francis of Francis Smyth's wife | 18 Nov. |
| Tho: of William Dinsdale | 18 Nov. |
| Edward of Edward Davis | 25 Nov. |
| Elizabeth of Tho: Bratle | 2 day 10 mo. |
| Hester of Capt Weldin | 2 day 10 mo. |
| Mary of Henry Phillips | 2 day 10 mo. |
| Lidia of Daniel Turand's wife | 2 day 10 mo. |
| Theophilus of Theophilus Frairy | 9 day 10 mo. |
| Eliah of Mordeca Nichols' wife | 9 day 10 mo. |
| Elizabeth of Crispus Brewer's wife | 9 day 10 mo. |

| | |
|---|---|
| Rachel of Mr. Howchin | 16 day 10 mo. |
| Samuel of Henry Bridgham | 20 day 11 mo. |
| Sarah of sister Peek | 20 day 11 mo. |
| John of Richard Wayt | 10 day 12 mo. |
| Ruth of William Davis | 17 day 12 mo. |
| Benjamin of John Marshall | 17 day 12 mo. |

## 1661.

### TOWN.

Elizabeth of Nathaniel and Mary Adams born Mar. 2
William of Henry and Mary Adams born May 30.
Benjamin of Hope & Rachel Allen born Jan. 10.
Edward of Edward & Martha Allen born Sept. 21.
Mary of John & Martha Amey born Oct. 10.
Mary of Angola & Eliza. (negros) born Oct. 11.
John of John & Mary Bowhanon born Aug. 23.
Hannah of John & Joanna Baker born Nov. 4.
Martha of Thomas & Leah Baker born Sept. 3.
Nathaniel of William & Pilgrim Baker born May 13.
Susanna of Edward & Patience Blake born July 20.
Benjamin of William & Hannah Ballantine born July 22.
Isaac of Stephen & Jane Butler born Oct. 9.
Mary of Orlando & Sarah Bagly born Jan. 5.
Hezekiah of Mr. Abraham & Rebecca Browne born Aug. 22.
Jonathan of Josiah & Ranus Belcher born Sept 1.
Mary of Thomas & Abigail Bill born Aug. 15.
Zakeus of Capt. Thomas & Mary Breden born July 1.
Anna of Henry & Frances Boyen born May 4.
Elizabeth of Richard & Martha Bowden born May 18.
Elizabeth of Alexander & Margaret Bogle born Apr. 2.
Ralph of Ralph & Ann Benning born June 24.
Thomas of Thomas Jr. & Mary Buttolph born Oct. 5.
Mary of Samuel & Mary Bedwell born Sept. 18.
Benjamin of Richard & Eliza. Barnard born Jan. 6.
Antipas of Antipas & Hannah Boyce born Feb. 8.
Andrew of Andrew & Elizabeth Cload born Apr. 28.
Hannah of David & Lydia Chappine born Oct. 23.
Samuel of John & Ann Checkley born Nov. 26.
David of David & Frances Carwithen born June 1.
Daniel of Christopher & Rebecca Clarke born Feb. 10.
Richard of Richard & Mary Collens born June 18.
David of David & Obedience Copp born Dec. 8.
Mary of James & Mary Dennis born June 5.
Sarah of Samuel & Sarah Davis born Sept. 11.
Elizabeth of John & Mary Dawes born June 24.
Jonathan of William & Susanna Dawes born Nov. 3.
Joseph of William & Martha Demsdall born Nov. 21.
Lydia of Edward & Sarah Ellis born Nov. 17.
Mary of Samuel & Mary Emons born Nov. 18.
Sarah of Thomas & Martha Fitch born June 14.
Theophilus of Theoph: & Hannah Frary born Jan. 30.
Ruth of John & Eliza. Ferniside born Aug. 20.
David of David & Mary Faulkner born June 7.
Samuel of Samuel & Anne Flack born Oct. 18.
Thomas of John & Sarah Faireweather born Sept. 5.
Joseph of Nathaniel & Margaret Gallop born Mar. 20.
Mary of John & Susanna Griffine born Jan. 21.
Samuel of William & Eliza: Greenough born Mar. 3.
Richard of Richard & Lydia Garret born Nov. 3.
Bartholmew of Thomas & Frances Gold born Oct. 27.
Susanna of Nathaniell & Mary Green born Apr. 29.
Zachariah of Zachariah & Phoebe Gillam born Nov. 4.

Thomas of Thomas & Eliza. Gwine born Nov. 3.
Susanna of Charles & Eunice Gleden born Nov. 16.
Samuel of James & Mary Hudson born Mar. 23.
Mary of Joseph & Frances How born Mar. 17.
Abraham of John & Persis Harrison born Sept. 3.
Mary of Thomas & Hannah Hull born Aug. 22.
Samuel of Ensign John & Judith Hull born Aug. 1.
Thomas of Richard & Mary Hicks born Feb. 23.
Hannah of William & Mary Hunter born Nov. 22.
Elizabeth of Ezekiel & Eliza. Hamlin born Oct. 24.
Ephraim of Samuel & Isabel Howard born Feb. 23.
Solomon ⎫ of David & Katharine Hitchbone born Dec. **14.**
David   ⎭ of David & Katharine Hitchbone born Dec. **14.**
Abraham of William & Mary Hambleton born Dec. 23.
Martha of Edmund & Eliza. Jackson born Feb. 11.
John of John & Emm Jepson born May 8.
Hannah of Capt. James & Abigail Johnson born June 12.
Samuel of David & Elizabeth Kelly born Nov. 30.
John of Thomas & Susanna Kelton born Aug. 15.
Samuel of John & Alice Lewes born Jan. 18.
———— son of John & Hannah Lowell born ————
Edward of Mr. Thomas & Elizabeth Lake born June 28.
Elizabeth of William & Mary Lane born Feb. 3.
Edward of Mr. Edward & Hannah Lane born Feb. 20.
Joseph of Joseph & Abigail Lowell born Aug. 1.
Lydia of Jeremiah & Sarah Murrell born Oct. 14.
Mary of John & Ruth Marshall born Jan. 2.
John of Robert & Mary Marshall born Jan. 7.
Elizabeth of John & Eliza. Megdaniel born Sept. 3.
Elizabeth of George & Hannah Manning born Oct. 13.
Mary of Samuel & Abigail Moore born May 2.
Sarah of Richard & Sarah Mason born Sept. 3.
David of Arthur & Joanna Mason born Oct. 24.
Mary of Samuel & Rebecca Mavericke born Oct. 2.
John of Richard & Elizabeth Martine born Oct. 2.
Margaret of Dorman & Margt. Mahoone born June 3.
Mary of Robert & Catharine Nanny born June 22.
Elizabeth of Joshua & Elizabeth Nash born Feb. 17.
Abigail of Coronell Peter & Sarah Oliver born Jan. 1.
Daniel of Henry & Eliza. Powning born Aug. 27.
Abigail of Nicholas & Hannah Phillips born Feb. 20.
Elizabeth of Zechariah & Eliza. Phillips born June 29.
Ebenezer of William & Esther Pearse born Mar. 16.
George of George & Mary Pearse born Jan. 27.
Mary of John & Mary Parker born May 20.
Mary of Peter & Mary Pue born June 17.
James of James & Mary Penniman born Sept. 27.
John of John & Susanna Rainsford born Mar. 5.
Elizabeth of Robert & Mary Right born July 9.
John of George & Mary Robinson born ————.
William of William & Alice Russell born Apr. 16.
Lydia of Mr. Joseph & Elizabeth Rocke born Apr. 21.
Samuel of Samuel & Margaret Rucke born Oct. 4.
Jonathan of Jonathan & Mary Rainsford born July 26.
John of Thomas & Judith Reap born Sept. 2.
Joseph of Richard & Exercise Rawser born Oct. 2.
John of William & Hopestill Shute born Mar. 7.
Joseph of Thomas & Sarah Stevens born April 17.
Elizabeth of Nicholas & Hannah Stone born Sept. 25.
Elizabeth of Thomas & Anne Saxton born June 8.
Sarah of Robert & Eliza. Sanford born Nov. 23.
Samuel of Samuel & Naomi Sherman born Oct. 3.
Sarah of William & Eliza. Sumner born Feb. 3.
Anna of John & Phillip Snell born Jan. 2.

Benjamin of John & Eliza. Studley born May 23.
Joseph of Mr. Anthony & Christian Stoddard born Dec. 1.
John of Capt. Thomas & Mary Savage born Aug. 15.
Abigail of David & Abigail Saywell born Sept. 12.
Comfort of John & Martha Starre born Feb. 4.
Christian of John & Sarah Tuckerman born July 8.
Hannah of Daniel & Esther Travis born Jan. 5.
Mary of William & Rebecca Thirrell born Apr. 6.
John of John & Sarah Tomline born Nov. 14.
Elizabeth of Richard & Elizabeth Tout born Dec. 4.
Samuel of Samuel & Abigail Towne born July 12.
John of John & Mary Verrin born July 11.
John of Lyonell & Elinor Wheatly born Oct. 6.
Margaret of Edward & Eliza. Wanton born Aug. 13.
Sarah of Sergt. Richard & Frances Woodde born May 21.
Mary of Mr. Thomas & Mary Walker born Aug. 9.
Hannah of John & Mary Williams born Apr. 27.
Thomas of Thomas & Anne Williams born Mar. 29.
Sarah of Thomas & Eliza. Watkins born Nov. 7.
Thomas of Thomas & Mary Webster born Jan. 11.
John of Edward & Sarah Winslow born June 18.
Francis Hopestill* dau. of Richard & Sarah Woodhouse born Mar. 8.
John of Peter & Sarah Warren born Sept. 8.
Thomas of Thomas & Naomi Wells born Dec. 4.
Mary of Nathaniel & Hannah Wilson of Muddy River born May 22.

Mr. Ralph Smith Pastor of the Church of Plymouth died the first of March.
John of John and Mary Glover died the 19th of Aprill.
Thomas of Thomas and Susanna Bumsteed deceased the 3d of May.
Thomas of Thomas and Abigail Wiborne deceased the 11th of May.
Seargent Nathaniell Williams deceased the 23d of Aprill.
Thomas of Thomas and Mary Read deceased the 11th of May.
Tabytha wife of Mathew Abday deceased————.
Joan Coffine deceased the 30th of May.
John of Edmund and Martha Allen deceased the 29th of Aprill.
Dorman Mahoon deceased the 2nd of Aprill.
Ann dau. of John Checkley died the 20th of June.
Susanna of Samson and Abigail Shore deceased the 22nd of June.    .
Ebenezer of Richard and Tomasin Collicott deceased the 24th of June.
Anne wife of Thomas Saxton deceased the 23d of June.
Benjamine of Mr. Joseph and Elizabeth Rocke deceased the 20th of June.
Anne of Mr. Edward and Anna Lane deceased the 27th of June.
Mercy of Richard and Johanna Knight deceased the 27th of July.
Nathaniell of ———— and Sarah Bucknell deceased the 22d of July.
Samuell of Symon and Christian Roberts deceased the 27th of July.
Ruth of William and Francis Param deceased the 4th of July.
Thomas of Joshua and Elizabeth Nash deceased first of July.
Mary of Robert and Mary Stroud deceased the 30th of June.
Mary of Zechariah and Phebe Gillam died the 14th of August.
Zechariah of Jeremiah and Sarah Fitch deceased the 13th of August.
Martha daughter of Robert Bradford deceased the 13th of August.
Sarah of Richard and Francis Woodee deceased the 23d of August.
John of Captain Thomas and Mary Savage deceased the 23d of August.
Seargent Evan Thomas deceased the 25th of August.
Abigail of William and Elizabeth Wardell died the 23d of August.
Edward of Mr. Thomas and Mary Lake deceased the 27th of August.
Nicholas of Nicholas and Hannah Phillips deceased the 18th of August.
Elizabeth of Samuell and Constant Mattocke deceased the 3d day of September.
Hannah of Mr. John and Hannah Paine deceased the 13th of September.
Arabella of Mr. John and Mary Palsgrave deceased the 9th of September.
John of John and Sarah Stone deceased the 12th of September.

---

*This is plainly so written in the oldest MS., but in the second MS. the double-named daughter is changed to twin sons, probably with reason. — W. S. A.

Robert Nash deceased the 13th of September.
Johanna of Richard and Johanna Knight deceased the 23d of September.
John of John and Sarah Warren deceased the 19th of September.
John Pearse died the 17th of September.
Mary of Madit and Joan Ings deceased the 5th of October.
Ephraim of Thomas Robinson deceased the 22nd of September.
Sarah of Richard and Sarah Mason deceased the 9th of September.
Sarah of Orlando and Sarah Bagly deceased the 30th of September.
Benjamin of James and Sarah Pemberton deceased the 29th of September.
William of William and Alice Russell deceased the 29th of August.
Sarah of Robert and Mary Feild deceased the 30th of September.
Thomas Snelling a ship-carpenter dying intestate living at Dartmouth in Eng. the 16th of October.
Elizabeth Habell deceased the 31st of August.
James Davis seaman deceased the 17th of October.
Nicholas Edwards a stranger living at Barbadoes near Spixes Bay deceased the 22nd of October.
William of Richard and Jane Drus deceased the 25th of July.
Mary wife of Thomas Robinson deceased the 26th of October.
Elizabeth of Francis and Mary Hudson deceased the 23rd of October.
Margery Elliott deceased the 30th of October.
Thomas of Thomas Jr. and Mary Buttolph deceased the 30th of October.
Thomas Barlow deceased the 23rd of October.
Temperance daughter of John and Susanna Sweete deceased the 28th of November.
James Sanford deceased the 2nd of November.
John of John and Mary Bowhonnon deceased the 14th of November.
Nathaniell Wales senior deceased the 4th of December.
Johanna wife of Thomas Ashly deceased the 27th of December.
Roger Wheeler deceased the 7th of December.
George Pearse deceased the 7th of December.
Hopestill daughter of Thomas Bill deceased the 28th of November.
Anne wife of William Munnings deceased the 4th of December.
John of John and Martha Saffine deceased the 11th of December.
Stephen of Robert and Elizabeth Meeres deceased the 10th of December.
Cecile wife of William Brisco deceased the 9th of December.
William of Samuell and Mary Gallop deceased the 28th of November.
Jane Wheeler deceased the 27th of December.
Solomon and David twins of David and Katherine Hitchbone deceased the 19th of December.
William of William and Elizabeth Pearse deceased the 4th of January.
Rice Jones deceased the 3d of January.
Isabell wife of Nathaniell Wales deceased the 18th of December.
John Paddy deceased the 8th of January.
Joseph of Mr. Anthony and Christian Stoddard deceased the 27th of December.
Elizabeth of Richard and Dorothy Graves deceased the 2d of January.
Elizabeth of John and Anne Cleare deceased the 23rd of Jan'y.
Thomas of the said John and Elizabeth Cleare deceased the 31st of January.
Samuell of Thomas Robbinson deceased the 16th of January.
Margaret wife of Alexander Bogle deceased the 22nd of February.
Mary of Thomas and Hannah Hull deceased the 19th of March.

John Reylean an Irishman & Margaret Brene an Irishwoman were married 15th March by John Endecott Governor.
Habbiah Savage & Hannah Ting daughter of Mr. Edward Ting of Boston were married 8th May by John Endecott Governor.
John Wampony an Indian & Anne Praske were married 21st May by Major Humphrey Atherton.
Mr. John Freake & Elizabeth Clarke daughter of Captain Thomas Clarke of Boston were married 28th May by Major Humphrey Atherton.
Edward Howard & Hannah Hawkins daughter of Thomas Hawkins of Boston were married 7th June by Mr. Thomas Danforth of Cambridge.
Joseph Benjamine of Bastable & Jemima Lumbard daughter of the late Thomas Lumbard deceased were married 10th June by Richard Bellingham Dep. Gov.

William Makepeace & Ann Johnson were married 23rd May by Major Humphrey Atherton.

John Preston & Susanna Read widow were married 28th May by Mr. Thomas Danforth of Cambridge.

Samuell Browne & Mary Mattocke daughter of James Mattocke of Boston were married 9th July by John Endecott Governor.

Christopher Mosse & Prudence Woodward daughter of Nathaniell Woodward of Boston were married.

Bryan Morfrey an Irishman & Margaret Mayhoone widow were married 20th July by John Endecott Governor.

John Cann & Ester Read daughter of William Read of Boston were married 30th July.

Josiah Cooper & Wayte-a-while Makepeace of Boston were married 13th September by John Endecott Governor.

William Clarke now resident in Boston & Martha Farr daughter of George Farr of Lynne were married 18th September by Mr. Richard Russell.

John Jarvis & Rebecca Parkman daughter of Elias Parkman of Boston were married 18th September by Richard Bellingham Dep. Gov.

Benjamin Richards & Hannah Hudson daughter of Lieutenant William Hudson of Boston were married 10th October by Mr. Richard Russell.

Gilbert Dallison & Margaret Story were married 24th October by Mr. Richard Russell.

James Greene & Rebecca Jones daughter of Thomas Jones of Dorchester were married 19th November by John Endecott Governor.

John Searle & Katherine Warner widow were married 26th November by John Endecott Governor.

Pilgrim Sympkins & Katherine Richardson were married 27th November by Richard Bellingham Dep. Gov.

John Drummond & Lydia Hallet widow were married 27th November by John Endecott Governor.

John Sparke & Mary Sennet daughter of Walter Sennet of Boston were married 26th November by John Endecott Governor.

John Curtis & Rebecca Wheeler daughter of the late Thomas Wheeler of Boston deceased were married 26th December.

John Butcher & Mary Deane were married 30th January by Mr. Thomas Danforth of Cambridge.

John Walley & Elizabeth Wing daughter of the late Robert Wing deceased were married 3d April.

Thomas Ashly & Hannah Broome widow were married the last of January by Mr. Thomas Danforth of Cambridge.

Mr. Henry Shrimpton & Mrs. Mary Fenn widow were married 27th February by Richard Bellingham Dep. Gov.

Peter Aspinwall of Muddy River & Remember Palfrey of Redding were married 12th February by John Endecott Governor.

John Combes & Elizabeth Barlow relict of Thomas Barlow were married 24th February by Captain Mason of Watertowne.

## FIRST CHURCH.

| | | |
|---|---|---|
| Joseph of Naomi Wells | 3 day | 1 mo. |
| Elizabeth of Elizabeth Brookin | 3 day | 1 mo. |
| John } of John Blackleach | 10 day | 1 mo. |
| Elizabeth } of John Blackleach | 10 day | 1 mo. |
| Sarah of Joseph How | 24 day | 1 mo. |
| Josua of Sister Kibby | 31 day | 1 mo. |
| John of Ann & Wm Ballantin | 14 day | 2 mo. |
| David of Ann & William Ballantin | 14 day | 2 mo. |
| Elizabeth of Ann & William Ballantin | 14 day | 2 mo. |
| Lydia of Mr. Rocke | 28 day | 2 mo |
| Mary of Mary & James Hudson | 28 day | 2 mo. |
| Thomas of Leah & Tho: Baker | 28 day | 2 mo. |
| John of Leah & Tho: Baker | 28 day | 2 mo. |
| Rachel of Leah & Tho: Baker | 28 day | 2 mo. |
| Rachel of Tho: Harwood's wife | 5 day | 3 mo. |

| | | |
|---|---|---|
| Sarah of Richard Woody of Ch. of Roxberry | 26 day | 3 mo. |
| Hannah of John Andrews' wife | 2 day | 4 mo. |
| Mary of John Andrews' wife | 2 day | 4 mo. |
| Martha of John Andrews' wife | 2 day | 4 mo. |
| Sarah Burgisse | 16 day | 4 mo. |
| William of Sarah Burgisse | 16 day | 4 mo. |
| Samuel of Sarah Burgisse | 16 day | 4 mo. |
| Hannah of James Johnson | 16 day | 4 mo. |
| Elizabeth of Thomas Saxton's wife | 7 day | 5 mo. |
| John of Edward Rawson | 14 day | 5 mo. |
| Thomas of Elizabeth & William Spowell | 21 day | 5 mo. |
| William of Elizabeth & William Spowell | 21 day | 5 mo. |
| Mehetabel of Elizabeth & William Spowell | 21 day | 5 mo. |
| Samuel of John Hull | 4 day | 6 mo. |
| John of Capt. Savag | 18 day | 6 mo. |
| Daniel of Henry Fowning | 1 day | 7 mo. |
| Abraham of        Harrison | 8 day | 7 mo. |
| Martha of Leah Baker | 8 day | 7 mo. |
| William of Hester & William Peirce | 15 day | 7 mo. |
| Nathaniel of Hester & William Peirce | 15 day | 7 mo. |
| Moses of Hester & William Peirce | 15 day | 7 mo. |
| Ebenezer of Hester & William Peirce | 15 day | 7 mo. |
| Hester of Hester & William Peirce | 15 day | 7 mo. |
| Ruth of Mr. Firniside | 29 day | 7 mo. |
| Elizabeth of George Manning | 20 day | 8 mo. |
| Hannah of David Chapin | 3 day | 9 mo. |
| Jonathan of Wm. Dawes | 10 day | 9 mo. |
| Lydia of William Ellis' wife | 24 day | 9 mo. |
| Jonathan of William Dinsdale | 24 day | 9 mo. |
| Sarah of Robert Sanford | 24 day | 9 mo |
| Benjamin of John Chickly | 1 day | 10 mo. |
| Joseph of Anthony Stoddard | 8 day | 10 mo. |
| Thomas of Ann & Tho: Wells | • 8 day | 10 mo. |
| Peter of John Looell | 26 day | 11 mo. |
| Daniel of Christopher Clark | 16 day | 12 mo. |
| Martha of Edmond Jackson | 16 day | 12 mo. |

## 1662.

### Town.

Elizabeth of John & Eliza. Alden born May 9.
John of Josua & Mary Atwater born Aug. 14.
John of John & Hannah Andrewes born Sept. 20.
Samuel of Peter & Remembrance Aspinwall of Muddy River born Nov. 10.
John of John & Eliza. Brookin born March 13.
James of Thomas & Abigail Bill born Feb. 28.
William of Mr. Thomas & Elizabeth Brattle born Nov. 22.
Nathaniel of Henry & Eliza. Bridgham born Apr. 2.
James of James & Hannah Breding born Apr. 1.
Sarah of Roger & Sarah Burgesse born Jan. 28.
Hannah of William & Hannah Ballentine born Nov. 15.
James of Samuel & Mary Browne born May 2.
Robert of Jonathan & Mary Bolston born Dec. 3.
Abigail of James & Sarah Balston born Aug. 20.
Sarah of John & Tabitha Blower born July 1.
Jane of John & Jane Bushnell born Dec. 18.
Thomas of Thomas & Mary Buttolph born Feb. 5.
William of Andrew & Elizabeth Cload born Feb. 16.
Joseph of John & Eliza. Conney born Apr. 27.
Hannah of Joseph & Hannah Chandler born Sept. 8.
Elizabeth of John & Elizabeth Combes born Nov. 30.
Ruth of Capt. William & Huldah Davis born Feb. 12.

Joseph of Joseph & Eliza. Davis born Jan. 26.
Hannah of John & Returne Davis born Jan. 24.
Samuel of John & Lydia Drummond born Aug. 23.
Elizabeth of Bernard & Eliza. Engles born July 15.
Martha of Obadiah & Alice Emons born Oct. 23.
Joseph of William & Sarah Eastis born Nov. 20.
Jacob of Jacob & Mary Eliott born Nov. 16.
Thomas of Thomas & Jane Edsell born Dec. 14.
David of John & Susanna Farnam born Oct. 30.
Zachariah of Jeremiah & Sarah Fitch born Feb. 19.
Deborah of Jeremiah & Sarah Fitch born Nov. 5.
Daniel of Robert & Mary Field born Sept. 6.
Abigail of Theoph: & Hannah Frarye born Sept. 5.
Solomon of Samuel & Anne Flacke born Dec. 3.
Daniel of Daniel & Sarah Fairfield born Sept. 18.
Penelope of John & Sarah Faireweather born Jan. 15.
Mary of Mr. John & Eliza. Freeke born Mar. 25.
Sarah of Matthew & Mary Grosse born Aug. 23.
Mary of William & Ruth Greenow born Nov. 28.
Rebecca of William & Rachel Griggs of Rumney Marsh born **Apr.** 3.
Mary of John & Mary Glover born Apr. 16.
Elizabeth of James & Rebecca Greene born Nov. 14.
Samuel of Nathaniell & Mary Greenwood born Sept. 24.
Hannah of Benja. & Hannah Gillam born Apr. 27.
John of John & Hazelpanah Gee born May 27.
Ebenezer of James & Mary Hudson born Mar. 4.
Matthew of Edward & Esther Howard born Mar. 15.
Samuel of Eliphalet & Ann Hett born May 13.
———— dau. of John and Persis Harrison born Feb. 2.
Thomas of Thomas & Hannah Hull born Jan. 16.
Samuel of Nathaniell & Sarah Hunn born Sept. 13.
Mary of Christopher & Anne Holland born Feb. 8.
Benjamin of Thomas & Rachel Harwood born Feb. 4.
Margaret of Jarret & Rebecca Ingram born Jan. 17.
John of John & Jane Jackson born Feb. 24.
Mary of Arthur & Jane Kinde born Apr. 27.
Richard of Richard & Joanna Knight born Apr. 30.
Joseph of John & Alice Lewis born Feb. 4.
Edward of Capt. Thomas & Mary Lake born July 15.
Elizabeth of Mr. Simon & Hannah Lynde born Mar. 25.
Susanna of Thomas & Mary Lambert born Feb. 28.
Patience of John & Elizabeth Lowell born Oct. 7.
Hannah of Joseph & Abigail Lowell born Jan. 31.
John of Mr. Hudson alias John & Sarah Leveret born Aug. **25.**
Thomas of Henry & Sarah Messenger born Mar. 22.
James of Samuel & Constance Mattock born Oct. 27.
Oliver of John & Martha Mellowes born Apr. 3.
Hannah of Thomas & Sarah Moore born Apr. 26.
Philip of Robert & Sarah Mason born July 16.
Jacob of Richard & Sarah Mason born Oct. 17.
Elizabeth of John & Katharine Maverick born Oct. 17.
John of John & Rebecca Maverick born July 28.
Prudence of Michael & Susanna Martine born Mar. 26.
Ruth of John & Elizabeth Morse born Dec. 18.
Sarah of Christopher & Prudence Mosse born Mar. 28.
Samuel of Samuel & Elizabeth Milles born Apr. 27.
Cotton of Mr. Increase & Mariah Mather born Feb. 12.
George of George & Lydia Nowell born Mar. 21.
William of William & Susanna Norton born Sept. 14.
John of John & Sarah Phillips born Mar. 4.
Mary of John & Isabel Pearse born Mar. 13.
Joyliffe of Richd. & Elizabeth Price born Mar. 2.
Sarah of Zechariah & Eliza. Phillips born Sept. **7.**
Sarah of Thomas & Eliza. Peck born June 5.

Ruth of John & Ruth Pearse born Nov. 22.
Mary of James & Sarah Pemberton born July 13.
Hannah of Mr. John & Sarah Paine born Mar. 31.
James of John & Sarah Parker born Aug. 13.
John of Timothy & Deborah Pratt born Dec. 3.
Mary of John & Kesia Perkins born Sept. 8.
John of James & Martha Robinson born Sept. 17.
Joseph of Simon & Christian Roberts born Sept. 18.
William of Wm. & Ruth Read born May 7.
Samuel of Mr. Joseph & Elizabeth Rocke born May 17.
Mary of John & Susanna Ransford born Jan. 10.
Prudence of Amos & Mary Richardson born Jan. 31.
Sarah of Robert & Betteris Risden born May 29.
Joseph of Simon & Susanna Rogers born July 29.
Abigail of Charles & Abigail Stockbridge born Feb. 24.
Elizabeth of John & Katherine Searle born Oct. 19.
Ann of Barthol: & Elzaphan Stretton horn Feb. 19.
Rebecca of Richard & Joice Staines born Dec. 26.
John of Charles & Abigail Stockbridge born Sept. 29.
Joseph of Mr. Habiah & Hannah Savage born Aug. 15.
Abigail of William & Hopestill Shute born Aug. 13.
William of Pilgrim & Catharine Symkins born Oct. 3.
Elizabeth of Arthur & Joane Scovell born Dec. 1.
John of Mr. John & Martha Saffine born Apr. 14.
Sarah of John & Sarah Stutche born Oct. 21.
Susanna of Thomas & Elizabeth Sheauer born Feb. 7.
Coleborne of Daniel & Mary Turell born Dec. 4.
Abigail of Richard & Grace Trevis born Jan. 8.
Martha of Richard & Martha Tewells born Sept. 8.
Mary of Benjamin & Elisha Thurston born Apr. 24.
Abigail of Samuel & Abigail Towne born Sept. 3.
Isaac of Isaac & Dorcas Wooddee born Apr. 6.
Susanna of Thomas & Susanna Walker born Feb. 20.
Charles of Thomas & Anne Williams born Sept. 20.
Sarah of William & Joanna Williams born Apr. 20.
Sarah of Robert & Rebecca Winsor born May 7.
Joanna of John & Josabeth Wing born Sept. 4.
John of Mr. John & Eliza. Woodmansey born Feb. 2.
Joseph of Peter & Sarah Wanyen born Feb. 19.
Mary of Eleazer & Mary Way born May 24.
Hannah of Richard & Esther Way born May 23.
John of John & Elizabeth Walley born Aug. 27.
James of James & Rebecca Whetcombe born Nov. 30.

Daniell of Christopher and Rebecca Clarke deceased the 16th of March.
Samuell of William and Elizabeth Greenough deceased the 21st of March.
Richard Garret deceased the 29th of March.
Mr. Samuell Haugh Pastor of the Church at Reading deceased at Mr. Heze-
    kiah Usher's house in Boston the 30th of March.
George of George and Lydia Nowell deceased the 30th of Aprill.
Nathaniell Wales deceased the 20th of May.
William Blanten deceased the fifteenth day of June.
Elizabeth of Mr. John and Elizabeth Aldin died the 14th of the 5th month.
Ruth of William and Ruth Read deceased July 17.
Richard of Richard and Joannah Knight died the 16th of the 5th month.
Ann of William and An Pollard died the 2nd of the 6th month.
Alice Griggs died being a widow the 19th of July.
Mr. William Coleborne deceased August first.
Henry Blake deceased the 26th day of July.
Hannah of John and Ruth Pearse died the 28th of July.
Elisabeth of Nathaniel and Mary Addams died the 17th of the 6th month.
William Robinson of Bermoodes died the third of September.
Debora of Jeremia and Sarah Fitch died January 14.
Edward of Mr. Thomas and Mary Lake deceased August 12.

Mary of Arthur and Jane Kind died August 28.
Prudence of Michael and Susanna Martyn died the 31st of the 5th month
Sarah of Samuell and Sara Bucknell deceased the 12th of the 5th month.
Richard of Richard and Elisabeth Hollingworth died the 31st of the 6th month.
Edward of Edward and Margrett Cowell deceased the 7th of the 7th month.
Zechariah of Zechariah and Phebe Gillam died the 1st of the 7th month.
Captaine Robert Clarke of Redriffe in Old England died in Boston at the
    house of Richard Staines in New England 16th of the 7th month.
Mary of Mr. John and Elisabeth Freake died the 25th of the 7th month.
James Lane of Plymouth in Old England carpenter died at Boston in New
    England October 3d.
Caleb of Caleb and Judeth Pendleton died the 1st of October.
Joanna of John and Joanna Baker died September 14th.
Nathaniel Wales died the 18th of May.
Elisabeth Cane widow died October 8th.
Elisabeth of John and Jane Bushnell died the 17th of the 2d month.
John Tum an Hamburgher died the 11th of October, at the house of Richard
    Bradley Boston in New England.
Debora daughter of Christopher Holland died the 20th of the 7th month.
Thomas Gold deceased the 26th of October.
Richard Woodcock died the 12th of November.
Jacob of Jacob and Mary Elliott deceased the 6th of the 10th month.
John of John and Jane Bushnell died the 10th of the 2nd month.
Mary        servant to Thomas Bligh deceased the 27th of November.
An Oliver widow deceased December 20th.
Sarah wife of Edmund Greenleife deceased January 18.
Mehittabell wife of Seth Perry died February 20th.
Captain John Cullick deceased the 23d of January.
Samuell of Samuell and Naomy Sherman died the 18th of the 7th month.
Jacob Ledger deceased the 24th of February.
Anna of Mr. Humphrey and Mary Davy deceased the 12th of September.
Joseph of Joseph and Elisabeth Davis died the 18th of the 12th month.
Mary of William and Mary Hunter died 15th of 1st month.
Nathaniell Ramsey servant to Alexander Addams died the 22nd of the 1st
    month.                          .


James Hill & Hannah Hincksman were married 10th April by Captaine Dan-
    iell Gookine of Cambridge.
Thomas Walker & Susanna Collins daughter of John Collins of Boston were
    married 25th March by Mr. Richard Russell of Charlestown.
Tego Ockonell & Philipa King servant to John Conney were married first
    May by Mr. Thomas Danforth of Cambridge.
Mr. John Woodmansey & Elizabeth Carr daughter of George Carr of Salis-
    bury were married first May by Mr. Thomas Danforth.
Richard Price & Grace Waite daughter of Gamaliell Wayte of Boston were
    married 6th May by Richard Bellingham Deputy Governor.
Joseph Davis & Elizabeth Saywell were married 7th May by Major Willard.
Edward Kilby & Elizabeth Yeomans widow were married 9th May by Major
    Generall Denison.
Jarrett Ingraham & Elizabeth Searles daughter of Edward Searles were mar-
    ried 28th May by John Endecott Governor.
Eliazer Fawre & Mary Preston daughter of Daniel Preston of Dorchester
    were married 28th May by John Endecott Governor.
Samuell Mason & Mary Holeman daughter of the late John Holeman of Dor-
    chester deceased were married 29th May by John Endecott Governor.
John Petty & Ann Canning were married 30th May by John Endecott Gov.
Mathew Abdy & Alice Cox were married 24th May by Richard Bellingham
    Deputy Governor.
Henry Raynor & Johanna Edwards widow were married 9th June by John
    Endecott Governor.
George Hisket & Sarah Clarke daughter of Thomas Clarke of Nodles Island
    were married 11th June by John Endecott Governor.

## FIRST CHURCH.

| | | |
|---|---|---|
| Ebenezer of Mary & James Hudson | 9 day | 1 mo. |
| John of Sister Brookin | 16 day | 1 mo. |
| Mary of John Peirce of church of Maldin | 16 day | 1 mo. |
| Thomas of Henry Messinger's wife | 23 day | 1 mo. |
| Edward of Edward Cowell's wife | 30 day | 1 mo. |
| James of Mr. Braden | 6 day | 2 mo. |
| Nathaniel of Henry Bridgham | 6 day | 2 mo. |
| Thomas of Dorcas Corbin | 6 day | 2 mo. |
| Mary of Dorcas Corbin | 6 day | 2 mo. |
| John of Dorcas Corbin | 6 day | 2 mo. |
| Robert of Benjamin Thurstone | 27 day | 2 mo. |
| Mary of Edward Davis | 27 day | 2 mo. |
| Sarah of Rebecca Windsor | 11 day | 3 mo. |
| Mary of        Read | 11 day | 3 mo. |
| Samuel of Mr. Rock | 18 day | 3 mo. |
| Mary of Sister Griggs | 18 day | 3 mo. |
| Mary of Mr. Way | 25 day | 3 mo. |
| Phillip of George Mongay | 1 day | 4 mo. |
| Joseph of Simon Rogers | 3 day | 6 mo. |
| Mary of James Pemerton | 17 day | 6 mo. |
| Samuel of Mrs. Droomer of Ch. of Wattertown | 31 day | 6 mo. |
| Sarah of James Richards | 7 day | 7 mo. |
| Abigail of Theophilus Frary | 7 day | 7 mo. |
| Daniel of Robert Feild | 7 day | 7 mo. |
| John of John Androwe | 21 day | 7 mo. |
| Benjamin of Tho: Savage | 12 day | 8 mo. |
| James of Constance & James Mattock | 26 day | 8 mo. |
| Samuel of Henry Phillips | 2 day | 9 mo. |
| William of Thomas Brattle | 23 day | 9 mo. |
| Jacob of Jacob Eliot | 23 day | 9 mo. |
| Colbrone of Daniel Turand's wife | 11 day | 11 mo. |
| Prudence of Amos Richisson's wife | 8 day | 12 mo. |
| Benjamin of Rachel & Thomas Harwood | 8 day | 12 mo. |
| Sarah of Sarah & John Burges | 8 day | 12 mo. |
| Cotton of Increase Mather | 15 day | 12 mo. |
| Rebecca of John Harrisson | 15 day | 12 mo. |

## 1663.

### TOWN.

John of John & Eliza Aldin born Mar. 12.
William of William & Mehitabel Aves born March 16.
Joseph of Nathaniel and Mary Adams born Dec. 19.
Experience of Henry and Mary Adams born Nov. 9.
Abigail of Mr. Josua and Mary Atwater born Jan. 23.
Robert of John & Betteris Alexander born Apr. 19.
Sarah of Orlando & Sarah Bagly born Mar. 2.
Elizabeth of Ambros & Mary Bennet born April 1.
Nathaniel of Nath. & Ruth Beltnap born April 1.
William of Benja. & Sarah Briscoe born Apr. 7.
Patience of Mr. Thomas & Mary Broughton born Apr. 14.
Abigail of Edward & Patience Blake born Nov. 10.
Nathaniel of Joseph & Ruth Beltnap born Aug. 13.
Rebecca of Mr. Abraham & Rebecca Browne born Aug. 26.
Abigail of Samuel & Sarah Bucknell born July 16.
Faith of Edward & Mary Belcher born May 15.
Elizabeth of Josiah & Ranis Belcher born July 10.
Benjamin of Jonathan & Mary Balston born Feb. 8.
Samuel of John & Sarah Buckman born Feb. 17.

Mary of Mathew & Mary Bernard born Aug. 5.
John of John & Mary Bull born July 14.
Elizabeth of Mr. Samuel & Mercy Bradstreet born Jan. 29.
David of David & Obedience Copp born Mar. 2.
Samuel of William & Martha Clarke born June 28.
Elizabeth of Christopher & Rebecca Clarke born Aug. 4.
Hannah of Henry & Hannah Crab born Apr. 8.
John of John & Mary Collins born Mar. 1.
Elizabeth of Josiah & Waitawhile Cooper born May 5.
William of Timothy & Phillippee Cann born July 21.
Elizabeth of Timothy & Phillippee Cann born July 21.
Robert of Mr. Robert & Elizabeth Couch born Nov. 2.
Mary of Samuel & Sarah Davis born Mar. 21.
John of Capt. William & Huldah Davis born June 10.
John of Mr. Robert & Jemima Drue born Oct. 17.
William of Samuel & Anne Dyer born Mar. 7.
Edward of Edward & Sarah Ellis born Mar. 16.
Jonathan of Mr. David & Mary Evans born Apr. 3.
Joseph of Jacob & Mary Eliott born Jan. 13.
Thomas of Thomas & Sarah Edwards born Feb. 6.
Sarah of Jeremiah & Sarah Fitch born Feb. 21.
Elizabeth of Mr. John & Eliza. Freake born June 13.
Jasper of Jasper & Eliza. Frost born Feb. 5.
Margaret of Eleazer & Mary Farr born Nov. 16.
Dorothy of William & Eliza. Greenough born Mar. 16.
Benjamin of Zachariah & Phoebe Gillam born Mar. 23.
Oliver of Oliver & Ann Griffine, born Sept. 6.
Thomas of Henry & Hannah Glover born June 25.
Mary of Nathaniell & Mary Greene born May 3.
Thomas of Richard & Mary George born Oct. 11.
Hezekiah of Henry & Joane Gidley born May 16.
Margaret of Mr. Robert & Elizabeth Gibbs born May 13.
William of John & Elizabeth Gill born Aug. 15.
Hannah of Elipha. & Anne Hett born Feb. 13.
Sarah of William & Mary Hunter born May 15.
Mary of Ezekiel & Eliza. Hamblinne born Nov. 10.
Thomas of George & Sarah Hiskett born Mar. 30.
Samuel of John & Eliza. Hunniborn born May 2.
John of Charles & Margaret Hopkinnes born July 5.
Abigail of Mr. Joseph & Ellen Hill born Feb. 5.
Arabella of Thomas & Exercise Hodges born Feb. 1.
Sarah of Francis & Hannah Hill born Jan. 26.
Jeremiah of William & Mary Ingram born Jan. 20.
Joanna of James & Joanna Inglish born Nov. 18.
Susanna of Edmund & Eliza. Jackson born Dec. 2.
Thomas of John & Emm Jepson born Nov. 5.
Elias of John & Rebecca Jarvis born Jan. 13.
Joanna of Richard & Joanna Knight born July 12.
Hannah of John & Mary Kneeland born July 18.
Zachariah of Henry & Mary Kemble born Oct. 7.
Samuel of Edward & Eliza. Lilly born Mar. 20.
Thomas of William & Mary Lane born March 8.
Ann of Capt. Thomas & Mary Lake horn Oct. 12.
Hannah of Edward & Mary Lilly born May 27.
Richard of Richard & Elizabeth Martin born Mar. 24.
Thomas of Thomas & Mary Matson horn Mar. 1.
Amey of John & Mary Matson born Mar. 12.
Robert of Robert & Mary Marshall born at Plymouth in New england Aug. 15.
Martha ⎫ of John & Eliza. Magdanell born Sept. 14.
Mary ⎭ of John & Eliza. Magdanell born Sept. 14.
James of George & Hannah Manning born Mar. 6.
Mary of John & Sarah Miriam born May 15.
Mary of Samuel & Mary Mason born Apr. 19.
Hannah of Mr. Samuel & Rebecca Mavericke born Oct. 25.

Hannah of Humphrey & Mary Milum born June 27.
Margaret of Christopher & Prudence Mosse born May 23.
Jonathan of John & Constance Merry born Sept. 3.
John of John & Mercy Meeres born Dec. 28.
Michael of George & Lydia Nowell born Mar. 24.
Elizabeth of Mr. Robert dec. & Catharine Nanney born Jan. 2.
Joseph of Samuel & Eliza. Norden born Feb. ult.
Sarah of Joshua & Elizabeth Nash born Feb. 20.
Daniel of Mr. Peter & Sarah Oliver born Feb. 28.
Benjamin of Thomas & Eliza. Peck born Mar. 1.
James of Benja & Wilmut Phippen born Jan. 30.
Gamaliel of Gamaliel & Sarah Phippen born Feb. 16.
Anna of Henry & Eliza. Powning born Feb. 29.
Phoebe of Nehemiah & Phoebe Pearse born Aug. 31.
Benjamin of William & Ann Pollard born Apr. 22.
Ruth of William & Frances Parham born Sept. 30.
Elizabeth of Mr. Richard & Elizabeth Price born Feb. 10.
Ebenezer of Richard & Grace Price born Apr. 6.
Paul of Edward & Elizabeth Page born May 2.
Elizabeth of John & Mary Parker born Aug. 14.
Samuel of George & Eliza. Person born Aug. 30.
Nathaniel of Nathaniell & Sarah Reynolds born Mar. 3.
Hezekiah of William & Ruth Read born July 6.
Benjamin of Mr. Joseph & Elizabeth Rock born Sept. 3.
Dorothy of Jonathan & Mary Rainsford born Sept. 11.
Sarah of Samuel & Sarah Ryall born May 18.
Mary of Francis & Elizabeth Smith born July 18.
Sarah of Richard & Lucretia Smith born Sept. 8.
Temperance of Thomas & Temperance Smith born May 26.
Francis of Benja & Hannah Smith born Dec. 14.
Sarah of Thomas & Sarah Stevens born Dec. 8.
Henry of Henry & Mary Stevens born May 25.
Benjamin of Nicholas & Hannah Stone born Feb. 17.
Hannah of John & Hannah Souther born Aug. 31.
Benjamin of John & Ann Sandy born Aug. 7.
John of John & Philippee Snell born Oct. 9.
John of Mr. Anthony & Christian Stoddard born Apr. 22.
Arthur of Capt. Thomas & Mary Savage born Feb. 26.
Arthur of Arthur & Joane Scovell born June 24.
Ann of Sampson & Abigail Sboare born Aug. 16.
Joseph of John & Mary Simmons born Aug. 31.
Samuel of William & Eliza. Spowell born Nov. 1.
Mary of Clement & Joanna Salmon born Jan. 12.
Rebecca of Robert & Mary Thornton born Sept. 1.
Sarah of Daniel & Mary Turell born Oct. 14.
Eliza. of Daniel & Mary Turell born Oct. 14.
Matthew of John & Sarah Tamlin born Oct. 13.
Stephen of Stephen & Hannah Talbye born Aug. 9.
Derlow of Ephraim & Sarah Turner born Dec. 3.
Thomas of John & Mercy Verinne born Oct. 15.
Joanna of Aaron & Joan Way born Mar. 5.
Thomas of Thomas & Ruth Wyburne born Aug. 10.
Rebecca of Richard & Rebecca Wayte born Jan. 3.
Mary of William & Joanna Williams born Jan. 15.
Rowland of Thomas & Eliza. Watkinnes born Dec. 5.
Mary of Capt. Richard & Anne Waldren born Sept. 14.
Esther of Thomas & Esther Woodward of Muddy River born ? ——
William of Mr. Richard & Bethiah Wharton born Apr. 16.
Elizabeth of Mr. Dean & Sarah Winthrop born July 9.
Sarah of Edward & Sarah Winslow born Apr. 10.
Abigail of Nathaniel & Hannah Wilson born Feb. 17.
Hannah ⎫ of Thomas & Hannah Wheeler born May 24.
Mary ⎭ of Thomas & Hannah Wheeler born May 24.
Joseph of Lawrence & Hannah Waters born Oct. 14.
Anna of John (the Indian) & Ann White born Feb. 7.

Elizabeth wife of John Purchase died the 16th of March.
Mr John Norton teacher of the Church of Christ at Boston deceased the 5th of Aprill.
Hannah of William and Mary Hunter died the 14th of May.
John of Mr. Anthony and Christian Stoddard died the 1st of May.
Mary of Christopher and Ann Holland died the 25th of 2nd month.
Maria a negro servant of John Blower died the 14th of the 3d month.
Sara wife of Orlando Bagly died the 18th of the 3d month.
Jonathan of Mr. William and Ann Alford died the 24th of the 3d month.
Mathew of Mathew and Mary Whiple died the 30th of the 4th month.
Joseph of Mr. Habia and Hannah Savage died June 30th.
Robert Lincoln deceased May 6th.
John Preston died June 6th.
Mary of Thomas and Hannah Wheeler deceased.
Mary of Mr Samuell and Abigail Moore died July.
Joanna wife of John Baker died the 21st of July.
Alice wife of Bartholomew Bernard died the 29th of June.
Phillip of Robert and Sara Mason died the 3d of the 6th month.
Thomas of Thomas and Hannah Hull died August 1.
Mr. David Evans deceased the 27th of July.
Joseph of Leiutenant Richard and Elizabeth Cook died the 2nd of July.
Jane wife of Thomas Edsell deceased the 9th of September.
Sara of William and Sara Hawkinnes died the 11th of the 7th month.
Sara of Deacon John and Millicent Wiswall died the 19th of the 7th month.
Rebecca of Mr. Abraham and Rebecca Brown died the 12th of the 7th month.
Susanna of Bartholomew and Damaris Thredneedles died the 2nd of June.
Thomas of Thomas and Ruth Wyborne died August 28.
Hannah daughter of John Hyland of Scituat died August 16.
Mary of John and Returne Davis died the 12th of the 6th month.
John of James and Martha Robinson died the 13th of the 6th month.
Robert of Jonathan and Mary Balston died the 3d of October.
Rowland of Thomas and Elizabeth Watkinnes died 20th of 7th month.
John Knowles servant to Mr. John Woodmansey died the 21st of the 10th month.
John White servant to Thomas Buttolph senior died the 22nd of the 7th month.
Elisabeth Hubberd died the 16th day of August.
Mr. Robert Nanny died the 27th day of August.
Samuell of Mr. George and Elizabeth Peirson died the 8th of the 8th month.
Phillippe daughter of John Snell died the 10th of October.
Sara Laurenc servant of Samuel Mattock died 15th October.
Ralph Benning deceased the 14th of November.
Sara & Elisabeth twins of Danieli and Mary Turell died the 22nd of October.
Elisabeth of Captain James and Abigail Johnson died the 23rd of 11th month.
Ellen wife of Mr. Joseph Hill deceased January 6th.
Andrew Cload deceased February the last.
Dorothy wife of John Sunderland died the 29th of January.
Thomas Leader deceased the 28th of October.
—— Paine of Canebeck deceased at the house of Captain Thomas Lake the 15th of February.
Sarah of William and An Cotton died the 22nd of January.
John of Mr. John and Elisabeth Woodmansey died February 1st.
Mary of Nathaniel and Sarah Rainolls died January 8th.
Mary wife of Robert Rainolls deceased January 18.
Rebecca of John and Persis Harrison died July 25th.
Samuell of Nathaniel and Sara Hunn died the 8d of September.
John Meeres deceased the 12th of November.

## FIRST CHURCH.

| | | |
|---|---|---|
| Benjamin of Goodman Pecke's wife | 8 day | 1 mo. |
| John of Mr. Atwater | 15 day | 1 mo. |
| Mary of Thomas Emmins' wife | 22 day | 1 mo. |

Aquilla of Sarah &          Gibson a Scotchman          5 day  2 mo.
John of Anthony Stoddard                                26 day  2 mo.
Jonathan of Mr. Alford                                  17 day  3 mo.
Mary of John Meriam                                     24 day  3 mo.
John of William Davice                                  14 day  4 mo.
Ann of Sister Keeby                                     14 day  4 mo.
Hezekiah of Will. Read                                  12 day  5 mo.
John of Henry Stevens                                   19 day  5 mo.
Marcy of Francis Smyth's wife                              26   July.
Elizabeth of Christopher Clark's wife                      9 August.
Elizabeth of Deane Winthorp's wife                     23 day  6 mo.
Ann of Sampson Shore's wife                            23 day  6 mo.
Nathaniel of sister Baker                              23 day  6 mo.
Mary of sister Baker                                   23 day  6 mo.
Benjamin of Joseph Rocke                                6 day  7 mo.
Marcy of Capt. Waldin                                      11   Oct.
James of James Dinnis                                      11   Oct.
Sarah of Sarah & Daniel Turant                            18   Oct.
Elizabeth of Sarah & Daniel Turant                        18   Oct.
Thomas of Sister Veerin                                   18   Oct.
Mehitabel of        Thurston                           15 day  9 mo.
Susanna of Edmond Jackson                               6 day 10 mo.
Francis of Benjamin Smyth of Ch. of Deadham           20 day 10 mo.
Rebecca of Richard Wayt                                 3 day 11 mo.
Joseph of Jacob Eliot                                  17 day 11 mo.
Arthur of Capt. Savag                                  28 day 12 mo.
Daniel of Peter Oliver                                 28 day 12 mo.

## 1664.

### TOWN.

William of John & Eliza. Aldin born Mar. 16.
Remembrance son of John & Martha Amey born Mar. 18.
James of John & Hannah Andrewes born Dec. 1.
Peter of Peter & Remember Aspinwall of Muddy River born June 14.
Martha of Hope & Rachel Allen born Mar. 30.
Eleazer of Edward & Martha Allen born Apr. 25.
William of Angola & Eliza. (negroes) born May 13.
Thomas of Matthew & Hannah Armestrong born June 3.
John of William & Mehetable Avis born Sept. 10.
Elizabeth of John & Desire ye Truth Akors born May 18.
Sarah of David & Sarah Adams born Mar. 7.
Nathaniel of Matthew & Esther Bunn born Mar. 23.
John of Thomas & Grace Berry born Mar. 3.
Patrick of John & Mary Bowhoman born Feb. 14.
John of John & Thankful Baker born Feb. 26.
Katharine of Mr Thomas & Elizabeth Brattle born Sept. 26.
James of Henry & Eliza. Bridgham born May 12.
Anna of Benja. & Sarah Brisco born Jan. 31.
Mary of James & Lydia Burgesse born June 9.
Sarah of William & Hannah Ballantine born Sept. 18.
Isaac of Stephen & Jane Butler born May 29.
Hannah of John & Eliza. Brookin born June 16.
Abigail of William & Lydia Browne born July 6.
Elizabeth of Mr Abraham & Rebecca Browne born Nov. 17.
Mary of Samuel & Mary Browne born Sept. 2.
Persis of William & Persis Browne born Aug. 16.
Thomas of Thomas & Abigail Bill born Dec. 24.
Lydia of Capt. Thomas & Mary Bredon born Aug. 8.
———— dant of Henry & Frances Bowen born Feb. 17.
Mary of Thomas & Mary Buttolph born Jan. 21.
Abigail of Abraham & Abigail Busby born Sept. 16.

Hannah of Jeremiah & Anna Bumsteed born Nov. 21.
Elizabeth of Phillip & Judith Bullis born Nov. 19.
Elizabeth of John & Susanna Cole born Mar. 4.
Samuel of Richard & Mary Collins born Mar. 7.
Ebenezer of David & Lydia Chaffinne born Apr. 6.
Thomas of Thomas & Abigail Clarke born July 7.
Elizabeth of John & Eliza. Conney born Apr. 2.
Jonathan of David & Obedience Copp born Feb. 23.
John of Anthony & Hannah Checkley born Dec. 30.
John of John & Elizabeth Combes born July 20.
Joseph of Joseph & Susanna Cocke born Aug. 24.
Elizabeth of Edward & Mary Cowell born Nov. 10.
Rowland of Umphri & Mary Davy born Mar. 23.
Joseph of Edward & Hannah Davis born Aug. 20.
Elizabeth of Samuel & Sarah Davis born Oct. 6.
Joseph of Joseph & Eliza. Davis born June 5.
Samuel of John & Mary Dawes born Sept. 18.
Mary of Ambrose & Mary Dawes born Sept. 24.
John of John & Dorothy Downes born Aug. 14.
Joseph of Ambrose & Esther Due born Feb. 7.
Elizabeth of Obadiah & Alice Emons born Jan. 12.
Samuel of Samuel & Mary Emōns born Nov. 9.
John of Robert & Hannah Earle born Nov. 19.
Elizabeth of Thomas & Martha Fitch born Aug. 2.
Mehetable of Theoph: & Hannah Frarye born Jan. 23.
Sarah of Daniel & Sarah Fairfield born Feb. 19.
Elizabeth of Jasper & Eliza. Frost born Feb. 24.
John of John & Sarah Frankes born May 26.
Susanna of John & Susanna Griffinne born Nov. 13.
Thomas of John & Mary Gilbert born Oct. 4.
Benjamin of Nathaniell & Margaret Gallopp born Jan. 3.
Abigail of Samuel & Mary Gallop born June 27.
Elizabeth of William & Eliza. Greenow born Nov. 30.
Benoni of Believe & Anne Gridley born Sept. 5.
Nathaniel of Nathaniell & Mary Green born Jan. 20.
James of James & Rebecca Green born Dec. 15.
Hezekiah of Henry & Joane Gidley born Feb. 14.
Abigail of Henry & Marah Gibbs born Apr. 12.
Purchase son of William & Sarah Gibson born Apr. 30.
John of John & Hannah Grover born June 23.
Hannah of Thomas & Hannah Hull born Mar. 1.
Ephraim of Thomas & Rebecca Hawkinnes born Apr. 5.
Isaac of John & Persis Harrison born June 18.
Samuel of Nathaniell & Sarah Hunn born Oct. 12.
George of George & Eliza. Hunniborne born Feb. 4.
George of George & Sarah Hollard born Jan. 12.
Hannah of James & Hannah Hill born Mar. 21.
Isaac of Edward & Elizabeth Jones born June 20.
John of John & Jane Johnson born Apr. 11.
Isaac of Edward & Elizabeth Jones born Dec. 1.
William of Arthur & Jane Kinde born Feb. 26.
Mary of Richard & Julian Knight born June 3.
Mary of Joseph & Mary Knight born Jan. 2.
Edward of Edward & Elizabeth Kelley born Nov. 4.
Joseph of Mr Simon & Hannah Lynde born Feb. 12.
Bezalell of Mr Hudson & Sarah Leveret born Sept. 1.
Rebecca of Major General John & Sarah Leveret born Dec.
Benoni of John & Alice Lewes born Jan. 25.
Simeon of Richard & Sarah Mason born Mar. 23.
John of John & Ruth Marshall born Oct. 2.
Christopher of John & Sarah Marshall born Aug. 18.
Joseph of John & Martha Mellowes born Dec. 6.
Rachel of Thomas & Sarah Moore born May 25.
Joanna of Arthur & Joanna Mason born Mar. 26.

John of Michael & Susanna Martyn born May 1.
Hannah of John & Elizabeth Morse born Feb. 28.
Mariah of Mr Increase & Mariah Mather born Mar. 17.
John of John & Mary Matson born Jan. 26.
Prudence of Christopher & Prudence Mosse born Feb. 6.
Mary of Richard & Ann Mortimore born May 28.
Edmund of Edmund & Eliza. Mumford born July 11.
Elizabeth of Thomas & Ann Michel born Oct. 19.
Elizabeth of Richard & Experience Miles born Dec. 22.
David of William & Susanna Norton born May 31.
Grace of Andrew & Grace Newcomb born Oct. 20.
Nathaniel of George & Eliza. Orris born Apr. 27.
William of Mr John & Sarah Payne born Mar. 15.
Zechariah of Zechariah & Eliza. Phillips born Oct. 22.
Ann of William & Ann Pollard born Oct. 18.
Richard of Richard & Grace Price born Apr. 9.
Thomas of Thomas & Hannah Paine born July 2.
John of Timothy & Deborah Pratt born Aug. 9.
Sarah of John & Kesia Perkinnes born Oct. 8.
William of John & Mary Pell born Apr. 1.
Elizabeth of Samuel & Deborah Pell born Dec. 5.
Mary of George & Eliza. Peirson born Nov. 19.
Ann of Robert & Rose Pegge born May 4.
Abigail of Richard & Abigail Patteshal born Sept. 29.
Abigail of Samuel & Margaret Ruck born June 5.
Joshua of Joshua & Bathsheba Rice born May 3.
John of John & Alice Ratcliffe born Nov. 16.
Elizabeth of Joseph & Eliza. Soper born Mar. 13.
Thomas of Mr John & Martha Saffinne born Mar. 18.
John of John & Sarah Snelling born Mar. 17.
Temperance of Thomas & Temperance Smith born Aug. 28.
Robert of Robert & Elizabeth Smith born June 1.
Nathaniel of Nathaniel & Mary Stone born Mar. 25.
Benjamin of Thomas & Mary Saxton born May 18.
Bridget of Bartho. & Elizabeth Stretton born Jan. 28.
Mary of Robert & Eliza. Sanford born Sept. 22.
Ann of Richard & Joice Staines born Jan. 29.
Ephraim of John & Sarah Seate born Nov. 18.
Samuel of Samuel & Naomi Sherman born Apr. 24.
Experience of William & Eliza. Sumner born Sept. 22.
Ebenezer of Mr Anthony & Christian Stoddard born July 1.
John } of John & Tamasin Scarlet born Apr. 16.
Samuel } of John & Tamasin Scarlet born Apr. 16.
Thomas of Abia & Hannah Savage born Oct. 19.
Dorothy of John & Mary Sunderland born Apr. 7.
John of John & Martha Starr born Dec. 7.
Thomas of Thomas & Hannah Shearer born Jan. 23.
John of John & Catharine Searle born Nov. 19.
Daniel of Daniel & Esther Trevis born Nov. 4.
Martha of Richard & Martha Tuell born Jan. 24.
Jonathan of John & Mary Tuttell born Aug. 25.
Gideon of William & Rebecca Thurrell born July 16.
Elizabeth of Capt. Richard & Martha Thurston born Sept. 29
Eleazer of Benja. & Elishal Thurston born Mar. 2.
James of James & Martha Talbott born Aug. 23.
James of John & Mary Tappin born July 4.
Joshua of William & Sarah Ustis born July 11.
James of John & Elizabeth Vyall born June 5.
Dorcas of Isaac & Dorcas Woodee born Aug. 10.
Joseph of Edward & Eliza. Wanton born May 9.
Sarah of John & Mary Williams born Aug. 4.
Thomas of Thomas & Anne Williams born Apr. 9.
Samuel of Robert & Rebecca Windsor born Sept. 18.
John of James & Mary Webster born Aug. 5.

Richard of Richard & Bethiah Wharton born Feb. 1.
Sarah of John & Joshabeth Wing born May 13.
Peter of Mr James & Rebecca Whetcombe born Mar. 1.
Thomas of Thomas & Hannah Wheeler born Dec. 9.
Richard of Mr John & Eliza. Winslow born Apr. 18.
Deliverance son of John & Deliverance Wakefield born Sept. 8.

Temperance of Thomas and Temperance Smith died the 10th of the 1st month.
Mary of John Barrell late of Boston and Mary died the 10th of the 1st month.
Mr. Samuell Maverick died March 10.
Henry Bishop deceased the 11th of May.
Thomas Emons deceased the 11th of May.
John of John and Thomasin Scarlet died May 7th.
Nathaniell Tucker seaman living in Old England servant to Captain Andrew
    Ashford died at Boston in New England May 19.
Lydia Balston widow deceased Aprill 25.
Ruth of John and Elisabeth Mosse died June 2nd.
Sarah of John and Josabeth Wing died June 15.
Joshua of Joshua and Bathsheba Rice died May 16.
Elisabeth of John and Katherine Searle died June 8.
Nathaniel of Nathaniel and Mary Sherman died June 1.
Alice wife of Deacon Thomas Marshall died May 20.
Sarah of John and Tabitha Blower died June 22d.
Elisabeth of Mr. Jeremiah and Elisabeth Eginton died June 25th.
William of John and Mary Pell died June 12th.
Rowland of Mr. Humphry and Mary Davy died June 17.
Samuell of John and Thomasin Scarlett died June 13th.
Thomas Munt deceased July 27.
William of William and Elisabeth Auldinne died the 7th of June.
Abigail of Josua and Mary Atwater died July 7.
Thomasin wife of Stephen Barrett died the 8th of July.
Anna of Samson and Abigail Shore died June 26.
Elisabeth of John and Elisabeth Conny died June 16.
Elisabeth of Mr. Robert and Katherin Nanny died July 1.
Jacob of John and Isabell Pearce died June 20.
William Feild a stranger died at John Sweet's in Boston July 11.
Steven of Steven and Hannah Tolbye died July 1st.
William Rogers died July 13.
Rebecca of Marshall and Rebeca Rayt.[1]

## FIRST CHURCH.

| | | |
|---|---|---|
| Hannah of Henry Powning | 6 day | 1 mo. |
| Ann of Tho: Hall's wife | 6 day | 1 mo. |
| Edward of Ed. Elice's wife | 20 day | 1 mo. |
| Rowland of Humphry Davy | 26 day | 1 mo. |
| Edward of Edward Allen | 3 day | 2 mo. |
| Sarah of Edward Alien | 3 day | 2 mo. |
| Ebenezer of David Chapin of Ch. of Sprinkfield | 3 day | 2 mo. |
| Martha of William Hesye's wife | 24 day | 2 mo. |
| Sarah of Mr. Firniser of Duxberie | 24 day | 2 mo. |
| Purchass son of Sarah Gibson | 1 day | 3 mo. |
| Josias of Josias Belcher | 3 day | 2 mo. |
| John of Josias Belcher | 3 day | 2 mo. |
| Jonathan of Josias Belcher | 3 day | 2 mo. |
| Elizabeth of Josias Belcher | 3 day | 2 mo. |
| James of Henry Bridgham | 15 day | 3 mo. |
| Sarah of Sarah & James Balston | 22 day | 3 mo. |
| John of Sarah & James Balston | 22 day | 3 mo. |
| James of Sarah & James Baiston | 22 day | 3 mo. |
| Abigail of Sarah & James Balston | 22 day | 3 mo. |
| James of John Vial | 12 day | 4 mo. |

---

[1] The rest is worn away, being last line of page in MS. — W. S. A.

| | | |
|---|---|---|
| Ann of Sister Brookin | 19 day | 4 mo. |
| Isaac of John Harisson | 26 day | 4 mo |
| Mary of Sister Burges | 26 day | 4 mo |
| Ebenezer of Anthony Stoddard | 17 day | 5 mo |
| John of John Tappin | 17 day | 5 mo |
| Joseph of John Tappin | 17 day | 5 mo |
| James of John Tappin | 17 day | 5 mo |
| William of John Chickly | 3 | July. |
| Elizabeth of Tho: Fitch of **Watertowne** | 7 day | 6 mo |
| Joseph of Edward Davis | 4 day | 7 mo |
| John of Mary Wheatly | 18 day | 7 mo |
| Jaine of Mary Wheatly | 18 day | 7 mo |
| Mary of Mary Wheatly | 18 day | 7 mo. |
| Abigail of Abram Busby | 18 day | 7 mo |
| Mary of Robert Sanford | 25 | Sep |
| William of Sister Windsor | 25 | Sep. |
| Kathrine of Mr. Brattle | 2 | Oct. |
| Mary of Mrs. Hicks | 16 | Oct. |
| Elizabeth of Mrs. Hicks | 16 | Oct. |
| Thomas of Mrs. Hicks | 16 | Oct. |
| Thomas of Tho: Matson's **wife** | 16 day | 8 mo. |
| Thomas of Abiah Savage | 30 | Oct. |
| Elizabeth of James Hudson | 6 day | 9 mo. |
| Samuel of Mary Emens | 13 day | 9 mo. |
| James of Mary Andrews | 4 day | 10 mo. |
| Rebecca of Maior Leveret | 11 day | 10 mo. |
| Mehitabel of Theophilus Frary | 29 day | 11 mo. |
| Renony of Sister Lewis | 29 day | 11 mo. |

## 1665.

### TOWN.

Edmund of John & Hannah Andrewes born Nov. 4.
Benjamin of Nathaniel & Mary Addams born Dec. 20.
Elizabeth of John & Eliza. Aldinne born Apr. 9.
John of Hugh & Anne Amos born July 16.
Mary of Benja & Sarah Brisco born Dec. 22.
John of Ambrose & Mary Bennet born Sept. 21.
Mary of Roger & Sarah Burges born May 3.
Elizabeth of Joseph & Ruth Beltnap born July 1.
William of William & Hannah Ballantine born Nov. 26.
James of Stephen & Jane Butler born Aug. 2.
Zurishaddai of William & Persis Browne born Sept. 20.
Elizabeth of John & Eliza. Brown born July 6.
Hannah of Samuel & Sarah Bucknell born May 7.
Mary of Edward & Mary Belcher born Feb. 7.
Joseph of Josiah & Ranis Belcher born Oct. 14.
Jonathan of James & Sarah Balston born Dec. 28.
Susanna of Thomas & Abigail Bill born Mar. 18.
Thomas of John & Tabitha Blower born May 19.
Esther of Matthew & Esther Bunn born Nov. 2.
Thomas of Richard & Eliza. Buckman born Dec. 15.
James of John & Mary Bull born July 16.
Annice of Mr. Samuel & Mercy Bradstreet born Nov. 17.
Edward of Edward & Dorothy Budd born May 31.
Elizabeth of Thaddeus & Hannah Berry born Nov. 24.[1]
Samuel of Thomas & Esther Brental born Dec. 2.[1]
Jonathan of David & Lydia Chapin born Feb. 12.
Jane of Shem & Deborah Chapen born Sept. 16.
John of Percival & Eliza. Clarke born Nov. 1.

---

[1] Only found in second MS. — W. S. A.

William of John & Eliza. Coney born July 5.
Benjamin of William & Ann Cotton born Mar. 18.
Joseph of Joseph & Hannah Chandler born Oct. 8.
Thomas of Josiah & Waitawhile Cooper born Apr. 5.
Elizabeth of Mr. Robert & Elizabeth Couch born Oct. 20.
Nicholas of Joseph & Susanna Cocke born Dec. 21.
James of Clement & Dorcas Corbinn born Mar. 31.
John of John & Susanna Crosse born Oct. 21.
Deborah of Capt. William & Huldah Davis born Apr. 13.
Mary of John & Returne Davis of Block Island born July 2.
Esther of Samuel & Sarah Davis born Jan. 19.
Rebecca of Ambrose & Mary Dawes born Feb. 25.
Frances of James & Frances Dowell born May 21.
Mary of James & Frances Ellis born Aug. 11.
Deborah of Jeremiah & Sarah Fitch born June 27.
Sarah of Robert & Mary Field born Mar. 25.
Mehetable of Theoph : & Hannah Frarye born Feb. 4.
Samuel of Samuel & Anne Flack born May 7.
Deborah of John & Grace Frank born Jan. 11.
Jonathan of Francis & Mary Franseco born Mar. 21.
Abigail of John & Mary Gilbert born Nov. 12.
Anna of William & Ruth Greenough born May 20.
Elizabeth of Joseph & Lydia Gridley born Dec. 5.
Nathaniel of John & Mary Glover born Oct. 6.
Rebecca of Richard & Rebecca Green born Aug. 7.
Ann of Benja. & Hannah Gillam born June 6.
Mary of Richard & Mary George born Jan. 26.
Robert of Mr. Robert & Elizabeth Gibbs born Sept. 20.
Elizabeth of Henry & Mary Gibbs born June 25.
Benjamin of Benja. & Lydia Gibbs born Aug. 22.
Sarah of William & Sarah Gibson born Feb. 5.
Mary of Jonathan & Mary Gatliffe born Dec. 14.
Martha of Peter & Jane Golding born Jan. 21.
Peter of Peter & Jane Golding born ——
Ephraim of Thomas & Rebecca Hawkinns born Oct. 15.
John of Eliphalet & Anne Hett born Feb. 9.
Mary of Thomas & Hannah Hull born Feb. 18.
Hannah of Joseph & Frances How born Apr. 15.
Rebecca of Richard & Mary Hickes born Mar. 26.
Mary of William & Mary Hunter born Apr. 25.
Benjamin of Ezekiel & Eliza. Hamlinn born Nov. 26.
Richard of Nicholas & Eliza. Hayward born Aug. 10.
William of Nathaniell & Eliza. Harwood born Mar. 28.
Elizabeth of Henry & Eliza. Harwood born Apr. 3.
John of George & Sarah Hiskett born May 14.
Experience of Jabez & Experience Heaton born June 15.
John of John & Joanna Howen born Nov. 12.
Israel of Israel & Arm Howen born Aug. 26.
John of John & Elizab. Jones born Nov. 8.
Anna of William & Rebecca James born Oct. 5.
Joseph of Joseph & Mary Knight born Mar. 3.
Elizabeth of Henry & Ruth Kiskeyes born May 3.
Henry of Henry & Mary Kembol born Feb. 25.
John of John & Mary King born May 24.
Susanna of Mr. Thomas & Abigail Kellond born Oct. 21.
John of Capt. Thomas & Mary Lake born Feb. 22.
Ruth of John & Naomi Lowell born July 11.
Joseph of Joseph & Abigail Lowell born Nov. 19.
Hosea of Jeremiah & Sarah Morrill born July 25.
Mary of Mr. Robert & Mary Marshall born Mar. 1.
Constance of Samuel & Constance Mattock born Sept. 10.
Hannah of Henry & Hannah Manning born Apr. 20.
Ann of Samuel & Mary Mason born July 4.
Sarah of John & Katharin Maverick born June 20.

Edward of Michael & Susanna Martyn born July 12.
Elizabeth ⎫ of Richard & Elizabeth Martin born Apr. 15.
Mary ⎬ of Richard & Elizabeth Martin born Apr. 15.
Ebenezer of Henry & Sarah Messenger born Oct. 25.
Stephen of Samuel & Mary Meers born Nov. 21.
William of William & Katharine Mansell born Sept. 14.
Simon of Simon & Mary Melin of Winnisimmett born Sept. 25.
William of William & Dorcas Morrice born Dec. 18.
Lydia of Robert & Lydia Miller born Jan. 25.
George of George & Lydia Nowell born Dec. 16.
Sarah of Andrew & Millicent Neale born Apr. 1.
Arthur of Robert & Mary Oakes born Mar. 17.
Ann of Mr. John & Sarah Paine born Mar. 24.
Elisha of Henry & Mary Phillippes born May 12.
Sarah of Nicholas & Hannah Phillips born Apr. 13.
Nicholas of Nicholas & Philippa Phillips born Nov. 30.
Ebenezer of Thomas and Eliza. Peck born July 11. .
Thankful of Thomas & Eliza. Peck born July 11.
Sarah of John & Isabel Pearse born Aug. 10.
Benjamin of James & Sarah Pemberton born Mar. 11.
Elizabeth of Mr. John & Sarah Paine born Feb. 19.
Hannah of John & Ruth Pease born Mar. 1.
Experience of Robert & Rose Pegg born Mar. 22.
Richard of Richard & Abigail Patteshall born Feb. 7.
Elias of Elias & Sarah Parkman born Nov. 13.
Mary of Joseph & Ann Penewell born Feb. 13.
William of Edward & Mary Right born Oct. 3.
Martha of George & Mary Robinson born Mar. 31.
Elizabeth of Simon & Christian Roberts born Dec. 28.
Sarah of William & Ruth Read born June 26.
William of William & Hannah Reade born Mar. 26.
Isaac of John & Susanna Ransford born Apr. 8.
Samuel of Samuel & Sarah Ryall born Feb. 17.
Mary of Samuel & Sarah Ryall born Feb. 17.
John of John & Eliza. Rowland born Sept. 4.
Samuel of Henry & Mary Stevens born Sept. 24.
Paul of Joseph & Elizabeth Souther born Jan. 30.
Mary of Thomas & Mary Saxton born Jan. 9.
Elizabeth of Caleb & Mary Stretton born Feb. 24.
Edward of Jonath: & Mary Shrimpton born Sept. 22.
Mary of Nathaniel & Mary Sherman born Mar. 28.
Hannah of Bartho & Hannah Sutton born Sept. 13.
Joseph of Joseph & Eliza. Soper born Mar. 23.
Dorothy of Mr. Anthony & Christian Stodderd born Nov. 24.
Thomas of Thomas Jr. & Elizabeth Savage born July 20.
William of William & Hopestill Shute born Aug. 28. ,
Mary of John & Thomasin Sunderland born July 15.
Elizabeth of Arthur & Joane Scovell born Sept. 18.
Rebecca of Pilgrim & Catharine Simkins born Mar. 14.
Elizabeth of Clement & Joanna Salmon born Feb. 26.
Henry of Thomas & Mary Swan born May 16.
Robert of John & Martha Sharp of Muddy River born May 17.
Rachel of Philip & Rachel Squire born Jan. 5.
Joseph of Alexander & Anne Simson born Jan. 17.
Mehetable of Richard & Grace Trevis born Mar. 2.
Benjamin of Daniel & Mary Turell born June 21.
Hannah of Mr. Henry & Mary Taylor born July 7.
Richard of Richard & Elizabeth Tout born Oct. 25.
Samuel of Stephen & Hannah Talbye born Jan. 9.
Robert of Ephraim & Sarah Turner born June 17.
Prudence of William & Frances Turner born Oct. 12.
John of Francis & Rebecca Thomas born Apr. 15.
William of William & Sarah Towers born July 19.
William of Bernard & Mary Trott born Nov. 23.

Joseph of Thomas & Mary Townsend born Dec. 23.
James of John & Mercy Verin born Mar. 4.
Sarah of Richard & Rebecca Wayt born June 23.
John of Thomas & Ruth Wyborne born Sept. 25.
Thomas of Thomas & Susanna Walker born May 31.
John of John & Jane Williams born Dec. 28.
Hannah of Thomas & Eliza. Watkinnes born Apr. 9.
Hannah of Thomas & Esther Woodward of Muddy River born **Apr. 11.**
Sarah of John & Jehosebath Wing born Feb. 9.
James of Mr. John & Eliza. Woodmansey born Dec. 7.
Mary of Edward & Sarah Winslow born Apr. 30.
Benjamin of Peter & Sarah Warren born July 25.
Mary of Thomas & Naomi Wells born Apr. 15.
Elizabeth of John & Elizabeth Walley born May 8.
Susanna of Joseph & Mary Wheeler born Dec. 25.
Hannah of Lawrence & Hannah Waters born Jan. 26.
Elizabeth of Mr. John & Eliza. Winslow born Mar. 14.
Mary of Mr. William & Mary Whitingham born May 26.
Hannah of Robert & Hannah Wakum born Dec. 3.
Samuel of Samuel & Joanna Ward born Nov. 16.
Mary of Samuel dec. & Bridget Wesselbee late of Norwich in England **born**
Jan. 10.

### FIRST CHURCH.

| | | |
|---|---|---|
| Nathaniel of Nathaniel Renolds | 26 day | 1 mo. |
| Sarah of Nathaniel Renolds | 26 day | 1 mo. |
| Sarah of Robert Feild | 26 day | 1 mo. |
| Deborah of Mr. Davis | 16 day | 2 mo. |
| Richard of Grace Price | 16 day | 2 mo. |
| Ann of Joseph How | 16 day | 2 mo. |
| Mary of Sister Wells | 16 day | 2 mo. |
| Ann of Humphrey Davy | 30 day | 2 mo. |
| Elishu of Henry Philips | 15 | May. |
| Mary of Nath: Renolds | 28 | May. |
| Ebenezer of Sister Peck | 18 day | 4 mo. |
| Thankful of Sister Peck | 18 day | 4 mo. |
| Saray of Sister Brookin | 18 day | 4 mo. |
| Sara of Sister Turand | 25 day | 4 mo. |
| Benjamin of Richard Waight | 25 day | 4 mo. |
| Timothy of Sister Hickes | 1 day | 5 mo. |
| Deborah of Jeremiah Fitch | 1 day | 5 mo. |
| Sarah of William Read | 1 day | 5 mo. |
| Mary of George Monioy | 9 day | 5 mo. |
| Ruth of John Looell | 16 day | 5 mo. |
| Sarah of John Peirce | 13 day | 6 mo. |
| Benjamin of Benjamin Gibbes | 27 day | 6 mo. |
| David of Arthur Mason's wife | 10 | Sept. |
| Mary of Arthur Mason's wife | 10 | Sept. |
| Joanna of Arthur Mason's wife | 10 | Sept. |
| Constance of Sister Mattock | 17 | Sept. |
| Joseph of Josia Belcher | 15 day | 8 mo. |
| Ebenezer of Sister Messinger. | 29 | Oct. |
| John of Mr. Saffin | 12 | Nov. |
| Thomas of Mr. Saffin | 12 | Nov. |
| ⎧ Joseph of Joseph Belknap | 12 | Nov. |
| ⎨ Elizabeth of Joseph Belknap | 12 | Nov. |
| ⎩ Mary of Joseph Belknap | 12 | Nov. |
| Joseph of Joseph Davis | 12 | Nov. |
| Ann of Mr. Broadstreet | 19 | Nov. |
| Deborah of Mr. Stoddard | 26 | Nov. |
| Robert of Mrs. Marshall | 3 day | 10 mo. |
| William of Sister Balentine | 3 day | 10 mo. |

| | | |
|---|---|---|
| ⌈ Elizabeth of Sister Norden | 10 day | 10 mo. |
| \| Susannah of Sister Norden | 10 day | 10 mo. |
| ⎬ Abigail of Sister Norden | 10 day | 10 mo. |
| ⌊ Joseph of Sister Norden | 10 day | 10 mo. |
| Joanna of John Wing | 10 day | 10 mo. |
| Jonathan of Sister Balston | 31 day | 10 mo. |
| Mehetabel of Theophilus Frayry | 11 day | 12 mo. |
| Sarah of John Wing | 11 day | 12 mo. |
| Sarah of Sister Gibson | 11 day | 12 mo. |
| ⌈ John of Martha & John Shaw | 4 day | 12 mo. |
| ⎬ Martha of Martha & John Shaw | 4 day | 12 mo. |
| ⌊ Joseph of Martha & John Shaw | 4 day | 12 mo. |
| ⌈ Nathaniel of Sarah & Nathaniel Hunn | 4 day | 12 mo. |
| \| John of Sarah & Nathaniel Hunn | 4 day | 12 mo. |
| ⎬ George of Sarah & Nathaniel Hunn | 4 day | 12 mo. |
| ⌊ Sarah of Sarah & Nathaniel Hunn | 4 day | 12 mo. |
| Mary of Hannah Hall | 18 day | 12 mo. |
| Jonathan of David Chapin | 18 day | 12 mo. |
| Mary of Mrs. Marshall | 25 day | 12 mo. |

## 1666.

### Town.

William of John & Eliza: Auldin born Mar. 5.
Martha of Edward & Martha Allen born Mar. 11.
Desire ye Truth of John & Desire ye Truth Akors of Muddy River born Mar. 9.
Sarah of Richard & Eliza. Bernard born Mar. 4.
John of John & Mary Cotton born Mar. 13.
Mary of Edward & Sarah Ellis born Mar. 28.
William of Clement & Mary Grose born Mar. 3.
Jacob of Edward & Elizabeth Jones born Mar. 10.
Ebenezer of William & Mary Lane born Mar. 27.
Henry of Edmund & Eliza. Mumford born Mar. 7.
William of William & Frances Parham born Mar. 16.
Thomas of Thomas & Temperance Smith born Mar. 5.
Mary of Richard & Lucretia Smith born April 2.
    [Only the foregoing births of this year are found in oldest MS., which ends here. — W. S. A.]
Mary of Henry & Mary Adams born Apr. 24.
Matthew ⎱ of Matthew & Hannah Armstrong born May 29.
John   ⎰ of Matthew & Hannah Armstrong born May 29.
Nathaniel of Peter & Remembr: Aspinwall born June 5.
Ruth of John & Martha Amey born June 24.
Jane als Grace of Joshua & Mary Atwater born Sept. 9.
Elizabeth of David & Sarah Adams born Dec. 26.
Elizabeth of Angola & Elizabeth (negroes) born Dec. 10.
John of John & Mary Adams born Jan. 21.
Zachariah of John & Elizabeth Alden born March 8.
James of John & Hannah Andrews born Mar. 17.
Grace of Francis & Joice Burgis born May 6.
Joseph of Samuel & Sarah Bucknell born May 10.
William of John & Jane Bushnell born June 28.
William of William & Lydia Browne born July 8.
Sarah of Phillip & Judith Bullis born July 21.
Joseph of Joseph & Eliza. Buckminister born July 3
Abigail of Thomas & Mary Buttolph born Jan.
Bethiah of Thomas and Elizabeth Brattie born Dec. 13.
John of Benja & Sarah Brisco born Jan. 20.
Thomas of Jeremiah & Anna Bumsteed born Feb. 22.
Mercy of James & Lydia Burges born Feb. 17.
John of William & Martha Clarke born Apr. 3.
Susanna of Ralph & Susanna Carter born Aug. 15.
John of Matthew & Elizabeth Coy born Sept. 2.

John of John & Susanna Cole born Jan. 17.
Caleb of Richard & Martha Coy born Aug. 15.
Timothy of Timothy & Elizabeth Crunmell born Nov. 12.
Mary of John & Elizabeth Coombs born Nov. 28.
Abigail of John & Susanna Cross born Feb. 1.
Mary of Christopher & Rebecca Clarke born Mar. 1.
William of David & Obedience Copp born Mar. 14.
David of David & Frances Carwithen born Apr. 27.
Mary of James & Mary Dennis born June 16.
John of Joseph & Eliza. Davis born Oct. 2.
Elizabeth of Anthony & Eliza. Davis born Oct. 26.
Sarah of Thomas & Sarah Deane born Oct. 27.
Susanna of John & Mary Dawse born Nov. 21.
John of Fathergon & Hannah Dinely born Dec. 28.
Elizabeth of James & Frances Dowell born Jan. 2.
Edward of Edward & Hannah Davis born Feb. 6.
Margaret of Humphrey & Mary Davie born Feb. 19.
Benjamin of William & Sarah Eustis born May 17.
John of Thomas & Sarah Edwards born Oct. 8.
John of John & Mary Ewell born Oct. 2.
Mary of Obadiah & Alice Emons born Jan. 16.
Obadiah of Samuel & Mary Emons born Jan. 19.
Hannah of Jacob & Mary Eliott born Mar. 17.
Joseph of John & Sarah Franks born June 14.
Clarke of John & Elizabeth Freake born Oct. 11.
Henry of Henry & Mary Floyd born Oct. 27.
Richard of Thomas & Margaret Forbush born Mar. 23.
Abigail of Jeremiah & Sarah Fitch born Aug. 5.
Mehetable of John & Ruth Gwinn born May 29.
Elizabeth of John & Ann Greenleafe born July 19.
Thomas of Thomas & Catharine Goodridge born July 2.
Mary of Believe & Anna Gridley born Dec. 4.
Thomas of James & Rebecca Green born Jan. 2.
Remember of John & Susanna Griffin born Feb. 5.
Thomas of John & Elizabeth Gill horn Sept. 16.
Temperance of Henry & Joane Gidley born Mar. 23.
Elizabeth of Nathanil & Mary Green born June 29.
Elizabeth of Isaac & Elizabeth Gross born May 22.
Hezekiah of Barnard & Mary Harris born Aug. 13.
Mary of Elisha & Hannah Hutchinson born Oct. 11.
Rebecca of Nicholas & Elizabeth Hayward born Nov. 19.
Melatiah of Thomas & Rebecca Hawkins born Nov. 12.
Joanna of Jabez & Experience Heaton born Dec. 18.
Elizabeth of John & Elizabeth Hooper born Jan. 22.
James of James & Hannah Hill born Feb. 21.
Henry of Henry & Elizabeth Harwood born Feb. 23.
Mary of William & Mary Ingram born June 26.
William of John & Rebecca Jarvis born Aug. 10.
Susanna of Edmund & Elizabeth Jackson born Sept. 19
Mary of John & Mary Kneeland born Apr. 13.
John of John & Mary King born Aug. 13.
Sarah of Thomas & Elizabeth Kemble born Apr. 19.
Susanna of Richard & Julian Knight born Jan. 21.
Elizabeth of Edward & Elizabeth Lillie born July 6.
Nathaniel of John & Alice Lewis born July 5.
Benjamin of Simon & Hannah Lynde born Sept. 23.
Ruth of Humphrey & Mary Milani born Apr. 26.
Benjamin of John & Mary Mann born May 26.
Michael of John & Isabel Magdaniel born July 26.
Arthur of Arthur & Joanna Mason born Apr. 16.
Sarah of James & Margery Maxwell born Oct. 19.
James of James & Elizabeth Meers born Dec. 21.
Mary of John & Mary Matson born Dec. 22.
Mary of George & Hannah Manning born Nov. 3.

Joseph of John & Sarah Marion born Oct. 14.
Elizabeth of Increase & Maria Mather born Jan. 6.
Edmund of Return & Sarah Munnings born Mar. 21.
Thomas of John & Ruth Marshall born Feb. 6.
Elizabeth of Robert & Sarah Mason born Feb. 23.
Mary of Andrew & Millicent Neale born June 6.
Joshua of Samuel & Elizabeth Norden born July 3.
Robert of Joshua & Elizabeth Nash born Dec. 3.
Hannah of Elisha & Abigail Odlin born Sept. 3.
Matthias of William & Mary Okington born Jan. 1.
Michael of Seth & Dorothy Perry born Apr. 11.
Jonathan of William & Ann Pollard born Apr. 12.
Ann of Gamaliel & Sarah Phippen born Apr. 28.
Timothy of Timothy & Deborah Prout born July 6.
John of John & Mary Pell born born June 30.
Rebecca of Benja. & ——— Phippen born Aug. 10.
Jonathan of Henry & Mary Phillips born Sept. 12.
Elizabeth of Edward & Elizabeth Page born Sept. 12.
Nathaniel of Thomas & Elizabeth Peck born Nov. 17.
Deliverance of John & Deliverance Pollard born Sept. 19.
Judith of John & Judith Parmiter born Feb. 14.
William of Samuel & Deborah Pell born Feb. 21.
Hannah of Jona. & Mary Rainsford born Apr. 5.
Daniel of Nathanll & Damaris Robinson born Feb. 10.
Peter of Samuel & Margaret Ruck born Jan. 25.
Elizabeth of William & Ruth Read born Dec. 22.
Thomas of John & Alice Ratliffe born Jan. 17.
Humphry of Humphry & Mehetable Richards born Jan. 12.
Elisha of Joseph & Elizabeth Rock born Feb. 16.
Thomas of Thomas & Sarah Rawlins born Jan. 20.
Symon of John & Martha Saffin born Apr. 4.
Anna of William & Martha Smith born Apr. 6.
Sarah of John & Ann Sawdy born Apr. 9.
Mary of John & Mary Symons born June 26.
Mary of Joseph & Mary Sanderson born July 6.
Elizabeth of John & Sarah Skeath born July 4.
Richard of Richard & Elizabeth Shute born Aug. 31.
Mary of John & Eliza. Skinner born Oct. 26.
Ebenezer of William & Eliza. Sumner born Oct. 30.
Daniel of Daniel & Deliverance Searle born Oct. 29.
Comfort of Comfort & Mary Starr born Nov. 15.
Mary of Samuel & Eliza. Shrimpton born Dec. 4.
Philip of Nathaniel & Mary Sherman born Dec. 30.
Thomas of Thomas & Mary Swann born Feb. 8.
Ebenezer of John & Catharine Searle born Mar. 6.
William of Bartho & Hannah Sutton born Mar. 3.
Mehetable of Benja. & Elishua Thurston born Nov. 11.
Eliza. of Capt. Richard & Mary Thurston born May 26.
Benjamin of Bartho : & Damaris Thredneedle born June 5.
Nathaniel of John & Joanna Turner born June 26.
Priscilla of John & Sarah Tuckerman born Aug. 5.
John of Henry & Mary Taylor born Aug. 4.
Elizabeth of William & Eliza. Talmage born Sept. 22.
Joseph of James & Martha Talbott born Sept. 21.
William of Peter & Lydia Townsend born Sept. 13.
David of Samuel & Abiga Townsend horn Sept. 29.
Isaac of John & Sarah Tomson born Oct. 21.
Sarah of Ephraim & Sarah Turner born March 24.
John of Aaron & Joane Way born May 8.
John of John & Hannah Wiswall born May 12.
Samuel of Nathanll & Hannah Wilson born June 10.
Lydia of Robert & Rebecca Winsor born Aug. 1.
Jose of Deane & Sarah Winthrop born May 3.
Humphry of Richard & Bethiah Wharton born Aug. 5.

Hannah of Thomas & Anne Williams born Mar. 22.
Anna of John & Deliverance Wakefield born Sept. 2.
Ann of Isaac & Dorcas Woodee born Nov. 21.
Hannah of Thomas & Elizabeth Watkins born Oct. 28.
Samuel of Thomas & Hannah Wheeler born Dec. 23.
Peter of James & Rebecca Whetcomb born Dec. 7.
John of William & Hannah Williams born Dec. 20.
Mary of Joseph & Mary Wheeler born Feb. 23.
Joseph of Joseph & Grace Webb born Mar. 10.
Elizabeth of William & Mary Whittingham born Dec. 24.

## FIRST CHURCH.

| | |
|---|---|
| James of        Allen | 11 day 1 mo. |
| Benjamin of Will. Cotton | 25 day 1 mo. |
| Mary of Sister Elice | 1 aprell. |
| Simon of        Saffin | 15 day 2 mo. |
| Michael of Seth Perry | 15 day 2 mo. |
| Ruth wife of John Marshall | 22 day 2 mo. |
| Sarah wife of John Centure | 22 day 2 mo. |
| Abigail of Arthur Mason | 22 day 2 mo. |
| Ann of Abigail Phipeny | 29 day 2 mo. |
| William of Nath. Harwood's wife | 29 day 2 mo. |
| ⎧ James of Mary Hawkins | 29 day 2 mo. |
| ⎨ Elizabeth of Mary Hawkins | 29 day 2 mo. |
| ⎩ Sarah of Mary Hawkins | 29 day 2 mo. |
| ⎧ James of Ruth Marshall | 29 day 2 mo. |
| ⎨ John of Ruth Marshall | 29 day 2 mo. |
| ⎩ Mary of Ruth Marshall | 29 day 2 mo. |
| Benjamin of James Pemerton | 6 day 3 mo. |
| Richard of Richard Crichly | 6 day 3 mo. |
| ⎧ Elizabeth of Nicholas Phillips' wife | 6 day 3 mo. |
| ⎪ Hannah of Nicholas Phillips' wife | 6 day 3 mo. |
| ⎨ Abigail of Nicholas Phillips' wife | 6 day 3 mo. |
| ⎩ Sarah of Nicholas Phillips' wife | 6 day 3 mo. |
| ⎧ John of John Centure's wife | 6 day 3 mo. |
| ⎩ Elizabeth of John Centure's wife | 6 day 3 mo. |
| John of Sister Marshall | 20 day 3 mo. |
| Amye of Ann Matson | 20 day 3 mo. |
| Ann of Martha Smyth | 3 day 4 mo. |
| ⎧ Mary wife of John Neeland | 10 day 4 mo. |
| ⎨ Mary of John Necland's wife | 10 day 4 mo. |
| ⎩ Ann of John Neeland's wife | 10 day 4 mo. |
| Joyce of Sister Winthorp | 10 day 4 mo. |
| ⎧ Elizabeth of Elizabeth Weeden | 17 day 4 mo. |
| ⎪ Sarah of Elizabeth Weeden | 17 day 4 mo. |
| ⎨ Mary of Elizabeth Weeden | 17 day 4 mo. |
| ⎪ Ann of Elizabeth Weeden | 17 day 4 mo. |
| ⎩ Edward of Elizabeth Weeden | 17 day 4 mo. |
| Mary of Mary Dennis | 17 day 4 mo. |
| Nathaniel of Sister Lewes | 8 day 5 mo. |
| Josua of Samuel Norden | 8 day 5 mo. |
| Josua of Henry Phillips | 22 day 5 mo. |
| ⎧ Bridget of Freegrace Bendall | 5 day 6 mo. |
| ⎨ Elizabeth of Freegrace Bendall | 5 day 6 mo. |
| ⎩ Ann of Freegrace Bendall | 5 day 6 mo. |
| Lydia of Sister Winsor | 5 day 6 mo. |
| Samuel of Sister Miles | 12 day 6 mo. |
| Abigail of Jeremy Fitch | 12 day 6 mo. |
| Sarah of John Cotton | 16 day 7 mo. |
| ⎧ Jerimiah of Mrs. Greene | 16 day 7 mo. |
| ⎪ Susannah of Mrs. Greene | 16 day 7 mo. |
| ⎨ Mary of Mrs. Greene | 16 day 7 mo. |
| ⎩ Elizabeth of Mrs. Greene | 16 day 7 mo. |

| | |
|---|---|
| Mary of Samuel Mason | 16 day 7 mo. |
| Anna of Samuel Mason | 16 day 7 mo. |
| Jacob of Hope Allen's wife | 16 day 7 mo. |
| Joseph of Hope Allen's wife | 16 day 7 mo. |
| Rachel of Hope Allen's wife | 16 day 7 mo. |
| Mary of Hope Allen's wife | 16 day 7 mo. |
| Benjamin of Hope Allen's wife | 16 day 7 mo. |
| Heiborne son of Rich: Wait | 23 day 7 mo. |
| Susanna of Edmond Jackson | 23 day 7 mo. |
| Elizabeth of Will: Talmage | 23 day 7 mo. |
| John of Joseph Davis | 14 day 8 mo. |
| Joseph of John Meriam | 21 day 8 mo. |
| Abigail of Samuel Mason | 21 day 8 mo. |
| Sarah of James Mackwell | 21 day 8 mo. |
| Robert of Robert Gibbs | 14 day 8 mo. |
| Margaret of Robert Gibbs | 14 day 8 mo. |
| Nathaniel of Sister Pecke | 18 day 9 mo. |
| Mary of George Manning | 25 day 9 mo. |
| Bethiah of Mr. Brattle | 16 day 10 mo. |
| Mary wife of Joseph Knight | 16 day 10 mo. |
| Elizabeth of William Read | 23 day 10 mo. |
| Tho: of Sister Sheerod | 23 day 10 mo. |
| Mary of Sister Sheerod | 23 day 10 mo. |
| Mary of Ambrose Dawes | 23 day 10 mo. |
| Susan of Ambrose Dawes | 23 day 10 mo. |
| Mary of Mrs Person | 30 day 10 mo. |
| Mary of John Matson's wife | 30 day 10 mo. |
| Susan of Ambrose Dawes' wife | 30 day 10 mo. |
| Anna of Ambrose Dawes' wife | 30 day 10 mo. |
| Elizabeth of Mr. Mather | 3 day 12 mo. |
| Obediah of Mary Emins | 3 day 12 mo. |
| Edward of Edward Davis | 9 day 12 mo. |
| Thomas of Ruth & John Marshall | 9 day 12 mo. |
| Elisha of Mr. Rocke | 17 day 12 mo. |
| Margaret of Mr. Davy | 24 day 12 mo. |
| Marcy of Sister Burges | 24 day 12 mo. |

## Town.

Abraham of William & Mehetable Avis born June 28.
Elizabeth of Nathanll & Mary Adams born Oct. 2.
Joseph of Henry & Mary Adams born Oct. 4.
Abraham of Abraham & Sarah Adams born Nov. 11.
Anna of Hugh & Ann Amos born Jan. 28.
Hannah of Matthew & Hannah Armstrong born Feb. 19.
Christian of John & Elizabeth Brookin born July 22.
Hannah of James & Hannah Brading born Aug. 1.
Samuel of Samuel & Sarah Bucknell born June 14.
Elizabeth of Richard & Elizabeth Barnam born Aug. 20
Isaac of Stephen & Jane Butler born Aug. 10.
Edward of Edward & Patience Blake born Oct. 16.
Alice of Free Grace & Mary Bendall born Oct. 4.
Mary of John & Mary Bull born Oct. 29.
Mercy of Samuel & Mary Bradstreet born Nov. 20.
Thomas of Ambrose & Mary Bennet born Nov. 10.
Mary of John & Sarah Buckman born Dec. 12.
Rebecca of Josiah & Ranis Belcher born Dec. 31.
Michael of Thomas & Abigail Bill born Dec. 27.
Elizabeth of Roger & Elizabeth Burges born Nov. 18.
John of George & Pearne Broughton born Jan. 22.
Susanna of William & Hannah Balentine born Feb. 2.

Mary of Edward & Dorothy Bird born Jan. 31.
Martha of James & Jemima Biss born Feb. 23.
Sarah of Abraham & Abigail Bashy born Jan. 7.
Abigail of John & Mary Bohannon born Sept. 26.
Samuel of Thaddeus & Hanna Berry born June 20.
Josiah of Josiah & Waitawhile Cooper born Apr. 4.
Susannah of Joseph & Susanna Cock born June 30.
Thomas of John & Elizabeth Coney born Sept. 26.
Mary of Percival & Elizabeth Clarke born Oct. 18.
Benjamin of Samuel & Jane Cane born Nov. 24.
John of John & Martha Clarke born Jan. 27.
Mary of Robert & Elizabeth Couci born Dec. 24.
Samuel of Matth: & Elizabeth Coy born Feb. 19.
Elizabeth of Timothy & Philippe Cunnell born Jan. 16.
Mary of John & Mary Cotta born Mar. 1.
Thomas of Leonard & Mercy Dowding born July 22.
Rebecca of Samuel & Sarah Davis born July 9.
Margaret of Capt. Wm. & Judith Davis born Nov. 18.
Elizabeth of Thomas & Sarah Deane born Dec. 29.
William of John & Dorothy Downes born Feb. 23.
Mary of William & Phoebe Eglin born July 8.
Mary of Edward & Sarah Ellis born Dec. 11.
Elizabeth of Samuel & Mary Emmons born Feb. 11.
Elizabeth of James & Frances Ellis born Feb. 1.
Jeremiah of Jeremiah & Sarah Fitch born Sept. 1.
Elizabeth of John & Susanna Farnham born Nov. 11.
Mary of Edward & Mary Farnham born Dec. 17.
John of John & Elizabeth Freake born Jan. 8.
Abigail of John & Ann Flacke born Feb. 21.
William of William & Maria Gard born July 13.
Ebenezer of John & Mary Gilbert born Jan. 24.
Nathaniel of Nathanll & Mary Greene born Jan. 24.
Luke of William & Ruth Greenough born Feb. 10.
Priscilla of William & Sarah Gibson born Feb. 12.
Sarah of Henry & Mary Gibbs born Jan. 28.
Frances of Peter & Jane Goulding born Feb. 22.
Joseph of Charles & Margaret Hopkins born Aug. 1.
Samuel of Thomas & Hannah Hull born Aug. 14.
William of William & Martha Holstead born Aug. 19.
Mary of Joshua & Hannah Hewes born May 27.
———— dau. of John & Sarah Heward born May 19.
Susanna of Daniel & Sarah Henchman born June 7.
Sarah of Joseph & Sarah Hurd born Oct. 1.
Sarah of George & Sarah Hisket born Sept. 27.
John of John & Joanna Hunlock born Oct. 7.
William of William & Mary Hamlin born Oct. 11.
Hannah of Ezekiel & Eliza. Hamlin born Nov. 2.
Mary of John & Mary Holman born Dec. 14.
Anna of Thomas & Jane Harding born Feb. 20.
Sarah of James & Sarah Harris born Mar. 2.
Lydia of Joseph & Frances How born Mar. 16.
Thomas of Eliphal & Ann Hett born Mar. 16.
Elisha of Elisha & Hannah Hutchinson born Mar. 16.
Elizabeth of John & Joanna Howen born Feb. 16.
John of James & Joanna Ingles horn Sept. 5.
Mary of James & Anna Johnson born Oct. 19.
Mercy of Richard & Joanna Knight born Mar. 31.
John of Thomas & Abigail Kellond born June 2.
Thomas of Thomas & Mary Kingston horn Sept 29.
Samuel of Joseph & Mary Knight born Jan. 11.
Sarah of Hudson & Sarah Leveret born June 6.
Hannah of John & Ursula Lawrance born June 10.
Margaret of John & Naomi Lowell born Oct. 20.
John of John & Hannah Luscomb born Jan. 2.

Thomas of Edward & Elizabeth Lillie born Jan. 10.
Abigail of Joseph & Abigail Lowell born Feb. 4.
Edward of John & Agnes Lux born Mar. 1.
Richard of Richard & Elizabeth Loft born Mar. 14.
Abigail of John & Elizabeth Morse born Mar. 30.
Elizabeth of Francis & Elizabeth Morse born July 23.
Elizabeth of Richard & Elizabeth Martin born July 25.
Elizabeth of Thomas & Sarah Moore born Apr. 27.
Sarah of James & Martha Mellows born Oct. 16.
Richard of Richd & Experience Miles born Oct. 10.
Felex dau. of James & Margery Maxwell born Sept. **22.**
Peter of Samuel & Kathar Mansell born Nov. 21.
Benjamin of Edmund & Eliza. Mountfort born Feb. **19.**
Francis of Thaddeus & Eliza. Maccarty born Mar. 21.
Joseph of George & Lydia Nowell born May 28.
Tabitha of Edward & Catharine Naylor born July 2.
Mary of John & Rebecca Nash born Nov. 26.
Mary of Robert & Mary Nokes born Dec. 5.
Mary of William & Susanna Norton born Feb. 5.
Richard of Richard & Elizabeth Price born Mar. 26.
Robert of William & Anne Pitts born Apr. 3.
Joseph of George & Elizabeth Parson born Aug. 18.
John of Nicholas & Philippa Phillips born May 3.
Samuel of Samuel & Mary Peacock born June 2.
Thomas of Nicholas & Hannah Phillips born Oct. **19.**
Kesiah of John & Kesiah Perkins born Oct. 7.
Elizabeth of Seth & Dorothy Perry born Jan. 15.
Mary of Robert & Rose Pegg born Jan. 17.
Elizabeth of John & Judith Parmiter born Feb. 8.
James of James & Martha Robinson born July 21.
Mary of William & Susanna Rogers born Apr. 9.
John of John & Ellener Sherrar born July 26.
John of Thomas & Hannah Sherrar born Aug. 18.
John of John & Sarah Starky born Sept. 23.
Mary ⎫ of Jona & Mary Shrimpton born Oct. 30.
Jona ⎭ of Jona & Mary Shrimpton born Oct. 30.
Elizabeth of John & Tomasin Scarlet born Nov. 18.
Elizabeth of Thomas & Mary Savage born Nov. 8.
Nathaniel of John Junr. & Mary Sunderland born Nov. **17.**
John of John & Elizabeth Skinner born Jan. 22.
Josiah of John & Martha Saffin born Jan. 31.
Robert of Robert & Eliza. Sanford born Apr. 15.
Elizabeth of Richard & Elizabeth Shute born Jan. 1.
Daniel of Daniel & Mary Sutton born Feb. 19.
Richard of John & Margaret Selly born Mar. 17.
Elizabeth of Arthur & Jane Scovell born Mar. 18.
Mary of Samuel & Mary Stocker born Apr. 25.
Simon of John & Hannah Snell born Aug. 22.
Benjamin of John & Martha Starr born Aug. 19.
Hannah of Abijah & Hannah Savage born Aug. 27.
Mary of Ahijah & Hannah Savage born Aug. 27.
Sarah of William & Sarah Towers born Apr. 16.
Elizabeth of Francis & Rebecca Thomas born Sept. **25.**
Thomas of Richard & Martha Tewell born Oct. 17.
Elizabeth of William & Rebecca Taylor born May 17.
Thomas of Thomas & Mary Townsend born Dec. 10.
Mary of William & Mary Tice born Sept. 4.
Mary of Benjamin & Elizabeth Thurston born Feb. **11.**
Susanna of Peter & Lydia Townsend born Feb. 22.
Samuel of John & Elizabeth Viall born Nov. 25.
Mercy of John & Mercy Veren born Jan. 8.
William of James & Mary Webster born Mar. 25.
Elizabeth of Aaron & Jane Way born June 23.
Mary of Thomas & Susanna Walker born July 30.

Elizabeth of John & Elizabeth Walley born July 28.
Thomas of Thomas & Martha Waler born July 26.
Elizabeth of Bartho & Amey Whitwell born June 6.
Elizabeth of Nathaniel & Eliza. Woodward born June 10.
Susanna of Thomas & Elizabeth Watts born July 1.
Martha of John & Mary Winsor born Aug. 22.
Mary of Sampson & Rebecca Waters born Aug. 28.
John of Samuel & Joanna Ward born Sept. 27.
Elizabeth of Thomas & Judith Woodward born June 24.
Lydia of Joseph & Lydia Wheeler born Sept. 16.
Joseph of James & Rebecca Whetcombe born Nov. 26.
Joshabeth of John & Joshabeth Wing born Dec. 15.
Elizabeth of Peter & Sarah Warren born Jan. 4.
Mercy of Nathanll & Mary Woodward born Jan. 17.
John of Lawrance & Hannah Waters born Feb. 10.
Mehetable of Thomas & Eliza. Watkins born Feb. 14.
Mercy of John & Eliza. Winsley born Feb. 14.
Elizabeth of Thomas & Anne Williams born Feb. 6.
John of John & Hannah Wiswall born Mar. 21.
Elizabeth of William & Mary Whittingham born Dec. 24.

## First Church.

| | | |
|---|---|---|
| Hannah of Jacob Eliot | 24 day | 1 mo. |
| James of Sister Andrewes | 24 day | 1 mo. |
| Robert of Robert Sanford | 14 day | 2 mo. |
| John of Sarah Franks | 21 day | 2 mo. |
| John of Sister Keyne | 21 day | 2 mo. |
| Jain of Sister Keyne | 21 day | 2 mo. |
| Abiel Evirell | 28 day | 2 mo. |
| John of John Aldin | 28 day | 2 mo. |
| Elizabeth of John Aldin | 28 day | 2 mo. |
| ⌈ Samuel of Mrs. Hannah Lynde born 1 Dec. 1653 | 5 day | 3 mo. |
| ⎢ John of Mrs. Hannah Lynde born 9 Nov. 1657 | 5 day | 3 mo. |
| ⎢ Nathaniel of Mrs. Hannah Lynde born 22 Nov. 1659 | 5 day | 3 mo. |
| ⎥ Elizabeth of Mrs. Hannah Lynde born 25 Mar. 1662 | 5 day | 3 mo. |
| ⎢ Joseph of Mrs. Hannah Lynde born 2 Aug. 1664 | 5 day | 3 mo. |
| ⌊ Benjamin of Mrs. Hannah Lynde born 23 Sept. 1666 | 5 day | 3 mo. |
| Zachary of John Aldin | 19 day | 3 mo. |
| Daniel of Collinell Scirle | 2 day | 4 mo. |
| Susanna of Mrs. Ilinksman of Ch. at Dublin in Ireland | 9 day | 4 mo. |
| Samuel of Sister Brookin | 16 day | 4 mo. |
| Elizabeth of Nath. Harwood's wife | 16 day | 4 mo. |
| Mehetabel of Henry Philips | 21 day | 5 mo. |
| Christian of Sister Brookin | 28 day | 5 mo. |
| James of Sister Robinson | 28 day | 5 mo. |

## 1668.

### Town.

Samuel of John & Hannah Andrews born May 18.
Elizabeth of Theodore Jr. & Eliza Atkinson born June 25.
Mary of Edward & Martha Allen born Aug. 14.
Elizabeth of John & Desire ye Truth Akers born Nov. 24.
Thomas of William & Mehetable Anis born Feb. 10.
Joseph of John & Martha Amey born Feb. 10.
Timothy of Timothy & Joanna Armitage born Feb. 20.
George of William & Elizabeth Browne born Apr. 5.
Mary of Jeremiah & Anne Bumstead born May 30.
Samuel of Francis & Jane Burges born July 5.
John of Moses & Eliza. Bradford born Aug. 15.
Mary of Thomas & Eliza. Brattle born Aug. 10.

Mary of Robert & Bathsheba Brunsdon born Sept. 22.
Ephraim of Mauassah & Mary Beck born Dec. 5.
Ruth of Joseph & Lydia Belknap born Nov. 27.
Deborah of George & Deborah Burrell born Dec. 17.
Elizabeth of Joseph Buckminister born ———.
Mary of John & Mary Briggs born Jan. 28.
Elizabeth of Edward & Dorothy Budd born Mar. 6.
Nicholas of Thomas & Mary Buttolph born Mar. 3.
Jonathan of James & Sarah Balston born Mar. 21.
Jeremiah of Jeremiah & Sarah Belcher born Oct. 31.
Peter of Richard & ——— Bennet born Oct 1.
Hannah of Thaddeus & Hannah Berry born Aug. 12.
Mary of William & Martha Clarke born March 22.
Sarah of Anthony & Hannah Checkley born June 18.
Daniel of Ralph & Susanna Carter born July 12.
John of Henry & Rebecca Cowley born Aug. 27.
Edward of John & Hannah Cowell born Sept. 12.
Hannah of John & Susanna Cole born Dec. 17.
Alice of John & Sarah Clarke born Nov. 11.
Samuel of John & Susanna Cross born March 18.
Sarah of David & Obedience Copp born March 1.
William of John & Margaret Courser born April 16.
Mary of John & Elizabeth Coney born March 10.
James of James & Frances Dawes born Apr. 13.
Thomas of John & Mary Drury born Aug. 10.
Elizabeth of Joseph & Elizabeth Davis born Dec. 13.
William of Fathergon & Hannah Dinely born Dec. 1.
Susanna of Ambrose & Mary Dawes born Mar. 19.
John of John Junr. & Abigail Davenport born Feb. 22.
James of John & Mary Ewell born Apr. 16.
Mary of Benj. & Mary Emōns born Oct. 14.
Mehetable of Thomas & Mary Eldridge born Nov. 23.
Mary of Henry & Urseley Edwards born Mar. 10.
James of James & Hannah Flood born Apr. 6.
Mary of Henry & Mary Floyd born May 29.
John of John & Eliza. Foster born July 31.
John of Theophilus & Hannah Frarey born Dec. 11.
John of John & Sarah Fayerweather born Jan. 22.
Thomas of Thomas & Martha Fitch born Feb. 5.
Rebecca of Jeremiah & Sarah Fitch born Feb. 19.
Sarah of John & Sarah Franks born Feb. 26.
Ann of Jesper & Elizabeth Frost born Mar. 7.
Samuel of Francis & Mary (Negroes) born Mar. 17.
Mary of Nathanll & Margaret Gallop borne June 25.
Catharine of Thomas & Catharine Goodridge born June 17.
Faith of Benjamin & Hannah Gillam born July 18.
Henry of Robert & Elizabeth Gibbs born Oct. 8.
Elizabeth of Thomas & Eliza. Gwinn born Oct. 16.
Mary of William & Maria Gard born Feb. 22.
Anna of William & Eliza. Greenough born Feb. 21.
Eleazer of John & Mary Gilbert born Mar. 1.
Jane of Thomas & Dorothy Grecian born Feb. 28.
Bethiah of Believe & Anna Gridley born Mar. 17.
Hannah of John & Hannah Greenleafe born Oct. 5.
Jonathan of George & Sarah Hollard born March 15.
Elizabeth of Jabez & Experience Heaton born Apr. 15.
Ann of William & Dorothy Hawkins born May 17.
Mary of Israel & Anne Howe born May 18.
Thomas of Thomas & Abigail Hatherly born July 1.
Eleazer of James & Mary Hudson born June 19.
John of Nicholas & Eliza. Howard born June 29.
Naomi of John & Naomi Henley born Nov. 11.
Ignatius of James & Hannah Hill born Nov. 6.
Elizabeth of John & Mary Hill born Nov. 10.

Richard of Eliakim & Sarah Hutchinson born & died Jan. **13.**
Phoebe of John & Mary Holman born Jan. 15.
Mary of William & Mary Hamken born Jan. 17.
William of William & Anne Hobby born Feb. 9.
Hannah of Henry & Eliza. Harwood born Jan. 17.
James of James & Eliza. Hewes born Feb. 7.
Elizabeth of William & Mary Ingram born Feb. 1.
William of John & Elizabeth Jones born June 19.
Samuel of John & Jane Johnson born Apr. 15.
Joseph of Edward & Elizabeth Jones born Oct. 9.
Edmond of Edmond & Eliza. Jackson born Oct. 5.
Elizabeth of Jonathan & Eliza. Jackson born Feb. **16.**
William of Samuel & Hannah King born Apr. 13.
David of Richard & Joanna Knight born Apr. 7.
Giles of Henry & Mary Kemble born July 14.
Rebecca of Thomas & Eliza. Kemble born July 12.
Richard of Richard & Julian Knight born Oct. 18.
John of John & Mary Kneeland born Nov. 29.
John of Thomas & Abigail Kellond born Feb. 13.
James of James & Elizabeth Laydon born Apr. 12.
John of John & Elizabeth Langburrô born Apr. 18.
Nathaniel of Thomas & Mary Lake born July 18.
John of John & Sarah Leveret born Aug. 20.
Simon of Simon & Hannah Lynde born Oct. 8.
James of Joseph & Abigail Lowell born Mar. 27.
Elizabeth of Thomas & Rachel Martin horn Apr. **10.**
Elizabeth of Samuel & Mary Meers born Apr. 9.
Bethiah of Simeon & Bethiah Messenger born May 24.
Margaret of Christopher & Prudence Morse born May **10**
Alice of Arthur & Joanna Mason born June 26.
Elizabeth of James & Elizabeth Meers born Aug. 1.
Zacheus of Samuel & Caylance Matlock born Sept. **15.**
Abigail of John & Mary Matson born Oct. 19.
Thomas of Samuel & Mary Mason born Dec. 6.
Ruth of John & Elizabeth Morse born Jan **13.**
Thomas of Thomas & Mary Matson born Jan. 13.
Sarah of George & Hannah Manning born Mar. 19.
William of Robert & Hannah Mokum born Mar. 14.
Ruth of Richard & Ruth Newport born Apr. 27.
Lydia of Edward & Catharine Nailor born July 26.
Andrew of Andrew & Mellicent Neale born Nov. 25.
Mary of Robert & Sarah Orchard born Mar. 26.
Nathaniel of John & Elizabeth Olden born July 9.
Susanna of John & Susanna Oliver born Aug. 27.
Margaret of Elisha & Abigail Odlin born Feb. 26.
Mehetable of Daniel & Sarah Phippen born Apr. 27.
Sarah of John & Ruth Pearse born June 1.
Hannah of John & Deliverance Pollard born Aug. **15.**
Mary of James & Mary Penniman born Sept. 17.
Ruth of Ezekiel & Ruth Padner born Sept. 12.
Jonathan of James & Sarah Pemberton born Aug. **28.**
William of Tobias & Sarah Paine born Jan. 21.
Richard of Samuel & Mary Peacock born Jan. 22.
John of Elias & Sarah Parkman born Jan. 24.
John of Henry & Mary Phillips born Jan. 22.
John of Timothy & Deborah Pratt born Feb. 23.
David of William & Ann Pollard born Apr. 18.
Mary of Nathanll & Damaris Robinson born June 22.
Edward of Jonathan & Mary Rainsford born June 27.
John of Nathanll & Priscilla Reynolds born Aug. 4.
Ann of Thomas & Temperance Smith born Apr. 29.
Mary of Anthony & Christian Stoddard born Mar. 25.
Samuel of Clement & Joanna Salmon born Apr. 5.
Samuel of John Senr & Tomasin Sunderland born Apr. **14.**

Joseph of John & Sarah Skeath born June 9.
John of John & Rebecca Scottow born June 25.
Nathaniel of Nathanll & Mary Sherman born June 15.
Martha of Robert & Elizabeth Smith born July 2.
Thomas of Thomas Junr. & Eliza. Savage born Aug. 2.
Sarah of Pilgrim & Cathar. Symkins born Sept. 21.
Silence of Henry & Mary Stevens born July 26.
Samuel of Col. Danl. & Deliverance Searle born Oct. 16.
Martha of William & Martha Snith born Jan. 16.
Mary of John & Sarah Stanbury born Feb. 14.
Thomas of Joseph & Elizabeth Soper born June 8.
Elizabeth of Capt. Thos. & Mary Savage born Feb. 24.
Joseph of Comfort & Mary Starr born Mar. 7.
Lydia of Paltiel & Lydia Sconer born July 8.
Grizell of Philip & Rachel Squire born May 14.
Ann of Thomas & Ann Shapcot born Jan. 18.
Mary of Henry & Mary Taylor born June 6.
Hannah of Stephen & Hannah Taylor born July 2.
Hannah of John & Joanna Turner born July 15.
Abigail of William & Leah Towers born Aug. 19.
Martha of John & Sarah Tuckerman born Aug. 28.
Jonathan of Samuel & Abigail Towsend born Sept. 10.
John of Daniel & Esther Trenis born Oct. 2.
William of James & Martha Talbot born Dec. 26.
Mary of William & Eliza Talmage born Jan. 13.
Nathaniel of John & Sarah Tomlin born Jan. 18.
Benjamin of Richard & Eliza. Tout born Sept. 16.
Ruth of Thomas & Ruth Weybourn born Apr. 22.
Thomas of John & Mary Weybourn born Sept. 13.
Susanna of Thomas & Elizabeth Wales born Sept. 8.
Ellener of Leonard & Ellener Wheatly born Aug. 8.
Sarah of John & Jane Williams born Nov. 28.
Elizabeth of William & Joanna Williams born Jan. 4.
John of John & Lydia Watts born Jan. 22.
John of John & Deliverance Wakefield born Jan. 27.
Richard of William & Mary Whittingham born Jan. 18.
John of Thomas & Susanna Walker born Feb. 2.
Constance of William & Constance Woster born Mar. 10.
Mary of Thomas & Esther Woodward born Jan. 13.

## FIRST CHURCH.

| | |
|---|---|
| John of Sister Kneeland | 13 day 10 mo. |
| Manasse of Sister Becke | 13 day 10 mo. |
| Ann of Samuel Mason | 13 day 10 mo. |
| John of Theophelous Frary | 20 day 10 mo. |
| Elizabeth of Joseph Davis | 20 day 10 mo. |
| Ann of Thomas Matson | 17 day 11 mo. |
| Martha of Martha & William Smyth | 17 day 11 mo. |
| John of Henry Philips | 24 day 11 mo. |
| John of Deliverance & John Wakfield | 31 day 11 mo. |
| Mary of William Talmage | 31 day 11 mo. |
| Thomas of Thomas Fitch | 7 day 12 mo. |
| Mehitabel of Mary Eldrige | 7 day 12 mo. |
| Rebecca of Jeremiah Fitch's wife | 22 day 12 mo. |
| Jeremiah of Jeremiah Belcher's wife | 28 day 12 mo. |
| Elizabeth of Thomas Savage | 28 day 12 mo. |
| Sarah of John Franks' wife | 28 day 12 mo. |

## 1669.

### TOWN.

Ellener of Joshua & Mary Atwater born Apr. 23.
Hannah of Thomas & Elizabeth Allin born June 21.
William of John & Elizabeth Alden born Sept. 10.
Theodore of Theodore & Elizabeth Atkinson born Oct. 3.
Samuel of Samuel & Hopestill Austins born Oct. 8.
Henry of Henry & Mary Adams born Jan. 15.
Jane of Abraham & Sarah Adams born Feb. 22.
Samuel of Samuel & Sarah Alcock born Mar. 2.
Rebecca of Samuel & Sarah Bucknell born Mar. 30.
Elizabeth of William & Elliner Baker born Mar. 29.
David of John & Hannah Buttolph born May 7.
Grace of Thomas & Grace Berry born June 1.
Jonathan of William & Hannah Ballentine born Sept. 19.
Richard of Free Grace & Mary Bendall born Sept. 10.
Jacob of Thomas & Abigail Bell born Oct. 31.
Sarah of Robert & Mary Brickenton born Sept. 3.
Mary of James & Hannah Braden born Jan. 11.
Mary of John & Elizabeth Brookin born Jan. 20.
Sarah of John & Agnes Bowden born Jan 28.
John of Phillip & Judith Bullis born Jan. 8.
Edward of Josias & Ranis Belcher born Jan. 19.
Rebecca of Benja. & Sarah Brisco born Feb. 20.
Mary of Robert & Elizabeth Burgis born Jan. 14.
Elizabeth of Robert & Priscilla Blumfield born Mar. 16.
Mehetable of John & Mary Bull born Jan. 1.
Samuel of Samuel & Mary Browne born Jan. 1.
Edward of Jeremiah & Sarah Belcher born Feb. 14.
Thomas of Thomas & Esther Brental born Nov. 1.
Augustine dau. of Samuel & Deborah Clement born Apr. 2.
Elizabeth of Ezekiel & Mercy Corneth born May 3.
Sarah of Edward & Sarah Cowell born Apr. 3.
John of John & Mary Clough born Apr. 11.
Abigail of Robert & Penelope Cooke born July 11.
Anthony of Josiah & Waitawhile Cooper born June 28.
Ann of John & Anne Checkley born Aug. 4.
Mary of John & Hannah Cowell born Nov. 20.
William of William & Mary Caswell born Dec. 15.
Rebecca of Henry & Rebecca Cooley born Nov. 25.
Union son of David & Lydia Chapin born Dec. 23.
Martha of Joseph & Martha Cox born Mar. 3.
Joseph of Joseph & Abigail Dudson born July 11.
Hannah of Edward & Hannah Davis born Sept. 12.
Nathaniel of Samuel & Sarah Davis born Nov. 26.
Mary of Anthony & Elizabeth Davis born May 3.
Thomas of Joseph & Rebecca Dudley born Feb. 26.
Sarah of William & Mary Dier born Feb. 17.
Joseph of Capt. Wm. & Huldah Davis born Sept. 3.
Rebecca of Obadiah & Rachel Emōns born Apr. 19.
Margaret of Robert & Hannah Earle born July 18.
Nathaniel of Samuel & Mary Emōns born Feb. 9.
Benjamin of Benja. & Mary Emōns born Jan. 24.
Daniel of Thomas & Sarah Edwards born Mar. 16.
Lydia of Edward & Lydia Ellis born Mar. 13.
Samuel of William & Phoebe Eglen born Mar. 14.
Jane of John & Elizabeth Freake born Oct. 26.
Elizabeth of Hopestil & Elizabeth Foster born July 26.
John of John & Mehetable Frost born Jan. 9.
Elizabeth of Edward & Mary Farnham born Feb. 5.
Richard of James & Rebecca Green born Apr. 7.

Isaac of Isaac & Mary Goose born May 5.
Anna of Nathanll & Mary Greenwood born Apr. 7.
John of John & Ruth Gwinn born Aug. 2.
Edmund of Clement & Anna Gross born Sept. 26.
Lydia of Benja. & Lydia Gibbs born Jan. 26.
Thomas of Stephen & Sarah Gates born Dec. 31.
Elizabeth of Peltiel & Lydia Grover born Feb. 13.
Mary of Joseph & Sarah Hurd born Apr. 29.
William of Daniel & Sarah Henchman born July 28.
Mary of Thomas & Mary Hutchins born Apr. 13.
Elizabeth of John & Elizabeth Harris born Sept. 7.
Mercy of Ezekiel & Elizabeth Hamlin born Sept. 5.
Benjamin of Charles & Margaret Hopkins born Aug. 21.
John of John & Elizabeth Hopper born Sept. 7.
Mary of James & Dinah Halsey born Jan. 2.
Susanna of John & Joanna Hare born Jan. 29.
Ruth of Joseph & Frances How born Mar. 4.
Elizabeth of Elisha & Hannah Hutchinson born Feb. 24.
Joanna of John & Joanna Henlock born Feb. 27.
Jane of James & Joanna Ingles born Mar. 31.
Anna of James Junr. & Anna Johnson born May 29.
Job of Samuel & Elizabeth Judkin born Sept. 24.
Abigail of Henry & Mary Kemble born Oct. 13.
John of Joseph & Mary Knight born Jan. 19.
Henry of Thomas & Eliza. Kemble born Mar. 14.
Samuel of John & Naomi Lowell born Aug. 1.
Martha ) of John & Agnes Lux born Sept. 20.
Mary  ) of John & Agnes Lux born Sept. 20.
Elizabeth of Richard & Elizabeth Loft born Feb. 24.
Samuel of Samuel & Deliverance Legg born Mar. 16.
Persis of Thomas & Ann Maynel born June 3.
Nathaniel of Increase & Maria Mather born July 6.
Samuel of Join & Ruth Marshall born July 14.
Elizabeth of Robert & Sarah Mason born July 29.
Sarah of Return & Sarah Manning born Apr. 7.
Thomas of Thomas & Sarah Moore born Sept. 2.
John of John & Sarah Marsh born Aug. 29.
Mary of Francis & Anna Morss born Sept. 26.
Hannah of Francis & Anna Morss born Sept. 26.
John of Samuel & Constance Mattock born Sept..14.
Mary of Daniel & Mary Matthews born Oct. 3.
Abigail of Richard & Elizabeth Martin born Nov. 14.
Deliverance dau. of James & Margaret Maywell born Jan. 15.
Mary of John & Martha Mellows born Mar. 19.
Edward of James & Eliza. Meeres born Mar. 22.
Elizabeth of Dego (negro) & Hagar Muntero born Oct. 1.
George of George & Lydia Nowell born Feb. 15.
Mary of Samuel & Eliza. Nordin born Mar. 22.
Mary of William & Mary Okinton born Sept. 7.
Samuel of Samuel & Mary Pettifur born May 28.
John of Nicholas & Philippa Phillips born June 21.
George of Edward & Elizabeth Pullin born July 22.
John of William & Elizabeth Pickerin born Apr. 17.
Joseph of Zechariah & Elizabeth Phillips born Sept. 4.
Thomas of George & Elizabeth Pearson born Oct. 30.
Margaret of Robert & Margaret Peard born Dec. 20.
Robert of Robert & Rose Pegge born Jan. 19.
Mary of William & Hopestill Pitts born ult. Feb.
Elizabeth of Obadiah & Anna Read born Mar. 23.
John of John & Mary Rice born May 9.
Edward of Join & Susanna Rainsford born Apr. 21.
Ann of Simon & Christian Roberts born July 18.
Elizabeth of William & Ruth Road born Apr. 22.
John of Samuel & Margaret Ruck born Aug. 17.

Grace of William & Elizabeth Robins born Sept. 19.
Elizabeth of Richard & Elizabeth Randall born Nov. 6.
Elizabeth of John & Alice Ratliffe born Jan. 1.
Elizabeth of Robert & Eliza. Reynolds born Jan. 2.
Mary of John & Elizabeth Russell born Sept. 15.
John of Humphrey & Mehetable Richards born Apr. 1.
John of John & Hannah Stiles born Mar. 31.
Hannah of Bartho. & Hannah Sutton born Apr. 12.
Moses of Thomas & Mary Saxton bore May 31.
Elizabeth of Nicholas & Elizabeth Stevens born June 21.
Jane of Anthony & Christian Stoddard born July 29.
Hannah of Thomas & Hannah Sherrar born Aug. 6.
Thomas of Edward & Mary Stevens born Apr. 15.
Thomas of Thomas & Temperance Smith born Aug. 1.
Deliverance of William & Hannah Sumner born Mar. 18.
Elizabeth of Thomas & Judith Snowsell born Sept. 8.
William of John & Emme Stepson born Sept. 4.
Sarah of Jonathan & Mary Shrimpton born Nov. 29.
John of Laomi & Deborah Simpson born Dec. 3.
Joseph of John & Elizabeth Skinner born Jan. 8.
Joseph of John & Martha Saffin born Feb. 2.
Thomas of Thomas & Susanna Stanbury born Jan. 17.
Elizabeth of Philip & Rachel Squire born Feb. 2.
Mary of Comfort & Mary Starr born Mar. 14.
Joseph of John & Sarah Snemy born Oct. 10.
Nicholas of John & Ellener Shern born May 14.
Abigail of Ephraim & Sarah Turner born June 8.
Buny son of Bernard & Mary Trott born June 20.
Humphrey of Daniel & Mary Turell born Sept. 10.
Hannah of John & Joanna Turner born Sept. 30.
Francis of Jonathan & Sarah Tyng born Dec. 11.
Susanna of Peter & Lydia Townsend born Feb. 20.
Elizabeth of Henry & Eliza. Thomson born Jan. 29.
John of Benja & Elishua Thurston born Mar. 15.
Elizabeth of John & Elizabeth Usher born June 18.
Edward of Edward & Jane Urin born June 2.
Joseph of John & Mercy Verin born Mar. 12.
Joseph of Thomas & Hannah Wheeler born Mar. 31.
Mary of William & Mary Whitwell born Mar. 28.
Priscilla of Deane & Sarah Winthrop born May 1.
John of John & Eliza. Winslow born May 22.
William of Thomas & Mary Walker born May 24.
Susanna of Thomas & Ann Williams born June 1.
Martha of John & Mary White born July 7.
John of Robert & Rebecca Winsor born Apr. 22.
Jane of Thomas & Rebecca Whetcombe born Aug. 31.
Edward of Edward & Eliza. Winslow born Nov. 1.
Rachel of John & Mary Williams born Dec. 15.
Martha of Isaac & Dorcas Woodee born Nov. 12.
Joseph of Joseph & Lydia Waler born Feb. 3.
Joseph of Joseph & Lydia Williams born Feb. 14.
Ebenezer of John & Joshabeth Wing born Oct. 15.
William of Sampson & Rebecca Waters born Mar. 3.
Eleazer of Samuel & Joanna Ward born Feb. 17.

FIRST CHURCH.

| | | |
|---|---|---|
| John of John Davenport Junr | 21 day | 1 mo. |
| Elizabeth of Theodore Atkinson's wife | 21 day | 1 mo. |
| Susanna of Ambrose Dawes' wife | 21 day | 1 mo. |
| Sarah of George Manning's wife | 21 day | 1 mo. |
| Richard of Robert Sanford | 28 day | 1 mo. |
| Jonathan of Jonathan Balsto's wife | 28 day | 1 mo. |

| | | |
|---|---|---|
| William of Richard Gibbs' wife | 28 day | 1 mo. |
| Hezekiah of James Burges' wife | 4 day | 2 mo. |
| Rebecca of John Bucknell's wife | 4 day | 2 mo. |
| Elizabeth of Sister Winsor | 25 day | 2 mo. |
| John of William Read | 25 day | 2 mo. |
| Priscilla of Deane Winthrop's wife | 16 day | 3 mo. |
| John of John Clough | 6 | Jun. |
| Samuel of John Marshall's wife | 18 day | 5 mo. |
| Hannah of James Allen Teacher | 25 day | 5 mo. |
| Jaine of Anthony Stoddard | 1 day | 6 mo. |
| William of Mr. Hinchman | 1 day | 6 mo. |
| Ann of John Chickly | 8 day | 6 mo. |
| Samuel of John Looell | 8 day | 6 mo. |
| Ann of Tho: Sheares' wife | 22 day | 6 mo. |
| Pitford of Freegrace Bendall | 12 day | Sept. |
| Humphrey of Daniel Turant's wife | 12 day | Sept. |
| Hannah of Edward Davis | 25 day | 7 mo. |
| Simon of Simon Broodstreet | 24 day | 8 mo. |
| John of Samuel Mattock | 24 day | 8 mo. |
| Theodore of Theodore Atkinson Junr | 31 day | 8 mo. |
| Thomas of Mrs. Person | 31 day | 8 mo. |
| Mary of John Cowell's wife | 21 day | 9 mo. |
| Vnion daughter of David Chapin | 19 day | 10 mo. |
| Mary of Sister Brookin | 23 day | 11 mo. |
| John of James Mackwell | 23 day | 11 mo. |
| Deliverance of Sister Knight | 23 day | 11 mo. |
| Joseph of Mr. Saffan | 6 day | 12 mo. |
| Nathaniel of Mary Emins | 13 day | 12 mo. |

## 1670.

### TOWN.

Martha of Angola (negro) & Elizabeth born Apr. 16.
Thomas of Eleazer & Hanna Armitage born Aug. 3.
James of James & Elizabeth Allin born Aug. 20.
John of Hope & Mary Allin born Nov. 24.
Ebenezer of William & Rebecca Allin born Sept. 25.
Mercy of Edward & Patience Blake born Mar. 26.
William of Ambrose & Mary Bennet born May 21.
Thomas of Joseph & Hannah Belknap born June 29.
Samuel of Samuel & Mercy Bosworth born July 9.
Elizabeth of Robert & Elizabeth Butcher born July 29.
Elizabeth of Robert & Bathsheba Bronsden born Aug. 27.
Mary of Robert & Bathsheba Bronsden born Aug. 27.
Rachel of George & Pearne Broughton born Sept. 1.
Ann of Samuel & Martha Bradstreet born Sept. 3.
Elizabeth of John & Elizabeth Barnes born Sept. 7.
James of John & Mary Bohannon born Oct. 20.
Jacob of Jacob & Sarah Bowry born Sept. 15.
Jeremiah of Jeremiah & Anna Bumstead born Nov. 25.
Elizabeth of Nathanll & Judith Blague born Dec. 5.
Edward of Thomas & Elizabeth Brattle born Dec. 18.
Ephraim of Manassah & Mary Beck born Dec. 28.
Mary of Samuel & Sarah Bucknel born Dec. 16.
Hannah of John & Hannah Buttolph born Jan. 15.
Moses of Moses & Eliza. Bradford born Nov. 24.
Newcombe of Phillip & Susanna Blague born Jan. 27.
Alexander of William & Ellener Baker born Feb. 8.
Jeremiah of John & Sarah Buckman born Feb. 5.
Ezekiel of Ezekiel & Rebecca Brisco born Feb. 23.
Elizabeth of Abraham & Abigail Busby born Dec. 27.

Thomas of Thaddeus & Hannah Berry born Sept. 20.
Joanna of William & Ellen Clarke born Aug. 22.
Jonathan of Jona & Margaret Copp born Apr. 6.
Elizabeth of Ralph & Susanna Carter born May 9.
Rebecca of John & Elizabeth Coney born June 18.
Samuel of Samuel & Deborah Clement born July 18.
Sarah of Edward & Sarah Cowell born July 29.
Jeremiah of John & Mary Cotton born July 17.
Elisha of Elisha & Elizabeth Cooke born Aug. 18.
Mary of John & Margaret Coaser born Aug. 22.
Thomas of John & Sarah Clarke born Sept. 22.
Joanna of John & Joanna Carthew born Jan 9.
William of John & Martha Clarke born Dec. 19.
Ebenezer of Timothy & Philippe Cunnell born Feb. 15.
John of John & Mary Chanterell born ult. Feb.
Robert of Robert & Sarah Cooke born Dec. 9.
John of John & Anne Dinsdall born Apr. 20.
Lydia of John and Mary Drury born July 11.
Addington of Eleazer & Rebecca Davenport born Aug. 3.
Mercy of Anthony & Elizabeth Davis born Dec. 12.
Elizabeth of Hicks & Sarah Dannyneg born Dec. 18.
Robert of John & Dorothy Downes born Feb. 10.
Abigail of Joseph & Elizabeth Davis born ——.
Abraham of John & Abiall Davenport born Mar. 18.
Richard of John & Bridget Davenport born Nov. 13.
Joanna of Henry & Joanna Ellis born May 8.
James of Henry & Ursely Edwards born June 2.
David of William & Sarah Eastis born May 31.
John of Thomas & Mary Eldredge born Nov. 12.
James of James & Susanna Ellis born Nov. 23.
Samuel of Robert & Hannah Earle born Mar. 10.
Elizabeth of John & Elizabeth Endecott born Dec. 17.
John of John & Sarah Fayrweather born Apr. 8.
Richard of James & Hannah Flood born June 8.
Thomas of Thomas & Margaret Forbush born July 8.
Prudence of Theophilus & Hannah Frarey born Aug. 23.
Esther of Jeremiah & Sarah Fitch born Sept. 29.
Thomas of John & Susanna Farnham born Sept. 17.
Mehetable of John & Elizabeth Freake born Oct. 5.
Mary of Samuel & Anne Flacke born Mar. 12.
Elizabeth of Richard & Mary George born Apr. 8.
Christian dau. of William & Mary Gard born May 31.
William of William & Sarah Gibson born Mar. 26.
Mehetable of John & Mary Gilbert born Aug. 27.
Patience of Henry & Mary Gidley born Oct. 13.
John of Matthew & Ellener Gross born Sept. 11.
Mary of John & Hannah Greenleafe born Jan. 23.
Thomas of Jonathan & Mary Gatlief born Feb. 10.
William of William & Ruth Greenough born Feb. 20.
Anna of Clement & Anna Gross born Mar. 18.
Mary of Eliphalet & Anne Hill born Apr. 1.
Elizabeth of William & Dorothy Hawkins born Apr. 1.
Richard of Eliakim & Sarah Hutchinson born Apr. 18.
Elizabeth of James & Hannah Hill born June 15.
Margaret of George & Sarah Hollard born June 23.
Mary of John & Joanna Howen born July 4.
Robert of Robert & Sarah Haughton born July 18.
Mary of James & Sarah Hains born July 4.
Hannah of Joseph & Sarah Hurd born Aug. 4.
Ann of William & Anne Hobby born Sept. 9.
Abigail of George & Sarah Hisket born ——.
John of John & Elizabeth Harris born Dec. 27.
Abigail of Thomas & Abigail Hatherly born Sept. 8.
Samuel of George & Hannah Henley born Jan. 9.

William of William & Hannah Hoare born Feb. 1.
Experience of Jabez & Experience Heaton born Nov. 27.
Robert of Israel & Anne Howen born Jan. 1.
Mary of John & Susanna Howlet born Jan. 22.
John of James & Dinah Halsy born Mar. 1.
Nathaniel of John & Rebecca Jarvis born May 25.
Phoebe of Samuel & Phoebe Johnson born Aug. 30.
Mary of Jonathan & Elizabeth Jackson born Dec. 3.
Jacob of Jacob & Elizabeth Jesson born Dec. 18.
Samuel of Samuel & Hannah Johnson born Jan. 24.
Edward of Samuel & Mary Jenkins born Mar. 18.
Rachel of Richard & Julian Knight born May 25.
Thomas of Thomas & Abigail Kellond born July 18.
Solomon of John & Mary Kneeland born Feb. 7.
John of John & Ursula Lawrance born April 16.
Thomas of Symon & Hannah Lynde born May 19.
Rebecca of Thomas & Mary Lake born July 6.
Margaret of Zebulon & Rachel Letherland born July 4.
Sarah of John & Sarah Leveret born June 30.
Samuel of John & Naomi Lowell born Jan. 30.
John of Edmund & Eliza. Mountfort born Mar. 28.
Martha of Peter & Martha Maverick born Feb. 8.
Francis of Samuel & Naomi Moore born July 15.
Elizabeth of Samuel & Constance Mattock born Aug. 18.
Benjamin of John & Sarah Marion born Aug. 25.
Thaddeus of Thaddeus & Eliza. Maccarty born Sept. 12.
Lydia of John & Lydia Mane born Sept. 26.
Rebecca of Return & Sarah Manning born Sept. 21.
Bethiah of John & Grace Matthews born Jan. 2.
John of John & Mary Messenger born Jan. 2.
Bethiah of John & Elizabeth Morse born Jan. 13.
Joseph of John & Sarah Marsh born Feb. 3.
John of Richard & Sarah Mason born Mar. 9.
Anna of John & Kathar Maverick born Sept. 21.
William of William & Susanna Norton born July 8.
Robert of Robert & Mary Noakes born July 10.
Elizabeth of Andrew & Mellicent Neale born Aug. 2.
Abigail of Elisha & Abigail Odlin born April 5
Hannah of John & Susanna Oliver born July 13.
Samuel of Samuel & Mary Peacock born Mar. 26.
Rachel of John & Kesia Perkins born Mar. 27.
Ell: of John & Ruth Pearse born Apr. 15.
Edward of Richard & Abigail Patishall born Apr. 27.
Robert of Robert & Sarah Petty born Apr. 14.
John of Henry & Mary Phillips born July 9.
Samuel of Samuel & Elizabeth Paine born Aug. 26.
John of John & Judith Parmiter born Oct. 31.
Elizabeth of Elias & Sarah Parkman born Dec. 29.
William of John & Deliverance Pollard born Feb. 1.
Ann of Thomas & Esther Platts born Feb. 28.
Tabitha of John & Joanna Porter born Dec. 13.
Hannah of John & Mary Pell born Mar. 24.
Zachariah of Timothy Junr. & Deborah Prout born Mar. 20.
Abigail of Roger & Abigail Rose born Apr. 25.
Nathaniel of Solomon & Priscilla Rainsford born Dec. 28.
Benjamin of John & Christian Roberts born Jan. 8.
Peter of Nathanll & Priscilla Reynolds born Jan. 26.
Ann of Robert & Elizabeth Reynolds born Aug. 11.
Catharine of Bartbo & Eliphal Sutton born Apr. 15.
Richard of Robert & Elizabeth Sandford born Mar. 27.
James of Arthur & Joanna Scovell born June 13.
Benjamin of John & Sarah Sloth born July 11.
William of Richard & Elizabeth Shute born Oct. 1.
John of John & Margaret Selly born Sept. 22.

Sarah of Francis & Mary Skinner born Nov. 24.
Mary of Thomas & Mary Skinner born Oct. 4.
Grace of Christopher & Agnes Skinner born Oct. 30.
Samuel of Joseph & Elizabeth Souther born Dec. 9.
James of William & Martha Smith born Feb. 9.
Samuel of Joseph & Elizabeth Soper horn Oct. 18.
Elizabeth of Stephe 1 & Dorothy Sergeant born Apr. 12.
Mary of Joseph & Sarah Shaw born Mar. 1.
Martha of Samuel & Mary Stocker born Sept. 12.
Elizabeth of Richard & Martha Tewell born Apr. 3.
James of Thomas & Mary Thompson born Apr. 10.
Benjamin of Benjamin & Abigail Thwing born July 24.
Sarah of John & Sarah Tucker born Apr. 19.
Damaris of Bartho & Damaris Thredneedle born Oct. 26.
Ephraim of Ephraim & Sarah Turner born Nov. 23.
Mary of Samuel & Abigail Tompson born Dec. 3.
Sarah of William & Leah Towers born Dec. 12.
Henry of Henry & Mary Taylor born Oct. 12.
Abigail of Benja. & Susanna Thompson horn Nov. 29.
Elizabeth of Jona. & Sarah Tyng born Dec. 28.
John of John & Maria Thwing born Oct. 16.
Henry of Bernard & Mary Trott born Jan. 18.
Abraham of John & Sarah Tuckerman born Dec. 3.
Elizabeth of John & Elizabeth Viali born Apr. 6.
Jonathan of Isaac & Mary Vergoose born July 23.
Nathaniel of Benja. & Rachel Williams born Apr. 13.
Mary of John Jr. & Hannah Wiswall born Apr. 21.
Rebecca of Joseph & Mary Wheler born Apr. 10.
Elizabeth of James & Mary Webster born May 14.
Nathaniel of John & Elizabeth Warren born May 27.
Edward of Edward & Ruth Willis born July 5.
Ann of John & Elizabeth Winslow born Aug. 7.
Martha of William & Mary Whittingham born July 24.
William of William & Mary Whitwell born Sept. 26.
Thomas of Thomas & Ruth Weybourne born Sept. 6.
Mary of John & Anna Williams born Oct. 2.
Elizabeth of John & Elizabeth White born Nov. 25.
Mary of John & Mary Wyborne born Dec. 9.
Mary of Thomas & Mary Waler born Dec. 31.
Robert of Peter & Sarah Warren born Dec. 14.
Samuel of John & Elizabeth Walley born Feb. 1.
Joseph of Thomas & Elizabeth Watkins born Jan. 15.
Joseph of Thomas & Susanna Walker born Feb. 19.
Rebecca of John & Lydia Watts born Feb. 22.
James of William & Johanna Williams born Sept. 18.
Elizabeth of Thomas & Susanna Wagget born Oct. 13.
Joseph of James & Mary Worden born Mar. 21.

### FIRST CHURCH.

| | | |
|---|---|---|
| Samuel of Mrs. Alcock of Ch. of Cambridge | 6 day | 1 mo. |
| Ruth of Joseph How | 6 day | 1 mo. |
| Marah of Samuel Norden | 27 day | 1 mo. |
| Elizabeth of Mrs. Tompson of Ch. of Cambridge | 27 day | 1 mo. |
| Elizabeth of John Viall | 10 day | 2 mo. |
| John of John Clough | 24 day | 2 mo. |
| John of Mary & Hudson Leveret | 8 day | 3 mo. |
| Bezaliell of Mary & Hudson Leveret | 8 day | 3 mo. |
| Mary of Mary & Hudson Leveret | 8 day | 3 mo. |
| Elizabeth of Mrs. Noushzwell | 8 day | 3 mo. |
| Ann of Ann Linde | 22 day | 3 mo. |
| { Joseph of sister Simmons now wife of John Button | 22 day | 3 mo. |
| { Mary of sister Simmons now wife of John Button | 22 day | 3 mo. |

| | | |
|---|---|---|
| Thomas of Sarah & John Fayerweather | 12 day | 4 mo. |
| Penellopye of Sarah & John Fayerweather | 12 day | 4 mo. |
| John of Sarah & John Fayerweather | 12 day | 4 mo. |
| Darlow of Ephraim Turner's wife | 12 day | 4 mo. |
| Robert of Ephraim Turner's wife | 12 day | 4 mo. |
| Sarah of Ephraim Turner's wife | 12 day | 4 mo. |
| Hannah of John Turner's wife | 12 day | 4 mo. |
| Hannah of Mary & John Hill | 12 day | 4 mo. |
| Elizabeth of John Usher | 19 day | 4 mo. |
| Sarah of Mai$^r$ Leveret | 3 day | 5 mo. |
| John of Henry Philips | 10 day | 5 mo. |
| Satisfaction of Mary Belcher | 31 day | 5 mo. |
| Faith of Mary Belcher | 31 day | 5 mo. |
| Mercy of Mary Belcher | 31 day | 5 mo. |
| Lydia of Lydia & John Drury | 31 day | 5 mo. |
| Samuel of John Warrin | 14 day | 6 mo. |
| John of John Warrin | 14 day | 6 mo. |
| Nathaniel of Lydia & Nathaniel Williams | 14 day | 6 mo. |
| James of James Allen Teacher | 21 day | 6 mo. |
| Joseph of Abigail Looell | 21 day | 6 mo. |
| James of Abigail Looell | 21 day | 6 mo. |
| Hannah of Abigail Looell | 21 day | 6 mo. |
| Elizabeth of Constance & James **Mattocke** | 21 day | 6 mo. |
| Hester Lockston aged 20 years | 28 day | 6 mo. |
| Benjamin of John Meriam | 4 day | 7 mo. |
| Temperance of Temperance Smith | | 9 of Oct. |
| Robert of Temperance Smith | | 9 of Oct. |
| Edmund of Elizabeth Mumford | | 9 of Oct. |
| Henry of Elizabeth Mumford | | 9 of Oct. |
| Benjamin of Elizabeth Mumford | | 9 of Oct. |
| John of Elizabeth Mumford | | 9 of Oct. |
| Elizabeth of Elizabeth Mumford | | 9 of Oct. |
| John of Lydia Parmeter | 6 day | 9 mo. |
| John of Hope Allen's wife | 20 day | 9 mo. |
| Moses of Moses Bradford | 26 day | 9 mo. |
| Ephraim of Ephraim Turner's wife | 26 day | 9 mo. |
| Ephraim of Manasse Beck's wife | 1 day | 11 mo. |
| Elizabeth of Abigail & Abram Busby | 1 day | 11 mo. |
| George of Lydia & George Newell | 22 day | 11 mo. |
| Michael of Lydia & George Newell | 22 day | 11 mo. |
| Joseph of Lydia & George Newell | 22 day | 11 mo. |
| Hannah of Lydia & George Newell | 22 day | 11 mo. |
| Peter of Nathl. Renold | 29 day | 11 mo. |
| Lydia of Lydia Millard | 29 day | 11 mo |
| Mary of John Greenleaf's wife | 29 day | 11 mo. |
| Samuel of John Lowell | 5 day | 12 mo. |
| Solomon of John Neeland's wife | 12 day | 12 mo. |
| James of Martha & William Smyth | 12 day | 12 mo. |

## 1671.

### TOWN.

Mehetable of William & Mehetable Avis born Apr. 10.
Benjamin of Nathanll & Mary Adams born May 27.
John of John & Sarah Atwood born May 23.
Edward of Edward & Sarah Allen born July 11.
John of William & Deborah Armstrong born Aug. 11.
Gideon of Gideon & Sarah Allen born Aug. 9.
Thomas of Samuel & Hope Aston born Sept. 12.
Elizabeth of Isaac & Eliza. Addington born Sept. 21.
Edward of Theodore & Elizabeth Atkinson born Sept. 8.

Joseph of Joseph & Rebecca Allen born Jan. 3.
Ruth of John & Martha Amey born Mar. 1.
John of James & Elizabeth Allen born Feb. 29.
Elizabeth of Edward & Lydia Allen born June 23.
Nathaniel of Thomas & Esther Brental born July 31.
John of Thomas & Mary Beard born Mar. 26.
Benjamin of Benja. & Sarah Brisco born May 2.
Martha of Edward & Dorothy Budd born June 19.
Thomas of Phillip & Judith Bullis born Aug. 3.
Martha of Edward Jr. & Mary Belcher born Sept. 15.
William of Stephen & Mary Butler born Oct. 10.
Abigail of John & Elizabeth Brucken born Oct. 8.
Elizabeth of Thomas & Mary Briges born Nov. 21.
John of John & Elizabeth Barnes born Dec. 14.
Roger of Roger & Elizabeth Burges born Dec. 6.
Anna of Josiah & Ramis Belcher born Feb. 13.
John of John & Mary Bull born Mar. 14.
Elizabeth of Joseph & Elizabeth Billing born Jan. 18.
Sarah of Jeremiah & Sarah Belcher born Feb. 23.
Faithful of Faithful & Margaret Bartlett born Sept. 30.
Samuel of David & Obedience Copp born Apr. 15.
David of David & Elizabeth Cumins born Apr. 28.
Hannah of John & Susanna Cross born May 1.
Richard of Richard & Sarah Crisp born May 16.
George of George & Judith Croswait born June 16.
Margaret of John & Esther Crary born Feb. 19.
Ezekiel of Ezekiel & Mary Carveth born July 7.
John of Robert & Martha Cox born Aug. 7.
Margaret of Thomas & Martha Cox born Nov. 3.
John of John & Mary Cotta born Nov. 23.
John of John & Hannah Cowell born Nov. 15.
Mary of William & Elizabeth Coleman born Dec. 3.
Francis of William & Mary Caswell born Dec. 23.
Joseph of Joseph & Hannah Calley born Feb. 18.
Mary of Henry & Rebecca Coolle born Feb. 24.
Elizabeth of John & Elizabeth Coney born Feb. 24.
Nathaniel of Preserved & Deborah Collecot born Feb. 6.
Ebenezer of John & Mary Clough born Dec. 8.
Elizabeth of Joseph & Susannah Cock born Mar. 20.
Edward of Robert & Elizabeth Couch born Mar. 22.
William of John & Susannah Cole born July 13.
Adam of Adam & Hannan Dinsdall born Mar. 29.
Joseph of Leonard & Mercy Dowding born July 23.
John of John & Anne Dinsdall born Aug. 9.
Mary of Humphry & Mary Davie born Nov. 4.
Sarah of James & Francis Dowell born Dec. 1.
William of Ambrose & Mary Daws born Dec. 19.
Robert of Joseph & Abigaile Dudson born Mar. 20.
Rebecca of George & Lydia Ellistone born Apr. 2.
John of Peter & Clemence Egerton born July 19.
Robert of Edward & Sarah Ellis born Sept. 24.
Catharine of Teasant & Sarah Estick born Dec. 12.
Thomas of Benja & Mary Emons born Jan. 4.
Mary of John and Mary Ewell born Mar. 22.
Obadiah of Obadiah & Alice Emons born Nov. 8.
Samuel of Obadiah & Alice Emons born Nov. 8.
Henry of Henry & Mary Floyd born May 20.
Mehetable of John & Mebetahle Frost born July 15.
Mary of Hopestill & Elizabeth Foster born July 22.
Hannah of Tremble & Elizabeth Gridley born Apr. 19.
Elizabeth of Thomas & Dorothy Greshan born Sept. 3
Mary of Nathanll & Mary Greenwood born Sept. 26.
Samuel of Ezekiel & Ruth Gardner born Aug. 1.
Joseph of William & Eliza Greenough born Jan. 22.

Esther of Andrew & Sarah Garner born Dec. 7.
Jacob of Robert & Elizabeth Gibbs born Feb. 18.
John of James & Rebecca Green born Feb. 24.
Nathaniel of William & Mary Hamlen born Mar. 27.
Abigail of Nicholas & Elizabeth Howard born Mar. 25.
Blanton of John & Mary Holman born May 22.
Benjamin of Charles & Margaret Hopkins born July 3.
John ⎫ of John & Joanna Harris born Sept. 17.
George ⎭ of John & Joanna Harris born Sept. 17.
Thomas of Humphrey & Mary Hodges born Sept. 16.
Elizabeth of Henry & Eliza. Harwood born May 17.
Mary of Eliakim & Sarah Hutchinson born Sept 30.
Mary of Thomas & Kathar. Hartwed born Oct. 18.
Mehetable of Joseph & Sarah Hurd born Nov. 19.
Mary of John & Sarah Hollard born Nov. 14.
Samuel of Samuel & Rachel Holman born Dec. 12.
Hannah of Elisha & Hannah Hutchinson born Jan. 20.
John of John & Joanna Hunlock born March 19.
Sarah of John & Sarah Howard born Mar. 21.
John of Joseph & Hannah Holman born June 23.
Elizabeth of James & Joanna Ingles born Oct. 23.
Joanna of James & Anne Johnson born July 6.
John of John & Elizabeth Jackson born Sept. 12.
Sarah of Thomas & Susanna Kelton born May 18.
Samuel of Thomas & Abigail Kellond born Sept. 11.
Elizabeth of Thomas & Elizabeth Kemble born Sept. 8.
Davis of Richard & Joanna Knight born Mar. 15.
William of William & Hannah Long born July 30.
Mary of John & Hannah Liscomb born Aug. 10.
Sarah of Thomas & Mary Lake born Sept. 14.
Richard of Edward & Elizabeth Lillie born Sept. 20.
Henry of Henry & Mercy Lowder born Dec. 7.
Benjamin of John and Agnes Luz born Dec. 29.
Abigail of Joseph & Abigail Lowell born Mar. 9.
Ruth of William & Ruth Mumford born Mar. 26.
Mary of Simeon & Bethiah Messinger born Mar. 25.
Samuel of Samuel & Mary Mason born Apr. 18.
Samuel of Samuel & Anne Mosely born Apr. 18.
Samuel of Samuel & Mary Meers born May 22.
William of John & Eliza. Magdaniel born Sept. 21.
John of George & Hannah Manning born Oct. 11.
Dennis of Dennis & Alice Magdaniel born Nov. 25.
Sarah of Increase & Maria Mather born Nov. 9.
William of Thomas & Elizabeth Mercer born Oct. 19.
Lydia of Richard & Elizabeth Martin born Feb. 8.
William of Nathanll & Deborah Man born Feb. 19.
Robert of James & Elizabeth Meers born Jan. 29.
Daniel of Darmon & Ellener Morris born Feb. 13.
Samuel of Samuel & Martha Maverick born Mar. 16.
Joshua of John & Martha Messenger born Jan. 2.
Hannah of Thomas & Hannah Narramore born Sept. 23.
Joseph of Robert & Mary Noakes born Oct. 16.
Elizabeth of Andrew & Mellicent Neale born Dec. 11.
Mary of William & Susanna Norton born Dec. 15.
Joseph of Joshua & Elizabeth Nash born Feb. 14.
John of John & Rebecca Nash born Mar. 9.
John of John & Joanna Prescot born Mar. 29.
Hannah of Moses & Elizabeth Paine born Apr. 20.
Joseph & ⎫ of Nicholas & Phillippe Phillips born May 14.
Benja. ⎭ of Nicholas & Phillippe Phillips born May 14.
Benjamin of William & Frances Parham born Apr. 30.
Elizabeth of William & Hopestill Pitts born July 5.
Hannah of Zechariah & Elizabeth Phillips born July 31.
William of William & Joane Phillips born Aug. 8.

Samuel of Samuel & Mary Pard born Sept. 25.
Thomas of Benja. & Ellener Phippen born Dec. 1.
Josiah of Timothy & Deborah Pratt born Jan. 11.
Anna of Richard & Elizabeth Price born Jan. 29.
Ellener of James & Sarah Pemberton born Feb. 3.
Mary of Samuel & Mary Prockter born Dec. 22
Sarah of Obadiah & Anna Reed born Apr. 16.
Abigail of Joshua & Abigail Rawlings born May 25.
Judith of Richard & Elizabeth Randall born July 19.
Robert of Nathanll & Damaris Robinson born July 28.
George of Humphry & Mehetable Richards born July 7.
Ruth of John & Hannah Ruggles born Nov. 3.
Margaret of Samuel & Margaret Ruck born Sept. 25.
Hannah of John & Susanna Rainsford born Nov. 15.
Elizabeth of Daniel & Hannah Remington born Oct. 22.
John of John & Elizabeth Russell born Nov. 9.
Nathan of Nathan & Mary Rainsford born Jan. 10.
Sarah of John & Sarah Starkey born Apr. 1.
Mary of Joseph & Ann Stocker born Apr. 10.
William of John & Sarah Snelling born Apr. 9.
James of Loamie & Deborah Simpson born July 13.
Jonathan of John & Sarah Smith born July 5.
Thomas of Thomas & Temperance Smith born July 28.
Thomas of Pilgrim & Catharine Simpkins born May 30.
Henry of Thomas & Judith Snowsell born Aug. 15.
John of Erasmus & Elizabeth Stevens born Aug. 16.
Clement of William & Eliza. Sunner born Sept. 6.
Elizabeth of Jabez & Elizabeth Salter horn Oct. 1.
Ann of John & Ann Sandys born Nov. 2.
Rebecca of Thomas & Rebecca Smith born Nov. 26.
Samuel of Jonathan & Mary Shrimpton born Dec. 10.
Mary of Ephraim & —— Savage born Nov. 19.
Mary of Comfort & Mary Starr born Jan. 18.
Hannah of Richard & Hannah Sharp born Feb. 14.
Samuel of William & Martha Smith born Mar. 6.
Philip of Philip & Rachel Squire born Mar. 20.
Martha of Samuel & Eliza. Shrimpton born Jan. 21.
Elizabeth of John & Ellener Shern born Feb. 9.
Ann of John & Ann Soames born Nov. 2.
John of Stephen & Hannah Tolby born May 4.
Nathaniel of Nathaniel & Deborah Thayer born Aug. 28.
Dorothy of Henry & Eliza. Tompson born Oct. 26.
Peter of Peter & Lydia Townsend born Oct. 9.
Rebecca of John & Sarah Tomlin born Dec. 8.
Elizabeth of Thomas & Mary Thatcher born Dec. 26.
Jonathan of Jonathan & Sarah Tyng born Jan. 29.
William of William & Mary Whittingham born Nov. 9.
Lydia of Samuel & Joanna Ward horn Mar. 30.
Jonathan of Lawrance & Hannah Waters born May 2.
Mary of William & Abigail Wright born May 17.
Rebecca of James & Rebecca Whetcomb born June 20.
Sarah of Richard & Sarah Wharton born Aug. 7.
Rachel of Thomas & Esther Woodward born.
Sarah of John & Mary White born Aug. 16.
Mary of Joseph & Grace Webb born Aug. 27.
Elizabeth of John & Joshabeth Wing born Sept. 19.
Mary of John & Anstis Williams born Sept 18.
William of Joseph & Mary Wheler born Sept. 26.
Thomas of John & Jane Williams born Oct. 22.
Hannah of Robert & Hannah Wacum born Nov. 15.
Martha of Lionel & Abigail Wheatly born Nov. 15.
Sarah of Bartho. & Amey Whitwell born Dec. 6.
Lydia of Joseph & Lydia Williams born Dec. 13.
Benjamin of Thomas & Hannah Wheeler born Jan. 18.
Mary of William & Mary Whitwell born Feb. 6.

## First Church.

| | | |
|---|---|---|
| Mary of sister Bucknell | 5 day | 1 mo. |
| Abram of Mr John Davenport | 19 day | 1 mo. |
| Comfort of sister Mary Starr | 19 day | 1 mo. |
| Mary of sister Mary Cotte | 19 day | 1 mo. |
| Mary of John Andrewes' wife | 9 day | 2 mo. |
| Samuel of David Copp | 16 day | 2 mo |
| Ruth of sister Ruth Mumford | 16 day | 2 mo. |
| Sarah Howard | 23 day | 2 mo. |
| Elizabeth Gross | 23 day | 2 mo. |
| Anna Gridly | 23 day | 2 mo. |
| Samuel of sister Ruth Bosworth | 7 day | 3 mo. |
| Sara of sister Sara Tucker | 7 day | 3 mo. |
| Lydia Moore, mother | 14 day | 3 mo. |
| Lydia of Lydia Moore | 14 day | 3 mo. |
| Elizabeth Lawson | 14 day | 3 mo. |
| Elizabeth of sister Foster | 14 day | 3 mo. |
| Thomas of sister Mary Wibourne | 28 day | 3 mo. |
| Mary of sister Mary Wibourne | 28 day | 3 mo. |
| Mary of sister Tewksberry | 18 day | 4 mo. |
| James of James Townesend | 2 day | 5 mo. |
| John of Elizabeth & John Skinner | 9 day | 5 mo. |
| Joseph of Elizabeth & John Skinner | 9 day | 5 mo. |
| Mary of Elizabeth & John Skinner | 9 day | 5 mo. |
| Mary of sister Elizabeth Foster | 23 day | 5 mo. |
| Thomas of sister Smyth | 30 day | 5 mo. |
| William of sister Long | 6 day | 6 mo. |
| William of sister Grace Webb | 6 day | 6 mo. |
| Elizabeth of sister Grace Webb | 6 day | 6 mo. |
| Henry of sister Mrs Knozell | 20 day | 6 mo. |
| Richard of sister Experience Miles | 20 day | 6 mo. |
| Mary of sister Mary Hewes | 20 day | 6 mo. |
| Ann of sister Mary Hewes | 20 day | 6 mo. |
| Mary of sister Elizabeth Weeb | 3 day | 7 mo. |
| Martha of sister Belcher | 17 day | 7 mo. |
| Thomas of sister Mary Butolph widow | 1 day | 8 mo. |
| Mary of sister Mary Butolph widow | 1 day | 8 mo. |
| Abigail of sister Mary Butolph widow | 1 day, | 8 mo. |
| Nicholas of sister Mary Butolph widow | 1 day | 8 mo. |
| Elizabeth of Elizabeth & Isaac Addington | 1 day | 8 mo. |
| Edward of Theodore Atkinson Junior | 1 day | 8 mo. |
| Robert of Robert Ellis' wife | 1 day | 8 mo. |
| Abigail of John Brookin | 15 day | 8 mo. |
| John of George Maninge | 15 day | 8 mo. |
| Dorothy of Henry Thomson | 29 day | 8 mo. |
| Mary of Humphrey Davie | 5 day | 9 mo. |
| Ruth of John Ruggles husband to our sister Ruggles sometime wife of Nicholas Phillips | 5 day | 9 mo. |
| Hazelelponi Gee | 19 day | 9 mo. |
| John of sister Cowell | 19 day | 9 mo. |
| John of sister Clerke | 19 day | 9 mo. |
| Mary of sister Clerke | 19 day | 9 mo. |
| Elizabeth of sister Clerke | 19 day | 9 mo. |
| John of John Cottie | 26 day | 9 mo. |
| Lydia of sister Williams Junior | 24 day | 10 mo. |
| Mary of sister Starre | 81 day | 10 mo. |

## 1672.

### Town.

Mackworth of Abraham & Hannah Adams born Apr. **17.**
Hannah of David & Hannah Adams born Apr. 23.
Elizabeth of Edward & Lydia Allen born Mar. 21.
Johnathan of Jonathan & —— Adams born May 29.
John of Theodore Sen. & Mary Atkinson born June **13.**
James ⎱ of Hope & Hannah Allen born Sept. 6.
Eliza. ⎰ of Hope & Hannah Allen born Sept. 6.
Sarah of William & Mehetable Avis born Oct. 15.
John of Henry & Mary Adams born Dec. 12.
Abigail of Theodore Junr & Eliza. Atkinson born Dec. **13.**
Elizabeth of Samuel & Sarah Alcock born Dec. 25.
Zachariah of John & Elizabeth Alden born Feb. 18.
Elizabeth of Thomas & Mary Atkins born Dec. 30.
William of John & Mary Briggs born Aug. 28.
Timothy of Timothy & Abigail Batt born Apr. 20.
Samuel of Samuel & Hannah Bridge born May 10.
Mary of Richard & Eliza. Barnum born May 7.
John of Joseph & Hannah Belknap born June 1.
Hannah of Samuel & Mary Brown born June 14.
Robert of Robert & Priscilla Blumford born June 21.
Peter of James & Hannah Brading born May 5.
Mercy of Benja & Bathshua Beale born July 17.
Mary of George & Perne Broughton born Aug. 10.
Joseph of Robert & Bathsieba Bronsden born Aug. 7.
Zaccheus of Samuel & Mary Bosworth born Aug. 2.
Benjamin of Ambrose & Mary Bennit born Oct. 2.
Sarah of Benja. & Hannah Breeme born Oct. 15.
Jane of Richard & Anne Burges born Nov. 2.
Moremercy dau. of Free Grace & Mary Bendall born July **30.**
Love of William & Elizabeth Baker born Dec. 16.
Elizabeth of John & Elizabeth Barnes born Dec. 7.
Thomas of Thomas & Susanna Bingley born Jan. 1.
James of James & Mehetable Bill born Nov. 23.
Manassah of Manassah & Mary Beck born Feb. 23.
Nathaniel of Nathanll & Judith Blake born Feb. 26.
John of Thomas & Esther Brental born Mar. 3.
Elizabeth of Anthony & Hannah Checkley born May **8.**
John of John & Mary Cox born May 12.
Mary of John & Mary Chanterel born May 24.
Thomas of Andrew & Mehetable Clarke born July **10.**
Moses of Jona. & Margaret Copp born June 19.
Edward of Edward & Sarah Cowell born Aug. 12.
Nathaniel of John & Sarab Clarke born Sept. 22.
Sarah of Richard & Sarah Crisp born Sept. 15.
Hannah of John & Hannah Cowell born Nov. 2.
Mary of Josiah & Deborah Cobbet born Oct. 29.
Samuel of John & Margaret Courser born Nov. 5.
David of David & Elizabeth Cumins born Oct. 30.
Sarah of Robert & Sarah Cooke born Mar. 10.
Joseph of Joseph & Mary Cowell born Mar. 7.
Elisha of Roger & Ann Doubleday born Apr. 5.
John of John & Bridget Davenport born June **13.**
Priscilla of Edward & Susanna Darby born June **20.**
Mary of John & Mary Drury born July 10.
Abigail of John & Abigail Davenport born Aug. 20.
Hannah of Henry & Hannai Deddicot born Oct. 23.
Thomas of Abraha: & Hannah Darby born Jan. **16.**
Peter of Peter & Clemence Edgerton born Oct. **6.**

William of Henry & Ursely Edwards born Nov. 28.
Thomas of Thomas & Mary Eldridge born Dec. 28.
Hannah of Samuel & Mary Emons born Mar. 1.
Lydia of Henry & Joanna Ellis born Mar. 10.
Elizabeth of Thomas & Margaret Farbush born Apr. 17.
Joanna of Benja. & Kathar. Francklin born July 12.
Lydia of James & Hannah Flood born July 10.
Elizabeth of John & Dorothy Foy born Sept. 21.
Thomas of John & Elizabeth Freeke born Nov. 29.
Susanna of Believe & Anne Gridley born Apr. 10.
Penelope of John & Mary Gilbert born May 5.
Esther of John & Mary Green born June 10.
Priscilla of John & Priscilla Green born Sept. 2.
Hannah of Thomas & Elizabeth Gross born Aug. 21.
Thomas of James & Mehetable Goodin born Oct. 20.
Walter of Thomas & Catharine Goodridge born Dec. 15.
Ann of Matthew & Ellener Gross born Jan. 5.
John of John & Hannah Greenleafe born Feb. 10.
Dionysia of Benja. & Hannah Gillam born Feb. 8.
John of William & Ruth Greenough born Feb. 17.
Benjamin of Benjamin & Lydia Gibbs born Feb. 26.
William of William & Hannah Harris born March 25.
Thomas of Thomas & Mary Hutchinson born March 25.
Sarah of Robert & Sarah Horton born April 27.
Ruth of Thomas & Ruth Hitchborn born June 22.
Naomi of John & Hannah Henley born July 27.
John of William & Dorothy Hawkins born Aug. 7.
Benjamin of John & Mary Homan born Aug. 14.
Thomas of John & Mary Hayward born Oct. 27.
Mercy of William & Anne Hobby born Oct. 4.
Bethiah of Josiah & Mary Hobart born Oct. 5.
Mary of Francis & Sarah Haselwood born Nov. 16.
Thomas of John & Johanna Howen born Dec. 15.
Sarah of Joshua & Hannah Hewes born Jan. 4.
Samuel of John & Abigail Howlet born Feb. 6.
Sarah of John & Elizabeth Hopper born Nov. 2.
Katharine of Elisha & Han: Hutchinson born Feb. 24.
George of George & Sarah Hiskett born Mar. 11.
Deliverance of Henry & Lydia Ingram born Oct. 5.
Rebecca of John & Rebecca Jarvis born Apr. 17.
Thomas of Thomas & Abigail Jolls born Apr. 25.
Sarah of Samuel & Phebe Johnson born June 10.
Sarah of John & Sarah Johnson born June 11.
Abraham of Jacob & Elizabeth Jesson born July 14.
Edmund of Edmund & Eliza. Jackson born Aug. 2.
John of John & Mercy Jaye born Sept. 30.
Jotham of John & Elizabeth Jones born Oct. 9.
Jonathan of Jonathan & Eliza. Jackson born Dec. 28.
Mary of Samuel & Hannah Johnson born Jan. 10.
Dinah of Joseph & Mary Knight born May 15.
Timothy of Henry & Mary Kemble born Aug. 29.
Mary of John & Rachel King born Dec. 19.
Rebecca of Richard King born Jan. 23.
Thomas of Francis & Elizabeth Lyford born Mar. 25.
Sarah of Simon & Hannah Lynde born May 5.
William of William & Naomi Lowle born Aug. 7.
Nicholas of Nicholas & Gartered Lash born Sept. 2.
Sibella of Samuel & Deliverance Legg born Sept. 2.
Jonathan of William & Hannah Long born Sept. 21.
Phillip of Richard & Elizabeth Loft born Nov. 13.
William of Zibeon & Rachel Letherland born Mar. 5.
Samuel of Samuel & Hannah Minot born Apr. 26.
Sarah of Edward & Eliza. Mumford born Apr. 22.
Joseph of John & Ruth Marshall born Apr. 14.

John of Francis & Ann Morse born June 6.
Nicholas of Nicholas & Christian Molder born June 21.
Joseph of John & Mary Mann born June 30.
Sarah of John & Martha Messenger born Oct. 1.
Lydia of William & Ruth Mumford born Nov. 17.
Mehetable of Samuel & Constance Mattock born Nov. 7.
Elizabeth of John & Abigail Muberry born Nov. 16.
Jane of John & Jane Matson born Feb. 2.
Elizabeth of William & Eliza. Middleton born Feb. 11.
Susanna of Michael & Susanna Martin born July 3.
Sarah of John & Sarah Noyes born Aug. 20.
Sarah of Thomas & Hannah Narramore born Sept. 26.
Lydia of George & Lydia Nowell born Nov. 1.
Isaac of Samuel & Eliza. Norden born Mar. 8.
Mary of John & Susanna Oliver born June 3.
John & ⎫ of John & Elizabeth Osborne born June 11.
Thomas ⎭ of John & Elizabeth Osborne born June 11.
Margaret of Elisha & Abigail Odlin born Aug. 5.
John of John & Sarah Orris born Aug. 5.
Elizabeth of Peter & Hannah Odlin born Nov. 9.
Hannah of Samuel & Mary Peacock born July 20.
Judith of John & Judith Parmiter born July 17.
Rebecca of John & Ruth Pearse born Aug. 12.
Elizabeth of Walter & Elizabeth Poor born Aug. 22.
Elizabeth of Henry & Mary Phillips born Aug. 29.
William of William & Eliza Parker born Nov. 10.
Mary of John & Joanna Fricot born Nov. 20.
Humility of Edward & Elizabeth Paige born Jan. 7.
Elizabeth of Thomas & Elizabeth Peck born Feb. 6.
Tabitha of Robert & Rose Pegge born Feb. 27.
Elizabeth of Nicholas & Philippa Phillips born June 5.
Elizabeth of Samuel & Elizabeth Rust born Apr. 4.
Michael of William & Elizabeth Robins born June 8.
Prudence of Edward & Sarah Ranger born Nov. 5.
Joseph of Simon & Christian Robarts born Jan. 24.
Anna of Obadiah & Anna Reed born Feb. 3.
Mary of Christo. & Dorcas Smith born Feb. 8.
Anthony of Sampson & Susanna Stoddard born May 24.
Deborah of Laomi & Deborah Simpson born May 31.
Benjamin of John & Martha Saffin born June 15.
Rebecca of John & Rebecca Scottow born June 27.
Abiel of John & Hannah Styles born July 18.
Elizabeth of John Junr & Sarah Shaw born Aug. 9.
Benjamin of John & Sarah Snelling born Aug. 18.
Samuel of Thomas & Temperance Smith born Aug. 23.
Elizabeth of John & Elizabeth Skinner born Oct. 6.
Abigail of Thomas & Susanna Stanbury born Oct. 26.
Jacob of Fearnot & Bethiah Shaw born Nov. 6.
Martha of Joseph & Ann Stocker born Dec. 25.
Frances of Edward & Elizabeth Shippen born Feb. 2.
Experience of John & Sarah Starkey born Feb. 3.
Samuel of Samuel & Mary Stocker born Mar. 28.
Thomas of Thomas & Ann Shapcot born July 9.
Mary of Daniel & Anna Turell born Apr. 4.
Lydia of Benjamin & Abigail Twing born Jan. 25.
John of John & Sarah Tucker born Aug. 22.
Elizabeth of Ephraim & Sarah Turner born Aug. 19.
Mary of William & Mary Thorn born Oct. 2.
Rebecca of Joseph & Dorothy Townsend born Oct. 13.
John ⎫ of Bradish Thayer born Oct. 3.
Susanna ⎭ of Bradish Thayer born Oct. 3.
Susanna of Thomas & Mary Townsend born Nov. 5.
John of James & Eliza. Townsend born Dec. 14.
**Anna of Samuel & Abiga. Townsend born Jan. 30.**

Matthew of Edward & Jane Uren born Nov. 16.
Mary of Isaac & Mary Vergoose born May 22.
John of John Junr & Mary Viall born Sept. 14.
Lydia of Thomas & Mary Varney born Oct. 6.
William of William & Constant Woster born May 7.
Martha of Robert & Margaret Williams born May 21.
Mercy of Dean & Sarah Winthrop born Jan. 18.
Katharine of Edward & Eliza. Winslow born June 2.
Martha of John & Mary Williams born Apr. 23.
Moses of Aaron & Joane Way born June 13.
Joseph of Richard & Bathsheba Williams born Dec. 3.
Bethiah of Richard & Sarah Wharton born Sept. 18.
Thomas of Isaac & Dorcas Woodde born Sept. 9.
Mary of Experience & Elizabeth Willis born Oct. 9.
Edward ⎫ of Edward & Ruth Willis born Nov. 5.
John　⎭ of Edward & Ruth Willis born Nov. 5.
Nathaniel of John & Ann Williams born Nov. 11.
Samuel of Peter & Mehetable Welcom born Oct. 15.
William of Thomas & Mary Waler born Dec. 20.
Mary of James & Mary Webster born Dec. 9.
William of Joshua & Sarah Winsor born Nov. 26.
William of William & Abigail Wright born Jan. 5.
John of Sampson & Rebecca Waters born Jan. 2.
Benjamin of Thomas & Elizabeth Walker born Jan. 2.
Benjamin of Benjamin & Ruth Williams born Jan. 2.
Richard of Joseph & Eliza Williams born Feb. 8.
Susanna of Isaac & Susanna White born Feb. 12.
Ebenezer of Peter & Sarah Warren born Feb. 11.
Jonathan of Jonathan & Abiga Woodberry born Feb. 22
Jonathan of Thomas & Ruth Wybourn born Mar. 19.
Joseph of John &. Eliza. White born Feb. 19.
Thomas of John & Eliza. Walley born Feb. 26.
Susanna of Giles & Ruth Young born July 5.

## FIRST CHURCH.

| | | |
|---|---|---|
| John Allen of our Teacher | 3 day | 1 mo. |
| Samuel of Wm. Smith | 10 day | 1 mo. |
| Robert of sister Dudson | 24 day | 1 mo. |
| Elizabeth of Edward Allen | 24 day | 1 mo. |
| Philip of sister Squire | 24 day | 1 mo. |
| A Child of John Violl | 14 day | 2 mo. |
| Ephraim of sister Phebe Egland | 14 day | 2 mo. |
| A child of sister Belshur of Rumney Marsh or Wenysement | 14 day | 2 mo. |
| A Child of sister Franckes | 28 day | 2 mo. |
| A Child of sister Faireweather | 28 day | 2 mo. |
| A child of | 28 day | 2 mo. |
| A child of Samuel Brugge | 12 day | 3 mo. |
| A child of bro Maxwell named —— | 12 day | 3 mo. |
| Child of Mary & Joseph Knight | 19 day | 3 mo. |
| Mary of Hannah Lynde | 26 day | 3 mo. |
| Martha of Robt. Williams | 26 day | 3 mo. |
| John of John Temple, buried 9 day 4 mo. | 2 day | 4 mo. |
| Hester of sister Greene | 17 day | 4 mo. |
| Moro-Mercy of Freegrace Bendall | 30 day | 4 mo. |
| Mary of sister Drywry the younger | 7 day | 5 mo. |
| Lydia of sister Permiter | 21 day | 5 mo. |
| Edmund of Edmund Jackson | 4 day | 6 mo. |
| Edward of sister Cowell | 18 day | 6 mo. |
| William of bro Lowell | 18 day | 6 mo. |
| Elizabeth of bro Phillips | 18 day | 6 mo. |
| Martha Walner | 18 day | 6 mo. |

| | | |
|---|---|---|
| John of sister Tucker | 25 day | 6 mo. |
| Elizabeth daughter[1] | 25 day | 6 mo. |
| Zechaus of our sister Bosworth | 25 day | 6 mo. |
| Thomas of sister Walner | 25 day | 6 mo. |
| Mary of sister Walner | 25 day | 6 mo. |
| Child of sister Smith | 1 day | 7 mo. |
| Abigail of John Davenport | 15 day | 7 mo. |
| Jonathan of sister Temperance Smith | 22 day | 7 mo. |
| Elizabeth of Sister —— | 16 day | 8 mo. |
| Lydia Mumforth | 17 day | 9 mo. |
| Mehetabel Mattocke | 17 day | 9 mo. |
| Ebenezer of brother Clough | 24 day | 9 mo. |
| Ruth of sister Chapin | 1 day | 10 mo. |
| John of sister Darby | 8 day | 10 mo. |
| Sara of sister Darby | 8 day | 10 mo. |
| Sara of sister Messinger | 8 day | 10 mo. |
| Abigail of sister Atkinson the younger | 15 day | 10 mo. |
| —— of James Townsend | 15 day | 10 mo. |
| Mary of sister Starkie | 29 day | 10 mo. |
| Sarai of sister Starkie | 29 day | 10 mo. |
| —— of —— | 29 day | 10 mo. |
| —— —— | 29 day | 10 mo. |
| —— of sister Waller | 22 day | 10 mo. |
| Sarai of sister Hewes | 5 day | 11 mo. |
| —— of bro. Norden | 5 day | 11 mo. |
| Jo —— & Jo —— sons of sister Gatline | 5 day | 11 mo. |
| —— son of sister Ruggles | 12 day | 11 mo. |
| Elizabeth of sister Alcocke | 26 day | 11 mo. |
| John of sister Greeneleaffe | 16 day | 12 mo. |
| Robert of Moyses Bradford | 16 day | 12 mo. |
| Hannah Maninge of sister Dinsdale | 23 day | 12 mo. |
| Adam Dinsdale of sister Dinsdale | 23 day | 12 mo. |
| John of sister Lowell | 23 day | 12 mo. |

## 1673.

### Town.

Jeremiah of James & Eliza. Allen born Mar. 29.
Benjamin of Joshua & Mary Atwater born May 16.
James of John & Sarah Atwood born June 3.
John of Edward & Lydia Allen born June 10.
Isaac of Nathanll & Mary Adams born Nov. 7.
Judith of Henry & Judith Allen born Nov. 26.
Eleazer of Timothy & Joanna Armitage born Feb. 18.
Theodore of Theodore Senr. & Mary Atkinson born Feb. 28.
Rebecca of Jonathan & Rebecca Adams born Mar. 9.
Barnabas of Timothy & Abigaile Batt born Apr. 14.
James of James & Hopestill Barnes born Apr. 6.
Robert of Moses & Eliza. Bradford born Feb. 12.
Mary of Thomas & Mary Beard born May 25.
Samuel of John & Hannah Buttolph born May 18.
Hannah of Joseph & Hannah Belknap born June 8.
Jane of Edward & Dorothy Budd born July 25.
Edward of George & Pearne Broughton born Oct. 12.
Hannah of Samuel & Hannah Bridge born Oct. 22.
Nathaniel of Jeremiah & Sarah Belcher born Oct. 27
Dorothy of Josiah & Ranis Belcher born Oct. 28.
Elizabeth of Joseph & Elizabeth Baster born Dec. 24.

---

[1] This should refer to Tucker or Bosworth; but the record is so bad as to leave it uncertain. — W. B. A.

Mary of Ezekiel & Rebecca Brisco born Dec. 17.
Sarah of Paul & Sarah Batt born Jan. 18.
John of John & Susanna Barnet born Dec. 15.
John of John & Elizabeth Baster born Dec. 1.
Rachel of Phillip & Judith Bullis born Sept. 28.
Benjamin of Phillip & Susanna Blague born Mar. 13.
Esther of Roger & Elizabeth Burges born Mar. 16.
Henry of John & Mary Bull born Mar. 12.
Joseph of Thomas & Esther Brental born Mar. 3.
Free Grace of Free Grace & Mary Bendall born Feb. 10.
Mary of John & Joanna Carthew born Mar. 27.
Robert of Persival & Elizabeth Clarke born Apr. 20.
Martha of Robert & Martha Cox born June 4.
John of David & Obedience Copp born June 9.
John of John & Mary Chrismas born June 12.
Joseph of John & Mary Chanterel born June 9.
John of Elisha & Elizabeth Cooke born July 11.
Margaret of Edward & Sarah Cowell born Aug. 2.
Mary of John & Mary Clough born Aug. 7.
Joseph of Joseph & Susanna Cock born Sept. 5.
Benjamin of John & Elizabeth Coney born Oct. 16.
Mary of Anthony & Hannah Checkley born Oct. 14.
Hannah of Samuel & Deborah Clement born Nov. 5.
Samuel of John & Martha Clarke born Nov. 10.
Benjamin of William & Elizabeth Coleman born Oct. 19.
Richard of Preserved & Deborah Collecot born Oct. 29.
Joshua of John & Mary Cotta born Nov. 10.
John of Richard & Jane Cleare born Feb. 10.
Jonathan of Jona. & Margaret Copp born Apr. 6.
John of William & Mary Castle born Feb. 11.
Susanna of Andrew & Mehetable Clarke born Mar. 12.
John of Henry & Rebecca Cowley born Feb. 13.
Thomas of Thomas & Martha Cox born Mar. 24.
Susanna of John & Susanna Cross born Nov. 27.
Roger of John & Esther Crary born Apr. 20.
Sarah of Adam & Hannah Dinsdall born Apr. 6.
Cornelius of Samuel & Sarah Davis born Apr. 1.
Humphry of Humphry & Mary Davie born June 10.
Leonard of Leonard & Mercy Dowding born July 18.
Susanna of John & Ann Dinsdall born Oct. 10.
Thomas of John & Mary Dyer born Sept. 18.
George of Samuel & Deborah Davis born Oct. 25.
Hannah of Stephen & Sarah Davis born Oct. 25.
Elizabeth of Joseph & Elizabeth Davis born Nov. 8.
Susanna of Ambrose & Mary Dawse bord Jan. 11.
Jethro of Roger & Ann Doubleday born Oct. 25.
George of Joseph & Elizabeth Dell born Jan. 25.
Mary of Jeremiah & Ann Dummer born Mar. 14.
Joseph of Joseph & Abigail Davis born March 23.
Thomas of Thomas & Ann Dean born Mar. 18.
Henry of Henry & Elizabeth Emes born May 4.
Jacob of Jacob & Mary Eliot born Apr. 16.
Robert ⎱ of Robert & Hannah Earle born May 15.
Roger ⎰ of Robert & Hannah Earle born May 15.
Susanna of James & Susanna Ellis born May 25.
Samuel of Samuel & Mary East born Sept. 26.
Rebecca of Benja. & Mary Emons born Dec. 23.
Phoebe of William & Phoebe Eglon born Mar. 17.
Samuel of Theophilus & Hannah Frarey born May 13.
Benjamin of Samuel & Anne Flack born May 23.
Martha of Thomas & Margt. Forbush born Aug. 22
Abigail of Daniel & Sarah Fairfield born Feb. 22.
Jonathan of Henry & Mary Floyd born Mar. 16.
James of James & Jane Fryer born Mar. 3.

Hannah of William & Hannah Gibson born May 5.
Lydia of Henry & Mary Gibs born July 3.
Ann of Joseph & Martha Gillam born July 15.
Thomas of Thomas & Dorothy Gretian born Aug. 30.
James of John & Emm Gypson born Sept. 20.
Elizabeth of Peter & Sarah Goulding born Oct. 6.
Mary of Samuel & Mary Greenwood born Dec. 30.
Joseph of Jonathan & Mary Gatleife born Feb. 15.
Sarah of Nathanll. & Mary Greenwood born Feb. 24.
Elizabeth of Thomas & Elizabeth Gross born Jan. 22.
William of Daniel & Mary Henchman born Mar. 29.
James of James & Sarah Harris born Apr. 4.
Joseph of John & Joanna Harris born Mar. 25.
John of Humphrey & Sarah Horrell born Apr. 8.
Nathll of Humphrey & Sarah Horrell born Apr. 8.
Sarah of John & Eliza. Harris born Apr. 14.
Samuel of William & Hannah Hoare born May 6.
Mary of Thomas & Abiga. Hatherly born May 11.
Mary of James & Mary Harrington born May 19.
John of John & Mary Hill born June 2.
Elizabeth of James & Dinah Halsey born June 24.
William of Samuel & Abigail Hudson born June 22.
Sarah of John & Sarah Horton born June 30.
Rebecca of George & Mary Hooper born July 29.
Elizabeth of Reuben & Hannah Hull born Sept. 9.
Sarah of John & Joanna Hunlock horn Sept. 10.
William of William & Dorothy Hawkins born Sept. 8.
Sarah of Eliakim & Sarah Hutchinson born Oct. 15.
Mary of John & Ann Hubbard born Oct. 25.
Elizabeth of Charles & Mcbetable Hopkins born Oct. 22.
Lydia of William & Lydia Huff born Nov. 14.
Michael of Timothy & Kathar. Hortman born Nov. 29.
Thomas of William & Decline Hollowell born Oct. 1.
Mary of Joseph & Sarah Hurd born Feb. 17.
Thomas of Robert & Joanna Harwood born Jan 31.
Henry of Henry & Eliza. Harwood born Jan. 2.
Thomas of Thomas & Ruth Hitchborn born Mar. 23.
Henry of Henry & Lydia Ingram born Nov. 1.
Hannah of Samuel & Mercy Jacklin born Apr. 5.
Elizabeth of John & Eliza. Jackson born Aug. 24.
Elizabeth of Samuel & Eliza. Judkin born Sept. 6.
Mary of Aaron & Mary Jeffords born Dec. 4.
Michael of Robert & Elizabeth Judd born Feb. 12.
Ruth of John & Mary Kneeland born July 30.
Elizabeth of Thomas & Abigail Kellond born Aug. 14.
Hannah of Thomas & Susanna Kellon born Sept. 19.
Sarah of John Esq & Sarah Leveret born June 15.
Elizabeth of Francis & Elizabeth Lyford born July 19.
Hannah of William & Hannah Long born Jan. 25.
John of Samuel & Decline Legg born Mar. 1.
Elizabeth of John & Naomi Lowell born Mar. 1.
Enoch of Simon & Hannah Lynde born Jan. 27.
Samuel of Samuel & Hannah Minot born Mar. 31.
Hannah of Edmund & Eliza. Mountfort born Apr. 14.
Bartholomew of John & Sarah Marsh born July 3.
Sarah of John & Lydia Moore born July 19.
Rachel of Henry & Rachel Mattock born July 24.
John of John & Elizabeth Morse born Aug. 28.
Mary of Samuel & Mary Meers born Nov. 26.
Mary of Samuel & Constance Mattock born Nov. 13.
Oliver of James & Elizabeth Meers born Dec. 3.
Samuel of Jeremiah & Sarah Merils born Dec. 10.
Mary of James & Margery Maxwell born Jan. 25.
John of John & Abigail Mulberry born Jan. 28.

John of Samuel & Mary Mason born Jan. 29.
Andrew of Oliver & Patty Mansfield born Feb. 17..
Huldah of Francis & Anne Morse born March 7.
Robert of Robert & Mary Noakes born Oct. 13.
Elizabeth of John & Elizabeth Osborne born Dec. 25.
John of John & Elizabeth Pole born Apr. 14.
John of Benja. & Ellener Phippen born June 1.
Edeth of Thomas & Esther Platts born June 11.
Ann of Robert & Mary Peard born July 9.
Mary of Nehemiah & Phoebe Pearse bore Aug. 21.
William of William & Eliza. Pickram born Aug. 24.
Samuel of William & Love Prout born Sept. 16.
Jonathan of Samuel & Mary Peacock born Oct. 15.
Edward of William & Elizabeth Porter born Dec. 20.
Mary of Samuel & Mary Pollard born Nov. 22.
Samuel of Samuel & Mary Pearse born Jan. 28.
Martha of Richard & Martha Patteshal born Jan. 31.
Mary of Humphry & Mehetable Richards born Apr. 9.
Solomon of Solomon & Priscilla Rainsford born May 14.
Andrew of Samuel & Margaret Ruck born Aug. 31.
Thomas of Caleb & Eliza. Rawlings born Sept. 15.
Thomas of John & Eliza. Russell born Sept. 15.
Samuel of Samuel & Sarah Ruggles born Oct. 1.
Mary of John & Charity Ricks born Jan. 13.
Ann of Richard & Elizabeth Randall born Feb. 18.
Jonathan of John & Susan Rainsford born Feb. 25.
Margaret of John & Margaret Selley born Mar. 25.
James of Sampson Negro & Susan his wife born Mar. 25.
Aeneas of Aeneas & Joane Salter born Apr. 7.
Mary of Ephraim & Mary Savage born Apr. 8.
Samuel of Samuel & Eliza. Shrimpton born Apr. 20.
Thomas of Robert & Elizabeth Sanford born Apr. 27.
Thomas of Joseph & Mary Shaw born Apr. 17.
Hannah of Ephraim & Alice Searle born May 15.
Phoebe of John & Mary Smith born June 27.
Benjamin of Joseph & Mary Swett born July 12.
Joseph of Benja. & Mercy Sanderson born Mar. 4.
Mary of Jabez & Elizabeth Salter born Aug. 28.
Jane of Christo. & Dorcas Smith born Aug. 27.
Samuel of John & Sarah Stanbridge born 15 ————.[1]
Mary of Rossemus & Elizabeth Stevens born ————.[1]
Lydia of John & Elizabeth Scott born ————.[1]
Hannah of John & Hannah Soames born ————.[1]
Philip of Philip & Margaret Stratton born ————.[1]
William of William & Catharine Simpkins born ————.[1]
Mary of Joseph & Elizabeth Soper born Dec. 1.
Sibella of John & Ann Sands born Oct. 22.
Deborah of John & Maria Thwing born Mar. 29.
James of Bartho. & Damaris Thredneedle born Apr. 17.
John of John & Elizabeth Tuder born Feb. 12.
Deliverance of Ephraim & Sarah Turner born Aug. 1.
Lydia of Peter & Lydia Townsend born Aug. 5.
John of Jona. & Sarah Tyng born Sept. 1.
Mary of William & Leah Towers born Sept. 2.
Mary of William & Mary Timberlake born Sept. 15.
Hannah of Walter & Hannah Thomas born Sept. 23.
Silvanus of George & Tabitha Tankersly born Sept. 24.
Thomas of Thomas & Mary Thatcher born Sept. 25.
Henry of Henry & Elizabeth Tompson born Oct. 23.
Samuel of John & Sarah Tucker born Dec. 22.
Isaac of John & Sarah Tuckerman born Feb. 6.
Sarah of John & Sarah Tomlin born Jan. 21.

[1] The corner of leaf is torn off. — W. S. A.

Thomas of William & Rebecca Taylor born Feb. 18.
Robert of John & Deliverance Tray born Mar. 20.
Benjamin of John & Mary Vering born Aug. 19.
Susanna of Isaac & Mary Vergoose born Mar. 3.
Joanna of William & Joanna Williams born Apr. 18.
Richard of James & Rebecca Whetembe born May 3.
Thomas of Samuel & Hannah Ward born June 25.
William of James & Mary Worden born July 9.
John of William & Ureth Whitway born Aug. 9.
Sarah of John & Elizabeth Wensley born Aug. 11.
Benjamin of Thomas & Hannah Wheeler born Sept. 10.
Jonathan of Robert & Margery Williams born Sept. 22.
John of Experience & Mary Willis born Aug. 29.
Robert of John & Josabeth Wing born Sept. 8.
Elizabeth of Thomas & Susanna Walker born Oct. 19.
John of Richard & Bathsheba Williams born Oct. 24.
Sarah of Joseph & Grace Webb born Oct. 14.
Sarah of Joshua & Sarah Winsor born Nov. 3.
Frances of Richard & Sarah Wharton born Oct. 6.
Priscilla of Cornelius & Priscilla White born Nov. 28.
Samuel of Peter & Mehetable Welcome born Dec. 22.
William of Lionel & Abigail Wheatly born Mar. 1.
—— Daugt. of Thomas & Susanna Wagget born Oct. 31.[1]
—— Daugt. of Edward & Elizabeth Winslow born Mar. 22.[1]
—— Son of Thomas & Esther Woodward born Sept. 10.[1]
—— Daugt. of Joseph & Joanna Wing born Mar. 2.[1]
—— of Thomas & Mary Wells born Dec. 10.[1]

## FIRST CHURCH.

| | | |
|---|---|---|
| Isaac of brother Norden | 9 day | 1 mo. |
| Sarai of brother Emons | 9 day | 1 mo. |
| Jeremiah of James Allen our Teacher | 30 day | 1 mo. |
| Sarah of sister Dinsdale | 13 day | 2 mo. |
| Hannah of sister Moumfforth | 20 day | 2 mo. |
| —— of our sister Clerke | 27 day | 2 mo. |
| Hannah of Ephraim Searle | 18 day | 3 mo. |
| Thomas of Robert Sanfford | 4 day | 3 mo. |
| Martha of sister Rachel Litherland | 4 day | 3 mo. |
| William of sister Rachel Litherland | 4 day | 3 mo. |
| John of sister Williams[2] | 8 day | 4 mo. |
| —— dau. of our bro. Douse[2] | 8 day | 4 mo. |
| John of Edward Allen | 15 day | 4 mo. |
| John of David Copp | 15 day | 4 mo. |
| Sarai Leveritt of John Leveritt Gover. | 22 day | 4 mo. |
| Humphrey of Humphrey Davie | 22 day | 4 mo. |
| Benjamin of sister Swete | 13 day | 5 mo. |
| Sarah of John Moore | 20 day | 5 mo. |
| —— of sister Neeland | 27 day | 5 mo. |
| —— of sister Turner | 3 day | 6 mo. |
| Mary of sister Balston | 10 day | 6 mo. |
| Mary of bro. Clough | 10 day | 6 mo. |
| Martha of Edw: Cowell | 10 day | 6 mo. |
| Benjamin presented by sister Douce aged about 6 or 7 yrs. | 10 day | 6 mo. |
| Mehetabel of Sarah Orchard | 17 day | 6 mo. |
| James of John Jepson | 21 day | 7 mo. |
| Tho: of John Dyer of Ch. of Weymoth | 19 day | 8 mo. |
| Ruth of sister Web | 19 day | 8 mo. |
| Henry of Henry Tompson | 26 day | 8 mo. |

[1] The corner of leaf is torn off. — W. S. A.
[2] Perhaps these lines should read " John of sister Williams, dau. of our bro. Douse." — W. S. A.

Hannah of Samuel Bridges            26 day  8 mo.
Hephzibeh of George Monioye       9 day  9 mo.
also Goody Baxter presented        9 day  9 mo.
—— of sister Belcher              23 day  9 mo.
Judith of Henry Allen Deacon      31 day  9 mo.
Mercy of sister Boswoorth         31 day  9 mo.
John of John Temple             31 day  9 mo.
Elizabeth presented by Sergent Jackson    8 day 10 mo.
Mary of sister Mattocke           8 day 10 mo.
Mary of Edward Davis           18 day 11 mo.
Enoch of Symond Lynde          1 day 12 mo.
Mary of brother Maxwell          1 day 12 mo.
John of Sam Mason              1 day 12 mo.
Hannah of sister Brookin         1 day 12 mo.
       It is since informed that the child presented by Goodman Brookin
       was the child of his sister Longe.
John of sister Gatliffe            15 day 12 mo.
Mercy of sister Brookin         22 day 12 mo.

## 1674.

### Town.

Deborah of Hope & Hannah Allen born Mar. 26.
William of Edward & Mary Ashly born June 24.
Elizabeth of Jonathan & Eliza. Armitage born Aug. 26.
Samuel of William & Mehetable Avis born Sept. 2.
David of David & Hannah Adams born Nov. 15.
Isaac of Abraham & Sarah Adams born Nov. 10.
Samuel of Henry & Judith Allen born Jan. 12.
Mary of Henry & Mary Adams born Feb. 12.
Thomas of Thomas & Mary Atkins born Feb. 26.
Anna of Thomas & Lydia Batt born July 22.
Joseph of George & Deborah Burrell born July 27.
Elizabeth of John & Susanna Bewers born Sept. 5.
Sarah of Jeremiah & Sarah Bumsteed born Sept. 8.
John of Benja. & Elizabeth Button born Oct. 7.
Sarah of Robert & Elizabeth Butcher born Oct. 28.
Joseph of Robert & Elizabeth Blumford born Oct. 22.
Sarah of William & Elener Baker born Dec. 3.
John of John & Mary Briggs born Dec. 20.
Robert of John & Susanna Bradish born Dec. 28.
Abigail of Richard & Elizabeth Barnam horn ——
Susanna of Benja. & Sarah Brisco born Feb. 9.
Mercy of John & Hannah Buttolph born Mar. 2.
Abigail of Josiah & Ranis Belcher born Mar. 10.
Mary of Samuel & Mercy Brackenbury born Feb. 26.
Mary of Manassah & Mary Beck born Mar. 12.
John of John & Lydia Ballantine born Mar. 15.
Rebecca of Richard & Elizabeth Critchley born Mar. 1.
Elizabeth of Sampson & Elizabeth Cole born June 7.
Samuel of Samuel & Bethiah Clarke born Mar. 27.
John of John & Ellener Comer born Aug. 12.
Mary of Peter & Rachel Codner born Sept. 3.
Phillip of David & Elizabeth Cumins born Nov. 1.
Joanna of John & Mary Courser born Sept. 18.
Sarah of Robert & Sarah Canon born Nov. 18.
Patience of Ralph & Susann Carter born Nov. 7.
Hannah of Robert & Anne Chelston born Dec 3.
Hannah of Anthony & Hannah Checkley born Dec. 19.
Susanna of John & Mary Clough born Jan. 27.
William of John & Elizabeth Clear born Jan. 20.

John of Ellis & Mary Callender born Jan. 30.
John of John & Hannah Cowell born Jan. 12.
Elizabeth of Thomas & Hannah Clarke born Feb. 11.
Phillip of John & Mary Cox born Feb. 9.
Thomas of John & Sarah Clarke born Feb. 22.
Thomas of Thomas & Jane Clarke born Feb. 15.
Eleazer of Eleazer & Rebecca Davenport Apr. 13.
Hugh of Hugh & Mary Drury born July 19.
Hannah ⎱ of William & Huldah Davis born Aug. 19.
Jane ⎰ of William & Huldah Davis born Aug. 19.
Giles of Giles & Hannah Dier born Oct. 30.
Isaac of Isaac Deschamps born Nov. 10.
David of Sampson & Sarah Dewer born Dec. 5.
William of Samuel & Sarah Davis born Nov. 17.
Thomas of Hix & Sarah Dening born Dec. 17.
Sarah of Roger & Ann Doubleday born Feb. 14.
Samuel of Francis & Martha Dudson born Feb. 14.
Mark of Mark & Mary Day born Mar. 24.
William of Henry & Elizabeth Emes born May 28.
Sarah of John & Mary Ewell born June 16.
John of Peter & Clemence Edgerton born May 30.
Mary of Simon & Mary Emry born June 30.
Sarah of Phesant & Sarah Eastwick born Apr. 24.
Mercy of Joseph & Mercy Eliot born Aug. 27.
Ann of John & Elizabeth Endecot born Oct. 7.
Ann of John & Mary Ely born Dec. 26.
John of James & Susanna Ellis born Jan. 13.
James of Edward & Sarah Ellis born Feb. 14.
Mary of John & Elizabeth Freake born May 6.
William of Joseph & Mary Farnham born June 29.
John of John & Dorothy Foy born June 28.
Sarah of Benj. & Katharine Franklin born Oct. 2.
Bethiah of Theophilus & Hannah Frarey born Dec. 5.
Hannah ⎱ of Alexander & Catharine Forbush born Feb. 10.
Eliza. ⎰ of Alexander & Catharine Forbush born Feb. 10.
Elizabeth of Nathanll. & Mary Fox born Dec. 27.
Joseph of James & Hannah Flood born Feb. 15.
Elizabeth of Daniel & Sarah Fairfield born Mar. 1.
Sarah of Patrick & Sarah Forset born Mar. 1.
Sarah of John & Priscilla Green born Mar. 29.
Benjamin of Benjamin & Lydia Gibbs born July 29.
Nathaniel of William & Rebecca Gilbert born Aug. 6.
Gillet of Jacob & Hannah Garner born Sept. 23.
Esther of James & Rebecca Green born Sept. 27.
Patience of Richard & Elizabeth Gibbs born Nov. 10.
Aquila of William & Hannah Gibson born Dec. 3.
Thomas of Matthew & Mary Grover born Jan. 16.
Mercy of William & Eliza. Greenough born Feb. 16.
John of Nathanll. & Mary Green born Feb. 22.
John of William & Maria Gard born Mar. 4.
Windsor of Peter & Sarah Goulding born Mar. 3.
Judith of William & Anne Hobby born May 8.
Jane of Daniel & Mary Henchman born May 25.
John of George & Hannah Henley born June 13.
Mary of James & Mary Harrington born July 1.
Irene of Joshua & Mary Hobart born Apr. 10.
John of John & Sarah Holland born July 20.
Sarah of John & Susanna Howlet born May 22.
Powell of Anthony & Margaret Hayward born Oct. 19.
Thomas of Thomas & Judith Hunt born Nov. 11.
Hannah of John & Sarah Howard born Oct. 29.
Mary of George & Sarah Hisket born Nov. 11.
Ephraim of Ephraim & Sarah Hall born Oct. 22.
Margaret of James & Sarah Harris born Jan. 16.

Thomas of Elisha & Susan Hutchinson born Jan. 30.
Hannah of Robert & Sarah Horton born Jan. 7.
Samuel of Joseph & Elizabeth How born Dec. 28.
Sarah of John & Anne Hubbard born Feb. 11.
John of James & Elizabeth Hewes born Aug. 25.
Ann of John & Joanna Howen born Feb. 12.
Joseph of William & Hannah Hoare born Mar. 15.
John of John & Mary Hayward born Mar. 22.
James of James & Joanna Ingles born May 24.
Edmund of John & Elizabeth Irons born Jan. 27.
Jonathan of Thomas & Abigail Jolls born Mar. 21.
Jacob of Jacob & Elizabeth Jesson born Sept. 18.
Samuel of Samuel & Mary Jenkins born Oct. 11.
Mary of Edward & Elizabeth Jackson born Dec. 22.
Mercy of Samuel & Mercy Jacklin born Dec. 24.
Sarah of Samuel & Elizabeth Judkin born Jan. 17.
Mercy of John & Elizabeth Jacklin born Mar. 12.
Thomas of Thomas & Abigail Kellond born Aug. 29.
Arthur of John & Rachel Kinde born Oct. 28.
Edward of John & Mary King born Feb. 27.
Skipper of John & Kathar. Maverick born May 4.
Elizabeth of Dennis & Alice Magdaniel born May 7.
Elizabeth of Daniel & Mary Matthews born June 30.
Edward of Samuel & Naomi Moore born July 5.
Mary of Richard & Sarah Middlecot born July 1.
Jeremiah of Return & Sarah Munnings born Apr. 5.
Honour of Dorman & Ellener Merris born Apr. 1.
John of John & Margaret Marsh born July 23.
Elizabeth of Jacob & Rebeccca Mason born July 29.
Samuel of Increase & Maria Mather born Aug. 28.
Thomas of Henry & Alice Mare born Oct. 8.
Mercy of John & Eliza. Magdaniel born Oct. 11.
Joseph of George & Hannah Manning born Nov. 6.
Dorcas of Edward & Jane Mortimore born Nov. 28.
Joseph of Joseph & Eliza. Marshal born Dec. 18.
Arthur of Arthur & Susanna Mason born Jan. 18.
Joshua of Edmund & Eliza. Mountfort born Feb. 6.
Nathaniel of Nathanll & Deborah Mann born Mar. 17.
James of Thomas & Hannah Narramore born May 4.
Mary of Andrew & Mellicent Neale born June 11.
John of John & Sarah Noise born Nov. 4.
John of Peter & Hannah Odlin born Feb. 5.
Elizabeth of John & Mary Pell born June 22.
Mary of Nicholas & Philippa Phillips born June 23.
Elizabeth of Thomas & Elizabeth Peck born June 29.
Wheelwright of George & Elizabeth Parson born Apr. 10.
Sarah of John & Sarah Place born July 11.
Robert of William & Rebecca Pasmore born June 29.
Lydia of Moses & Elizabeth Paine born Aug. 23.
John of William & Hopestill Pitts born Aug. 28.
Joseph of James & Mary Peniman born Oct. 8.
Margaret of Timothy & Deborah Prout born Nov. 11.
John of John & Judith Parmiter born Nov. 17.
Sarah of Seth & Dorothy Perry born Nov. 24.
Peter of William & Elizabeth Porter born Dec. 24.
Mary of Samuel & Mary Pearse born Feb. 5.
Elizabeth of John & Elizabeth Poole born Dec. 29.
Elizabeth of John & Elizabeth Peck born Feb. 26.
David of David & Abigail Rainsford born May 20.
John of Edmund & Sarah Ranger born Apr. 16.
Mary of Samuel & Elizabeth Rust born Apr. 14.
Ann of William & Anne Rawson born Apr. 11.
Philip of Nathanll & Priscilla Renalls born Sept. 15.
Elisha of Thomas & Sarah Rix born Oct. 30.

Damaris of Nathanll & Damaris Robinson born Dec. 29.
Elizabeth of Samuel & Elizabeth Shrimpton born Apr. 21.
Nathan of Thomas & Susanna Stanbury born May 3.
Thomas of Thomas & Margaret Stevens born May 6.
Benjamin of Benja. & Mercy Sanderson born May 25.
Jane of Philip & Rachel Squire born June 9.
Elizabeth of Thomas & Temperance Smith born June 7.
Samuel of John & Sarah Smith born June 4.
Solomon of William & Martha Smith born July 9.
Mary of John & Mary Smith born July 20.
Martha of John & Sarah Starkey born Mar. 25.
Ann of Laomi & Deborah Simpson born July 28.
Elias of Elias & Mary Stiff born Aug. 13.
Martha of Thomas & Ann Shapcot born Aug. 4.
Daniel of Joseph & Elizabeth Souther born Aug. 12.
Samuel of Samuel & Sarah Snow born Aug. 24.
Thomas of Thomas & Mary Smith born Sept. 8.
Habijah of Thomas & Elizabeth Smith born Sept. 10.
John of Aeneas & Joane Salter born Sept. 24.
Richard of Richard & Hannah Sharp born Sept. 12.
Edward of Edward & Elizabeth Shippen born Oct. 2.
Ephraim of Ephraim & Alice Searle born Nov. 4.
Thomas of John & Sarah Skeath born Oct. 23.
William of William & Mary Spowell born Dec. 7.
John of Ephraim & Mary Savage born Nov. 30.
Sarah of Joseph & Sarah Showell born Jan. 27.
Phoebe ⎫ of Joseph & Mary Swett born Feb. 7.
Anna  ⎭ of Joseph & Mary Swett born Feb. 7.
Elizabeth of Benja. & Mary Stowe born Jan. 29.
John of John & Sarah Shaw born Jan. 28.
Mercy of William & Elizabeth Sumner born Jan. 6.
Joshua of John & Rebecca Scottow born Feb. 22.
Elnathan of William & Abigail Stevens born Feb. 18.
Margaret of Stephen & Dorothy Sergeant born Mar. 10.
Anna of Daniel & Anna Turell born Mar. 31.
Mary of Timothy & Experience Thornton born Apr. 2.
Pen of Pen & Sarah Townsend born July 31.
Silvanus of George & Tabitha Tankersly born Sept. 17.
John of Richard & Elizabeth Tout born Sept. 5.
John of John & Kesiah Tucker born Oct. 1.
Elizabeth of James & Elizabeth Taylor born Oct. 24.
Ann of Joseph & Dorothy Townsend born Oct. 21.
Thomas of John & Elizabeth Tuder born Nov. 11.
Anna of Richard & Anna Travis born Oct. 2.
Joshua ⎫ of Thomas & Mary Townsend born Nov. 21.
Caleb  ⎭ of Thomas & Mary Townsend born Nov. 21.
John of John & Rebecca Taylor born Nov. 22.
John of Thomas & Mary Thatcher born Jan. 22.
Hannah of John & Maria Thwing born Mar. 4.
Nathaniel of John & Mary Viall born Oct. 8.
Obadiah of Obadiah & Susannah Wakefield born May 4.
Samuel of Bartho. & Amey Whitwell born May 17.
Elizabeth of John & Mary Williams born May 22.
Timothy of William & Constant Worcester born June 2.
John of John & Austis Wilkins born Apr. 30.
John of Richard & Hannah West born May 29.
Hannah of Joseph & Lydia Williams born May 20.
Susanna of Agnes & Patience White born Apr. 4.
John of John & Mary White born July 2.
Michael of Experience & Elizabeth Willis born July 9.
Elizabeth of John & Elizabeth Woodmansey born Aug. 13.
John of John & Susanna Wilkins born Sept. 15.
Mary of Joseph & Sarah Winslow born Sept. 25. *
Catharine of Richard & Sarah Wharton born Oct. 6.

Anna of John & Anna Williams born Nov. 4.
Sarah of Thomas & Elizabeth Weaver born Nov. 6.
Jonathan of Lawrence & Hannah Waters born Oct. 8.
William of John & Hannah Wiswall born Oct. 10.
Joseph of Joseph & Abigail Walker born Dec. 8.
Anna of Isaac & Susanna White born Jan. 10.
Abigail of William & Abigail Wright born Jan. 15.
Henry of James & Mary Warden born Jan. 20.
Richard of Isaac & Dorcas Woodde born Feb. 1.
John of John & Elizabeth Wensley born Feb. 8.
Martha ⎫ of John & Elizabeth Webber born Feb. 18.
Mary  ⎭ of John & Elizabeth Webber born Feb. 18.
Sarah of Henry & Sarah Wright born Feb. 19.
William of William & Joanna Williams born Feb. 25.
Mehetable of Thomas & Mary Waller born Feb. 18.
Sarah of John & Deliverance Wakefield born Mar. 1.
Joseph of Joseph & Mary Wheeler born Mar. 15.
Joanna of Samuel & Joanna Ward born Mar. 24.
Mary of Timothy & Naomi Yeale born Jan. 11.

## FIRST CHURCH.

| | |
|---|---|
| Elizabeth of John Lowell | 8 day 1 mo. |
| Henry of sister Elizabeth Bridgham | 15 day 1 mo. |
| Phebe of sister Eglon | 22 day 1 mo. |
| Joseph of sister Dudson | 29 day 1 mo. |
| Deborah of Hope Allen's wife | 29 day 1 mo. |
| of sister Starkey | 29 day 1 mo. |
| Freegrace of Freegrace Bendall | 5 day 2 mo. |
| of Timothy Thornton | 5 day 2 mo. |
| Thomas of sister Wheeler | 10 day 3 mo. |
| Joseph of sister Wheeler | 10 day 3 mo. |
| Samuel of sister Wheeler | 10 day 3 mo. |
| Benjamin of sister Wheeler | 10 day 8 mo. |
| Rebecca of bro: Crichley | 10 day 3 mo. |
| children of sister Johanna Ward | 24 day 3 mo. |
| of sister Leveritt | 7 day 4 mo. |
| of Samuel Williams | 21 day 4 mo. |
| of sister Squire | 21 day 4 mo. |
| of William Smith | 12 day 5 mo. |
| Pen of Pen Townsend | 2 day 5 mo. |
| Philip of Nathaniel Renolds | 20 day 7 mo. |
| children of John Butolph | 8 mo. |
| of Ephraim Searle | 1 day 9 mo. |
| child of sister Travise | 1 day 9 mo. |
| child of bro: Manninge | 1 day 9 mo. |
| of sister Parmiter | 22 day 9 mo. |
| ⎰ John of John Thwinge | 6 day 10 mo. |
| ⎱ —— his sister | 6 day 10 mo. |
| Sarah of sister Winsor | 6 day 10 mo. |
| Mary of brother Jackson | 27 day 10 mo. |
| Samuel of bro: How | 3 day 11 mo. |
| John of brother Griggs | 3 day 11 mo. |
| Mary of James Townsend | 10 day 11 mo. |
| Samuel of Deacon Allen | 17 day 11 mo. |
| John of sister Cowell | 17 day 11 mo. |
| Susanna of bro: Clow Junior | 81 day 11 mo. |
| Phebe of bro: Sweat | 14 day 12 mo. |
| Anne of bro: Sweat | 14 day 12 mo. |

## 1675.

### TOWN.

Ebenezer of Henry Allin born Jan. 30.
Mehetable of Samuel & Mary Emōns born Feb. 6.
Madett of Samuel & Mary Eings born Sept. 25.
John of Lott Gorden born May 4.
Samuel of Samuel & Anna Haugh born Feb. 1.
John of John & Martha Hunt born Mar. 24.
Hephzibah of Gershom & Sarah Hobart born Feb. 16.
John of John Mellowes born Mar. 5.
Samuel of Caleb Stretton born Mar. 3.
Elizabeth of John & Eliza. Woodmansey born Mar. 3.
Mary of Robert Williams born Dec. 2.
Elizabeth of Samuel Wakefield born Mar. 2.
Elisha of Joseph & Grace Webb born Feb. 13.
Nathll. of Nathll. & Mary Williams born Aug.

### FIRST CHURCH.

| | |
|---|---|
| Martha of sister Jackson | 14 day  1 mo. |
| John of sister Williams | 21 day  1 mo. |
| Elizabeth of sister Williams | 21 day  1 mo. |
| John of John Ballantine | 4 day  2 mo. |
| Hannah of Elisha Audlin | 4 day  2 mo. |
| Abigail of Elisha Audlin | 4 day  2 mo. |
| Elisha of Elisha Audlin | 4 day  2 mo. |
| another | 4 day  2 mo. |
| William of sister Ruth Younge | 11 day  2 mo. |
| Elisha of Elisha Audlin | 25 day  2 mo. |
| James of sister Mavericke | 25 day  2 mo. |
| Martha of sister Mavericke | 25 day  2 mo. |
| William of John Brookinges | 16 day  3 mo. |
| Joseph of sister Belsbar of Winesimet | 6 day  4 mo. |
| ——— presented by Henry Messenger | 6 day  4 mo. |
| William of sister Greeneleaffe | 13 day  4 mo. |
| Mary of sister Bosworth | 13 day  4 mo. |
| another | 13 day  2 mo. |
| Peletiah ⎱ of George Munioye | 20 day  4 mo. |
| Gershon ⎰ of George Munioye | 20 day  4 mo. |
| John of sister Alcocke | 20 day  4 mo. |
| Samuel of Samuell Bridges | 20 day  4 mo. |
| William of John Ballentine | 20 day  4 mo. |
| Hannah of Edward Allen | 20 day  4 mo. |
| Mercy of Jonathan Bridgham | 12 day  7 mo. |
| Samuel of sister Skinner | 12 day  7 mo. |
| of John Dyer | 19 day  7 mo. |
| Moore | 26 day  7 mo. |
| sister Orchard | 26 day  7 mo. |
| Tho: son of David Coppe | 10 day  8 mo. |
| Thomas of Timothy Thornton | 21 day  9 mo. |
| Edward of Edward Thwinge | 28 day  9 mo. |
| Presented by Mr Stoddard name Phebe | 28 day  9 mo. |
| Gamaliel of Persival Clerke | 12 day 10 mo. |
| Scarlet of Freegrace Bendall | 19 day 10 mo. |
| John of Henry Tompson | 19 day 10 mo. |
| Ebenezer of Henry Allene | 6 day 12 mo. |
| Robert ⎱ of sister Wakum | 6 day 12 mo. |
| William ⎰ of sister Wakum | 6 day 12 mo. |
| Hannah ⎱ of sister Wakum | 6 day 12 mo. |
| James ⎰ of sister Wakum | 6 day 12 mo. |

Elizabeth of sister Hannah Wakum       27 day 12 mo.
Elisha of bro: Web       27 day 12 mo.
Susanna of John Clough
Thomas of James Allen       May 22.
Hannah of John Moore
John Ruggles       March 16.

## 1676.

### Town.

Mary of Edward Ash born Apr. 28.
David of David Adams born May 23.
Mary of Jonathan Adams born Apr. 26.
Rachel of Hope Allen born May 16.
Peter of Peter Andle born' May 8.
Samuel of Samuel Aliack born Aug. 18.
Hannah of William & Mehetable Avis born Sept 28.
Ephraim of Henry & Judith Allen born Jan. 4.
Elizabeth of James & Elizabeth Allison born Dec. 11.
Jane of Timothy & Joanna Armitage born Nov. 10.
Deborah of Arthur Brancum born May 11.
Margaret of John Bull born May 19.
Mary of Mary Buckway born July 14.
Mary of Edward & Dorothy Budd born July 14.
Lydia of John & Lydia Ballentine born June 2.
Robert of Robert & Elizabeth Butcher born Aug. 15.
Manassah of Manassah & Mary Beck born Oct. 6.
Thomas of Thomas & Lydia Batt born May 22.
Sarah of Jeremiah & Sarah Bumsteed born Aug. 15.
Benjamin of Roger Burges born Nov 20.
Robert of John & Susanna Bowers born Oct. 24.
Thomas of Thomas & Mary Bishop born Dec. 19.
William of William & Ellener Baker born Feb. 12.
Susanna of Peter & Mary Bennet born Aug. 23.
Ruth of Joseph & Hannah Belknap born Mar. 17.
Mercy of John & Eliza Brooking born Dec. 15.
Henry of Joseph & Sarah Bridgham born Dec. 16.
John of John Clough born May 2.
William of William Clarke born Apr. 29.
Sarah of William Coleman born June 5.
Joshua of John Cott born June 27.
Sarah of John Comes born July 13.
Henry of Henry Coole born July 27.
Jeremiah of John Cowell born July 25.
Mary of William Castle born July 11.
Naomi of Matthew & Naomi Collins born Sept. 15.
Ann of Joseph & Susanna Cock born June 10.
Elizabeth of Richard & Jane Cleare born May 28.
George of Charles & Judith Crosthwayt born Mar. 3.
Mehetable of Andrew & Mehetable Clarke born Dec. 8.
Elizabeth of David & Eliza. Comins born Nov. 26.
Josiah of Josiah & Deborah Cobham born Dec. 7.
Sarah of John & Sarah Clarke born Jan. 17.
Abigail of Robert Dudson born Mar. 25.
Thomas of Thomas Duglas born July 11.
William of Mary Day born Aug. 9.
Mary of John Davenport born Aug. 23.
Rebecca of Eleazer & Rebecca Davenport born Aug. 7.
Mary of Francis & Martha Dudson born Apr. 16.
Elizabeth of John & Mary Drewry born July 9.
Sarah of Sampson & Sarah Dewer born Oct. 22.

William of William & Hannah Downe born Feb. 2.
John of John & Mary Davis born Apr. 19.
Thomas of Peter Edgerton born Sept. 16.
Mehetable of Thomas & Mary Eldredge born Oct. 8.
Susanna of David & Mary Edwards born Oct. 29.
Lydia of George & Lydia Ellistone born May 24.
Robert of Robert & Bethiah Emõns born Mar. 23.
Mary of Joseph Farnham born May 14.
Ellener of Jeremiah & Sarah Fitch born Aug. 20.
Benjamin of James & Hannah Flood born Feb. 1.
Samuel of Hopestill & Elizabeth Foster born Dec. 27.
Benjamin of Benjamin & Kathar Franklyn born Jan. 28.
Sarah of William Greenhalgh born May 2.
Hannah of Erasmus Garrett born May 20.
Ebenezer of Nathanll. Green born June 12.
Bethiah of Enoch Greenleafe born Aug. 11.
Elizabeth of John Gilbert born Sept. 2.
Samuel of William & Ruth Greenough born Aug. 31.
Susanna of Joseph & Eliza. Gridley born Aug. 10.
James of William & Hannah Gibson born Mar. 24.
Elizabeth of Edward & Eliza. Goodin born Nov. 25.
Henry of William & Ann Gerrish born Aug. 18.
Joseph of Joseph & Martha Gillam born Mar. 30.
John of John Hagget born May 1.
Lydia of William Huffe born June 20.
Elizabeth of William & Ann Hobby born Oct. 18.
Francis of Samuel & Abigail Hudson born Aug. 15.
Mary of Elisha & Han: Hutchinson born Oct. 1.
Abigail of Experience & Abigail Harris born Nov. 28.
Richard of Richard & Mary Hunt born Aug. 4.
John of John & Anne Hubbard born Jan. 9.
Samuel of Ephraim & Sarah Hall born Dec. 25.
Anna of Samuel & Anna Haugh born Jan. 27.
Mary of James & Sarah Harris born Feb. 3.
John of John & Martha Hunt born Mar. 24.
Elizabeth of Benja. & Elizabeth Hord born Feb. 28.
Josiah of Josiah & Hannah Helman born Sept. 28.
Abigail of Eliakim & Sarah Hutchinson born Mar. 7.
George of George & Abigail Hatherly born Oct. 28.
Hannah of William & Hannah Harris born July 1.
Archiball of James Ingles born Sept. 25.
John of Samuel Jackson born May 1.
Mary of William James born Apr. 25.
Samuel of Samuel & Pnoebe Johnson born Dec. 15.
Mary of Andrew & Martha Judson born Apr. 20.
Thomas of Samuel & Mary Jenkins born Dec. 29.
Hannah of Samuel & Elizabeth Judkin born Feb. 14.
John of John & Elizabeth Jackson born Mar. 12.
Mary of Peter & Mary King born Feb. 4.
Ebenezer of John Liscum born Apr. 29.
Thomas of John Larkin born May 9.
Patience of Samuel & Deliverance Legg born Aug. 29.
William of John & Naomi Lowell born Jan. 3.
William of William & Margaret Lovering born Feb. 26.
Samuel of John Mosse born Nov. 13.
Elizabeth of Jacob Mason born Apr. 23.
Fairbanck of Samuel Mattock born Feb. 11.
Katherine of John Materick born Sept. 16.
Hannah of James & Elizabeth Meers born Jan. 28.
Margaret of Thaddeus & Elizabeth Maccarty born Feb. 25.
Hannah of John & Lydia Moore born Feb. 23.
Edward of Edward & Jane Mortimore born June 10.
Samuel of Samuel & Ruth Marshall born Oct. 7.
David of James & Selphina Morgan born Nov. 10.

Susanna of William Norton born June 25.
John of Richard & Ann Narramore born Sept. 10.
Thomas & ⎱ of Nicholas Neales born May 20.
Henry     ⎰ of Nicholas Neales horn May 20.
Sarah of John Orris born Aug. 14.
Joseph of William Porter born June 15.
William of William Palfrey born July 22.
Lydia of Joseph Pearce born Aug. 11.
Joseph of Benja. & Ellener Phippen born Nov. 30.
Joanna of John & Joanna Prescot born Jan. 6.
Joseph of John & Mary Pell born Mar. 5.
Lydia of John & Judith Parmiter born Jan.
John of James Richards born July 3.
William of John Ruggles born July 22.
John of John Ricks born Aug. 16.
John of Samuel Ruggles born Mar. 15.
Mary of Thomas Ricks born Oct. 1.
Margaret of William & Ann Rawson born Aug. 1.
Charles of Humphry & Mehetable Richards born Oct. 8.
Joseph of Nathanll. & Priscilla Reynolds born Dec. 29.
Mary of William & Sarah Rouse born Dec 29.
Benjamin of John Shaw born Mar. 24.
Elizabeth of Joseph Sweat born July 7.
Sarah of Constantine Sams born May 21.
Hannah of Ephraim Savage born Aug. 7.
Sarah of Æneas Salter born Aug. 1.
Elizabeth of Edward Shippen born Aug. 21.
William of Philip & Rachel Squire born Oct. 15.
Elizabeth of Savil & Sarah Sympson born Nov. 4.
Mehetable of Robert & Mehetable Smith born June 24.
Mary of Joseph & Elizabeth Soper born May 28.
Sarah of Samuel & Sarah Snow born June 21.
Robert of Robert & Elizabeth Streeto born Apr. 5.
Elizabeth of Robert & Ann Shelstone born Nov. 19.
Obadiah of Ephraim & Alice Sale born Dec. 9.
Sarah of John & Sarah Stanbridge born Jan. 23.
Sarah of John & Elizabeth Skinner born Jan. 4.
Richard of Richard & Margaret Smith born Jan. 6.
Rebecca of John & Rebecca Scottow born Mar. 1.
Peter of Elias & Mary Stiffe born Feb. 23.
Martha of Thomas & Ann Sheepscot born Mar. 16.
Joseph of John & Martha Saffin born Jan 24.
William of Robert & Sarah Sedgewick born June 9.
Rebecca of Thomas & Rebecca Smith horn Mar. 24.
Mary of John & Sarah Skeath born Mar. 22.
William of John Taylor born May 21.
Mary of Jonathan Tyng born Jan. 16.
Solomon of Samuel Townsend born Aug. 1.
Robert of John & Sarah Tucker born May 14.
Mary of George & Mary Tucker born Aug. 20.
Joanna of John & Kesiah Tucker born Dec. 20.
Martha of John & Martha Temple born Feb. 14.
Benjamin of Edward Vein born May 25.
Mary of John & Mary Viall born Oct. 10.
John of Thomas & Mary Varnee born Dec. 1.
John of John Winchester born Apr. 17.
Abigail of John Warren born May 10.
Experience of Experience Willis born May 28.
Hannah of Nathaniel Whiteing born July 3.
John of John Winchcomb born July 22.
Austis of John & Anstis Wilkins born Aug. 17.
Sarah of Thomas & Mary Waller born Nov. 5.
Simon of Samuel & Abigail Willard born Dec. 6.
Thomas of Thomas & Elizabeth Williams born Jan. 1.

Peter of Peter & Sarah Warren born Apr. 20.
Daniel of Joseph & Lydia Williams born Dec. 25.
Mary of Henry & Sarah Wright born Feb. 14.
William of John & Hannah Wiswall born Jan. 27.
John of George & Rachel Waldron born Aug. 21.


## FIRST CHURCH.[1]

| | |
|---|---|
| John of John Cotte | 2 day 5 mo. |
| Mary of John Davenport | 17 day 7 mo. |
| Lydia of sister Travis | 17 day 7 mo. |
| John of William Griggs | 24 day 7 mo. |
| David of sister Duer | 8 day 8 mo. |
| Deborah of sister Litherland | 8 day 8 mo. |
| Child of Edward Goodwin | 3 day 10 mo. |
| Simon of Samuel Willard | 10 day 10 mo. |
| Elizabeth of Ephraim Sale | 10 day 10 mo. |
| ——— Allen | 7 day 11 mo. |
| ——— Lowell | 7 day 11 mo. |
| Hutchinson Thomas Jr. | 9 day 11 mo. |
| John Temple | 9 day 11 mo. |
| Edward Ashley | 9 day 11 mo. |
| ——— Moore | 25 day 11 mo. |
| Hannah of William Griggs | Sept. 22. |
| Elisha of Elisha Hutchinson | 22 Jan. |
| Elizabeth of Elisha Hutchinson | 22 Jan. |
| Hannah of Elisha Hutchinson | 22 Jan. |
| Thomas of Elisha Hutchinson | 22 Jan. |
| Martha of John Temple | Feby. 15. |
| Hannah of John Moore | |


## 1677.

### TOWN.

Hope of Hope & Hannah Allen born June 18.
Jonathan of Jonathan & Eliza. Armitage born Aug. 24.
Nathan of John & Elizabeth Alden born Oct. 17.
Mary of Nathanll. & Mary Adams born Sept. 23.
Rebecca of Jeremiah & Sarah Belcher born Apr. 11.
Lydia of Charles & Elizabeth Benmur born Feb. 27.
Nathaniel of James & Hannah Brading born June 17.
Susanna of Philip & Susanna Blake born June 26.
Amy of Thomas & Amy Bridge born June 9.
Mary of Nathanll. & Mary Barnes born June 4.
Joseph of Samuel & Mercy Bosworth born July 22.
Sarah of John & Rebecca Bully born July 26.
Ellen of Samuel & Hannah Bridge born Aug. 4.
Perne of George & Perne Broughton born June 15.
Sarah of John & Aphra Bennet born June 13.
Mary of Thomas & Esther Bucknel born Aug. 26.
Sarah of Samuel & Anne Burnell born Aug. 20.
Thomas of Thomas & Christian Baker born Sept. 16.
Elizabeth of John & Elizabeth Barrell born Apr. 4.
Abigail of John & Susanna Bennet born Sept. 24.
Elizabeth of John & Abigail Broughton born Sept. 22.
Nathaniel of Nathanll. & Deborah Byfield born Nov. 14.

---

[1] For several years the records were so carelessly kept as to be very uncertain and of little value. — W. S. A.

Henry of Jonathan & Eliza. Bridgeham born Nov. 2.
Mary of John & Anne Balston born Dec. 8.
James of James & Sarah Burroughs born Jan. 28.
Stephen of Stephen & Abigaile Burton born Aug. 8.
Nathaniel of Nathanll. & Mary Barnes born Mar. 20.
Mary of Arthur & Deborah Branscomb born July 25.
James of Thomas & Mary Beard born Jan. 30.
Elizabeth of Robert & Martha Cox born Apr. 15.
Martha ⎫ of Joseph & Mary Clement born Apr. 13.
Mary  ⎭ of Joseph & Mary Clement born Apr. 13.
Frances of Francis & Mary Cooke born May 15.
Sarah of John & Hannah Courser born Apr. 13.
John of John & Anne Collins born May 26.
Sarah of John & Susanna Cross born May 21.
Sarah of Elisha & Elizabeth Cooke born July 31.
Elizabeth of John & Elizabeth Cleare born Aug. 15.
Samuel of John & Martha Clarke born Sept. 21.
Sarah of Nicholas & Esther Crarey born Nov. 14.
Jacob of Thomas & Martha Cox born Jan. 4.
Uriah of Uriah & Joanna Clarke born Oct. 5.
Samuel of John & Mary Clough born Nov. 22.
Sarah of William & Sarah Clarke born Jan. 27.
Hannah of John & Hannah Cowell born Mar. 9.
Hannah of Peter & Rachel Codner born Feb 1.
John of William & Sarah Cooke born Mar. 8.
Mary of John & Mary Dafforn born Apr. 15.
Elijah of Roger & Ann Doubleday born Apr. 13.
Mary of John & Anne Dinsdall born May 19.
John of John & Mary Davis born July 24.
Mary of Thomas & Sarah Dolberry born Apr. 13.
Benjamin of John & Mary Dyer born July 15.
Mary of Giles & Hannah Dyer born June 28.
William of Adam & Hannah Dinsdall born Aug. 24.
Elizabeth of Henry & Elizabeth Dering born July 18.
Joseph of Ambrose & Mary Dawes born Oct 21.
Mercy of John & Mary Drewry born Oct. 25.
Rebecca of Thomas & Ann Deane born Dec. 7.
Hannah of John & Elizabeth Dare born Dec. 18.
Paul of Paul & Mary Dudley born Mar. 4.
Samuel of Edward & Hannah Davis born Feb. 28.
Hannah of Robert & Hannah Earle born May 1.
Mary of Joseph & Mary Emerson born July 13.
John of William & Phoebe Eglin born May 15.
Samuel of Henry & Elizabeth Eems born Aug. 26.
Mercy of Joseph & Mercy Eliot born Aug. 31.
Edmund of Peter & Clement Edgerton born Oct. 17.
Thomas of Thomas & Hannah Eliot born Oct. 14.
Henry of Henry & Joanna Ellice born Sept. 11.
Mary of John & Eliza. Faireweather born Apr. 23.
Elizabeth of John & Mehetable Frost born July 12.
Abigail of Daniel & Sarah Fairfield born Nov. 6.
Samuel of Patrick & Sarah Facit born Dec. 29.
Charles of Joseph & Mary Farnham born Feb. 8.
Olive of John & Olive Furnell born Mar. 24.
Deliverance of Thomas & Margaret Forbush born Dec. 18.
William of William & Hannah Gibson born Apr. 14.
Jacoh of Jacob & Mercy Gully born June 5.
Benjamin of Benj. & Hannah Gillam born June 5.
Abigail of Thomas & Elizabeth Gross born Oct. 25.
Obadiah of Obadiah & Elizabeth Gill born Oct. 8.
Thomas of Peter & Sarah Goulding born Jan. 23.
Nathaniel of William & Rebecca Gilbert born Jan. 6.
Knight of Joseph & Martha Gillam born Jan. 30.
Samuel of Samuel & Mary Greenwood born Mar. 6.

Consider son of William & Ruth Greenough born Mar. 7.
Stephen of John & Anna Greenleafe born Mar. 5.
Elizabeth of Edmond & Hannah Gatch born June 5.
Susanna of John & Susanna Harrison born Mar. 28.
George of George & Mary Hooper born Apr. 14.
Joseph of William & Decline Holowel born May 5.
Mary of Jeremiah & Mehetable Howard born June 7.
Daniel of Daniel & Mary Henchman born June 16.
Robert of John & Sarah Howard born May 26.
John of John & Hannah Harwood born June 7.
Mary of John & Silence Hayward born June 5.
Ann of John & Joanna Howen born July 3.
Sarah of John & Elizabeth Harris born Aug. 2.
Samuel of Joshua & Hannah Hews born Sept. 8.
George of George & Mary Hare born Sept. 15.
Sarah of John & Sarah Holland born Sept. 21.
Thomas of Thomas & Joanna Hunt born Sept. 30.
Mary of Thomas & Sarah Harris born Oct. 3.
Dorothy of Gershom & Sarah Hobart born Dec. 6.
Ephraim of Thomas & ——— Hunt born Apr. 17.
Rachel of Samuel & Rachel Holman born Sept. 20.
Atherton of Samuel & Anne Haugh born Jan. 12.
George of William & Prudence Harrison born Feb. 26.
Elizabeth of James & Elizabeth Howard born Feb. 6.
Samuel of Samuel & Lydia Holmes born Nov. 14.
Rachel of James & Elizabeth Hews born Nov. 1.
Thomas of John & Elizabeth Indicot born Feb. 21.
Mary of John & Rebecca Jarvis born Apr. 12.
Jeremiah of Jeremiah & Faith Jackson born June 11.
Mary of John & Sarah Johnson born Sept. 2.
Hannah of Samuel & Hannah Johnson born Jan. 22.
Robert of Thomas & Susanna Jolls born June 2.
Elizabeth of Roger & Elizabeth Judd born Mar. 3.
John of William & Hannah Long born May 15.
Francis of Francis & Elizabeth Lyford born May 31.
William of William & Jane Lancaster born Sept. 10.
Susanna of Phillip & Mary Langden born Oct. 23.
Jane of Charles & Bethiah Lidgett born June 14.
Henry of Henry & Jane Lunt born Dec. 5.
Samuel of Samuel & Mary Lynde horn Nov. 27.
Mehetable of John & Naomi Lowell born Jan. 7.
Abigail of Increase & Maria Mather born Apr. 13.
Ann of John & Abigail Mulberry born Aug. 26.
Rachel of Henry & Rachel Maddox born Sept. 2.
Mercy of Joel & Rebecca Madever born Aug. 12.
William of William & Ruth Mumford born June 2.
Sarah of John & Elizabeth Morse born Nov. 24.
Elizabeth of John & Margaret Marsh born June 7.
Dorcas of James & Dorcas Maxwell born Feb. 27.
Joseph of Samuel & Mary Mason born Nov. 24.
Lydia of Arthur & Rebecca Mosier born Feb. 25.
Paul & } of Edward & Sarah North born Aug. 14.
Sarah  } of Edward & Sarah North born Aug. 14.
Samuel of John & Mehetable Newton born Jan. 23.
Rebecca of Experience & Abigail Orris born Mar. 11.
Sarah of Thomas & Sarah Pemberton born June 7.
Abigail of Seth & Abigail Perry born June 23.
Mary of Samuel & Mary Pearse born Aug. 3.
Courtney of John & Elizabeth Poole born Nov. 9.
George of William & Elizabeth Porter born Nov. 21.
Elizabeth of John & Hannah Peas born Jan. 15.
Mary of John & Mary Pollard born Mar. 8.
Andrew of Samuel & Margaret Ruck born Apr. 14.
Edward of William & Ann Rawson born Sept. 6.

Samuel of Samuel & Sarah Ruggles born Sept. 14.
Susanna of Thomas & Sarah Rootes born Sept. 30.
Nathan of John & Susanna Rainsford born Jan. 14.
Solomon of John & Charity Ricks born Jan. 10.
Sarah of Solomon & Priscilla Rainsford born Feb. 4.
Mary of Caleb & Eliza. Rawlins born Mar. 10.
Obadiah of Obadiah & Susanna Read born Nov. 29.
Mary of Simeon & Mary Stoddard born Apr. 15.
Dinah of Joseph & Eliza. Souther born Apr. 13.
Rebecca of Thomas & Martha Squire born Apr. 8.
John of Samuel & Hannah Sewall born Apr. 2.
Nathaniel of John & Sarah Shaw born May 15.
Edward of Robert & Mehetable Smith born June 7.
Catharine of Richard & Hannah Sharp born May 9.
Joseph of Richard & Joyce Smith born June 9.
Elizabeth of James & Sarah Stevens born June 11.
Ann of Joseph & Ann Stocker born July 26.
Bethiah of Rowland & Bethiah Storey born July 15.
Elizabeth of Thomas Junr. & Eliza. Savage born Aug. 4.
Hannah of John & Jane Sparrey born Sept. 15.
Isaac of Thomas & Susanna Stanbury born Oct. 31.
Sarah of Robert & Sarah Sedgewick born Dec. 19.
Mehetable of Sampson & Mehetable Sheafe born Dec. 10.
Mary of Benja. & Mercy Sanderson born Nov. 29.
Rebecca of Thomas & Elizabeth Skinner born Jan. 22.
Samuel of Ephraim & Alice Sale born Feb. 11.
Edward of Edward & Elizabeth Shippen born Feb. 10.
Rebecca of Joseph & Rebecca Smith born Dec. 17.
Sarah of Arthur & Sarah Smith born Aug. 12.
Mary of Stephen & Dorothy Sergeant born July 5.
John of Pilgrim & Catharine Simpkins born Mar. 22.
Margaret of William & Margaret Snelling born June 20.
Simon of Cyprian & Mary Stevens born Aug. 13.
Sarah of Penn & Sarah Townsend born Apr. 3.
Margaret of Peter & Margaret Townsend born June 13.
Nathan of Thomas & Mary Townsend born July 5.
Alice of Henry & Eliza. Thompson born Sept. 8.
Nathaniel of Theophilus & Hannah Thornton born Aug. 15.
Mary of Richard & Elizabeth Tout born Oct. 15.
Maria of John & Maria Thwing born Apr. 12.
Dorothy of Joseph & Dorothy Townsend born Nov. 17.
Thomas of Edward & Elizabeth Thwing born Dec. 14.
Joseph of James & Elizabeth Townsend born Jan. 24.
Ruth of Bartho: & Damaris Threeneedle born Feb. 27.
Elizabeth of Timothy & Experience Thornton born Nov. 17.
Lydia of Daniel & Anne Turell born Jan. 17.
Elizabeth of William & Mary Trowte born Mar. 3.
Abigail of Edward & Abigail Tuttle born Feb. 14.
Peter of Isaac & Mary Vergoose born Feb. 17.
Stephen of Lawrance & Hannah Waters born Apr. 3.
Joanna of Joseph & Abigail Walker born May 5.
Abigail of Lionel & Abigail Wheatly born June 9.
Rebecca of Sampson & Rebecca Waters born May 28.
Thomas of John & Mary Wells born June 30.
Joseph of Joseph & Sarah Winslow born June 16.
Hannah of Richard & Bethiah Way born July 13.
Isaac of Isaac & Priscilla Waldron born June 23.
Hannah of Richard & Hannah West born July 6.
Eunice of John & Eunice Wayt born July 11.
William of Joshua & Sarah Winsor born Sept. 2.
John of John & Sarah Walley born Nov. 7.
Joanna of John & Mary Williams born Nov. 22.
Mercy of Thomas & Susanna Walker born Jan. 7.
Jonathan of Joseph & Mary Wheeler born Dec. 26

Samuel of John & Delivera. Wakefield born Jan. 15.
John of John & Eliza. Williams born Feb. 8.
Samuel of William Jr. & Abigail Wright born Feb. 17.
James of Robert & Margery Williams born Feb. 20.
Samuel of William & Constant Wooster born Dec. 23.
John of John & Elizabeth Warren born Feb. 10.
Elizabeth of Experience & Elizabeth Willis born Dec. 8.
Joseph of Peter & Eliza. Welcome born Feb. 2.
Obadiah of Obadiah & Susanna Wakefield born Nov. 11.
Elizabeth of Nathnll. & Mary Williams born Feb. 28.
Thomas of John & Susanna Wilkins born Jan. 18.
Joseph of Richard & Bathshua Williams born Mar. 7.
Hannah of John & Hannah Walker born Apr. 25.

## FIRST CHURCH.

| | |
|---|---|
| James of William Gibson | 5 day 1 mo. |
| ———— of bro: Saffin | 12 day 1 mo. |
| Elizabeth of sister Jackson | 18 day 1 mo. |
| John of sister Jackson | 18 day 1 mo. |
| ———— of sister Pecke | 25 day 1 mo. |
| Pen of Pen Townsend | 8 day 2 mo. |
| ———— sister Cox | 8 day 2 mo. |
| a Grandchild of Henry Messenger | 15 day 2 mo. |
| a Grandchild of John Viall | 15 day 2 mo. |
| John of John Ballentine | 6 day 3 mo. |
| William of sister Dinsdale | 26 day 6 mo. |
| Ellen of Samuel Bridge | 5 day 6 mo. |
| Mary of John Thwing | April. |
| Samuel Ruggles | Sept. 15. |

## 1678.

### TOWN.

Mehetable of David & Hannah Adams born Apr. 17.
Mary of John & Constant Alcock born May 3.
Elizabeth of Bozoune & Rachel Allen born July 17.
Dorcas of Jonathan & Rebecca Adams born June 27.
Isaac of William & Mehetable Avis born May 1.
John of John & Desire Amce born Nov. 3.
Joseph of Henry & Judith Allen born Sept. 15.
Stephen of Charles & Eliza: Benmore born May 25.
Mary of Nicholas & Elizabeth Boone born June 19.
Richard of Samuel & Mary Boswell born June 9.
Martha of John & Mary. Bull born Aug. 7.
Dorothy of Edward & Dorothy Bud born July 23.
John of John & Susanna Butler born June 29.
Jacob of Thomas & Sarah Baker born Sept. 25.
Judith of Nathaniel & Judith Blague born Sept. 23.
Thomas of Moses & Eliza. Bradford born Nov. 20.
Ebenezer of Jeremiah & Sarah Belcher born Feb. 21.
Ebenezer of Timothy & Abigail Batt born Dec. 15.
Ruth of Josiah & Ranis Belcher born Dec. 21.
Abigail of Joseph & Hannah Belknap born Jan. 27.
Mehetable of Manassah & Mary Beck born Jan. 13.
Deborah of Nathanll. & Deborah Byfield born Feb. 2.
Sarah of Oliver & Gartright Berry born Jan 28.
Jonathan of John & Mary Briggs born Mar. 22.
Jeremiah of Jerem. & Sarah Bumsteed born Oct. 14.

Jonathan of John & Eliza. Brooking born Oct. 18.
Edward of George & Mary Briggs born Aug.
John of Ralph & Susanna Carter born May 8.
Mary of William & Eliza. Coleman born May 10.
Sarah of Matthew & Naomi Collins born Dec. 7.
Emm of John & Mary Chantrel born Apr. 15.
Jane of Thomas & Jane Clarke born Mar. 20.
Rebecca of Samuel & Deborah Clement born July 10.
Elizabeth of Nathanll. & Elizabeth Cane born Aug. 22.
James of David & Elizabeth Cumins born Sept. 19.
John of John & Sarah Coney born Sept. 17.
Jonathan of John & Anne Carter born June 9.
Mercy of Thomas & Anne Cooke born Nov. 11.
William of John & Ellener Comer born Nov. 28.
Elizabeth of Jonathan & Elizabeth Corwin born May 5.
Sarah of Matthew & Naomi Collins born Dec. 7.
Elisha of Elisha & Elizabeth Cooke born Dec. 20.
Charles of Charles & Judith Crosthwayt born Feb. 3.
Richard of Richard & Sarah Cowell born Oct. 5.
Ruamma of Perciful & Elizabeth Clarke born Apr. 4.
Samuel of Gilbert & Frances Cole born Nov. 30.
Joanna of John & Mary Cotta born Nov. 13.
George of George & Mary Cray born Aug. 15.
Benjamin of John & Mary Crary born Mar. 30.
Benjamin of Leonard & Mercy Dowding born May 20.
Nathaniel of Eleazer & Rebecca Davenport born June 20.
John of John & Mary Dafforne born Aug. 3.
Anthony of Anthony & Anna Dious born July 27.
William of William & Mary Dinsdall born Sept. 5.
Ann of Sampson & Sarah Dewer born Sept. 25.
John of John & Mary Drury born Dec. 26.
Samuel of Joseph & Elizabeth Davis born Mar. 3.
Jane of William & Jane Deane born Mar. 12.
Martha of Francis & Martha Dudson born Mar. 18.
Joseph of Joseph & Elizabeth Eldredge born Apr. 16.
Nathaniel of Samuel & Mercy East born Apr. 2.
Elizabeth of William & Sarah Eustis born July 4.
Mary of Robert & Hannah Earle born Dec. 20.
Deborah of John & Susanna Ellice born Feb. 22.
Mary of Henry & Elizabeth Emes born Nov. 23.
Abigail of Thomas & Jane Eliot born Feb. 12.
Elizabeth of Peter & Mary Edgerton born Mar. 5.
Samuel of Samuel & Mary Eings born Aug. 17.
William of William & Elizabeth Fisher born July 10.
Joseph ⎫ of John & Dorothy Foy born Aug. 11.
Benja. ⎭ of John & Dorothy Foy born Aug. 11.
Ellener of Edward & Sarah Fowle born July 26.
Mary of John & Lydia Foster born Mar. 13.
Thomas of John & Joane Gee born May 15.
Ruth of Matthew & Ellener Gross born May 12.
William of William & Hannah Griggs born June 23.
Benjamin of William & Hannah Gibson born Sept. 8.
William of Gyles & Mary Goddard born Aug. 4.
Agnes of Edmund & Joanna Gatch born Jan. 23.
Elizabeth of William & Sarah Greene born Jan. 29.
Lydia of Samuel & Lydia Holmes born Mar. 26.
George of George & Hannah Henley born May 9.
Thomas of William & Dorothy Hawkins born May 22.
Martha of John & Martha Hunt born June 5.
Edward of Elisha & Eliza. Hutchinson born June 18.
Thomas of Nicholas & Mary Hall born July 3.
Samuel of John & Joanna Hunlock born July 26.
James of James & Mary Harrington born May 9.
Samuel of Thomas & Abigail Hatherly born Mar. 17.

William of John & Ann Hubbard born at Ipswich Dec. 15.
Lydia of Henry & Lydia Ingram born Apr. 18.
Joseph of James & Joanna Ingles born May 23.
Elizabeth of John & Elizabeth Jackson born Jan. 30.
John of Thomas & Abigail Kellond born June 15.
Sarah of Nicholas & Sarah Knell born June 29.
John of Benja. & Phoebe Langdon born May 20.
Samuel of Joseph & Abigail Lowle born July 13.
Deborah of Zibeon & Rachel Lytherland born Oct. 2.
John of William & Jane Lancaster born Oct. 3.
Hannah of Jacob & Rebecca Mason born May 25.
Hannah of James & Elizabeth Meers born June 2.
Sarah of Richard & Sarah Middlecot born May 20.
Jonathan of Edmund & Eliza Mountfort born June 15.
John of John & Lydia Meers born July 5.
Elizabeth of Hosea & Grace Mellot born Apr. 19.
Lucey of Arthur & Joanna Mason born Aug. 11.
Elizabeth of Edward & Jane Mortimore born Aug. 19.
John of John & Martha Morton born Jan. 13.
John of John & Margaret March born Jan. 8.
John of Samuel & Ruth Marshal born March 19.
John of Thomas & Anna Norton born Aug. 14.
Rachel of John & Mary Neeland born Sept. 2.
John of John & Susanna Nichols born Feb. 28.
John of Elisha & Abigail Odlin born May 25.
Elizabeth of Peter & Hannah Odlin born Nov. 21.
Sweet of John & Susanna Oliver born Jan. 16.
Nathaniel of John & Ruth Peirce born Apr. 10.
Elizabeth of George & Elizabeth Purkis born May 16.
Elizabeth of Thomas & Hannah Pemberton born June 17.
Elizabeth of Thomas & Susannah Plimly born June 20.
Nathaniel of John & Mary Pittum born July 8.
Edmund of Edmund & Susanna Perkins born May 8.
William of Thomas & Esther Platts born Aug. 1.
Thomas of Thomas & Elizabeth Peck born Sept. 12.
Thomas of William & Constant Palfrey born Oct. 5.
Elizabeth of John & Elizabeth Playstead horn Nov. 7.
Mehetable of William & Sarah Penny born Nov. 21.
Ann of Richard & Martha Pattishal born Dec. 11.
Joseph of Joseph & Hannah Priest born Mar. 18.
Elizabeth of William & Elizabeth Porter born Feb. 23.
William of William & Sarah Rouse born May 25.
Ruth of John & Mary Ross born Apr. 9.
Obadiah of Obadiah & Susanna Read born Nov. 29.
Edward of William & Anne Rawson born Aug. 29.
Isaac of Abraham & Abigail Spencer born Mar. 17.
Thomas of Thomas & Rebecca Smith born May 13.
Mary of Philip & Margaret Stratton born May 10.
Rebecca of John & Rebecca Scottow born June 21.
Mary of Sampson & Susanna Stoddard born June 13.
Mary of Robert & Ann Shelstone born June 1.
Samuel of Samuel & Hannah Sewall born June 11.
Thomas of Thomas & Margaret Stapleford born June 29.
Samuel of Samuel & Mary Snow born July 20.
Jabez of Jabez & Elizabeth Salter born July 8.
John of Robert & Elizabeth Street born Dec. 9.
Simon of Cyprian & Mary Stevens born Aug. 13.
Anthony of Simeon & Mary Stoddard born Sept. 24.
Sarah of Ephraim & Sarah Savage born Oct. 27.
Samuel of Samuel & Susanna Sexton born Jan. 25.
Peter of Æneas & Joan Salter born Feb. 13.
John of Philip & Rachel Squire born Aug. 16.
Elias of Thomas & Sarah Smith born Mar. 6.
Mary of John & Margaret Spry born July 12.

Rebecca of John & Sarah Skeath born Mar. 4.
John of Fearnot & Bethiah Shaw born Mar. 30.
Richard of Constantine & Elizabeth Sams born Oct. 7.
John of Thomas & Mary Tauley born Apr. 7.
John of John and Mary Trough born Mar. 28.
Benjamin of John & Sarah Tucker born June 21.
Lydia of Daniel & Anne Turell born Jan. 17.
Deborah of Nathaniel & Deborah Thayer born Aug. 22.
William of William & Leah Tower born.Aug. 29.
John of Joseph & Mariana Tapping born Aug. 12.
Robert of Henry & Mary Tarleton born Oct. 6.
Benjamin of Benja: & Abigail'Thwing born July 20.
Benjamin of Richard & Martha Tewell born Nov. 13.
Elias of Samuel & Abigail Townsend born Mar. 2.
Elizabeth of William & Mary Timberlake born Mar. 3.
Jane of John & Elizabeth Usher born Mar. 2.
Joseph of John & Mary Viall born Jan 5.
Jane of Thomas & Mary Waller born June 23.
Solomon of Benjamin & Rebecca Williams born July 4.
John of John & Josabeth Wing born Aug. 7.
Elizabeth of John & Mary Winchcombe born Sept. 8.
Mary of Thomas & Mary Wells born Mar. 25.
Benjamin of George & Constant Waldron horn Apr. 24.
John of John & Elizabeth Webber born Mar. 23.
Mary of Jacob & Mary Wilkins born Jan. 2.
Ebenezer of Henry & Sarah Wright born Jan. 1.
Elizabeth of John & Elizabeth Webber born Jan. 25.
Ann of Edward & Elizabeth Winslow born Aug. 7.
Priscilla of Isaac & Priscilla Waldron born Dec. 6.
Arabella of John & Elizabeth Whaley born Mar. 5.
Henry of Obadiah & Susannah Wakefield born Sept. 17.
Mary of Samuel & Hannah Winslow born June 8.

### First Church.

| | |
|---|---|
| Edward of Elisha Hutchinson | 23d June. |
| John of John Odlin | 28 May. |
| William of William Griggs | June. |
| John of John Moore | Feb. |

## 1679.

### Town.

Bridget of John & Bridget Aires born June 20.
John of John & Hannah Aulgar born Aug. 13.
Jane of Timothy & Joanna Armitage born Oct. 6.
Eleazer son of Jona: & Elizabeth Armitage born Oct. 20.
Sarah of James & Sarah Allen born Sept. 13.
Joseph of Joseph & Elizabeth Arnold born Mar. 21.
Jeremiah of Samuel & Mercy Bosworth born May 13.
Mary of John & Susannah Bradish born May 12.
Jonathan of Jona. & Elizabeth Balston born July 10.
Samuel of Samuel & Anne Burnell born Oct. 9.
Thomas of Thomas & Sarah Baker born Jan. 3.
John of John & Esther Barnell born Aug. 13.
William of Samuel & Hannah Bridge born Aug. 31.
Nicholas of Nicholas & Elizabeth Boone born Aug. 10.
Ruth of Thomas & Mary Barber born Feb. 4.
Josias of Thomas & Mary Beard born Dec. 4.

William of John & Lydia Ballentine born Aug. 23.
Rebecca of Joseph & Rebecca Brisco born Sept. 16.
John of John & Mehetable Benjamin born Sept. 4.
Samuel of William & Persis Browne born Sept. 25.
Rebecca of Robert & Rebecca Brousdou born Oct. 7.
John of John & Sarah Burgis born Oct. 21.
Isabell of Nathanll. & Mary Barnes Oct. 23.
Mary of James & Sarah Burroughs born Oct. 30.
Josiah of Thomas & Mary Beard born Dec. 4.
James of Jonathan & Eliza. Bridgeham born Jan. 12.
John of John & Sarah Balston born Jan. 31.
Caleb of Thomas & Esther Brental born Feb. 29.
Mary of George & Sarah Briggs born Dec. 6.
Ruth of Josiah & Deborah Cobham born Mar. 30.
Joanna of John & Joanna Carthew born Apr. 4.
Humphry of Robert & Rebecca Combey born Sept. 3.
Joseph of Joseph & Susanna Cock born Sept. 15.
Jonathan of John & Margaret Courser born Sept. 29.
Sarah of Richard & Sarah Covell born Oct. 21.
John of John & Hannah Clap born Nov. 11.
Elizabeth of Sampson & Elizabeth Cole born Nov. 19.
Thomas of Uriah & Joanna Clarke born Nov. 29.
Robert of John & Sarah Coney born Dec. 12.
Mercy of John & Susanna Cross born Dec. 28.
William of William & Rachel Clarke born Dec. 30.
Jane of Thomas & Jane Clarke born Mar. 16
John of John & Deliverance Corpe born Mar. 18.
Joseph ⎰ of John & Anne Dinsdall born May 25.
Hannah ⎱ of John & Anne Dinsdall born May 25.
Elizabeth of John & Elizabeth Dyer born July 1.
Mary of Richard & Mary Drew born Oct. 14.
Anna of Sampson & Sarah Dewer born Nov. 7.
Robert of Robert & Sarah Darbey born Nov. 30.
Elizabeth of Henry & Elizabeth Dering born Jan. 5.
Mary of Leonard & Mercy Dowding born Jan. 24.
Benjamin of Benja. & Mary Dunning born Mar. 3.
Elizabeth of Joseph & Elizabeth Eldredge born July 30.
Sweet of David & Mary Edwards born Sept. 9.
Elizabeth of John & Elizabeth Emett born Sept. 24.
Mary of Thomas & Mary Eldridge born Nov. 19.
Elizabeth of Asaph & Elizabeth Eliott born Feb. 14.
James of Thomas & Mary Farney born May 21.
Solomon of Samuel & Anne Flack born June 15.
Mary of John & Sarah Flood born Aug. 14.
Abigail of James & Hannah Flood born Sept. 25.
Christian of John & Eliza. Fayerweather born Sept. 20.
Edward of Edward & Eliza. Goodwin born Apr. 9.
Grace of John & Joane Gee born May 25.
Thomas of Benjamin & Hannah Gillam born Aug. 10.
Elizabeth of Daniel & Elizabeth Greenland born May 28.
Sarah of Peter & Sarah Goulding born Aug. 19.
John of John & Hannah Goffe born Sept. 18.
Samuel of Obadiah & Elizabeth Gill born Nov. 23.
Rebecca of William & Rebecca Gibson born Jan. 20.
Elizur of Elizur & Mary Holyoke born Mar. 28.
Ann of Thomas & Judith Hunt born May 11.
John natural son of John Hudson & Mary Mitchelson born Aug. 2.
Elizabeth of John & Elizabeth Herbert born Sept. 1.
Marke of John & Mary Hands born Oct. 27.
Rebecca of William & Prudence Harrison born Oct. 31.
Mary of George & Sarah Hiskett born Nov. 14.
Powell of Anthony & Margaret Haywood born Nov. 18.
Eliakim of Eliakim & Sarah Hutchinson born Dec. 3.
William of William & Judith Hasey born Dec. 21.

Rebecca of John & Rebecca Hagget born Jan. 16.
James of James & Lydia Hawkins born Jan. 22.
Martha of Joseph & Sarah Hurd born Jan. 25.
Mary of Joseph & Sarah Hurd born Jan. 25.
Mehctable of Elisha & Eliza. Hutchinson born Feb. 6.
Hannah of Nicholas & Mary Hale born Mar. 1.
Joanna of John Jennings & Joanna Holland born Jan. 31.
John of Henry & Lydia Ingram born Jan. 3.
Sarah of John & Elizabeth Indecot born Mar. 15.
Edward of Samuel & Phoebe Johnson born Aug. 1.
Mary of Samuel & Mary Jenkins born Aug. 23.
Sarah of Jonatha. & Eliza. Jackson born Oct. 9.
Rebecca of John & Rebecca Jarvis born Jan. 27.
Jonathan of Samuel & Mercy Jackline born Feb. 28.
David of Roger & Elizabeth Judd born Mar. 3.
Jane of Peter & Mary King born Feb. 9.
Benjamin of John & Naomi Lowle born Nov. 5.
Rebecca of Joseph & Rebecca Lawrance born Nov. 13.
Hannah of Samuel & Elizabeth Lynde born Jan. 1.
Thomas of Arthur & Rebecca Mosier born Sept. 22.
David of James & Dorcas Maxwell born Aug. 31.
Elizabeth of William & Ruth Mumford born Sept. 2.
Sarah of Thomas & Elizabeth Mercer born Oct. 21.
Abigail of Joshua & Elizabeth Matson born Nov. 3.
James of John & Mary Mills born Nov. 10.
Thomas of John & Lydia Moore born Nov. 26.
Mary of Henry & Rachel Maddocks born Dec. 21.
Catharine of Thaddeus & Elizabeth Maccarty born Jan. 23.
Nathaniel of Nathaniel & Deborah Man born Jan 27.
John of John & Mary Nevil born Sept. 14.
Ebenezer of John & Elizabeth Paine born Apr. 25.
Hannah of John & Sarah Place born July 10.
Mehetable of Lisle & Esther Palmer born Apr. 13.
John of John & Elizabeth Palmer born Aug. 28.
Lydia of John & Mary Pell born Sept. 7.
Rebecca of Job & Rebecca Prince born Nov. 12.
William of William & Catharine Paine born Nov. 14.
John of John & Mary Price born Jan. 2.
William of John & Elizabeth Poole born Jan. 7.
Elizabeth of Hugh & Mary Perrin born Jan. 12.
Samuel of John & Mary Pollard born Jan. 16.
Rebecca of John & Ruth Peirce born Feb. 15.
Elizabeth of Joseph & Sarah Peck born Feb. 29.
Mary of Thomas & Susanna Plimble born Mar. 6.
Rebecca of William & Rebecca Pasmore born Oct. 26.
Mary of Peter & Joane Papillaus born Jan. 29.
Elizabeth of John & Charity Ricks born Oct. 3.
Rachel of William & Ann Rawson born Oct. 16.
Ann of Caleb & Elizabeth Rawlins born Oct. 25.
Elizabeth of William & Sarah Rowse born Dec. 20.
Margaret of William & Eliza. Robins born Dec. 22.
Nathaniel of Solomon & Priscilla Rainsford born Feb. 23.
James of Obadiah & Anne Read born Feb. 29
John of Thomas & Eliza. Skinner born Apr. 2.
Abigail of Rowland & Bethiah Storey born Apr. 3.
Martha of Thomas & Martha Squire born May 22.
Joseph of John & ——— Stanbridge born June 10.
Isabella of George & Esther Sigsworth born Sept. 23.
Mary of Philip & Rachel Squire born Oct. 12.
John of John & Elizabeth Skinner born Oct. 13.
Nathaniel of Ephraim & Alice Sale born Oct. 21.
William of William & Hannah Sumner born Nov. 22.
William of Jabez & Elizabeth Salter born Jan. 5.
Hannah of Samuel & Hannah Sewall born Feb. 3.

Joseph of John & Jane Sparrey born Feb. 16.
Anna of Robert & Ann Shelstone born Feb. 22.
Abraham of Abraha. & Abigail Spencer born Mar. 5.
John of Nathanll & Elizabeth Togood born Apr. 20.
Lydia of Benja. & Abigail Thwyng born July 20.
Priscilla of Thomas & Mary Townsend born Sept. 20.
Joshua of William & Ruth Turner born Sept. 28.
Mary of John & Martha Temple born Oct. 6.
Sarah of Joseph & Sarah Turell born Oct. 31.
John of William & Leah Towers born Nov. 1.
Ann of Timothy & Experience Thornton born Nov. 7.
Sarah of Bartbo. & Damaris Threeneedle born Nov. 9.
Abigail of John & Kesiah Tucker born Nov. 10.
Robert of Edward & Elizabeth Thwyng born Jan. 9.
Mary of Thomas & Mary Thatcher born Jan. 28.
Mary of Thomas & Mary Tough born Mar. 11.
Edward of Edward & Abigail Tuttle born Jan. 2.
Hannah of Joseph & Lydia Williams born May 26.
Benjamen of George & Rachel Waldron born May 22.
Anna of Richard & Martha Wharton born May 26.
Samuel of John & Elizabeth Walley born Aug. 4.
Oliver of Nathanll & Mary Williams born Aug. 21.
John of Wait & Mary Winthrop born Sept. 12.
Charles of John & Mary Winchcomb born Sept. 29.
Richard of Richard & Martha Wells born Nov. 2.
Joshua of Joshua & Sarah Winsor born Nov. 7.
Elizabeth of John & Anna Williams born Dec. 5.
Sarah of Samuel & Sarah Walker born Dec. 10.
Jacob of Robert & Margery Williams born Dec. 19.
Susanna of John & Susanna Wilkins born Dec. 22.
Return of Return & Martha Wait born Dec. 28.
Sarah of John & Eliza. Woodmansey born Jan. 8.
Ephraim of Henry & Sarah Wright born Mar. 4.

### FIRST CHURCH.

| | |
|---|---|
| Mehetabel of Elisha Hutchinson | Feb. 8. |
| Sarah of James Allen | Sept. 14. |
| Joseph of John Fayreweather | Dec. 24. |
| Mary of John Fayreweather | Dec. 24. |
| Christian of John Fayreweather | Dec. 24. |
| Mary of John Temple | Oct. 7. |
| William of Samuel Bridge | 31 day 6 mo |
| Elizabeth Dyer | 6 day 5 mo. |
| John Skinner | 19 day 8 mo. |
| Mary Emmons | 2 day 9 mo. |
| Benjamin Thornton | |
| Thomas of John Moore | Nov. |
| Elizabeth of bro. Dering | Jan. |
| Joseph Orchard | Aug. |

## 1680.

### TOWN.

John of Daniel & Mariana Allin born June 19.
Henry of Henry& Judith Allen born July 8.
Milam of John & Constance Alcock born Aug. 8.
Mary of Matthew & Martha Aulgar born Jan. 19.
Sarah of Thomas & Sarah Barnes born May 24.
John of William & Mary Bodkyn born Mar. 25.

Elizabeth of Nathaniel & Deborah Byfield born Apr. 1.
William of William & Ellener Baker born May 30.
Alexander of Josiah & Mary Baker born June 8.
John of Thomas & Mary Barber born Feb. 14.
John of James & Frances Blackborn born July 11.
Brocke of Thomas & Mary Baker born July 28.
Elizabeth of Charles & Mary Blinco born Aug. 12.
Matthew of John & Esther Bernard born Aug. 26.
James of James & Temperance Barnes born Sept. 28.
—— daughter of Stephen & Abigail Burton born Oct. 16.
Ann of John & Ann Balston born Nov. 27.
Samuel of John & Mary Bull born Dec. 19.
Theophilus of Samuel & Lois Bligh born Dec. 23.
Mehetable of Manassah & Mary Beck born Dec. 27.
Hugh of Hugh & Susanna Babel born Mar. 3.
Benjamin of Josiah & Ranis Belcher born Mar. 20.
Mary of Jonas & Mary Clay born Apr. 27.
William of William & Elizabeth Coleman born May 2.
John of Charles & Jeduthan Crosthwayt born May 7.
Ruth of Thomas & Anne Cooke born May 18.
Thomas of Gilbert & Frances Cole born June 14.
Thomas of John & Ellener Comer born Sept. 6.
William of George & Mary Cray born Sept. 27.
Mehetable of John & Hannah Cowell born Oct. 3.
Staines of Robert & Anne Cole born Jan. 19.
Deliverance of John & Elizabeth Cotta born Jan. 26.
Sarah of John & Sarah Cragg born Feb. 9.
Naomi of Matthew & Naomi Collins born May 1.
Hannah of John & Hannah Clap born Feb. 14.
Margaret of John & Palti Dorrell born July 21.
Abigail of William & Abigaile Davis born Mar. 28.
Mary of Joseph & Hannah Dious born Apr. 20.
Sarah of Benja. & Sarah Davis born May 20.
Thomas of Thomas & Mary Davis born July 10.
Thomas of Ambrose & Mary Dawes horn Nov. 1.
Rachel of John & Rachel Drake born Nov. 21.
Isaac of John & Mary Dafforne born Nov. 30.
Elizabeth of Leonard & Mercy Dowding born Feb. 22.
Anna of Gershom & Sarah Davis born Mar. 20.
Sarah of Henry & Joanna Ellis born Oct. 17.
John of John & Catharine Eades born Oct. 25.
Elizabeth of Robert & Hannah Earle born Nov. 16.
John of Henry & Elizabeth Emes born Nov. 30.
Elizabeth of George & Ruth Edwards born Dec. 20.
Hannah of Thomas & Hannah Eliott born Mar. 8.
Mary of Samuel & Mary Eings born May 23.
Lydia of John & Lydia Foster born Oct. 22.
Daniel of Daniel & Ruth Fairfield born Dec. 1.
Elizabeth of John & Frances Francis born Jan. 15.
William of John & Dorothy Foy born Mar. 6.
Mary of Jacob & Mary Gulley born Apr. 18.
Sarah of James & Sarah Goffe born May 2.
Abraham of Lott & Elizabeth Gourden born June 4.
Priscilla of Samuel & Mary Greenwood born June 13.
John of John & Hannah Green born June 23.
Joseph of Nathanll & Mary Green born July 13.
Samuel of James & Rebecca Green born July 20.
John of Valentine & Mary Giles born Aug. 10.
Elizabeth of William & Hannah Gibson born Nov. 27.
Joshua of John & Joane Gee born Jan. 19.
Samuel of John & Hannah Greenleafe born Feb. 26.
Mary of Thomas & Elizabeth Gross born Jan. 18.
Sarah of Richard & Elizabeth Harris born June 17.
Isaac of James & Elizabeth Hughs born June 20.

Samuel of Thomas & Rebecca Harris born July 23.
James of James & Abigail Howard born Aug. 7.
Bridget of Humphrey & Sarah Horrel born Sept. 1.
Benjamin of William & Hannah Hoare born Sept. 5.
Edward of Elizur & Mary Holyoke born Sept. 30.
Mary of Richard & Mary Hunt born Oct. 3.
Nathaniel of John & Ann Hubbard born Oct. 13.
Asaph of James & Sarah Harris born Nov. 10.
Robert of John & Joanna Howen born Dec. 17.
Sarah of James & Dinah Halsey born Dec. 23.
Edward of Ephraim & Sarah Hall born Jan. 29.
Ephraim of Thomas & Judith Hunt born Feb. 17.
Elizabeth of William & Hannah Harris born Sept. 11.
John of John & Jane Jacob born May 12.
William of William & Lydia Jeffery born July 12.
Desire of Aaron & Mary Jeffers born Dec. 13.
Elizabeth of John & Hannah Jones born Dec. 18.
Daniel of Samuel & Mary Jenkins born Jan. 18.
Rebecca of Richard & Hannah Knight born Oct. 14.
Joseph of Henry & Elizabeth Kerbey born Jan. 4.
William of Jane Lancaster born May 6.
Elizabeth of James & Susanna Lindall born July 16.
Elizabeth of John & Sarah Larkin born Aug. 29.
Mary of Samuel & Mary Lynde born Nov. 16.
Grace of Thomas & Grace Levenworth born Feb. 8.
Nathaniel of John & Naomi Lowle born Feb. 25.
Mary of Isaac & Mary Lewis born Mar. 1.
Jacob of Jacob & Rebecca Mason bon Apr. 23.
John of James & Elizabeth Meers born May 12.
Hannah of William & Hannah Milbourn born May 19.
Abigail of William & Eliza. Middleton born Mar. 22.
Hannah of Increase & Maria Mather born May 30.
Joshua of Joshua & Elizabeth Matson born June 30.
Richard of Edward & Jane Mortimore born Aug. 10.
Catharine of Robert & Joane Mansfield born Sept. 12.
Jonathan of James & Salphin Morgan born Nov. 19.
Abigail of John & Abigail Mulberry born Jan. 1.
Moses of Paul & Jemina Maverick born Feb. 8.
Elisha of John & Sarah Mellows born Mar. 16.
Elizabeth of John & Elizabeth Needham born Nov. 23.
John of George & Mary Newby born Dec. 25.
Elias of Elias & Joanna Oakeman born Apr. 21.
Elizabeth of Nathanll & Mary Oliver born ——.
Hannah of Peter & Hannah Odlin born Mar. 3.
Sarah of George & Elizabeth Purkis born Apr. 1.
Yelverton of Seth & Dorothy Perry born Apr.12.
Mary of William & Elizabeth Porter born Apr. 30.
Elizabeth of Joseph & Lydia Peirse born May. 5.
Mary of John & Mary Pittom born May 18.
James of Thomas & Hannah Pemberton born June 4.
Sarah of Moses & Mary Peirse born June 19.
Mary of John & Elizabeth Peck born July 5.
John of Edmund & Susanna Perkins born Oct. 14.
Moses of Moses & Hannah Patrick born Nov. 3.
Job of Job & Rebecca Prince born Nov. 10.
Thomas of William & Sarah Payne born Nov. 15.
Joanna of John & Sarah Place born Jan. 7.
John of John & Mary Price born Mar. 12.
John of George & Sarah Ripley born Mar. 31.
Thomas of Jeremiah & Martha Raper born July 16.
Sarah of James & Sarah Ropes born Nov. 20.
George of George & Elizabeth Robinson born Dec. 28.
Thomas of John & Charity Rix born Jan. 22.
Christian of Sampson & Susanna Stoddard born May 11.

Jane of Samuel & Dorcas Stocker born July 1.
Habakuk of Thomas & Rebecca Smith born July 7.
Samuel of Thomas & Rebecca Smith born July 7.
Sarah of Edward & Mary Smith born July 16.
John of Obadiah & Sarah Sale born July 23.
Jane of Savil & Sarah Simpson born Sept. 13.
Arthur of Thomas & Elizabeth Savage born Mar. 29.
Mary of Ephraim & Sarah Savage born Nov. 10.
Mehetable of Sampson & Mehetable Sheafe born Nov. 27.
Mary of Edward & Esther Stevens born June 15.
John of John & Hannah Somes born Jan. 14.
Ruth of Joseph & Ruth Shaw born Feb. 3.
Elizabeth of Simeon & Mary Stoddard born Feb. 10.
Hannah of Thomas & Mary Tawley born Apr. 16.
Richard of William & Mary Tout born May 8.
William of James & Mary Twisdell born June 11.
John of John & Mary Trough born July 13.
Nicholas of Nicholas & Christian Tribah born Aug. 31.
Elisha of Thomas & Mary Townsend born Sept. 9.
Sarah of Penn & Sarah Townsend born Sept. 14.
Rachel of John & Maria Thwyng born Jan. 31.
Elizabeth of Edward & Elizabeth Thwyng born Feb. 7.
Josiah of Josiah & Sarah Torrey born Feb. 9.
Elizabeth of John & Rebecca Tayler born ——.
Anthony of John & Elizabeth Underwood born May 2.
John of John & Eunice Wayt born Apr. 2.
William of James & Eliza. Whetcombe born Apr. 21.
Hannah of Peter & Hannah Warren born May 19.
Lydia of Jacob & Mary Wilkenson born May 30.
Henry of William & Persis Way born June 7.
Priscilla of Isaac & Priscilla Waldron born June 23.
Edward of Samuel & Eunice Willard born July 6.
Hannah of John & Sarah Walley born July 23.
John of John & Mary White born Aug. 12.
Joanna of John & Jehosheba Wing born Nov. 25.
Joseph of Michael & Elizabeth Willis born Jan. 4.
Sanderson of Richard & Hannah West born Feb. 5.
Benjamin of Benja. & Palsg: Walker born Jan. 4.
Naomi of Giles & Ruth Young born Dec. 16.
John of Roger & Elizabeth Yelings born Aug. 30.

John Harker & Patience Fowler were married by John Richards Esq. Assist.
    Dec. 14.

### First Church.

| | |
|---|---|
| Rebecca Gibson | |
| Mary Eldridge | |
| Jonathan of Sam Jacklin | May 11. |
| Christian dautr. of Sampson Stoddard | May |
| Jsack of James Hughes | |
| Mary of Jo: Pecke | July 5. |
| John of John Wayte | April 2. |
| Henry of Henry Allin | July 8. |
| John of Obadiah Sale | July 23. |
| Joseph of Nathan Green | July 23. |
| Sarah of Pen Townsend | |
| Sarah of John Moore | Nov. |
| Margaret of Palti Dorrell | |
| Rebecca of Rich. Knight | |
| Thomas of Ambrose Dawes | |
| Daniel of Daniel Fayrefeild | |
| Margaret of sister Dorrell born July 21 | July 25. |
| William Fisher born 25 Jan. 168– | Feb. 4. |

## 1681.

Mary of Daniel & Mariana Allin born June 30.
Isaac of David & Hannah Adams born Aug. 7.
Mary of Thomas & Mary Ashley born Sept. 1.
Sarah of John & Elizabeth Alden born Sept. 27.
Elizabeth of Timothy & Joanna Armitage born Oct. **17.**
Nathaniel of Jonathan & Rebecca Adams born Nov. **21.**
Lydia of Bozoun & Lydia Allen born Mar. 7.
Joanna of Robert & Joanna Breck born June 12.
Abigail of Nathanil & Mary Barnes born Apr. 2.
Stephen of Stephen & Tabitha Butler born Apr. 22.
Abraham of Joseph & Hannah Belknap born Apr. 26.
Mary of Thomas & Mary Bridle born June 25.
Ann of William & Susanna Baker born July 1.
Elizabeth of Thomas & Elizabeth Barnard born July 4.
Mary of James & Sarah Burgis born July 2.
William of John & Eliza. Brooking born Sept. **17.**
Thomas of Aaron & Hannah Beard born Sept. 23.
Abigail of Samuel & Hannah Bridge born Sept. 27.
John of John & Esther Barnard born Nov. 6.
Hannah of Moses & Elizabeth Bradford born Nov. **15.**
George of Thomas & Sarah Baker born Dec. 30.
Martha of John & Elizabeth Brown born Jan. 8.
Joseph of Joseph & Rebecca Brisco born Jan. 4.
Elizabeth of Jonathn. & Eliza. Bridgeham born Jan. 22.
John of Thomas & Mary Baker born Feb. 14.
Elizabeth of Josiah & Mary Baker born Feb. 26.
Charles of Charles & Mary Blinco born Jan. 12.
William of William & Rebecca Clarke born Mar. 31.
Mary of John & Mary Clarke born May 3.
Thomas of Thomas & Jane Clarke born June 3.
Sarah of Samuel & Rachel Clarke born July 14.
Jane of John & Hannah Coller born July 20.
John of John & Margaret Courser born Aug. 29.
Bartholomew of Richard & Abigail Cheever born Sept. **9.**
Theodore of Elnathan & Tomasin Chauncey born Oct. **1.**
Hannah of Caleb & Sarah Chapin born Jan. 4.
John of Uriah & Joanna Clarke born Feb. 10.
Elizabeth of Mungo & Mary Crafford born May 19.
Martha of Peter & Rachel Codner born Sept. 7.
Nathaniel of John & Elizabeth Dyer born Oct. 17.
Margaret of Benja. & Sarah Davis born Oct. 28.
Samuel of Gershom & Sarah Davis born Nov. 11.
Thomas of Sampson & Sarah Dewer born Nov. 23.
Elizabeth of Griffin & Elizabeth Edwards born June **17.**
Rachel of Samuel & Mary East born Jan. 5.
Christopher of Richard & Jane English born Jan. 27.
Thomas of Francis & Sarah Ellis born Feb. 1.
John of John & Mary Frost born May 16.
John of James & Hannah Flood born Aug. 3.
John of John & Lydia Foster born Feb. 5.
Dorothy of Thomas & Dorothy Gretian born Mar. 29.
Newman of William & Eliza. Greenough born Apr. **2.**
Edmund of Edmund & Joanna Gage born July 3.
Nathaniel of John & Susanna Gardner born July 20.
Obadiah of Obadiah & Elizabeth Gill born Dec. 2
Ellener of William & Hannah Gibson born Jan. 22.
Sarah of John & Elizabeth Herbert born Apr. 12.
Lydia of James & Lydia Hawkins born Aug. 24.

Richard of George & Mary Hooper born May 3.
Elizabeth of Thomas & Anne Hill born Apr. 28.
Mary of Joseph & Sarah Hurd born May 8.
Elisha of Elisha & Eliza. Hutchinson born May 16.
Samuel of Samuel & Rachel Holman born June 7.
Thomas of Thomas & Mary Hunt born Aug. 21.
Mary of Elizur & Mary Holyoke born Sept. 1.
Sarah of Joseph & Hannah Hasey born Sept. 13.
Sarah of Robert & Elizabeth Howard born Sept. 17.
Rebecca of Thomas & Rebecca Harris born Nov. 8.
Thomas of William & Sarah Hunt born Mar. 23.
Sarah of John & Patience Harker born Sept. 21.
Aaron of Henry & Lydia Ingraham born Oct. 31.
Jane of John & Jane Jacob born Sept. 8.
Thomas of John & Eliza. Jackson born Oct. 5.
Richard of Thomas & Susanna Kellond born Sept. 26.
Elizabeth of John & Rachel Kinde born Nov. 30.
William of William & Hannah Milborne born May 28.
Robert of Hugh & Ellener Mullegin born Aug. 9.
Naomi of William & Ruth Mumford born Aug. 18.
Rebecca of Jacob & Rebecca Mason born Aug. 24.
Sarah of John & Sarah Mason born Aug. 25.
Susanna of James & Dorcas Maxwell born Aug. 27.
Thomas of Samuel & Ruth Marshall born Nov. 1.
John of Samuel & Hannah Marion born Dec. 25.
Catharine of John & Lydia Moore born Feb. 5.
John of John & Sarah Melleson born Dec. 20.
John of Elisha & Abigail Odlin born Nov. 18.
Sarah of Nathanll & Eliza. Oliver born Jan. 7.
John of Seth & Dorothy Perry born Aug. 23.
Elizabeth of Samuel & Elizabeth Philps born Sept. 5.
Nathaniel of Nathanll & Christian Peirse born Oct. 2.
Thomas of Samuel & Elizabeth Parris born Oct. 25.
William of Thomas & Esther Platts born Nov. 24.
Jane of Samuel & Mary Peacock born Dec. 19.
Ruth of William & Ruth Penney born Dec. 15.
Mary of Moses & Mary Peirse born Jan. 22.
John of Thomas & Susanna Plimley born Jan. 25.
William of William & Constance Palfrey born Feb. 17.
Peter of Peter & Jone Papillaus born Mar. 6.
Hannah of Samuel & Hannah Phillips born Mar. 8.
Hannah of Joseph & Hannah Priest born Mar. 20.
Sarah of Samuel & Sarah Phillips born Mar. 21.
Samuel of Edmund & Mary Ranger born Mar. 29.
Dyonisia of Samuel & Dyonisia Ravenscroft born Apr. 12.
John of John & Mary Roberts born July 16.
Dorothy of William & Ann Rawson born Aug. 8.
Jemina of Samuel & Jemina Ruggles born Aug. 12.
Hannah of Nathanll & Priscilla Reynolds born Jan. 15.
William of John & Charity Ricks born Feb. 6.
Sarah of John & Sarah Strange born Apr. 6.
Jacob of John and Sarah Stanbridge born Apr. 17.
Anna of William & Anna Smith born May 10.
John of Thomas & Rebecca Smith born July 6.
Abigail of Obadiah & Sarah Sale born Aug. 6.
Martha of Thomas & Martha Squire born Aug. 9.
Mary of Ephraim & Mary Sale born Aug. 21.
Joanna of John & Sarah Skeath born Aug. 24.
Joseph of Joseph & Ann Stocker born Sept. 18.
Thomas of Robert & Esther Scott born Oct. 13.
Savil of Savil & Sarah Simpson born Oct. 15.
Rebecca of Thomas & Rebecca Smith born Oct. 20.
Ebenezer of Philip & Rachel Squire born Nov. 3.
Abigail of Eleazer & Martha Starr born Nov. 26.

Abigail of Samuel & Hannah Sewall born Dec. 29.
Samuel of John & Elizabeth Sawdey born Feb. 8.
Susanna of Robert & Ann Shelstone born Feb. 12.
Jacob of Sampson & Mehetable Sheafe born Feb. 18.
Humphrey of Joseph & Sarah Turell born May 21.
Timothy of Timothy & Experience Thornton born May 6.
Sarah of William & Leah Tower born June 10.
Nathaniel of Nathanll & Deborah Thayer born July 11.
Sarah of James & Sarah Twisdell born Aug. 11.
Samuel of John & Kesiah Tucker born Sept. 7.
John of John & Lucey Turner born Nov. 1.
Mary of David & Joanna Thomas born Jan. 2.
Sàrah of John & Martha Temple born Jan. 7.
Eliza. of Edward & Elizabeth Thwyng born Feb. 19.
Peter of George & Rebecca Thomas born Feb. 6.
Mary of Edward & Abigail Tuttle born Aug. 31.
John of John & Austis Wilkins born April 2.
Humphry of Jonathan & Sarah Wade born May 1.
Josiah of Samuel & Eunice Willard born June 21.
Joseph of William & Constance Wooster born June 22.
Mercy of Samuel & Sarah Walker born July 5.
Priscilla of Isaac & Priscilla Waldron born July 12.
Martha of Return & Martha Wayt born Aug. 4.
John of Wait & Mary Winthrop born Aug. 26.
William of James & Eliza. Whetecombe born Sept. 9.
Prudence of Samuel & Mary White born Oct. 5.
Thomas of Joseph & Mary Wheeler born Nov. 1.
Elizabeth of Robert & Margery Williams born Nov. 8.
Ann of Gabriel & Mary Warner born Dec. 3.
Elizabeth of Cornelius & Priscilla White born Dec. 29.
John of John & Mary Winchcombe born Jan. 3.
Elizabeth of Nathaniel & Mary Williams born Jan. 22.
John of John & Eliza. Woodmansy born Jan. 28.
Grace of John & Eunice Wayt born Feb. 7.
Jane of Jacob & Mary Wilkinson born Feb. 13.
Abigail of Michael & Elizabeth Willis born Mar. 12.
Mehetable of Henry & Sarah Wright born Mar. 22.

### FIRST CHURCH.

| | |
|---|---|
| John of John Odlin | 20 Nov. |
| Sarah Tucker | Sept. 25. |
| Wates. of John Fayreweather | Dec. 11. |
| Hannah of Wm Griggs | May 30. |
| Sarah of John Temple | January. |
| Abigail of Samuel Bridge | 20 day 8 mc |
| Rachel of John Thwing | Feby. 6. |
| Catharine of John Moore | Dec. |
| Vertue Orchard | Sept. |

### 1682.

#### TOWN.

Benjamin of Henry & Judith Allen born Apr. 4.
Samuel of John & Sarah Aulgar born Apr. 8.
Hannah of John & Constance Alcock born Nov. 5.
Thomas of Thomas & Mary Ashley born Dec. 3.
Katharine of Daniel & Mariana Alline born Dec. 15.
Elizabeth of William & Mary Bodkin born Aug. 15.
Mary of Josias & Mary Baker born May 26.

Benjamin of Nathanll & Mary Barnes born Mar. 30.
Ruth of Samuel & Lois Bligh born Mar. 31.
Peter of James & Temperance Barnes born May 1.
John of John & Anne Balston born May 16.
Sarah of Samuel & Mary Bodman born June 2.
Joseph of John & Charity Baily born Aug. 21.
Ebenezer of Manassah & Mary Beck born Aug. 23.
William of Samuel & Hannah Bickner born Sept. 20.
Mary of James & Mehetable Bill born Oct. 10.
Lydia of John & Lydia Ballantine born Oct. 24.
John of Thomas & Mary Buck born Feb. 27.
Mary of Thomas & Mary Barber born Feb. 25.
Joseph of Thomas & Esther Barnell born Dec. 18.
Edward of Edward & Mary Bicknell born Dec. 20.
Elizabeth of Thomas & Mary Beard born Apr. 9.
Thomas of Charles & Mary Blinco born Dec. 12.
Mary of Philip & Sarah Bass born May 15.
Dorothy of Richard & Sarah Covel born Mar. 27.
John of John & Sarah Carter born Aug. 8.
Susanna of Richard & Abigail Cheever born Aug. 27.
Elizabeth of Francis & Sarah Carlile born Oct. 2.
Staines of Robert & Anne Cole born Dec. 10.
Jeremiah of William & Elizabeth Condey born Jan. 2
William of John & Hannah Cowell born Jan. 25.
John of John & Susanna Cross born Mar. 3.
John of John & Sarah Center born Aug. 8.
Hannah of Caleb & Sarah Chapin born Jan. 4.
Paul of Paul & Mary Dudley born Apr. 26.
Mary      } of Henry & Elizabeth Dering born May 18.
Martha   } of Henry & Elizabeth Dering born May 18.
Margaret of William & Abigail Davis born May 29.
Elizabeth of Richard & Mary Drew born July 23.
Joseph of Joseph & Hannah Dions born Oct. 2.
Sarah of Charles & Mary Dumery born Oct. 20.
Mary of William & Mary Downe born Nov. 21.
John of John & Elizabeth Davis born Dec. 11.
Hannah of William & Mary Davis born July 15.
John of John & Catharine Eyre born Mar. 27.
John of George & Ruth Edwards born Mar. 30.
Mary of William & Sarah Eustis born May 4.
Thomas of Joseph & Eliza. Eldridge born Mar. 7.
Mary of Henry & Elizabeth Emes born Nov. 26.
Mary of John & Frances Francis born Jan. 29.
Hannah of John & Dorothy Foy born Feb. 4.
Mary of Robert & Eliza. Fethergill born Jan. 18.
Rebecca of Thomas & Mary Goodridge born Aug. 10.
Elizabeth of Robert & Mary Gutteridge born Apr. 9.
Samuel of John & Hannah Green born. Apr. 14.
Jacob of Robert & Sarah Gilbert born Apr. 30.
Hannah of William & Thankful Griggs born May 30.
Mary of Benja. & Hannah Gillam born June 9.
Miles of Samuel & Mary Greenwood born Sept. 12.
William of Phillip & Hanna Goss born Oct. 6.
Elizabeth of John & Hannah Goodwin born Dec. 16.
Aquilla of William & Hannah Gibson born Feb. 5.
Joseph of Samuel & Hannah Green born Feb. 21.
Samuel of Thomas & Abigail Hatherly born Apr. 16.
Anna of James & Sarah Harris born Apr. 22.
William of William & Ann Hollowell born May 1.
Benjamin of Joshua & Hannah Hewes born June 9.
Thomas of Margaret Halsey born Aug. 18.
Elizabeth of Thomas & Mary Hitchborn born Sept. 19.
Samuel of Samuel & Mary Holmes born Oct. 7.
Margaret of Edward & Margaret Hunlock born May 7

Rebecca of James & Elizabeth Hughs born Oct. **14.**
Rebecca of James & Dinah Halsy born Nov. 26.
Samuel of Nicholas & Mary Hale born Dec. 2.
Jonathan of John & Joanna Hunlock born Dec. **12.**
Paul of William & Hannah Hoar born Dec. 23.
Mercy of William & Hannaɪ Harris born July 26.
John of William & Elizabeth Ireland born Sept. 17.
David of Roger & Elizabeth Judd born Jan. 17.
Hannah of John & Hannah Jones born Jan. 17.
John of Philip & Mary Langdon born Aug. 27.
Deodat of Deodat & Jane Lawson born Sept. 1.
Elizabeth of Henry & Rachel Mattock born May 16.
Elizabeth of Robert & Eliza. Mason born June 4.
Nathaniel of Joshua & Eliza. Matson born Sept. 14.
Nathaniel of James & Eliza. Meeres born Oct. 7
Mary of Isaac & Phoebe Marion born Dec. 4.
James of James & Eliza. Marshal born Dec. 2.
Samuel of Arthur & Rebecca Mosier born Jan. 21.
Martha of Francis & Martha Marshal born Feb. 6.
Jonathan of William & Hannah Milbourn born Nov. 10.
William of William & Hannah Negro born Nov. **14.**
Mary of Peter & Hannah Odlin born Nov. 6.
John of Richard & Rebecca Ormes born Nov. 17.
Joseph of Joseph & Lydia Pearce born June 23.
Elizabeth of John & Eliza. Playsteed born July 15.
James of Thomas & Hannah Pemberton born Sept. **3.**
Sarah of John & Ruth Pearce born Sept. 9.
Thomas of Thomas & Amce Penant born Nov. 26.
Elizabeth of Samuel & Elizabeth Parris born Nov. **28.**
Anna of James & Anne Pecker born Feb. 13.
Abial of Edward & Abial Paige born Mar. 5.
James of James & Susanna Pryer born Jan. 1.
Samuel of Samuel & Dyonisia Ravenscroft born Apr. **12.**
Solomon of George & Sarah Ripley born Nov. 18.
William of William & Ann Rawson born Dec. 2.
Mercy of John & Mercy Rowlstone born Feb. 15.
Caleb of Caleb & Elizabeth Ray born Feb. 19.
Benjamin of Æneas & Joanna Salter born May 8.
Elizabeth of Samuel & Dorcas Stocker born May **9.**
Hannah of John & Hannah Somes born June 9.
Jabez of Jabez & Elizabeth Salter born July 4.
Samuel of Robert & Mary Saunders born Mar. 23.
Peter of Ponett & Eugene Stelle born July 22.
Faith of Thomas & Elizabeth Savage born Aug. **11.**
Richard of Ephraim & Sarah Savage born Sept. 15.
Simeon of Simeon & Mary Stoddard born Oct. 20.
Benjamin of Joseph & Ruth Shaw born Oct. 26.
Elizabeth of Michael & Mary Shute born Dec. 19.
Mary of John & Jane Sparrey born Dec. 27.
Samuel of Samuel & Elizabeth Sendall born Jan. 20.
Hopestill of Ephraim & Mary Sale born Feb. 14
Samuel of Savil & Sarah Simpson born Feb. 23.
Sarah of Obadiah & Sarah Sale born Mar. 3.
Sarah of William & Anne Sydenham born Mar. 10.
Mary of William & Abigail Seeres born Mar. 23.
Abigail of Edward & Frances Shore born Feb. 23.
Abraham ⎱ of Samuel & Abigail Townsend born May 20.
Isaac ⎰ of Samuel & Abigail Townsend born May 20.
Mehetable of James & Sarah Twisdell born Nov. 25.
Benjamin of Thomas & Mary Townsend born Jan. 10.
Jane of Thomas & Mary Tawley born Mar. 2.
Jane of Nicholas & Christian Tribah born Mar. 11.
Israel of John & Eliza. Underwood born Jan. 13.
John of Isaac & Mary Vergoose born July 26.

Elizabeth of John & Mary Viall born Nov. 12.
Anna of Richard & Anna West born June 2.
John of Obadiah & Susanna Wakefield born July 4.
Samuel of Experience & Elizabeth Willis born Aug. 31.
Martha of Richard & Martha Wharton born Oct. 25.
Peter of Peter & Elizabeth Weare horn Nov. 28.
Elizabeth of Sampson & Rebecca Waters born Feb. 1.
Anna of Henry & Esther Webster born Feb. 9.
Priscilla of Cornelius & Priscilla White born Mar. 4.
Thomas of Samuel & Mehetable Worden born Oct. 6.
Elizabeth of Benja. & Palsg: Walker born Apr. 29.
John of John & Eliza. Welch born July 22.
David of Roger and Eliza. Yelings born Aug. 12.

### FIRST CHURCH.

| | |
|---|---|
| Benjamin of John Thwing | Oct. 8. |
| James of James Barnes | May. |
| Rachel of John Moore | Feb. |
| Mary of bro. Dering ⎫ twins | May. |
| Martha of bro. Dering ⎭ | May. |

## 1683.

### TOWN.

Esther of John & Esther Agard born July 16.
John of Henry & Judith Allen born Sept. 17.
Daniel of Daniel & Mariana Alline born Dec. 6.
Eliza. of John & Bridget Aires born Sept. 28.
Mary of Benjamin & Mary Alford born Sept. 15.
Samuel of Samuel & Elizabeth Bill born ———.
Martha of John & Susanna Beales born Mar. 29.
Persis of Samuel & Hannah Bridge born Mar. 30.
Abigail of Joseph & Rebecca Brisco born Apr. 2.
Hannah of William & Hannah Bryant born June 26.
Dorothy of Samuel & Lois Bligh born July 17.
Elizabeth of Grimstone & Elizabeth Bowde born Aug. 22.
Elizabeth of John & Sarah Birge born Sept. 20.
Nathaniel of Nathanll & Elizabeth Barnes born Sept. 24.
James of John & Esther Barnard born Sept. 28.
Abraham of Abraham & Martha Blish born Oct. 3.
Abigail of Jeremiah & Sarah Bumsteed born Nov. 4.
John of James & Temperance Barnes born Nov. 21.
Mary of Josiah & Mary Baker born Feb. 7.
Thomas of Thomas & Mary Bidle born Feb. 9.
John of John & Charity Baily born Jan. 5.
Mary of James & Grace Butler born Feb. 21.
Jonathan of John & Mary Bull born Feb. 24.
Thomas of Thomas & Sarah Baker born Mar. 22.
James of James & Sarah Burges born Dec. 22.
Mary of David & Mary Basset born Feb. 20.
Robert of Robert & Joanna Breck born Apr. 30.
Mary of Samuel & Mary Checkley born Apr. 12.
Mary of Thomas & Jane Clarke born May 12.
Ann of Thomas & Ann Cooke born Aug. 27.
Katharine of Matthew & Naomi Collins born Sept. 10.
Rachel of Jonas & Mary Clay born Oct. 3.
David of Sampson & Elizabeth Cole born Dec. 21.
Mary of Gilbert & Joanna Cordey born Dec. 15.
Lydia of Caleb & Sarah Chapin born Mar. 15.

Rebecca of Robert & Rebecca Cumbey born Dec. **8.**
Mary of John & Elizabeth Dyer born June 3.
Martha of John & Rachel Drake born June 19.
Mary of Ebenezer & Dorcas Davenport born July **15.**
Sarah of Benja. & Sarah Davis born Aug. 16.
John of Charles & Mary Demurry born Nov. 26.
Abigail of William & Elizabeth Day born Dec. 29.
Samuel of Henry & Abigail Dawson born Aug. **17.**
Hannah of Giles & Hannah Dyer born Aug. 8.
Ebenezer of Samuel & Mary Emons born Apr. **18.**
Sarah of Andrew & Sarah Eliott born June 9.
John of Henry & Joanna Ellis born Aug. 18.
Catharine of John & Catharine Eyre born Dec. 10.
John of Asaph & Hannah Eliott born Dec. 18.
Ruth of John & Mary Fairfield born Sept. 1.
Sarah of Thomas & Elizabeth Fox born Nov. 15.
James of John & Eliza. Fayerweather born Dec. **8.**
Charles of John & Mary Frost born Dec. 26.
Mary of Giles & Elizabeth Fyfield born Mar. **1.**
Mary of John & Joane Gee born Apr. 11.
Priscilla of John & Susanna Gardner born Apr. **15.**
Sarah of John & Hannah Greenleafe born Sept. 3.
Mary of Lot & Elizabeth Gourding born Sept. 30.
William of William & Hannah Gibson born Dec. **16.**
Jane of Peter & Sarah Goulding born Jan. 1.
Benjamin of John & Martha Goodwin born Jan. **17.**
Sarah of Joseph & Sarah Greenleafe born Feb. 3.
Sarah of Roger & Sarah Gilbert born Feb. 22.
Samuel of John & Hannah Goffe born June 19.
Charles of George & Mary Hooper born Apr. 30.
John of Joseph & Sarah Hurd born May **7.**
Elizabeth of Richard & Elizabeth Harris born June **19.**
James of James & Lydia Hawkins born Aug. 8.
Asa of Joseph & Anna Hasey born Aug. 14.
John of John & Christian Herridge born Aug. 31.
Silence of John & Experience Hayward born Dec. 9.
Samuel of Samuel & Elizabeth Ho per born Dec. 19.
Robert of Robert & Elizabeth Howard born Dec. 22.
Jacob of James & Elizabeth Hewes born Feb. 23.
Martha of Edward & Margaret Hunlock born Feb. 7.
Moses of Henry & Lydia Ingram born July 9.
John of John & Mary Ireland born July 27.
Elizabeth of Aaron & Mary Jeffers born May 13.
Sarah of Joseph & Elizabeth Jackson born Aug. 26.
William of Thomas & Elizabeth Johnson born Sept. 4.
Mary of Samuel & Mary Jenkins born Sept. 21.
John of George & Mary Jones born July 28.
Abigail of Humphrey & Susanna Luscombe born June **12.**
Joseph of James & Grizzell Lloyd born Aug. 11.
Isaac of Isaac & Mary Lewis born Aug. 31.
John of Samuel & Deliverance Legg born Jan. 16.
Hannah of Robert & Hannah Mare born Sept. 16.
Nathaniel of James & Elizabeth Meers born Sept. 26.
George of George & Lucey Monk born Nov. 7.
Ephraim of Samuel & Ruth Marshal born Jan. 3.
Joseph of Jacob & Rebecca Mason born Feb. 9.
Samuel of John & Sarah Melleson born July 16.
Margaret of John & Eliza. Needham born Nov. 8.
Sarah of William & Sarah Payne born Mar. 25.
Edmund of Richard & Martha Patteshal born Mar. 31.
Jane of John & Sarah Place born Apr. 18.
Dominicus of Moses & Catharine Patrick born July **7.**
Edmund of Edmund & Susanna Perkins born Sept. 6.
Ruth of John & Mary Pell born Sept. 27.

Mary of Samuel & Mary Pearce born Dec. 1.
Obadiah of Obadiah & Elizabeth Read born Mar. 27.
Paulus Emilius of John & Eunice Robinson born Jan. 7.
Jonathan of Solomon & Priscilla Rainsford born Dec.11.
David of William & Ann Rawson born Dec. 13.
Charity of John & Charity Ricks born Jan. 29.
George of Samuel & Dyonisia Ravenscroft born Mar. 20.
Samuel of John & Mary Roberts born Dec. 25.
Sarah of Samuel & Elizabeth Stocker born Dec. 8.
Gideon of Joseph & Rebecca Smith born Apr. 1.
Jabez of Jabez & Elizabeth Salter born June 1.
Roger of Roger & Elizabeth Stayner born July 23.
William of William & Mary Slack born July 25.
Mary of Samuel & Mary Smith born July 29.
Sampson of Sampson & Mehetable Sheafe born Aug. 14.
Mary of Ebenezer & Martha Savage born Aug. 15.
Sarah of Edward & Esther Stevens born Aug. 20.
Rowland of Rowland & Anne Storey born Sept. 3.
Faith of Thomas & Elizabeth Savage born Oct. 3.
Mercy of John & Hannah Somes born Oct. 22.
Rebecca of Thomas & Rebecca Smith born Oct. 27.
Hezekiah of William & Hannah Sumner born Feb. 21.
Ann of John & Anne Soley born Mar. 8.
Sarah of Edward & Esther Stevens born Aug. 20.
Anna of John & Rachel Todd born Apr. 14.
Catharine of Timothy & Mary Thornton born Apr. 16.
Martha of George & Rebecca Thomas born Sept. 22.
Margaret of Josiah & Sarah Torrey born Apr. 19
Zachariah of Nathanll & Deborah Thayer born May 29.
Joanna of David & Joanna Thomas born Sept. 15.
Elias of Elias & Mary Tatenham born Dec. 2.
John of Edward & Abigail Tuttle born Nov. 24.
Mary of John & Mercy Veren born May 20.
Silvanus of George & Lucey Vickars born June 13.
Elizabeth of James & Eliza. Whetcombe born Apr. 2.
Elizabeth of Wait & Mary Winthrop born May 11.
Mary of John & Eliza. Woodmansey born July 21.
Jeremiah of Joseph & Lydia Williams born Aug. 22.
Mary of Peter & Hannah Warren born Nov. 21.
Abigail of Thomas & Susanna Walker born Dec. 22.
Anna of John & Sarah Ware born Jan. 5.
Joseph of Experience & Elizabeth Willis born Feb. 2.
James of John & Hannah Williams born Mar. 25.
Edward of Edward & Sarah Wadkins born Jan. 10.
Samuel of Samuel & Sarah Walker born Apr. 25.

FIRST CHURCH.

| | |
|---|---|
| Clarke of Elisha Hutchinson | July 8. |
| Mercy of John Clough | |
| James of John Fayreweather | Dec. 8. |
| Persis of Samuel Bridge | 1 day 2 mo. |
| John of James Barnes | Nov. |

## 1684.

### TOWN.

Elizabeth of John & Grace Alliset born June 19.
Ann of Tobias & Anne Atkins born July 2.
Dorcas of Jonathan & Rebecca Adams born July 7.

Ann of Thomas & Mary Ashley born Sept. 17.
Samuel of John & Sarah Aulgar born Sept. 28.
Sarah of John & Constance Alcock born Jan. 28.
Mary of Thomas & Mary Buck born Sept. 2.
Mary of John & Sarah Blake born May 11.
Bethiah of James & Mehetable Bill born May 6.
Thomas of Thomas & Mary Burroughs born June 4.
William of William & Hannah Billings born July 8.
Robert of Robert & Rebecca Bronsdon born July 28.
Abraham of Daniel & Sarah Ballard born Aug. 27.
Sarah of Daniel & Sarah Ballard born Aug. 27.
John of Edward & Mary Bicknell born Sept. 11.
John of Samuel & Anne Beighton born Sept. 19.
· Thomas of Thomas & Elizabeth Barnard born Oct. 10.
Thomas of Edward & Mary Burtles born Jan. 27.
Susanna of George & Mercy Bearstow born Nov. 2.
Elizabeth of William & Secunda Browne born Nov. 17.
Mary of Joseph & Deborah Belknap born Nov. 24.
Jacob of Thomas & Mary Baker born Jan. 5.
John of Joseph & Rebecca Brisco born Jan. 30.
Benjamin of Samuel & Hannah Bridge born Feb. 18.
Abigail of Jeremiah & Sarah Bumsteed born Feb. 12.
John of John & Martha Clough born Apr. 16.
Samuel of John & Mary Cole born Sept. 16.
Bartholomew of Richard & Abigail Cheever born Dec. 2.
Elizabeth of Thomas & Jane Clarke born Dec. 22.
Rebecca of Samuel & Mary Checkley born Sept. 2.
Hannah of William & Hannah Coleman born Jan. 19.
Richard of Robert & Anne Cole born Jan. 21.
Jonathan of John & Mary Center born Feb. 8.
Jennet of Mungo & Mary Crafford born Nov. 2.
Elizabeth of Charles & Mary Coole born Aug. 23.
Thomas of Sampson & Sarah Dewer born Apr. 13.
Henry of Henry & Elizabeth Dering born Oct. 6.
Elizabeth of Edmund & Sarah Dolbeer born Oct. 28.
Elizabeth of William & Mary Downe born Jan. 9.
Elizabeth of John & Elizabeth Davis born Sept. 25.
Joanna of William & Susanna Dennis born Sept. 16.
Free Love of William & Mary Davis born July 8.
Mary of Francis & Sarah Ellis born May 6.
David of David & Mary Edwards born Aug. 29.
Ruhama of Thomas & Ruhama Eldridge born Dec. 16.
George of George & Ruth Edwards born Oct. 15.
Abigail of William & Abigaile Everden born Jan. 11.
John of John & Lydia Foster born July 27.
Hannah of Abraham & Mary Francis born Dec. 19.
Mary of John & Mary Frost born Jan. 22.
Sarah of John & Sarah Fosdike born Feb. 19.
Robert of Robert & Elizabeth Fethergill born Aug. 19.
John of John & Anne Figg born Nov. 5.
William of William & Eliza- Greenough born July 8.
William of William & Thankful Griggs born July 26.
Elizabeth of Robert & Mary Gutteridge born Aug. 7.
Rachel of Isaac & Sarah Griggs born Dec. 15.
Nicholas of Nicholas & Mary George born Feb. 7.
Abigail of Benjamin & Abigail Gillam born Feb. 22.
Hannah of Ezekiel & Ruth Gardner born Mar. 13.
Nathaniel of Joseph & Mary Grafton born Nov. 7.
Richard of Richard & Abigail Gridley born Aug. 16.
John of Nicholas & Mary George born Feb. 6.
Sarah of Humphrey & Sarah Horrell born June 1.
Lydia of Edward & Lydia Hilliard born June 5.
Thomas of Thomas & Rebecca Harris born July 16
Jacob of William & Judith Hasey born Aug. 26.

Richard of John & Anne Hubbard born Aug. 27.
Hezekiah of William & Hannah Harris born Apr. 8.
Mary of Jacob & Martha Howen born Aug. 21.
Richard of Richard & Elizabeth Harris born Oct. 2.
Ephraim of James & Sarah Harris born Dec. 17.
Edward of William & Prudence Harrison born Feb. 9.
William of William & Hannah Hoare born Mar. 1.
Elizabeth of John & Joanna Hunlocke born Mar. 12.
John of John & Patience Harker born July 21.
Nathaniel of Samuel & Mary Ings born July 27.
Sarah of John & Sarah Jenkins born Mar. 25.
Abigail of Samuel & Mercy Jackline born Mar. 25.
Abigail of John & Rebecca Jarvis born Sept. 2.
Mary of John & Jane Jacob born Oct. 7.
Matthew of Matthew & Susanna Jones born Jan. 19.
John of Thomas & Eliza. Johnson born Jan. 16.
Abigail of John & Abigail Keech born June 5.
William of William & Deborah King born Oct. 1.
Peter of Peter & Mary King born Jan. 8.
Elizabeth of John & Emm Kelly born Nov. 27.
John of Joshua & Sarah Lane born Mar. 26.
James of James & Susanna Lindall born May 28.
Elizabeth of Samuel & Deliverance Legg born Oct. 29.
Peter of Charles & Mary Lidget born Jan. 2.
Thomas of William & Mary Lackey born Sept. 9.
Alice of William & Eliza. Middleton born July 4.
Abigail of William & Mary Morto born June 25.
Susanna of John & Susanna Mulberry born Apr. 3.
Paul of Paul & Elizabeth Miller born May 30.
Elizabeth ⎫ of Nathanll. & Deborah Man born July 18.
Sarah    ⎭ of Nathanll. & Deborah Man born July 18.
Abraham of Henry & Rachel Maddocks born Aug. 9.
John of John & Anna Marion born Aug. 17.
Robert of Robert & Sarah Mason born Jan. 14.
John of Archibald & Elizabeth Morris born Feb. 9.
James of James & Dorcas Maxwell born Feb. 15.
Benjamin of Benja. & Rebecca Marshal born Oct. 20.
Mary of William & Hannah Milbourn born Nov.
Samuel of John & Hannah Orris born Nov. 2.
Sarah of William & Elizabeth Parkman born Apr. 5.
Joseph of Joseph & Bridget Phillips born May 17.
Sarah of John & Sarah Pomrey born June 21.
Mary of James & Tomasin Penniman born Aug. 18.
Richard of William & Constance Palfrey born Aug. 19.
Elizabeth of Joseph & Lydia Pearse born Aug. 22.
Sarah of John & Elizabeth Plaisteed born Oct. 22.
Judith of George & Elizabeth Pordage born Feb. 26.
Hannah of John & Hannah Pitcher born Mar. 5.
Moses of Moses & Mary Peirce born Apr. 17.
Thomas of Thomas & Hannah Pemberton born Mar. 17.
Ann of James & Susanna Pryer born Jan. 13.
Mary of Obadiah & Elizabeth Reed born May 4.
John of John & Experience Roberts born June 13.
Matthew of Richard & Sarah Rycroft born July 7.
John of George & Elizabeth Robinson born June 19.
Sarah of Philip & Margaret Squire born Mar. 27.
Prudence of Robert & Anne Shelstone born May 3.
Hull of Samuel & Hannah Sewall born July 8.
Sarah of Obadiah & Sarah Sale born Aug. 27.
William of Fearnott & Bethiah Shaw born Nov. 4.
Mary of Thomas & Mary Simcock born July 16.
Mary of Simeon & Mary Stoddard born Sept. 19.
Joseph of Robert & Elizabeth Sanderson born Oct. 10.
Hephzibah of Ephraim & Mary Sale born Dec. 24.

Matthew of Sampson & Mehetable Sheafe born Jan. 1.
Elizabeth of Ephraim & Sarah Savage born Jan. 8.
Elizabeth of Savil & Sarah Simpson born Mar. 5.
Elizabeth of Edward & Mary Sumers born June 8.
Mary of Constan: & Elizabeth Sams born Dec. 2.
Sarah of Richard & Sarah Talley born Apr. 16.
Ebenezer of William & Leah Tower born May 2.
Elizabeth of James & Elizabeth Townsend born July 18.
Elizabeth of John & Martha Temple born July 28.
Cornelius of Nathaniel & Deborah Thayer born Nov. 14.
Jeremiah of Jeremiah & Mercy Tay Jan. 19.
George of George & Rebecca Thomas born Mar. 16.
Prudence of Isaac & Mary Vergoose born Apr. 21.
Roger & ⎫ of Richard & Anne West born May 22.
Anna    ⎭ of Richard & Anne West born May 22.
Lydia of Jehu & Eunice Wayt born June 5.
Ann of John & Eliza Woodmansey born July 20.
Sarah of Joln & Elizabeth Walley born Aug. 25.
Ebenezer of Samuel & Elizabeth Wakefield born Sept. 12.
John of Richard & Martha Wharton born Sept. 29.
Deliverance of Michael & Elizabeth Willis born Nov. 1.
Nathan of Cornelius & Priscilla White born Nov. 5.
Peter of Peter & Mehetable Welcome born Nov. 8.
Robert of Peter & Abigail Warren born Dec. 27.
Hannah of Peter & Abigail Wyar born Jan. 3.
William of Waitstil & Mary Winthrop born Jan. 4.
Benjamin of Thomas & Susanna Walker born Mar. 13.
Joshua of Joshua & Sarah Winsor born Mar. 16.
Samuel of Samuel & Mehetable Worden born Feb. 10.
John of John & Sarah Wheatly born May 18.
William of Samuel & Sarah Walker born Dec. 8.
John of Benja. & Palsg: Walker born Mar. 18.
Cornelius of Cornelius & Faith Waldo born Nov. 17.

### FIRST CHURCH.

| | |
|---|---|
| William of Wm. Griggs | July. |
| Elizabeth of John Temple | July. |
| Benjamin of Samuel Bridge | Feb. 22. |
| Francis of John Moore | Nov. |
| Henry of brother During | Oct. |
| Ann of sister Dorrell born Apr 25 | Apr. 29. |
| Thomas Fisher born Sept. 28 | Oct. 5. |
| John of John Marion | Aug 31. |

## 1685.

### TOWN.

Mary of Bozoun & Lydia Allen born July 13.
James of James & Elizabeth Adlington born Dec. 14.
Katharine of Daniel & Mariana Alline born Feb. 18.
John of Benja. & Mary Alford born July 5.
John of Roger & Sarah Burges born Apr. 5.
Joseph of John & Mary Briggs born Apr. 7.
Benjamin of John & Mary Briggs born Apr. 7.
Abigail of Samuel & Hannah Bicknel born Apr. 14.
Joseph of Grinstone & Elizabeth Bowde born Apr. 27.
Philip of Philip & Sarah Bass born May 2.
Sarah of John & Sarah Barnard born May 3.
Grace of James & Grace Butler born May 2.
Ellener of Thomas & Esther Bulkley born Sept. 16.

Elisha of Edmund & Elizabeth Browne born Sept. 16.
Mehetable of Thomas and Esther Brental born Nov. 14.
Joseph of Joseph & Deborah Belknap born Nov. 18.
John of John & Mary Bonner born Jan. 10.
Elizabeth of Nathanll. & Elizabeth Barnes born Jan. 22.
Joseph of James & Temperance Barnes born Feb. 7.
Richard of Samuel & Elizabeth Bill born Mar. 25.
Abigail of Thomas & Mary Beard born Sept. 18.
John of William & Joanna Bolderson born Dec. 28.
Sarah of John & Sarah Blake born Feb. 2.
Mary of Thomas & Mary Bossinger born Feb. 2.
Mary of Charles & Mary Blinco born Mar. 7.
Samuel of Samuel & Mary Checkley born Sept 23.
John of John & Susanna Cross born Sept. 28.
William of William & Elizabeth Colman born Nov. 3.
Mary of John & Ellener Comer born Dec. 15.
Sarah of John & Sarah Clarke born July 9.
James of John & Sarah Coney born Oct. 12.
Matthew of Matthew & Naomi Collins born May 1.
Job of Job & Joanna Chamberlain born May 16.
Abigail of John & Hannah Clap born Nov. 21.
William of David & Mary Couch born Jan. 25.
Richard of Robert & Anne Cole born Jan. 21.
Elizabeth of James & Elizabeth Correll born Feb. 9.
Sarah of William & Martha Davis born Apr. 22.
Elizabeth of Benja. & Sarah Davis born May 23.
John of John & Rachel Drake born June 12.
Sarah of John & Sarah Davis born July 1.
Abigail of Henry & Abigaile Dawson born Aug. 27.
John of John & Palti Dorrell born Aug. 28.
Samuel of John & Elizabeth Dyer born Oct. 13.
Giles of Giles & Hannah Dyer born Dec. 5.
Sampson of Sampson & Sarah Dower born Mar. 13.
Ebenezer of Richard & Mary Ellis born June 19.
William of William & Abigail Everden born Dec. 17.
Joseph of Joseph & Elizabeth Eldridge born Dec. 23.
Elizabeth of John & Elizabeth Eustis born Jan. 30.
Sarah of Stephen & Mary Feilder born May 30.
Joseph of John & Dorothy Foy born Aug. 21.
Josiah of Josiah & Ann Franklin born Aug. 23.
John of John & Sarah Fosdike born Mar. 6.
Huldah of Thomas & Elizabeth Gross born Sept. 13.
John of Isaac & Sarah Griffin born Sept. 2.
Jane of Samuel & Hannah Greene born June 12.
Peter of Samuel & Mary Greenwood born July 7.
Elizabeth of Lot & Elizabeth Gourding born Aug. 10.
Thomas of Thomas & Mary Goodridge born Dec. 16.
Elizabeth of Samuel & Susanna Gray born Dec. 21.
Joseph of John & Hannah Goffe born Mar. 8.
Grace of John & Joane Gee born Sept. 4.
Abraham of Abraham & Elizabeth Gourding born Jan. 3.
Mary of George & Mary Hooper born May 2.
Martha of Edward & Lydia Hilliard born May 23.
Martha of John & Elizabeth Howen born June 23.
William of William & Mary Hough born July 18.
Hannah of Samuel & Rachel Holman born Aug. 5.
Joseph of Joseph & Susanna Hiller born Sept. 9.
Hannah of Isaac & Hannah Hallom born Jan. 25.
Hannah of Elizur & Mary Holyoke born Feb. 12.
Mary of Edward & Margaret Hunlock born Feb. 15.
Ann of William & Sarah Hunt born Feb. 23.
Charles of John & Mary Hewes born Feb. 26.
Thomas of Thomas & Mary Hunt born Mar. 15.
Elizabeth of William & Elizabeth Hewes born Apr. 26.

Susanna of Thomas & Meldred Inglesby born Aug. 27.
George of Nathanll. & Ellener Jewell born Apr. 28.
William of Samuel & Mercy Jacklin born Apr. 29.
Thomas of John & Sarah Jenkins born Jan 12.
Elizabeth of Joseph & Elizabeth Jackson born Jan. 27.
William of Roger & Anne Kilkup born June 4.
John of John & Emmin Kelly born Nov. 23.
John of Elizabeth Lane born May 8.
Theophilus of Samuel & Mehetable Lillie born June 10.
James of Philip & Mary Langdon born Aug. 15.
David of David & Martha Langdon born Sept. 20.
Joseph of Isaac & Mary Lewis born Nov. 16.
Henry of James & Grizzell Lloyd born Nov. 28.
Sarah of Joshua & Sarah Lane born Feb. 6.
John of John & Anna Marion born May 30.
Hannah of Samuel & Hannah Marion born June 23.
Zachariah of John & Sarah Melleson born June 18
Andrew of Francis & Martha Marshal born July 26.
Margaret of Andrew & Ruth Mariner born Sept. 7.
Mary of Benja. & Rebecca Marshal born Nov. 17.
Ann of John & Phoebe Marshal born Dec. 28.
Bethiah of Joshua & Elizabeth Matson born Jan. 18.
John of Paul & Elizabeth Miller born Feb. 17.
Zachariah of John & Elizabeth Needham born Oct. 1.
Samuel of Peter & Hannah Odlin born May 6.
Richard of Richard & Rebecca Ormos born Aug. 17.
Robert of Richard & Martha Patteshal born Mar. 26.
Ann of Samuel & Sarah Phillips born May 20.
Dorothy of John & Rachel Pasco born July 19.
Jonathan of Edward & Abial Paige born July 20.
Mary of Hugh & Mary Price born July 25.
Amy of Thomas & Amy Penant born Oct. 5.
John of John & Elizabeth Peck born Oct. 6.
Benjamin of Joseph & Bridget Phillips born Oct. 18.
Cotton of Thomas & Dorothy Palmer born Nov. 11.
William of William & Elizabeth Parkman born Dec. 19.
Abigail of John & Elizabeth Palmer born Feb. 6.
Jane of Thomas & Hannah Pemberton born Mar. 18.
William of Joseph & Bethiah Parson born Dec. 29.
Anna of Daniel & Anna Quinsey born June 1.
Ann of Abraham & Sarah Quiddington born Jan. 30.
Jeremiah of Thomas & Martha Raper born Apr. 27.
Mary of Stephen & Judith Robino born July 29.
John of John & Charity Rickes born Aug. 30.
Jeremiah of Samuel & Sarah Ruggles born Nov. 14.
Margaret of Samuel & Hannah Ruck born Jan. 3.
Sarah of John & Experience Roberts born Jan. 28.
Gershom of John & Judah Rawlins born Jan. 29.
Joseph of Rowland & Anne Storey born Mar. 31.
Anthony of Anthony & Susanna Stokes born June 18.
Mary of Robert & Mary Saunders born July 12.
Benoni of Charles & Elizabeth Salter born July 17.
Abigail of Robert & Abigail Seers born July 24.
Elizabeth of John & Hannah Somes born Aug. 31.
Elisha of Jabez & Elizabeth Salter born Sept. 22.
Arthur of Arthur & Sarah Smith born May 23.
David of Simeon & Mary Stoddard born Dec. 5.
Henry of Samuel & Hannah Sewall born Dec. 8.
Mary of Stephen & Esther Swasy born Dec. 10.
Sarah of William & Hannah Sunner born Dec. 29.
Sheffield of Joseph & Anne Stocker born Jan. 12.
Nathaniel of Joseph & Rebecca Smith born Feb. 1.
Elizabeth of Thomas & Elizabeth Smith born Feb. 14.
Thomas of Thomas & Rebecca Smith born Feb. 17.

Elizabeth of Ralph & Susanna Straker born Aug. 31.
Joseph of Joseph & Hannah Souther born Feb. 27.
Hezekiah of Thomas & Mary Townsend born Apr. 13.
John of Thomas & Mary Talley born June 21.
Thomas of Thomas & Miriam Tyler born Aug. 15.
Rebecca of Penn & Sarah Townsend born Aug. 15.
Nathaniel of William & Leah Tower born Oct. 11.
Richard of·Richard & Sarah Talley born Dec. 21.
Sarah of John & Maria Thwing born Feb. 22.
Sarah of John & Martha Tuttle born Jan. 8.
Mary of Francis & Mary Whitman born Apr. 10.
Elizabeth of Michael & Judith Wrong born May 9.
Sampson of Sampson & Rebecca Waters born June 20.
Sarah of John & Sarah Ware born July 12.
Cyrus of William & Abigail Wright born Aug. 4.
Sarah of Ephraim & Elizabeth Warren born Aug. 10.
John of Experience & Elizabeth Willis born Sept. 4.
John of Gabriel & Mary Warner born Nov. 22.
Samuel of Edward & Sarah Wadkins born Dec. 13.
Sarah of Griffin & Sarah Williams born Jan. 2.
Robert of Robert & Margery Williams born Jan. 13.
Thomas of Thomas & Sarah Wheatly born Jan. 8.
Abraham of Gregory & Sarah Wakeman born Nov. 8.

### FIRST CHURCH.

| | |
|---|---|
| Samuel of Elisha Hutchinson | Oct. 25. |
| John of John Fayreweather | Dec. 3. |
| Sarah of John Thwing | Feb. 28. |
| Joseph of James Barnes | Feb. |
| James Howard aged 5 years | May. |
| Abigail Howard aged 2 years | May. |
| Elizabeth Howard aged 1 month | May. |
| Catharine of Joun Moore | March. |
| John of sister Dorrell born Aug. 28 | Aug. 29. |
| John Squire | May 3. |
| Margaret Squire | Aug. 16. |
| Jeremiah Ruggles | Nov. 14. |
| John of John Marion | July 5. |

## 1686.

### TOWN.

Hannah of Matthew & Martha Aulgar born May 22.
Anne of John & Elizabeth Allen born May 28.
Grace of John & Grace Allisct born May 24.
Hannah of John & Sarah Alguer born July 4.
Benjamin of Benja. & Mary Alford born Oct. 5.
Elizabeth of David & Hannah Adams born Oct. 8.
William of Thomas & Mary Ansell born Dec. 24.
James of Jonatha. & Rebecca Adams born Jan. 7.
Jane of John & Avis Adams born Feb. 21.
Rebecca of Joshua & Rebecca Atwater born Feb. 25.
Rebecca of John & Mary Arnold born Feb. 26.
Ann of Bozoun & Lydia Allen born Mar. 11.
John of Robert & Joanna Bell born Mar. 27.
Joseph of John & Susanna Butler born May 28.
Elizabeth of Phillip & Margaret Barger born June 10.
Samuel of Thomas & Sarah Banister born July 11.
Edward of Edward & Mary Bromfield born May. 7.
Joseph of Thomas & Mary Barber born July 9.

Samuel of Thomas & Rebecca Bayley born July 19.
Benjamin of William & Hannah Bryant born July 16.
Hannah of Ambrose & Hannah Berry born July 30.
Martha of Charles & Elizabeth Benmore born Aug. 4.
Sarah of Joseph & Rebecca Brisco born Aug. 1.
Sarah of John & Sarah Benjamin born May 8.
Benjamin of John & Anne Balston born May 3.
Elizabeth of Peter & Elizabeth Bonyot born June 19.
Thomas of Edward & Esther Bennet born Aug. 19.
Sarah of John & Mary Boyes born Aug. 22.
Sarah of Thomas & Elizabeth Barnard born Aug. 23.
Benjamin of Robert & Rebecca Bronsdon born Aug. 30.
John of James & Margaret Barton born Sept. 5.
Mary of Peter & Elizabeth Butler born Sept. 26.
Andrew of John & Sarah Borland born Sept. 26.
Thomas of Thomas & Mary Bill born Oct. 4.
Ann of Samuel & Anne Burnell born Oct. 7.
Samuel of Samuel & Martha Burrell born Oct. 30.
Robert of Thomas & Joanna Barnes born Dec. 3.
John of John & Mary Barber born Dec. 10.
Elizabeth of James & Grace Butler born Dec. 23.
Susanna of William & Elizabeth Burt born Dec. 31.
Thomas of Thomas & Esther Bulkley born Nov. 1.
Susanna of John & Jane Boderitt born Nov. 27.
Jeremiah of Joseph & Deborah Belknap born Jan. 1.
Mary of Henry & Rebecca Bushell born Jan. 16.
Daniel of John & Esther Barnard born Jan. 24.
Thomas of Jeremiah & Sarah Bumsteed born Feb. 1.
Charity of John & Charity Bayly born Feb. 4.
John of Abrah. & Martha Blish born Feb. 6.
Edward of Edward & Mary Bertles born Feb. 13.
Mary of John & Sarah Balston born Feb. 16.
Sarah of Thomas & Sarah Baker born Feb. 25.
Mercy of John & Mercy Bowker born Feb. 26.
John of Thomas & Mary Beetle born Feb. 28.
Elizabeth of Nathaniel & Mary Baker born Mar. 9.
Thomas of Robert & Elizabeth Butcher born Mar. 11.
Samuel of Samuel & Anne Beighton born Apr. 6.
Mary of Gilbert & Joanna Cordey born Mar. 27.
Caleb of Caleb & Sarah Chapin born Apr. 2.
Thomas of John & Mary Cole born Apr. 23.
Martha of John & Martha Clough born June 10.
John of Thomas & Anne Cooke born June 12.
Sarah of Andrew & Sarah Cunningham born Sept. 5.
Rebecca of Jonathan & Rebecca Charles born Sept. 5.
Jonathan of Sampson & Elizabeth Cole born Sept. 2.
William of William & Susanna Critchfield born Oct. 13
Hannah of Joshua & Elizabeth Cobbett born Oct. 18.
John of William & Lydia Clough born Oct. 27.
Dean of John & Mary Chantrel born Nov. 1.
Elizabeth of George & Elizabeth Clarke born Nov. 12.
Mary of Richard & Abigaile Cheever born Dec. 24.
Deborah of John & Martha Cornish born Dec. 24.
William of Job & Joanna Chamberlain born Jan. 16.
John of Mungo & Mary Crafford born Feb. 18.
Abigail of John & Mary Clough born Mar. 15.
Sarah of Robert & Rebecca Cumbey born Apr. 16.
Thomas of Charles & Mary Damaree born May 13.
William of Humphrey & Sarah Davie born June 27.
Thomas of John & Elizabeth Davis born July 24.
William of William & Susanna Dennis born Dec. 2.
Sarah of William & Sarah Dinsdal born Dec. 15.
William of Benja. & Sarah Davis born Jan. 22.
Zachariah of Zachariah & Sarah Davis born Feb. 16.

Joseph of John & Elizabeth Dyer born Mar. 2,
Mary of Thomas & Hannah Eliot born July 25,
Rebccca of Samuel & Mercy East born Aug. 16.
Martha of Henry & Joanna Ellis born Sept. 3.
Richard of Richard & Mary Ellis born Sept. 9.
William of Samuel & Mary Eings born Apr. 9.
William of William & Elizabeth Endecot born Sept. 25.
John of John & Katharine Eades born Nov. 6.
Esther of Edward & Sarah Everett born Jan. 24.
Jonathan of Jonathan & Martha Farnum born May 6.
Mary of John & Mary Fairfield born Apr. 3.
Gabriel of Gabriel & Catharine Fishlock born July 15.
Thomas of Thomas & Elizabeth Fathom born June 24.
Hannah of Hugh & Ellener Floyd born Nov. 5.
Ann of Josiah & Anne Franklin born Jan. 5.
Sarah of James & Mary Ferryes born Jan. 18.
Sarah of John & Lydia Foster born Jan. 29.
Joseph of John & Anne Figg born Mar. 6.
Bartholomew of Bastian & Elizabeth Gazeau born Apr. 23.
Elizabeth of William & Elizabeth Greenough born June 8.
Susanna of Robert & Mary Gutteridge born Aug. 19.
Enoch of Joseph & Sarah Greenleafe born Sept. 2.
Sarah of Isaac & Sarah Griggs born Aug. 9.
Samuel of William & Thankful Griggs born Sept. 26.
Mercy of Peter & Sarah Golding born Sept. 8.
Elizabeth of Obadiah & Elizabeth Gill born Sept. 28.
Zachariah of Benja. & Elizabeth Gillam born Oct. 11.
Joseph of Richard & Abigail Gridley born Nov. 6.
Solomon of John & Hannah Green horn Nov. 14.
Thomas of Thomas & Elizabeth Gross born Dec. 6.
Nathaniel of Joseph & Hannah Gallop born Jan. 14.
Ann of William & Hannah Gibson born Feb. 5.
Mary of Nicholas & Mary George born Feb. 5.
Isaac of Isaac & Mary Girrard born Mar. 24.
Samuel of John & Martha Goodwin born Jan.—
Mary of Francis & Johanna Holland born Apr. 15.
William of John & Experience Hayward born May 25.
Susanna of John & Susanna Hills born June 13.
Sarah of James & Elizabeth Hues born July 16.
Ruth of Samuel & Esther Huxford born July 22.
John of Abraham & Elizabeth Harrison born July 26.
John of Thomas & Annis Hill born Aug. 5.
John of William & Hannah Harris born Aug. 9.
Thomas of Thomas & Rebecca Harris born Aug. 10.
Mary of James & Sarah Harris born Oct. 11.
Ann of William & Patience Hodon born Oct. 27.
John of John & Mary Holbrooke born Nov. 4.
Susanna of Joseph & Susanna Hiller born Nov. 5.
Anne of John & Anne Hubbard born Dec. 5.
Elizabeth of Thomas & Judith Hunt born Dec. 21.
Sarah of Joshua & Hannah Hewes born Dec. 23.
William of John & Deborah Hurd born Jan. 17.
Samuel of John & Hannah Haughton born Jan. 31.
William of William & Mary Hough born Feb. 2.
Hannah of Elizur & Mary Holyoke born Feb. 15.
William of William & Mary Hopper born Feb. 18.
Abigail of Ambrose & Hanna Honywell born Feb. 27.
Hannah of William & Hannah Hoare born Mar. 5.
Zachariah of Ephraim & Sarah Hall born Mar. 6.
John of John & Elizabeth Indicot born Apr. 2.
Elizabeth of Henry & Lydia Ingram born July 17.
Abigail of Thomas & Meldred Inglesby born Feb. 10.
Samuel of Samuel & Mary Jenkins born Apr. 4.
Mary of William & Mary Jarvis born July 5.

Mary of William & Sarah Joyce born Sept. 15.
Thomas of Matthew & Susanna Jones born Oct. 8.
Ebenezer of Roger & Elizabeth Judd born Oct. 21.
Hannah of John & Hannah Jones born Nov. 3.
Ann of Thomas & Dorothy Jennings born Jan. 13.
William of William & Jane Keen born May 2.
Susanna of John & Mary King horn Sept. 3.
Elizabeth of John Kilby born Sept. 15.
John of William & Deborah King born Sept. 22.
John of John & Emm Kally born Sept. 15.
George of George & Martha Lawson born Apr. 10.
Elizabeth of Charles & Mary Lidget born June 8.
Mercy of Thomas & Mary Lincoln born June 6.
Elizabeth of John & Elizabeth Langdon born ———.
Elhanan of Elhanan & Mary Lyon born July 27.
William of William & Mary Lackey born July 29.
Samuel of Samuel & Mehetable Lillie born Nov. 12.
Samuel of David & Martha Langdon born Nov. 13.
Samuel of James & Dorcas Maxwell born May 12.
Joseph of John & Anne Marion born June 10.
Jane of Samuel & Elizabeth Mansell born June 19.
Ruth of Samuel & Ruth Marshal born July 2.
Jane of Edward & Jane Mortimore born July 12.
Sarah of Stephen & Sarah Mason born July 27.
Susanna of Robert & Anne Moore born Aug. 6.
Phoebe of William & Phoebe Manly born Sept. 1.
William of George & Lucey Monk born Aug. 17.
Susanna of John & Margaret Marsh born Oct. 10.
John of Richard & Mary Marrett born Oct. 26.
Tomasin of John & Joanna Mills born Oct. 30.
Robert of John & Abigail Mulberry born Nov. 17.
Christopher of Christopher & Mary Monk born Dec. 16.
Rebecca of Benjamin & Rebecca Marshal born Jan. 15
Ruth of Andrew & Ruth Mariner born Feb. 6.
Sarah of John & Sarah Melleson born Feb. 3.
Joseph of Henry & Alice Mare born Mar. 13.
Susanna of John & Sarah Mason born Mar. 19.
Joseph of Joseph & Mary Moss born Mar. 22.
Elizabeth of Thomas & Elizabeth Messenger born Mar. 28
Sarah of Thomas & Hannah Narramore born Aug. 10.
Michael of Michael & ——— Nowell born Aug. 18
John of John & Susanna Nichols born Dec. 6.
Sarah of John & Sarah Oliver born May 4.
Samuel of Peter & Hannah Odlin born May 6.
Mary of John & Mary Okey born Oct. 8.
Martha of John & Hannah Orris born Oct. 15.
Regnal of Regnal & Priscilla Odal born Jan. 20.
Hannah of Nathaniel & Hannah Parkman born Mar. 30.
William of Moses & Mary Peirce born Apr. 11.
Mary of Thomas & Mary Parris born May 27.
Elizabeth of William & Sarah Paine born June 21.
Peter of Roger & Hannah Prouse born May 1.
Mary of Edward & Elizabeth Perry born ———
Joseph of Joseph & Sarah Peck born June 8.
Gillam of Samuel & Hannah Phillips born Sept. 25.
Elizabeth of Thomas & Elizabeth Pike born Oct. 29.
Sarah of Job & Rebecca Prince born Nov. 23.
James of James & Tomasin Peniman born Dec. 11.
Bethiah of Joseph & Bethiah Parson born Jan. 1.
Edeth of William & Catharine Paine born Feb. 8.
Hannah of George & Elizabeth Pordage born Feb. 13.
John of Samuel & Mary Pearse born Feb. 17.
Elizabeth of Nathanll & Mary Pulman born Feb. 11.
Jane of Edmund & Susanna Perkins born Feb. 25.

Elias of William & Eliza. Parkman born Feb. 27.
Joseph of Joseph & Lydia Pearse born Mar. 24.
Sarah of Richard & Sarah Ricraft born May 10.
Dorothy of William & Ann Rawson born June 19.
Christian of John & Eunice Robinson born June 11.
Thomas of John & Mercy Rowlistone born July 28.
Thomas of Thomas & Mary Rowe born July 27.
Edward of Edward & Huldah Rainsford born July 18.
Nathaniel of Obadiah & Elizabeth Read born Aug. 23.
Elizabeth of Thomas & Sarah Robinson born Sept. 26.
Mercy of Thomas & Mercy Raper born Oct. 8.
Elizabeth of Joseph & Eliza. Rogers born Oct. 10.
Sarah of Samuel & Dyonisia Ravenscroft born Nov. 20.
Edmond of John & Mary Roberts born Dec. 7.
Judith of Stephen & Judith Robino born Jan. 1.
John of Daniel & Ruth Royce born Jan. 23.
Lydia of Charles & Mary Raven born Jan. 23.
Esther of Robert & Ann Shelstone born May 4.
Mary of Henry & Purchase Spray born May 22.
Ann of Arthur & Sarah Smith born June 15.
Mary of William & Mary Shortrigs born Apr. 29.
Mary of Josiah & Mary Stone born Apr. 4.
John of William & Mary Slack born Apr. 19.
John of John & Mary Stevens born July 2.
Rebecca of Alexander & Rebecca Seers born Aug. 12.
Prudence of Philip & Margaret Squire born Aug. 15.
Joanna of John & Jane Smith born Aug. 28.
Lydia of Thomas & Eliza. Savage born Sept. 6.
Elisha of Jabez & Eliza. Salter born Oct. 9.
Christopher of Joseph & Hanna Souther born Oct. 1.
Grace of William & Mary Starling born Oct. 28.
Ann of Rowland & Anne Storey born Oct. 28.
Susanna of Robert & Mary Saunders born Dec. 15.
Benjamin of John & Hannah Somes born Jan. 8.
William of William & Martha Smallage born Jan. 13.
Benjamin of Ralph & Susanna Straker born Jan. 15.
John of Ephraim & Mary Sale born Jan. 17.
Gifford of John & Mary Squire born Jan. 22.
Hannah of Ephraim & Sarah Savage born Jan. 17.
Sarah of John & Ann Symonds born Jan. 25.
Stephen of Samuel & Hannah Sewall born Jan. 31.
Hannah of William & Hannah Smith born Feb. 1.
Daniel of Daniel & Elizabeth Stoddard born Mar. 6.
Samuel of Matthias & Elizabeth Smith born Mar. 21.
Mary of William & Mary Thwing born Apr. 7.
Benjamin of Edward & Eliza. Thwing born Apr. 14.
Richard of John & Mary Trow born July 29.
Mary of Joseph & Tomasin Tailor born Oct. 30.
Woodward of Jeremiah & Mercy Tay born Feb. 12.
Mehetable of John & Penelope Verin born Feb. 25.
Susanna of Isaac & Mary Vergoose born May 5.
Mary of Samuel & Mehetable Worden born May 4.
Samuel of Samuel & Hannah White born July 7.
Mary of James & Mary Webster born July 15.
John of Henry & Sarah Wright born Aug. 3.
Elizabeth of Return & Martha Wayte born Aug. 6.
Joshua of Samuel & Elizabeth Wakefield born Aug. 19.
Elizabeth of Joseph & Lydia Williams born Aug. 22.
Abiel of John & Elizabeth Walley born Aug. 30.
Rebecca of Thomas & Rebecca Walker born Sept. 6.
Gamaliel of John & Eunice Wayt born Sept. 24.
Mercy of Richard & Ann West born Sept. 28.
Mary of Samuel & Sarah Walker born Oct. 2.
Barachiah of John & Elizabeth Webber born Oct. 4.

Dorothy of Richard & Martha Wharton born Oct. 26.
Francis of Francis & Mary Williams born Oct. 12.
John of James & Elizabeth Worth born Jan. 27.
John of John & Sarah Ware born Feb. 18.
James of Nathanll & Mary Williams born Mar. 3.
Obadiah of Michael & Elizabeth Willis born Mar. 5.
Samuel of Obadiah & Susanna Wakefield born Mar. 15.
Eliza. of Cornelius & Faith Waldo born Jan. 7.
Thomas of John & Eliza. Welch born Jan. 9.
Elizabeth of William & Juda Youres born May 2.

William Weeler & Ann Phippen were married May 16.

### FIRST CHURCH.

Samuel of Wm. Griggs                                 Sept. 26.
Joseph of Lydia Clough                               Feby. 13.
John of Lydia Clough                                 Feby. 13.
Elizabeth Fisher born Oct. 1685                       Oct.
Joseph of John Marion                                June 13.

## 1687.

### TOWN.

Benjamin of Daniel & Mariana Allin born Apr. 26.
Samuel of John & Sarah Atwood born May 18.
Dorothy of Edward & Mary Ashley born July 11.
John of Thomas & Mary Atwood born July 17.
Hopestill of Henry & Judith Allen born July 16.
John of Josiah & Hannah Abbot born Aug. 22.
Rebecca of John & Constance Alcock born Aug. 29.
Isaac of Joseph & Mary Alberry born Sept. 16.
Elizabeth of John & Elizabeth Allen born Oct. 31.
John of John & Mary Alberry born Jan. 4.
Elizabeth of John & Elizabeth Alden born Nov. 7.
Abigail of Abraham & Abigail Adams born Jan. 25.
Elizabeth of James & Eliza. Adlington born Feb. 5.
Samuel of Joshua & Mary Atwater born Mar. 3.
William of Jona. & Frances Bill born May 17.
John of John & Mary Blake born May 28.
Kathar. of John & Margt. Besheau born June 10.
Mary of John & Sarah Birge born June 9.
Mary of Thomas & Mary Baker born June 14.
Sarah of Joshua & Sarah Bradbent born June 14.
Peter of Peter & Sarah Bradshaw born June 9.
Tabitha of Stephen & Tabitha Butler born June 16.
Peter of John & Joanna Bennit born June 17.
Jonah of John & Mary Bonner born July 8.
Nathaniel of Jonath. & Susanna Balston born July 27.
Ebenezer of Samuel & Hannah Bridge born Aug. 2.
John of John & Sarah Bushnell born Aug. 4.
Richard of Richard & Margaret Beedon born Aug. 9.
John of Thomas & Lydia Burrington born Aug. 21.
Mary of Edward & Mary Bromfield born Aug. 23.
Elizabeth of Henry & Sarah Bennet born Aug. 23.
Sarah of William & Secunda Brown born Aug. 24.
Joseph of Joseph & Lydia Bill born Aug. 26.
David of David & Mary Bassett born Sept. 3.
Lydia of Thomas & Rebecca Bayly born Sept. 6.
Benjamin of James & Sarah Burgis born Sept. 10.
John of John & Abiga. Brookings born Sept. 23.
Hannah of James & Mehetable Bill born Sept. 27.

William of William & Hannah Bryant born Oct. 5.
William of Clampet & Jane Beer born Oct. 11.
Benjamin of James & Temperance Barnes born Oct. 25.
John of Thomas & Esther Bulkeley born Nov. 9.
Mary of Samuel & Martha Burril born Dec. 10.
Mary of Jonathan & Eliza Bridgeham born Dec. 16.
John of William & Hannah Billing born Jan. 13.
Thomas of Thomas & Elizabeth Burton born Jan. 16.
John of Peter & Elizabeth Butler born Jan. 21.
Elizabeth of George & Elizabeth Beard born Jan. 23.
Ann of Samuel & Ann Beighton born Jan. 29.
John of William & Joan Badlam born Feb. 8.
Sarah of James & Elizabeth Burgis born Mar. 18.
Phillip of Phillip & Ann Blackley born Feb. 16.
Katharine ⎫ of Timothy & Sarah Clarke born Apr. 6.
Sarah ⎭ of Timothy & Sarah Clarke born Apr. 6.
Sarah of Peter & Penelope Clarke born Apr. 7.
William of William & Martha Cole born Apr. 14.
Thomas of Edward & Sarah Cowell born Apr. 15.
William of Samuel & Mary Checkley born Apr. 18.
Jonathan of Jona. & Joanna Cockcroft born May 15.
William of Duncan & Susanna Campbell born May 27.
Ann of Samuel & Elizabeth Checkley born May 30.
Lydia of Richard & Ann Christophers born July 1.
Edward of Edward & Sarah Collins born July 3.
Mary of David & Mary Crouch born July 4.
Ellener of John &·Ruth Center born July 6.
John of John & Ann Cotton born Sept. 4.
Mary of William & Mary Clap born Sept. 18.
Sarah of John & Joanna Carthew born Oct. 13.
Joanna of George & Sarah Callender born Oct. 23.
Mercy of Peircy & Elizabeth Clarke born Oct. 29.
John of Robert & Mary Clap born Nov. 7.
Mary of John & Sarah Coney born Nov. 8.
Join of John & Mary Curtis born Nov. 8.
Ann of Henry & Mary Cole born Nov. 9.
Edward of Edward Pepper & Sarah Crague born Dec. 6.
Joshua of Thomas & Sarah Cheever born Jan. 6.
Rachel of Jonas & Mary Clay born Jan. 28.
Ann of John & Hannah Clap born Jan. 30.
Elizabeth of John & Martha Cornish born Feb. 15.
Elizabeth of Ellis & Mary Callender born Feb. 20.
Thomas of James & Mary Cornish born Mar. 18.
Joanna of Jonathan & Hannah Dawes born Apr. 21.
Mary of Joseph & Anna Dease born May 22.
Thomas of Thomas & Martha Davis born July 3.
Elizabeth of Robert & Elizabeth Dawson born July 10.
George of Join & Hannah Davis born July 22.
Rebecca of Nicholas & Rebecca Davis born Dec. 21.
Mary of Henry & Abigaile Dawson born Jan. 14.
Mary of Sampson & Sarah Dewer born Feb. 1.
William of Charles & Rachel Deale born Feb. 5.
John of David & Mary Edwards born May 19.
Thomas of John & Catherine Eyre born June 21.
Samuel of Benja. & Mary Emons born July 28.
Ellener of John & Mary Earle born Sept. 3.
Nicholas of William & Elizabeth Edees born Sept. 21.
Mary of William & Abigail Everdon born Oct. 7.
Mary of Andrew & Sarah Eliott born Dec. 23.
Abigail of John & Mary Earthy born Dec. 28.
Christopier of Richard & Jane English born Jan. 27.
Elias of Richard & Mary Ellis born Mar. 14.
Susanna of David & Dorothy Farnam born Apr. 7.
Giles of Giles & Elizabeth Fyfield born Apr. 18.

Ebenezer of William & Elizabeth Fisher born May 19.
James of John & Sarah Fosdike born July 28.
Elizabeth of Thomas & Elizabeth Fox born Sept. 6.
John of Thomas & Mehetable Ford born Dec. 27.
John of Jonathan & Sarah Franklin born Dec. 21.
Joseph of Josiah & Ann Franklin born Jan. 5.
Samuel of John & Dorothy Foy born Feb. 15.
Susanna of Robert & Elizabeth Fethergill born Feb. 22.
Lydia of John & Lydia Foster born Feb. 25.
James of John & Amey Figg born Feb. 13.
Joseph of Enoch & Kate Greenleafe born Apr. 4.
Jotham of Jotham & Margaret Grover born Apr. 11.
James of Joseph & Lydia Griffin born Apr. 12.
James of James & Joanna Grant born June 16.
Thomas of Thomas & Experience Gold born June 19.
Thomas of Thomas & Frances Gold born July 4.
William of Bastian & Elizabeth Geffeere born Aug. 19.
Elizabeth of Samuel & Grace Goodman born Aug. 29.
William of John & Hannah Goffe born Sept. 29.
Elizabeth of Samuel & Elizabeth Greenwood born Oct. 18.
William of John & Hannah Greenleafe born Nov. 4.
Hannah of John & Martha Goodwin born Dec. 18.
Elizabeth of Robert & Elizabeth Gelgris born Dec. 29.
Martha of Samuel & Mary Greenwood born Jan. 8.
William of James & Elizabeth Glass born Jan. 11.
John of William & Anne Gibbins born Jan. 11.
Margaret of William & Hannah Gibson born Jan. 22.
Lately of John & Joane Gee born Feb. 4.
Joseph of Samuel & Susanna Gray born Dec. 6.
Hannah of John & Susanna Herod born Mar. 31.
Nicholas of Thomas & Bridget Hay born June 13.
Elizabeth of Richard & Elizabeth Harris born July 1.
Rachel of Benja & Mehetable Harwood born July 3.
William of John & Elizabeth Higgs born Aug. 15.
Samuel of Samuel & Abigail Hudson born Sept. 20.
Martha of Jacob & Martha Hewens born Oct. 1.
Sarah of Daniel & Sarah Harris born Oct. 18.
Mercy of James & Lydia Hawkins born Oct. 29.
Mary of William & Ann Hollowell born Dec. 26
James of James & Elizabeth Hobson born Jan. 1.
Elizabeth of Thomas & Judith Hunt born Jan. 4.
Lydia of William & Patience Heyden born Jan. 9.
John of Arthur & Mary Hale born Jan. 16.
Ebenezer of John & Deborah Hurd born Jan. 7.
Benjamin of Joseph & Susanna Hiller born Jan. 19.
Mary of Thomas & Rebecca Harris born Jan. 30.
Benjamin of Thomas & Abigail Hatherly born Jan. 31.
John of Abraha. & Elizabeth Harrison born Feb. 5.
Remember of William & Elizabeth Hewes born Mar. 7.
George of George & Anne Hollard born Mar. 19.
Hannah of Job & Hannah Ingram born June 24.
Joseph of Henry & Lydia Ingram born Aug. 18.
Joseph of John & Elizabeth Indecot born Nov. 1.
Elizabeth of William & Elizabeth Ireland born Feb. 24.
John of John & Mary Jarvis born May 8.
Mary of Isaac & Mary Jones born Apr. 9.
Thomas of Thomas & Temperance Jackson born May 29.
Jane of David & Elizabeth Jeffreys born July 4.
Thomas of Thomas & Elizabeth Johnson born Aug. 2.
John of John & Ruth Jepson born Aug. 24.
Susanna of Samuel & Mary Jones born Aug. 27.
Benjamin of Samuel & Elizabeth Johnson born Sept. 22.
Joseph of Joseph & Elizabeth Jackson born Nov. 3.
Robert of David & Priscilla Johnson born Nov. 24.

John of John & Sarah Jenkins born Nov. 27.
James of John & Rachel Kind born May 21.
Mary of John & Abigail Keech born May 24.
John of Peter & Mary King born July 26.
Elizabeth of Thomas & Elizabeth Kellond born Aug. 6.
Elizabeth of Roger & Anne Kilkup born Aug. 10.
Zachariah of Thomas & Mary Kirke born Nov. 6.
Elizabeth of John & Elizabeth Leech born Apr. 7.
John of John & Mary Leech born Apr. 17.
Elizabeth of John & Elizabeth Lane born May 10.
Mary of Thomas & Opportunity Lane born June 14.
Mary of Richard & Susanna Leatherer born July 14.
Jane of Thomas & Jane Larkin born July 16.
Richard of Lawrance & Catharine Lott born Sept. 3.
Charles of Charles & Mary Lidgett born Sept. 28.
John of John & Esther Lowell born Nov. 6.
Samuel of Philip & Mary Langdon born Dec. 22.
Jonathan of David & Martha Langdon born Jan. 2.
Susanna of Thomas & Susanna Lane born Jan. 23.
Josiah of John & Elizabeth Langdon born Jan. 28.
John of Isaac & Mary Lewis born Feb. 25.
Francis of John & Lydia Moore born Apr. 8.
George of George & Hannah Matthews born May 1.
Mary of Samuel & Hannah Marion born June 18.
William of Francis & Martha Marshal born July 10.
Thomas of Thomas & Sarah Martin born Aug. 9.
Rebecca of Stephen & Mercy Minot born Aug. 20.
Abigail of Cotton & Abigail Mather born Aug. 22.
John of John & Ann Marion born Aug. 29.
Rebecca of Henry & Rachel Maddux born Oct. 9.
Mary of William & Mary Morto born Oct. 12.
William of John & Phoebe Marshal born Oct. 12.
Peter of Thomas & Catharine Moussett born Oct. 18.
Joanna of William & Eliza. Middleton born Nov. 8.
Phoebe of William & Phoebe Manly born Nov. 29.
Elizabeth of Florence & Eliza. Maccarty born Dec. 25.
John of James & Eliza. Marshal born Jan. 12.
Joseph of Paul & Elizabeth Miller born Jan 27.
Joseph of John & Dorothy Matton born Feb. 2.
Henry of Henry & Ruth Mountfort born Feb. 12.
Samuel of James & Hannah Merrick born Jan. 29.
Abigail of William & Susanna Millborn born Apr. 28.
Mehetable of John & Eliza. Needham born Dec. 17.
John of John & Susanna Nichols born Jan. 14.
James of Nathanll. & Elizabeth Oliver born Oct. 27.
James of Thomas & Martha Oakes born Oct. 30.
Samuel of Regnal & Priscilla Odall born Jan. 29.
John of John & Sarah Oliver born Feb. 20.
John of John & Rachel Fascho born Apr. 1.
Grace of Samuel & Elizabeth Phelps born Apr. 5.
James of Alexander & Sarah Prindle born Apr. 24.
Ann of William & Elizabeth Porter born June 15.
Benjamin of Benja. and Mary Peck born July 22.
Thomas of John & Eliza. Plaistead born Aug. 17.
Hannah of James & Susanna Prior born Sept. 1.
Mary of Thomas & Mary Parris born Sept. 25.
Edward of Edward & Elizabeth Pell born Oct. 19.
James of Thomas & Ruth Prince born Nov. 23.
Joshua of William & Constance Palfroy born Dec. 19.
William of William & Margaret Pollard born Dec. 21.
Sarah of Ebenezer & Sarah Plumb born Dec. 23.
Samuel of John & Elizabeth Peck born Dec. 27.
Susanna of Samuel & Elizabeth Parris born Jan. 9.
Nathaniel of Moses and Mary Peirse born Jan. 11.

Arimnel of John & Eliza. Palmer born Mar. 4.
Mercy of Joseph & Mercy Pennywell born Mar. 7.
Tabitha of Nathaniel & Tabitha Peck born Mar. 14.
Eliza. of John & Elizabeth Pearse born Dec. 19.
Mary of Richard & Joanna Read born Mar. 26.
Richard of Solomon & Priscilla Rainsford born June 25.
Ebenezer of William & Ann Rawson born July 24.
Martha of George & Eliza. Robinson born Aug. 8.
Michael of William & Sarah Rowse born Oct. 12.
Mary of William & Elizabeth Robie born Oct. 19.
Sarah of Nathanll. & Sarah Reynolds born Oct. 23.
Joseph of Joseph & Mary Russell born Dec. 12.
Samuel of Samuel & Anne Ruck born Dec. 14.
Richard of Richard & Sarah Ricroft born Jan. 22.
James of James & Sarah Robe born Jan. 30.
Sarah of Obadiah & Elizabeth Read born Jan. 26.
Elizabeth of Abraham & Elizabeth Rue born Mar. 10.
Thomas of Samuel & Susanna Sexton born Apr. 8.
Samuel of Epaphras & Rebecca Shrimpton born Apr. 9.
Lancelot of Francis & Catharine Stepney born Apr. 13.
Elizabeth of Roger & Elizabeth Stayner born Apr. 13.
Elizabeth of William & Elizabeth Stretton born Apr. 20.
Hannah of Joseph & Hannah Simpson born June 18.
Mercy of Constant & Elizabeth Sams born July 3.
Abigail of Robert & Abigail Seers born July 12.
Sarah of James & Mary Smith born July 24.
Charles of Edward & Mary Summer born Aug. 12.
James of John & Mary Shory born Aug. 21.
Joseph of Eleazer & Martha Starr born Aug. 26.
Sarah of John & Martha Symons born Aug. 31.
John of Nathanil & Mary Saunders born Sept. 2.
Sarah of Thomas & Eliza. Skinner born Sept. 18.
Hannah of Joseph & Anne Stocker born Sept. 27.
Rebecca of John & Jane Smith born Oct. 16.
Mary of Thomas & Rebecca Smith born Nov. 9.
Rebecca of Thomas & Rebecca Smith born Dec 22.
Pilgrim of William & Jane Shipreve born Dec. 25.
Lydia of Henry & Purchase Spry born Jan. 4.
Thomas of Thomas & Jane Stedman born Jan. 8.
Thomas of Joseph & Ruth Shaw born Jan. 15.
John of Rowland & Ann Storey born Feb. 3.
Abigail of Richard & Rachel Skinner born Feb. 2.
Jonathan of Simeon & Mary Stoddard born Feb. 5.
Samuel of William & Mary Slack born Jan. 22.
William of Michael & Sarah Shaller born Feb. 29.
Ann of John & Ruth Soul born Mar. 10.
Lydia of Edward & Esther Stevens born Mar. 20.
Mary of Arthur & Sarah Smith born Mar. 21.
Rebecca of George & Rebecca Thomas born Mar. 25.
John of Nathanll & Deborah Thayer born Apr. 2.
Eleazer of Samuel & Sarah Tely born June 10.
John of Samuel & Lydia Turell born July 3.
John of Thomas & Miram Tyler born July 14.
Hannah of John & Martha Temple born July 28.
Isaac of Penn & Sarah Townsend born Aug. 14.
Joshua of William & Ruth Turner born Aug. 20.
Mary of James & Eliza. Townshend born Oct. 27.
Hannah of Peter & Ann Townsend born Oct. 27.
Anna of Daniel & Anna Turell born Oct. 30.
Sarah of William & Sarah Thompson born Nov. 20.
Samuel of James & Rebecca Taylor born Dec. 5.
Abigail of Richard & Sarah Talley born Jan. 18.
Priscilla of Timothy & Experience Thornton born Feb. 28.
Joshua of Edward & Abigail Tuttle born July 20.

Elizabeth of David & Mary Vaughan born Apr. 6.
Mary of Samuel & Mary Veazy born June 17.
Susanna of Isaac & Mary Vergoose born Mar. 8.
Dorothy of Edward & Jane Weeden born Apr. 22.
Elizabeth of Benjamin & Rachel Williams born May 7.
William of Francis & Mary Whitman born May 9.
Ebenezer of Benja. & Palsg. Walker born May 23.
Samuel of William & Mary Wilson born July 5.
Henry of John & —— Wooddee born July 19.
Susanna of Richard & Phœbe Whitridge born Aug. 10.
Ruth of Richard & Eliza. Willee born Oct. 13.
Susanna of Timothy & Susanna Wadsworth born Oct. 29.
Sarah of John & Ruth Weeden born Nov. 16.
Joseph of William & Sarah Williams born Nov. 30.
Margaret of Samuel & Eunice Willard born Dec. 3..
Mary of Return & Martha Wayt born Dec. 24.
William of John & Elizabeth Walley born Dec. 23.
Elizabeth of Jonathan & Sarah Wales born Jan. 19.
Thomas of Thomas & Sarah Wheeler born Jan. 31.
Joseph of Andrew & Dorothy Wood born Mar. 4.
Thomas of Thomas & Rebecca Walker born Mar. 13.
Andrew of Andrew & Elizabeth White born Mar. 12.
Maudlin of Robart & Luce Ward (Negros) born Oct. 9.


Thomas Cushing & Deborah Thaxter were married by the Rev. Samuel
    Willard Oct. 17.
John Darling & Ann Rocket were married Jan. 2.
John Farnun & Deborah Mean were married Sept. 16.
Thomas White & Mehitabel Thornton were married Dec.


### FIRST CHURCH.

| | |
|---|---|
| Giffard Squire | Jan. 30. |
| Abigail of John Clough | 2d mo. |
| Francis of John Moore | Apr. |
| Ebenezer Fisher born 19 May | May 22. |
| John of John Marion | Sept. 4. |
| William Peck | |
| John of John Harrison aged 1 year. | June 18. |
| Mary of Samuel Mirian aged about 2 or 3 days. | June 18. |
| Elizabeth of Richard Harris' wife aged 2 days. | July 2. |
| Hopestill of Henry Allin Deacon aged 2 days. | July 17. |
| Dorothy of brother Ashley aged about 1 week. | July 17. |
| John of sister Arnold | July 17. |
| George of brother Davies | July 24. |
| Hannah of John Temple aged about 3 days. | July 21. |
| Judith of sister Vee aged 1 year. | July 21. |
| Isaack of Pen Towsend born August 13. | Aug. 13. |
| Joseph of sister Ingram | Aug 21. |
| John of John Miriam Junior | Sept 4. |
| Benjamin Burgesse | Sept 11. |
| Elizabeth Foxe | Sept. 11. |
| Benjamin Barnes | Oct. 30. |
| Hannah Townsend | Oct. 30. |
| Mary Townsend | Oct. 30. |
| Mercy Hawkins | Oct. 30. |
| Mercy Clarke | Oct. 30. |
| William Groenleife | Nov. 6. |
| Henry Wooddy | Nov. 6. |
| John Bulkly of sister Esther Bulkly | Nov. 13. |
| Jeremiah Peck son to a sister belonging to Mr. Wills | Nov. 27. |
| Sarah Blake | Dec. 25. |
| John of Sarah Blake | Dec. 25. |

| | |
|---|---|
| Mary of Sarah Blake | Dec. 25. |
| Sam Pecke | Jan. 1. |
| Susannah Parris | Jan. 15. |
| Samuel Flack | Jan. 22. |
| Richard Ricott | Jan. 29. |
| Margaret Gibson | Feb. 5. |
| Mary Diore | Feb. 5. |

## 1688.

### TOWN.

Mary of John & Sarah Aulgar born Apr. 19.
Priscilla of Bozoun & Lydia Allen born Apr. 22.
Lydia of William & Phillis Arnold born Apr. 22.
Abigail of Thomas & Mary Atkins born June 3.
Elizabeth of John & Grace Allisett born July 5.
Judeth of Benja. & Mary Alford born Sept. 13.
Daniel of Daniel & Mariana Allen born July 27.
Sarah of John & Sarah Atwood born Nov. 14.
John of John & Elizabeth Allen born Nov. 25.
Hannah of John & Elizabeth Alden born Nov. 20.
Eliphal of Tobias & Anne Atkins born Dec. 4.
Lydia of Jona. & Rebecca Adams born Dec. 24.
Ann of John & Avis Adams born Feb. 16.
Abigail of Oliver & Gantrig Berry born May 10.
Elizabeth of Thomas & Sarah Baker born June 5.
Lydia of John & Ann Balston born June 22.
Jarvis of Jarvis & Martha Ballard born July 10.
Sarah of John & Sarah Birge born July 15.
Joseph ⎫ of Daniel & Sarah Ballard born July 16.
Benja. ⎭ of Daniel & Sarah Ballard born July 16.
John of Edward & Mary Bertles born July 28.
Benjamin of William & Elizabeth Burt born Aug. 9.
Mary of Grimstone & Elizabeth Bond born Aug. 13.
Mary of John & Esther Barnard born Aug. 14.
Mary of John & Susanna Butler born Aug. 15.
Joseph of Samuel & Hannah Bickner born Aug. 17.
James of James & Grace Butler born Aug. 21.
———— son of William & Joanna Boulderson born Sept. 18.
Hannah of Thomas & Sarah Banister born Sept. 30.
Elizabeth of Peter & ———— Barber born Oct. 8.
Lydia of Phillip & Sarah Bass born Dec. 6.
John of John & Mercy Booker born Dec. 18.
Mary of William & Mary Browne born Dec. 30.
William of William & Mary Browne born Dec. 30.
Ann of George & Ann Beaverly born Jan 2.
Joanna of John & Joanna Bennet born Jan. 7.
James of James & Rachel Barrey born Jan. 8.
Hannah of William & Hannah Billing born Jan. 26.
Mary of John & Mary Bonner born Jan. 28.
Ebenezer of Samuel & Martha Burrell born Feb. 1.
Ann of William & Mary Barnsdale born Feb. 1.
Elizabeth of Samuel & Anne Burnell born Feb. 5.
James of Robert & Eliza. Butcher born Feb. 8.
Robert of Thomas & Joanna Barnes born Feb. 15.
John of Phillip & Margaret Barger born Feb. 17.
Sarah of Peter & Sarah Bradshaw born Mar. 3.
Ebenezer of James & Sarah Burgis born Mar. 10.
Thomas of Thomas & Mary Bossinger born Mar. 10.
William of William & Secunda Browne born Mar. 21.
James of James & Sarah Balston born July 29.
Abigall of Francis & Frances Buckitt born Oct. 8.

Mary of Jonathan & Rebecca Charles born Apr. 6.
Hannah of Mungo & Mary Crafford born Apr. 7.
Mary of John & Kathar. Carlton born Apr. 26.
Mary of John & Mary Cole born May 9.
James of James & Mary Correll born May 15.
Mary of ———— & Mary Cooke born May 25.
Richard of Matthew & Naomi Calline born June 25.
Thomas of Thomas & Mehetable Cooper born June 27.
Joseph of Nathanll & Anne Callo born July 10.
Thomas of Thomas & Anne Cooke born Aug. 2.
Ezekiel of Charles & Mary Coully born Aug. 27.
John of Thomas & Deborah Cushing born Sept. 6.
Hannah of John & Hannah Collins born Sept. 18.
Mary of John & Martha Clough born Sept. 23.
William of Stephen & Margaret Clifford born Sept. 25.
Lydia of William & Lydia Clough born Nov. 4.
Henry of Richard & Ann Christophers born Nov. 16.
Andrew of Andrew & Sarah Cunningham born Nov. 29.
Sarah of William & Susan Critchfield born Dec. 7.
Grace of Jonathn & Joanna Cockcroft born Nov. 10.
David of David & Mary Crouch born Dec. 18.
John of John & Eliza. Cranmer born Dec. 21.
Henry of Henry & Mary Cole born Jan. 2.
John of John & Elizabeth Coombs born Jan. 7.
Elizabeth of Job & Joan Chamberlain born Jan. 11.
Sarah of John & Mary Cotta born Jan. 10.
William of William & Christian Condey born Jan. 12.
Edward of Robert & Mary Calef born Jan. 30.
Joshua of Samuel & Mary Checkley born Feb. 8.
Rebecca of Samuel & Eliza. Checkley born Feb. 4.
Martha of William & Martha Cole born Feb. 7.
Archbald of Duncan & Susanna Campbell born Feb. 10.
David of David & Eliza. Carwithen born Mar. 8.
Paul of Paul & Mary Collings born Aug. 15.
Mary of Eleazer & Mary Darby born Apr. 3.
Joseph of Charles & Sarah Demaree born Nov. 12.
Jacob of Jacob & Susanna Davis born Nov. 2.
Abigail of Thomas & Martha Davis born Nov. 20.
Mary of William & Mary Down born Dec. 24.
James of John & Elizabeth Davis born Jan. 15.
Mary of Henry & Abigail Dawson born Mar. 7.
Benjamin of Henry & Elizabeth Emes born Apr. 6.
Sarah of John & Elizabeth Eustis born Apr. 6.
Mary of John & Mary Earle born July 10.
Martha of John & Catharine Eyre born Jan. 28.
Elizabeth of John & Catharine Eades born Feb. 11.
Martha of Francis & Elizabeth Foxcroft born Mar. 26.
Thomas of Thomas & Elizabeth Fenton born Apr. 14.
Thomas of Thomas & Elizabeth Fox born July 15.
Susanna of John & Dorothy Farnham born Aug. 1.
Abraham of Abraham & Mary Francis born Sept. 10.
Abigail of John & Mary Fairfield born Oct. 20.
John of Jonathan & Martha Farnum born Jan. 4.
Eleazer of Gibson & Rebecca Farr born Jan. 15.
Susanna of Giles & Elizabeth Fifield born Jan. 17.
Sarah of Hugh & Ellener Floyd born Jan. 28.
Susanna of David & Elizabeth Falkner born Mar. 14.
William of William & Thankful Griggs born Apr. 6.
Jeremiah of John & Susanna Gardner born Apr. 12.
Anna of William & Eliza. Greenough born May 5.
Rebecca of James & Anna Green born May 19.
Mary of Nicholas & Mary George born June 28.
Abigail of Richard & Abigail Gridley born July 17.
William of Isaac & ———— Gross born Sept. 8.

Ezekiel of Ezekiel & Mary Grazillier born Oct. 8.
Rachel of Enoch & Catharine Greenleafe born Nov. 10.
Thomas of Anthony & Dorcas Gretian born Nov. 18.
Hannah of Joseph & Hannah Gallop born Dec. 2.
Ann of Benja. & Abigail Gillam born Dec. 11.
Dean of Jotham & Margaret Grover born Jan. 7.
Susanna of Samuel & Susanna Gray born Jan. 3.
Nicholas of Nicholas & Mary George born Jan. 23.
Sarah of Henry & Sarah Gibbs born Jan. 19.
Abigail of Christopher & Abigail Goffe born Jan. 21.
Thomas of Thomas & Experience Gold born Jan. 29.
Mercy of William & Hannah Gibson born Feb. 11.
Rachel of Joseph & Sarah Greenleafe born Feb. 17.
Elizabeth of Joseph & Hannah Hasey born Mar. 28.
Isaac of Isaac & Hannah Hallom born Apr. 8.
Priscilla of Thomas & Mary Hunt born Apr. 11.
Christopher of John & Sarah Holland born May 22.
Ephraim of James & Sarah Harris born July 11.
John of Francis & Joanna Holland born Aug. 19.
Samuel of William & Hannah Harris born Oct. 23.
James of James & Hannah Hawkins born Nov. 18
Mary of William & Mary Hough born Dec. 31.
Joseph of James & Elizabeth Hews born Jan. 7.
Daniel of Hezekiah & Abigail Henchman born Jan. 21.
Elizabeth of Ephraim & Sarah Hall born Jan. 21.
Martha of Sarah Harris & Henry Lilly born Jan. 20
Hannah of William & Experience Heyden born Jan. 31.
James of Thomas & Esther Hamlen born Feb. 6.
Martha of Edward & Lydia Hilliard born Feb. 8.
William of John & Hannah Hobbey born Mar. 14.
Mary of Robert & Martha Ireland born Apr. 26.
Grace of John & Grace Ireland born May 3.
Samuel of Thomas & Mildred Inglesby born June 16.
Michael of Robert & Susanna Ireland born Aug. 14.
Margaret of Job & Hannah Ingram born Aug. 27.
Sarah of William & Sarah Johnson born May 20.
Joseph of Aaron & Mary Jeffers born June 9.
Samuel of Thomas & Elizabeth Johnston born Sept. 19.
Susanna of Mathew & Susanna Jones born Oct. 31.
Sarah of Thomas & Dorothy Jennings born Dec. 9.
Samuel of William & Lydia Jeffrey born Dec. 24.
John of John & Hannah Jones born Jan. 22.
John of David & Elizabeth Jeffries born Feb. 5.
Samuel of Samuel & Mary Jones born Feb. 9.
Daniel of Moses & Susanna Jacth born March 16.
Elizabeth of Thomas & Temperance Jackson born Mar. 14.
Emm of John & Emm Kally born May 6.
John of William & Jane Keen born Aug. 31.
Elizabeth of John & Abigail Keech born Aug. 31.
John of John & Rebecca Kilbey born Dec. 24.
James of William & Deborah King. born Jan. 27.
Susanna of Elhanan & Mary Lyon born July 11.
Zibeon ⎱ of Zibeon & Rachel Letherland born Aug. 23.
Rachel ⎰ of Zibeon & Rachel Letherland born Aug. 23.
Sarah of Thomas & Jane Larkin born Sept. 28.
Joseph of James & Grizzell Lloyd born Oct. 8.
Richard of Richard & Anne Leekey born Dec. 17.
Thomas of Thomas & Mercy Lesenby born Jan 21.
Emm of Thomas & Susanna Lane born Jan. 28.
Joanna of James & Elizabeth Loper born Feb. 6.
Elizabeth of Robert & Rebecca Lewis born Feb. 12.
Hannah of Samuel & Mehetable Lilly born Feb. 4.
Thomas of Florance & Eliza. Maccarty born Feb. 5.
Ebenezer of Ebenezer & Rose Messenger born Mar. 30.

Margaret of John & Margaret Mila born Apr. 9.
Sarah of Thomas & Eliza. Messenger born Apr. 17.
Jacob of John & Margaret Marsh born Apr. 18.
Priscilla of Andrew & Ruth Mariner born May 1.
Wiseman of Richard & Sarah Mussenan born May 3.
Joseph of John & Abiga. Mulberry born May 16.
John of Nathanil & Deborah Man born June 26.
Robert of Edward & Jane Mortimore born July 31.
Christopher of Benjamin & Rebecca Marshal horn Sept. 9.
John of Thomas & Eliza. Mercer born Sept. 6.
Samuel of James & Dorcas Maxwell born Sept. 30.
Hannah of George & Hannah Matthews born Oct. 6.
Stephen of Stephen & Mercy Minot born Oct. 24.
Samuel of Samuel & Ann Mattock born Dec. 17.
Joanna of Samuel & Ruth Marshal born Dec. 24.
Elizabeth of Robert & Eliza. Mogridge born Jan 8.
Joseph of Joseph & ——— Moss born Jan. 18.
William of John & Sarah Mellison born Jan. 13.
Elizabeth of Francis & Martha Marshal born Feb. 21.
Susanna of David & Tempera. Norton born Sept. 29.
William of William & Lamey (negroes) born Feb. 9.
John of Peter & Rebecca Noseter born July 16.
Tacey of John & Mary Okey born May 9.
Martha of John & Hannah Orris born Nov. 26.
William of Samuel & Sarah Phillips born Apr. 1.
William of William & Sarah Paine born June. 10.
Edward of Edward & Abial Paige born Aug. 11.
Elizabeth of John & Hannah Parmiter born Sept. 3.
John of John &.Hannah Pitcher born Sept. 23.
Elizabeth of Nathanll & Mary Pulman born Sept. 20.
Sarah of William & Elizabeth Porter born Nov. 7.
Nehemiah of Samuel & Mary Pearce born Nov. 11.
Mary of Thomas & Hannai Pemberton born Oct. 26.
Thomas of John & Rachel Fascho born Dec. 4.
Josiah of Job & Rebecca Prince born Dec. 5.
Elias of William & Deborah Parkman born Oct. 9.
Nathaniel of Nathaniel & Hannah Parkman born Oct. 29.
Samuel of Benja. & Mary Peck born Jan. 19.
Sarah of Thomas & Ama Pennant born Jan. 31.
Sarah of John & Sarah Pynm born Mar. 8.
Stephen of Thomas & Martha Raper born June 16.
Thomas of Samuel & Dyonisia Ravenscroft born June. 29.
Sarah of John & Eunice Robinson born Aug. 6.
Susanna of Stephen & Jude Robino born Nov. 24.
Joseph of John & Mercy Rowlstone born Nov. 28.
Susanna of Joseph & Eliza. Rogers born Dec. 4.
Mary of Edmund & Barbary Robins born Dec. 6.
Mary ⎱ of John & Experience Roberts born Dec. 25.
Joseph ⎰ of John & Experience Roberts born Dec. 25.
Jane of Gamaliel & Mary Rogers born Jan. 3.
David of David & Hannah Rainsford born Jan. 29.
Hannah of John & Hannah Ridgeaway born Feb. 12.
John of John & Mary Robinson born Feb. 21.
Thomas of William & Elizabeth Robie born Mar. 20.
Mary of John & Elizabeth Strade born Apr. 6.
Ralph of Ralph & Susanna Straker born May 9.
Sarah of Josiah & Mary Stone born May 3.
John of Gregory & Jane Sugars born May 26.
Jeremiah of Hugh & Mary Sampson born June 4.
Clorinda of Daniel & Chariot Streing born June 13.
Hannah of Philip & Margaret Squire born July 28.
Sampson of Thomas & Anne Shapcott born Aug. 5.
Sarah of Alexander & Rebecca Seers born Aug. 11.
Abigail of Bryant & Abigail Smith born Aug. 22.

Joseph of Samuel & Hannah Sewall born Aug. 15.
Robert of Robert & Mary Saunders born Oct. 5.
Samuel of Joseph & Hannah Souther born Dec. 1.
John of John & Anne Simons born Dec. 26.
Mercy of Constant. & Elizabeth Sams born Jan 12.
Peter of John & Ann Smith born Jan. 21.
Alexander of Joseph & Hannah Simpson born Jan. 25.
Richard of Jabez & Elizabeth Salter born Feb. 3.
Henry of Henry & Purchase Spry born Feb. 7.
Hannah { of Thomas & Rebecca Smith born Feb. 18.
Abial    { of Thomas & Rebecca Smith born Feb. 18.
John of Daniel & Elizabeth Stoddard born Mar. 7.
Joseph of Joseph & Rebecca Smith born Mar. 9.
Jonathan of Samuel & Sarah Snow born Mar. 14.
John of Richard & Anne Story born Mar. 20.
Sarah of Samuel & Sarah Tely born Apr. 22.
Ann of George & Rebecca Thomas born Apr. 30.
Elizabeth of Matthew & Susanna Taunton born May 2.
Benjamin of John & Maria Thwing born June 6.
Joseph of Richd. & Hannah Tout born June 10.
John of Nathanll & Deborah Thayer born July 2.
Susanna of Bartho. & Damaris Threeneedle born Aug. 8.
John of John & Hannah Tapper born July 11.
John of John & Martha Tuttle born July 5.
John of Edward & Elizabeth Thwing born July 29.
Christopher of Samuel & Lydia Turell born Dec. 17.
Ebenezer of Nathanll & Deborah Thayer born Feb. 1.
William of Thomas & Mariam Tyler born Mar. 15.
John of Martha & John Tuttle born July 5.
Sarah of Edward & Abigail Tuttle born Jan. 5.
David of David & Mary Vaughan born July 19.
George of Edward & Sarah Wadkins born Apr. 14.
Robert of Sampson & Rebecca Waters born May 5.
Susanna of Thomas & Elizabeth Wagget born May 23.
Samuel of Samuel & Hannah White born June 7.
Hannah of Michael & Elizabeth Willis born June 14.
Edward of Edward & Jane Weeden born July 3.
John of John & Elizabeth Walley born July 19.
Experience of Experience & Elizabeth Willis born Aug. 19.
James of James & Mary Webster born Aug. 27.
Joseph of Richard & Anna West born Sept. 22.
John of Henry & Esther Webster born Sept. 28.
Hephzibah of Robert & Margery Williams born Nov. 1.
Elizabeth of Samuel & Sarah Walker born Nov. 16.
William of Francis & Mary Whitman born Nov. 21.
Elizabeth of Joseph & Lydia Williams born Dec. 9.
Elizabeth of Benja. & Rachel Williams born Jan. 7.
Elizabeth of Benja. & Susanna Worthilake born Jan. 2.
John of John & Mary Wooddee born Jan. 25.
Nathaniel of Thomas & Abigail Walter born Jan. 30.
Dorcas of Samuel & Elizabeth Wakefield born Feb. 5.
Susanna } of John & Richard Weekes born Feb. 22.
John    } of John & Richard Weekes born Feb. 22.
Elizabeth of John & Eunice Wayte born Feb. 26.
William of John & Ann Wyllys born Mar. 1.
Recompence of Timothy & Susanna Wadsworth born Mar. 19.

Jushua Gee & Eliza. Harrise were married by Rev. Joshua Moody Sept. 25.

## FIRST CHURCH.

Samuel Atwater                                          April 1.
William Grigges                                         April 8

| | |
|---|---|
| Priscilla **Allin** | April 22. |
| Susannah **Langdone** | May 13. |
| Philip Langdone | May 13. |
| John Langdone | May 13. |
| James Langdone | May 13. |
| Samuel Langdone | May 13. |
| Peirce Fitchlocke | May 20. |
| Mary Morter | June 3. |
| Benjamin **Twinge** | June 10. |
| Joseph Toute | June 10. |
| Joseph Giffards | June 10. |
| Anna Willis | June 17. |
| John Man | July 1. |
| Sarah Hughes | July 8. |
| John Twing | July 29. |
| Thomas Fox | Aug. 5. |
| Mary Clow | Sept. 23. |
| Joseph West | |
| Hannah Matthews | Oct. 7· |
| Samuel Maxwell | Oct. 7· |
| Hephzibah Williams | Nov. 4· |
| Lydia Clough | Nov. 4· |
| Abigaile Davises | Nov. 25· |
| Joseph Rowliston son of Bosworth yt was now Rowliston. | Dec 2 |
| Josiah Prince | Dec. 9· |
| Mary Bridgham | Dec. 18. |

## 1689.

### TOWN.

Joseph of Thomas & Mary Ashley born Apr. 7.
Joseph of Joseph & Anne Allen born Oct. 22.
Richard of Thomas & Abigail Adkins born Oct. **12.**
John of William & Hannah Bryant born Mar. 25.
Sarah of Thomas & Mary Bedell born Apr. 2.
Mary of Gilbert & Mercy Bant born Apr. 28.
Elizabeth of John & Charity Bayly born May 1.
Thomas of Henry & Abial Brightman born May 11.
Mary of Edward & Mary Bromfield born June 2.
Richard of John & Sarah Blake born May 23.
John of Joseph & Rebecca Briscoe born July 2.
Elizabeth of Thomas & Eliza. Barnerd born Aug. 6.
Joseph of Abraham & Martha Blish born July 24.
Mary of Nathaniel & Mary Baker born Sept. 12.
Mary of Edward & Mary Bricknall born Sept. 15.
John of Samuel & Hannah Bridg born Oct. 5.
Esther ⎱ of Thomas & Esther Buckley born Oct. 11.
Elinor ⎰ of Thomas & Esther Buckley born Oct 11.
Richard ⎱ of Richard & Mary Brown born Oct. 13.
Mary ⎰ of Richard & Mary Brown born Oct. 13.
John of John & Theodora Belcher born Dec. 11.
Mary of Edward & Mary Bartles born Jan. 1.
Constantine of Henry & Sarah Bennet born Dec. 25.
Elizabeth of John & Mary Boyes born Jan. 15.
Samuel of Thomas & Sarah Baker born Sept. 9.
Sarah of Richard & Abigail Cheever born Apr. 15.
Sarah of Francis & Sarah Cole born Apr. 29.
John of John & Sarah Coney born May 19.
Deborah of Edward & Sarah Cowel born Sept. 26.
Samuel of Samuel & Ruth Clough born Sept. 29.
Mary of John & Anna Cotton born Nov. 5.
Ezekiel of Ezekiel & Sarah Cleasby born **Nov. 25.**

Samuel of John & Sarah Coniball born Jan. 16.
Eliza. of John & Anna Clay born Feb. 28.
Sarah of Zachar & Sarah Davis born Apr. 19.
Elizabeth of Lawrence & Elizabeth Drisco born Apr. 18.
Edward of Edward & Hannah Dissater born June 13.
Samuel of Jeremiah & Anna Duñer born Apr. 16.
John of Richard & Mary Drew born July 21.
Mary of Thomas & Mary Down born July 27.
Rachel of Charles & Rachel Deale born Sept. 13.
Anne of Eliezur & Mary Darby born Sept. 1.
William of Joseph & Ann Dios born Sept. 6.
John of John & Rachel Draper born Sept. 29.
Lydia of Samuel & Lydia Dyer born Nov. 17.
Abigail of Joseph & Abigaile Eustis born Apr. 1.
Joanna of Lewis & Absiah Elleir born Apr. 26.
Jonathan of Jona & Mary Evans born July 7.
Mary of Joseph & Silence Eliot born July 23.
Eliza. of William & Eliza. Eades born Sept. 24.
Susanna of Henry & Joanna Elise born Nov. 25.
Hannah of John & Eliza Eustice born Oct. 9.
Richard of John & Martha Edwards born Nov. 20.
William of William & Susanna Ellise born Nov. 27.
Samuel of Benja. & Mary Emmons born Feb. 14.
Samuel of John & Dorothy Foy born Mar. 26.
Joseph of Josiah & Anne Franklin born June 30.
Lydia of Robert & Eliza. Fethergill born Oct. 6.
John of John & Mary Fairfeeld born Oct. 20.
Rebecca of Joseph & Rebecca Fuller born Nov. 6.
Charity of Gabril & Catharine Fitchlock born Feb. 9.
Lydia of Gibson & Rebecca Faur born Jan. 16.
John of Philip & Hannah P.[1] Finnah born Oct. 1.
Rebecca of Thomas & Mary Goodridge born Apr. 21.
Edward of Edward Gouge & Martha Staples born Apr. 25.
Rebecca of Samuel & Susanna Gray born Jan. 26.
John of Bastian & Eliza. Gosier born Aug. 4.
Abigail of Richard & Abigail Gridley born Oct. 21.
Mary of Aaron & Mary Geaffalls born Oct. 25.
Sarah of Isaac & Sarah Griffin born Feb. 21.
James of Joseph & Lydia Griffin born Feb. 16.
Mercy of John & Martha Goodwin born Feb. 24.
Peter of Joshua & Eliza. Gee born Dec. 16.
Ann of William & Elizabeth Hall born Apr. 10.
John of John & Alice Hurst born Apr 22.
Mehetable of Benja. & Mehetable Harwood born Apr. 25.
Thomas of Thomas & Rebecca Harris born Apr. 29.
Joseph of Thomas & Annis Hill born May 24.
Sarah of Thomas & Bridget Hay born May 26.
Mary of John & Rebecca Hacket born June 26.
Samuel of Robert & Elizabeth Howard born Apr. 5.
Edward } of Elizur & Mary Holyoke born June 26.
Samll  } of Elizur & Mary Holyoke born June 26.
Hannah of John & Eliza. Higgs born Aug. 8
Eliza. of Samuel & Abigail Hudson born Aug. 9.
Joseph of John & Johanna Hunlock born Oct. 18.
Abigail of James & Lydia Hankins born Oct. 13.
Hannah of Thomas & Sarah Hill born Oct. 27.
Mary of Richard & Eliza. Harrise born Nov. 7.
Elizabeth of Eliakim & Sarah Hutchinson born Nov. 5.
Ebenr. of John & Patience Harker born Feb. 26.
Daniel of Hezekiah & Abigail Henchman born Jan. 1.
Nicholas of Nicholas & Ruhamah Inglesby born Apr. 6.

---

[1] This seeming initial was written as a query if the name should **not begin** with Ph., under which the same parents appear in 1692. — W. S. A.

Joseph of Henry & Lydia Ingram born Apr. 30.
Sarah of William & Mary Jarvis born Mar. 30.
Isaac of Isaac & Mary Jones born May 28.
Ruth of John & Ruth Jepson born June 7.
Mary of David & Priscilla Johnston born May 5.
Richard of John & Susanna Jacobs born Sept. 15.
Samson of John & Mary Jarvise born Jan. 6.
James of John & Sarah Jenkins born Jan. 10.
Elizabeth of Richard & Sarah Knight born May 8.
Elizabeth of John & Mehetable Keen born June 7.
Daniel of Joseph & Ruth Knight born July 4.
Nathaniel of John & Rachel Kinde born Sept. 1.
Mary of Andrew & Susanna Knot born Sept. 28.
Mary of Richard & Susanna Kennet born Oct. 8.
John of Roger & Ann Kilkup born Nov. 6.
Eliza. of Thomas & Eliza. Kellon born Dec. 5.
Luke of Elias & Elizabeth Lipsey born May 15.
Ephraim of John Langdon born Jan. 25.
Richard of Richard & Martha Ladd born Sept. 7.
Abigail of David & Martha Landon born Aug. 26.
Jonathan of John & Joanna Mills born May 3.
Samuel of Samuel & Mary Marion born June 7.
John of John & Ann Marion born June 28.
Joseph of Joseph & Hannah Milam born June 22.
Henry of Ebenezer & Rose Messenger born July 8.
Samuel of John & Sarah Mason born July 31.
John of John & Lydia Moor born Aug. 27.
Mary of Willm & Phoebe Manley born Sept. 11.
Sarah of Willm & Olive Macloughlin born Oct. 29.
Joseph of Edward & Mary Morse born Nov. 14.
Sarah of John & Abigail Mulbery born Jan. 2.
Thomas of Christopher & Mary Monck born Jan. 2.
George ⎱ of Andrew & Ruth Marriner born Jan. 19.
Andrew ⎰ of Andrew & Ruth Marriner born Jan. 19.
Thomas of Thomas & Dorcas Marshall born Aug. 3.
Susanna of William & Susanna Milhorn born July 11.
Manassah of Samuel & Ruth Marshall born Jan. 30.
Susanna of John & Susanna Nichols born Apr. 4.
David of David & Temperance Norton born Nov. 4.
Brattle of Nathanll & Elizabeth Oliver born June 1.
Josiah of Thomas & Martha Oakes born May 3.
Bethiah of John & Sarah Oliver born Jan. 13.
Nathaniel of Joseph & Bridget Phillips born Mar. 30.
Samuel of George & Elizabeth Pordage born Apr. 15.
Jane of Nathanll & Tabitha Peck born May 11.
John of Richard & Rachel Procter born June 10.
Joseph of Robert & Hannah Price born July 4.
Thomas of Joseph & Bethiah Parsons born Aug. 11.
John of Benja. & Eliza. Pemberton born Nov. 27.
George of Thomas & Hannah Pemberton born Nov. 18.
Nathaniel of Nathaniel & Mary Pulman born Jan. 10.
Bariah dau. of Samuel & Mary Pearse born Feb. 7.
John of Daniel & Anna Quinsie born July 21.
Nathanll of George & Eliza. Robinson born June 22.
Eliza. of John & Eliza. Richards born June 24.
Ruth of Nathaniel & Ruth Renalls born Sept. 11.
Martha of Thomas & Martha Raper born Nov. 18.
Thankful of Ephraim & Mary Sale born May 18.
Mary of William & Mary Shortrigs born June 16.
James of James & Prudence Smith born June 12.
Joseph of Joseph & Ruth Shaw born May 31.
William of William & Mary Starling born June 20.
Martha of Simeon & Mary Stoddard born Dec. 14.
Abigail of John & Mary Stevens born July 9.

Martha of William & Martha Smallage born Aug. 24.
Mary of Michael & Mary Shute born Aug. 17.
William of John & Mary Smith horn Sept. 20.
Thomas of Thomas & Rebecca Smith born Sept. 11.
Robert of Robert & Abigail Seers born Oct. 7.
Eliza. of Josiah & Mary Stone born Dec. 22.
Nathaniel of Nathll & Eliza. Shannon born Dec. 9.
Sarah of John & Jane Snelling born Feb. 1.
Benjamen of Benja. & Joanna Stone born Jan. 16.
John of John & Jane Smith born Jan. 26.
Richard of Roger & Eliza. Stainer born Mar. 8.
————ah ⎱ dautrs of Samuel & Susanna Saxton born July 4.
Elizabeth ⎰ of Samuel & Susanna Saxton born July 4.
Joseph of Joseph & Mary Thaxter born May 7.
William of Jeremiah & Mercy Tay born June 16.
Samuel of Samuel & Sarah Tyley born July 19.
Mary of John & Mary Trow born Aug. 9.
Anna of Pen & Sarah Townsend born ————.
Joseph of Samuel & Lydia Turel born Nov. 29.
Anne of James & Eliza. Townsend born Feb. 26.
Sarah of John & Sarah Vickars born Apr. 23.
Isaiah of Samuel & Elizabeth Verry born June 28.
Samuel of Samuel & Mary Veazie born June 23.
John of John & Penelopee Verein born Sept. 28.
David of David & Mary Vaughan born Dec. 7.
Thomas of Thomas & Hannah Verein born Jan. 26.
James of James & Elizabeth Worth born Apr. 7.
Elizabeth of John & Elizabeth Welch born June 3.
Hannah of Thomas & Sarah Wheeler born July 27.
John of Andrew & Bethiah Wilson born Sept. 1.
Mary of William & Mary Wilson born Sept. 7.
Richard of Richard & Phebee Whiteridge born Sept. 26.
Joseph of Waite & Mary Winthrop born Sept. 10.
Mary of Joseph & Lydia Williams born Nov. 6.
Eliza. of John & Eliza. Webb born Dec. 3.
Ebenr. of Experience & Eliza Willise born Dec. 23.
Eliza. of Joshua & Sarah Winsor born Dec. 23.
Eliza. of Thomas & Deborah Walker born Feb. 3.
Nicholas of Return & Martha Waite born Feb. 6.
William of Ebenr & Deliverance Weeks horn Feb. 20.
Eliza. of Samuel & Eliza. Worden born Feb. 19.


John Barnard & Hannah Hoksey were married Nov. 21.
Thomas Buttolph & Abiel Sanders were married by Rev. Samuel Willard
    Dec. 3.
Andrew Belcher & Hannah Walker were married by Thomas Danforth Esq.
    Feb. 13.
John Cook & Ruth Greenliefe were married by the Rev. Theodate Lawson
    Dec. 16.
Thomas Davise & Hannah Allen were married by Elisha Cook Esq. Assist.
    Sept. 12.
Andrew Dolbery & Eliza Condey were married by Willm. Johnson Esq.
    Assist. Dec. 31.
Richard Draper & Sarah Kilbey were married by the Rev. Theodate Lawson
    Oct. 22.
Jeremiah Fitch & Martha Messenger were married by Rev. James Allen
    Sept. 5.
John Foster & Abigail Kellond were married by John Richards Esq. Assist.
    Nov. 28.
Josiah Franklin & Abiah Foulger were married by the Rev. Sam. Willard
    Nov. 25.
Thomas Gwin & Johanna Armitage were married by Rev. Saml. Willard
    Nov. 21.

Thomas Linkoln & Mehetable Frost were married by Rev. Joshua Moody
Aug. 3.
William Lay & Mary Howen were married by John Richards Esq. Assist.
Jan. 11.
John Mico & Mary Brattle were married by Rev. Samuel Willard Aug. 20.
Paul Mylham & Eliza Tay were married by Elisha Cook Esq. Assist. Dec. 17.
William Phillips & Deborah Long were married by the Rev. Saml. Willard
Nov. 13.
George Rayson & Eliza Dyer were married by Isa. Addington Esq. Assist.
May 21.
Thomas Scudder & Sarah Phillips were married by Rev. James Allen Nov. 4.
William Turner & Hannah Jacklin were married by the Rev James Allen
Aug. 28.
Andrew Waker & Eliza. Allen were married by the Rev. Theodate Lawson
Aug. 8.
Richard Way & Hannah Knight were married by Nath Salstinstall Esq. Assist.
Aug. 13.

William Hewes & Eliza. Grafton were married Nov. 25.[1]

Mary of John & Mary Bonner died July 28.
Samuel of Thomas & Sarah Baker died Sept. 27.
Esther of Thomas & Esther Buckley died Nov. 2.
Benjamen Briscow died Dec. 19.
Richard of Richard & Mary Brown died Dec. 24.
Mary of John & Martha Clough died June 29.
Eliza. of Will. & Eliza. Condey died Sept. 18.
Eliza. Cushing widow died Nov. 23.
Eliza. Cummins died Nov. 13.
John of Richard & Mary Drew died Aug. 16.
Joseph of Joseph & Ahigal Dudson died May 1.
James of John & Eliza. Davise died Sept. 15.
John Dinsdale died Aug. 31.
Edward of Edward & Hannah Disiter died Sept. 14.
Bridget Gwin died Nov. 13.
Mercy of Will. & Hannah Gibson died Dec. 2.
John of John & Eliza. Harrise died Aug. 14.
Abigall wife of Capt. Edward Hutchinson died Aug. 10.
Nathaniel of John & Rachel Kind died Sept. 25.
William Lamb died Jan. 15.
Jacob of John & Margaret Marsh died Aug. 21.
Rachel of John & Lydia Moor died Sept. 8.
Mary of Will. & Phebee Manley died Sept. 22.
Mary of Sam. & Constance Mattocks died Nov. 12.
Thomas Moor died Jan. 5.
John Needham died Jan. 14.
Eliza. of Samuel & Eliza. Paine died Sept. 27.
Lydia Pearse died Nov. 11.
Samuel Ruggles died Dec. 12.
John Shaw died July 23.
Edward Stevens died Oct. 5.
Phillippi widow of Ralph Samis died Jan. 8.
Jeremiah of Hugh & Mary Samson died Feb. 12.
Samuel of John & Sarah Tucker died May 5.
Sarah of John & Sarah Tucker died July 31.
John of John & Hannah Tapper died Oct. 15.
Joseph of Andrew & Dorothy Wood died Dec. 3.
Warner Wisendonk died Sept. 14
Mary of William & Mary Wilson died Oct. 16.
Sarah Wheatley died Nov. 26.
Thomas Watkins died Dec. 16.

---

[1] This marriage took place before 1690, but the fourth figure of the date is illegible. —
W. S. A.

Eliza. dau. of Thomas Watkins died Dec. 26.[1]
Eliza. dau. of Thomas Watkins died Jan. 8.[1]
Edward Wright died Jan. 21.

### FIRST CHURCH.

| | |
|---|---|
| Sarah Cotte | Jan. 13. |
| John Combs | Jan. 13. |
| Mary Loveringe | Jan. 13. |
| Moses Peirce | Jan 27. |
| William Peirce | Jan. 27. |
| Nathaniel Peirce | Jan. 27. |
| Mary Peirce | Jan. 27. |
| Sarah Peirce | Jan. 27. |
| John Woody | Jan. 27. |
| Mercy Gibson | Feb. 17. |
| Hannah Ingram a woman | Feb. 25. |
| Elizabeth Coggshall | March 3. |
| Sarah Coggshall | March 3. |
| Margaret Coggshall | March 3. |
| Elizabeth Wayte | March 3. |
| Rachell Ingram | March 3. |
| Elizabeth Jackson | March 17. |
| Ebenezer Gibson | March 10. |
| Hannah Cogshall | March 10. |
| Joseph Ingram | May 5. |
| Thankful Sale | May 19. |
| Samuel Mattocks | May 19. |
| Richard Blake | May 26. |
| Prudence of Bosoon Allin ⎫ twins | Aug. |
| Ann of Bosoon Allin ⎭ | Aug. |
| Samuel Moore | Sept. |
| John Bridge | Oct. 6. |
| Nathaniel Fisher | Oct. 6. |
| Esther Bulkley | Oct. 13. |
| Elenor Bulkley | Oct. 13. |
| Isaac Griggs | Oct. 13. |
| Abigail Hawkins | Oct. 20. |
| Mary Giffords | Oct. 27. |
| Anne of Pen Townsend | Nov. 10. |
| Mary Harris of Brantry | Nov. 10. |
| Susannah Willis | Dec. 1. |
| Ezekiel Clesby | Dec. 1. |
| Hannah Warner alias Mortar | Dec. 15. |
| Hannah Winsor | Dec. 29. |
| Ebenezer Willis | Dec. 29. |

## 1690.

### TOWN.

Esther of Edward & Mary Ashley born Mar. 25.
Mary of Abrm: & Abigall Adams born June 11.
John of John & Eliza. Alden born Sept. 20.
Mary of William & Mary Arnold born Nov. 17.
Anna of Thomas & Mary Ashley born Jan. 8.
Esther of Lewise & Ahigal Allaire born Jan. 27.
Hannah of John & Sarah Alger born Dec. 10.
Jabish of John & Eliza. Allen born Jan. 6.
George of George & Mary Burrel born Mar. 19.
Martha of George & Mercy Bearstow born Mar. 6.

---

[1] One of these was probably the wife, but the record is as printed above. — W. S. A.

Samuel of Peter & Eliza Butler born Mar. 26.
John of Elisha & Dorothy Bennet born Apr. 4.
William of Jonathn & Frances Bill born Apr. 7.
Samuel of William & Eliza. Burt born May 16.
John of John & Susana Baster born June 13.
James of Samuel & Ann Beighton born Mar. 28.
Sarah of Peter & Sarah Barbour born June 27.
Hannah of John & Susana Butler born Aug. 27.
Thomas of Edward & Mary Bromfield bꭐru Sept. 2.
Henry of John & Charity Bayley born Sept. 8.
Sarah of George & Sarah Briggs born Oct. 30.
Katherine of Richard & Katherine Barnerd born Nov. 8
Peter of William & Joanna Bolderson born Dec. 20.
Deliverance of William & Eliza. Brown born June 19.
Sarah of George & Sarah Briggs born Oct. 13.
Deborah of Samuel & Martha Burrel born Jan. 3.
Joseph of Thomas & Sarah Baker born Jan. 20.
Sarah of John & Sarah Blake born Dec. 17.
Phillip of Phillip & Margaret Barger born Feb. 10.
James of James & Rachel Barry born Feb. 12.
Mary of Thomas & Sarah Bannister born July 10.
Jacob of John & Mercy Bucker born Jan. 13.
Beatrix of John & Sarah Bourland born Dec. 31.
Thomas of Joseph & Abigall Belknap born Jan. 24.
William of Francis & Frances Buckitt born Jan. 20.
Mary of John & Mary Cole born Mar. 4.
James of James & Mary Cornish born Apr. 9.
Lydia of Samuel & Mary Checkley born Mar. 31.
Deborah of Thomas & Deborah Cushing born Apr. 15.
Michael of Edward & Sarah Collings born May 2.
Rachel of John & Eliza. Cranmer born Apr. 18.
James of Mongo & Mary Crafford born Apr. 26.
Sarah ⎱ of William & Susanna Crutchfeeld born June 18.
John ⎰ of William & Susanna Crutchfeeld born June 18.
Eliza. of Andrew and Sarah Cuningham born June 17.
Abiah of Ellis & Mary Callender born June 22.
Abigail of Thomas & Sarah Cheever born May 20.
Mary of Matthew & Naomie Collings born July 27.
Mary of Jonathn & Joanna Cockcroft born Sept. 17.
Aaron ⎱ of Job & Joanna Chamberlin born Jan 7.
Moses ⎰ of Job & Joanna Chamberlin born Jan 7.
David of Caleb & Sarah Chapen born July 2.
Jonas of Jonas & Mary Clay born Dec. 29.
Edward of Edward & Sarah Cruff born Dec. 30.
Ruth of Samuel & Ruth Clough born Jan. 26.
John of John & Eliza. Clark born Feb. 18.
Jonas of Timothy & Sarah Clark born Sept. 8.
John of Samuel & Eliza. Checkley born Dec. 2.
Matthew of Duncan & Susanna Campbell born Feb. 14.
Mary of Robert & Rebecca Cumbey born Dec. 15.
Thomas of Thoms & Hannah Davise born Aug. 13.
Sarah of Richard & Sarah Draper born Aug. 3.
Mary of William & Mary Davise born Sept. 6.
Sarah of Charles & Sarah Demerey born Dec. 4.
Samson of Samson & Sarah Dewer born Jan. 28.
Christian dau. of John & Eliza. Egbeer born June 30.
Elizabeth of William & Eliza. Endecot born July 26.
Joseph of Joseph & Abigail Eustice born Jan. 29.
Abigail of John & Eliza. Eustice born Feb. 21.
Benjamen of Willm & Sarah Eustice born Feb. 20.
Hannah of Thomas & Hannah Fairwether burn June 30.
Elizabeth of Gyles & Eliza. Fifield born June 13.
John of Josiah & Abia Franklin born Dec. 7.
John of David & Dorothy Farnum born Dec. 12.

Ebenezer of Hugh & Elenor Floyd born Feb. 21.
James of James & Johanna Grant born Mar. 31.
Abigail of Samuel & Mary Greenwood born Apr. 13.
Lydia of Isaac & Mary Goose born May 18.
Daniel of Christopher & Abigail Goff born May 27.
John of Jotham & Margaret Grover, born July 2.
Abigail of Luke & Abigail Greenough born Sept. 17.
Eliza. of Bastian & Eliza. Gosier born Sept.
Solomon of John & Hannah Green born Nov. 10.
Sarah of Obediah & Eliza. Gill born Jan. 3.
Eliza. of Joshua & Eliza. Gee born Nov. 22.
Samuel ot Samll & Eliza. Greenwood born Aug. 15.
Sarah of Edward & Lydia Hillard born May 6.
Sarah of William & Anne Hollowel born June 7.
Eliza. of Thomas & Bridget Hayes born July 25.
Richard of John & Alice Hurst born Oct. 4.
Mary of Thomas & Mary Hunt born Oct. 11.
Mehetable of Thomas & Rebecca Harrise born Feb. 8.
David of David & Eliza. Jefferyes born June 15.
Mary of David & Priscilla Johnson born June 30.
William of William & Sarah Johnson born Aug. 18.
Experience ot Roger & Eliza. Judd born Dec. 16.
James of Matthew & Susanna Jones born Dec. 19.
John of John & Mary Jenkins born June 4.
Ruth of John & Ruth Jepson born June 28.
Mary of Philip & Mary Langdon born Mar. 24.
James of James & Ann Lablond born May 31.
James of James & Anna Lablond born Apr. 17.
Zachary of Zachary & Eliza. Long born June 13.
Samuel of Samuel & Mary Landman born June 29.
Mehitable of Thomas & Mehitable Lincoln born Jan. 25.
Susanna of William & Mary Lay born Aug. 6.
Robert of Francis & Martha Marshall born Sept. 4.
Sarah of George & Barbary Mitchell born Oct. 19.
Stephen of James & Eliza. Mears born May 15.
John of John & Sarah Meryfeeld born Dec. 12.
Mary of Robert & Ann More born Feb. 4.
John ⎱ of John & Joanna Mills born Feb. 22.
James ⎰ of John & Joanna Mills born Feb. 22.
Isaac of George & Hannah Mathews born Dec. 1.
John of Stephen & Mercy Minot born Dec. 23.
William of Florence & Eliza. Maccarty born Feb. 3.
Zacheus of John & Margaret Marsh born Feb. 10.
Catharine of Samuel & Mary Maryon born Sept. 15.
John of John & Lydia Moor born Feb. 4.
John of Thomas & Dorcas Marshall born Dec. 27.
Robert of Francis & Martha Marshal born Sept. 4.
Thomas of Thomas & Eliza. Mesenger born Jan. 18.
Thomas of Regnal & Priscilla Odell born Apr. 8.
Anna of Joseph & Mary Penewel born Mar. 8.
Ruth of Thomas & Ruth Prince born Mar. 6.
Bryant of Bryant & Hannah Parrot born Mar. 19.
Samuel of William & Eliza. Porter born May 18.
John of Edward & Eliza. Pell born July 14.
Hannah of Thomas & Hannah Phillips born Sept. 7.
Eliza. of William & Eliza. Parkman born Sept. 12.
William of William & Deborah Phillips born Nov. 17.
William of William & Margaret Pollard born Apr. 2.
Rebecca of Richard & Sarah Rycroft born Mar. 2.
Joseph of John & Charity Ricks born Apr. 15.
Thomas of Samuel & Ann Ruck born June 23.
Alice of Philip & Alice Richards born Aug 10.
Mary of John & Mercy Rowlston born Sept. 29.
George of George & Eliza. Raylin born Feb. 11.

Joseph of Joseph & Mary Russell born Nov. 21.
Mary of John & Experience Roberts born Nov. 7.
Joseph of Joseph & Sarah Robinson born Sept. 15.
Eliza. of John & Mary Roberts born Jan. 5.
Nathanll of George & Eliza. Robinson born Feb. 7.
Richard of Roger & Eliz. Stainer born Mar. 8.
Judith of Samuel & Hannah Sewall born Aug. 13.
Hugh of Hugh & Mary Samson born Sept. 13.
Mary of Alexander & Rebecca Seers born Sept. 27.
Jane of Philip & Margaret Squire born Jan. 29.
John of John & Hanniball Salsbery born Jan. 5.
Thomas of Bryant & Abigail Smith born Nov. 13.
Thomas of John & Ann Simons born Feb. 4.
Abigail of John & Abigail Turner born June 29.
Thomas of John & Sarah Tenny born June 15.
William of Willm & Mary Thwing born July 8.
Dorothy of George & Rebecca Thomas born Dec. 20.
Anne of Pen & Sarah Townsend born Nov. 10.
Joseph of Richard & Hannah Tout born Dec. 12.
Abigail of James & Rebecca Taylor born Aug. 2.
Nathaniel of Edward & Abigail Tuttle born Nov. 20.
Phebee of Edward & Abigail Tuttle born Aug. 12.
John of John & Sarah Vicars born Mar. 12.
Mary of Andrew & Eliza. Veech born Aug. 19.
William of Edward & Sarah Watkins born Apr. 6.
Susanna of John & Susanna Wilkins born Apr. 9.
Abigail of Edward & Eliza. Wilton born May 23.
Eliner of James & Esther White born Sept. —.
Sarah of Francis & Mary Whitman born Nov. 2.
Mary of William & Mary Wilson born Nov. 4.
Richard of Richard & Phebee Whiteridge born Jan. 29.
Eliza. of James & Mary Webster born Aug. 14.
Susanna of Samuel & Sarah Walker born Jan. 28.
Rachel of Cornelius & Faith Waldo born Apr. 20.
Mary of Thomas & Tryphana Woodward born May 16.

John Atwood & Mary Smith were married by James Russell Esq. Assist.
Oct. 27.
Joseph Belknap & Abigail Buttolph were married by Isa. Addington Esq.
Assist. Apr. 1.
Richard Barnerd & Katherine Wilson were married by Rev. Charles Morston
Apr. 3.
Alex. Bulman & Margaret Taylor were married by Rev. John Bayley Dec. 22.
Samuel Bridg & Christian Peirse were married by Isa. Addington Esq. Assist.
Dec. 3.
Isaac Biscou & Ann Brooks were married by Saml. Sewall Esq. Assist.
Nov. 20.
George Clark & Ann Lutterell were married by Saml. Sewall Esq. Assist.
Feb. 3.
John Darbey & Rachel Codner were married by Saml. Sewall Esq. Assist.
Oct. 9.
Thomas Fox & Esther Jarvise were married by Simon Bradstreet Esq. Gov.
Mar. 21.
Theophelus Frarey & Mary Greenwood were married by Saml. Sewall Esq
Assist. June 12.
William Gayer & Maria Gaurd were married by William Johnson Esq. Assist.
July 4.
John Grantham & Martha Bant were married by Saml. Sewall Esq. Assist.
Dec. 8.
John Hooper & Mary Litchfeeld were married by Mr. Emblim Baptist Minis.
Jan. 27.
Thomas Jackson & Priscilla Grafton were married by Isa. Addington Esq.
Assist. Oct. 15.

Theodat Lawson & Deborah Allen were married by Isa. Addington Esq. Assist. May 6.
Israel Lyon & Hannah Hewen were married by Saml. Sewall Esq. Assist. Mar. 25.
Thomas Moorhouse & Mary Hill were married by Saml. Sewall Esq. Assist. Apr. 3.
John Mayn & Mary Peacok were married July 24.
Nathanl: Orrise & Mary Ivet were married by Saml. Sewall Esq. Assist. Sept. 11.
William Paseo & Ruth Hetchbone were married by Isa. Addington Esq. Assist. Oct. 20.
John Pim & Mary Orchard were married by Isa. Addington Esq. Assist. Feb. 5.
William Shute & Martha Budd were married by Saml. Sewall Esq. Assist. May 19.
Thomas Savage & Mehitabel Harwood were married by Thos. Danforth Esq. Dep. Gov. Feb. 5.
David Stevens & Eliza Webster were married by the Parson of the Church of England Jan. 29.
John Scolly & Lydia Grover were married by Benja. Swaine Dec. 22.
Joseph Townsend & Elizabeth Berry were married by Jeremiah Swain Esq. Assist. May 22.
Peter Virgue & Sarah Johnson were married by Isa. Addington Esq. Assist. Jan. 21.
William Warren & Abiel Rogers were married by Rev. Thomas Cheever Nov. 1.
Robert Watson & Susanna Prior were married by Saml. Sewall Esq. Assist. Feb. 13.


Joseph of Thomas & Mary Ashley dyed March 12th.
Nathaniel Adams dyed March 30.
Mary of Edward & Mary Ashley dyed July 11.
Joseph of Joseph & Ann Allen dyed Aug. 12.
Samuel of John & Sarah Alger dyed Janry. 24.
Samuel of Peter & Eliza. Butler dyed May 18.
John of Joseph & Rebecca Briscow dyed July 2.
Elinor of Thoms. & Esther Buckley dyed July 8.
Hannah wife of Wm. Bryant dyd. July 14.
Ebenr of Samll & Martha Burrel dyed July 21.
Hanna of Josiah & Mary Baker dyed Aug. 1.
Katherine of Richard & Eliza. Bason dyed July 21.
John of John & Sarah Blake dyed Aug. 7.
Sarah dau. of James Burges dyed Aug. 25.
Hanna wife of Samll Bridg dyd. June 11.
Hanna of Samuel & Hannah Bridg dyed July 21.
Willm. of Samuel & Hannah Bridg dyed Aug. 16.
John of Samll & Hannah Bridg dyed Aug. 29.
James Burges dyed Novr. 27.
Benjamen of James & Sarah Burges dyed Febry. 6
Hannah of Thomas & Sarah Bannister dyed Aug.
Thomas Buttolph dyed Novr. 30.
Mary of James & Sarah Balston dyed Janry 2.
Eliza. Bridgham Widdo dyed Janry. 19.
Beatrix of John & Sarah Borland dyed Janry. 11.
Eliza. wife of George Clark dyed March 18.
Ann of Thoms & Jane Clark dyed Aprill 23.
Mary of Willm & Mary Clap dyed June 18.
Henry of Richd & Anna Christophers dyed July 15.
Lydia of Richd & Anna Christophers dyed July 20.
James of John & Sarah Coney dyed July 15.
John Cox dyed July 3.
John of John & Mary Cole dyed Septr. 25.
Thomas of Thoms & Ann Cook dyed Octbr.
Mrs Eliza Clark dyed Janry. 10.

Moses of Job & Joanna Chamberlin dyd. Febry. 5.
Aaron of Job & Joanna Chamberlin dyd Febry. 15.'
Capt. Roger Clap dyed Febry 2.
James Cook dyed Deer 15.
David Cummins dyd Deer 12.
Mr John Clark dyed Deer 17.
John Coney Senr dyed Deer 24.
Mary wife of Benja Dyer dyed March 15.
Sarah Darbey dyed June 15.
Anne of Eliezur & Mary Darbey dyed July 3.
Samuel Dwight dyed July 5.
Roger Dubbleday dyed Novr. 22.
Joseph of Joseph & Abigail Eustice dyed Janry 29.
Mary of Benja & Mary Emmons dyed June 23.
Mary wife of Benja Emmons dyed Septr 12.
Samuel of Henry & Mary Emmons dyed July 27.
Lydia of Gibson & Rebecca Faur dyed July 22.
Joseph Foard dyed Novr 2.
Eliza of Gyles & Eliza Fyfield dyed Septr 2.
John Fairfield dyed Janry 23.
Prudence Frary widdo dyed Febry 24.
Abigall of Christopher & Abigall Goff dyed March 14.
Sarah Grant dyed March 25.
Sarah wife of Joseph Greenliefe dyed June 4.
Sarah wife of Isaac Griffin dyed July 10.
William of John & Hannah Greenliefe dyed Aug. 9.
Abigail of Richd & Abigail Gridley dyed Aug. 26.
Josiah Grice dyed Janry 2.
Mary of Thomas & Mary Hunt dyed Aprill 11.
Thomas Hobbs dyed June 18.
Mary Helgeson daur of Mary Small dyed Octobr 21.
Nicholas Hale dyed Deer 14.
Thomas Hitt dyed Deer 6.
Benjamen of Joseph & Mabel Hill dyed July 19.
John Hurd Senr dyed Septr 23.
Anna Jennings dyed June 4.
William of Wm. & Sarah Johnson dyed Septr 9.
James of Matthew & Susana Jones dyed Janry 13.
Francis Johnson dyd Febry 3.
William King dyed May 1.
William Kent dyed June 9.
Theophelus of Samll & Meehitabel Lillie dyed May 31.
Henry Lane dyed June 4.       .
John of Thoms & Mary Lake dyed June 27.
Luke of Elias & Eliza. Lipsey dyed Septr 16.
Mary of Samll & Martha Landman dyed Octor 10.
Hanna Harden daur of Joseph & Mary Long dyed Janry 7.
James Meryfeeld dyed July 3.
Samuel Marshall dyed July 7.
Sarah wife of mr. Samll Marshall of Barnst dyed July 22.
Sarah daur of Samuell Marshall dyed Aug. 2.
Sarah of John & Sarah Morrise dyed Septr 22.
Thomas Madson dyed Deer 29.
William Monek dyed Aug. 2.
Lucey Monek dyed Septr 21.
John of John and Anna Maryon dyed Aug. 15.
Experience Milles dyed Janry 26.
Daniel of Danll & Susana Morey dyed June 7.
William Needham Senr dyed Deer 30.
Samuel of John & Hannah Orrise dyed June 9.
Samuel Peacock dyed March 30.
Ebenr Plumb dyed July 26.
Ruth of Thomas & Ruth Prince dyed Sept. 12.
John of Benja. & Eliza. Pemberton dyed Octor 4.

Hannah wife of Thomas Phillips dyed Octor **13.**
Moses Payn Senr dyed Deer 15.
William Pollard junr dyed Janry 24.
Joseph of William & Ann Pollard dyed Decr 30.
Joseph of Joseph & Mercy Rowlston dyed July **21.**
Sarah of John & Experience Roberts dyed Septr 9.
Nathanll of George & Eliza. Robinson dyed Deer. **16.**
John Ragland dyed Nov. 28.
Peter of Samll & Margaret Ruck dyed Deer 9.
Michael of Willm & Eliza. Robbins dyed Deer **3.**
Margaret wife of Samll Ruck dyed Janry 1.
Abiather of Samll & Ann Scarlet dyed March 10.
Bethia of Rowland & Ann Storey dyed June 8.
Henry Stevens dyed June 11.
Abigail of Robt & Abigail Seers dyed July 3.
Henry of Henry & Purchace Spry dyed Aug. 6.
Judeth of Samll Sewall Esqr. & Hannah his wife dyed Aug. **13.**
Mary Smith dyed July 11.
William of Wm. & Mary Smith dyed Septr 26.
Thoms Skinner Bakr dyed Deer 28.
Samll of Joseph & Hannah Souther dyed Febry 21.
Mr. Ephram Sale dyed Deer 2.
Robert of Thoms & Temperence Smith dyed Deer **15.**
James Thomas a strangr dyed May 29.
Mary of James & Eliza. Townsend dyed Aug. 5.
Ann of James & Eliza. Townsend dyed Aug. 18.
Jeremiah of Samuel & Abigall Townsend dyed Septr 6.
Elizabeth Tille widdo dyed Novr 26.
Samuel Vezey dyed Decr.
John of John & Sarah Vickers dyed March 22.
Francis wife of Samll Ward dyed June 10.
Mrs. Mary Winthrop wife of Waite Winthrop Esqr. dyed June **14.**
Sarah of John & Eliza. Walley dyed June 29.
Nicholas of Return & Martha Waite dyed July 19.
Henry of Isaac & Susana White dyed July 15.
Sarah of Isaac & Susana White dyed Aug. 15.
Eliza White Widdo. dyed Deer 23.
Sarah of Barthll & Amy Whitwell dyed Janry 11.
Robert of Robt & Margery Williams dyed Septr 7.

## First Church.

| | |
|---|---|
| Daniel Hincksman | Jan. 5. |
| Sarah Courser | Jan. 5. |
| John Courser | Jan. 5. |
| Ebenezer Thornton | Jan. 12. |
| Sarah Burgesse | Jan. 12. |
| Christian Holdenour | Jan. 26. |
| Jerusha Grosse | Feb. 9. |
| Beriah Peirce | Feb. 9. |
| William Harrison | Feb. 9. |
| John Yellings ⎫ | Feb. 9. |
| David Yellings ⎬ the mother now Combs | Feb. 9. |
| Elizabeth Yellings ⎭ | Feb. 9. |
| Charitie of sister Fitchlocke | Feb. 16. |
| Elizabeth Worden | Feb. 23. |
| Anna Townsend | March 2. |
| John Proctor | March 9. |
| Rebecca Ricott | March 16. |
| Esther Ashley | March 30. |
| Mary Landale | March 30. |
| Sarah Reynolds | May 11. |
| Ruth Reynolds | May 11. |

| | |
|---|---|
| Thomas Tenny | June 15. |
| Sarah Browne | Aug. 31. |
| Samuel Atwater | Sept. 21. |
| Mary Rolleston | Oct. 5. |
| Hannah Gibson | Nov. 2. |
| Mary Arnold | Nov. 23. |
| Judith Ford | Dec. 7. |
| Deliverance Browne | Dec. 7. |
| Isaac Matthews | Dec. 7. |
| Elizabeth Gee | Dec. 28. |
| Sarah Blake | Dec. 28. |

## 1691.

### TOWN.

James of Benja. & Mary Alford born July 19.
Mary of Joseph & Anne Allen born July 28.
Samuel of Abrm. & Abigall Adams born Feby 11.
Joseph of William & Phillippi Arnall born Oct. 2.
Mathew of James & Elizabeth Adlington born Jan. 6.
Abigall of John & Hannah Adams horn Oct. 6.
Josiah of Jonathan & Mary Adams born Nov. 29.
Mary of John & Eliza. Alden born Dec. 15.
Elizabeth of John & Sarah Alger born Feb. 4.
Mary of James & Eliza. Burges born Mar. 13.
Elizabeth of Joseph & Hannah Biiling born July 14.
Eliza. of Peter & Eliza. Butler born May 21.
Margaret of Jonathan & Susana Balston born Nov. 17.
Samuel of William & Mary Brown born Dec. 3.
William of Phillip & Sarah Bass born Mar. 29.
Hannah of Nathanll & Mary Baker born Apr. 18.
Hannah of John & Mary Boyes born May 18.
Henry of Henry & Abiel Brightman born May 23.
Bartholl. of Daniel & Sarah Ballard born May 6.
Eliza of William & Sarah Burrage born June 10.
Eliza of William & Mary Barnsdale born Aug. 20.
Josiah of Josiah & Mary Baker born Aug. 20.
Elizabeth of George & Mary Burrel horn Sept. 25.
Nathaniel of Nathanll & Rebecca Balston born Sept. 6.
Sarah of William & Hannah Billin born Oct. 31.
John of Richard & Eliza Barson born Dec. 30.
John of John & Charity Balie born Feb. 24.
Mary of Edward & Mary Bartles born May 1.
Elizabeth of Joseph & Rebecca Briscoe born June 24.
Peter of James & Temperence Barnes born Aug. 21.
Lydia of John & Sarah Balston born Aug. 25.
Edward of Jarvise & Martha Ballard born July 26.
Benjamen of Samuel & Hannah Bickner born Nov. 22.
Eliza. of Thomas & Mary Beedle born Dec. 4.
Hannah of Samuel & Christian Bridg born Nov. 29.
Abigal of Joseph & Abigal Belknap born Feb. 29.
Samuel of William & Mary Brown born Apr. 24.
Abigall of Thomas & Sarah Cheever burn Mar. 20.
Sarah of John & Hannah Cerlile born Mar. 8.
Eliza. of Thomas & Deborah Cushing born Nov. 4.
Sarah of John & Sarah Coney born May 9.
Daniel of Robert & Mary Calef born Deer. 27.
Richard of John & Ruth Cook born Jan. 7.
Mary of John & Martha Clough born Apr. 15.
Elizabeth of John & Martha Clough born Apr. 15.
Thomas of Thomas & Ann Cook born July 27.
Sarah of Timothy & Sarah Clark born Oct. 18.
Elizabeth of James & Mary Cornish born Nov. 30.

Mary of Richard & Mary Cheever born Jan. 2.
Mary of John & Sarah Clark born Feb. 12.
Jonathan of Jonathn & Hannah Dawes born Apr. 11.
Thomas of Thomas & Hannah Davise born Oct. 24.
Thomas of Henry & Abigail Dawson born Nov. 25.
Mary of Peter & Susanna Devaulx born Mar. 9.
Ann of Samuel & Ann L.[1] Drew born Apr. 26.
Elizabeth of William & Susanna Dennise born Oct. 16.
Rachel of John & Rachel Draper born Novr. 9.
Mary of Charles & Sarah Demery born Feb. 16.
Samuel of Zachry & Sarah Davise born Oct. 15.
Eliza of Simon & Eliza. Eyre born Oct. 30.
Savil of Thomas & Ann Eyre born Dec. 13.
Nathanll of John & Mary Earl born Dec. 20.
Mary of Joseph & Eliza. Eldridge born Mar. 25.
Benjamen of John & Mary Endecot born June 27.
Sarah of John & Hannah Edwards born Nov. 30.
John of John & Elizabeth Eustis born Dec. 20.
John of John & Eliza. Egbcer born Dec. 9.
Eliza. of Jonathan & Martha Farnum born Oct. 13.
Joseph of Joseph & Hannah Grant born June 22.
David of William & Hannah Gibson born Nov. 20.
Hannah of John & Hannah Goff born July 24.
John of Samuel & Bethiah Goodenhous born Oct. 3.
Martha of David & Martha Gwin born Oct. 15.
Lydia of Richard & Abigail Gridley born Dec. 21.
Mercy of James & Lydia Hawkins born July 20.
Joseph of William & Mary Hough born July 11.
William of William & Eliza. Hewes born June 27.
Hephsiba of John & Patience Harker born June 27.
Isaac of John & Eliza. Hurd born Dec. 22.
Thankful of John & Experience Howard born Feb. 17.
Abraham of Abram & Eliza. Harrison born Feb. 29.
Samuel of Hezekiah & Abigail Henchman born Feb. 5.
Mary of Henry & Mary Hill born Jan. 23.
Eliza. of Henry & Lydia Ingram born Sept. 4.
John of Isaac & —— Jones born Oct. 24.
Thomas of Thomas & Priscilla Jackson born July 18.
Eliza. of David & Eliza. Jefferyes born Feb. 12.
Susanna of Andrew & Susanna Knot born Nov. 2.
John of William & Jane Keen born Apr. 15.
John of John & Lydia Kelton born Aug. 17.
Susanna of Moses & Margaret Kenny born Feb. 13.
James of James & Anna Lablond born June —.
Benjamen of Thoms & Mercy Leasonbee born Aug. 27
Mary of Richard & Martha Ladd born Nov. 2.
Benjamen of Joshua & Mary Lee born Feb. 18.
Abraham of Isack & Mary Lewis born June 9.
John of John & Margaret Mila born Mar. 3.
Mark of Joseph & Hannah Maylim born Mar. 23.
Edmund of Edmund & Eliza. Mountfort born May 14.
John of John & Eliza. Mullegan born Dec. 20.
Eliza. of William & Olive Macloughlin born Sept. 10.
Sarah of Paul & Eliza. Millar born Feb. 21.
Eliza. of Samll & Ann Mattocke born Sept. 20.
Joseph & } of Alexr. & Dorcas Millar born Sept. 15.
Benjamen } of Alexr. & Dorcas Millar born Sept. 15.
Sarah of John & Sarah Marshall born Sept. 12.
Jonathan of John & Sarah Mason born Jan. 4.
Eliazur of Christopher & Mary Monck born Jan. 30.
Israel of John & Susanna Morey born July 3.
Eliza. of John & Sarah Morrise born July 20.

---

[1] This was probably not intended for an initial, though it so appears. — W. S. A.

Benjamen of John & Abigail Mulbery born Nov. 21.
Mercy of Archibald & Eliza. Morrise born Jan. 7.
Christian of William & Susanna Milhorn born Oct. 31.
Elias of Elias & Susanna Nean born Apr. 2.
William of David & Temperence Norton born Dec. 14.
Mary of Peter & Rebecca Noscter born June 23.
Thos ⎱ of David & Temperance Norton born July 31.
John ⎰ of David & Temperance Norton born July 31.
Mary of Richard & Rachel Proctor born May 21.
Judeth of George & Eliza. Pordage born Sept. 16.
Eliza. of Benjamen & Eliza. Pemberton born Nov. 12.
Rebecca of Job & Rebecca Prince born Nov. 21.
Joseph of Thomas & Eliza. Person born Feb. 16.
David ⎱ of William & Eliza. Porter born Nov. 25.
John ⎰ of William & Eliza. Porter born Nov. 25.
Thomas of Thomas & Eliza. Pike born Dec. 15.
Grace of William & Mary Painter born Dec. 18.
John of John & Eliza. Pearse born Dec. 4.
Abigail of Robert & Hannah Price born Nov. 19.
Joseph of Joseph & Eliza. Rogers born Oct. 2.
Mercy of Thomas & Martha Raper born Oct. 23.
Mary of Nathanll & Ruth Renalls born Aug. 21.
Mary of Caleb & Mary Ray born Aug. 28.
David of David & Hannah Ransford born Oct. 20.
John of John & Mary Robinson born Sept. 2.
Ann of Rowland & Ann Storey born Mar. 14.
Mary of Gregory & Jane Sugers born Mar. 17.
Purchace of Henry and Purchace Spry born Mar. 14.
Mary of Francis & Mary Smith born Mar. 19.
John of John & Mary Sunderland born Apr. 2.
Abigail of William & Martha Shute born July 31.
John of Thomas & Rebecca Smith born Oct. 20.
Mary of Samuel & Hannah Sewall born Oct. 28.
Elizabeth of Edward & Rebecca Shippen born Oct. 20.
William of Robert & Eliza. Smith born Jan. 22.
Lydia of John & Lydia Scolly born June 6.
Deborah of Robert & Ann Shelston born Oct. 14.
John of John & Jane Snelling born Oct. 21.
Mary of John & Jane Smith born Nov. 28.
David of John & Mary Stevens born Jan. 22.
Hannah of Michael & Mary Shute born Aug. 31.
Joseph of Joseph & Hannah Simson born July 30.
Mary of David & Eliza. Stephens born Oct. 16.
Thomas of Samuel & Sarah Tyley born Mar. 9.
Mary of Joseph & Eliza. Townsend born Feb. —.
Isabella of William & Isabella Tylly born May 23.
Deborah of Nathanll & Deborah Thayer born Oct. 14.
John of Isaac & Sarah Taylor born Jan. 16.
Mercy of William & Hannah Turner born Feb. 19.
Samuel of John & Martha Tuttle born Mar. 20.
Samuel of Valentine & Susanna Use born Sept. 14.
Mary of John & Sarah Vicars born Mar. 4.
Hannah of Thomas & Hannah Verein born Sept. 17.
Mary of Thomas & Sarah Webb born June 4.
Mary of William & Abiel Warren born Sept. 24.
Michael of Samuel & Hannah White born Nov. 11.
Thomas of Return & Martha Waite born Dec. 14.
David of Andrew & Bethiah Wilson born Dec. 25.
Francis of Francis & Mary Whitman born Jan. 14.
Ann of James & Eliza. Worth born Oct. 16.
Robert of Robert & Margery Williams born Apr. 3.
John of John & Eunice Waite born Sept. 13.
Samuel of Richard & Mary White born Dec 15.
Moses of Thomas & Rebecca Walker born Dec. 26.

Rebecca of James & Mary Webster born Dec. 3.
Lydia of Experience & Eliza. Willise born Feb. 21.
Judeth of Cornelius & Faith Waldo born Jan. 25.
Rose of Robert & Luce Ward (Negros) born Oct. 26.


William Alden & Mary Drewrey were married by Samuel Sewall Esq. Assist.
May 21.
Nathaniel Alden & Hepsiba Mountjoy were married by Samuel Sewall Esq.
Assist. Oct. 1.
William Adams & Sarah Nostock were married by Mr. Emblim Bapt. mins.
Dec. 10.
George Beard & Abiel Buttolph were married by Samuel Sewall Esq. Assist.
Dec. 17.
Thomas Clark & Rebecca Smith were married by Isa. Addington Esq. Assist.
Apr. 30.
John Clark & Sarah Shrimpton were married by Isa. Addington Esq. Assist.
Apr. 30.
Richard Cobb & Esther Bates were married by Saml Sewall Esq. Assist.
Sept. 16.
William Crow & Eliza Sergent were married by Simon Bradstreet Esq. Gov.
Dec. 10.
Benja. Dyer & Hannah Odlin were married by Saml Sewall Esq. Assist.
Dec. 10.
Samuel Durham & Eliza. Reed were married by Saml. Sewall Esq. Assist.
July 6.
Amos Fisher & Ruth Adams both of Dedham were married by Saml. Sewall
Esq. Assist. Dec. 22.
Richard Flood & Eliza. Harmon were married by Saml. Sewall Esq. Assist.
Dec. 1.
Thomas Gwin & Sarah Dixey were married by Isa. Addington Esq. Assist.
Nov.
Samuel Grice & Priscilla Green were married by Rev. —— Whitman Minist
of Hull July 14.
John Hurd & Eliza. Webb were married by Mr. Emblim Baptist Minister
Mar. 16.
Nathaniel Holmes & Sarah Thaxter were married by Rev. John Norton
Minist. of Hingham Oct. 1.
William Joyce & Sarah Cleverly were married by Saml. Sewall Esq. Assist.
Sept. 24.
Nathanl. Jarvise & Eliza. Salter were married by Saml. Sewall Esq. Assist.
Sept. 28.
Moses Kenny & Margaret Letherland were married by Isa. Addington Esq.
Assist. July 24.
Edward Kettow & Mercy Belcher were married by Mr. Emblin Bapt. Minst.
Dec. 4.
Christopher Kilbey & Sarah Simkins were married Mar. 20.
Isaac Loreing & Sarah Young were married by Isa. Addington Esq. Assist.
Aug. 5.
James Loyd & Rebecca Leveret were married by Isa. Addington Esq. Assist.
Nov. 3.
Thomas Lawreson & Eliner Loe were married by Saml. Sewall Esq. Assist.
Aug. 26.
James Pitts & Eliza. Hough were married by Elisha Hutchinson Esq. Assist.
Mar. 10.
Edward Proctor & Eliza. Cock were married by Isa. Addington Esq. Assist.
Nov. 24.
William Phillps & June Butterfeeld were married by Isa. Addington Esq.
Assist. Apr. 2.
John Pasco & Eliza Loft were married by Mr. Emblim Baptist Minis. May 25.
William Painter & Mary Messenger were married by Saml. Sewall Esq.
Assist. May 28.
Mark Pilkinton & Faith Cross were married by Saml. Sewall Esq. Assist.
Nov. 18.

John Prat & Margaret Maverick were married by Elisha Hutchinson Esq. July 29.

William Randoll & Eliza. Hill were married by Saml. Sewall Esq. Assist. Dec. 10.

John Smith & Sarah Scudder were married by Saml. Sewall Esq. Assist. Sept. 16.

Benj. Tout & Mary Winsor were married Aug. 29.

Samuel Thorn & Abigail Barber were married by Saml. Sewall Esq. Assist. Dec. 17.

Samuel Veazey & Mary Virgoose were married by Saml. Sewall Esq. Assist. Nov. 25.

Saml Ward & Mary Sale were married by Isa. Addington Esq. Assist. Dec. 10.

Samuel Wentworth & Eliza Hopson were married by Isa. Addington Esq. Assist. Nov. 12.


Jabez of John & Eliza. Allen dyed Aug. 18.

Mary Beard dyed April 31.

Peter of John & Joanna Bennet dyed April 22.

Joseph Brunning dyed Aprill 8th.

Susanna Brunning dyed March 26.

Rainess Belcher dyed Octobr 2.

Nicholas Baxter dyed Janry 10.

Deborah of Thomas & Deborah Cushing dyed July 23.

Edward Cowel dyed Septr 12.

Mary of John & Martha Cornish dyd. Sept. 14.

Katherine wife of Henry Clark dyed Febry 26.

Eliza. Colman dyed Sept. 17.

Mary of John & Martha Clough dyed Aprill 22.

Eliza. of John & Marth Clough dyd. Aprill 25.

James of James & Mary Dennise dyed May 7.

Thomas Dewer Senr. dyed Febry 1.

Nicholas George dyd. April 9th.

Joseph of William & Mary Hough dyed July 31.

John Hurd dyed Febry 18.

Mary Lumsden dyed Febry 24.

Saml Mason Senr. dyed Sept. 20.

Abigail of Samll. & Mary Mason dyed Febry 20.

Nehemiah Pearce dyed March 10.

Mary of Stephen & Judeth Robineau dyed March 11.

David Ransford dyed Novr 28.

Joseph of Joseph & Eliza Rogers dyed Novr 27.

John of John & Ann Smith dyed Octor 3.

Mary of John & Sarah Vickers dyed March 19.

Samuel Walker dyed Octor 12.

Samuel Worden dyed Janry 12.


## First Church.

| | |
|---|---|
| Martha of Sampson Stoddard aged 16 years | Jan. 18. |
| Sampson of Sampson Stoddard aged 12 years | Jan. 18. |
| Mary of Sampson Stoddard aged 8 years | Jan. 18. |
| Mercy of Sampson Stoddard aged 6 years | Jan. 18. |
| Isabella of Deliverance Legg aged 14 years | Feb. |
| Daniel of Deliverance Legg aged 9 years | Feb. |
| John of Deliverance Legg aged 8 years | Feb. |
| Sampson Duer aged 1 week | Feb. |
| John More aged 3 weeks | Feb. 22. |
| Peter Butler aged 8 years | Feb. 22. |
| John Butler | Feb. 22. |
| Jane a Negro | Feb. 22. |
| Elizabeth Egerton aged 9 or 10 years | March 8. |
| Mary Burgesse | March 15. |

| | |
|---|---|
| Elizabeth Fransis | Apr. 5. |
| John Mirick | Apr. 5. |
| Joseph Mirick | Apr. 5. |
| Bartholmew Chevers  aged about **6 ys.** | Apr. 19. |
| Sarah Chevers | Apr. 19. |
| Susannah Chevers | Apr. 19. |
| Benjamin Willis | Apr. 26. |
| William Arnold | May 3. |
| Mary Arnold | May 3. |
| Robert Williams | May 3. |
| Ebenezer Mumford | May 31. |
| Elizabeth Butler | May 31. |
| Mary Proctor | May 31. |
| Thomas of Mr. Jackson | July 26. |
| Mercy Hawkins | Aug. 2. |
| Peter Barnes | Aug. 23 |
| Mary Reynolds | Aug. 23 |
| Elizabeth Ingram | Sept. 6. |
| John Wayte | Sept. 13 |
| Sarah Clough | Sept. 27. |
| Deborah Thare | Oct. 18. |
| David Gibson | Nov. 22. |
| Rebecca Prince | Nov. 22. |
| Hannah Bridge | Dec. 6. |
| Boozone of Capt Boozone Allin | Dec. 20. |
| Samuel of        White | **Dec. 20.** |

## 1692.

### TOWN.

Mary of Edward & Mary Ashley born Apr. 13.
John of Lewise & Abigail Allaire born Dec. 5.
Eliza. of Theoder & Mary Adkinson born Nov. 28.
Mary of Nathaniel & Hephsiba Alden born Aug. 20.
Barakiah of Barakiah & Abigall Arnall born Oct. 10:
Constantine of Henry & Sarah Bennet born Mar. 8.
Hannah of Thomas & Sarah Banister born Mar. 10.
Margaret of Thomas & Margaret Berry born June 25.
Allexander of Allexr & Margaret Bulman born Jan. 16.
Christian of John & Sarah Blake born Sept. 16.
Ehenr of Samuel & Ann Beighton born Sept. 30.
John of William & Eliza. Burt born Jan. 5.
William of George & Mercy Bearstow born Jan. 10.
John of John & Eliza. Benmore born Feb. 3.
John of Edward & Mary Bartles born Oct. 10.
Sarah of Edward & Mary Bromfeeld born Oct. 11.
Sarah of John & Mercy Bucker born Dec. 19.
Sarah of Phillip & Sarah Bass born June 13.
James of James & Eliza. Barry born June 14.
Mary of Peter & Sarah Barbour born June 14.
Ruth of Nathaniel & Mary Biker born June 13.
Jonathan of John & Hannah Barnerd born Jan. 14.
Ezekiel of Thomas & Sarah Cheever born Mar. 7.
Alice of Richard & Hannah Clark born Mar. 1.
William of William & Martha Cole born Jan. 10.
Elisha of Ellise & Mary Callender born Apr. 27.
———— son of Samuel & Susan Collins born Aug. 30.
Mary of Willm & Susanna Critchfeeld born Sept. 27.
John of John & Martha Cornish born Mar. 27.
Andrew of Andrew & Sarah Cuningham born Aug. 17.
Thomas of John & Eliza. Coombs born Sept. 10.
Nathaniel of Willm & Lydia Clough born Nov. 22.

Joseph of John & Mary Cotta born Jan. 9.
William of William & Eliza Crow born Jan 18.
Alice of George & Mary Clark born Feb. 13.
Sarah of John & Sarah Carey born June 13.
Christopher of Christor & Tamozine Capril born Oct. 26.
Samuel of Saml & Eliza. Durham born Mar. 1.
Samuel of Jacob & Susanna Davise born Feb. 7.
Samuel of Edward & Ann Durant born Apr. 4.
Hannah of Benja. & Hannah Dyer born Sept. 27.
Sarah of John & Elizabeth Dyar born Feb. 6.
Mary of Thomas & Ann Dean horn Aug. 20.
Mercy of John & Grace Elliset born Aug. 20.
Mary of Jonathan & Mary Evans born Dec. 4.
John of Joseph & Silence Eliott born Mar. 17.
John of John & Mary Edicott born Feb. 17.
William of William & Sarah Evstiss born Apr. 11.
Mary of David & Eliza. Faulkner born Mar. 7.
John of John & Dorothy Farnum born Apr. 23.
Mary of David & Dorothy Farnum born Oct. 14.
Elinor of Hugh & Elinor Floyd horn Feb. 12.
Richard of Richard & Mary Fifeeld born May 12.
Thomas of Thomas & Hannah Fairwether born Nov. 7.
Peter of Josiah & Abia Franklin born Nov. 22.
Henry of Henry & Sarah Franklin born June 24.
John of Samuel & Susanna Gray born Aug. 16.
Joshua of Joshua & Eliza. Gee born Aug. 18.
Hannah of Richard & Hannah Green born Feb. 8.
Henry of Hezekiah & Annis Gidley born Apr. 5.
Ann of John & Joan Gee born Apr. 27.
Anna of Thomas & Lydia Gilbert born June 9.
Robert of James & Eliza Glass born Sept. 19.
Priscilla of Samuel & Priscilla Grice born Apr. 12.
Henry of William & Patience Gibbons born Aug. 18.
Nathaniel of John & Susanna Gardener born Nov. 20.
Jeremiah of Nathanll & Elizabeth Green born Feb. 6.
Eliza. of William & Elizabeth Gill born Jan.
Eliza. of Thomas & Sarah Gwin born Sept. 3.
Mary of Bartho: & Mary Green born Oct. 13.
Jacob of Robert & Mary Gibbs born Mar. 6.
Nathanll of William & Judeth Hasic born Mar. 13.
Sarah of Thomas & Mary Hunt born Dec. 9.
Nathaniel of Ephraim & Sarah Hall born Aug. 14.
Sarah of Nathanll & Sarah Holmes born Aug. 27.
Grace of John & Grace Ireland born Jan. 15.
William of William & Fortune Inglesfeeld born Dec. 19.
Margaret of Elias & Margaret Jarvise born Mar. 24.
John of John & Mary Jarvise born Feb. 14.
Anna of Matthew & Susanna Jones born Apr. 30.
Richard of Thomas & Hannah Jepson born Apr. 16.
John of John & Ruth Jepson born Aug. 15.
Ann of John & Esther Jose born Aug. 18.
Richard of Richard & Sarah Jenkins born Apr. 11.
Thomas of Thomas & Priscilla Jackson born July 18.
Sarah of John & Rebecca Kilbey born Mar. 8.
George of Roger & Anne Kilcup born Apr. 5.
Samuel } of John & Emme Kelly born Apr. 11.
Mary } of John & Emme Kelly born Apr. 11.
Mary of John & Mary Kneland born Sept. 12.
Rachel of Zibion & Rachel Letherland born July 30.
William of Willm & Eliza. Lavise born July 17.
Lydia of Robert & Lydia Login born Feb. 13.
James of Samuel & Mary Landman born Mar. 27.
John of Thomas & Elinor Lawreson born Sept. 10.
James of James & Rebecca Loyd born Aug. 16.

Mary of Isaac & Sarah Loreing born June 7.
Samuel of Samuel & Mehitable Lillie born June 5.
Mary of Thomas & Mehitable Lilcoln born Mar. 16.
Samuel of Deodat & Deborah Lawson born Feb. 9.
Joseph of David & Martha Landon born Nov. 22.
Joseph    } of Robert & Eliza. Maugridge born Mar. 3.
Benjamen } of Robert & Eliza. Maugridge born Mar. 3.
Rebecca of Francis & Martha Marshall born Feb. 7.
Mary of Joseph & Hannah Maylim born Jan. 22.
Susanna of Robert & Ann Moor born Feb. 6.
Margaret of John & Margaret Marsh born Apr. 6.
Abigail of Thomas & Eliza. Mosamy born Nov. 12.
Mary of Joseph & Ann Marsh born Dec. 29.
Edward of Samuel & Mary Maryon born Dec. 2.
Eliza. of Thomas & Eliza Mesenger born Oct 7.
Michael of Edward & Sarah Martine born Feb. 25.
Michael of Edward & Sarah Martin born Feb. 25.
Isabella of Nathanll & Sarah Newgate born Feb. 8.
John of John & Keziah Needham born Dec. 22.
William of John & Susanna Nicholls born May 9.
Rebecca of Christor. & Sarah Osgood born May 3.
——— son of John & Sarah Oliver born Aug.
John of John & Lydia Osment born Mar. 12.
Sarah of William and Deborah Phillips born Dec. 28.
Alexander of Alexr & Sarah Prindle born Apr. 17.
Eliza. of John & Christian Pitts born Apr. 25.
Susanna of William & Eliza. Parkman born Sept. 4.
Thomas of Edward & Susanna Phillips born Aug. 29.
John of William & Constance Palfrey born Nov. 20.
Mary of Mark & Faith Pilkinton born July 27.
John of Thomas & Margaret Powel born Aug. 25.
Hannah of Philip & Hannah Phinney born June 22.
Bridget of Samuel & Sarah Philips born Feb. 4.
Eliza. of Thomas & Mary Pratt born Jan. 24.
Nathaniel of Benja. & Eliza. Quelch born Dec. 9.
John of John & Mary Russell born Aug. 25.
——— son of John & Mary Russell born Aug. 25.
Mary of Joseph & Mary Russell born Feb. 12.
Robert of George & Eliza. Robinson born Jan. 23.
Mary of John & Mary Roberts born Aug. 16.
Sarah of Edmund & Mary Ranger born Sept. 15.
Joseph of Willm & Eliza. Randoll born Sept. 15.
Benjamen of Eliazur & Martha Starr born Mar. 7.
Samson of Jabez & Eliza. Salter born Mar. 21.
John of Samuel & Susanna Saxton born Mar. 7.
John of Cyprian & Eliza. Southhack born July 15.
Joyce of Alexander & Rebecca Seers born Nov. 26.
John of Richard & Tamozine Skinner born Jan. 6.
Hannah of Joseph & Margaret Soper born Apr. 13.
Sarah of Robert & Abigail Seers born Aug. 11.
Luke of Josiah & Mary Stone born Aug. 30.
Ryal of Henry & Purchace Spry born Feb. 20.
John of John & Ann Smith born July 7.
Eliza. of Joseph & Eliza. Townsend born Oct. 1.
Grace of William & Isabella Tylly born Nov. 4.
Samuel of Samuel & Abigail Thorn born Oct. 25.
Michael of John & Hannah Tapper born Dec. 6.
John of John & Mary Tucker born Dec. 12.
John of William & Mary Thwing born June 18.
Ann of James & Rebecca Taylor born Nov. 13.
Eliza. of Benja. & Mercy Tout born ———
John of David & Mary Vaughan born Apr. 10.
Joanna of John & Sarah Vickers born Sept. 25.
Samuel of Samuel & Ayme Winslow born June 28.

Sarah of Nathanll & Mary Williams born Sept. 30.
Joanna of Saml & Mary Ward born Oct. 31.
Joshua } of Thomas & Rachel Winsor born Dec. 29.
Caleb } of Thomas & Rachel Winsor born Dec. 29.
Jane of Ebenezer & Deliverance Weeks born Mar. 29.
Sarah of Thomas & Sarah Wheeler born Apr. 10.
Eliza. of William & Mary Wilson born Oct. 4.
Timothy of Timothy & Susanna Wadsworth born Nov. 3.
Mary of James & Eliza. Worth born Dec. 10.
Daniel of Daniel & Hannah Ware born Nov. 26.
Thomas of Thomas & Tryphana Woodard born Sept. 26.
Ann of William & Ann Wheeler born July 19.


Moses Bradford & Eliza. Allen were married by Rev. James Allen Dec. 8.
Charles Beuford & Hannah Bickner were married by Rev. Saml. Willard
Feb. 10.
William Bryant & Hannah Disiter were married by Samuel Sewall Esq.
Assist. June 9.
John Bull & Mary Woodward were married by Samuel Sewall Esq. Assist.
Apr. 21.
Zachery Bignell & Hannah Smith were married by Jer. Dummer Esq.
Nov. 24.
Samuel Buckner & Mary Bille were married by the Parson of the Church of
Engld. Oct. 27.
William Colman & Margaret Haywood were married by John Phillips Esq.
Assist. June 30.
Joshua Cornish & Susanna Bennet were married by Rev. John Bayley Nov. 8.
Stephen Cross & Mary Lawrence were married by Rev. Cotton Mather
· Jan. 23.
Samuel Clark & Sarah Avise were married by John Eyer Esq. J. Pac.
Sept. 8.
William Copp & Ann Ruck were married by John Philips Esq. Assist.
May 24.
Moses Draper & Mary Thatcher were married Nov. 3.
Capt. John Fairwether & Mary Hewes were married by Rev. James Allen
Nov. 17.
Richard Green & Hannah Sherrar were married by Saml. Sewall Esq. Assist.
June 1.
Robert Gyles & Margaret Barret were married by Rev. James Allen Feb. 17.
John Green & Bethiah Messenger were married by Saml. Sewall Esq. Assist.
Jan. 17.
Abram Gourden & Abigail Towers were married by Rev. Cotton Mather
Jan. 5.
John Gerrish & Lydia Watts were married by Simon Bradstreet Esq. Gov.
Apr. 19.
Robert Gibbs & Mary Shrimpton were married by John Richards Esq. Assist.
May 19.
Henry Gibbs & Mercy Greenough were married June 9.
William Gill & Eliza. Scarlet were married May 3.
Benja. Hallawell & Mary Stocker were married May 12.
Eben. Holmes & Sarah Withington were married by Saml. Sewall Esq.
Assist. Feb. 2.
John Hallaway & Mary Grant were married by Saml. Sewall Esq. Assist.
Feb. 2.
Saml. Hood & Rebecca Thwing were married by John Eyer Esq. J. Pac.
July 17.
Nathl Kettle & Joanna Ellise were married by John Eyre Esq. J. Pac. Oct. 5.
Joseph Lobdale & Eliza Townsend were married by John Joylife Esq. J. Pac.
Sept. 1.
Joseph Marsh & Ann Thurogood were married by Saml. Sewall Esq. Assrt.
Mar. 2.
Thomas Okes & Eliza Danson were married by Rev. James Allen Feb. 2.
Thomas Phillips & Mary Howard were married by Isa. Addington Esq. Assist.
Mar. 1.
Stephen Palmer & Eliza. Cheever were married by Rev. James Aller Jan. 19.

Joylieffc Price & Rebecca Coney were married by John Joylieffe Esq. J. Pac. Dec. 7.

Francis Parnell & Dorothy Fowles were married by John Phillips Esq. Assist. Aug. 15.

Richard Prat & Mercy —— were married March 16.

Andrew Rankin & Grace Butler were married by Simon Bradstreet Esq. Gov. Apr. 5.

James Rayner & Eliza. Andrews were married by William Bond Esq. J. Pac. Oct. 25.

Joseph Skeath & Hannah Davise were married by Isa. Addington Esq. Assist. Apr. 18.

Richard Skinner & Tamozine Taylor were married by Saml. Sewall Esq. Assist. Apr. 21.

Abrm. Tuckerman & Constance Worster were married by John Eyer Esq. J. Pac. July 15.

Edward Taylor & Jane Payn were married by John Richards Esq. Assist. Aug. 4.

Philip Voden & Abigail Kemball were married by Rev. Cotton Mather Dec. 22.

Isaac Virgoose & Eliza. Foster were married by James Russell Esq. Assist. July 5.

Christopher Vale & Joanna Heifernan were married by Jeremiah Dummer Esq. Sept. 21.

Benja. Webb & Susana Ballintine were married by Saml. Sewall Esq. Assist. Nov. 21.

Jonathn. Waldo & Hannah Mason were married by Saml. Sewall Esq. Assist. Nov. 28.

Thomas Walley & Christian Johnson were married by John Eyer Esq. J. Pac. Sept. 22.


Eliza of John & Sarah Alger dyed Febry 26.
Eliza wife of Nathll. Barnes dyd. Septr. 20.
Moses Bradford Scnr. dyed March 23.
Lydia of John & Sarah Balston dyed Aug. 12.
Margaret wife of John Clough dyed Febry. 10.
Mercy of John & Grace Ellisct dyed Sept. 17.
Jeremiah Fitch dyed May 3.
Thomas Grubb dyed July 25.
Joshua of Joshua & Eliza Gee dyed Aug. 18.
Ralph Hewes dyed Novr. 13.
Thankfull of John & Experience Howard dyed Octobr. 1.
James of James & Rebecca Loyd dyed Aug. 25.
Mary of Isaek & Sarah Lowrin died Aug. 20.
John Magor dyed July 15.
Grace of Thomas & Bethulea Mighell dyed May 25.
Thomas of Tho. & Elizabeth Mesenger died July 26.
Rebecca of Nathanll & Hannah Parkman dyed Aug. 9.
Samll Smith dyed June 15.
Ketura Savery dyed April 15.
Margaret wife of Thomas Smith dyed Octor. 7.
Abigail of Wm. & Martha Shoot died Sept. 27.
Eliza. of Samuel & Mehitabel Worden dyed May 18.
Mary of Isaek & Sarah Lowrin died Aug. 20.
Thomas of Tho. and Elizabeth Mesenger died July 26.
Abigail of Wm. and Martha Shoot died Sept. 27.


## FIRST CHURCH.

| | |
|---|---|
| Mary of sister Chevers the younger | Jan. 10. |
| Judith of sister Waldo | Jan. 31. |
| Lydia of bro. Experience Willis | Feb. 28. |
| Hannah of Mr. Bannister aged 2 days. | Mar. 20. |
| Cornelius } twins of sister Pecke the younger now Waldo | Mar. 27. |
| Jonathan } | Mar. 27. |

| | |
|---|---|
| · Abigail of John Moore | Apr. 10. |
| Shubael Dummer | Apr. 17. |
| Mary Ashley | Apr. 17. |
| Catharine George Grand child to Mr. Lee aged 8 days | June 4. |
| James Berry aged 4 days | June 19. |
| John Clow | June 26. |
| John Tu son. she was daughter Leatherlands wife[1] . | Aug. 7. |
| James Lloyde | Aug. 21. |
| Joshua Gee | Aug. 21. |
| Henry Gibbons | Aug. 21. |
| Sarah Anger | Sept. 18. |
| Thomas Coombes | Sept. 18. |
| Christian Blake | Sept. 18. |
| Hannah of Benjamin Dyer | Oct. 3. |
| Elizabeth Messenger aged not 1 week. | Oct. 10. |
| Benjamin Pecke aged some years | Oct. 10. |
| Samuel Pecke aged some years | Oct. 10. |
| Priscilla Gardiner | Oct. 23. |
| John Gardiner | Oct. 23. |
| Jeremiah Gardiner | Oct. 23. |
| Samuel Thorne | Oct. 30. |
| Joanna Ward | Nov. 6. |
| Nathaniel Gardiner | Nov. 27. |
| Elizabeth Atkinson | Dec. 4. |
| Nathaniel Quelch | Dec. 11. |

## 1693.

### TOWN.

Mary of William & Mary Alden born Feb. 14.
William of Joseph & Ann Allen born Sept. 22.
John of John & Hannah Adams born Nov. 4.
John of John & Mary Atwood born Feb. 16.
Peter of Nicholas & Margaret Allen born Mar. 21.
Susanah of Joseph & Comfort Alison born Jan. 4.
Rebecca of John & Grace Alliset born Oct. 19.
Abraham of Abraham & Abigail Adams born July 14.
Sarah of Benja. & Mary Alford born Mar. 17.
Thomas of Jacob & Theodosia Bill born Mar. 30.
Susanah of Joseph & Rebecca Brisco born Apr. 15.
Saml of Samll & Hannah Burrell born Apr. 18.
Hanah of Joseph & Hanah Billings born Mar. 15.
Eliz. of John & Elizabeth Buckanau born Mar. 1.
Margaret of John & Susanah Buttler born June 1.
Eliz. of John & Sarah Banister born July 21.
Joseph ⎱ of Ambros & Hanah Berry born July 11.
Benja. ⎰ of Ambros & Hanah Berry born July 11.
Samuell of Saml & Mary Bucknel born June 4.
Rebecka of Nathll & Rebecka Bolston born July 3.
Joseph of Henry & Abiell Brightman born July 19.
Sarah of Daniel & Sarah Ballard born Sept. 6.
John of Moses & Elizabeth Bradford born Septr. 18.
Peter of Francis & Frances Buckitt born Apr. 24.
Eliz. of Richard & Catharine Barnard born Sept. 5.
Mary of Willm & Mary Browne born Sept. 10.
George of George & Ruth Badcock born July 28.
William of Samuel & Christian Bridge born Sept. 14.
Robert of Jarvis & Martha Ballard born Oct. 15.
William of William & Mary Brown born Nov. 18.
John of Richard & Elizabeth Bearson born Dec. 31.

---

[1] Perhaps Mrs. Tu was a daughter of Mrs. Leatherland, or possibly Mrs. Leatherland had a daughter baptized the same day. — W. S. A.

Mergeret ⎱ of Alexander & Margaret Bulman born Jan. **4.**
Elizabeth ⎰ of Alexander & Margaret Bulman born Jan. **4.**
Mercy of John & Charity Baley born Jan. 29.
Merget of Peter & Sarah Barber born Feb. 12.
Merget of Isaac & Ann Biscon born Jan. 30.
Oliver of Oliver Berry born Feb. 26.
John of William & Sarah Burrage born Feb. 11.
Samuel of Edward & Mary Bartells born Mar. 11.
Mary of Peter & Elizabeth Buttler born Feb. 21.
Kathrine of Josiah & Mary Baker born Mar. 23.
Sarah of Philip & Sarah Bass born Apr. 5.
Thoms. of Thomas & Lydia Burington born Apr. 13.
Susana of William & Mary Barnsdell born Apr. 18.
Thomas of Thomas & Mary Bosenger born June 18.
John of David & Mary Basset born June 9.
Mary of Thomas & Margaret Bomer born June 6.
Dorcas of Nicholas & Dorcas Bose born Dec. 5.
Rachel of John & Hannah Carlile born Mar. 7.
Ann of William & Ann Copp born Mar. 17.
Susanah of Nicholas & Sarah Cocke born Mar. 23.
Mary of Samuel & Ruth Clough born Apr. 4.
Eliz. of Ebenezer & Eliza. Chafein born Apr. 5.
William of John & Sarah Cooper born Mar. 12.
Philip of Edward & Sarah Cruff born May 22.
Mary of John & Ruth Cooke born June 27.
Alexander of Alexander and Eliza. Clomy born July **11.**
Sarah of Edward & Sarah Clarke born May 25.
Sarah of John & Sarah Clarke born Sept. 17.
Susanna of Job & Joanna Chamberling born Nov. **23.**
Mary of John & Priscilla Chadwick born Dec. 1.
Rachel of Edward & Sarah Coilings born Dec. 9.
Eliza of Francis & Sarah Cole born Jan. 9.
Thomas of Thomas & Deborah Cushing born Jan. 30.
Ebenezer of Caleb & Sarah Chafin born Jan. 29.
James of James & Elizabeth Crockford born Feb. 20.
John of James & Mary Cornish born Aug. 29.
Eliz. of Samuel & Mary Chickley born Sept. 3.
Mary of Paul & Mary Collings born July 15.
Thomas of Thomas & Mary Downe born Aug. 28.
Ann of Richard & Sarah Draper born July 7.
Joseph of Henry & Abigall Dawson born Sept. 3.
Thomas of Benjamin & Hannah Dyer born Nov. 7.
William of John & Rachel Draper born Dec. 27.
Sarah of Henry & Elizabeth Dickerson born Jan. **29.**
Sarah of Thomas & Hannah Davis born May 12.
Martha of Edmun & Sarah Dolebear born Feb. 23.
Moses of Moses & Mary Draper born Sept. 12.
Elizabeth of Zachary & Sarah Davise born Nov. 11.
Benjamin of Benjamin & Mary Emms born June 24.
Eliza. of John & Elizabeth Egbear born Oct. 1.
Eliza. of Benja. & Elizabeth Emons born Nov. 8.
Rachel of Rachel & David Eustiss born Feb. 16.
John of William & Eliza. Endicutt born Dec. 23.
Eliza. of William & Abigail Everdon born Feb. 7.
James of Richard & Elizabeth Flood born June 11.
Penelophe of Joseph & Rebecca Fuller born July 20.
Eliza. of John & Sarah Fosdick born Sept. 16.
Joseph of Jonathan & Martha Farnum born Oct. 19.
John of Gyles & Elizabeth Fifield born Sept. 11.
Eliza. of John & Catharine Fowle born Oct. 20.
Peter of William & Esther Frothingham born Oct. 24.
Hannah of David & Eliza. Faulkner born Jan. 19.
Benjamin of Benjamin & Mary Fitch born Jan. 13.
Jacob of Robert & Mary Gibbs born Mar. 6.

Margaret of David & Martha Gwin born Mar. 6.
Christopher of Christopher & Abigail Goffe born July 13.
Susanna of John & Susanna Garrett born July 3.
Mary of Samuel & Elizabeth Gaskell born Aug. 20.
Mehitable of William & Hannah Gibson born Aug. 28.
James of James & Hannah Gooch born Oct. 12.
John of Abraham & Abigail Gorden born Oct. 15.
Ann of Benjamin & Abigail Gillam born Nov. 7.
Eliza. of John & Lydia Geerish born Oct. 19.
Mary of John & Bethiah Green born Nov. 11.
Anna of Samll & Prisilla Grice born Feb. 14.
John of John & Elizabeth Gaud born Mar. 13.
Mary of Joshua & Elizabeth Gee born Jan. 25.
Lydia of Thomas & Lydia Gilbert born Aug. 14.
John of Joseph & Hannah Grant born Sept. 22.
Mary of Benja. & Mary Hollowell born Mar. 17.
Hannah of Ambrose & Hannah Honnowell born June 7.
Mary of James & Lydia Hawkins born May 17.
John of John & Ann Hobby born July 2.
William of William & Ann Holowell born July 31.
Eliza. of William & Elizabeth Hall born May 16.
George of Herculus & Jane Hewitt born Mar. 27.
Eliza. of Nathanll & Elizabeth Hatch born Aug. 2.
William of John & Elizabeth Higgs born Aug. 23.
Margaret of Hesеciah & Abigail Henchman born Jan. 7.
Benjamin of Benja. & Mehitable Hopkins born Jan. 20.
Abigail of John & Doreos Hiscot born Jan. 29.
Abigail of William & Mary Haugh born Feb. 8.
Job } of Job & Hannah Ingraham born Apr. 19.
Jere } of Job & Hannah Ingraham born Apr. 19.
Nathll of Thomas & Priscilla Jackson born May 15.
Nathll of Nathll & Elizabeth Jarvis born Nov. 9.
Rebecca of David & Elizabeth Jefferies born Dec. 9.
Hannah of Thomas & Hannah Jepson born Dec. 29.
David of John & Mary Jenkins born Feb. 20.
Nathanll of Nathanll & Joanna Kettle born Oct. 14.
Christopher of John & Rebecca Kilbee born Dec. 9.
George of George & Agnis Lourcin born June 27.
Cromwell of Joseph & Elizabeth Lobdell born June 12.
Sarah of Isaac & Sarah Lorin born Aug. 26.
Paul of Philip & Mary Langdon born Sept. 12.
Solomon of Solomon & Sarah Legeree born Sept. 17.
Richard of Richard & Mary Lowden born Jan. 9.
Mehitable of Samuel & Mehitable Lilly born Feb. 2.
Ann of James & Ann Leblond born Apr. 8.
Benjamen of David & Martha Landon born Dec. 18.
Samuel of John & Martha Morton born Aug. 3.
Thomas of Thomas & Elizabeth Muligan born Apr. 27.
Ebenezer of Daniel & Susanna More born July 22.
Joseph of Cotton & Abigail Mather born Mar. 28.
Ann of William & Mary Morer born Aug. 18.
Abraham of Robert & Elizabeth Maugridge born Nov. 1.
Sarah of Robert & Elizabeth Maugridge born Nov. 1.
Mary of Duncan & Mary Mackfarland born Jan. 22.
Johanna of Samuel & Ruth Marshall born June 26.
Sarah of Nathaniel & Rest Newhall born Mar. 14.
Eliza. of George & Elizabeth Newby born Jan. 29.
Bass of Bass servant of Samuel Lilly (negro) born Feb. 4.
Eliza. of William & Sarah Owen born Aug. 1.
Eliza. of Stephen & Eliza. Palmer born Mar. 2.
Eliza. of Thomas & Mary Parris born July 10.
John of William & Eliza. Parkeman born Jan. 19.
Mary of Edward & Eliza. Procter born June 16.
Samuel of Richard & Dorothy Poutland born July 4.

Samuel of Samuel & Hannah Philips born May 26.
Marget of Thomas & Margaret Powell born July 18.
Hannah of ——— & Hannah Porter born July 12.
Mehitable of Job & Rebecca Prince born Sept. 3.
Hannah of Robert & Hannah Prise born Sept. 12.
Francis of Francis & Dorothy Pornall born Sept. 26.
Eliza. of James & Elizabeth Pitts born Dec. 30.
Thomas of Thomas & Rachel Parker born Feb. 19.
Benjamin of Thomas & Ruth Prince born Feb. 28.
Joseph of Thomas & Elizabeth Pyke born Mar. 7.
Benjamin of John & Charity Ricks born June 9.
Andrew of Andrew & Grace Rankin born July 13.
Eliza. of Joseph & Martha Ransford born May 17.
James of James & Elizabeth Rayner born Sept. 28.
Hanah of Kaleb & Hanah Ray born Oct. 2.
Sarah of George & Elizabeth Robinson born Feb. 5.
Nathll. of Nathll. & Ruth Raynolds born Jan. 14.
Hannah of John & Bridget Rylee born Sept. 10.
Mary of John & Mary Robinson born Oct. 30.
Abigail of Rowland & Ann Storey born Mar. 11.
John of John & Rebecca Smith born Feb. 20.
John of Joseph & Hannah Simpson born June 12.
Elizabeth of David & Elizabeth Stephens born June 22.
James of James & Edy Seward born June 29.
Thomas of Samuel & Hannah Smith born Aug. 6.
Joanna of Michael & Hannah Sale born Aug. 27:
William of William & Martha Shute born Mar. 22.
Jane of Samuel & Hannah Sewell born Aug. 7.
Benjamin of Francis & Mary Smith born Aug. 17.
John of John & Margaret Soaper born Nov. 16.
William of Simeon & Mary Stodard born Nov. 6.
Abraham of John & Jane Snelling born Dec. 5.
Joanna of Benjamin & Joanna Stone born Dec. 20.
Thomas of Thomas & Mehetable Savage born Jan. 20.
Joseph of Joseph & Hannah Skeath born Nov. 28.
Mary of John & Mary Sunderlin born Feb. 2.
Hannah of John & Lydia Seally born Mar. 5.
William of William & Eliza. Straton born Feb. 1.
Mary of John & Martha Tuttle born Nov. 9.
John of Daniel & Anna Turrell born Apr. 18.
John of John & Martha Twing born June 2.
Eliza. of George & Rebecca Tomas born July 28.
Jeremiah of Jeremiah & Mercy Toy born Oct. 30.
Hannah of Samuel & Hannah Tulley born Feb. 16.
Hannah of William & Hannah Turner born Feb. 25.
Eliza. of Richard & Hannah Tout born Mar. 12.
John of Edward & Abigail Tuttel born Mar. 11.
Eliza. of Benja. & Mercy Tout born May 7.
Katharine of James & Elizabeth Vpduke born June 7.
Eliza. of Isaac & Elizabeth Vergoose born May 5.
Mary of Thomas & Hannah Vering born Nov. 5.
Mary of Christopher & Joanna Vale born June 20.
Eliza. of Andrew & Elizabeth Veach born Aug. 5.
Abigail of Philip & Abigail Voden born Aug. 13.
Jacob of James & Abigail Woodmansey born Mar. 1.
Edward of Edward & Hannah Winslow born Apr. 15.
Charles of Andrew & Elizabeth Waker born Apr. 17.
Eliza. of John & Abigail Winslow born Apr. 2.
Mildred of Michael & Elizabeth Willis born May 7.
Eliza. of John & Elizabeth Walley born May 4.
Samuel of Francis & Mary Whitman born May 19.
Susanna of James & Mary Webster born June 7.
Anna of John & Sarah Ware born June 11.
Eliza. of Amos & Elizabeth Wedland born Sept. 14.

William of William & Eliza. Wheeler born Oct. 19.
Richard of Return & Martha Wait born Oct. 21.
James of James & Esther White born Nov. 12.
John of John & Abigail Winslow born Dec. 31.
Mary of Richard & Phebe Whitridge born Feb. 8.
Ebenezer of Ebenezer & Deliverance Weeks born Nov. 23.
Edward of Samuel & Elizabeth Wentworth born Feb. 5.
Thomas of Thomas & Sarah Wheeler born Feb. 18.
Mercy of Andrew & Bethiah Willson born Feb. 17.
Rachel of John & Eliza. Welch born Jan. 12.

Walter Allen & Elizabeth Middleton were married by Jer. Dummer Esq. Dec. 11.
Edward Bear & Mary Hale were married by Saml. Sewall Esq. Assist. May 19.
John Battis & Mary Kelley were married by Samuel Sewall Esq. Assist. June 15.
John Barrel & Sebella Legg were married by Rev. John Bayley Sept. 14.
Thomas Blower & Eliza Gridley were married by Saml. Sewall Esq. Assist. Sept. 21.
Francis Brooker & Sarah Hubbert were married by Rev. James Allen Nov. 9.
James Bahage & Eliza Davise were married by Rev. Cotton Mather Oct. 9.
John Benmore & Mary Richards were married by Rev. Cotton Mather Nov. 16.
Benjamin Blackleech & Mary Bucknell were married by Mr. Theodot Lawson minister Sept. 18.
Joseph Calef & Mary Ayer were married by Rev. James Allen Mar. 24.
Thomas Carter & Ruth Mountfort were married by Rev. James Allen May 2.
Jeremiah Cushing & Judeth Parminter were married by Rev. Saml. Willard Mar. 29.
John Clough & Mary Beard were married by Saml. Sewall Esq. Assist. Apr. 12.
Ebenezer Clough & Martha Goodwin were married by Rev. Cotton Mather Mar. 28.
John Child & Hannah French both of Watertown were married by Rev. John Bayley Sept. 5.
Samuel Capen & Ann Stone both of Dorchester were married by Rev. John Bayley Nov. 16.
Daniel Collings & Rebecca Clemans were married by Rev. John Bayley Dec. 13.
Robert Cook & Submit Weeks both of Dorchester were married by Rev. James Allen Oct. 26.
Henry Champney & Eliza Worthylake were married by Rev. Cotton Mather Dec. 8.
Joseph Clerk & Sarah Wells were married by Rev. James Allen Dec. 11.
James Dowell & Eliza Wing were married by Rev. Saml. Willard Apr. 27.
Henry Dickeson & Eliza. Castle were married by Saml. Sewall Esq. Assist. Oct. 25.
Simon Dewolfe & Alice Bolt were married by Saml. Sewall Esq. J. Pac. Jan. 19.
Robert Davise & Jane Alger were married by Rev. Cotton Mather Feb. 19.
John Edwards & Amey Warren were married by Saml. Sewall Esq. Assist. Mar. 2.
Edward Edlington & Phebey Holman were married by Saml. Sewall Esq. Assist. June 27.
William Eame of Long Iseland & Mary Balston of Muddy River were married by Rev. James Allen July 12.
Arthur Eastmead & Mary Hix were married by Rev. Saml. Willard Aug. 4.
Edward Egleston & Phebee Holman were married July 27.
Benja. Fitch & Mary Hett were married by Rev. Cotton Mather March 2.
John Fairfield & Eliza. Badson were married by Rev. James Allen Apr. 18.
John Flack & Mary Varney were married by Saml. Sewall Esq. Asst. Dec. 23.
Samuel Gardener & Eliza. Goodwin were married by Rev. Cotton Mather May 11.
John Greenough & Eliza. Gross were married by Rev. James Allen Oct. 18.
Robert Griffin & Mary Ruddock were married by Rev. Saml. Willard Feb. 1.

Edmund Gross & Dorothy Belcher were married by Rev. Cotton Mather Feb. 19.

Samuel Gurney & Sarah Shapley were married by Pen Townsend Esq. Oct. 26.

William Hough & Mary Bricknell were married by Rev. Cotton Mather March 24.

Nathl. Halsie & Hannah Gross were married by Rev. Cotton Mather June 22.

Michael Homer & Mary Burroughs were married by Rev. Cotton Mather July 13.

Joseph Hall & Mary Bill were married by Saml. Sewall Esq. Assist. July 13.

John Homer & Margery Stephens were married by Rev. Saml. Willard July 13.

Obadiah Haws & Rebecca Cowen were married by Saml. Sewall Esq. J. Pac. Dec. 19.

John Hewson & Susanna Norden were married by Rev. Cotton Mather Aug. 17.

Nathl. Henchman & Hannah Green were married by Rev. Cotton Mather Jan. 11.

Francis Holmes & Rebecca Wharfe were married by Rev. Cotton Mather Feb. 15.

Samuel Hooper of Marblehead & Mary White of Boston were married by Rev.Cotton Mather Feb. 16.

Job. Hilliard & Mary Fowl were married July 4.

John Hudson & Susanna Norden were married Aug. 17.

Thomas Hatherly & Lydia Green were married by Thomas Danforth Esq. Aug. 1.

Joseph Hasie & Hannah Buckman were married by Mr. Thomas Cheever Jan. 12.

Thomas Hammond & Mehitabel Veray were married by Jer. Dummer Esq. June 15.

John Johnson & Margaret Cowell were married by Rev. Saml. Willard Aug. 2.

Thomas Lyon & Anne Case were married by Saml. Sewall Esq. J. Pac. Nov. 1.

Joshua Linkoln & Hannah Palmer both of Hingham were married by Rev. James Allen Feb. 12.

Eliezur Morton & Rebecca Marshall were married by Rev. Saml. Willard Apr. 11.

Thomas Mellens & Mary Thredneedle were married by Rev. Saml. Willard Sept. 28.

David Mason & Eliza Clark were married by Rev. Saml. Willard. Dec. 12. .

John Mountfort & Mary Cock were married by Saml. Sewall Esq. J. Pac. Jan. 17.

Robert Mason & Mary Ridman were married by Rev. James Allen Jan. 31.

Robert Mason & Mariot Redman were married Jan. 30.

George Nowell & Eliza. Johnson were married by Rev. Cotton Mather Oct. 13.

Jabez Negus & Sarah Brown were married by Rev. James Allen Jan. 9.

William Owen & Sarah Vitterell were married by Rev. Cotton Mather Apr. 28.

Samuel Oake & Joanna Phillips were married by Rev. Samuel Willard Oct. 4.

Robert Oliver & Elizabeth Burey were married by Rev. Cotton Mather Sept. 14.

Jonathan Pollord & Mary Winslow were married by Rev. Saml. Willard Dec. 26.

William Perram & Martha Penewell were married by Rev. Cotton Mather Nov. 16.

Arthur Power & Sarah Makaset both of Brantrey were married by Rev. James Allen Jan. 17.

Samuel Ruck & Hannah Nicholson were married by Rev. James Allen Apr. 4.

Joseph Russell & Susanna Cheever were married by Rev. James Allen June 5.

Thomas Salter & Mary Habberfeeld were married by Rev. Saml. Willard May 4.

Joseph Snelling & Sarah Sedgwick were married by Rev. Cotton Mather June 8.

Josiah Sanders & Rachel Holman were married by Rev. James Allen Dec. 4.

Joseph Scott & Eliza. Winslow were married by Rev. Saml. Willard Jan. 18.

Robert Sanderson & Sarah Crow were married by Saml. Sewall Esq. J. Pac. Dec. 21.

Digory Sargent of Worster & Constance James of Boston were married by Rev. Cotton Mather Oct. 13.

Samuel Swetman & Margaret Peard were married by Rev. Cotton Mather Oct. 26.

Seth Smith & Mehitable Heath were married by Rev. Cotton Mather Jan. 10.

Simon Tainter & Joanna Stone both of Watertown were married by Rev. John Bayley May 9.

Henry Tomson & Mary Keeffe were married by Saml. Sewall Esq. Assist. Aug. 8.

Henry Tomson & Mary Vocory were married by Saml. Sewall Esq. Assist. Sept. 11.

James Townsend & Mary Lynck were married by Rev. James Allen Nov. 7.

John Tuckerman & Susanna Chamberline were married by Rev. James Allen Nov. 14.

Benja. Thaxter & Susanna Molton were married by Rev. James Allen Dec. 4.

Anthony Thoring & Sarah Courser were married by John Eyer Esq. J. Pac. Nov. 3.

John Turner & Susanna Kennet were married by Rev. Cotton Mather Feb. 14.

Samuel Thayer & Susanna Scant both of Brantrey were married by Rev. James Allen Jan. 17.

Samuel Townsend & Elizabeth ——— were married Mar. 15.

Thomas Veakin & Zipora Arra (negroes) were married by Rev. Cotton Mather Nov. 20.

Joseph Withington & Deliverance Leadbetter were married by Saml. Sewall Esq. Assist. Mar. 29.

Saml. Warkman & Martha White were married by Rev. James Allen Aug. 3.

John Wakefeeld & Eliza. Walker were married by Rev. Cotton Mather Nov. 23.

Ezra Whitmarsh & Bathsheba Richards both of Weymouth were married by Rev. Cotton Mather Jan. 20.


Edward of Jarvice & Martha Ballard dyed March 25.

Edward Allen Died May 31.

Abraham of Abraham Adams Died July 16.

Josiah of Jonathan & Rebecca Adams Died Sept. 15.

Mary Allen Died Octor. 11.

Abigall of Abrah. & Abigail Adams Died Decemr 31.

Mary Wife of Edward Belcher Died March 21.

Mary Wife of Robart Browne Died March 16.

Christian Blake Died May 1.

Joseph of Ambrose Berry Died July 24.

Benjamin of Ambrose Berry Died July 16.

Sarah of John & Mercy Booker Died Aug. 26.

Mary wife of John Bennet Died Aug. 8.

John Bennet of Nodles island Died Augt. 4.

Mary Relect of mr. John Blake Died Janry 7.

Hanah of Nathll & Hanah Baker Died Sept. 10.

Alexander Clemy Died Augt. 9.

Mary of John & Sarah Clarke Died Octor. 8.

Sarah of John & Sarah Clarke Died Octor. 16.

Caleb of Caleb Chapin Died Feb. 14.

Richard Cornish Died Febr. 6.

Sarah wife of Richard Cornish Died Aug.

John Cowell Died Decemr.

Left. Bartho. Chiveer Died Deer. 18.

Hanah Wife of Edward Drinker Died May 14.

Rebecca Elistone Died June 8.

Capt. Jacob Eliott Died July.

Joan Wife of John Gee Died July 17.

John Gee Died July 25.

Capt. William Greenoug Died Aug. 6.

Isack Grifin Died July 30.

Hanah wife of Michaell Homer Died Aprill 28.

Esther Houchin Died July 2.

William Hawkins died Sept. 27.

John Higgs Died Octr. 22.

Hanah wife of Joseph Hasey died Augt. 18.
Mary Wife of William Hough Died June 27.
Mary of William & Mary Hough Died Sept. 29.
William How Esquire died Deer. 22.
Elizabeth wife of Joseph How Died Sept. 9.
John of John & Ruth Jepson Died Feb. 7.
Joana Johnson Died May 24.
Jonathan Jackson Died Aug. 28.
Richard Kennet Died Aprill 1.
Thomas of Tho. & Elizabeth Kellen Died Feb. 28.
Mr. James Loyd Died July.
Rachell Letherland Died Sept. 1.
John Lawranc Died Apr. 16.
Isaek Lewes Died Aprill 6.
Joseph of Cotton Mather Died Apr. 1.
Joseph of James & Hanah Miriack Died Sept. 19.
Ebinezer of Daniell & Susana Morey Died Sept. 17.
John Moor Died July 7.
Rachell Daugt. of John Moor Died Janry 14.
John of John & Kesiah Nedam Died July 29.
John of David Norton Died Augt. 20.
Besse of Besse Negro Svt Samll Lilly Died Febry 18.
Mary Relect of Samuell Nowell Died Aug. 14.
Bethiah Oliver Died July 27.
Thomas Pemberton Died July 26.
Elizabeth Parkeman Died Aug. 22.
Mary Parris Died Aug. 13.
Elizabeth Parris Died Aug. 22.
Ruth of Nathll & Ruth Raynols Died March 16.
Benjamin of John & Charity Ricks Died June 16.
William Robins Died May 7.
Samuell Sexton Died July 21.
Sarah Sneling Died Augt. 4.
Jane of Samll & Hanah Sewell Died Sept. 13.
Deacon Robart Sanderson Died Octor 7.
Mary wife of Capt. John Smith Died Janry 24.
Thomas Smith Died Novr. 1.
John of Daniell & Anna Turrell Died Dec. 1.
Elizabeth wife of Joseph Townsand Died Febr. 27.
Margaret Thatcher Died Febr. 23.
Eliza. of Isack & Elizabeth Vergoose Died May 20.
Sarah wife of Thomas Warren Died May 4.
Lawrence Waters died Sept. 26.
Sarah Willet died Octor 21.
Daniell of Daniell & Hanah Ware died Janry 8.
Nathaniell of Samuell Wentworth Died Sept. 10.
Ebinezer of Ebinezer Weeks died Deer 8.
Sampson Waters died Augt 14.
James Woodmancy died Feb. 26.

## FIRST CHURCH.

| | |
|---|---|
| Joseph Cotta | Jan. 14. |
| Jeremiah Green | Feb. 12. |
| Isabella Newgate | Feb. 12. |
| Sarah Dyer | Feb. 12. |
| Sarah Manning | Feb. 26. |
| Job Ingram | Apr. 23. |
| Jeremiah Ingram | Apr. 23. |
| Hannah Ingram | Apr. 30. |
| Mildred Willis | May 7. |
| Nathaniel Jackson | May 21. |
| Mary Hawkins | May 21. |
| Joseph Howard | May 21. |

| | | |
|---|---|---|
| John Kinge | June | 4. |
| Catharine Fitchlocke | June | 11. |
| Mary of Portsmouth | July | 2. |
| Mary Cooke | July | 2. |
| Elizabeth Bannister | July | 23. |
| John Draper | July | 23. |
| Elizabeth Draper | July | 23. |
| Andrew Raglin | July | 23. |
| Benjamin Smith | Aug. | 20. |
| Mary Warner | Aug. | 20. |
| Mehitable Prince | Sept. | 3. |
| Mehitable Gibson | Sept. | 3. |
| Matthew Collins | Sept. | 3. |
| Sarah Collins | Sept. | 3. |
| Naomy Collins | Sept. | 3. |
| Rebecca Collins | Sept. | 3. |
| William Bridge | Septr. | 17. |
| Paul Langdon | Septr. | 17. |
| Elizabeth Windeline | Septr. | 17. |
| Abigail Hatherley a maid | Septr. | 24. |
| John Bradford a child | Septr. | 24. |
| John Davis | Oct. | 8. |
| David Copp | Oct. | 22. |
| James Goneh | Oct. | 22 |
| Thomas Dyer | Nov. | 1? |
| William Draper | Dec. | 3· |

## 1694.

### TOWN.

Elizabeth of John & Constant Alcock born Apr. 3.
Ann of Bozoon & Lydia Allin born Mar. 18.
Nathaniel of Nathaniel & Hephsibah Alden born Aug. 6.
Avis of John & Hannah Adams born Feb. 6.
Eliz. of Willm & Phillis Arnell born Aug. 19.
Enoch of Silence & Esther Allen born Nov. 11.
Frances of Edward & Mary Bromfield born June 8.
Mary of John & Isabella Barrell born June 30.
Bathsheba of James & Elizabeth Babagge born July 22.
James of John & Joanna Bennitt born Sept. 4.
Jacob of John & Mercy Booker born Sept 3.
William of Thomas & Mary Beetle born Oct. 10.
Willm of Willm & Mercy Browne born Oct. 31.
Robart of Robart & Mary Blabour born Dec. 5.
Sarah of Saml & Sarah Barrett born Jan. 8.
Thomas of Thomas & Margaret Berry born Mar. 19.
Benja. of Thomas & Sarah Baker born May 7.
Eliz. of Philip & Elizb. Bass born Apr. 23.
Nathl of Nathl & Mary Baker born May 7.
Lilingston son of Peter & Mary Bowden born Sept. 10.
John of George & Ruth Badcock born May 5.
Joseph of Joseph & Hanah Billings born May 17.
Samuel of Thomas & Mary Baker born June 26.
Eliz. of Daniell & Mary Bassett born July 15.
Anna of Benja. & Elizabeth Bream born July 23.
Kathrine of Richard & Eliz. Bason born Aug. 12.
William of Peter & Sarah Barbour born July 12.
Mary of Isaac & Hannah Biscon born July 1.
Kathrine of Saml & Martha Burrell born Sept. 11.
Gilbert of Gilbert Bant born Oct. 30.
Mary of Joseph & Abigall Belknap born Oct. 15.
Judith of Thomas & Judith Barnard born Oct. 23.
Margaret of Thomas & Margaret Bomer born Jan. 29.

William of Thomas & Mehetable Cooper born Mar. 20.
John of Ebenezer & Martha Clow born Mar. 1.
Abigail of Richard & Abigail Cheever born Apr. 7.
Mary of John & Martha Cornish born Mar. 22.
Ann of George & Mary Clarke born Apr. 26.
{ George of Richard & Hannah Clarke born May 8.
{ John of Richard & Hannah Clarke born May 8.
Nathan of Thomas & Sarah Cheveer born Mar. 16.
Mary of Thomas & Sarah Curtess born Apr. 20.
Stephen of Jonas & Mary Clay born May 16.
Mary of Matthew & Mary Carey born May 15.
Mary of Ebenezer & Elizabeth Chapin born July 1.
Joseph of Joseph & Ann Cooke born July 30.
Daniel of Daniel & Rebecca Collings born Aug. 31.
Eliza. of Henry & Elizabeth Chamlet born Sept. 30.
Ann of Thomas & Rebecca Clarke born Sept. 2.
Richard of Samuel & Mary Chickley born Oct. 4.
Samuel of Samuel & Mary Clarke born Oct. 11.
Eliza. of William & Elizabeth Crow born Oct. 27.
Thomas of Thomas & Priscilla Comings born Oct. 24.
Peter of John & Elizabeth Coombs born Aug. 9.
Eliza. of John & Hannah Carlile born Dec. 19.
William of Andrew & Hannah Cuningham born Nov. 17.
Priscilla of John & Priscilla Clough born Dec. 18.
Lydia of James & Mary Cornish born Nov. 22.
Joseph of Charles & Sarah Dameere born Apr. 1.
John of James & Elizabeth Dowell born Apr. 2.
Thomas of Thomas & Jane Dean born Nov. 28.
Eliza. of Samuel & Elizabeth Durham born Nov. 26.
Edmund of Joseph & Hannah Days born Dec. 14.
Esther of Richard & Sarah Draper born Jan. 13.
Ann of Eliezer & Mary Darby born Feb. 1.
Sarah of John & Sarah Dingly born Feb. 13.
Mary of Moses & Ann Dry born Feb. 5.
Thomas of Thomas & Ann Dean born Nov. 28.
John of John & Mary Earle born July 21.
Mary of John & Elizabeth Eustiss born May 11.
Sarah of William & Sarah Eustiss born May 7.
Mary of Edward & Phebe Eglington born Jan. 22.
Mary of Benjamin & Elizabeth Emons born Mar. 25.
Jonathan of Jonathan & Mary Evans born Apr. 6.
Catherine of John & Catherine Eyre born July 20.
Thomas of Thomas & Ann Eyre born July 13.
Mary of Richard & Mary Fiefield born May 7.
Alexander of Alexander & Mary Fulerton born June 16.
Edward of Joseph & Rebecca Fuller born Aug. 1.
Mary of Josias & Abiah Franklin born Sept. 26.
Rebecca of Gibson & Rebecca Fawer born Oct. 9.
Eliza. of Richard & Elizabeth Flood born Jan. 13.
Susana of Henry & Susanna Faray born Mar. 11.
John of William & Elizabeth Fox born July 29.
Francis of Francis & Elizabeth Foxcraft born Jan. 26.
Sarah of Henry & Sarah Franklin born May 15.
Mary of Thomas & Mary Frost born Dec. 15.
Joanna of James & Joanna Grant born July 20.
Eliza. of John & Martha Goodwin born Sept. 9.
Samuel of Bartholomew & Mary Green born Sept. 7.
Henry of Robart & Mary Gibbs born Nov. 7.
John of Anthony & Darcos Gretian born Feb. 6.
Eliza. of ——— & Elizabeth Green born Feb. 10.
Thomas of David & Martha Gwin born Dec. 13.
Rachel of Christopher & Abigail Goffe born Mar. 2.
Eliza. of Thomas & Experience Gould born Feb. 11.
Mehitable of Obidiah & Elizabeth Gill born Jan. 1.

Duncan of Duncan & Margaret Garnock born Mar. 28.
Elizabeth of John & Eliza. Greenogh born Nov. 13.
John of John & Aniball Henderson born ———
Richard of Richard & Elizabeth Harris born Mar. 2.
Samuel of Eliezer & Mary Holioake born Mar. 21.
Rebecca of William & Rebecca Hill born Apr. 18.
Agnis of John & Aniball Henderson born May 8.
Eliza. of Daniel & Joanna Harris born Mar. 5.
Richard of Richard & Elizabeth Henderson born June 20.
Margett of Herculus & Jane Hewitt born June 23.
John of John & Margett Homes born Aug. 8.
Mary of Samuel & Mary Hooper born Aug. 22.
Anna of Henry & Mary Hill born Sept. 9.
Rachel of John & Experience Haywood born July 20.
Benjamin of Thomas & Rebecca Harris born ———
Ann of Benja. & Mary Holeway born Jan. 28.
John of Jacob & Mary Holeway born Dec. 9.
Abigail of Heseciah & Abigail Henchman born Jan. 1.
James of James & Bethiah Hewes born Aug.
Ruhamah of Nicholas & Ruhamah Ingolsdby born May 8.
Jonathan of William & Elizabeth Ireland born Jan. 5.
Eliza. } of Richard & Sarah Jenkins born Mar. 5.
Mary } of Richard & Sarah Jenkins born Mar. 5.
Anna of John & Ruth Jepson born Apr. 9.
Rebecca of William & Elizabeth Jarvis born May 22.
John of John & Margaret Johnson born June 11.
Nathanll of Christopher & Sarah Kilbee born Mar. 20.
John of Moses & Margett Kenny born July 1.
Henry of Henry & Elizabeth Kerby born Feb. 20.
John of John & Mary Kneland born Nov. 14.
Thomas of John & Lydia Kelton born Feb. 14.
Jane of Thomas & Eliza. Kellen born Oct. 11.
Peter of James & Ann Leblond born Jan. 1.
William of Richard & Mary Lux born Mar. 1.
Hannah of Peter & Hannah Leech born Nov. 14.
Edward of Robert & Bridget Ladd born Oct. 10.
Joseph of Thomas & Mercy Lazinby born Aug. 20.
Rebecca of James & Rebecca Loyd born May 4.
William of William & Susanna Milhorn born Apr. 27.
Joseph of Joseph & Hannah Mariner born Mar. 23.
Mary of William & Olef Macloughlin born Mar. 22.
John of John & Sarah Marshall born Mar. 22.
Abigail of Cotton & Abigail Mather born June 14.
James of Thomas & Mary Mellins born May 1.
Margaret of Paul & Elizabeth Milner born Sept. 15.
Sarah of James & Hannah Mirick born Oct. 11.
Mary of Archibell & Sarah Mackgudy born Oct. 17.
Dorcas of Thomas & Dorcas Marshall born May 17.
Edmund of John & Mary Mountfort born Oct. 19.
Nathaniel of Robert & Marya Mason born Oct. 25.
Susanna of Daniel & Susanna Morey born Oct. 18.
Isack of Samuel & Mary Marion born Nov. 8.
James of Samuel & Ann Mattock born Sept. 4.
James of John & Elizabeth Muligan born Dec. 4.
Thomas of William & Rebecca Mann born Feb. 25.
Mary of Christopher & Mary Monek born Mar. 26.
Joseph of Joseph & Ann Marsh born Dec. 21.
Mary of Edward & Sarah Martin born Mar. 14.
Robert of Michell & Lydia Nowell born Aug. 22.
Hannah of Thomas & Sarah Negus born Jan. 1.
Joseph of Maybe servant to James Cornish (negro) born Feb. 18.
Jenne of Secundas & Peggy (Negroes) born ———
Rebecca of Timothy & Mary Nash born Feb. 13.
William of John & Sarah Oliver born Nov. 5.

Margett of John & Marget Pratt born Mar. 1.
Sarah of Benjamin & Elizabeth Pemberton born Mar. 8.
Rachel of Thomas & Hannah Pecke born Nov. 28.
Sarah of Alexander & Sarah Prinly born Feb. 13.
Joseph of Edward & Elizabeth Procter born Feb. 20.
Sarah of Mark & Faith Pintinton born Jan. 3.
Stephen of Stephen & Elizabeth Palmer born Mar 2.
Ann of Thomas & Mary Pratt born Feb. 11.
Susanna of William & Mercy Farram born Mar. 14.
William of Edward & Elizabeth Pell born May 11.
Mercy of Samuel & Mary Pearse born Sept. 20.
Hannah of Nathll & Hannah Purdue born Oct. 5.
Benjamin of Benja. & Eliza. Quelch born Aug. 25.
Ezechiel of Joseph & Susanna Rusell born May 6.
Ennis of John & Annis Robinson born May 27.
Edward of David & Eliza Robinson born Sept. 19.
Eliza. of James & Elizabeth Rainer born Oct. 28.
Jane of John & Mary Roberts born Oct. 14.
William of William & Mary Ruck born Jan. 15.
Eliza. of Joseph & Sarah Robinson born Feb. 20.
Mary of John & Mary Russell born Apr. 13.
Mary of Thomas & Rebecca Smith born Jan. 15.
Mary of John & Elizabeth Stratford born Apr. 22.
Eliza. of Daniel & Elizabeth Stodard born June 8.
Joseph of Joseph & Ruth Shaw born June 24.
Elizabeth of John & Mary Stevens born Mar. 29.
Eliza. of Thomas & Margaret Savage born Aug. 1.
Samuel of Rowlen & Ann Storey born Aug. 20.
Nicholas } of John & Anibell Salsbury born Aug. 20.
James   } of John & Anibell Salsbury born Aug. 20.
Joseph of Seth & Mehetable Smith born Oct. 12.
Rebecca of Nicholas & Sarah Stoughton born Sept. 10.
Sarah of Samuel & Hannah Sewell born Nov. 21.
Joseph of Joseph & Elizabeth Scott born Nov. 23.
Phineas of Henry & Purchase Spry born Dec. 5.
Ann of Alexander & Rebecca Sears born Dec. 13.
Richard of Richard & Sarah Sherin born Nov. 25.
Margaret of John & Jane Smith born Jan. 28.
Benjamin of Benjamin & Susanna Thaxter born Augt. 22.
William of Samuel & Abigail Thorn born Dec. 23.
John of John & Sarah Tenny born Jan. 12.
Susanna of John & Mary Tucker born Jan. 25.
Liddia of John & Hannah Tapper born Jan. 28.
Mary of James & Mary Townsand born Feb. 11.
John of Samuel & Sarah Tiley born Mar. 2.
Maverick of George & Rebecca Thomas born Feb. 24.
Eliza. of Isaac & Elizabeth Virgoose born May 27.
Susanna of Andrew & Elizabeth Veach born Jan 19.
Joseph of William & Charity Webb born Mar. 7.
Hannah of Daniel & Hannah Ware born May 5.
Michael of Michael & Elizabeth Willis born July 11.
Maudlin of Robard & Lucey Ward born ——
Eliza. of John & Humillis Williams born Oct. 14.
Eliza. of Ebenezer & Deliverance Weeks born Oct. 25.
John of John & Elizabeth Wakefield born Aug 14.
George of Daniel & Mary Willard born Oct. 22.
Edward of John & Abigail Wilson born Dec. 6.
Joshua of Edward & Hannah Winslow born Feb. 12.
Mary of William & Elizabeth Wheeler born Feb. 17.
Mary of Samuel & Mary Ward born Nov. 27.
Triphena of Thomas & Triphena Woodward born Jan. 30.

John Adams & Hannah Checkley were married by Rev. John Bayley Oct. 19
Joseph Adams & Elizabeth Hewes were married by Rev. James Allen May 3.

Henry Adams & Martha Hewen were married by Rev. Cotton Mather Jan. 10.

Matthew Armstrong & Margaret Halce were married by John Phillips Esq. June 7.

Thomas Belknap & Jane Cheeney both of Cambridg were married by Saml. Sewall Esq. J. Pac. Mar. 6.

Samuel Barrat & Sarah Manning were married by Rev. James Allen Mar. 8.

William Brown of Salem & Rebecca Bayley of Boston were married by Rev. John Bayley Apr. 26.

Jabez Beers & Elizabeth Barber both of Watertown were married by Rev. John Bayley. May 17.

Robert Bronsdon & Hannah Bream were married by Rev. Cotton Mather Apr. 12.

Benjamen Bream & Eliza Clemy were married by Rev. Cotton Mather May 24.

William Brown & Mercy Jacklin were married by Rev. James Allen Oct. 29.

John Banks & Mehitabel Mattox were married by Rev. Samuel Willard Aug. 29.

John Beer & Mary Eades were married by Rev. Saml. Willard Sept. 21.

Theophelus Burrel of Lyn & Lydia Gethercole of Boston were married by Rev. Cotton Mather July 5.

Titus Brooks & Eliza Noaks were married by Samuel Sewall Esq. J. Pac Nov. 20.

Nathanl. Beedle & Eliza Sharp were married by Rev. Thomas Cheever Jan. 30.

Benjamin Bream & Eliza Clemmy were married by Rev. Cotton Mather May 28.

David Copp & Patience Short were married by Rev. James Allen Dec. 27.

Edward Camden & Ruth Pasco were married by Rev. Saml. Willard Sept. 25.

Mongo Crawford & Susanna Kennet were married by Rev. Saml. Willard Jan. 29.

John Colman & Judith Hobbey were married by Rev. Cotton Mather July 19.

John Cunniball & Lydia Beighton were married by Rev. Cotton Mather Nov. 2.

John Coney & Mary Clark were married by Jer. Dummer Esq. Nov. 8.

Samuel Daniel & Deborah Ford were married by Saml. Sewall Esq. J. Pac. Mar. 15.

Edward Drinker & Mary Emmons were married by Rev. James Allen Mar. 6.

John Dyer & Hannah Morton were married by Rev. Saml. Willard June 6.

Joseph Dowding & Ann Sands were married by Rev. Cotton Mather Sept. 21.

John Dinsdale & Hannah Banford were married by Rev. Thomas Cheever Sept. 19.

Samuel Earl & Lydia Flood were married by Rev. Saml. Willard Apr. 20.

Benja. Emmons & Mary Amory were married by Rev. Saml. Willard Sept. 10.

Benjamen Easterbrook & Abigail Willard were married by Rev. Saml. Willard Nov. 29.

Roger Earl & Lydia Travise were married by Rev. Cotton Mather Oct. 25.

John Edwards & Sibella Newman were married by Saml. Sewall Esq. J. Pac. Oct. 29.

John Evans & Mary Clap were married by Rev. Thomas Cheever Jan. 7.

Thomas Fitch & Abiel Daunforth were married by Rev. Saml. Willard Apr. 12.

Joseph Gallop & Elizabeth Dwight were married by Timothy Dwight Esq. Mar. 1.

Philip Goodwin & Eliza. Luxford both of Cambridge were married by Saml. Sewall Esq. J. Pac. June 14.

Thomas Gray of Plymouth & Anna Little of Marshfeeld were married by Rev. John Bayley July 3.

Benja. Gallop & Hannah Sharp were married by Rev. Samuel Willard Nov. 1.

Richard Gridley & Hannah Dawes were married by Rev. Samuel Willard Feb. 27.

Peter Grant & Sarah Scarlet were married by Rev. Cotton Mather July 25.

Richard Gull & Rebecca Hill were married by Rev. Cotton Mather Jan. 24.

Terrence Henley & Eliza. Weeks were married by Rev. James Allen Apr. 2.

Thomas Hunt & Susanna Saxton were married by Rev. Cotton Mather June 21.

Robert Hawkins & Esther Hughs were married by Rev. Saml. Willard June 7.

Thomas Hall & Hannah Paine were married by Rev. Saml. Willard Feb. 15.

Erasamus Harrison & Mary Rouse were married by Rev. Cotton Mather Jan. 3.

James Jarvise & Penelopee Waters were married by Rev. James Allen July 18.

George Jefferyes of Piscattiqua & Hannah Porter of Boston were married by Rev. John Bayley Nov. 28.

Eben. Jones & Lydia Norcot both of Dorchister were married by Rev. Saml. Willard May 17.

Christopher Killiowe & Eliza Foster were married by ye Parson of —— May 28.

Ebenr. Liscombe & Mehitable Curtice were married by Rev. Cotton Mather Oct. 18.

Ebenr. Lowle & Elizabeth Shaler were married by Rev. James Allen Jan. 30.

John Levensworth & Mary Brown were married by Rev. Samuel Willard Aug. 21.

William Mansell & Rebecca Jacobson were married by Saml. Sewall Esq. J. Pac. June 29.

Henry Mountfort & Sarah Dasset were married by Rev. James Allen Sept. 27.

Joseph Marshall & Mercy Short were married by Rev. Cotton Mather July 29.

Timothy Nash & Mary Foster were married by Rev. James Allen Apr. 2.

George Negro & Ruth Negro were married by Rev. John Bayley Aug. 14.

Thomas Owen & Eliza Chinny were married by Rev. James Allen Sept. 10.

Francis Fumery & Mehitabel Orchard were married by Mr. Emblim Bapt. Minis. Feb. 7.

Michael Perry & Joanna Breck were married by Rev. James Allen July 12.

William Payn & Mary Taylor were married by Rev. James Allen Oct. 11.

John Parmunter & Eliza East were married by Rev. James Allen Nov. 1.

Matthew Pool & Sarah Blake were married by Rev. John Bayley May 29.

Thomas Perkins & Remember Woodman were married by Rev. Cotton Mather July 26.

William Porter & Eliza Gale were married by Rev. Cotton Mather Jan. 31.

Elias Purrington & Sarah Orris were married by Mr. James Sherman July 7.

William Ruicks & Mary Ellise were married by Rev. James Allen Mar. 29.

Henry Roads & Eliza Paul were married by Rev. Thomas Cheever Feb. 27.

Winsor Sandey & Mehetabel Bull were married by Samuel Sewall Esq. J. Pac. Feb. 12.

John Stevens & Grace Gammon were married by Rev. Cotton Mather June 6.

Robert Smith & Deborah King were married by Rev. Saml Willard July 12.

Joseph Snelling & Rebecca Adams were married by Rev. Samuel Willard July 19.

John Street & Sarah Wing were married by Rev. Saml. Willard Sept. 10.

Benjamen Snelling & Jamina Andrews were married by Rev. Saml. Willard Jan. 29.

William Sutton & Mary Johnson were married by Rev. Saml. Willard Jan. 31.

Abijah Sherman & Sarah Franks were married by Rev. Cotton Mather July 12.

Nicholas Sparry & Sarah Sams were married by Rev. Cotton Mather Aug. 20.

Samuel Sarson & Ann Clay were married by Rev. Cotton Mather Jan. 3.

John Sweeting & Elinor Evans were married by Saml. Sewall Esq. J. Pac. Feb. 7.

Peter Townsend & Mary Welcome were married by Rev. James Allen Nov. 15.

Francis Thresher & Eliza Hicks were married by Rev. John Bayley Aug. 9.

Joseph Tounsend & Judith Woodman were married by Rev. Cotton Mather Aug. 9.

James Townsend & Rebecca Mosely were married by Parson Hatton Jan. 22.

Phillip Villarock & Eliza Wilcot were married by Rev. James Allen May 3.

John Vial & Mary Adams were married by Rev. Cotton Mather Dec. 27.

Josiah Wilcot of Salem & Mary Freek of Boston were married by Rev. James Allen May 1.

Jonathan Whitaker & Sarah Toothaker both of Chelmsford were married by Rev. James Allen Nov. 15.

John Wiburn of Scituate & Esther Ripple of Boston were married by Rev. James Allen May 10.

Benja. Watson & Ann Drue were married by Rev. John Bayley Sept. 15.

John Wiat & Hannah Garret were married by Rev. John Bayley Feb. 7.

Benedict Webber & Sarah Rice were married by Rev. Cotton Mather May 14.

James Williams & Sarah Salsbury were married by Rev. Cotton Mather Aug. 7.

Thomas Warren & Sarah Fitch were married by Rev. Cotton Mather. Dec. 14.

Moses Way & Sarah —— were married by Mr. Thomas Cheever Apr. 5.
William Young & Sarah Whiteache were married by Rev. Cotton Mather
Oct. 11.

William of Joseph Allen Died March 17.
Ann of Bozoon & Lidia Allen Died July 26.
Eliza daugt. of Willm Arnold died Sept. 8.
John of Richd & Elizabeth Bason Died June 27.
Samuel of Edward Barrells Died Aug. 19.
Willm. of William and Mary Bennet Died Novr 4.
Willm. of Thomas and Mary Beetel Died Octor 11.
Tho. of Thomas and Eliza. Blore Died Janr. 2.
Samll of Samll and Mary Bucknell Died Janr. 29.
Darcis daugt. of Nicholas Bow died July 20.
Mary daugt. of Henry Cole Died Aprill 12.
Sarah wife of John Conny Died Aprill 17.
Eliza. daugt. of Ebin. Chapin Died Aug. 23.
Rachell of John & Hannah Carlile Died Aug. 7.
Willm of Willm & Elizabeth Crow Died Aug. 8.
Martha Coy Died Augt.14.
Peter of John & Elizabeth Coombs Died Aug. 19.
Philip of Edward & Sarah Cruff Died July 14.
John of Ebinezer Clough Died Decr. 5.
John Downing died Aprill 29.
Sarah of Thomas and Hanab Davis Died July 25.
Edmun of Joseph Dayes Died Janr. 21.
Mercy Dowden died March 11.
Mary of John and Elizabeth Eustis died July 7.
John of John and Mary Endicutt died Aug. 8.
Deborah Edmunds died Octo. 5.
William Euestis died Novr. 27.
Hanah wife of James Gouge died March 15.
Christopher of Christopher & Abigall Goffe died June 8.
Abigall wife of Richard Gridly Died Aug. 18
Joseph of Edward & Elizabeth Goffe Died Decemr 10.
Martha daugt. of William Hawkins died Sept. 16.
Mary wife of Francis Hudson died Sept. 25.
John Lowell died June 7.
John Mayn Died March 27.
John Mershall Died Apr. 18.
Mary of Tho. and Elizabeth Merier Died Aug. 8.
William Milbourn Died Aug.
James of Samuell Matox Died Sept. 3.
Relect of Patrick Ohogen Died June 5.
Prisila daughter of Regnall Odall Died July 27.
Nathll of Nathll & Hanah Parkeman Died Aprill 27.
Abigall of Tho. and Mary Philips Died Augt 6.
Gillam of Samll and Hanah Philips Died Octor 17.
Sarah of Willm & Deborah Philips Died Sept. 9.
Hanah wife of Thomas Pecke Died Decr 7.
Jane of Daniell & Dorcas Peck died Janr. 23.
Elizabeth wife of Benjamin Quelch Died Sept. 4.
James of James & Elizabeth Raymer Died May 12.
Hanah of John & Jane Rayly Died Augt 15.
Mary of John and Ann Smith Died July 30.
Ann Stephens died Augt 15.
Aniball wife of John Salsbury Died Sept. 7.
Eliza. of Thomas & Margaret Savage dyed Dec. 19.
Hanah of Samuel & Mary Tiley dyed March 15.
Wife of Timothy Thornton died March 23.
Benjamin Taylor died Augt 3.
John of Tho. and Miriam Tyler Died Janr. 3.
Samll of Samuell and Mary Veazy died Apr. 17.
Jonathan of Jonathan & Hannh Waldo Died Augt 18.

Sarah of Samll and Eunice Willard Died July 28.
Mehitabell Wife of Peter Welcome died Octor 23. ;
Edward of John and Abigall Wilson Died Janr. 20.
Nathll of Edward and Sarah Watkins died Decr 31.

### FIRST CHURCH.

| | |
|---|---|
| Thomas Savage | Jan. 21. |
| Nathaniel Reynolds | Jan. 21. |
| Mary Gee | Jan. 28 |
| Elizabeth Nuby | Feb. 4. |
| Mary Butler | Feb. 25. |
| Richard Harris | Mar. 4. |
| Anne of Bosone Allin | Mar. 25. |
| Abigail Chevers | Apr. 8. |
| Mary Moseley aged 17 years | Apr. 29. |
| Rebecca Loyde | May 6. |
| Ezekiel Russell | May 6. |
| Mary Eustace | May 13. |
| Job Fisher | June 17. |
| David Langdane | June 17. |
| Abigail Langdane | June 17. |
| Joseph Langdane | June 17. |
| Benjamin Langdane | June 17. |
| John Cooke | July 8. |
| Mary Cooke | July 8. |
| Sarah Cooke | July 8. |
| Thomas Cooke | July 8. |
| Michael Willis . | July 15. |
| Sarah Cary | Aug. 26. |
| Benjamin Thaxter | Aug. 26. |
| . Elizabeth Ranger | Sept. 2. |
| Benjamin Quelch | Sept. 9. |
| Rebecca Stanton | Sept. 16. |
| Mercy Pierce | Sept. 23. |
| John Collins | Oct. 7. |
| Joseph Marriner | Nov. 4. |
| Sarah Miricke | Nov. 11. |
| Mary Ward | Nov. 25. |
| John Banister | Dec. 2. |
| Rachel Pecke | Dec. 2. |
| James Mattocks | Dec. 9. |
| Priscilla Clow | Dec. 23. |
| William Thorne | Dec. 23. |

## 1695.

### TOWN.

Eliz. of Willm & Mary Alden born Mar. 10.
Eliz. of Joseph & Elizabeth Adams born Mar. 27.
Ebenezer of Joseph & Ann Allen born May 8.
Deliverance of John & Grace Alleset born Oct. 12.
Thomas of Benjamin & Mary Alford born Oct. 6.
Hannah of Barachiah & Abigall Arnold born Dec. 20.
Joseph of John & Hannah Adams born Dec. 20.
Mary of John & Hannah Adams born Dec. 20.
Eliz. of William & Phillis Arnel born Feb. 4.
Joseph of Henry & Martha Adams born Aug 19.
John of James & Rachell Barry born Oct. 12.
Nicholas of Joseph & Abigall Belknap born Oct. 15.
Sarah of James & Elizabeth Babagge born Oct. 15.
Willm of Henry & Abigall Brightman born Feb. 1.
Mary of John & Elizabeth Bucanan born Dec. 2.
Jarvis of Peter & Mary Bowden born Feb. 24.
John of Thomas & Mary Bedell born Feb. 28.

Mary of Joseph & Rebecca Brisco born Apr. 7.
Edward of Edward & Mary Brumfield born Nov. 5.
Hezekiah of Peter & Elizabeth Buttler born June 10.
William of Nathll & Mary Baker born July 2.
Zacheriah of Philip & Sarah Basse born July 8.
George of George & Abigall Beard born July 22.
Thomas of Thomas & Dorothy Bennet born July 27.
Robart of William & Mercy Brown born Aug. 20.
Isaac of Isaac & Hanah Biscon born Aug. 23.
Thomas of Edward & Mary Brattell born Sept. 17.
Eliz. of Edward & Hannah Ball born Sept. 27.
Eliz. of Samll & Martha Burrell born Sept. 22.
Hanah of Edward & Mary Boylston born Sept. 30.
Sarah of William & Sarah Burrage born Sept. 24.
Samuel of Samuell & Sarah Boyles born Oct. 4.
Abigall of William & Mary Barnsdell born Oct. 26.
Mary of George & Mary Bearston born Nov. 1.
Timothy of Edward & Mary Bartells born Dec. 2.
Eliz. of John & Sibillo Barrell born Nov. 21.
Thornton of Samll & Sarah Barratt born Nov. 6.
John of John & Eliz. Buckanan born Dec. 25.
William of John & Mercy Booker born Dec. 24.
Lydia of John & Sarah Balston born Nov. 16.
Mary of Josiah & Mary Baker born Jan. 12.
Deborah of Richard & Ann Colicutt born Mar. 4.
William of Samuel & Ruth Clough born Mar. 9.
Martha of John & Sarah Clarke born Mar. 25.
Priscilla of William & Lydia Clow born Apr. 18.
Deborah of John & Sarah Cunabell born May 5.
Martha of Ebenezer & Martha Clough born May 20.
Sarah of John & Ruth Coock born Aug. 11.
Eliza. of John & Mary Cuttler born Sept. 7.
Joanna of William & Ann Copp born Sept. 7.
John of John & Priscilla Chadwick born Oct. 1.
Mary of Job & Joanna Chamberling born Nov. 30.
Mary of John & Elizabeth Coombs born Nov. 25.
Mary of John & Mary Conney born Nov. 7.
David of David Crouch born ———
Eliza. of John & Sarah Carey born Jan. 11.
Eliza. of John & Mary Cambell born Feb. 6.
Sarah of Edward & Sarah Cruff born Oct. 6.
Ann of Matthew & Mary Cary born Feb. 10.
Samuel of Samuel & Mary Chickley born Feb. 11.
Martha of George & Mary Clarke born Feb. 18.
Susanna of Duncan & Susanna Cambell born Feb.
John of Paul & Mary Collings born Sept. 20.
Eliza. of Christor. & Tamzine Capril born June 16.
Edward of Edward & Ann Durant born Mar. 2.
John of Samuel & Deborah Daniel born Mar. 20.
Abigail of Benja. & Hannah Dyar born Apr. 7.
Joseph of Sampson & Sarah Dewer born Apr. 3.
Samuel of Jacob & Susanna Davis born May 25.
Samuel of Samuel & Mary Dyer born May 23.
Martha of Charles & Sarah Demeret born June 6.
Leonard of Joseph & Ann Dowden born July 1.
Mary of Robert & Jane Davis born Aug. 29.
Jane of William & Mary Davis born Sept. 29.
Mary of John & Rachel Draper born Oct. 11.
James of Henry & Abigail Dawson born Feb. 7.
Hannah of John & Hannah Dinsdill born June 10.
Daniel of Daniel & Dorothy Deusberry burn Mar. 18.
Eliza. of Philip & Eliza. Delaruck born Dec. 2.
Eliza. of Benja. & Mary Emms born Mar. 31.
Bagworth of John & Mary Endicutt born Apr. 2.

Aniball of Adam & Elizabeth Eve born June 20.
William of William & Elizabeth Endicutt born Dec. 23.
Bethiah of John & Catharine Eyre born July 24.
Joseph of William & Elizabeth Endicutt born Nov. 28.
Samuel of Robert & Bethiah Eames born Feb. 24.
Mary of Thomas & Abiell Fitch born Apr. 21.
Esther of William & Esther Fratingham born Oct. 13.
Eliphalet of Benjamin & Mary Fitch born Oct. 29.
Thomas of Joseph & Rebecca Fuller born Dec. 11.
John of Henry & Sarah Franklin born Feb. 26.
Elizabeth of Nathll & Elizabeth Green born Apr. 10.
Mary of Thomas & Lydia Gilbert born May 20.
William of Elizabeth & William Gill born Apr. 6.
Sarah of Thomas & Sarah Gwin born Apr. 21.
Eliza. of Joseph & Jane Gleden born Aug. 1.
John of John & Susanna Garrett born Aug. 12.
Eliza. of James & Elizabeth Glass born Nov. 6.
Hannah of Benjamin & Hannah Gallop born Sept. 20.
John of Richard & Hannah Gridley born Nov. 23.
Samuel of Samuel & Susanna Grice born Jan. 24.
Eliza of Samuel & Eliza. Gardner born Feb. 4.
John of John & Lydia Gerish born Jan. 22.
William of Richard & Rebecca Gull born Jan. 16.
Ann of Thomas & Bridget Hayes born Mar. 1.
Joanna of Thomas & Mary Hunt born Mar. 29.
James of Nathaniel & Hannah Halsey born April 10.
Nathaniel of Nathaniel & Anna Henchman born Mar. 31.
Samuel of Samuel & Deborah Hood born Aug. 10.
Lydia of Thomas & Lydia Hatherly born Oct. 20.
Ebenezer of William & Ann Holoway born Nov. 15.
Eliza. of Nathll & Sarah Holms born Sept. 15.
Eliza. of Richard & Elizabeth Harris born Dec. 24.
Archelus of Archelus & Jane Hewitt born Jan. 27.
William of William & Mary Hough born Feb. 1.
Charles of Torrence & Elizabeth Henly born Apr. 13.
Sarah of Eliezer & Mary Holoake born Feb. 2.
Nathaniel of Nathaniel & Eliza. Hatch born Oct. 22.
Alis of Henry & Lydia Ingraham born Aug. 7.
Eliza. of Thomas & Priscilla Jackson born Mar. 10.
John of James & Penelophe Jarvis born Mar. 2.
Sarah of David & Elizabeth Jefferies born May 4.
Rebecca of John & Mary Jarvis born Aug. 23.
Emme of Thomas & Hannah Jepson born Feb. 9.
David of David & Priscilla Johnson born Dec. 15.
John of Nathll & Joanna Kettell born Mar. 26.
Richard of John & Rebecca Kilbee born Jan. 2.
Mary of Isaac & Sarah Lorin born Mar. 26.
John of William & Elizabeth Lavis born Sept. 3.
Sarah of Solomon & Sarah Legeree born July 18.
Eliza. of Joseph & Elizabeth Lobdell born July 19.
Mary of Robert & Mary Lash born Nov. 25.
Eliza. of Samuel & Mehitable Lilly born Feb. 29.
Martha of Thomas & Mehitable Lincoln born July 18.
Joseph of John & Abigail Mulberry born June 10.
Henry of Thomas & Elizabeth Mesenger born Feb. 28.
Sarah of Francis & Martha Marshall born Feb. 11.
John of Joseph & Hannah Maylam born Jan. 14.
Eliza. of Edmund & Elizabeth Mountfort born Apr. 25.
Mary of Joseph & Mercy Marshall born May 20.
Dorcas of Alexandr & Dorcas Miller born May 29.
William of William & Ann More born July 28.
Mary of Philip & Mary Miritt born Aug. 31.
Nathaniel of Joseph & Hannah Mariner born Oct. 9.
Duncan of Duncan & Mary Mackfarland born Oct. 22.

Benjamin of John & Sarah Mason born Dec. 23.
Sarah of John & Sarah Mills born Dec. 9.
Mary of Edward & Sarah Martine born Mar. 14.
Sarah of Samuel & Ruth Marshall born Oct. 11.
Child Alis Richard of Samuel & Peggee (Negro) born Mar. 15.
Eliza. of Richard & Elizabeth Newland born Oct. 12.
James of Nathll & Rest Newell born Dec. 29.
Alis of John & Susanna Nichols born Aug. 18.
Samuel of David & Temperance Norton born Jan. 10.
Sarah of William & Sarah Owen born Feb. 26.
Samuel of Rignall & Priscilla Odall born Aug. 20.
Hannah of William & Sarah Paine born Apr. 21.
Remember of John & Sarah Parker born May 2.
Edward of Thomas & Remember Perkins born May 1.
William of John & Elizabeth Peck born July 27.
Nicholas of Thomas & Mary Phillips born July 25.
Sarah of Elias & Sarah Purington born Aug. 13.
Thomas of Thomas & Margett Powell born Aug. 28.
Rachel of John & Jane Potter born Oct. 20.
Abigail of John & Sarah Pimm born Oct. 10.
Gillam of Samuel & Hannah Phillips born Oct 4.
Benjamin of Robert & Hannah Price born Oct. 20.
Samuel of William & Elizabeth Parkeman born Nov. 19.
Eliza. of Michael & Johanna Perry born Sept. 6.
William of William & Mary Pain born Nov. 23.
Simon of John & Experience Roberts born May 21.
John of John & Rebecca Ransford born May 15.
Charles of Charles & Mary Robarts born Oct. 15.
Sarah of Joseph & Mary Russell born June 19.
Mary of Ralph & Martha Ransford born June 21.
John of William & Elizabeth Randall born June 10.
Stephen of Thomas & Martha Rayper born June 14.
Joseph of Joseph & Susanna Russell born Oct. 24.
Martha of George & Elizabeth Robinson born Jan. 7.
John of Sampson & Mary Shore born Mar. 25.
Joseph of Joseph & Hannah Snelling born Apr. 20.
Jonathan of Simeon & Mary Stodard born May 4.
William of Henry & Elizabeth Sharpp born Mar. 24.
Eliza. of Cyprean & Elizabeth Southwick born May 2.
Margaret of Robert & Deborah Smith born June 1.
Robert of Nathll & Elizabeth Siannon born June 7.
William of John & Ann Smith born July 10.
Samuel of Joseph & Hannah Simson born Aug. 9.
John of Benjamin & Joanna Stone born Aug. 12.
Sarah of Robert & Esther Saunderson born Aug. 27.
Hannah of Winsor & Mehitable Sandy born Sept. 6.
James of James & Edy Steward born Oct. 30.
Habijah of Thomas & Mehitable Savage born Oct. 22.
Mehitable of Seth & Mehitable Smith born Oct. 27.
Jane of John & Jane Snelling born Nov. 9.
Elizabeth of Joseph & Margaret Soaper born Dec. 18.
Francis of Francis & Mary Smith born Jan. 13.
Brigett of William & Elizabeth Straton born Jan. 19.
Eliza. of John & Mary Sunderland born Feb. 7.
Jemima of Benjamin & Jemina Sneling born Mar. 22.
Ebenezer of Fearnot & Bethiah Seele born May 19.
John of John & Lydia Selly born Feb. 8.
John of Anthony & Sarah Thorning born May 26.
Samuel of James & Rebecca Townsand born Aug. 30.
John of John & Miriam Tyler born June 11.
Mary of John & Martha Twing born Sept. 4.
Margaret of Richard & Margett Tewell born Feb. 6.
John of Nicholas & Hannah Trerice born Mar. 7.
Mercy of Benja. & Mercy Tout born May 5.

Eunise of Edward & Abigail Tuttle born Jan. 30.
Sarah of James & Rebecca Taylor born May 19.
Abigail of Philip & Abigail Voden born Mar. 1.
Edward of Christopher & Joanna Vale born Apr. 7.
Samuel of John & Sarah Vickers born Aug. 7.
Rebecca of Thomas & Hannah Verring born Jan. 17.
Sarah of Francis & Mary Whitman born Mar. 3.
Samuel of Samuel & Mary Warkman born Mar. 15.
Lydia of James & Elizabeth Worth born Apr. 4.
Temperance of Experience & Elizabeth Willis born Apr. 8.
Sarah of John & Elizabeth Walley born Apr. 27.
Sarah of Andrew & Susanna Willis born May 4.
Margaret of John & Martha Wharfe born May 15.
Eliza. of James & Sarah Williams born May 15.
Eunice of Samuel & Eunice Willard born June 16.
Christopher of Christopher & Mary Weeks born Sept. 24.
Susanna of Timothy & Susanna Wodsworth born Oct. 16.
Elias of Daniel & Hannah Weare born Oct. 20.
John of John & Eliza Wakefield born Sept. 19.
Daniel of Samuel & Elizabeth Wentworth born Nov. 21.
Mary of Benjamin & Susana Worthlake born Nov. 21.
Hannah of Ebenezer & Deliverance Weeks born Jan. 5.
Allis of Thomas & Sarah Wheeler born Feb. 7.
Hannah of William & Ann Wheeler born Mar. 18.
Mary of Daniel & Mary Willard born Nov. 16.


Jeremiah Allen & Mary Caball were married by Rev. James Allen June 25.
Edward Boston & Mary Dasset were married by Rev. James Allen May 27.
William Briggs & Rebecca Dyer were married by Rev. John Bayley June 10.
John Cleverly & Sarah Cowel were married by Jer. Dummer Esq. Oct. 17.
Jonathan Elliston & Eliza. Wesendonck were married by Rev. John Bayley June 27.
Robert Edmunds & Rebecca Pasmore were married by Rev. Cotton Mather Mar. 26.
Robert Fitchue & Hannah Man were married by Rev. John Bayley Apr. 4.
Samuel Gray of Salem & Susanna Baster of Boston were married by Rev. Saml Willard Apr. 15.
Nathanl Hubbert & Mary Stowel both of Hingham were married by Rev. James Allen May 31.
Robert Hannah & Hannah Matson were married by Rev. John Bayley May 2.
William Harrise & Sarah Crisp were married by Rev. Saml Willard Apr. 11.
Andrew Hethrington & Hannah Briggs were married by Rev. Saml Willard Apr. 11.
Thomas Hall & Hannah Payn were married by Mr. Saml Willard Feb. 14.
Thomas Jacobs & Mary Dinnis were married by Rev. Cotton Mather Mar. 21.
Thomas Joy & Elizabeth Stoddard were married by Samuel Sewall Esq. J. Pac. Mar. 6.
Roger Kilcup & Abigall Dudson were married by Mr. James Allen July 4.
Samuel Letherbee & Lydia Biss were married by Jeremiah Dummer Esq. Nov. 15.
Samuel Moodey & Esther Green were married by Rev. James Allen Apr. 4.
John Monsir of Charlestown & Mary Mirick of Boston were married by Rev. James Allen Apr. 24.
John Manning & Joanna Lash were married by Rev. Cotton Mather May 9.
Duncan Maycome & Mary Smith were married by Mr. Saml Willard Apr. 18.
Llias Maverick & Sarah Smith were married by Mr. John Bayley Feb. 3.
Richard Roe & Margery Benbow were married by Rev. Cotton Mather June 20.
Samuel Sprague of Wooborn & Luise Burrell of Lyn were married by Rev. James Allen June 5.
John Simson & Rely Holmes were married by Mr. Samuel Willard June 4.
Richard Thomas & Mary Mason were married by Mr. John Baley July 16.
Jonathn Townsend & Elizabeth Walton were married by Mr. Jonathan Pearpoint Mar. 22.

James Walcom & Eliza. Hopkins were married by Rev. James Allen May 27.
John Whitehart & Martha Ladd were married by Rev. James Allen June 6.
Joseph Wheeler & Jane Hodges were married by Mr. Emblim ye Baptist
   Minister July 1.

Deacon Henry Allin died Janry 9.
Robart of Robart and Mary Blaber Died March 7.
George Badcock died Sept. 2.
John of Thomas and Mary Beetel Died Decemr 22.
Eliza. of Samuel and Mary Chickley Died June 6.
Tho. of Thomas & Prisilla Cumins Died June 2.
Prisilla wife of Jonathan Elasson Died March 5.
Wife of William Fuller died ————.
Mary of Thomas & Abiell Fitch Died May 11.
Sarah of Thomas and Sarah Gwin Died Deer. 7.
Judith Hull died June 22.
Rachell wife of Thomas Harwood died ————.
Elizabeth Harris died Sept. 17.
Ruth wife of John Jepson died Octor. 17.
Thomas of John & Lidia Kelton died May 9.
Jenne of Secundas Pegges — Negro Died Febr. 26.
Edwd. of Tho. and Remember Perkins Died May 2.
Frances Wife of William Parram Died Sept. 3.
Marget of Robt & Marget Smith Died June 8.
John of Sampson & Mary Shoar Died July 17.
John of John & Elizabeth Wakefield Died Mar. 13.
Eliza. of Ebin. and Deliverance Weekes Died Apr. 5.
Elizabeth daughter of Sampson Waters Died July 5.
Robart Williams died Augt. 25.
Edward of Samll & Elizabeth Wentworth died July 24.

## FIRST CHURCH.

| | |
|---|---|
| Hannah Negroes (Negus) | Jan. 6. |
| John Tenney | Jan. 13. |
| Sarah Barrett | Jan. 13. |
| William Rucke | Jan. 20. |
| Jane Pecke | Jan. 27. |
| Edward Tucker | Feb. 17. |
| Elizabeth Tucker | Feb. 17. |
| Christopher Clarke | Feb. 21. |
| Sarah Clarke | Feb. 24. |
| Sarah Ashley | Feb. 24. |
| Henry of Thomas Messenger | Mar. 3. |
| Elizabeth Jackson | Mar. 10. |
| Jonathan Cawley | Mar. 10. |
| John Daniel | Mar. 24. |
| Abigail Duer | April 7. |
| Joseph Dyer | April 7. |
| Abigail Payne | April 7. |
| Elizabeth Greene | April 14. |
| Temperance Willis | April 14. |
| Richard White | June 16. |
| Abiel Eves | June 23. |
| William Pecke | July 28. |
| John Arnold | Aug. 4. |
| Alice Ingram | Aug. 11. |
| Sarah Cooke | Aug. 11. |
| Rachel Proctor | Sept. 8. |
| Mary Twinge | Sept. 15. |
| Mary Cony | Sept. 22. |
| Thomas Hatherly Junr. | Sept. 29. |
| Nathaniel Mariner | Oct. 6. |
| Mary Draper | Oct. 13. |

| | |
|---|---|
| Lydia Hatherly | Oct. 20. |
| Nabia Savage | Oct. 27. |
| Joseph Russell | Oct. 27. |
| Mary Combs | Nov. 10. |
| Anne Allin | Dec. 1. |
| Samuel Waldo | Dec. 22. |
| Elizabeth Harris | Dec. 29. |

## 1696.

### TOWN.

Mary of Jeremiah & Mary Allen born Apr. 7.
Mary of Matthew & Margaret Armstrong born May 19.
Jonathan of Jonathan & Rebecca Adams born Feb. 6.
Sarah of Edward & Mary Ashley born Feb. 22.
Sarah of John & Deborah Burnet born Feb. 21.
Jacob of Francis & Frances Backit born Aug. 14.
Anna of Thomas & Lydia Barnes born Oct. 8.
John of Oliver & Gertrade Berry born Feb. 4.
Isaac of Richard & Eliz. Bason born Jan. 18.
Nathll of Thomas & Sarah Baker born Feb. 16.
Eliza. of Ebenezer & Elizabeth Chaplin born Mar. 2.
John of Francis & Sarah Cole born Mar. 27.
Sarah of Samuel & Sarah Clarke born Mar. 30.
Eliza. of Jonas & Mary Clay born May 12.
Susanna of Samuel & Susanna Colings born July 6.
Marget of William & Elizabeth Crow born May 26.
Marget of Thomas & Deborah Chushing born July 15.
Daniel of Richard & Abigail Cheever born Aug. 8.
Mary of Henry & Elizabeth Chamlet born Sept. 5.
Sarah of Thomas & Priscilla Comings born Sept. 15
Jeremiah of Jeremiah & Judith Cushing born Oct. 8.
Rebecca of Daniel & Rebecca Collings born Sept. 18.
John of John & Mary Coleworthy born Sept. 18.
Sarah of William & Lydia Clough born Nov. 9.
Mary of James & Mary Cock born Nov. 3.
Eliza. of John & Elizabeth Clow born Nov. 2.
Ann of Matthew & Naomi Collins born Dec. 30.
Abraham of Daniel & Elizabeth Champanell born Sept. 30.
Anna of John & Mary Conny born Jan. 23.
John of John & Elizabeth Cronenshild born Jan. 19.
John of John & Judith Coleman born Feb. 27.
Jeremiah of John & Ruth Center born Feb. 15.
Joshua of John & Hannah Doan born Mar. 5.
Sarah of Joseph & Hannah Dayes born May 21.
Jane of Thomas & Jane Dean born June 17.
William of William & Susanna Denis born July 4.
Rebecca of Richard & Sarah Draper born July 20.
Marget of Benja. & Hannah Dyar born Nov. 21.
Edward of Read & Hannah Elding born Nov. 18.
David of David & Rachel Evstiss born May 5.
Eliza. of Jonathan & Mary Evans born Oct. 20.
John of John & Sabella Edwards born Jan. 3.
Mary of William & Sarah Eustice born Aug. 11.
Martha of Jonathan & Martha Farnum born Mar. 27.
Abraham of Giles & Elizabeth Fifield born Apr. 2.
Mehetable of Richard & Mary Fifield born July 7.
Sarah of William & Elizabeth Fox born Aug. 11.
John of Alexander & Mary Fulerton born Sept. 30.
Dorothy of David & Dorothy Farnum born Sept. 30.
James of Josiah & Abiah Franklin born Feb. 4.
Hannah of Benjamin & Mary Frost born Oct. 28.
Noah of John & Rachel Floyd born May 24.

Thomas of Francis & Eliza. Foxcroft born Feb. 26. '
Bartbo. of Thomas & Experience Gould born Apr. 4.
Charles of John & Mary Gyles born June 12.
Eliza. of David & Martha Gwin born July 31.
Gamaliel of William & Hannah Gibson born Aug. 8.
Sarah of Henry & Mary Gibbs born Sept. 13.
Robert of Robert & Mary Gibbs born Nov. 29.
Eliza. of James & Elizabeth Gooch born Jan. 10.
Eliza. of Bartho. & Mary Green born Aug. 24.
Samll of Samuel & Elizabeth Greenwood born Aug. 15.
Sarah of Thomas & Sarah Gwin born Feb. 19.
Samuel of Richard & Hannah Gridley born Jan. 5.
James of James & Marget Goodwin born Dec. 27.
Abigail of Abraham & Abigail Gourdin born Aug. 22.
Nathil of Nathll & Elizabeth Goowin born Nov. 23.
John of Joseph & Hannah Grant born Nov. 25.
Mercey of John & Eliza. Greenough born Aug. 11.
Mary of John & Esther German born Oct. 3.
Mary of John & Eliza. Greenough born Aug. 15.
Nathll of Torrence & Eliza. Henly born Apr. 26.
Thomas of Thomas & Hannah Hall born May 2.
Martha of Thomas & Mary Hunt born Jan. 26.
William of William & Mary Healy born July 19.
Lydia of Nathll & Sarah Holmes born Nov. 19.
Mary of Nathll & Hannah Halsey born Nov. 11.
William of John & Anna Hobby born Nov. 11.
Francis of Francis & Rebecca Holmes born Mar. 20.
Augustine of Arthur & Mary Hale born June 14.
Mary of John & Grace Ireland born Mar. 5.
Henry of Henry & Lydia Ingraham born Feb. 13.
Thomas of Thomas & Mary Jacobs born Apr. 27.
Sarah of Matthew & Susanna Jones born June 9.
Frances of David & Elizabeth Jefferies born July 12.
Eliza. of Nathll & Elizabeth Jarvis born July 21.
Eliza. of David & Maybell Jenner born July 27.
Ann of Andrew & Susanna Knott born Dec. 16.
Samuel of John & Mary Kneeland born Jan. 31.
Miriam of Christopher & Sarah Killby born Dec. 5.
John of Richard & Sarah Lowden born Apr. 16.
Mary of Thomas & Mary Lazenby born Apr. 22.
Peter of Peter & Hannah Leech born June 21.
Ruth of Isaac & Sarah Lorin born Dec. 19.
Joseph of Joseph & Patience Lowell born Jan. 3.
Elizabeth of David & Martha Landon born May 15.
Benjamin of John & Mary Mountfort born Apr. 5.
Sarah of Robert & Maria Mason born Apr. 20.
Susanna of Christopher & Mary Monk born May 16.
Mary of Thomas & Mary Melings born May 17.
Edward of Edward & Elizabeth Mills born Sept. 16.
Charles of Mathew & Faith Midleton born Oct. 5.
Ebenezer of James & Hannah Mirack born Oct. 12.
Samuel of Alexander & Dorcas Miller born Nov. 25.
Duncan of Duncan & Mary Maicum born Nov. 29.
Eliza. of Samuel & Mary Marion born Nov. 21.
Jonathan of William & Rebecca Mann born Jan. 25.
John of Joseph & Ann Marsh born Aug. 2.
Richard of James & Hannah Mathews born Dec. 13.
Josiah of John & Eliza. Mullegan born Nov. 25.
Abigail of Thomas & Betty Mosemy born Feb. 18.
Sarah of Joseph Savages Mary Negro born Jan. 22.
Eliezar of William & Experience Norcut born Oct. 12.
Benjamin of Benjamin & Elizabeth Pemberton born Mar. 13.
Sarah of William & Deborah Phillips born Mar. 6.
Thomas of Thomas & Remember Perkins born Apr. 24.

John of John & Elizabeth Pitts born May 5.
Ann of Nathll & Ann Pether born May 10.
Elizabeth of William Jr. & Elizabeth Porter born Apr. 24.
Abigail of John & Margaret Pratt born May 17.
Eliza. of George & Elizabeth Pordade born May 16.
Rebecca of Nathanll & Hannah Parkman born June 6.
Ebenezer of Thomas & Johanna Peck born May 8.
Elizabeth of Ebenezer & Elizabeth Peck born June 4.
Thomas of Thomas & Elizabeth Person born July 13.
James of James & Elizabeth Pitts born July 23.
Benjamin of Jonathan & Mary Pollard born June 6.
Daniel of Daniel & Elizabeth Phipeny born Oct. 18.
Edward } of Edward & Abiell Porter born Dec. 5.
Abigail } of Edward & Abiell Porter born Dec. 5.
Margaret of Alexander & Sarah Prindle born Jan. 29.
Ann of Charles & Elizabeth Pimm born Aug. 19.
Thomas of Thomas & Elizabeth Procter born Dec. 19.
John of Richard & Mary Prat born May 18.
John of Nathanll & Ruth Raynolls born Mar. 29.
Samuel of Joseph & Esther Robarts born Apr. 30.
Humpery of Humpery & Susanna Richards born Sept. 3.
Eliza. of John & Elizabeth Rainger born Oct. —
E——— son of John & Mary Robinson born Oct. 27.
Elizabeth of Charles & Mary Roberts born Nov. 2.
Bartbo. of William & Mary Sutton born Apr. 20.
Nathll of John & Sarah Souther born Mar. 29.
Elizabeth of Joseph & Elizabeth Skinner born Apr. 27.
John of Joseph & Elizabeth Salter born Apr. 6.
Rebecca of Roland & Ann Story born May 2.
Mary of Sampson & Mary Shore born Apr. 18.
Hannah of Joseph & Hannah Skeith born Jan. 18.
Sarah of Alexander & Sarah Sherer born July 7.
John of John & Grace Stephens born July 12.
Sarah of John & Mary Stephens born June —.
Richard of William & Mercy Shoot born Aug. 12.
Sarah of John & Sarah Street born Sept. 9.
Anna of Samuel & Anna Smith born Oct 2.
Place of Thomas & Sarah Stevens born Jan. 19.
Margaret of Henry & Elizabeth Sharp born Dec. 11.
Jonathan of Joseph & Rebecca Sneling born Dec. 29.
Hannah of Alexander & Rebecca Seers born Jan. 14.
Thomas of Thomas & Sarah Stevens born Jan. 19.
Robert of Robert & Esther Sanderson born Jan. 16.
Cyprian of Cyprian & Elizabeth Southack born Feb. 22.
John (?) of Robert & Deborah Smith born Feb. 10.
Mary of William & Mary Turner born Mar. 29.
Abigail of Samuel & Abigail Thorne born June 11.
Isaiah of Jeremiah & Mercy Toy born Sept. 5.
Sarah of Samuel & Sarah Tiley born Sept. 1.
Hannah of John & Mary Trow born Oct 4.
Humpery of Daniel & Anna Turrell born Sept. 22.
Mosely of James & Rebecca Townsand born Dec. 2.
Mary of Peter & Mary Townsand born Jan. 25.
Elizabeth of John & Martha Tuttle born Dec. 14.
William of James & Rebecca Taylor born June 19.
Abigail of David & Mary Vaughan born Mar. 7.
Ann of Isaac & Elizabeth Virgoose born July 1.
Ann of Samuel & Ann White born Mar. 2.
Susanna of Richard & Phebe Whitridge born Mar 3.
John of John & Martha Whitehead born Aug. 6.
Ruth & } of Joshua & Ruth Wells born Apr. 2.
Abigail } of Joshua & Ruth Wells born Apr. 2.
John of John & Anna Wait born June 2.
Samuel of Samuel & Mary Ward born June 22.

Samuel of Samuel & Mary Way born July 12.
James of James & Elizabeth Wackum born July 2.
Thomas of James & Esther White born Oct. 14.
James of William & Charity Webb born Nov. 13.
Eliza. of William & Elizabeth Wheeler born Nov. 17.
William of William & Penelope Way born Dec. 24.
Susanna of John & Eliza. Welch born Apr. 29.
Samuel of Jonathan & Hannah Waldo born Aug. 7.

Samuel Bridg & Sarah Smith were married by Mr. James Allen Dec. 24.
Samuel Clark & Elizabeth Crafts were married by Mr. Nehemiah Walter
   May 5.
John Cleverly & Elizabeth Glover were married by Mr. James Allen Nov. 5.
Joseph Cowel & Eliza Williams were married by Mr. Miles Aug 6. ......
John Down & Ruth Badcock were married by Mr. Miles Aug. 30.
John Diggens & Rebecca Man were married by Mr. Miles Jan. 19. ....
Walter Gutridge & Anna Gross were married by Mr. Cotton Mather Nov. 12.
Edward Gilling & Mary Thortes were married by Mr. Miles Dec. 25.
Daniel Hodson & Sarah Sherman were married by Mr. James Allen Oct. 20.
Timothy Hammant & Melatiah Clark were married by Pen Townsend Esq.
   Jan. 19.
William Marlton & Sarah Whaly were married by Mr. Miles Jan. 1. ......
Thomas Palmer & Abigail Hutchinson were married by Mr. James Allen
   Jan. 29.
Joseph Rayner & Sarah Davis were married by Mr. Miles Feb. 3.
Robert Sample & Eliza Bourn were married by Mr. Miles Oct. 12.
Thomas Smith & Mary Shurah were married by Mr. Miles Mar. 10. ......
James Studson & Susanna Townsend were married by Pen Townsend Esq.
   Nov. 26.
John Tully & Eliza. Eldridg were married by Mr. James Allen Jan. 20.
Willm. Webster & Mary Mosely were married by Mr. James Allen Nov. 25.

Francis of David and Mary Perry Died May 3.
Hanah wife of Thomas Hall Died May 8.
Pasitians Cole daught Richd and Darcos died May 13.
Peter Townsand Senor died May 14.
Lidia Wife to Samll Earle died May 29.
Elizabeth Weeden the Midwife Died June 11.
John Diar Senior Died June 2.
Mary Daugt. of Thomas Cooper Died June 17.
Samll of Samll and Mary Blackden Died June 9.
Mary of Joseph and Eliz. Eldridge died June 13.
Thomas of Tho. and Hanah Hall Died July 16.
Cromell Son of Joseph Lobdell Died June 23.
Wm. of Wm. and Mary Ruck Died June 26.
Job of Wm. and Eliza. Fisher Died June 27.
Eliza. wife of Florance Macarty Died July 6.
Susanah wife of Joseph Bridgham Died July 11.
John of Wm. and Eliza. Lanis Died July 22.
Eliza. wife of Christopher Flegg Died Augt 10.
John of John and Martha Whitehead Died Augt 13.
Rebecca of Timo. and Mary Nash Died Augt 13.
Martha wife of William Dinsdell Died Augt. 7.
James of Robart & Eliza. Butcher Died Augt 23.
Nathll Peck Died Augt 24.
Eliza. daught. of Ebinezer Lowell Died Augt 26.
John of John and Sew. Garrett Died Sept. 3.
Mehitabell Daughter of Richd Fyfield Died Sept. 5.
John of Francis and Sarah Cole Died Sept. 13.
John Bradish died Octor 12.
John Rogers Died Novr 2.
Ann of Jonathan & Ann Bowers Died Novr. 18.
Sarah wife of Michaell Shaler Died Novr 20.
Mary Fauckner Died Novr 22.

Sarah of Wm and Lidia Clow Died Novr 26.
Peter of Peter and Mary Chardon Died Novr 29.
Susanah Hudson died Novr 14.
Paul Si n nons Died Novr 16.
John of John & Katherine Eyres Died Decemr 1.
Willm of Nathll and Eliza Oliver Died Novr. 13.
Mary wife of James Denise Died Novr 16.
Edward Eglington Died Novr 17.
Eliza. of Samll & Martha Buriall Died Decemr 4.
Marget of Benja. & Sarah Davis Died December 12.
Esther Latomie wife of Peter Dally Died Decemr 14.
Eliza of John and Elisa Ranger Died Decemr 16.
Eliza of Charles and Mary Robarts Died Decemr 16.
Hanab Rugles Died Janr. 3.
Rachell Wife of John Mershall Died Janry 15.
Jabis of Thomas & Jemina Butler Died Jan. 22.
Tho. of Duncan and Marget Garnick Died Feb. 6.
Humpery of Daniell & An Turrell Died Feb. 11.
Benja. of Thomas and Mary Baker Died Sept. 28.
Thomas Bill Died Octor 29.
Abigail wife of Thomas Bill Died Novr 7.
Robart of Robart Brinsdon Died Octor 13.
Joanah of Willm and Ann Copp Died March 20.
Susana of Duncan & Susanah Cambell Died Febr.
Joanah daugt. of John Carthew Died Novr. 13.
Hananiah Son of Samuell Dodge Died Novr 5.
David Edwards Died Octor 1.
John Glover died Sept. 23.
Hanah Gridly Died Janr. 15.
Abigall Wife of Abraham Gourden Died Sept. 6.
John Hill Died Janry 31.
Mary wife of Henry Kemball Died Jull. 4.
A child of Tong (negro) Died Janr. 28.
Ann daughter of Nathll Feather Died May 29.
John Peck Died May.
James Pemberton Died Octor 11.
Edwd of Edwd and Abiell Porter Died Deer 7.
Abigail of Edwd & Abiell Porter Died Decr 13.
Sarah Parkeman Died Deer 26.
Dorothy of Wm. & Elizabeth Robinson died Deer.
Abraham Smith Died March 26.
Sarah of Robart & Esther Saunderson Died Apr. 20.
Anna wife of Peter Salamon Died May 26.
Mary widow of Abraham Smith Died Aug. 23.
Sarah of Samll & Hanah Sewell Died Decer 23.
Joseph Souther died Janr. 2.
Sarah of John and Mary Stevens died Septr 25.
Mary Varny died Septr 28.
Sarah of John and Sarah Waite Died May 16.
A negro Child of mr. Waters died Jan. 2.
Eliza. dau. of Charles Roberts died Jan. 4.

## FIRST CHURCH.

| | |
|---|---|
| John Eustace | Jan. 5. |
| Elizabeth Cary | Jan. 12. |
| Francis Smith | Jan. 26. |
| Elizabeth Simmonds | Feb. 16. |
| Thomas Windsor | Feb. 23. |
| Joshua Windsor | Feb. 23. |
| Caleb Windsor | Feb. 23. |
| Solomon Windsor | Feb. 23. |
| William Holloway Junr. | Mar. 22. |
| John Reynolds | April 5. |

| | |
|---|---|
| John Slacke | April 5. |
| John Kettle | April 5. |
| Joseph Kettle | April 5. |
| Mary Allen aged 5 days | April 12. |
| William Daniels | May 10. |
| Hezekiah Butler | June 14. |
| Abigail Thorne | June 14. |
| Nathaniel Balston | June 14. |
| Rebecca Balston | June 14. |
| Elizabeth Langdane | June 21. |
| William Welsteed | June 28. |
| Samuel Ward | June 28. |
| Sarah Sheerer | July 12. |
| Gamaliel Gibson | Aug. 2. |
| Daniel | Aug. 9. |
| Abigail Waldo | Aug. 16. |
| Gatliffe Ranger | Aug. 23. |
| Mary Mattocks | Aug. 30. |
| Mercy Hawkins | Sept. 20. |
| John Endicott | Sept. 20. |
| William Endicott | Sept. 20. |
| Joseph Endicott · | Sept. 20. |
| Ebenezer Mirecke aged 1 week | Oct. 18. |
| Margaret Wright aged 15 years | Oct. 18. |
| Eleanor Pallow a negro | Oct. 25. |
| Richard of Eleanor Fallow | Oct. 25. |
| Robin of Eleanor Pallow | Oct. 25. |
| Eleanor of Eleanor Pallow | Oct. 25. |
| Thomas Davis | Nov. 15. |
| John Davis | Nov. 15. |
| James Davis | Nov. 15. |
| Thomas Barret | Nov. 15. |
| Margaret Dyer | Nov. 22. |
| Elizabeth Clow | Nov. 29. |

## 1697.

### TOWN.

Samuel of Joseph & Ann Allen born Apr. 8.
John of Joseph & Elizabeth Adams born Apr. 10.
Samuel of Samuel & Mary Avis born Apr. 13.
Thomas of Thomas & Mary Arnold born May 10.
Ann of John & Mary Atwood born June 19.
William of William & Mary Alden born July 23.
Katharine of John & Elizabeth Alden born Aug. 19.
Bethiah of John & Hannah Adams born Aug. 20.
Comfort of Joseph & Comfort Alliston born Oct. 24.
James of Jeremiah & Mary Allen born Dec. 25.
Constance of John & Constance Alcock born Jan. 17.
Daniel of Silence & Esther Allen born Feb. 8.
Moses of Moses & Eliza Aires born Aug. 12.
John of John & Abial Brightman born Mar. 30.
Newcomb of Newcomb & Mary Blaque born Mar. 22.
Eliza. of Benja. & Elizabeth Brame born Apr. 10.
Abial dau. of Jacob & Jerusa Bill born Apr. 11.
Mary of Nathaniel & Rebecca Balstone born May 6.
Katharine of Jarvis & Martha Ballard born Apr. 20.
John of Thomas & Elizabeth Blore born June 18.
Seth of Nathaniel & Mary Baker born June 20.
John of Ambros & Hannah Berry born Aug. 3.
John of Joseph & Hannah Billings born July 29.
Juda of Isaac & Ann Biscon born Aug. 27.
Nich. of Samuel & Martha Burrel born Oct. 1.

Jemina of John & Febbee Brenton born July 4.
Martha of Joseph & Rebecca Brisco born Nov. 26.
Thomas of Moses & Elizabeth Bradford born Dec. 24.
William of William & Ann Brown born Sept. 1.
William of Samuel & Sarah Bridge born Dec. 20.
Mary of William & Rebecca Briggs born Jan. 10.
Buttalph of Joseph & Abigail Belknap born Dec. 29.
James of John & Sarah Boreland born Feb. 15.
Peter of Peter & Sarah Barbour born Nov. 10.
Sebellah of Thomas & Lydia Burrington born Aug. 8.
Mary of John & Mary Clark born Mar. 15.
John of John & Hannah Carlile born Apr. 6.
Sarah of William & Ann Copp born Apr. 10.
John of Francis & Sarah Cole born July 29.
Mary of Ebenezer & Martha Clough born July 19.
Mary of Samuel & Mary Checkley born June 26.
Joshua ⎱ of Joshua & Mary Cornish born Sept. 1.
Mary ⎰ of Joshua & Mary Cornish born Sept. 1.
David of Andrew & Sarah Cuningham born Sept. 17.
Samuel of Samuel & Hannah Copp born Sept. 13.
John of John & Elizabeth Coombs born Oct. 3.
David of David & Patience Copp born Oct. 21.
Ann of John & Jane Collins born Oct. 25.
James of Samuel & Sarah Clark born Dec. 2.
Ebenezer of William & Liddiah Clough born Dec. 11.
Sarah of Thomas & Sarah Cox born Feb. 27.
John of John & Jane Coffy (negroes) born Feb. 15.
Hannah of John & Sarah Cunnibell born Aug. 5.
Margaret of Timothy & Sarah Clark born Apr. 4.
Jeremiah of John & Ruth Centor born Feb. 15.
Thomas of Christor. & Tamzine Capril born Nov. 3.
John of Edward & Sarah Dolbear born Mar. 2.
John of Edward & Hannah Durant born Mar. 29.
Hannah of Samson & Sarah Dewer born Aug. 21.
Eliazer of Eliazer & Mary Darby born Apr. 14.
Elizabeth of Thomas & Jane Dean born Sept. 20.
John of William & Dorothy Dusebury born Nov. 8.
Keziah of John & Rachel Draper born Jan. 20.
Joseph of Joseph & Hannah Dolbear born Jan. 10.
Joseph of Seth & Abigail Dwight born Feb. 3.  .
Ann of Joseph & Ann Dowden born Jan. 1.
Ruth of William & Sarah Eustice born Feb. 2.
Martha of Benja. & Elizabeth Emons born Mar. 3.
Robert of Robert & Bethiah Emes born Mar. 21.
John of Robert & Sarah Earle born Aug. 21.
Mary of John & Catharine Eyre born Sept. 15.
George of John & Lucey Elliston born Sept. 29.
Read of Read & Hannah Elden born Dec. 11.
Dorothy of Joseph & Rebecca Fuller born Mar. 15.
Richard of Richard & Elizabeth Flood born Mar. 6.
John of Henry & Susanna Farry born June 16.
Dorothy of John & Dorothy Farnum born June 11.
Thomas of Thomas & Abial Fitch born Sept. 21.
Mary of William & Esther Frothingham born Dec. 3.
Abigail of Christopher & Abigail Goffe born Mar. 13.
James of John & Bethiah Green born June 9.
Samuel of Joshue & Elizabeth Gee born June 10.
Mary of Nathaniel & Elizabeth Green born Aug. 8.
Joseph of Joseph & Jane Glidden born July 19.
Thomas of Thomas & Hannah Gilberd born Aug. 24.
Samuel of Richard & Hannah Green born Sept. 13.
Jane of Samuel & Priscilla Grice born Oct. 28.
John of Henry & Mary Gibbs born Dec. 14.
William of John & Lydia Gerrish born Dec. 28.

Ruth of Samuel & Elizabeth Gardner born Jan. 23.
William of William & Elizabeth Goddard born Jan. 24.
Thomas of David & Martha Gwin born Feb. 1.
Bartholomew of Barthol. & Mariah Green born July 12.
John of William & Elizabeth Gill born Oct. 3.
Hannah of Joseph & Hannah Grant born Jan. 15.
Nathll. of Joshua & Eliza. Hewes born Mar. 2.
Martha of William & Martha Hannah born Mar. 20.
Mary of Nathaniel & Ann Henchman born Apr. 13.
John of Torrence & Elizabeth Henly born Apr. 28.
Ruth of John & Abigail Hilton born June 29.
Mary of Joseph & Mary Heath born July 6.
Richard of Samuel & Deborah Hood born June 20.
Thomas of Thomas & Bridget Hays born Aug. 7.
John of Herculus & Jane Hewit born Sept. 1.
Ann of Jacob & Mary Holloway born Sept. 7.
John of John & Ruhamah Hill born Nov. 24.
Jacob of Elizur & Mary Holioke born Nov. 6.
John of Henry & Mary Hill born Jan. 4.
Lydia of William & Mary Hough born Feb. 2.
Eliza. of Robert & Hannah Hannah born Apr. 24.
John of Francis & Rebecca Holmes born Mar. 4.
Richard of John & Ann Hobby born Jan. —
Mary of James & Penellope Jarvis born Mar. 25.
Samuel of John & Sarah Jenkins born May 8.
Ruth of William & Sarah Johnson born Nov. 16.
Peter of David & Elizabeth Jeffries born Nov. 18.
Mary of Daniel & Elizabeth Jackson born Jan. 20.
James of John & Lydia Kelton born Mar. 5.
Samuel of Samuel & Mary Kneeland born Apr. 26.
Mary of Thomas & Elizabeth Kellen born July 4.
Jonathan of Jonatha. & Elizabeth Lambert born Mar. 20.
Eliza of William & Elizabeth Lavis born June 1.
Abigail of Thomas & Abigail Larramore born Aug. 2.
Margaret of John & Elizabeth Langdon born Aug. 23.
Ebenezer of Ebenezer & Eliza. Lowell born Oct. 21.
Thomas of Thomas & Mehitable Lincolne born Nov 12.
Gabril of James & Ann Lablond born Mar. 5.
Edward of Samuel & Mehitable Lilly born Feb. 25.
Joseph of Joseph & Elizabeth Lohden born Mar. 18.
Christopher of Thomas & Dorcas Marshal born May 22.
Robert of Robert & Ann More born June 19.
Ebenezer of Thomas & Elizabeth Messenger born June 2.
William of Joseph & Hannah Marriner born July 26.
Ralph } of Henry & Hannah Mayer born Aug. 8.
Henry } of Henry & Hannah Mayer born Aug. 8.
Grace of Francis & Mary Marshal born Oct. 15.
Sarah of John & Elizabeth Maxwell born Oct. 25.
Ann of John & Sarah Miles born Jan. 1.
Elizabeth of John & Mary Mountfort born Feb. 25.
John of John & Sarah Mason born Nov. 1.
Sarah of Edward & Sarah Martin born May 27.
Rebecca of Stephen & Mercy Minot born ———
Temperance of David & Temperance Norton born Mar. 16.
Lewis of Nathaniel & Sarah Newdigate born Jan. 31.
Samuel of John & Sarah Oliver born Mar. 6.
William of Rignal & Priscilla Odall born July 19.
Mary of John & Sarah Parker born Apr. 30.
Mary of Garrot & Sarah Pursly born Apr. 27.
Eliza. of William & Constance Palfree born Apr. 80.
Mary of William & Sarah Pain born May 16.
Sarah of Elias & Sarah Purington born June 29.
Sarah of Thomas & Elizabeth Pike born June 9.
Jacob of Jacob & Ann Parker born July 24.

Esther of Thomas & Hannah Platt born Aug. 11.
Sarah of Thomas & Mary Pratt born Aug. 10.
Thomas of Thomas & Abigail Palmer born Oct. 4.
Mary of Mark & Faith Pilkinton born Oct. 4.
Thomas of Thomas & Member Perkins born Oct. 19.
Ann of Jonathan & Mary Pollard born Jan. 22.
Abigail of William & Elizabeth Parkman born Jan. 8.
Obediah of Obediah & Mary Perry born May 28.
Elizabeth of Edward & Elizabeth Pell born Dec. 6.
Martha of John & Martha Ruggles born Mar. 31.
Eliza. of John & Experience Roberts born Apr. 18.
Sarah of Ralph & Martha Ransford born May 27.
Sarah of James & Elizabeth Raymer born May 15.
John of Joseph & Elizabeth Rogers born July 13.
William of William & Elizabeth Randal born July 24.
Elizabeth of Richard & Nagor Richards (negroes) born ——.
Elizabeth of Joseph & Mary Russell born Aug. 1.
Sarah of Thomas & Martha Raper born Sept. 30.
John of Humphry & Susanna Richards born Nov. 15.
Jane of John & Mary Roberts born Dec. 25.
Edmund of John & Elizabeth Ranger born Dec. 12.
Cyprian of Cyprian & Elizabeth Southack born Feb. 21.
Jane of John & Jane Smith born Mar. 6.
John of John & Rely Simpson born May 4.
Thomas of Thomas & Edeth Seward born May 2.
Samuel of Seth & Mehitable Smith born May 23.
John of Simeon & Mehitable Stoddard born June 3.
Joseph of Joseph & Hannah Souther born Feb. 7.
Joseph of Joseph & Elizabeth Skinner born July 26.
Henry of Henry & Sarah Smith born Apr. 30.
Hannah of Thomas & Mehitable Savage born Sept. 20.
Elizabeth of William & Martha Shoot born Sept. 18.
Ann of Joseph & Hannah Simpson born Sept. 19.
Thomas of Thomas & Margaret Savage born Apr. 20.
Nicholas of John & Bridget Salsbury born Oct. 28.
Susanna of James & Susanna Studson born Dec. 19.
Rebecca of Joshua & Rebecca Scottow born Jan. 26.
Abigail of John & Jane Snelling born Feb. 9.
Alce of John & Ann Smith born Jan. 28.
Abigail of Benja. & Susanna Stone born Feb. 16.
Sarah of Benja. & Jamina Snelling born Feb. 27.
Dorothy of John & Mary Stover born Oct. 16.
Abigail of Briant & Abigail Smith born Aug. 26.
Richard of Richard & Mary Thomas born Apr. 10.
James of James & Mary Townsend born Apr. 13.
Samuel of James & Mary Truworthy born Jan. 24.
John of John & Hannah Tapper born Nov. 1.
William of Samuel & Sarah Tily born Nov. 30.
Jonathan of Jona. & Elizabeth Townsend born Jan. 1.
Susanna of Benja. & Susanna Thaxter born Feb. 1.
Mary of William & Mary Turner born Feb. 28.
John of Samuel & Abigail Thorne born Feb. 10.
Mary of Benjamin & Mercy Tout born May 6.
Damarus of Edward & Abigail Tuttle born Nov. 20.
Mary of John & Sarah Vickers born Oct. 25.
Abigail of Thomas & Hannah Veering born Feb. 19.
Rebecca of Thomas & Rachel Winsor born Mar. 19.
John of Richard & Ann West born Mar. 26.
Sarah of Thomas & Sarah Warren born Mar. 8.
John dau. of Eperence & Eliza. Willis born Apr. 29.
Hannah of Edward & Hannah Winslow born Mar. 8.
Ebenezer of Michael & Elizabeth Willis born Apr. 9.
Abigail of Jobon & Abigail Wilson born May 14.
Jona. of Jonathan & Hannah Waldo born June 4.

Sarah of John & Martha Whitehead born July 21.
Mary of Christoper & Mary Weeks born Sept. 29.
Sarah of Samuel & Eunis Willard born June 10.
John of John & Tripena Woodard born Sept. 11.
Mary of John & Mary Wells born Nov. 22.
Seward of William & Abigail Waters born Jan. 6.
Joseph of Joseph & Hannah Wodsworth born Jan. 25.
Elizabeth of James & Eliza. Wacomb born Feb. 9.
Susannah of John & Elizabeth Wilkin born Feb. 26.
James of James & Sarah Williams born May 19.
William of William & Ann Wheeler born Apr. 27.
Ann of Obediah & Susanna Wakefield born Feb. 20.


John Allen & Elizabeth Edwards were married by Mr. James Allen July 22.
William Ambross & Elizabeth Mattock were married by Mr. Woodbridg Jan. 6.
Daniel Berry & Mary Mayer were married by Mr. James Allen July 8.
David Buckly & Hannah Tally were married by Mr. Cotton Mather June 3.
Samuel Burrel of Lyn & Margaret Jarvis of Boston were married by Mr. Cotton Mather Sept. 17.
Andrew Bondman of Cambridg & Eliza Tuesdell of Boston were married by Mr. Benja Wadsworth Dec. 16.
William Brattle of Cambridg & Eliza Hayman of Boston were married by Mr. Saml. Willard Nov. 3.
John Briggs & Sarah Curtis were married by Mr. Saml. Willard Jan. 11.
Joseph Belcher & Hannah Bill were married by Mr. Thomas Cheever Jan. 7.
Thomas Bowes & Sarah Bowes were married by Mr. Miles June 21.
William Barkly & Mary Miriour were married by Mr. Miles Jany 13.
William Bedford & Hannah Briant were married by Mr. Miles Feb. 22.
John Briggs & Elizabeth Allen were married by Pen Townsend Esq. Apr. 27.
Thomas Creese & Rookby Greenleaf were married by Mr. James Allen June 30.
William Codner & Sarah Young were married by Mr. James Allen Nov. 21.
Thomas Cocker & Sarah Waldren were married by Mr. Cotton Mather May 3.
John Collins & Jane Loyd were married by Mr. Saml Willard Apr. 22.
Abra. Cole & Ann Townsend were married by Mr. James Allen Sept. 30.
Joseph Chantril & Amie Gardner were married by Mr. Saml Willard Dec. 13.
John Cairness & Eliza Mortimor were married by Mr. Miles June 24.
David Dewer & Jannet Neal were married by Mr. Benja. Wodsworth July 29.
Henry Dee & Hannah Hillard were married by Mr. Miles Sept. 30.
Peter Dearlove & Jone Mullikin were married by Mr. Miles Oct. 27.
Elijah Dubbledee & Sarah Pain were married by Mr. Miles Jan. 23.
Thomas Davis & Grace Hult were married by Mr. Miles Jan. 27.
Joseph Eliot & Sarah Collins were married by Mr. James Allen July 29.
Jonathan Everrard & Penelope Clark were married by Mr. James Allen Aug. 9.
Rich. Frankin & Abigail Stanbury were married by Mr. James Allen Sept. 29.
Daniel Floyd & Mary Hallewel were married by Mr. Cotton Mather Jan. 18.
Robert Fletcher & Susanna Worthileg were married by Mr. Miles Jan. 13.
David Griffin & Catharine Howard were married by Mr. Saml Willard June 14.
William Goddard & Eliza. Fayrefield were married by Mr. James Allen Oct. 29.
Nicho. Green & Rebecca Clay were married by Mr. Miles Mar. 22.
Samuel Haugh & Margaret Johnson were married by Mr. Saml. Willard Sept. 30.
Joseph Humphry & Sarah Smith were married by Mr. Saml. Willard Oct. 28.
Joseph Halsey & Elizabeth Eldredg were married by Mr. James Allen Jan. 29.
Richard Henchman & Esther Webster were married by Mr. Cotton Mather Dec. 24.
William Hepworth & Mary Lock were married by Mr. Woodbridge Jan. 3.
Thomas Hudson & Sarah Crocker were married by Mr. Miles Oct. 24.
James Humphryes & Thankful White were married by Pen Townsend Esq. Nov. 4.
Daniel Jackson & Elizabeth Johnson were married by Mr. Cotton Mather Apr. 2.
James Jones & Joanna Williams were married by Mr. Cotton Mather Apr. 2.
Joshua Kent & Agnes Okeman were married by Mr. Saml. Willard Nov. 4.
John Kitt & Margaret Murrel were married by Mr. Miles Sept. 23.

Isaac Lobdale & Hannah Bishop were married by Mr. Cotton Mather Aug. 12.

John Leveret of Cambridge & Margaret Berry of Boston were married by Mr. Cotton Mather Nov. 25.

John Lathrop of Barnstable & Joanna Prince of Boston were married by Mr. Benja. Wadsworth Jan. 21.

Cornelius Loreson & Abiel Faig were married by Mr. Tho Cheever Nov. 4.

Thomas Marshall & Mary Chantril were married by Mr. Saml Willard June 18.

Stephen Mumford of Rode Island & Mary Timberlake were married by Mr. Saml Willard Aug. 30.

Thomas Mellous & Sarah Mumfort were married by Mr. James Allen Nov. 3.

Samuel Mears & Mariah Gross were married by Mr. Cotton Mather Dec. 7.

Florene Macartie & Sarah Newwork were married by Mr. Miles Aug. 24.

James & Savadorah (Negro) were married by Mr. Sam. Willard Dec. 11.

John Osland & Sarah Hide of New Town were married by Saml Sewell Esq. Oct. 14.

John Oliver & Hannah Mather were married by Mr. Increase Mather Jan 28.

Elisha Odlen & Mary Colburn were married by Mr. Saml Willard Dec. 30.

Joseph Pelham & Rebecca Barber were married by Mr. James Allen Mar. 19.

Theophilus Philpot & Rebecca Chonor were married by Mr. Miles Sept. 22.

John Pitts & Elizabeth Lindall were married by Mr. James Allen Sept. 10.

William Parsons & Martha Baldwin were married by Mr. James Allen Sept. 15.

John Perkins & Mary Mackfarland were married by Mr. Saml Willard Dec. 11.

Isaac Royall & Elizabeth Eliot were married by Mr. Benja Wodsworth July 1.

John Ruch & Hannah Hutchinson were married by Mr. James Allen Apr. 29.

Josiah Sanders & Rebecka Smith were married by Mr. Sam. Willard Apr. 7.

John Stiler & Mary Bull were married by Mr. Cotton Mather June 9.

Daniel Souther & Elizabeth Boden were married by Mr. Cotton Mather June 15.

John Sharp & Mary Brooks were married by Mr. James Allen Sept. 6.

Philip Slow & Barbary Hitchil were married by Mr. Miles Feb. 24.

Georg Siry & Jane Fall were married by Mr. Miles Mar. 16.

William Thornton of Salam & Ann Hanet of Charis Town were married by Mr Cotton Mather Aug. 17.

Thomas Tomlin & Sarah Sreet were married by Mr. Saml. Willard Dec. 30.

Richard Tally & Elizabeth Gross were married by Mr. Saml. Willard Jan. 27.

Joshua Tucker & Hannah Cleverly were married by Saml. Sewell Esq. Nov. 2.

John Wilkins & Elizabeth How were married by Mr. Cotton Mather Apr. 27.

John Wells & Mary Peck were married by Mr. Benja. Wodsworth Feb. 18.

Jonthon Williams & Mary Hunlock were married by Mr. Benja. Wodsworth July 12.

Samuel Weaver & Elizabeth Cravath were married by John Bayley Mar. 27.

Richard Ward & Mary Gusteen were married by Mr. James Allen Oct. 22.

Joseph Wood & Judieth Hely were married by Mr. Cotton Mather Oct. 20.

Nathl. Wheeler & Mary Bridges were married by Mr. Cotton Mather Nov. 9.

Elish. Webb & Lydia Scottow were married by Mr. Cotton Mather Nov. 18.

Joseph Wheeler & Elizabeth Pell were married by Mr. Cotton Mather Dec. 14.

John Winter & Ann Phenix were married by Mr. Miles Apr. 2.


Samuel King Dyed 9th march.

John Bendall Dyed the 30 April.

Hopestil Bryer Dyed the 20 April.

Newcomb of Newcomb Blaque Dyed 18 June.

Richard Son of Capt. Smithson Dyed 23 June.

Sarah Messenger Dyed 6 June.

Hannah Daugth. of Edward Boylstone Dyed 27 June.

Richard Willard Dyed 29 June.

Mr. Joshua Moody minister Dyed 6 July.

John of John & rely Simpsbn Dyed ———.

Sarah Lohden dyed the 22 march.

John Wilson was drowned the 10 March.

Samuel King Dyed the 11 March.
John of John & Susanna Bayly Dyed 11 March.
Eliza. of James & Elizabeth George Dyed 11 March.
Samuel Howard dyed the 11 March.
Sarah of Joseph & Hannah Day Dyed 17 March.
Deborah Paddy dyed 22 March.
Timo. Cunnel Dyed 3 April.
John Boder. Dyed 4 April.
John Marshall Dyed 12 April.
Richard Harris Dyed 12 April.
Mary Saxton dyed 12 April.
John of John Colman dyed 12 April.
Thomas of Edward Procter Dyed 12 April.
John of John Woody Dyed 17 April.
Hopestil Bryer Dyed the 28 April.
John Bendol Dyed 30 April.
Mary daugt. of John Parker Dyed 13 May.
William Esset Dyed 24 May.
Thomas Walker Dyed 30 May.
The wife of Daniel Wire dyed the 4 May.
Nathaniel of Nathll Baker Dyed June 13.
Rebecca daugt. of Roland Story Dyed 16 June.
Thomas of Thomas Perkins Dyed 10 June.
Mrs. Jerusha Saltonstal the wife of mr. Saltonstal of New London minister
    dyed 20 June.
Richard of Richard Smithson Dyed 23 June.
Old mrs. Messenger Dyed the 6 June.
Hannah Daugt. of Edwd Boylstone Dyed 6 June.
Maycome Dyed the 26 June.
Richard of mr. Samuel Willard Dyed 29 June.
Lt. Richard Way Dyed the 23 June.
Seth of Nathll. Baker Dyed July 14.
Mary wife of John Briggs Dyed 18 July.
John of John Eustus Dyed 11 July.
Abigail Daugtr of John Wilson Dyed July 16.
Mr. Joshua Moody minister Dyed 25 July.
Joseph of Joseph Lowle junr Dyed 10 July.
Mrs. Eliza. Jackson of Nevis dyed 11 July.
Mr. Hezekiah Vsher Dyed the 14 July.
Robert Adams dyed the 16 July.
Robert of Benja. Emms Dyed 25 July.
Elizabeth wife of George Robinson Dyed 7 July.
Sarah Daughtr. of mr Samuel Willard Dyed 23 July.
John of John Simpson dyed Augt. 9.
James of Philip Langdon dyed 18 Aug.
Sarah wife of Richard Tally Dyed 5 Aug.
Ann Daught. of Sampson Dewer Dyed 11 Aug.
Abigail Daugtr. of Samll. Thorne Dyed 3 Aug.
John Blore Dyed 8 Aug.
Eliza. daugtr of George Pordage Dyed 24 Aug.
Mary wife of William Habberfield Dyed 30 Aug.
Sarah wife of John Auger Dyed 6 Aug.
Jacob of Jacob Parker Dyed 6 Aug.
Mr. Thomas Grafford Dyed 6 Aug.
Ralph of Henry Mare Dyed 25 Aug.
Mary daughtr. of Sampson Shore Dyed 18 Aug.
Agnis Scaley Dyed the 5 Aug.
Isaac of Isaac Biscon Dyed 6 Septembr.
Samuel of Samuel Ward Dyed 6 Sept.
John Howard at Capt. Verrys Dyed 25 Sept.
Hannah Winchester Dyed 18 Sept.
Mis. Curwin Dyed 23 Sept.
John of Henry Brightman Dyed 6 Octobr.
Sarah daught of William Copp Dyed 20 Oct.

Ebenezr. of Michael Willis Dyed 30 Octor.
Mary Daught of Christopr Monk Dyed 25 **Oct.**
William Bryant Dyed 7 Oct.
Susanna Hill Dyed 18 Oct.
Jonathan Elieston Dyed 6 Novembr.
Samuel Johnson Dyed 18 Nov.
Christopher Slegg Dyed 25 Nov.
Philippy Philips Dyed 13 Decemr.
Mr. John Bayley Dyed 12 Dec.
Abigail Gorden Dyed 13 Dec.
Phil'p Langdon Dyed 11 Dec.
Margaret Roberts Dyed 14 Dec.
Lidia wife of John Gerrish Dyed **8 Janr.**
Eliza. Tucker Dyed 7 Jan.
Samll of Samll Copp Dyed 24 Jan.
William of John Gerrish Dyed 20 Jan.
Thomas Harris Butcher Dyed 5 Jan.
Joseph of Joseph Dolbear Dyed 25 Jan.
Mary daughtr of Samll. Hooper Dyed 22 Jan.
John son of Tadourneau Dyed 29 Jan.
Mabell wife of Joseph Hill Dyed 12 Jan.
Rebecca Winsor an Antiant wido. Dyed 28 Jan.
Rebecca Daughtr of Gipson Farr Dyed 22 Jan.
John of Edward Gouch Dyed 22 Jan.
Mary wife of Jarbis Coley Dyed 22 Jan.
Deborah wife of John Barrel Dyed 22 Jan.
Mis. Mary Turrel wife of Capt. Daniel Turrel Dyed 23 **Jan.**
Thomas Baker Senr. Dyed 3 Jan.
Eliza. Earle Dyed 24 Jan.
Dennis Mackdaniel Dyed 20 Jan.
John of Joseph Wadsworth Dyed Febr. 6.
James of James Grant Dyed 18 Feb.
Constant Daughtr of John Alcock Dyed **18 Feb.**
Mis. Brookhaven Dyed 2 Feb.
Mis. Wardel an Antiant wido. Dyed 22 Feb.
Thomas of Thomas & Margaret Savage died July **13.**

## First Church.

| | |
|---|---|
| Hannah Collins aged one week | Jan. 3. |
| Samuel Bill | Jan. 3. |
| Richard Bill | Jan. 3. |
| Hannah Bill | Jan. 3. |
| Abraham Bill | Jan. 3. |
| Ephraim Howard | Jan. 10. |
| Samuel of Samuel Marshall | Jan. 10. |
| John of Samuel Marshall | Jan. 10. |
| Thomas of Samuel Marshall | Jan. 10. |
| Ephraim of Samuel Marshall | Jan. 10. |
| Manasseh of Samuel Marshal' | Jan. 10. |
| Ruth of Samuel Marshall | Jan. 10. |
| Joannah of Samuel Marshall | Jan. 10. |
| Sarah of Samuel Marshall | Jan. 10. |
| Lydia Pollow a negro Child | Jan. 10. |
| John of Rev. John Bayly | Jan. 17. |
| Elizabeth Gooch | Jan. 17. |
| John Parke | Jan. 31. |
| Anna of John & Mary Coney | Jan. 31. |
| Joseph Lowel | Feb. 7. |
| Elizabeth Delvier | Feb. 7. |
| Henry Ingram | Feb. 14. |
| John Parker | Feb. 14. |
| Remember Parker | Feb. 14. |

| | |
|---|---|
| Enoch Greenleafe adult | Feb. 28. |
| Mary Gooch adult | Feb. 28. |
| Mary Thwing | Feb. 28. |
| William Thwing | Feb. 28. |
| John Thwing | Feb. 28. |
| Lydia Thwing | Feb. 28. |
| Hannah Green | Mar. 14. |
| Elizabeth Green | Mar. 14. |
| Isaiah Verry | Mar. 21. |
| Rachel Windsor | Mar. 21. |
| Mary Veach | Mar. 28. |
| Susanna Veach | Mar. 28. |
| Abigail Temple | April 4. |
| Ebenezer Willis | April 11. |
| Mary Goldsmith | April 11. |
| Joanna Willis | May 2. |
| Mary Parker | May 2. |
| Mary Balston | May 9. |
| Edmund Neagers | May 30. |
| Jonathan Waldo | June 6. |
| Ebenezer Messenger | June 6. |
| Edward of Ezekiel Clesbie | June 13. |
| William Marriner | Aug. 1. |
| Mary Green of N. G. Junr. | Aug. 8. |
| Sarah Ashley | Aug. 22. |
| Anna Dewer | Aug. 22. |
| Samuel Copp | Sept. 19. |
| David Cuningham | Sept. 19. |
| Samuel Green | Sept. 19. |
| Hannah Savage | Sept. 26. |
| John Coomes | Oct. 10. |
| David of David Copp | Oct. 24. |
| Margaret Robberts | Nov. 21. |
| Mary Wells | Nov. 28. |
| Edmund Ranger | Dec. 12. |
| James of Jeremiah & Mary Allen | Dec. 26. |
| Thomas Bradford | Dec. 26. |
| Chuzziah Draper | Dec. 26. |

## 1698.

### TOWN.

Matthew son of Matthew & Margaret Armstrong born April 17.
Josiah of Jonathan & Rebecca Adams born May 8.
James of John & Elizabeth Allen born Apr. 11.
Abigail of Thomas & Abigail Adkins born Nov. 19.
Mary of Samuel & Mary Avis born Dec. 4.
Elisha of Elisha & Eliner Andrews born Dec. 13.
Philips of Natha. & Hephzibeth Alden born Dec. 31.
Elizabeth of John & Mary Atwood born Aug. 21.
Eliza. of William & Elizabeth Ambross born Dec. 14.
Mary of Elisha & Mary Andling born Oct. 6.
Mary of Samuel & Christian Bridge born Mar. 13.
Newcomb of Newcomb & Mary Blaque born Apr. 21.
John of John & Mary Bears born May 19.
Rachel of James & Rachel Barry born July 14.
Rachel of Nathaniel & Mary Baker born July 29.
Thomas of Edward & Mary Brumfield born July 25.
Samuel of William & Mercy Brown born Aug. 30.
Lydia of Thomas & Lydia Barnes born Aug. 30.
Hannah of Edward & Hannah Ball born Aug. 30.
Margaret of Peter & Sarah Barbour born Aug. 30.
George of George & Mary Burrel born Sept. 24.

Joseph of Joseph & Hannah Belcher born Oct. 25.
Priscilla of Phillip & Sarah Bass born Jan. 18. .
Alford of Peter & Elizabeth Butler born Feb. 3.
Sarah of Randol & Sarah Broughton born Jan. 12.
William of Gilbert & Mercy Bant born Feb. 4.
Huldy of John & Elizabeth Bucanon born Feb. 5.
Edward of Edward & Mary Boylston born Nov. 22.
James of James & Eliza. Babbidge born Mar. 9.
Zechery of John & Elizabeth Banks born July 15.
Hannah of Daniel & Mary Berry born Apr. 27.
Samuel of Samuel & Deliverance Bayley born Dec. 24.
Mary of Samuel & Mary Barrat born Feb. 28.
Richard of Richard & Catharine Barnerd born Mar. 20.
John of John & Elizabeth Carnes born Apr. 3.
Thomas of Thomas & Rooksby Creesee born Apr. 1.
Hannah of Jonas & Mary Clay born May 28.
Margaret of George & Dorcus Courtney born June 5.
William of William & Ann Copp born June 9.
Ruth of John & Ruth Cook born July 1.
Margaret of James & Mary Cock born Aug. 21.
Richard of George & Mary Clark born Oct. 22.
James of Richard & Abigail Cheever born Nov. 22.
William of John & Juda Coleman born Dec. 15.
John of John & Sarah Clark born Dec. 15.
Mary of Edward & Sarah Cruff born Dec. 22.
William of William & Eliza. Crow born Dec. 8.
Sarah of Edward & Sarah Collins born Jan. 15.
James of Andrew & Sarah Cuningham born Feb. 15.
Elizabeth of Samuel & Eliza. Clark born Feb. 10.
Sarah of Matthew & Mary Cary born Feb. 14.
Prudence of Timo. & Sarah Clark born Dec. 31.
Esther of Paul & Mary Collings born Apr. 10.
William of William & Mary Davis born Mar. 25.
Sarah of Thomas & Hannah Davis born Mar. 27.
Hannah of Henry & Abigail Dawson born Mar. 11.
Ann of David & Jannet Dewer born May 15.
Jane of Thomas & Jane Danc born Sept. 2.
James of Robert & Jane Davis born Oct 17.
John of Benja. & Hannah Dyer born Nov. 21.
Abigail of Elijah & Sarah Dubbleday born Oct. 10.
Anna of Samuel & Elizabeth Durrum born Nov. 22.
Joseph of Joseph & Sarah Eliot born July 10.
Eliza. of Davis & Rachel Eustis born Aug. 6.
Antipas of John & Sybill Edwards born Nov. 23.
Eliza. of William & Eliza. Endicot born Jan. 2.
John of John & Catharine Eyre born Jan. 17.
Richard of Roger & Lydia Earle born Feb. 5.
Edward of Roben & Eliza. Ellis born Feb. 23.
Joseph of Joseph & Silence Eliot born May 1.
Mary of Benjamin & Mary Fitch born May 28.
Rubanas of Joseph & Rebecca Fuller born Aug. 20.
Lydia of Joseph & Joanna Flood born Jan. 5.
Sarah of Richard & Mary Fyfield born Jan. 10.
Benja. of Richard & Eliza. Flood born Feb. 3.
Eliza. of James & Eliza. Gooch born Mar. 17.
Hannah of Walter & Hannah Goodridge born Mar. 21.
Eliza. of Samuel & Elizabeth Greenwood born Apr. 21.
Hannah of Thomas & Sarah Gwin born Apr. 14.
Joshua of Joshua & Elizabeth Gee born June 29.
William of John & Mary Gyles born July 7.
Deborah of Barthol. & Mary Green born Aug. 2.
Benja. of Benja. & Hannah Gallop born Nov. 11.
Margar. of James & Margar. Gooding born Nov. 11.
Nathaniel of Nathaniel & Eliza. Green born Nov. 27.

Mary of Samuel & Elizabeth Gardner born Dec. 15.
James of Samuel & Susanna Grey born Jan. 4.
Samuel of Thomas & Lydia Gilbert born Feb. 21.
Elizabeth of Abraham & Sarah Gourden born Feb. 27.
Barthel. of Thomas & Experience Gold born May 24.
Martha of Barthol. & Mariah Green born Jan. 28.
John of John & Esther German born Apr. 24.
Jabez of Thomas & Mary Hunt born Apr. 5.
William of William & Sarah Harrison born Mar. 8.
Benja. of John & Margary Homer born May 8.
Mary of Samuel & Mary Hooper born June 1.
Mary of Samuel & Mary Hunting born June 4.
Elizabeth of Torrance & Eliza. Henly born Aug. 24.
Jane of Herculus & Jane Hewet born Oct. 30.
Keziah of Arthur & Mary Hale born Sept. 14.
Hannah of Nathanll & Hannah Hasey born Nov. 10.
Mary of William & Ann Holowell born Nov. 28.
Bridget of Thomas & Bridget Hays born Dec. 21.
Natha. of Natha. & Sarah Holmes born Dec. 14.
Eliza. of William & Martha Hannah born Jan. 16.
Benja. of Benja. & Mary Holowell born Jan. 20.
Samuel of Samuel and Margaret Hough born May 27.
Sarah of Thomas & Sarah Hudson born Jan. 31.
Sarah of Thomas & Eliza. Holmes born Feb. 22.
Natha. of John & Grace Irland born July 12.
Joanna of James & Love Ingles born May 2.
Mary of Thomas & Priscilla Jackson born May 24.
William of John & Mary Jarvis born Sept. 14.
Apfier of John & Apfier Jepson born Jan. 1.
Samuel of Joseph & Anna Johnson born Feb. 12.
Priscilla of David & Priscilla Johnson born Jan. 5.
James of Thomas & Mary Jacobs born Mar. 13.
William of John & Rebecca Kilby born Apr. 6.
Abigail of Roger & Abigail Kilcup born Jan. 3.
Joshua of Joshua & Agnes Kent born Sept. 14.
Solomon of Solomon & Mary Kneeland born Sept. 23.
Joseph of John & Mary Kneeland born Jan. 29.
Mary of David & Martha Langdon born Apr. 4.
Deborah of Edward & Deborah Lyde born Sept. 14.
John of John & Elizabeth Langdon born Oct. 17.
Joanna of John & Joanna Lathrop born Dec. 28.
Benja. of Joseph & Elizabeth Lobden born Dec. 27.
Gabril of James & Ann Lablond born Mar. 5.
Thomas of Thomas & Mary Mellens born Aug. 30.
Mary of Samuel & Mary Mears born Sept. 12.
Diana of Henry & Diana Mattox born Nov. 27.
Priscilla of Joseph & Hannah Marriner born Dec. 4.
Joseph of Samuel & Mary Marion born Dec. 18.
Patience of Henry & Hannah Mare born May 17.
Sarah of Florance & Sarah Mackarty born May 13.
Betty of Thomas & Betty Mosemy born Mar. 7.
John of Philip & Mary Marret born Dec. 19.
Priscilla of Ezekiel & Priscilla Needham born July 2.
Ezekiel of Natha. & Rest Newhall born Aug. 19.
Mary of John & Dorothy Nicholson born Jan. 20.
Lydia of John & Lydia Osment born Aug. 30.
Ann of Elias & Ann Oris born Feb. 18.
Nathanll of Nathanll & Hannah Parkman born June 12.
William of James & Elizabeth Pitts born June 13.
Stephen of Jacob & Rachel Price born June 22.
Mary of Daniel & Elizabeth Phippen born July 2.
Thomas of John & Elizabeth Pitts born June 28.
Mary of Thomas & Elizabeth Pearson born Sept. 20.
Joanna of Thomas & Joanna Peck born Oct. 20.

Mary of Thomas & Remember Perkins born Dec. 13.
Mary of John & Margaret Pratt born Aug. 22.
James of Benja. & Elizabeth Pemberton born Nov. 13.
Eliza. } of Alexander & Sarah Prinly born Jan. 24.
Mary } of Alexander & Sarah Prinly born Jan. 24.
Ann of Jacob & Ann Parker born Jan. 28.
Benja. of Edward & Elizabeth Procter born Feb. 8.
Sarah of John & Sarah Parker born Jan. 30.
Hannah of Thomas & Hannah Platts born Jan. 30.
Benja. of Joseph & Susanna Russell born Mar. 10.
Esther of Joseph & Esther Roberts born Mar. 25.
Mercy of John & Rebecca Ransford born May 12.
Abigail of Ralph & Martha Ransford born Nov. 2.
Sarah of William & Elizabeth Robie born Dec. 6.
Elizabeth of William & Eliza. Randall born Dec. 15.
Hannah of James & Eliza. Raymer born Jan. 19.
Esther of Isaac & Sarah Robinson born Feb. 14
Mehitable of Winsor & Mehitable Sandy born Mar. 10.
Hannah of Alexander & Sarah Sherrod born Mar. 19.
William of Rowland & Ann Story born Mar. 30.
Eliza. of Henry & Elizabeth Spurham born Mar. 13.
Rachel of Francis & Rachel Smith born Mar. 24.
John of John & Mary Sharp born May 10.
Alexander of Roben & Abigail Sears born May 28.
Eliza. of Josiah & Rebecca Sanders born July 11.
Sar.uel of Samuel & Ann Scadlock born July 18.
Abigail of Seth & Mehitable Smith born Aug. 17.
Margaret of Thomas & Margaret Savage born Sept. 10.
John of Joseph & Eliza Skinner born Oct. 3.
Eliza of Daniel & Eliza Souther born Oct. 16.
Mary of Jeremiah & Mary Smith born Dec. 4.
Catharine of Thomas & Margaret Simpkin born Dec. 23.
John of James & Edde Seward born Jan. 10.
Samuel of Natha. & Elizabeth Shannon born Jan. 16.
Joseph of Robert & Esther Sanderson born Jan. 26.
Susanna of Sampson & Mary Shore born Feb. 13.
John of Henry & Sarah Smith born Jan. 31.
Hannah of John & Elizabeth Sunderland born May 17.
Agnes of James & Mary Townsend born June 26.
Samuel of James and Mary Truworthy born Aug. 20.
John of Richard & Elizabeth Tally born Dec. 8.
Barnet of Richard & Margar. Tuel born Jan. 10.
Peter of Peter & Mary Townsend born Aug. 26.
Christopher of Christopher & Joanna Vail born Mar. 19.
Eliza. of David & Mary Vaughan born July 30.
Jonathan of Jonathan & Mary Williams born Apr. 26.
Ann of John & Ann Wiot born July 6.
Mary of Richard & Mary Ward born Sept. 19.
Andrew of Andrew & Susanna Willit born Oct. 18.
Susanna of Thomas & Rebecca Walker born Nov. 18.
Zechery of Zechery & Mary Wier born Dec. 7.
Rebecca of Joseph & Elizabeth Wheeler born Dec. 21.
John of William & Penelope Way born Jan. 24.
Benja. of Benja. & Ann Wotson born Feb. 16.
Esther of Thomas & Christian Wallis born Feb. 14.
William of William & Elizabeth Wheeler born Feb. 23.
Joseph of Joseph & Lydia Webb born Feb. 18.
Ann of William & Mary Webstrer born Feb. 24.
Samuel of Thomas & Sarah Wheeler born Feb. 26.
John of Edward & Hannah Winslow born Dec. 24.
Thomas of John & Elizabeth Wakefield born Jan. 5.
Mary of Richard & Ann West born Feb. 26.
Mary of Samuel & Ann White born Feb. 18.
John of James & Esther White born Oct. 8.
William of John & Elizabeth Welch born Sept. 18.

William Avery of Dedham & Methitabel Worden of Boston were married by Mr. James Allen Aug. 25.

David Adams & Loves Collins were married by Mr. James Allen Dec. 15.

William Adkinson & Sarah White were married by Mr. Miles Aug. 31.

John Brown of Salem & Sarah Burroughs of Boston were married by Mr. Saml Willard Apr. 21.

James Boulderson & Joanna Grey were married by Mr. Saml Willard May. 19.

Roger Burges & Esther Palmer were married by Mr. Cotton Mather Aug. 3.

Alwin Bucher & Elizabeth Barnard were married by Mr. Willard Dec. 15.

Jonathan Barret & Abigail Tuttle were married by Mr. Tho. Cheever Dec. 8.

Thomas Bedle & Mary Harington were married by Mr. Benja. Wodsworth Sept. 20.

James Blin & Margaret Dennison were married by Mr. James Allen Dec. 6.

Daniel Buff & Mary Emblem were married by Mr. Miles May 12.

Francis Brock & Mary Butler were married by Mr. Miles July 29.

John Cotta & Sarah Wharton were married by Mr. James Allen May 4.

Ezekiel Cravath & Elizabeth Hooks were married by Mr. James Allen June 14.

David Crage & Deborah Man were married by Mr. James Allen July 3.

Samuel Clark & Hannah Fairweather were married by Mr. Willard June 23.

John Comer & Mary Pittom were married by Mr. Saml. Willard Feb. 9.

George Courtney & Dorcas Selly were married by Mr. Miles June 2.

John Cox & Joanna Brown were married by Mr. Miles Nov. 18.

John Dolbear & Sarah Comer were married by Mr. Cotton Mather June 9.

John Downing & Hannah Ridgaway were married by Mr. Cotton Mather Sept. 27.

Abner Dole of Newbery & Sarah Belcher of Boston were married by Mr. Tho. Cheever Jan. 5.

Samuel Drown & Elizabeth Morrell were married by Mr. Benja. Wodsworth Feb. 3.

Alexander Dunkan & Eliza. Turnerr were married by Mr. Miles July 6.

John Ellis of Medfield & Mary Hill of Sherbourn were married by Samuel Sewell Esq. Apr. 7.

Robert Ellis & Eliza. Pemberton were married by Mr. James Allen June 4.

Samuel Earle & Mary Condage were married by Mr. Cotton Mather Dec. 13.

Nathaniel Emons & Mary Warmal were married by Mr. Benja. Wodsworth Sept. 15.

William Egleton & Dorcas Greetian were married by Mr. Miles Sept. 28.

John Elves & Jane Brock were married by Mr. Miles Oct. 6.

John Frissel & Dorothy Parnel were married by Mr. Cotton Mather July 22.

Joseph Flood & Joanna Mitchill were married by Mr. Woodbridge Mar. 10.

John Furs & Jane Wilson were married by Mr. Miles Sept. 21.

Benja. Gold of Hull & Mary Dinely of Boston were married by Mr. Saml. Willard May 5.

Abra. Gourden & Sarah Hodder were married by Mr. Cotton Mather May 12.

John Gill & Elizabeth Parsons were married by Mr. Cotton Mather June 1.

Joseph Green & Mary Beck were married by Mr. Cotton Mather July 30.

Jeremiah Gipson & Mary Hunter were married by Mr. Miles Apr. 13.

Winsor Golden & Eliza Ingolsby were married by Mr. Miles May 14.

Jonathan Hall & Margaret Seward were married by Mr. James Allen June 21.

Joseph Hubbert of Boston & Thankful Brown of Sudbury were married by Elisha Cook Esq. Aug. 4.

John Humphry & Kate Johnson were married by Mr. Cotton Mather June 2.

John Hughes & Deliverance Pallard were married by Mr. Benja. Wodsworth Sept. 15.

Joseph Hill & Elizabeth Peck were married by Mr. James Allen Dec. 22.

Arthur Hughes & Ruth Boulton were married by Mr. Woodbridge Aug. 15.

Isaac Jarvis & Abigail Voden were married by Mr. Woodbridge Jan. 19.

Samuel Jackson & Hannah Mare were married by Mr. Wodsworth Dec. 7.

Isaac Jarvis & Abigail Rowden were married by Mr. Woodbridge Jan. 19.

Samuel Johnson & Mary Stevens were married by Mr. Miles Dec. 20.

Timo. Kemble & Katharine Fowle were married by Mr. James Allen Aug. 18.

Timothy Kimball & Catharine Fowle were married by Mr. Woodbridge Aug. 18.

Samuel Lowel & Rachel Williams were married by Mr. James Allen July 22.

Samuel Lynde & Mary Richardson were married by Mr. James Allen Sept. 15.

Barnabas Lathrop & Abigail Dudson were married by Mr. James Allen Nov. 15.
Thomas Lilly & Elizabeth Hobby were married by Mr. Cotton Mather June 2.
Daniel Loring & Priscilla Man were married by Mr. Benja. Wodsworth Feb. 2.
Simon Lee & Theodor Belcher were married by Mr. Miles Dec. 9.
Henry Mattock & Diana Souther were married by Mr. Cotton Mather Mar. 3.
Duncan Makcum & Mary Hore were married by Mr. Willard Dec. 2
Thomas Miller & Sarah Day were married by Mr. James Allen July 8.
Thomas Miller of Dartmouth & Sarah Day of Boston were married by Saml
    Sewell Esq. Aug. 8.
Nathaniel Prisbury & Elizabeth Ganson were married by Mr. Saml. Willard
    Feb. 16.
Matthew Pauling & Susanna Walker were married by Mr. Saml Willard
    June 15.
John Pain & Bethia Hodge were married by Mr. Cotton Mather July 5.
Jonah Perry & Susanna Shaw were married by Mr. Cotton Mather June 9.
Theoder Percivah & Elizabeth Morss were married by Mr. Saml Willard
    Jan. 12.
John Peirce & Mary Cobet were married by Mr. Miles Nov. 9.
John Plaisted & Sarah Worthilake were married by Mr. Saml Willard Mar. 25
George Robinson & Sarah Maverick were married by Mr. Cotton Mather Apr. 7.
Walter Rost & Rebecca Harris were married by Mr. Willard Dec. 29.
Solomon Ridgeway & Bethia Wit were married by Mr. Miles Apr. 25.
Joseph Rud & Deborah Areland were married by Mr. Miles May 19.
Nathanl Shaw & Margaret Jackson were married by Mr. James Allen July 12.
Clement Sumner & Margaret Harris were married by Mr. Cotton Mather
    May 18.
Samuel Shipard & Alice Mason were married by Mr. Willard July 14.
John Simkins & Elizabeth Page were married by Mr. Willard Dec. 28.
John Sanders & Susanna Tomson of Brantry were married by Samuel Sewell
    Esq. May 24.
Solomon Townsend & Elizabeth Jarvis were married by Mr. Willard June 20.
William Twing & Ruth Chapin were married by Mr. Willard Jan. 26.
George Vaughn of Portsmouth & Mary Belcher of Boston were married by
    Mr. Willard Dec. 8.
John Woodward & Hannah Hide were married by Saml. Sewell Esq. Apr. 11.
John Wharton & Sarah Ballentine were married by Mr. James Allen Oct. 14.
Daniel Wear & Lydia Hillier were married by Mr. Cotton Mather Oct. 31.
Robert Wells of Weathersfield & Mary Stoddard of Boston were married by
    Mr. Willard Oct. 13.
John Wells & Eliza Bickford were married by Mr. Benja. Wodsworth Oct. 31.
Joseph Williams & Sarah Layton were married by Mr. James Allen Dec. 9.


Rebecca wife of Jolliff Price Dyed 3 March.
Sarah wife of Henry Tite Dyed 31 March.
Francis Ingraham Dyed 31 March.
Goodman Salter Dyed 25 March.
John Ransford Dyed April 5.
Sarah Samson Dyed 19 April.
Arthur Fustman Dyed 11 April.
Katharine Dowse an Antiant wido Dyed 14 April.
Mary wife of Thomas Bedle Dyed 2 April.
Elizabeth Smith Dyed 11 May.
Rebecca Daugth. of Rich. Draper Dyed 11 May.
Eliazer Heaton Dyed 28 May.
Thomas Merser senr. Dyed 28 May.
Rachel daugthr of Francis Smith Dyed 17 May.
William Lavis Dyed 6 May.
David Websbee Dyed 14 May.
Jane Barnard Dyed 31 May.
Goody fox at the Alms-house Dyed 10 May.
Elizabeth Richardson Dyed 18 May.
Goody Langly at the Almes-house Dyed 20 May.
Abigail daugthr of William Parkman Dyed 5 June.
Agnis daugthr of James Townsend Dyed 30 June.
James son of Eliza. Allen Dyed 28 June.

Joseph How dyed 9 June.
Elizabeth wife of David Jeffries Dyed 17 June.
Christoper of John Kilby Dyed 10 June.
Mary wife of James Townsend Dyed 8 July.
William of Wm. Randall Dyed 15 July.
George Burrel senr. Dyed 5 July.
Joseph Townsend shopkeeper Dyed 6 July.
Joseph of Josias & Sarah Byles Dyed 15 July.
Margaret of Benja. & Hanna Gallop Dyed 11 angt.
Mis. Eliza. Vsher wife of John Vsher Esqr. Dyed 17 **Aug.**
George Monk Dyed 7 Septembr.
Goodman Bodwell Dyed 6 Sept.
Sarah threeneedles Dyed 26 Sept.
Peter of David Jeffries Dyed 14 Septemr.
Jane wife of Herculus Hewet Dyed 3 Octor.
Samll Truworthy Dyed 8 Oct.
Samll of Samll & Priscilla Grice Dyed 10 Oct.
Joseph Webb Dyed 9 Oct.
Thomas Smith Dyed 13 Oct.
Robert Earle Dyed 18 Oct.
John Allen Dyed 18 Oct.
Mr Sampson Stoddard Dyed 4 Novemr.
Samuel Curwin Dyed 16 Nov.
Philip Wharton at the alms house Dyed 10 **Decemr.**
Mary wife of Jeremiah Smith Dyed 14 Dec.
Rebecca Allen widdow Dyed 25 Dec.
Ann wife of Samll Smith Dyed 9 Jaur.
Mary Stratton widdow Dyed 3 Februr.
Sarah of Alexandr & Sarah Prinly Dyed 14 Feb.
Thomas Greetian Dyed 3 Feb.
Thomas of Thomas & Abigall Palmer died **Dec. 1.**

## FIRST CHURCH.

| | |
|---|---|
| Mehitable of John & Mary Conney | Jan. 16. |
| Benjamin Indicot | Jan. 16. |
| Susannah Thaxter | Feb. 6. |
| John Thorn | Feb. 20. |
| Benjamin Pool | Mar. 6. |
| Mary of Samuel Bridge | Mar. 13. |
| Andrew Veach | Mar. 13. |
| Benjamin Russell | Mar. 13. |
| Elizabeth Goueh | Mar. 20. |
| Hannah Sherrerd | Mar. 20. |
| Sarah Davis | Mar. 27. |
| Rachel Smith | Mar. 27. |
| James of John & Elizabeth **Allen** | Apr. 17. |
| Jonathan of Jonathan Williams | May 1. |
| Ann of Thomas Messenger | May 8. |
| Mary of Brother Jackson | May 29. |
| Mehitabel Lyon | June 19. |
| Ruth Cook | July 3. |
| Theodor Atkinson | July 10. |
| Joshuah Moodey | July 17. |
| John of Abigail Hodsden of Ch. of Berwick | July 24. |
| Catharine of Mary Morehouse of Ch. of **Fairfeild** | Aug. 7. |
| Elizabeth Lowel | Nov. 13. |
| John of Benjamin Dyer | Nov. 27. |
| James Chevers | Nov. 27. |
| Marcy of Wm Hallowel | Nov. 27. |
| Nathaniel of Nat Green | Dec. 4. |
| Joanna of Joanna Lathrop | Dec. 4. |
| Priscilla Marriner | Dec. 11. |

## 1699.

### Town.

Jeremiah of John & Eliza. Allen born June 11.
Gillam of John & Elizabeth Alden born July 7.
Ann of John & Elizabeth Alden born July 7.
Benjn. of Joseph & Ann Allen born Aug. 15.
Joseph of Joseph & Eliza. Adams born Sept. 20.
Hannah of David & Lois Adams born Feb. 21.
Jane of Timo. & Rebecca Burbank born Mar. 24.
Joanna of James & Joanna Boulderston born Mar. 20.
Adoni of Adoni & Abigail Bulfinch born Mar. 23.
Benaniwell of Janna & Ann Bowers born Apr. 13.
Joseph } of James & Elizabeth Babbage born June 8.
Mary } of James & Elizabeth Babbage born June 8.
Rebecca of William & Rebecca Briggs born June 30.
Lydia of Thomas & Lydia Barnes born Aug. 18.
Ellis of Elisha & Doraty Bennet born Aug. 9.
William of William & Mary Barndell born Aug. 24.
Sarah of Benjamin & Elizabeth Brame born Aug. 22.
Robert of Moses & Elizabeth Bradford born Aug. 30.
Richard of Joseph & Hannah Billings born Aug. 7.
Grace of John & Mercy Booker born Sept. 3.
Rebecca of Thomas & Rebecca Burrington born Sept. 5.
Ann of Samuel & Sarah Brodge born Sept. 29.
John of Samuel & Martha Burrel born Oct. 19.
Elizabeth of Joshua & Esther Barnes born Oct. 19.
James of Josias & Sarah Byles born Oct. 7.
James of John & Phebee Brintnal born Nov. 18.
Rebecca of Peter & Sarah Barbour born Dec. 27.
Nathaniel of Joseph & Abigail Belknap born Dec. 18.
Henry of Daniel & Sarah Berry born Jan. 19.
James of James & Margaret Blin born Jan. 17.
Peter of George & Lucy Boose (negroes) born Aug. 12.
Sarah of William & Mary Bowen born June 10.
Rebecca of Alexander & Margaret Bulman born Feb. 18.
Agnen of Dundean & Susana Campbell born Mar. 2.
James of Samuel & Ruth Clough born Mar. 12.
Deborah of Daniel & Rebecca Collins born Mar. 4·
John of Jeremiah & Juda Cushing born Mar. 12.
Richard of William & Mary Cole born Mar. 10.
Ebenr. of Ebenezer & Martha Clough born Mar. 19.
Cluttebuck of Ezekiel & Elizabeth Cravath born Apr. 1.
Samuel of Samuel & Hannah Clark born Apr. 25.
Abigail of John & Mary Cutler born May 30.
Joseph of David & Mary Crouch born May 24.
Deborah of Thomas & Deborah Cushing born June 17.
Hannah of Thomas & Mehitable Cooper born Sept. 4.
Richard Carter of Joseph & Elizabeth Cowell born Sep. 6.
John of Samuel & Sarah Clark born Oct. 19.
Mary of Thomas & Sarah Cox born Nov. 19.
Sarah of John & Sarah Cotta born Dec. 2.
Mary of John & Mary Clough born Dec. 27.
Cleford of John & Elizabeth Cronenfield born Dec. 10.
Henry of Henry & Elizabeth Camler born Jan. 17.
Hannah of Richard & Abigail Cheever born Jan. 27.
John of John & Sarah Cary born Jan. 27.
Ann of James & Mary Cock born Feb. 10.
Thomas of David & Patience Copp born Feb. 26.
Mary of John & Mary Coney born Nov. 11.
John of John & Mary Carpenter born March 8.
Tamozine of Christor. & Tamzine Capril born Nov. 17.

Elizabeth of Patrick & Elizabeth Dudgeon born Mar. **23.**
David of Edmund & Sarah Dolbear born Mar. **25.**
Mary of Samuel & Mary Dyer born Apr. 20.
Thomas of Sampson & Sarah Dewer born June **2.**
Edmund of Joseph & Hannah Dolbear born June 14.
John of John & Sarah Dolbear born July 29.
Lydia of Nathaniel & Elizabeth Draper born July 31.
Richard of Richard & Sarah Draper born Sept. 9.
Ebenezer of Edward & Ann Durant born Sept. 20.
Elizabeth of Leonard & Elizabeth Drown born Nov. 2.
Jethro of Elijah & Sarah Doubleday born Nov. 10.
Jonathan of Jonathan & Penelopy Everard born Mar. 19.
Benjamen of Robert & Bethiah Emes born Mar. 30.
Eliza. of John & Elizabeth Eustis born Apr. 6.
Hannah of William & Sarah Eustis born May 23.
Robert of Jonathan & Mary Evans born June 14.
Hezekiah of William & Dorcas Egglestone born July **2.**
Nathaniel of Nathaniel & Mary Emons born July 2.
Elizabeth of Jonathan & Martha Farnum born Mar. **28.**
Rebecca of Samuel & Rebecca Foster born Apr. 10.
Dorathy of John & Dorathy Farnum born· Apr. 27.
Nathan of Richard & Abigail Franklin born July 6.
John of John & Abia Flagg born Oct. 20.
Mary of Joseph & Rebecca Fuller born Oct. 13.
Mary of Alexander & Mary Fullerton born Jan. 9.
Sarah of Josiah & Abiah Frankling born July 9.
Mary of Benjamin & Mary Goold born Mar. 10.
Mary of Samuel & Priscilla Grice born Apr. 1.
Mary of Joseph & Mary Green born May 6.
Mary of Robert & Mary Gibbs born May 28.
John of Nathaniel & Elizabeth Goodwin born July 14.
Elizabeth of Walter & Ann Goodridge born July 30.
John of James & Eliza. Gooch born Oct. 23.
Nathaniel of Samuel & Eliza. Greenwood born Oct. **10.**
John of John & Susanna Garret born Jan. 9.
Jacob of Jacob & Elizabeth Goulding born Jan. 11.
Sarah of William & Mary Gold born Feb. 25.
John of Joshua & Eliza. Gee born Feb. 27.
John of John & Eliza Greenough born July 17.
Obediah of John & Elizabeth Gill born Oct. 12.
Esther of John & Esther German born Nov. 28.
Elizabeth of Joseph & Judith Hood born Mar. 29.
Richard of Richard & Elizabeth Hubbert born Apr. 14.
John of Samuel & Deborah Hood born May 18.
Nathaniel of William & Elizabeth Hughs born Aug. 3.
Nathaniel of Nathaniel & Ann Henchman born Nov. 2.
Ann of Jacob & Mary Holoway born Nov. 29.
Thankful of Joseph & Thankful Hubberd born Dec. **25.**
Thomas of Robert & Hannah Hannah born Jan. 6.
Naomie of William & Margaret Heppe born Feb. 22.
Hannah of John & Elizabeth Humphrys born Feb. 12.
Eben of William & Mary Hughs born Feb. 7.
Ann of Francis & Rebecca Holmes born July 4.
Charles of John & Ann Hobbie born Apr. 3.
Edward of Samuel & Margaret Haugh born Sept. 19.
Joseph of Joseph & Eliza. Halsey born Mar. 21.
Thomas of Job & Hannah Ingraham born Apr. 4.
David of David & Mabell Jenner born July 4.
Sarah of Samuel & Hannah Jackson born Nov. **5.**
Ruth of John & Margaret Jones born Jan. 7.
Abigail of John & Aphiah Jepon born Feb. 17.
Thomas of Thomas & Elizabeth Kellen born Mar. **4.**
Katharine of Timo. & Katharine Kemble born July **17.**
John of Christopher & Sarah Kilby born Aug. 24.

Katharine of John & Rebecca Kilby born Feb. 10.
Katharine of Timothy & Katharine Kamble born July 17.
Andrew of Andrew & Susanna Knott born July 18.
Michael of Ebenezer & Elizabeth Lowle born Mar. 5.
Margaret of Thomas & Mercy Lazenby born Mar. 27.
Isaac of Isaac & Sarah Loring born Apr. 20.
Benja. of Jonathan & Elizabeth Lambert born June 1.
Timothy of James & Hannah Mireck born Apr. 6.
Benjamen of John & Elizabeth Mulligin born Apr. 1.
Antipas of Thomas & Dorus Marshall born May 3.
Isaac & } of Robert & Elizabeth Maugridg born June 5.
Rebecca } of Robert & Elizabeth Maugridg born June 5.
Incease of Cotton & Abigail Mather born July 9.
Joseph of Daniel & Mary Mory born July 20.
Joseph of Robert & Maria Mason born Dec. 19.
Rebecca of William & Rebecca Man born Jan. 11.
Catharine of John & Sarah Miles born Jan. 17.
Christopher of Christopr & Joyce Mynges born Feb. 11.
Elizabeth of John & Elizabeth Maxwell born Feb. 9.
Edward of Edward & Sarah Martin born Oct. 22.
Timothy of Timothy & Ann Mackue born Oct. 20.[1]
Michael of George & Elizabeth Nowell born Mar. 18.
Joanna of David & Temperance Norton born July 2.
Thomas of Thomas & Martha Nichols born Sept. 8.
Hamond of John & Sarah Oliver born June 8.
Abigail of Edward & Abia Porter born Mar. 9.
Thomas of Thomas & Mary Pratt born May 6.
Elizabeth of William & Deborah Philips born June 3.
Sarah of William & Mary Pain born July 16.
Sarah of John & Sarah Plasted born July 21.
Jacob of Jacob & Rachel Peirce born Oct. 27.
Sarah of Jonah & Rebecca Perry born Oct. 10.
Sarah of Mathew & Sarah Pauling born Nov. 25.
Nathan of Nathan & Elizabeth Presbery born Dec. 20.
Lydia of Robert & Hannah Price born Jan. 17.
John of Obediah & Mary Perry born Feb. 23.
John of John & Bethiah Pain born Apr. 18.
Aseph of Isaac & Elizabeth Royal born May 1.
John of John & Martha Ruggles born May 9.
John of Gyles & Margaret Roberts born Aug. 26.
Joseph of Mark & Sarah Round born Sept. 4.
Abigail of John & Hannah Ruck born Sept. 11.
Joseph of Joseph & Sarah Rayner born Sept. 28.
Walter of Walter & Rebecca Rost born Oct. 6.
Samuel of Samuel & Mary Russell born Oct. 26.
Abigail of Joseph & Mary Russell born Oct. 30.
Simeon of Joseph & Elizabeth Rogers born Feb. 18.
John of Josiah & Mary Stone born Mar. 2.
Rebecca of Joseph & Rebecca Snelling born Mar. 5.
Mary of William & Martha Shute born Mar. 1.
Dorothy of John & Mary Stover born Mar. 23.
William of Clement & Margaret Summers born Mar. 18.
Henry of Richard & Sarah Sherren born Mar. 28.
Hannah of Cyprian & Elizabeth Southack born Apr. 10.
Rely of John & Rely Simpson born Apr. 4.
Eliner of Sanders & Rebecca Seers born May 7.
Margaret of Natha. & Margaret Shaw born May 12.
Nathaniel of John & Mary Sunderland born June 15.
Thomas of Daniel & Elizabeth Stoddard born July 13.
David of John & Jane Smith born Aug. 19.
Thomas of Thomas & Deborah Smith born Aug. 17.
James of James & Susanna Studson born Sept. 11.

---

[1] By a slip of the pen this birth was recorded as of 1669. — W. S. A.

Benja. of Thomas & Mehitable Savage born Oct. 8.
Elizabeth of Joseph & Elizabeth Simpson born Oct. 3.
Benjamin of John & Ann Smith born Nov. 5.
Benjamin of John & Bridget Salsbury born Nov. 7.
Ann of Joseph & Hannah Simpson born Nov. 9.
Sarah of Joshua & Sarah Sectow born Nov. 8.
Samuel of Benja. & Joanna Stone born Dec. 30.
Isaac of John & Jane Snelling born Jan. 3.
Rebecca of Rowland & Ann Story born Feb. 1.
Paul of George & Jane Siry born Feb. 7.
Sarah of Samuel & Ann Scadlock born Feb. 8.
Benja. of Benjamin & Jemina Snelling born Feb. 14.
Martha of John & Martha Thwing born Mar. 24.
Mary of Thomas & Elizabeth Townsend born Mar. 28.
Samuel of Samuel & Lydia Turel born Apr. 8.
Jonathan of Jonathan & Elizabeth Townsend born June 25.
Benjamin of William & Ruth Thwing born Sept. 22.
Abigail of Thomas & Sarah Thomlin born Oct. 31.
William of William & Hannah Turner born Dec. 12.
Benja. of Benjamin & Mercy Tout born Feb. 27.
James of James & Rebecca Townsend born Feb. 21.
John of Christopher & Joanna Veal born Mar. 13.
Febee of Richard & Febee Vitterridge born Apr. 9.
Mary of John & Mary Vial born May 22.
Amos of Amos & Elizabeth Wadland born Mar. 1.
Elizabeth of Nathll & Mary Wheeler born Mar. 7.
Robert of Rachel & Thomas Winsor born Apr. 16.
Hannah of Joseph & Hannah Wodsworth born May —
Thomas of Thomas & Sarah Warren born June 11.
Abraham of James & Sarah Williams born June 21.
Davis of Francis & Mary Whiteman born July 13.
Deliverance of John & Elizabeth Wakefield born Aug. 17.
Abigail of William & Abigail Waters born Sept. 6.
Ebenezer of Ebener & Deliverance Weeks born Sept. 17.
Thomas of Thomas & Sarah Webb born Sept. 14.
Joseph of Joseph & Sarah Williams born Sept. 21.
John of John & Elizabeth Wilkins born Oct. 20.
Hannah of James & Elizabeth Wakecom born Oct. 21.
Hannah of Thomas & Triphene Woodword born Nov. 9.
Mary of Samuel & Mary Ward born Nov. 19.
Catharine of Jonathan & Catharine Wardall born Dec. 21.
Jonathan of Jonathan & Mary Williams born Jan. 8.
Matthew of Matthew & Jane Walter (negroes) born Feb. 7.
Allen ⎫ of Andrew & Elizabeth Waker born Feb. 19.
Eliza. ⎭ of Andrew & Elizabeth Waker born Feb. 19.

The following birth was not recorded till 1705, and therefore not found in time for its proper place. — W. S. A.

Joseph of Timothy and Margaret Prout born Feb. 4, 1651.

These two births, recorded in 1719, unfortunately missed their proper places. — W. S. A.

Phebee of John & Phebee Brentnall born Nov. 22, 1691.
John of John & Phebee Brentnall born Nov. 3, 1693.

The following births happened between 1690 and 1700, but the year is in no case written. — W. S. A.

Eliza. of Nathaniel & Hebhsibah Alden born ———.
Hebhsibah of Nathaniel & Hebhsibah Alden born ———.
Richard of George & Elizabeth George born Mar. 30.
Nathanll of Samuel & Mary Greenwood born Apr. 29.
Thomas of Thomas & Elizabeth Kellen born July 1.
Christian of Robert & Christian Mason born Feb. 22.
Abigail of John & Sarah Mason born Apr. 12.
Sarah of John & Experience Roberts born Apr. 17.
Joseph of Joseph & Elizabeth Rogers born ———

Francis Alexander & Sarah Kirk were married by Mr. Miles Mar. 13.

John Ashbury & Eleanor Griffen were married by Mr. James Allen Oct. 18.

David Anderson of CharlsTown & Hannah Philips of Boston were married by Mr. Samuel Willard Jan. 5.

Isaac Adams & Martha Stocker were married by Mr. Samuel Willard Jan. 4.

Jonathan Blake & Elizabeth Candage were married by Mr. Cotton Mather Feb. 16.

Nicholas Buttolph & Mary Guttridge were married by Mr. James Allen June 28.

Timothy Batt & Sarah Tudman were married by Mr. Saml Willard Aug. 3.

John Bonner & Persis Wanton were married by Mr. Saml Willard Sept. 28.

John Bennet & Sarah Harris were married by Mr. Saml Willard Oct. 25.

John Barret & Sarah Eustace were married by Mr. Cotton Mather Sept. 28.

Richard Bignell & Abigail Lawrance were married by Mr. Cotton Mather Nov. 2.

Joseph Bond & Elizabeth Prentice were married by Saml Sewell Esq. Nov. 13.

Samuel Baker & Febee Eglington were married by Saml. Sewell Esq. Dec. 19.

Thomas Bill & Agnis Batchelder were married by Mr. Woodbridge Nov. 23.

Francis Bruno & Sarah Vringe were married by Mr. Miles Jan. 26.

Alexander Chamberlin & Sarah Tinny were married by Mr. James Allen Apr. 20.

Robert Calfe & Margaret Barton were married by Mr. James Allen Dec. 23.

Charles Chancy & Sarah Wally were married by Mr. Saml. Willard Oct. 19.

Mathias Clark & Ann Barton were married by Mr. Saml. Willard Dec. 25.

Micah Coars & Rachel Short were married by Mr. Cotton Mather July 7.

Richard Collier & Mary Jarvis were married by Mr. Cotton ·Mather Jan. 25.

John Carter & Filippe White were married by Mr. Benj. Wodsworth Nov. 6.

William Cotton & Ama Carter were married by Mr. Benja. Wodsworth Nov. 6.

William Clear & Bethiah? Greenleaf were married by Mr. Benj. Wodsworth. Dec. 21.

Edmund Cross & Martha Dammon were married by Saml. Sewell Esq. Apr. 21.

Abioe Christen & Sarah Tylestone were married by Saml. Sewell Esq. Jan. 18.

Francis Caswell & Priscilla Tapril were married by Mr. Miles Aug. 18.

Thomas Copeland & Mary Arnold were married by Pen Townsend Esq. May 17.

Ebenezer Dennis & Damaris Robinson were married by Mr. Cotton Mather May 3.

Barret Dyer & Hannah Stewart were married by Mr. Cotton Mather June 29.

William Danil & Dorothy Bud were married by Mr. Benj. Wodsworth Sept. 27.

Isaac Decoster & Mary Temple were married by Mr. Benja. Wodsworth Nov. 2.

Thomas Degresha & Agnes Cracker were married by Mr. Cheever Mar. 16.

Jonathan Eustice & Sarah Scholly were married by Mr. Cotton Mather Nov. 16.

Obadiah Emons & Judith Hubberd were married by Mr. Benj. Wodsworth Nov. 7.

John Foy & Sarah Lynde were married by Mr. Saml. Willard Nov. 16.

Nathaniel Freeman & Alice Penuel were married by Mr. Cotton Mather Jan. 18.

William Francis & Triphena Yelling were married by Mr. Miles Apr. 29.

Daniel Fize & Sarah Lambert were married by Mr. Miles Nov. 6.

John Forbee & Penelope Leigh were married by Mr. Miles Dec. 4.

Jeremiah Fenwick & Eliza. Steadford were married by Mr. Miles Jan. 3.

Samuel Gidings of Ipswich & Elizabeth Sample of Boston were married by Mr. Samuel Willard Nov. 8.

Tobias Green & Mary Gent were married by Mr. Samuel Willard Nov. 17.

Benjamin Gipson & Mehitable Astin were married by Mr. Cotton Mather Jan. 4.

Edward Gipson & Ruth Comer were married by Mr. Cotton Mather Jan. 11.

John George & Hannah Grover were married by Mr. Benja. Wodsworth Aug. 22.

Thomas Gyles & Martha Bill were married by Mr. Cheever Jan. 18.

William Gold & Mercy Harris were married by Mr. Miles Apr. 16.

Edward Gray & Susanna Harrison were married by Pen Townsend Esq. Aug. 11.

Benjamin Hobart & Susanna Newcomb of Brantry were married by Saml. Sewell Esq. Apr. 5.

Elias Heath & Eliza Eldridge were married by Mr. James Allen May 13.

Atherton Haugh & Mercy Winthrop were married by Mr. Saml. Willard July 11.

Peter Hoxworth & Elizabeth Stephens were married by Mr. Saml. Willard Feb. 27.

Williams Hicks & Christian Harper were married by Mr. Miles Nov. 27.

Thomas Hayne & Rebecca Green were married by Mr. Miles Jan. 9.

Edward Hill & Mary Archer were married by Mr. Miles Feb. 15.

John Hog & Eliza Lewis were married by Mr. Miles Feb. 22

William Huse & Ann Russell were married by Pen Townsend Esq. Aug. 17.

Samuel Hinckley & Martha Lathrop were married by Pen Townsend Esq. Sept. 29.

John Jackson & Susanna Hayden were married by Mr. Benja. Wodsworth May 19.

John Jones & Margaret Bull were married by Saml. Sewell Esq. May 29.

John Jordon & Mary Frizell were married by Pen Townsend Esq. Oct. 4.

Samuel Keeling & Elizabeth Oliver were married by Mr. Samuel Willard Sept. 14.

Thomas Loring of Plimouth & Deborah Cushing of Cituate were married by Saml Sewell Esq. Apr. 19.

Thomas Lamere & Hannah Hodge were married by Mr. Cotton Mather Aug. 11.

John Lowery & Mary Davis were married by Mr. Benja. Wodsworth Nov. 13.

Benja. Loyd & Mary Dinsdell were married by Mr. Benja. Wodsworth Jan. 17.

John Lawson & Ann Eyers were married by Mr. Miles Dec. 28.

Timo. Mackhew & Ann Dry were married by Mr. Saml. Willard May 15.

John Marshall & Sarah Webb were married by Mr. James Allen May 26.

Joseph Merrifield & Mary Rogers were married by Mr. Benja. Wodsworth Apr. 6.

John Noyes & Susanna Edwards were married by Mr. Sam. Willard Mar. 16.

Robert Nokes & Mary Emerson were married by Mr Samuel Willard Aug. 17.

William Oorson & Mary Ellis were married by Mr. Miles June 27.

Obadiah Procter & Margaret Gardner were married by Mr. James Allen Aug. 24.

Joseph Plimpton & Priscilla Parterage or Parteridg were married by Pen Townsend Esq. Aug. 22.

Thomas Perry & Ruth Ripley were married by Pen Townsend Esq. Jan. 29.

John Richardson & Margaret Woodmansey were married by Mr. James Allen June 22.

Nathaniel Rogers of Portsmouth & Sarah Perkis were married by Mr. Saml. Willard Oct. 26.

William Randol & Elizabeth Skerry were married by Mr. Saml. Willard Dec. 21.

Nathaniel Roring & Susannah Butler were married by Mr. Cotton Mather Dec 13.

Adam Read & Margaret Denkin were married by Mr. Miles Jan. 11.

Benja. Stapils & Mary Cox were married by Mr. James Allen May 26.

Wigleworth Switser & Ussillah Coles were married by Mr. James Allen Feb. 2.

John Sparhawk of Bristol & Elizabeth Pool were married by Mr. Saml. Willard June 22.

William Snowton & Rachel Woodward were married by Mr. Saml. Willard June 28.

Jeremiah Smith & Ann Peather were married by Mr. Saml. Willard Dec. 21.

John Smallpeice & Olive Furnel were married by Mr. Miles Apr 7.

John Stodder & Mary Jay were married by Mr. Miles Nov. 14.

William Smith & Mary Perry were married by Mr. Miles Jan. 8.

William Taylor & Sarah Byfield were married by Mr. Sam. Willard Mar. 2.

Samuel Torry & Abigail Bridge were married by Mr. James Allen June 20.

John Titchborn & Sarah Allin were married by Mr. James Allen Aug. 17.

Peter Thatcher of Milton & Susanna Bayley of Boston were married by Mr. Saml. Willard Dec. 25.

James Talbot & Elizabeth Blore were married by Mr. Saml. Willard Dec. 25.

John Tyler & Deborah Leatherland were married by Mr. Cotton Mather Nov. 2.

James Thornbury & Lydia Curtice were married by Mr. Woodbridge Sept. 14.

Francis Traveres & Mary Burgess were married by Mr. Miles Jan. 27.

James Turberfeeld & Mercy Campball were married by Jeremiah Dummer Esq. Dec. 6.

John Venteman & Elizabeth Smith were married by Mr. Cotton Mather July 13.

Samuel Wentworth & Abigail Goffe were married by Mr. James Allen Oct. 28.

Richard Wale & Hannah Skerry were married by Mr. Saml. Willard Dec. 21.

Joshue Wells & Sarah Savage were married by Mr. Saml. Willard Dec. 25.

Richard Whites & Elizabeth Rust were married by Mr. Saml. Willard Jan. 4.

William Webber & Mary Sumer were married by Mr. Cotton Mather Sept. 19.

Nathaniel Witherly & Sarah Burgis were married by Mr. Cotton Mather Dec. 10.

George Walker & Rebecca Davenport were married by Benja. Wodsworth Oct. 5.

Joshua Week & Comfort Hubberd were married by Mr. Benja. Wodsworth Nov. 7.

Joseph Webb & Deborah Bass were married by Saml. Sewell Esq. Nov. 29.

Francis Whitmore & Ann Peirce were married by Mr. Woodbridge Dec. 7.

James Wiborn & Mary Graford were married by Mr. Miles Jan. 11.

Joshua Wight & Elizabeth Spowel were married by Pen Townsend Esq. Oct. 4.

Thomas Sudder & Sarah Phillip were married by Mr. James Allen Nov. 3.[1]

John of Samll & Hannah Marion Dyed 1 March.

Jonathan of Jona. & Martha Williams Dyed 22 March.

Joanna Rawlings Dyed 22 March.

James of William Thornton Dyed 15 April.

Susanna wife of Jona. Balston Dyed 17 April.

Rebecca Daugthr of Jer. Belcher of Rumney Marsh Dyed 21 April.

John of Edward Winslow Dyed 22 April.

Sarah Mosure Daught. of Wido. Mosure Dyed 23 April.

Samll of Joseph & Ann Johnson Dyed 22 April.

Cristopher Goffe Dyed 1 May.

Ann wife of William Copp Dyed June 6.

Sarah Daugth. of Constant Alcock Dyed 11 June.

Elizabeth of Ephraim & Sarah Savage Dyed 25 June.

Mary Buck Dyed 21 June.

Nathon of John & Mary Sanderson Dyed 22 June.

Nathon Belcher Dyed 3 July.

Thomas of Thomas & Hanna Eaton Dyed 9 July.

Michael of Ebenr & Elizabeth Lowle Dyed 7 July.

David of David & Mabell Jenners Dyed 22 July.

John of Jeremiah & Judeth Cushing Dyed 27 July.

Mr. Peter Butler Dyed 11 Aug.

Mary of Samll & Eliza. Gardner Dyed 25 Aug.

Eliza of William & Mary Wilson Dyed 31 Aug.

Capt. Laurance Hammond Dyed ye 29 Aug.

Ann of Jacob & Mary Holoway Dyed 16 Aug.

Samll of William & Mercy Brown Dyed 9 Septemr.

Ann of Joseph & Hannah Simpson Dyed 3 Septemr.

Abigail wife of William Waters Dyed 12 Sept.

Samll Baker was drowned 24 Sept.

Mary of Simeon & Mary Stoddard Dyed 20 Sept.

Tamazon Scarlet dyed 20 Octor.

Joanna of John & Joanna Lathrop Dyed 1 Octobr.

William of Roland & Ann Story Dyed 7 Oct.

Mary of Samll & Mary Ward Dyed 29 Novembr.

---

[1] This marriage took place before 1700, but the year is illegible. — W. S. A.

Ann of Joseph & Hannah Simpson Dyed 20 Nov.
Ebenezer of Ebenr & Martha Clough Dyed 6 Nov.
Elizabeth of Joseph & Eliza Simpson Dyed 6 Decemr.
Mary Daughtr of Thomas Perkins Dyed 1 Janr.
John Orris Dyed 19 Jan.
Thomas of John & Sarah Vickers Dyed 21 Jaur.
Jacob Smith Dyed 12 Jan.
Joseph of Daniel & Susanna Mory Dyed 24 Jan.
George Ball Dyed 15 Jan.
Thomas Peck senr. Dyed 3 Februr.
Joseph of Joseph & Elizabeth Halsey died 29 March.
Nathaniel of Samuel & Eliza Greenwood died 6 Jan.

The following death, recorded in 1710, unfortunately missed its proper place. — W. S. A.

Eliza. of Samuel & Eliza. Greenwood dyed within its moneth 2 Nov. 1687.

The following death was not recorded till 1714. — W. S. A.

Margaret wife of Timothy Prout died 29 Oct. 1685.

## FIRST CHURCH.

| | |
|---|---|
| Elizabeth Endicott | Jan. 1. |
| Samuel Baylie | Jan. 8. |
| Hannah of Eleanor Follow (negro) | Jan. 15. |
| Alford of Peter Butler | Feb. 5. |
| Sarah of John Parker | Feb. 5. |
| James Cunningham | Feb. 19. |
| Nicholas of Mary Phillips | Feb. 19. |
| Anna of Mary Webster | Feb. 19. |
| Abigail of James Hawkins | Feb. 26. |
| Amos Wadlin | Mar. 5. |
| Mary Barret | Mar. 5. |
| Jonathan of Jonathan Everard | Mar. 26. |
| Martha of John Twing | Mar. 26. |
| Thomas Ingram | April 9. |
| Elizabeth Eustice | April 9. |
| Timothy Myrick | April 9. |
| Samuel of James & Mary Ferres | April 9. |
| Mary of James & Mary Ferres | April 9. |
| Sarah of James & Mary Ferres | April 9. |
| Anna of James & Mary Ferres | April 9. |
| Katharine of Wm Welsted | April 23. |
| Robert of Tho. Windsor | April 23. |
| Ebenezer Delver | April 23. |
| Thomas of Samson Dure | June 4. |
| Jeremiah of John & Elizabeth Allen | June 11. |
| Ebenezer Reynolds | June 25. |
| Mary Waldo | Aug. 6. |
| John of John & Elizabeth Ranger | Aug. 20. |
| John of Giles & Margaret Roberts | Aug. 27. |
| Robert of Moses & Elizabeth Bradford | Sept. 3. |
| Benjamin of Thomas Savage the Goldsmith | Oct. 8. |
| John of James Gooch | Oct. 29. |
| Joseph Hill a varnisher's son | Nov. 5. |
| Mary of John & Mary Coney | Nov. 12. |
| Mary Ward a coopers daughter | Nov. 26. |
| James Thorn a carpenter's son | Dec. 31. |
| Thankfull of Joseph & Thankfull Hubbard | Dec. 31. |

# INDEX.

# INDEX OF NAMES.

Deddicot, 122.
Dee, 235.
Degresha, 250.
Delarock, 221.
Dell, Dill, } 20, 25, 29, 37, 39, 53, 127.
Delver, Delvier, } 238, 253.
Damaree, Dameere, Demaree, Demeret, Demerey, Demery, Demurry, Dumery, } 157, 160, 168, 179, 189, 196, 214, 221.
Dening, 43, 132.
Denkin, 251.
Denis, Denise, Dennis, Dennise, Dennys, Dinis, Dinnis, } 9, 10, 13, 14, 18, 19, 21, 23, 27, 28, 32, 41, 47, 50, 52, 54, 57, 64, 66, 67, 73, 77, 78, 91, 100, 102, 162, 168, 196, 199, 224, 226, 230, 250.
Denison, Dennison, } 72, 86, 243.
Dering, 141, 148, 150, 157, 159, 162, 164.
Deschamps, 132.
Deuce, 60.
Devaulx, 196.
Devotion, 29, 34, 63, 72.
Dewer, Duer, Dure, } 37, 50, 53, 54, 132, 137, 140, 145, 148, 154, 162, 165, 173, 189, 199, 221, 225, 232, 235, 237, 239, 240, 247, 253.
Dewolfe, 209.
Dexter, 73.
Deeble, Dible, } 27, 28, 32.
Dickerson, Dickeson, } 206, 209.
Diggens, 229.
Dineley, Dinely, Dyneley, } 3, 4, 5, 6, 7, 47, 100, 107, 243.
Dingly, 214.
Demsdall, Dinsdale, Dinsdall, Dinsdell, Dinsdill, } 18, 27, 33, 60, 63, 73, 75, 77, 78, 83, 114, 118, 126, 127, 130, 141, 144, 145, 148, 168, 187, 217, 221, 229, 251.
Diore, 178.
Dios, Dious, } 145, 151, 157, 184.
Disitor, Dissater, } 184, 187, 203.
Dixey, 198.
Doan, 226.
Dobson, 44.
Dod, Dodd, } 26, 33, 40, 42, 59, 73.
Dodge, 230.
Dolbear, Dolbeer, Dolobear, } 162, 206, 232, 238, 243, 247.
Dolberry, Dolbery, } 141, 186.
Dole, 243.
Doling, 43.
Doue, 42.
Dorrell, 151, 153, 164, 165, 167.
Doubleday, Dubbleday, Dubbledee, } 122, 127, 132, 141, 193, 235, 240, 247.
Douglas, Duglas, } 21, 24, 76, 137.
Doves, 69.
Dowden, Dowding, } 104, 118, 127, 145, 148, 151, 217, 210, 221, 232.
Dowell, 96, 100, 118, 209, 214.
Down, Downe, } 138, 157, 162, 179, 184, 206, 229.
Downam, 27.
Downes, 36, 45, 56, 64, 92, 104, 114.

Downing, 219, 243.
Douce, Douse, Dowse, } 13, 14, 18, 19, 20, 21, 22, 23, 27, 31, 33, 35, 41, 45, 48, 50, 53, 59, 63, 64, 68, 71, 130, 244.
Drake, 48, 151, 160, 165.
Draper, 184, 186, 189, 196, 203, 206, 213, 214, 221, 225, 226, 332, 239, 244, 247.
Drew, Drue, } 57, 73, 88, 148, 157, 184, 187, 196, 218.
Drinker, 211, 217.
Drisco, 184.
Drown, 243, 247.
Droomer, Drummond, } 82, 84, 87.
Drewrey, Drewry, Drury, } 24, 28, 107, 114, 117, 122, 132, 137, 141, 145, 198.
Drus, Druse, } 73, 81.
Dry, 214, 251.
Drywry, 125.
Dudgeon, 247.
Dudley, 2, 3, 8, 34, 38, 43, 110, 141, 157.
Dudson, 110, 118, 125, 132, 135, 137, 145, 187, 224, 244.
Due, 34, 46, 92.
Dumer, Dummer, } 127, 184, 203, 204, 205, 209, 210, 217, 224, 252.
Duncan, Duncun, Dunkan, Dunkin, } 33, 47, 51, 56, 63, 64, 67, 69, 72, 243.
Dunning, 148.
Durant, 201, 221, 232, 247.
Durham, Durrum, } 198, 201, 214, 240
Deusberry, Dusebury, } 221, 232.
Ditchfield, Dutchfield, } 17, 20, 21.
Dwight, Dwite } 63, 193, 217, 232.
Diar, Dier, Dyar, Dyer, } 3, 88, 110, 127, 130, 132, 136, 141, 148, 150, 154, 160, 165, 169, 184, 187, 193, 198, 201, 205, 206, 212, 213, 217, 221, 224, 225, 226, 229, 231, 240, 245, 247, 250.
Eades, 151, 169, 179, 184, 217.
Earl, Earle, } 92, 110, 114, 127, 141, 145, 151, 173, 179, 196, 214, 217, 229, 232, 238, 240, 243, 245.
Earthy, 173.
East, 7, 10, 13, 14, 18, 19, 24, 25, 30, 35, 39, 55, 58, 65, 67, 70, 127, 145, 154, 169, 218.
Easterbrook, 217.
Eastmead, 209.
Eastwick, Estick, } 118, 132.
Eaton, 4, 7, 15, 43, 252.
Eddington, 34.
Edees, 173.
Edgerton, Egerton, } 118, 122, 132, 138, 141, 145, 190.
Edicott, for Endicott, 201
Edindin, 49.
Edmonds, Edmunds, } 62, 219, 224.
Edsell, Edzall, } 38, 46, 84, 90.
Edwards, 42, 62, 81, 86, 88, 100, 107, 110, 114, 123, 138, 148, 151, 154, 157, 162, 173, 184, 196, 209, 217, 226, 230, 235, 240, 251.
Edye, 56.
Egbear, Egbeer, } 189, 196, 206.
Eggington, Eginton, Edlington, } 53, 55, 56, 94.
Eggleston, Egleston, Egleton, Eglington, } 209, 214, 230, 243, 247, 250.

Letherbee, 224.
Leatherland,
Letherland, } 115, 123, 130, 140, 146, 180, 198,
Litherland, } 201, 205, 212, 252.
Lytherland,
Levensworth, 218.
Levenworth, 152.
Leaverit,
Leveret, } 2, 9, 10, 11, 12, 15, 16, 24, 28, 30,
Leverett, } 34, 37, 39, 49, 51, 56, 58, 84, 92,
Leverit, } 95, 104, 108, 115, 116, 117, 128,
Leveritt, } 130, 135, 198, 236.
Lewes, } 32, 61, 71, 79, 84, 92, 95, 100, 102, 152,
Lewis, } 160, 166, 175, 180, 196, 212, 251.
Ley, 60.
Lidget, } 142, 163, 170, 175.
Lidgett,
Lillie, } 88, 100, 105, 119, 166, 170, 180, 193,
Lilly, } 202, 207, 212, 222, 233, 244.
Lilcoln,
Lincoln,
Lincolne, } 90, 170, 187, 190, 202, 210, 222, 233.
Linkoln,
Lindall, 152, 163, 236.
Lindon, 42.
Linn,
Linne, } 4, 6, 8, 20, 26, 76.
Lynne,
Lippincot, } 17, 19, 23, 25.
Lippincott,
Lipsey, 185, 193.
Litchfeeld; 191.
Little, 217.
Lloyd,
Lloyde, } 77, 160, 166, 180, 198, 201, 204, 205,
Loyd, } 212, 215, 220, 235, 251.
Loyde,
Lobdale, } 203, 207, 222, 229, 236.
Lobdell,
Lobden, 233, 236, 241.
Lock, 235.
Lockston, 117.
Loe, 198.
Loft, 105, 111, 123, 198.
Login, 201.
Long, } 36, 37, 39, 62, 119, 121, 123, 128, 131,
Longe, } 142, 187, 190, 193.
Looe, 42, 47.
Loper, 180.
Lord, 33, 40, 42, 44.
Loreson, 236.
Loreing,
Lorin, } 198, 202, 204, 207, 222, 227, 244,
Loring, } 248, 251.
Lowrin,
Lothrop, 22.
Lott, 175.
Lourcin, 207.
Love, 38.
Lovering, } 138, 188.
Loveringe,
Lowden, 207, 227.
Lowder, 119.
Loell, } 43, 50, 54, 60, 61, 63, 74, 76, 79, 83,
Looell, } 84, 96, 98, 104, 105, 108, 111, 113,
Lowel, } 115, 117, 119, 123, 125, 126. 128,
Lowell, } 135, 138, 140, 142, 146, 149, 152,
Lowle, } 175, 218, 219, 227, 229, 233, 237,
} 238, 243, 245, 248, 252.
Lowery, 251.
Loyall, 6, 8, 9, 12.
Ludkin, } 20, 37.
Ludkine,
Lugg, } 6, 8, 13, 14, 19, 67.
Lugge,
Lumbard, 81.
Lumsden, 199.
Lunerus, 38.
Lunt, 142.
Liscomb,
Liscombe, } 104, 119, 138, 160, 218.
Liscum,
Luscomb,
Luscombe,

Lutterell, 191.
Lux, 105, 111, 215.
Luxford, 217.
Luz, 119.
Lyde, 241.
Lyford, 123, 128, 142.
Lynck, 211.
Linde, } 38, 41, 50, 52, 60, 66, 84, 92, 100, 106,
Lynd, } 108, 115, 116, 123, 125, 128, 131,
Lynde, } 142, 149, 152, 243, 250.
Lyon, 170, 180, 192, 210, 245.
Lysle, 8, 9, 10, 16.

Macartie,
Macarty, } 105, 115, 138, 149, 175, 180, 190,
Maccarty, } 229, 236, 241.
Mackarty,
Mackfarland, 207, 222, 236.
Mackgudy, 215.
Mackhew, } 248, 251.
Mackue,
Mackwell, 103, 113.
Macloughlin, 185, 196, 215.
Madever, 142.
Madson, 193.
Mackdaniel,
Magdanell, } 67, 69, 71, 79, 88, 100, 119,
Magdaniel, } 133, 238.
Megdaniel,
Megdaniell,
Magor, 204.
Mahoon,
Mahoone, } 23, 27, 56, 79, 80, 82.
Mahoonne,
Mayhoone,
Makaset, 210.
Makepeace, 52, 57, 82.
Mane, 115.
Manley, } 170, 175, 185, 187.
Manly,
Man, } 100, 119, 124, 133, 149, 163, 181, 183,
Mann, } 215, 224, 227, 229, 243, 244, 248.
Maning, } 15, 17, 26, 28, 32, 39, 43, 50, 52,
Maninge, } 54, 61, 67, 69, 73, 75, 79, 83, 88,
Manning, } 96, 100, 103, 108, 111, 112, 115,
Manninge, } 119, 121, 126, 133, 135, 212, 217,
} 224.
Mansell, 97, 105, 170, 218.
Mansfield, 129, 152.
Manyard, 42.
Marble, 23.
March, 146.
Mare, 133, 160, 170, 237, 241, 243.
Mariner, } 166, 170, 181, 185, 215, 220, 222,
Marriner, } 225, 233, 239, 241, 245.
Marion, } 101, 115, 155, 158, 163, 164, 166, 167,
Maryon, } 170, 172, 175, 177, 185, 190, 193,
} 202, 215, 227, 241, 252.
Marlton, 229.
Marret, } 170, 241.
Marrett,
Marsh, 111, 115, 128, 133, 142, 170, 181, 187,
190, 202, 203, 215, 227.
Marshal, } 4, 7, 17, 20, 54, 58, 69, 72, 74, 78, 79,
Marshall, } 88, 92, 94, 96, 98, 99, 101, 102,
} 103, 111, 113, 123, 133, 138, 146,
} 155, 158, 160, 163, 166, 170, 175,
} 181, 185, 190, 193, 196, 202, 207,
} 210, 215, 218, 222, 223, 233, 236,
} 237, 238, 248, 251.
Martin, } 44, 50, 57, 59, 62, 70, 71, 75, 76, 79,
Martine, } 84, 86, 88, 93, 97, 105, 108, 111,
Martyn, } 119, 124, 175, 202, 215, 223, 233,
} 248.
Mason, 5, 9, 17, 25, 42, 52, 55, 60, 61, 62, 70, 72,
77, 79, 81, 82, 84, 86, 88, 90, 92, 96, 98,
100, 101, 102, 103, 108, 109, 111, 115,
119, 129, 131, 133, 138, 142. 146, 152,
155, 158, 160, 163. 170, 185, 196, 199,
204, 210, 215, 223, 224, 227, 233, 244,
248, 249.
Materick, 138.
Mather, 57, 84, 87, 93, 101, 103, 111, 119, 133,
142, 152, 175, 203, 204, 207, 209, 210,

Plimpton, 251.
Plumb, 175, 193.
Pole, 129.
Pollard, } 18, 20, 27, 36, 46, 59, 69, 85, 89, 93,
Pollord, } 101, 108, 115, 129, 142, 149, 175,
      190, 194, 210, 228, 234.
Pallow, } 231, 238, 253.
Pollow, }
Pomrey, 163.
Pool, } 14, 15, 133, 142, 149, 218, 245, 251.
Poole, }
Poor, 124.
Pope, 63.
Pordade, 228.
Pordage, 163, 170, 185, 197, 237.
Pormort, }
Pormott, } 3, 4, 6, 7, 10, 13, 26, 38, 40, 44, 57.
Purmit, }
Purmott, }
Porter, 15, 16, 17, 25, 29, 67, 115, 129, 133, 139,
      142, 146, 152, 175, 181, 190, 197, 208,
      218, 228, 230, 248.
Portis, 71.
Potter, 5, 58, 223.
Poutland, 207.
Powel, } 29, 63, 71, 202, 208, 223.
Powell, }
Power, 210.
Pownening, } 31, 35, 45, 49, 54, 58, 61, 64, 66,
Fowning, } 67, 69, 72, 79, 83, 89, 94.
Powter, 48.
Praske, 81.
Prat, } 71, 74, 85, 93, 108, 120, 199, 202, 204,
Pratt, } 216, 228, 234, 242, 248.
Prentice, 250.
Presbery, 248.
Prescot, 119, 139.
Preston, 33, 41, 82, 86, 90
Pretious, 44, 45.
Price, 52, 71, 74, 84, 86, 89, 93, 98, 105, 120,
      149, 152, 166, 185, 197, 204, 223, 241,
      244, 248.
Fricot, 124.
Priest, 146, 155.
Prince, 76, 149, 152, 170, 175, 181, 183, 190,
      193, 197, 200, 208, 213, 236.
Prindle, 175, 202, 228.
Prinly, 216, 242, 245.
Prior, 175, 192.
Prisbury, 244.
Prise, 208.
Prockter, } 43, 76, 120, 185, 194, 197, 198, 200,
Procter, } 207, 216, 225, 228, 237, 242, 251.
Proctor, }
Prouse, 170.
Prout, } 20, 21, 25, 26, 29, 32, 40, 44, 50, 53,
Proute, } 56, 63, 70, 101, 115, 129, 133, 249,
      253.
Pryer, 158, 163.
Pue, 79.
Pullen, } 76, 111.
Pullin, }
Pulman, 170, 181, 185.
Pumery, 218.
Purchase, 34, 50, 52, 55, 70, 90.
Purdue, 216.
Purington, } 218, 223, 233.
Purrington, }
Purkis, 146, 152.
Pursly, 233.

Quarlls, 48.
Quelch, 202, 205, 216, 219, 220.
Quiddington, 166.
Quinsey, } 166, 185.
Quinsie, }

Rachell, } 36, 41, 64, 77.
Ratchell, }
Ragland, 194.
Raglin, 213.
Rainsford, } 1, 2, 3, 4, 6, 7, 11, 12, 18, 19, 25,
Ransford, } 29, 32, 33, 35, 49, 52, 57, 69, 79,
Raynsford, } 85, 89, 97, 101, 108, 111, 115,

      120, 129, 133, 143, 149, 161, 171,
      173, 181, 197, 199, 208, 223, 234,
      242, 244.
Ramsey, 86.
Randal, }
Randall, } 112, 120, 129, 199, 202, 223, 234,
Randol, } 242, 245, 251.
Randoll, }
Rainger, } 124, 133, 155, 202, 220, 228, 230, 231,
Ranger, } 234, 239, 253.
Rankin, 204, 208.
Raper, } 152, 166, 171, 181, 185, 197, 223, 234.
Rayper, }
Rashley, 22.
Raser, } 76, 79.
Rawser, }
Ratcliffe, } 93, 101, 112.
Ratliffe, }
Raven, 171.
Ravenscroft, 155, 158, 161, 171, 181.
Rawlings, } 21, 28, 37, 39, 50, 52, 56, 75, 101,
Rawlins, } 120, 129, 143, 149, 166, 252.
Rawson, 33, 35, 38, 45, 46, 49, 54, 56, 60, 62,
      63, 68, 83, 133, 139, 142, 146, 149,
      155, 158, 161, 171, 176.
Ray, 158, 197, 208.
Raylin, 190.
Rayly, 219.
Raymer, 219, 234, 242.
Rainer, }
Rayner, } 86, 204, 208, 216, 229, 248.
Raynor, }
Rayson, 187.
Rayt, 94.
Read, } 24, 25, 29, 32, 42, 44, 46, 47, 48, 49, 51,
Reade, } 54, 55, 56, 58, 60, 63, 66, 68, 70, 71,
      72, 74, 76, 77, 80, 82, 85, 87, 89, 91,
      97, 98, 101, 103, 111, 113, 143, 146,
      149, 161, 171, 176, 251.
Reap, } 77, 79.
Reape, }
Redman, 210.
Reed, 120, 124, 163, 198.
Remington, 120.
Rex, 20, 24, 55.
Reylean, 81.
Rainolls, }
Raynolds, }
Raynolls, } 63, 69, 70, 74, 89, 90, 98, 108, 112,
Raynols, } 115, 117, 133, 135, 139, 155, 176,
Renalls, } 185, 194, 197, 200, 208, 212, 220,
Renold, } 228, 230, 253.
Renolds, }
Reynolds, }
Rice, 5, 8, 13, 93, 94, 111, 218.
Richards, 33, 48, 67, 82, 87, 101, 112, 120, 129,
      139, 153, 185, 186, 187, 190, 203,
      204, 209, 211, 228, 234.
Richardson, } 1, 27, 30, 37, 39, 46, 49, 59, 60,
Richeson, } 63, 70, 73, 82, 85, 87, 243, 244,
Richison, } 251.
Richisson, }
Ricker, 49.
Rickes, } 24, 26, 29, 45, 59, 61, 66, 129, 133,
Ricks, } 139, 143, 149, 152, 155, 161, 166,
Rix, } 190, 208, 212.
Ricott, 178, 194.
Ridder, }
Rider, } 30, 35, 45, 50.
Ryder, }
Ridgaway, }
Ridgeaway, } 181, 243, 244.
Ridgeway, }
Ridman, 210.
Right, 60, 65, 79, 97.
Riland, 76.
Ripley, 43, 152, 158, 251.
Ripple, 218.
Risden, } 46, 70, 85.
Risdon, }
Rissing, 62.
Roads, 218.
Robarts, 124, 223, 228, 230.
Robe, 176.

# INDEX OF. PLACES.

Lightning Source UK Ltd.
Milton Keynes UK
UKHW012246140219
337323UK00011B/738/P

9 781332 295395